Praise for

Goose Creek
A Definitive History
Volume One
Planters, Politicians and Patriots

Mike Heitzler's most interesting and readable history is an extraordinary gift, not only to the current and future residents of Goose Creek, but also to the people of this region and all of South Carolina. The sense of place that comes with knowledge of our past can help us build a better future and Mike Heitzler has splendidly given us a vivid understanding of a special place in South Carolina.

Joseph P. Riley Jr.
Mayor, City of Charleston, South Carolina

Dr. Michael Heitzler traces the development of a unique section of South Carolina from the earliest land grants to the emergence of a modern city. His work is a major history, replete with an abundance of tables, graphs and maps. His chronicle describes the everyday trials and challenges of thousands of Goose Creekers and provides a valuable resource for those conducting genealogical research into many Lowcountry and South Carolina family names.

Anne Propst
President of the Berkeley County Historical Society

Mike Heitzler takes us on a fascinating trip through Goose Creek's long history by explaining the community's settlement, its two-hundred-year prosperity, its almost total disappearance and its revival one hundred years later. I was born in Berkeley County and have a lifelong love for my home, thus I consider Mike's extensive research into the cultural and social evolution of Goose Creek as a personal gift to me, and my family. It's an awesome read!

Elaine Morgan
Chief Executive Director of the Berkeley County Chamber of Commerce

Michael J. Heitzler has spent four years compiling his wonderful two-volume history of Goose Creek, a community that fundamentally shaped the early political, agricultural and social history of South Carolina. Using in-depth research and analysis, the author has crafted one of the state's finest local histories, which will be of great interest to both scholars and laymen.

W. Eric Emerson, PhD
Executive Director, South Carolina Historical Society

Goose Creek
A Definitive History
Volume One
Planters, Politicians and Patriots

Michael J. Heitzler

The History Press

Published by The History Press
Charleston, SC 29403
www.historypress.net

Front cover: This photograph shows the ruins of the Elms Plantation circa 1930. The photograph is in the *Johnson Scrapbook, Volume I. Courtesy of the South Carolina Historical Society*.

Back cover: "Raising my eyes ever and anon to look down that dark and silent Goose Creek Avenue, my thoughts would run ever upon olden stories..." *Courtesy of the South Carolina Historical Society*.

The photograph on the back cover shows the gate and avenue of oaks at the Oaks Plantation in Goose Creek, South Carolina, *c.* 1904. The photograph is among the photographic collections of the South Carolina Historical Society, Charleston, South Carolina.

The quotation on the title page is taken from *The Olden Time in South Carolina* by Elizabeth A. Poyas.

First published 2005
Second printing 2010
Third printing 2015

Manufactured in the United States

ISBN 1.59629.055.2
ISBN-13 978.1.59629.055.6

Library of Congress Cataloging-in-Publication Data

Heitzler, Michael J. (Michael James), 1947-
Goose Creek, South Carolina : a definitive history 1670-2003 / Michael J. Heitzler ; edited by Nancy Paul Kirchner.
p. cm.
Includes bibliographical references (p.) and index.
ISBN 1-59629-055-2 (alk. paper)
1. Goose Creek (S.C.)--History. I. Kirchner, Nancy Paul. II. Title.
F279.G66H447 2005
975.7'91--dc22
2005014513

***Facing and following page*: *Mr. Manigault's Seat at Goose Creek, 1802,* from *A Charleston Sketchbook, 1796–1806,* by Charles Fraser. *Courtesy of Mrs. Caroline Cohen*.**

To you, my neighbors, across town and near,
Who I have known forever, or have yet to meet.
All of you bring truth to the old axiom,
"There's no place like home!"

Contents

Acknowledgements and Credits

THIS WORK WOULD HAVE BEEN impossible without the assistance and encouragement of many who shared my love and enthusiasm for Goose Creek. I appreciate the kindness of Goose Creek City Council for authorizing municipal staff to provide assistance copying and acquiring many municipal documents for research. I appreciate the scrutiny of city councilman Mark Phillips who edited some of the final draft. His analytical training as an engineer kept the document logical and simple throughout. Many friends, as well as colleagues at Westview Elementary School read sections of the manuscript and provided editorial suggestions. No assistance has gone unappreciated.

I thank John Tienken, chief executive officer and Jerry Squires, reproduction specialist of the South Carolina Public Service Authority (Santee Cooper) for digitizing the Henry A.M. Smith plats to facilitate their use in several of the chapters. I also thank Terrence Larimer, natural resource supervisor for the Naval Weapons Station in Charleston for his kindness and patience while showing me many historical relics in the restricted sections of the military property.

I also acknowledge the kindness and skilled assistance of Eric Emerson, PhD, executive director of the South Carolina Historical Society, as well as Mike Coker and other helpful and enthusiastic members of that organization. Additionally, I thank the staff of the South Carolina Department of Archives and History, and the United States Library of Congress for their assistance in searching and granting permission to reproduce illustrations, plats, maps, photographs and drawings. I also thank the skilled personnel at the Goose Creek and Moncks Corner branches of the Berkeley County Library and the South Carolina Room of the Charleston County Library for their patience and kindness.

My appreciation extends to Frances Etling Roberson for searching her private collection of family photographs and permitting me to use several of them. I also thank Mrs. Caroline Cohen for graciously allowing me to use a copy of a selected Charles Fraser art piece.

I offer my sincerest gratitude to Linda Sineath, dear friend and colleague, who sat by my side for dozens of hours and consistently found ways to improve the English sentence. What we sowed during those hours of toil heaped a bounty upon the content of this book and my understanding of friendship.

Finally, I thank Nancy Paul Kirchner for editing the book. She teaches English at the College of Charleston. As an enthusiastic editor, she worked with a well-stocked toolbox and the experience to aptly employ each instrument. That she did without exception. She brought clarity to the Goose Creek story and prepared the end product for public scrutiny.

List of Illustrations

Facsimiles

Drawings/Paintings

Maps

Map 4.1: The 1839 *Burr Map* shows the waterways and wetlands in the eastern part of the St. James, Goose Creek Parish.
Map 6.1: This map is an enhanced version of Mills' Atlas of 1825. The Goose Creek Road is shown as it continued northwest from Charleston.
Map 6.2: The partial map shows the section of the Walker and Abernethie, 1787 map that describes the road from Charleston to the Goose Creek Bridge.
Map 6.3: The partial map shows the section of the Walker and Abernethie map that describes the road to the Goose Creek Bridge and from the bridge to Red Bank Road.
Map 6.4: This map is an enhanced section of Mills' Atlas, 1825 showing the road system and selected plantations on the north side of Goose Creek, on Foster Creek and the Cooper River.
Map 6.5: The map describes the road from Goose Creek toward Moncks Corner in 1787.
Map 6.6: The Mills' Atlas of 1825 map has been enhanced for this publication to show the location of selected plantations on Back River and its headwaters.
Map 6.7: The map shows a section of the Mills' 1825 Atlas of the central part of the St. James, Goose Creek Parish.
Map 6.8: The map shows a section of the Mills' 1825 Atlas of the upper part of the St. James, Goose Creek Parish.
Map 7.1: This is a segment of a *Map Showing the Plantations along the Cooper River as they were in the year 1842.*
Map 7.2: William Henry Johnson drew a map from his collection of plats. A section of the map shown here describes some of the estates on the Neck and on the south side of Goose Creek.
Map 7.3: The partial map shows Sineath Station on the South Carolina Railroad near Windsor Hill.
Map 7.4: The partial map shows "Sineath's" on the public road.
Map 7.5: William Henry Johnson drew a map from his collection of plats.

Photographs

Photograph 4.1: The photograph shows a water reserve pond.
Photograph 6.1: The photograph shows a family fishing the water reserve at Ingleside (The Hayes).
Photograph 6.2: The photograph shows the Hilton House in Sandridge.
Photograph 7.1: The photograph shows the main house at the Marsh Land Plantation. John Ball, a wealthy rice planter, built it in 1810.
Photograph. 7.2: The photograph shows the Otranto clubhouse circa 1924.
Photograph 7.3: The photograph shows the double tub indigo vat located at the entrance to Mobay Industry at Bushy Park.
Photograph 7.4: The 1930 photograph shows the gravestone of Lamb Stevens.
Photograph 7.5: The photograph shows the Hayes Plantation situated on the headwaters of Goose Creek.
Photograph 7.6: The photograph shows Francis Holmes in his study at the Ingleside's main house.
Photograph 7.7: The photograph shows John Parker's burial monument at the Hayes Plantation.
Photograph 7.8: The photograph shows the Hayes ruins in April 2003.
Photograph 7.9: The photograph shows the ruins of the Elms Plantation circa 1930.
Photograph 7.10: The photograph shows the ruins of the Capital Brick Mansion at Crowfield as it appeared in the 1930s.

Plats

Plat 4.6: This plat is a tracing of a section of a plat of Yeamans Hall drawn by John Purcell from a 1786 survey.
Plat 4.7: The plat shows John C. Ball's White Hall Plantation on the headwaters of Back River as surveyed by Joseph Purcell in 1789.
Plat 4.8: The plat was drawn from the archaeological study conducted by Brockington and Associates Inc. in 1998 and 1999.
Plat 6.1: The partial plat shows the St. James, Goose Creek Church, Parsonage and Glebe.
Plat 6.2: The plat represents 109 acres of land conveyed by William Laughton Smith to Lewis Breaker at the 18-Mile House in February 1810.
Plat 6.3: The partial plat shows the Moncks Corner Road at the chapel and 23-Mile House.
Plat 6.4: The partial plat shows lands in the upper Back River section of the Goose Creek Parish.
Plat 6.5: The plat shows the plan of five hundred acres near Black Tom Bay owned by Captain Richard Gough.
Plat 7.1: The plat shows the Retreat Plantation when James Wright owned it in 1758.
Plat 7.2: The plat shows land sold to the United States government for the Charleston Navy Yard.
Plat 7.3: The partial plat is not dated but it shows that the number of acres in each parcel of Oak Grove Plantation amounted to 1,079 acres.
Plat 7.4: The partial plat shows a section of Yeamans Hall Plantation.
Plat 7.5: The plat shows Yeamans Hall Plantation as surveyed by "J.P.," probably Joseph Purcell, in 1786.
Plat 7.6: The plat shows lands south of Goose Creek and near the Neck.
Plat 7.7: The partial plat shows Cannon's "Settlement" near the public road to Goose Creek.
Plat 7.8: The partial plat drawn from a survey made in 1805 describes the estate of Cyprian Bigelow.
Plat 7.9: The partial plat was made from a survey conducted in 1805 for the estate of Cyprian Bigelow.
Plat 7.10: John Purcell drew the partial plat from a 1785 survey.
Plat 7.11: Henry A.M. Smith traced the Brick House plat from the original.
Plat 7.12: A partial plat of the Elms was drawn from a survey of 925 acres in 1796.
Plat 7.13: The plat of Bloomfield Plantation was surveyed and drawn in 1784 by John Fenwick.
Plat 7.14: The partial plat shows the Oaks Plantation as drawn from a survey made in 1817 by William Brailsford.
Plat 7.15: The plat describes the eight hundred-acre plantation named Mt. Pleasant as drawn by Joseph Purcell in 1790.
Plat 7.16: The partial plat was made from three surveys to show the accumulation of acreage that made up "Ravenel's" estate in 1857.
Plat 7.17: The partial plat shows the eight- to ten-acre tract on the Cooper River called Red Bank Landing.
Plat 7.18: The partial plat was drawn from a survey made in 1797 by John Diamond. The plat shows 662 acres of land called Red Bank at the confluence of the Cooper and Back Rivers.
Plat 7.19: The partial plat shows the southern lands owned by the Tennents.
Plat 7.20: The partial plat shows an "Old Brick Works," "Brick Yard" and "Landing" at Parnassus on Back River.

Tables

Table 4.2: The table is entitled *Some Typical Costs of Establishing a Plantation in Carolina, 1775.*
Table 4.3: The table is entitled *Comparative Private Wealth in 1774.*
Table 4.4: The table compares the percent of slave holdings in the Goose Creek Parish for the years 1745 and 1790 and gives the differences.
Table 4.5: The table is entitled *Top Ten Charleston Exports, 1747-1748.* Michael Trinkley adapted the table in 1995.
Table 4.6: The table lists some Goose Creek medical doctors during the plantation era.
Table 5.1: The table shows the representation assigned to each parish according to the 1721 Election Act as well as the number of representatives according to the population. The table also lists the number of acres per parish, the average number of acres per taxpayer, the number of slaves in the parish and the number of taxpayers in each parish.
Table 5.2: The table shows the number of acres of land and slaves owned in each parish in 1722.
Table 6.1: The table shows the 1790 *Census Enumeration Report* for St. James, Goose Creek Parish in the order of visitation.
Table 6.2: The table shows the households residing on the Neck in 1790.
Table 6.3: The table shows heads of households identified with the south side of Goose Creek in 1790.
Table 6.4: The table shows the heads of households residing on the North Side of Goose Creek.
Table 6.5: The table shows the heads of households identified with Cooper River.
Table 6.6: The table shows the heads of households residing in the Foster Creek neighborhood in 1790.
Table 6.7: The table shows the heads of households identified with Back River in 1790.
Table 6.8: The table shows the landowners in Wassamasaw between the years 1775 and 1789 that were not included on the 1790 census.
Table 6.9: The table shows the heads of households listed on the 1790 census that were identified with Wassamasaw.
Table 6.10: The table shows the names of landowners in the Upper Parish who owned land from 1775 to 1788 according to the records in the South Carolina Department of Archives and History but did not appear on the 1790 Census.
Table 6.11: The table shows the heads of households identified with the Upper Parish in 1790.
Table 6.12: The table shows the heads of households listed on the 1790 St. James, Goose Creek census that were not associated with a specific neighborhood within the parish.
Table 6.13: The table shows a summary of findings of all eight neighborhoods in St. James, Goose Creek Parish in 1790.
Table 7.1: The table lists eighty-three estates in the respective Goose Creek neighborhoods with the total shown for each neighborhood.

Preface

Man's creative struggle, his search for wisdom and truth, is a love story.

Iris Murdoch (1919–1999).

Here is Volume One of the two-volume updated edition to *Historic Goose Creek, South Carolina 1670–1980*. I published the first edition in 1983 to satisfy my curiosity about a community to which I had recently arrived and to provide orientation for thousands of new residents swelling the population of the burgeoning City of Goose Creek. Twenty years later, I felt compelled to revisit the subject that had changed dramatically during the intervening two decades. When I started the rewriting process, I thought I would simply add a chapter or two to explain the most recent decades and change the title to show the additions. But I found early in the rewriting process that this simple plan would not succeed because the work on the second edition required a different writing approach than planned, resulting in a project that was much more comprehensive than anticipated. Early in the writing, the project broadened. First, I found errors and omissions in the first edition that needed to be corrected. Additionally, I discovered that important research had been completed during the last twenty years and that some of the findings needed to be included in the second edition of the Goose Creek story. Recently published and unpublished accountings of changes in wealth, slave life, Native American culture, plantation society and land ownership by small farmers could add valuable insights into the local story and to the broader history of the state. Furthermore, land deeds and titles had been indexed during the last two decades for convenient and more thorough referencing. These sources provided important information that was more accessible than before and could not be ignored. Also, the 1920 and 1930 decennial enumeration census became available for public viewing and held many familiar family and place names and information that needed to be included in the second edition.

Remarkably, during the last twenty years, in compliance with the Coastal Zone Management Acts of 1972 and 1976, there have been more than sixty archaeological studies conducted on sites within or near the current city limits of Goose Creek. These studies supplied new information, as well as fresh interpretations to previously discovered data. Brockington and Associates Incorporated conducted archaeological testing at the Naval Weapons Station in the City of Goose Creek in 1998 and 1999. As a result of their work, Brockington suggested that three sites be recommended to the National Register of Historic Places and that the Parnassus Plantation Historic District be established to protect those locations. They also proposed that six other sites be recommended to the National Register of Historic Places as contributing elements to the Foster Creek Discontiguous Historic District. The findings from this archaeological work added to the understanding of the early brick and indigo industries in Goose Creek, in addition to the important rice culture. Such valuable new information was included in *Goose Creek, South Carolina: A Definitive History, Volume One, Planters, Politicians and Patirots,* to help explain the components of early industry and agriculture and the accumulation of wealth.

As the project grew, I found that improved technology greatly simplified data gathering and the processing and compiling of information into understandable chapters that heretofore would have required exhausting searches. Today, databases that are widely accessible by way of the Internet allow researchers to pour over records from the comfort of home computers. The South Carolina Historical Society has greatly expanded its holdings and improved access to them by way of the Internet during the last twenty years, as have some libraries. The South Carolina Department of Archives and History comprised an index of almost three hundred thousand documents now available online. This index simplified the search for Goose Creek documentations of property holdings and grants, petitions of various commissions and findings of a multitude of legal proceedings. Assistance from the trained researchers and staff members at libraries and other depositories were readily available via e-mail saving hundreds of hours searching false leads. Additionally, digital cameras and scanners allowed images to be conveniently saved and carefully studied, and e-mail contacts with historical scholars far and near made the project enjoyable and much less isolated, as was the case twenty years ago when I searched information for the first edition.

Although technology was helpful, the second edition became more complicated as the project grew. Many value judgments were required to determine what was to be included or left out of the story. History is never complete and can never be made so, but there is always the need to include all that is meaningful, useful and helpful to the interpretation of the data. The task of composing the first book, covering the years 1670 to 1980, began by collecting the secondary information that was widely scattered throughout the Lowcountry and the state, and assembling lost, misplaced or disjointed data and documents and putting them together to tell the story. The majority of the information in the first edition was derived from secondary sources augmented with data from census lists, commission reports and personal stories. The first undertaking required finding and interviewing the few remaining Goose Creekers who lived in the titled location near the dawn of the last century. Those seniors provided scattered bits and pieces of oral history that helped to explain the past one hundred years. In contrast, research for *Goose Creek, South Carolina: A Definitive History,* focused almost entirely on finding and interpreting volumes of primary data from public and private collections to uncover trends and truths about the full 333-year span. The large volumes of primary statistics augmented by a large collection of private papers resulted in a local history that contributes much to the story of South Carolina and the nation as a whole.

Adding to the challenges of writing this history were the complications caused by my personal involvement in the most recent three decades. I have lived over thirty-five years in the titled location and have known many of the historical personalities. Most of those who contributed to the drama during the second half of the twentieth century were still living and sometimes offered conflicting interpretations of events. Also, a concerted effort was required to consider readers' feelings about families and friends without adulterating the truth that is essential to the integrity of the second edition. In addition, how was I to treat myself in the last chapters of this saga? Since 1976, I have been fortunate to play a role in the guiding and shaping of Goose Creek as a member of city council and as the mayor. I was challenged to find the appropriate way to write about myself. My sense of history as science and truth prevailed. This sense required that I put myself in the last chapters as accurately as I could despite my inevitable biases. History has always been recorded from the point of view of writers within the context of their culture and value system. It seems the best that writers can do is be true to themselves and risk pitfalls and pratfalls that come whenever they pen their thoughts to published words.

I finished researching *Goose Creek, South Carolina: A Definitive History* by perusing twenty years of *The Goose Creek Gazette*'s weekly newspaper publications for general ideas as to what was important to readers during those decades. The other daily and weekly publications were studied, as well as nearly one thousand city council meetings' minutes and scores of official publications. I found this to be a task of synthesizing data into trends or focusing segments to bring clarity and meaning. It was especially rewarding to reread the weekly editorials written by Joyce Odum, *The Goose Creek Gazette*'s founder. Joyce spoke to us through her weekly column as if she was talking over a cup of coffee or chatting at the Bi-Lo produce aisle. She wrote from her heart about what was important at that time, and her editorials were needed to understand the optimism of the young city and to make the second edition more human and enjoyable.

When I attempted to discover Goose Creek for the first edition, I was thrilled to find plantation ruins and old land grants or letters from the colonial schoolteachers, but I was also careful not to give more meaning to discoveries than was due. Still those discoveries were not personal in as much as I never visited a living plantation nor spoke to any of the first settlers to know the full breadth of their lives. In contrast, the second edition differs from the first because it is personal in many ways. In the last decades, I found features that made Goose Creek intimate to me and perhaps to others as well. I have learned more about its summer nights, such as the "thinning of the fireflies." There are far fewer fireflies now than twenty years ago, which begs the question whether we have done something dreadfully wrong to the delicate ecological system that we all depend upon. On those same summer evenings, I could hear homerun cheers from Felkel Baseball Field more than a mile away, but in recent years, the cheers have been muffled by additional sounds of traffic and sirens on those sultry nights. In the spring, the killdeer still hide their eggs in plain view, if you know where to look, and recently I have seen geese in Goose Creek for the first time in memory, but sadly, the otter family that lived near my home has been gone for many years. I have learned to love the rumble of the nearby trains, and I would sleep less soundly if somehow the engines and wheels stopped passing near. Years ago, I found a wild berry patch near that same track. I still go to it and know quite well when the berries are ready for picking. I know I am not alone in caring about the many things big and small that make Goose Creek a uniquely personal place that many call home.

Unlike the city of Charleston, Goose Creek's charming neighbor, the City of Goose Creek has done little to share its long and rich history with residents and visitors. A few contemporary indicators tell some details of the past. For example, many of today's local roads share names with the colonial era, and nineteenth century routes can be easily traced on current roadways. Also a modern power line easement follows a colonial road route (See appendix 2 for past and present road routes). There are historical markers that give some information about three of the state's oldest sites: Medway House, the St. James, Goose Creek Church and the Otranto Plantation (see appendix 3 for the text of the historical markers). In addition, there are numerous cemeteries with descriptive and informative stone markers. There is a heavy granite marker indicating the site of an ancient French Church and there are ruins of colonial homes, brick kilns, indigo vats and garden walls. There are durable impressions discernable on aerial photographs that were left in the landscape by black and white laborers. Free and enslaved men and women worked hundreds of thousands of man-hours to convert dense forests, swamps and marshes into productive lands. There is also a complete original brick indigo vat available for public viewing. Sections of this research record and explain the cemetery stones and memorials, as well as the messages and locations of historical markers. Some chapters show and describe archaeological relics and ruins and explain their importance to the lives of Goose Creekers, but despite the importance of my work, this book is merely one of many initiatives needed to adequately tell the story.

Unfortunately, there has been little effort to present the historical relics in a useful manner. Therefore, Goose Creek's rich history has remained well hidden. Little has been done to preserve the history of black Carolina and even less to preserve the rich history of Goose Creek African Americans. Widespread illiteracy among Goose Creek blacks and the failure on the part of the literate Goose Creek whites to record day-to-day events have resulted in a shortage of information for African American Goose Creekers. Little physical evidence of the rural history remains and the older residents are passing from this world, taking with them countless stories of old Goose Creek in the early twentieth century.

Tourism and marketing studies consistently find that heritage and history attract visitors, homebuyers and investors and impact the perceptions of the community. Also, a *Southern Living* magazine survey found that historic sites were the first interests of readers when they toured, and a thorough study conducted for the South Carolina Department of Parks, Recreation and Tourism found that the most important criteria for visitors to South Carolina included interests in architecture and history.[1] Unfortunately, few understand the rich and interesting history of Goose Creek.

Goose Creekers miss opportunities to show their history to residents and visitors. We should develop strategies that take advantage of this untapped resource, such as the establishment of an historic commission composed of interested citizens to continue the research begun by this book because so much remains to be discovered, organized and shared. The commission could oversee the maintenance of a historic Web site and other media releases recalling significant Goose Creek events and contributions. The commission could design and erect historic markers indicating to tourists and residents that they are in a historically important part of South Carolina and the United States. Such strategies could result in a cost effective basis for improved public relations that emphasizes conservation and protection of historic resources. Also, initiatives to share and explain the community's long and rich heritage could be a way of finding a marketable brand name at a low cost. *Historic Goose Creek* could be that brand name. The city and the greater Goose Creek community should seize opportunities to improve the livability of the residential and commercial areas, and the city should develop strategic initiatives for enjoying local history and reaping the benefits that come with it.

Preface

Thus, this two-volume updated edition, entitled *Goose Creek, South Carolina: A Definitive History*, is merely one of many initiatives needed to help Goose Creekers and others understand, appreciate and benefit from the community's long and interesting past. Volume One of this work tells the story of the Europeans and Africans who settled in the wilderness and created successful plantations from the forests and wetlands of a small section of South Carolina. Volume Two traces the economic, social, and political systems that depended upon the bounty from approximately six-dozen large estates during the heady colonial era, and then relied upon increasingly meager returns from lands that eventually divided into more than eight hundred small farms by the advent of the twentieth century. Volume Two also explains the suburbanization of those small farms and the emergence of a dynamic municipality on the same lands that nourished Goose Creekers since the seventeenth century. Both volumes of this story are vital to the understanding of one of the most intriguing sections of the United States, but to be fully successful, this book must be truthful and fair to all participants in Goose Creek's past, present and future. With this in mind, I can only hope that the truth will prevail and that the text will pass the test of scrupulous readers. Moreover, I hope this updated and definitive history will help make Goose Creek more complete by keeping the residents and visitors better informed and inspire those who build and protect this place today and tomorrow. But mostly this work is a labor of love.

Chapter I
The Name and Place
1670–2003

Goose Creek is a name, a place and a destination with a story to tell. The City of Goose Creek takes its name from one of the oldest places in South Carolina and shares that name with no other municipality in the United States. According to the United States Mapping Service, there are dozens of places named Goose Creek in the United States but only one incorporated city or town (See appendix 4 for a listing of ninety places named Goose Creek). "Just a little bit and you're in the country," observed Goose Creek resident A.L. Collier during an interview with the *Charleston Evening Post* in 1978. Residents have long enjoyed the semi-rural character of their community, the "country" sounding name and the stretches of wetlands and forests that separate it from the surrounding suburban areas, but the population has doubled since Mr. Collier's remark and Goose Creek remains a country town in name only.

The City of Goose Creek is a suburban community located in the southernmost section of Berkeley County, South Carolina. Thirty years ago, it was nestled among vast acreages of undeveloped swamp, forests and cropland. Those open spaces gave the community a semi-rural character but also supplied the developmental resources that accommodated rapid population growth of the greater Charleston area. Since 1960, Goose Creek has been one of the fastest growing municipalities in South Carolina.[2] The area's population burgeoned as a result of the spread of urbanization and industrial development that radiated from Charleston, and from the preference of many wanting to live in a suburban or semi-rural environment. According to a population and economic survey conducted in 1975 by the Berkeley, Charleston and Dorchester Regional Planning Council, Goose Creek was expected to rapidly add to its population as the urbanization process continued, and so it did during the last three decades. Today more than 30,000 people call the City of Goose Creek home.

Today, as shown on Table 1.1, Goose Creek is the eleventh most populous city in South Carolina and its thirty-two square miles make it the sixth largest incorporated area in the state. Unfortunately, the origin of the name has been lost. The search for the original name of the creek and the source of its present name uncovered no documented origins. There are theories that attempt to explain the origin and many interesting speculations, but no proof. Thus, after centuries, the name keeps its mysterious charm.

Names of towns and cities are interesting to geographers and historians. Names not only offer an introduction to regional investigations, but they can also provide insights into the history of settlements, migration patterns, heritage and landscape elements. Names of places in South Carolina

Table 1.1

Rank	Name of City	Population	Number of Square Miles	Percentage Change in Population 1990–2000
1	Columbia	116,278	128	+19%
2	Charleston	96,650	114	+20%
3	North Charleston	79,641	62	+13%
4	Greenville	56,002	26	-4%
5	Rock Hill	49,765	31	+20%
6	Mount Pleasant	47,609	50	+58%
7	Spartanburg	39,673	19	-9%
8	Sumter	39,643	27	-8%
9	Hilton Head	33,862	56	+43%
10	Florence	30,248	18	+1%
11	**Goose Creek**	**29,208**	**32**	**+18%**
12	Summerville	27,752	15	+23%
13	Anderson	25,514	14	-3%
14	Aiken	25,337	16	+28%
15	Myrtle Beach	22,759	17	-8%

such as DeKalb, Marion and Sumter have originated from personalities in the state's military history. Names such as 10-Mile, Great Falls, Little Mountain and Myrtle Beach indicate type of terrain or location. The name "Goose Creek" provides little indication of the community history except the physical location of a creek, which meanders through the area until it flows into the Cooper River. There are similar names in South Carolina. Goose Mash is located near the Society Hill Bridge along the Pee Dee River and Gooseplatter Creek is located near the Aiken County line.[3] Also a plat drawn from a survey made in 1856 shows a creek named "Goose Creek" in the old Abbeville District.[4] There are other interesting place names located near Goose Creek. Daisy is a local name given to a swamp located in the northwest corner of Goose Creek near the junction of U.S. Highway 176 and State Highway 45. This swamp derived its name from the Deas family who owned Thorogood, Mt. Holly and other plantations in that area during the colonial era. "Daisy" is simply the corruption of the name "Deas."[5] Groomsville, located north of Goose Creek near the junction of State Highways 9 and 375, is one of the oldest known communities in Berkeley County with a family name as its designation. The name is derived from the Grooms family who lived and farmed in the area. Reference to this community is found in Joseph I. Waring's history of St. James, Goose Creek Church. The vestry of St. James established a school there in 1828. In addition there is Groomsville Road, a local name given to State Highway 9, between U.S. Highway 52 and 17-A.[6]

Strawberry, a small community situated where old State Highway 52 crosses the Atlantic Coastline Railroad, is also located north of Goose Creek. This community was situated on a road leading to an important crossing of the nearby Cooper River called Strawberry Ferry, from which it takes its name. The ferry took its name from Strawberry Plantation, owned by John C. Ball located at the ferry crossing. Strawberry appears on early maps as a station on the Atlantic Coastline Railroad. As late as 1940, a railroad station, post office, sawmill, two stores and five houses were located at Strawberry. The sawmill, post office and the railroad station went out of business in the 1940s.[7]

Map 1.1 This map shows Berkeley County in the 1895 South Carolina Atlas published by the Rand McNally Company. Rail stops at Woodstock, Ladson, Otranto, Mt. Holly and Strawberry are noted in the St. James, Goose Creek Parish.

Mount Holly takes its name from Mount Holly Plantation. The village began as a railway stop on the Atlantic Coastline Railroad during the early nineteenth century. There was a post office until 1990, but the sawmill has been gone for decades and the last general store closed in the early 1980s. Only a few homes and outbuildings remain. Mount Holly, located at the intersection of State Highway 45 (Old Mt. Holly Road) and U.S. Highway 52 (Goose Creek Boulevard) is currently within the incorporated limits of the City of Goose Creek. Map 1.1 shows the rail stops in Berkeley County in 1895. These stations were flag stops that required a wave of a flag to halt the train. By the turn of the twentieth century, the villages near these rail stops had supplanted Goose Creek, as a place. The name "Goose Creek," which once identified the most prosperous neighborhood in the British Colonies, appeared nowhere on the South Carolina Atlas.

Casey (Cayce, Caice), the largest of several black communities once located in central Goose Creek, does not appear on the 1895 atlas. Some sources indicate that "Casey" was the name of a former slave who started a small religious assembly that eventually developed into a well-populated and important settlement. The name was shared with the Casey school, Casey Assembly Hall and Casey Church. The church was the last of the remaining structures, which unfortunately burned

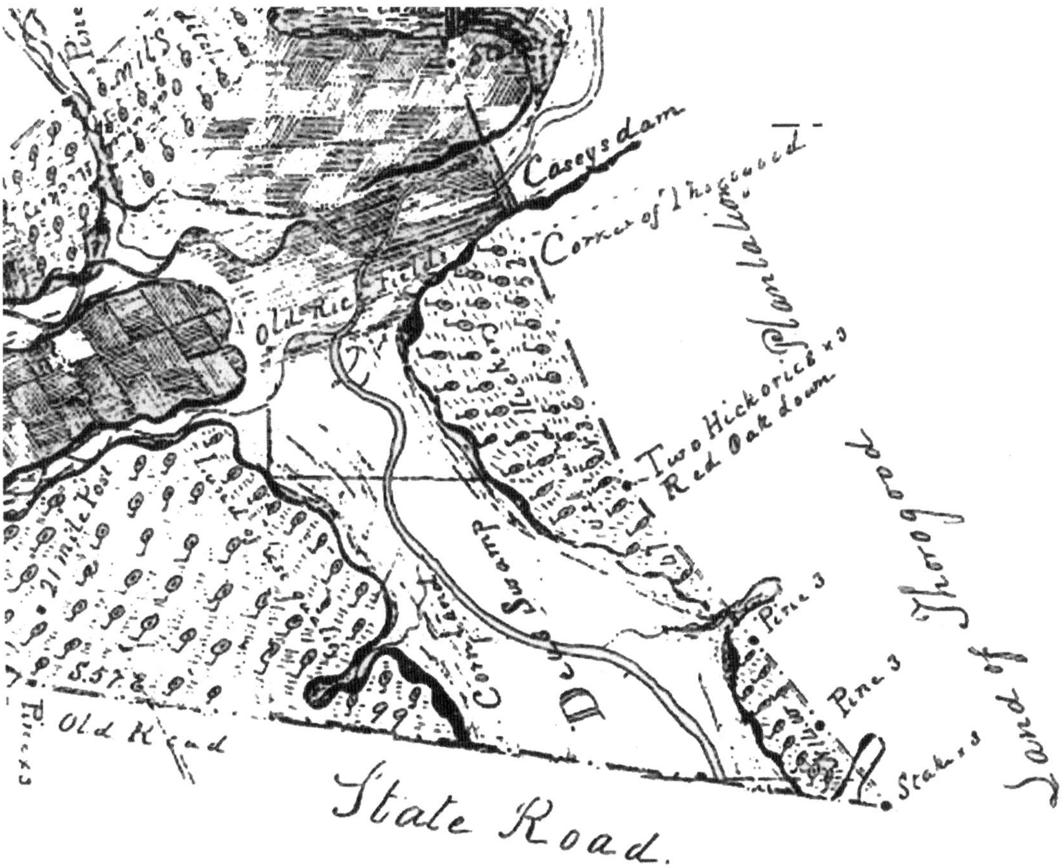

Plat 1.1 "Casey's Dam" is shown on this plat drawn from a survey made by Sam W. Joyner in 1850. The plat is included with the Hutchinson Papers among the collections of the South Carolina Historical Society.

to the ground in 1977. "Casey's Dam" appears in the upper right quadrant of an 1850 plat of Old Barn Plantation. The notation of the dam documents the presence of the name in the area prior to the Civil War. Plat 1.1 shows Casey's Dam on the plat of Old Barn Plantation.

"Wassamasaw" is another interesting local name. Wassamasaw Swamp, located in the central section of the St. James, Goose Creek Parish, was named by the native tribe of that area and was the site of one of the St. James, Goose Creek Church vestry schools. The native meaning of the word Wassamasaw is "connecting water."[8] This "connecting water" is a swamp beginning at Black Tom Bay near Lake Moultrie that flows into Cypress Swamp and then merges with the upper waters of the Ashley River.

There are a number of place names connected with outstanding personalities in the local history. Villeponteaux Branch is a small body of water that flows into Back River and is named for Zachariah Villeponteaux, a wealthy Huguenot vestryman of St. James, Goose Creek Church. He became well known for the gray brick he made at his Parnassus Plantation on Back River. Chicken Creek is one of several creeks flowing into the upper reaches of Back River. It was named for the Chicken family who owned the plantation lands on those headwaters. One member of the family, George Chicken was the captain of the Goose Creek militia and a commissioner of the Indian trade during the early colonial period.

Names of the various neighborhoods in contemporary Goose Creek also have an interesting history. Some are merely advertising phrases that enhance the marketability of the site, such as Boulder Bluff, Beverly Hills, Forest Lawn and Greenview Acres but others can be traced to specific origins. The Oaks residential area was named for the old Middleton Plantation with its stately avenue of oaks. Menriv Park is a portmanteau word formed from the name of U.S. Representative L. Mendel Rivers. Sedgefield may have been named for a field of coarse grass common in that area. There is also Pineview Terrace with many pines but no terrace. Camelot Village is named for King Arthur's legendary castle. Names of other subdivisions, such as Deerfield and Foxborough connote rural settings like hunting areas. A colonial landowner's name is used for Gibbes Forest subdivision. Crowfield, Bloomfield and Bushy Park are names of former grand plantations. Place names in England have been borrowed, as evidenced by Stratford Forest and Bedford Chase.

The origin of the name "Goose Creek" is difficult to ascertain. The Etiwan, Sewee and Wando Indians who inhabited the lands certainly had one or more names for the creek but the native name for Goose Creek has never been satisfactorily determined. The early European settlers ignored most of the Native American place names and immediately supplanted them with English or French names borrowed from places or influential leaders at home or abroad. The Native American name for Goose Creek was supplanted almost immediately after the first European settlement, making it necessary to determine the original name through deduction.

The records indicate that only once did the Europeans give a Native American name directly to any part of Goose Creek. An early record refers to the water as "Adthan Creek." At the 1678 grand council meeting, just eight years after the earliest Charleston settlement, a resolution stated that Mr. Edward Middleton would "take up his great lott [sic] of land on the upper part of Adthan Creek…"[9] Judge Henry A.M. Smith, one-time president of the South Carolina Historical Society, investigated the word "Adthan" used in the resolution. After examining the original manuscript, he interpreted the spelling as "Adthau" not "Adthan." Words ending with consonants referring to water are very rare among coastal Indian names. The endings "e," "ee," "au" and "aw" could have been the original intention when recorded in the grand council journal. The suffix "e" or "ee" among the coastal Indian languages indicated a river or body of water. Some examples are Pee Dee, Combahee, Santee, Congaree and Wateree. The local natives called Foster Creek, "Appeebee." The creek was later named after John Foster who settled on the banks of that waterway.[10]

Another Native American name for Goose Creek may be found in land warrants for Yeshoe, now called Otranto Plantation. Arthur Middleton came to Carolina with his brother, Edward, in 1678 and received a warrant for 1,780 acres of land, located at the head of Yeamans Creek, now called Goose Creek.[11] In 1682 he married Mary Smith, widow of John Smith, the owner of Booshoo Plantation on the Ashley River. According to the marriage settlement Arthur Middleton conveyed property named "Yeshoe" to his intended wife:

> *Mrs. Mary Smith late wife of John Smith of Booshooe in Ashley River in this Province, Esq. Decd. And for her joynture the Plant'n on wch ye sd Arthur Middleton now lives nigh Goose Creek in ye province afsd called Yeshoe containing 1780 acres…with ten Negroes.*[12]

The name Yeshoe, like Booshooe, is obviously a Native American name. The "e" suffix indicates a reference to water but whether it referred to the creek or the locality is uncertain. Thus it appears that there may have been two Native American names, Adthan (Adthau) and Yeshoe, one or both of which may have been the original name of Goose Creek.

The translation of these Indian names is nearly impossible to determine. There is no remaining vocabulary of the coastal tribes, but Oscar Lieber compiled a partial Catawba tribe vocabulary while working as a geologist for the state in 1856. With the help of his camp servant, a Catawba Indian, he compiled a vocabulary list of the Catawba language, which was a Siouan language.[13] They Siouan were closely allied with the coastal Indians, which increased the possibility of commonality of language and place names. Relying on this list, Judge Henry A.M. Smith delivered an address on the history of St. James, Goose Creek Church suggesting that the name "Goose Creek" referred to as Yeshoe or Yeowee by the coastal tribes, could be translated to "green water" from the Catawba word "ya-hah."[14] Although it was a mere supposition, this translation was tenable. Using the same analogy, it is also possible that Yeshoe meant snake creek, from the Catawba word "yah," meaning snake, referring to the snake-shape bends and curves of the creek's course. There is no Catawba word in Lieber's vocabulary resembling the name "Adthan," found in the early grant to Edward Middleton. Adthan may well have been an Etiwan or Wando word having no connection with the Catawba language. Contradictions to Judge Smith's reasoning are found in Eugene Waddell's *Indians of the South Carolina Lowcountry.* He claims that "Adthan" probably derives from the Woccan word "auhaun," which means, "goose." Woccan is a recognized Siouan dialect and he further states that the Catawba word for goose is "ahha," which may further strengthen his position. If the theory is correct, the Woccan word meaning goose is the origin of the name.[15]

In early grants the creek was known as Yeamans' Creek, the name of the second proprietary governor, Sir John Yeamans, whose estate lay along the creek near its junction with the Cooper River. A 1674 warrant was issued to Lady Margaret Yeamans and servants for 1,070 acres. This land was granted in 1675 and described as bordering upon "Yeamans his Creeke in Ittawan River."[16] Ittawan was the Indian name for the Cooper River, but it appears that Sir John Yeamans's name replaced the Indian name for Goose Creek. An estate with a plantation house built shortly after 1691, known as "Old Goose Creek," was established upon this site.[17] "Old Goose Creek" was used to refer to the mansion house and the estate until well into the nineteenth century. Mrs. Elizabeth Poyas wrote in her book, *Olden Time in Carolina* published in 1855, that Leize F.B. Lockwood married the house owner, George Henry Smith, in 1850. She renovated the old house and renamed it Yeamans Hall. The Yeamans Hall Plantation home and outbuildings were situated on a peninsula formed by a gooseneck turn in the creek. The creek bends and turns all along its course but at Yeamans Hall a full gooseneck turn occurs. At Yeamans Hall, the creek winds along a northern route until it turns and bends due south. This entire section of the creek was often referred to as the "neck." The original home on this site was called Goose Creek, as was the plantation in general. It is not clear whether the home and plantation were named after the creek or vice versa but some believe the creek was named because of the gooseneck turn in its course.

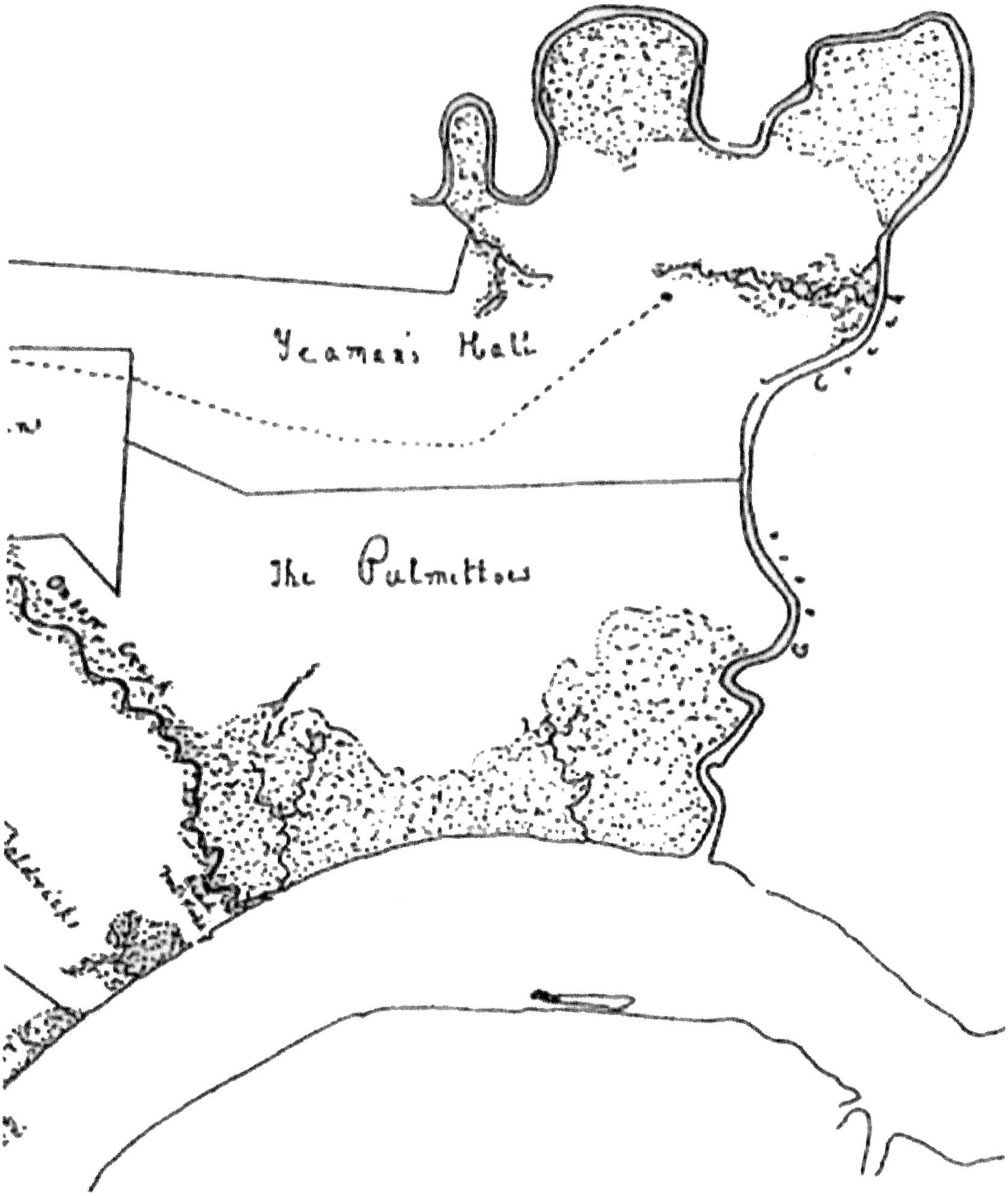

Plat 1.2 This partial plat shows The Palmettoes (Palmettos) Plantation and part of Yeamans Hall Plantation drawn by H.A.M. Smith. The gooseneck turn of Goose Creek provides the eastern and northern boundary of Yeamans Hall. The plat appeared in the 1918 edition of the *South Carolina Historical and Genealogical Magazine*.

Mrs. St. Julien Ravenel's book *Charleston: the Place and the People* credits the source of the name to the winding course and the gooseneck turn in the creek. This is a reasonable explanation, but there is no clear documentation for this claim except occasional reference to the "neck" in records of land on that winding section of the creek. A deed recorded for William Withers dated May 21/22, 1767, is one of several that refer to the "neck."[18] Wither's property was located on the north side of Goose Creek across the water from Yeamans Hall where the gooseneck turn occurs. By the nineteenth century it was common practice to refer to this location as "the neck."[19] Plat 1.2, drawn by Henry A.M. Smith and published in the *South Carolina Historical and Genealogical Magazine*, shows the Palmettos Plantation on the banks of the Cooper River and Yeamans Hall north of it. The drawing clearly illustrates the gooseneck turn in the creek from which the name Goose Creek may have been derived.

Maurice Mathews, an early settler, reported in 1680 the unsubstantiated claim that the name was derived from the abundance of geese on the creek. He reported that, "the creek is notted [sic] for plenty of game in the winter as goose, ducks..."[20] Other than Mathews's journal entry, there are no indications that geese were abundant at the time the area was given its present name. Additionally, the lists of foods comprising the native diet in the Goose Creek area did not include geese, and the early European settlers did not list geese as part of their diet nor include geese in cookbooks or recipes.

An untenable explanation for the source of the name relies on an early probate court record. The Reverend Robert Wilson, writing in 1922, stated that the source of the name came from "Goes" Creek, which he found in records describing a transfer of land on a creek called Goes Creek.[21] Reverend Wilson reasoned that the Dutch pronunciation of Goes Creek would be "Goose" Creek, hence the name. It is most likely that the word "Goes" in the record was simply a misspelling of the word "Goose." A look at almost any early document reveals multiple spellings for most words, depending on the writer's command of the language. One can easily find multiple spellings of "Goose Creek" in early records, such as Goes Creek, Goose Creeke, Goose Crick, Goos Creek and Goosegrick. In the 1695 will of Anthoine Prudhomme, a French spelling was applied: "L'Eglise Francoise qui assemble sur Gouscrick." Reverend Wilson's argument is furthered weakened by the fact that there were no probate courts in South Carolina and few German or Dutch settlers in Carolina in the 1670s when Goose Creek was given its present name.

The native name and the source of its present name may never be satisfactorily determined. Even the borders of the territory were vague at first. By 1700, all the lands on both sides of the creek, as far north as Back River and Foster's Creek and even to the headwaters of Goose Creek within five miles of the present town of Summerville, were settled. At that time this entire area was usually referred to as Goose Creek and the settlers were known as the "Goose Creek Men" or "Goose Creek people."

The Church Act of 1706 more clearly defined the territory, dividing the settled coastal region of South Carolina into nine parishes. The St. James, Goose Creek Parish was one of the original nine parishes.[22] Map 1.2 shows that the Goose Creek Parish was one of eighteen in 1768. Like the parishes of the established Church of England, the divisions were political, as well as ecclesiastical. The area was commonly referred to as the Parish of Goose Creek, but was properly known as the Parish of St. James, Goose Creek. The name "Goose Creek" was used to distinguish it from the Parish of St. James, Santee that was created the same year. As noted, the people residing along the

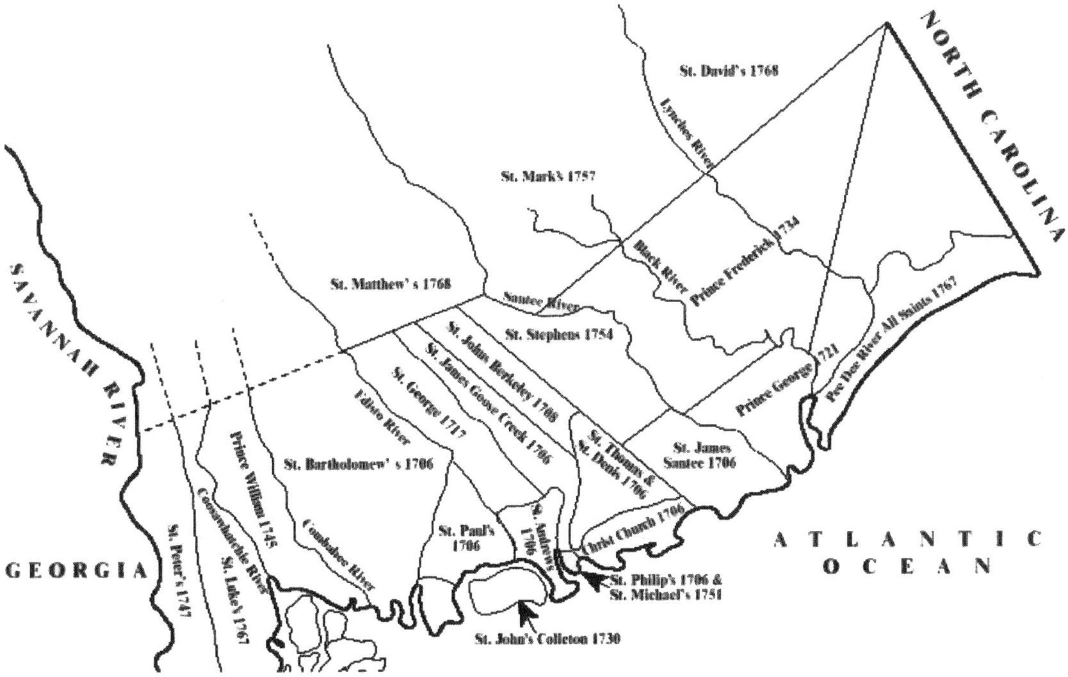

Map 1.2 This map shows the South Carolina parishes as they appeared in 1768. The map was borrowed from Edgar and Bailey, 1974.

four waterways in the eastern part of the parish (Goose Creek, Foster Creek, Back River and Cooper River) were generally known as the Goose Creek people, but the political boundaries forming the parish lines provided a political organization for those residing in the parish from the Cooper River to the western parish boundary at Four Hole Swamp. The parish lines were also used for enumeration every ten years beginning with the 1790 census and continuing until zip code districts were created in the 1960s. Table 1.2 gives population counts and percentages in the parish. The parish lines were adjusted by acts of the general assembly and the size of the Goose Creek Parish was reduced several times. These size reductions explain some of the fluctuation in population counts.

The original Parish of St. James, Goose Creek, as defined in the Church Act of 1706, included parts of what is North Charleston today, as well as all of the town of Hanahan. The parish reached east to the Cooper River and north to Back River. From the point where Back River branches from the Cooper River, the parish line follows Back River to its source. The line then runs west, from south of Pimlico and Fairlawn Barony, to the unsettled Carolina frontier. The southern boundary runs west-northwest parallel with the northern parish line to the frontier. The parallel boundary lines remain nearly eight miles apart. The Church Act did not define the western boundary, and at first the parish lines extended indefinitely into the western frontier.

In 1768, the province of South Carolina was divided into seven judicial districts.[23] This act made Berkeley County a part of Charleston District and created St. Matthews Parish, which set the western boundary of Goose Creek. This arrangement lasted with minor adjustments until 1799. One minor adjustment was made in 1786, when the line between St. Phillips, St.

Year	South Carolina Population	Charleston District Population	St. James, Goose Creek Parish Population	Parish Percent of State	Parish Percent of District
1790	249,073	66,985	2,787	1%	4%
1800	345,591	50,791	4,685	1%	9%
1810	415,115	63,179	3,354	.8%	5%
1820	490,309	80,212	5,499	1%	7%
1830	581,185	76,293	8,574	2%	11%
1840	594,398	82,661	4,131	.7%	5%
1850	668,507	72,805	3,435	.5%	5%
1860	703,708	70,100	5,867	.8%	8%
1870	705,606	88,863	7,783	1%	9%
1880	995,577	102,800	9,070	.9%	9%
Year	South Carolina Population	Berkeley County Population	St. James Goose Creek Parish Population	Parish Percent of State	Parish Percent of County
1890	1,151,149	55,428	Records destroyed by fire	Not available	Not available
1900	1,340,316	30,454	10,300	.8%	34%
1910	1,515,400	23,487	5,620	.3%	24%
1920	1,683,724	22,558	6,100	.4%	27%
1930	1,738,765	22,236	4,659	.3%	21%
1940	1,899,804	27,128	5,008	.3%	18%
1950	2,117,027	30,251	6,715	.3%	22%
Year	South Carolian Population	Berkeley County Population	Mount Holly District	Mount Holly District Percent of State	Mount Holly District Percent of County
1960	2,382,594	38,196	11,573*	.5%	30%
Year	South Carolina Population	Berkeley County Population	City of Goose Creek Population	City Percent of State	City Percent of County
1970	2,590,713	56,199	3,656	.1%	7%
1980	3,120,729	94,727	17,899	.6%	19%
1990	3,486,703	128,776	24,692	.7%	19%
2000	4,012,012	142,651	29,208	.7%	21%

Andrews and St. James, Goose Creek parishes was modified to follow redrawn property lines in the Charleston neck area.[24]

In 1799, the state was divided into districts, counties and parishes in accordance with another act, passed by the South Carolina general assembly a year earlier.[25] Under the provisions of this act, Charleston District was divided into the parishes of St. Michael; St. Philip; Christ Church; St. Thomas; St. Dennis; St. James, Santee; St. Stephen; St. John's Berkeley; St. James, Goose Creek; St. Andrew and St. John's, Colleton. By this act the parishes, including St. James, Goose Creek, were independent units regulating themselves under district law and sending representatives to the state legislature. At the time of the first federal census in 1790, a large western section of the parish had been placed in the newly established Orangeburg County, and by this action the parish was further reduced.

The population counts fluctuated widely for the census years of 1820, 1830 and 1840. Approximately 2,600 more slaves were counted in 1830 than in 1820 and almost 4,400 fewer slaves were counted ten years later in 1840. The parish lines remained unchanged during this period, and the records do not explain this unusual fluctuation in slave counts. The new state constitution, enacted after the Civil War, abolished the parish electoral system but parish lines continued to serve as census enumeration districts. The districts were referred to as "parish townships." In 1882, the act creating Berkeley County included part of St. James, Goose Creek. This new political division divided the old parish between Berkeley and Charleston Counties. The southern parish line was designated from the mouth of the confluence of Goose Creek with the Cooper River to a point on the Ashley River at the Colleton County line. This new designation placed a significant eastern section of the parish into Charleston County, including all lands east of Remount Road. In 1896, the area of Berkeley County was again reduced in size by cutting off another small portion of the former St. James, Goose Creek Parish.[26] This placed the entire town of Summerville outside the parish. By the same act, Orangeburg County acquired more sections of the western part of the Goose Creek Parish.[27] A year later, Dorchester County was created, taking Summerville and other sections in the vicinity.

The 1910 census excluded all of the area in the newly designated Orangeburg boundary from the Goose Creek count, including Holly Hill and Peck's Town. These new census zones left 194 families east of Dean's Swamp to be counted in the Goose Creek Parish. The same census also excluded Lincolnville and parts of Ladson from the St. James, Goose Creek Parish. The old St. James, Goose Creek Parish was again divided politically in 1921. That act moved more territory to Charleston County. A line was drawn at the intersection of Charleston and Berkeley Counties where the Atlantic Coastline Railroad crosses Remount Road today. The division line followed the railroad north to the waters of Goose Creek at the Highway 52 Bridge. At the bridge, the line follows the waters westward to the Dorchester County line. The total parish population was 4,659 in 1930, 5,008 in 1940 and

Opposite page: Table 1.2 Parish census tracts were not used after 1950. The census tract was divided into divisions. The 1960 Mt. Holly Division included all of Berkeley County west of the Cooper River and south of Moncks Corner. The Goose Creek District in Charleston County included 12,515 people and was composed of the area between the Berkeley County line and the Ashley River beyond the boundaries of North Charleston. The Goose Creek city limits defined the census tract beginning in 1970.

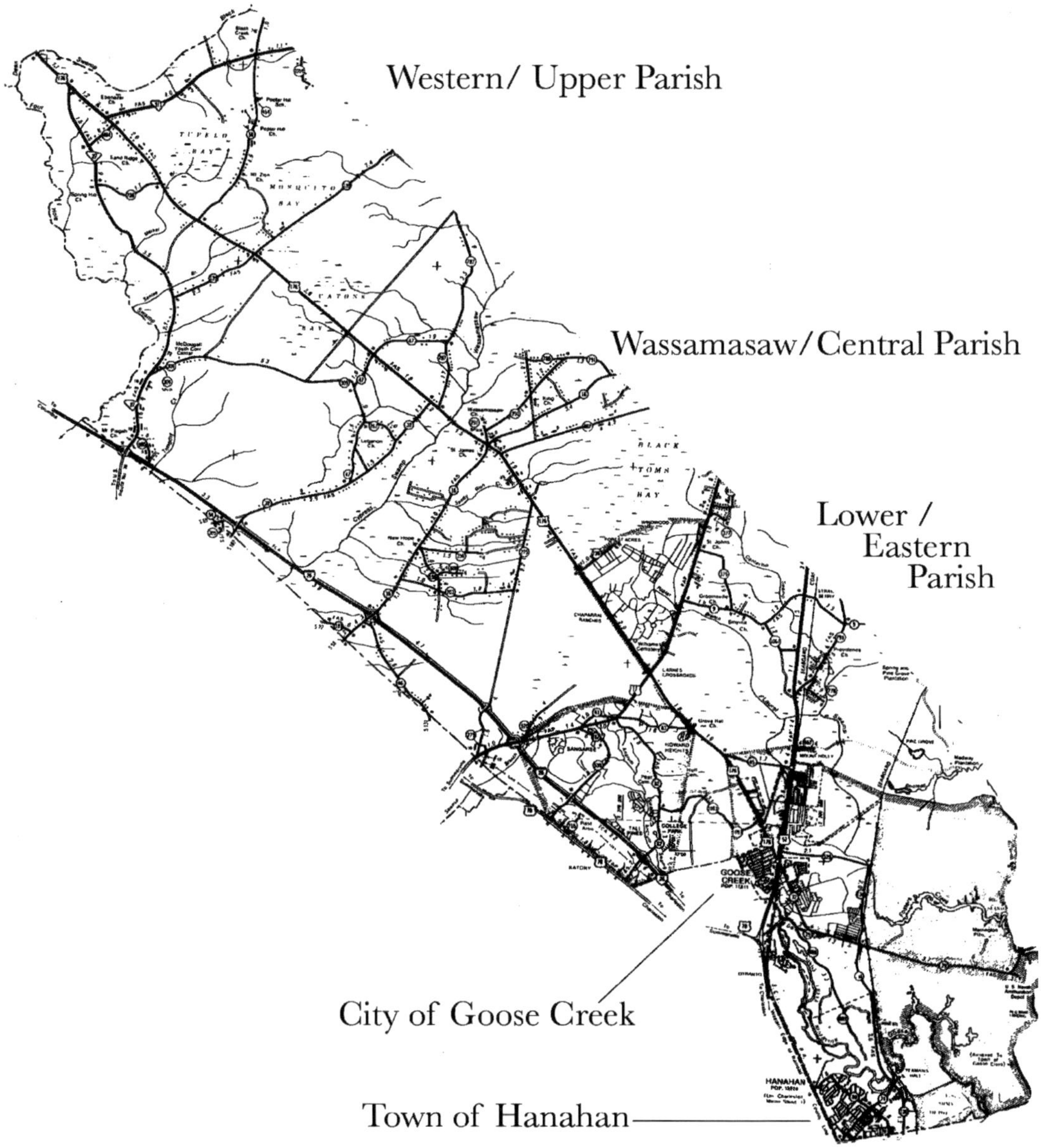

Map 1.3 This map from *Historic Resources of Berkeley County, South Carolina* shows the St. James, Goose Creek Parish section of a 2000 map of Berkeley County. (The sections of the parish were labeled for this publication.) *Courtesy of the Berkeley County Historical Society.*

6,715 in 1950. Parish census tracts were not used after 1950, and the census tract was divided into divisions, with Goose Creek included in the Mount Holly Division. The 1960 Mount Holly Division included all of Berkeley County west of the Cooper River and south of Moncks Corner. That census year there was also the Goose Creek District in Charleston County, which included 12,515 people and was composed of the area between the Berkeley County line and the Ashley River beyond the boundaries of North Charleston.

A survey mistake dating back to the early 1900s misplaced the Dorchester/Berkeley County line from Four Hole Swamp to Summerville. This mistake put three thousand acres of the St. James, Goose Creek Parish into Dorchester County. County officials are still negotiating the proper location of the political boundary line.

Map 1.3 is a contemporary map of the Goose Creek Parish, which can be divided into three sections: Western/Upper, Wassamasaw/Central and the Eastern/Lower. The eastern section kept the Goose Creek identity and most of that area is incorporated in the modern city boundaries. The mid-section, known as Wassamasaw and the far western area near Four Hole Swamp remain rural today. Today, the name Goose Creek is generally used in reference to the city and some unincorporated subdivisions nearby.

The city is young, having been chartered in 1961, but the corporate limits take in a much greater amount of land than did the original boundaries. Additional lands are being annexed and new families are moving to the inviting neighborhoods almost weekly. Even though the origin of the name has not been satisfactorily determined, Goose Creek as a place has become well known. Today, the name refers to a city and its environs, which include the eastern section of the parish lands that bind three tributaries to the Cooper River.

Chapter II
A Carolina Wilderness
1670–1719

During the first decades of settlement, Goose Creek was a wilderness where exposure to the elements, as well as starvation and illness were a persistent concern. In addition to these foreboding circumstances, were the constant threats of Spanish invasion and the almost complete absence of community protection. Safety was achievable to the extent to which men could provide for themselves and their families, thus making the Goose Creek wilderness a stark change from their former homeland. The overpowering isolation from friends, family and in many cases, from other European settlers caused severe hardship and forced upon these people a strong sense of independence. The slowness of communication, the difficulties of travel, continuing inflation, shortages of essentials and the absence of everyday necessities were regularly endured, but untreated minor injuries or common disease could mean death. Crop failures resulted in starvation and those without resourcefulness were doomed to fail in an environment where survival was a daily trial. The well-to-do Barbadians, the persecuted French Protestant, the land seeking Europeans and their enslaved Africans together confronted the challenges of the wilderness. The records show many years of problems and challenges, before the marsh and pinelands were shaped into prosperous plantations. What remains today are the records, chronicles and correspondence of the Goose Creek frontiersmen that tell of the hardships faced by all. The extant records document "starving times," "wild Indians," "pestilence," "a witch," "superstitions" and "slave revolts." Despite all the obstacles, the frontier was conquered, plantations were established and Goose Creek became a leading community in colonial South Carolina.

The Settlers

In the seventeenth century, Barbadian islanders sold their tropical farms, sailed to Carolina and settled near the waters of Goose Creek. Adverse economic conditions forced these farmers to leave their home island of Barbados in the West Indies. Once in Carolina, they used their colonial experience to transplant an agrarian system because the water, soil and climate were ideal for plantations, slaves and landed gentry. Others soon joined the people from Barbados. These additional arrivals were primarily from England, but some came from various other European countries including many Protestants from France, commonly known as the French Huguenots. Most came with a vision and a hope for a better life in the Carolina frontier.

The first two decades of the seventeenth century were periods of English experimentation in colonization. The English colonial designs proved successful in establishing new colonies in Virginia, Newfoundland, New England, South America and on the islands in the West Indies. Barbados, an English colony located in the Caribbean Sea just north of Trinidad, was an important origin of the Goose Creek settlement. Theoretically, Barbados and all the British islands in the Caribbean were the feudal possession of one man, the Earl of Carlisle. He was one of eight proprietors who owned vast expanses of land. Under the proprietary form of colonial government, the proprietor could govern as he saw fit, but a representative parliamentary government evolved for the practical administration of these colonies. The legislative assemblies on these small islands were composed of men elected by all the landowners in the parishes. This political arrangement grew progressively democratic and was later transplanted to Carolina by the independent-minded settlers.

At first, Barbados was a successful colony and between 1620 and 1640 its population swelled to eighteen thousand.[28] Tobacco was the first profitable crop grown in Barbados, but as it became more difficult to compete with the better-smoking Virginia tobacco, other crops were sought for experimental planting. In 1640, Pieter Brower, a Dutchman, introduced sugarcane in Barbados.[29] His experiments proved successful and by 1660 sugarcane replaced tobacco as the primary staple crop. Sugarcane planting brought significant changes to the island's economy because it required large capital investments, large plantations and a large labor force. The expense of land and slaves required for the cultivation of sugarcane forced many Barbadians to sell their farms and seek homes elsewhere. Some sailed to Charleston Bay.

There was a marked decline in the number of Barbadian farms and farmers as the small tracts were sold and consolidated into larger holdings, and as more landowners left Barbados in search of opportunity elsewhere. A contemporary estimate placed the number of farms and plantations at 11,200 in 1645. By 1667, only 745 farms and plantations were in operation.[30] By 1670, the number of white inhabitants declined to near twenty thousand, with approximately forty thousand slaves on the 166 square mile island.[31] Finally, an unexpected decline in sugar prices further discouraged more Barbadian farmers at a time when the British government began the earnest enforcement of navigation laws. Enforcement of the laws raised the cost of manufactured goods and thus the cost of living. Political crises, floods, crop damage and other natural catastrophes added to the plight of the Barbadians in the 1660s. Amidst the many problems and obstacles, many listened to promises of opportunities and left with hope for a better life in Carolina.

In 1671, the infant English colony at Charleston welcomed 106 new settlers from Barbados. Many of these Barbadians ventured up the Cooper River to the Goose Creek area. The desire to settle upon the fertile land along these rivers and the lesser creeks was a formative influence upon the development of Goose Creek. Some of the best lands were found on the banks of Goose Creek, and because it was navigable for much of its length and was fed by fresh water swamps that reached far inland, it was ideal for crop irrigation and transportation of people and products.

The Goose Creek Barbadians had much in common with each other and quickly became political allies. The Barbadian settlers were generally of a higher class than the other European settlers and shared similar colonial experiences. Also, they were wealthy members of the Anglican Church and held common political views and expectations. The Barbadian people of Goose Creek looked down upon the other settlers, whom they considered poor novices from England and "plain people" who were mostly dissenters from the Church of England. Many other Carolinians thought the Goose Creek Barbadians were arrogant, overbearing and not nearly as valuable to the colony as they were.[32] Consequently, a sense of rivalry resulted between the Barbadians and the Europeans.[33] Colonial Governor Joseph West wrote an uncomplimentary opinion of the Barbadians in a 1671 letter to Proprietor Lord Ashley. He stated:

> *Wee find that one of our servants brought out of England is worth 2 of ye Barbadians, for they are soe much addicted to Rum, that they will doe little whilst the bottle is at their nose...* [34]

Lord Ashley seemed to believe that the self-supporting Barbadians could provide colonial expertise, money and leadership during the first difficult years of colonization and that they were more valuable to the colony than the poor arriving from England. He disagreed with the governor and wrote, "The poorer settlers serve only to fill up numbers and live upon us."[35]

Until 1696, practically every ship entering Charleston harbor brought people of varying means who sought new homes in Carolina.[36] By the year 1700, small settlements of farms and plantations dotted both sides of the Cooper, Wando and Ashley Rivers, as well as Goose Creek, but it is difficult to accurately account for all the people who first settled the frontier. Some lands along Goose Creek were settled by Europeans as early as 1672 and 1673, and it appears as if all the lands along both sides of the creek, as well as nearby Back River and Foster Creek, were occupied within seven or eight years after the first 1670 landing at Charles Towne.[37] Maurice Mathews, a Goose Creek settler and Charleston merchant reported in 1680 that 115 men had started plantations on Goose Creek and Back River.[38]

During the 1680s, many other immigrants ventured to Goose Creek. Some emigrated from Jamaica and other islands of the West Indies. A small number of Anabaptists came directly from England, and a few from other European countries found their way to Charleston and eventually up the Cooper River to its tributaries. The lord proprietors arranged for land to be granted to the immigrants and advertised in Europe to encourage immigration because the proprietors owned vast reaches of land in Carolina and intended to reap profits by granting land and charging perpetual rents called "quit-rents." They planned for the lands to be granted systematically and they hoped to develop the province contiguously for safety, order and protection of their investments. The early settlement of the Goose Creek lands, however, went counter to the wishes of the lord proprietors because the Barbadians applied for and received grants for rich non-contiguous properties along the tributaries of the Cooper. The properties on Goose Creek were distant from the settled tracts in Charleston, but nevertheless some of the earliest settlers in Goose Creek were Edward Middleton, Robert Howe and Gabriel Manigault—three of the most influential men in early South Carolina.

Warrants were issued prior to the grants to authorize the award of the land. The warrants recorded the date, size and warrant number, as well as the name of the grantee and recipient. The location of the land was also given, and in some cases, other information such as the need for the land or the reason for the request. One warrant was for Sir John Yeamans who arrived in Carolina in 1671. His warrant appears to be one of the earliest in the Goose Creek area. Although he never lived in Goose Creek, another warrant was issued upon his death in 1674 for his widow, Lady Margaret Yeamans authorizing 1,070 acres for her and her servants.[39] The grant for this land was issued in 1675 and described it as being upon "Yeamans his Creek in Ittiwan River."[40] The name of "Yeamans Creek" was later changed to "Goose Creek."

The tracts bordering Yeamans's lands were granted a few years later to some of South Carolina's first families. William Murele arrived one year after the landing at Charles Towne and received 400 acres in his first grant. Nearby, a warrant was issued to "lay out 920 acres of land" for William Perryman in 1679.[41] In 1681, he received a grant for 574 acres on Yeamans Creek. In 1694–95, a grant was issued to Samuel Hartley for 400 acres on the south side of Goose Creek. His plantation was later named "Bigelow's" and was the Carolina origin of the famous Moultrie family.[42] In 1704, a warrant was issued for 500 acres of land to Lewis Lansac. According to later deeds, a grant was made in 1707 to Lansac for 600 acres on the south side of Goose Creek, also adjacent to Samuel Hartley.[43]

A former London merchant, Arthur Middleton, together with his brother, Edward, came to Carolina in 1678. That year a warrant was issued for 1,780 acres of land for both men.[44] This warrant was followed by a 1679 grant to them, for 1,780 acres at the head of Yeamans Creek. This was the original grant for the famous Otranto Plantation, originally referred to as "Yeshoe." The next year a warrant was issued to lay out acreage for Middleton and in 1680, an additional formal grant was issued to him for 1,000 acres at the head of Goose Creek. This plantation was originally called Broom Hall (later Bloomfield). Other Goose Creek lands were granted to Edward Middleton. Some of his lands were named Crowfield Plantation, eventually considered one of the best-landscaped plantations in the province. Another grant of 1,630 acres to Middleton was the Oaks Plantation, which is still recognized today by its stately tree lined avenue near the old St. James, Goose Creek Church. Edward Middleton developed the Oaks plantation and conveyed his share of the original Otranto grant to his brother, Arthur, in 1680.

The Hayes Plantation, on the headwaters of Goose Creek, west and contiguous to Otranto, is the original home of the Parker family. John Parker, who emigrated from Jamaica in 1694/95, received a warrant but died before the grant was issued. The warrant was subsequently reissued to Parker's widow.[45] His son John Parker became the original owner of the Hayes Plantation. Parker's widow married John Barker, immigrant of the Barker family who ten years later received a twelve hundred acre grant, which was made to John Barker's son, Thomas. Brick House or Martindale's was the name of the original plantation settlement of the Barkers.[46]

The original settlement of the Izard family in South Carolina was situated northwest of Otranto and northeast of Hayes. Ralph Izard, the immigrant, arrived in the province in 1682.[47] Ralph Izard, the son, devised a collection of grants and conveyances to form the beautiful Elms Plantation, which stayed in the family for many years. In 1683, Captain James Moore was granted twenty-four hundred acres of land that was formerly known by the native name of Boo-chaw-a and Wapensaw. These grants were the origin of Howe Hall, Button Hall and Liberty Hall Plantations.[48] James Moore later served as governor of the province. Nearby Job Howe of Howe Hall received a number of land grants dating as early as 1683.[49] He, like Ralph Izard and others, received several grants and amassed a large estate. Some early arrivals assembled thousands of acres. A warrant dated 1692 resulted in a grant for twenty-one hundred acres, which was part of the twelve thousand acres given to the Dutchman, John D'Arrsens Seigneaur de Wernhant by the lord proprietors.[50] This tract came to be known as Medway Plantation and is still a historical landmark in Goose Creek. Arrsens arrived in the colony as the leader of a small group of settlers from Holland. He built a brick home in 1688 on Back River, which remains today as one of the oldest houses in South Carolina. Arrsens died soon after his arrival to Carolina, and his widow married Thomas Smith, who later became governor.

George Cantey arrived on the first expedition in 1670. He and his son Tiege, who arrived two years later, were from Barbados. George Cantey received a warrant and later a grant for 300 acres between Goose Creek and the Ashley River.[51] In 1704, another grant was issued to John Sanders for 300 acres on the south side of Goose Creek.[52] John Ouldfield, born in Chester, England, immigrated to Goose Creek in 1709 and received two land warrants for 1,000 acres. Between 1716 and 1736, he received land grants amounting to 1,750 acres. He was elected to the Thirteenth Assembly for Berkeley County and served as Commissioner of High Roads for Goose Creek.[53]

Some early English settlers sought land in the Wassamasaw/Cypress Swamp section in the central part of the parish and even farther west to Dean's Swamp. These lands never developed into grand estates as did many of the plantations in the eastern parts of the parish, but they augmented the production and in some cases sustained many of the early frontier families. Governor James Moore received several land grants at Wassamasaw as early as 1680. After his death from what was probably yellow fever, his widow, Madam Margaret Moore, received a warrant for five hundred acres adjoining the Wassamasaw Plantation. She added her own grant in 1706–07. Captain David Davis purchased Wassamasaw lands in 1712. Tilney Coachman owned land at Wassamasaw in 1705 and Ralph Izard acquired four thousand acres there. Arthur Middleton owned one thousand Wassamasaw acres in 1706.[54] John Monck and later his son, Stephen, received a proprietary grant in that area in 1682.[55]

Some early immigrants to Goose Creek were French. To escape religious persecution, many French Huguenot Protestants took refuge in England in the latter part of the seventeenth century. The Edict of Nantes granted religious toleration to Protestants in France but the French King, Louis XIV, revoked the Edict in 1685. Before the revocation, the Huguenots lived freely without abuses and restrictions, but after the revocation, the Catholic majority inflicted religious and civil persecution on the Protestants. Soldiers were stationed in Protestant homes, children were taken from parents and thousands of French Protestants were tortured and killed. The revocation law also prohibited emigration from France, but many Huguenots escaped to Holland and from there journeyed to England. It was from England that the emigrant Huguenots sailed for the New World. In 1680, King Charles IV of England gave free passage to some Huguenot families on the ship *Richmond*. The ship arrived in Charles Towne that year with forty-five French refugees.[56] The lord proprietors promised free land to the Protestant refugees because it was hoped that they would introduce the cultivation of vines for wine, orchards for olives and mulberry trees for silk. This production was needed to advance the self-sufficient goals of the British mercantile system. Ironically, wine, olives and silk were never successfully produced in the colony because of climatic conditions and because the French immigrants were mostly tradesmen, weavers, mechanics or farmers without the required experience. Nevertheless, the French proved to be valuable additions to the struggling young colony. Nine years after the arrival of the first Huguenots, Peter Girard compiled a list showing that thirty-one French families were located in Goose Creek.[57] Among the French families prominent in Goose Creek during these early years were the families of Anthoine Prudhomme, Abraham Dupont, John Dupont, John Goble, Peter Bacot, Henry Bruneau, Pierre

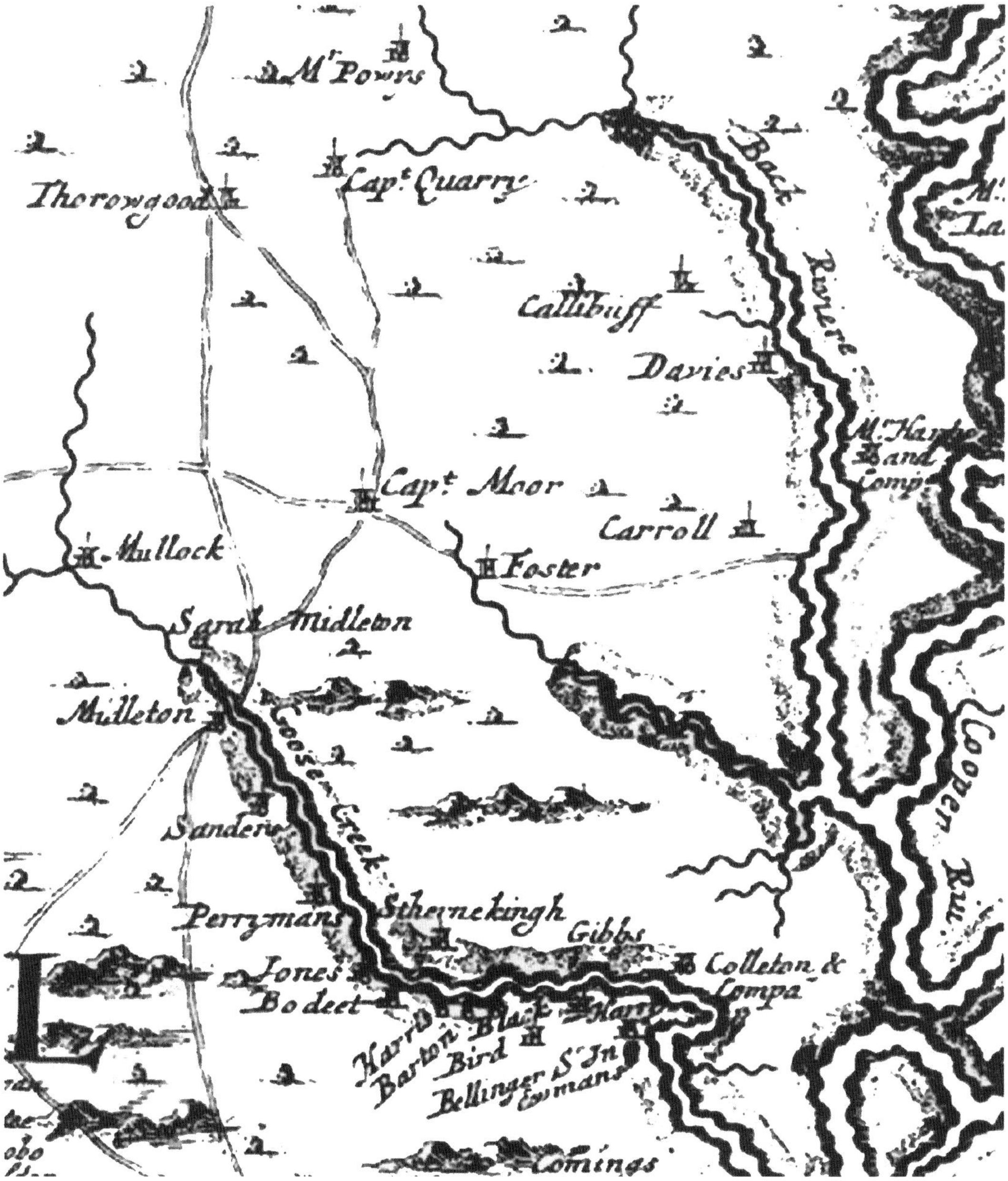

Map 2.1 This partial map entitled *Carte Particuliere De La Caroline*, Amsterdam, Chez Pierre Martier Libraire, 1688, shows Goose Creek, Foster Creek, Back River and a section of the Cooper River. *Courtesy of the United States Library of Congress.*

Dassex, Isaac Fleury (alias De France), Gideon Faucheraud, Elias Prioleau, Anthony Bonneau, Charles Franchomme, Francis Guerin, Benjamin Marion, John Postell, Dr. Isaac Porcher, J. Du Gue, Philip Trouillort, Paul Mazyck, Isaac Perronneau, Ann Le Brasseur, Elie Horry and Zachariah Villeponteaux.

Other heads of French families included George Gouden (Gourdin), who received a grant of 300 acres dated 1680 that states that he was already in possession of the land.[58] Two French Huguenot brothers immigrated to Carolina after the revocation of the Edict of Nantes. One brother, Abraham Fleury Sieur de la Plaine, settled on the headwaters of Goose Creek with his daughter, Marianne, in 1680. A warrant was issued to him for 140 acres of land.[59] Isaac Fleury, brother of Abraham, seemed to have been granted land in Goose Creek as early as 1694. Another Frenchman, Benjamin Marion, the grandfather of Francis Marion, settled near the Fleurys and nearby, Gideon Faucheraud acquired a tract of 150 acres in 1707. He eventually possessed more than 3,000 acres. Other Frenchmen acquired land in that vicinity too including John Filbein and Benjamin Goden.[60] John Boisseau obtained large grants near the headwaters of Goose Creek and close to today's Summerville. He received his first grant for 210 acres in 1696 at the head of "Yeamans Creek" and his properties adjoined the land of Abraham de la Plaine. Dr. Isaac Porcher, the ancestor of the South Carolina Porcher family, obtained a grant for 150 acres adjoining Abraham Fleury's property.[61] He eventually amassed an estate of over 4,400 acres. This tract remained in the family until 1848.

In addition to settling in the eastern parish, the French comprised an important part of the early population in the Wassamasaw section.[62] Isaac Porcher owned two tracts of land containing 570 and 600 acres near Wassamasaw Swamp as early as 1711.[63] Other French settlers in that area were Vincent and Thomas Gareing and Daniel Couriere, who jointly received a warrant for 3,000 acres near the lands of Robert Flood at "Wassam-issau Swamp."[64] The Legare family also owned large tracts in this area and remained here after most of the French relocated from Wassamasaw to the fertile banks of the Santee River.[65]

The abundance of French names is apparent in an incomplete enumeration preserved in *The Olden Time of Carolina*, compiled by Elizabeth Poyas in 1855. Her list indicated that approximately 12 percent of the early settlers were of French origin. According to that source, there were ninety-five taxpayers in Goose Creek in 1694 with personal worth ranging from £44 to £4,000.[66] More names of early Goose Creek settlers are found in the records of land grants, wills, correspondence, plats and newspaper accounts of births, deaths and marriages. The *Abstracts of the Wills of the State of South Carolina, 1670–1740*, contained the names of many of the planters in the Goose Creek community during the earliest years of settlement. Some of the recorded names were Nathaniel Snow, John Foster, Robert Gibbes, John Emporer, Peter Lamb, David Davis, Thomas Barker, Anthoine Prudhomme, John Goodby, John Sanders, Daniel Mackdaniel, John Bauyly, Benjamin Marion and Wilson Sanders.

Mapmakers of the period also noted prominent family names to identify locations. Map 2.1, drawn in 1688, indicates some additional family names not included in other records. The map notes the location of Powers, Cattebuss, Mullock, Quarry, Carroll, Bodeet (Dr. Bodett?), Jones and Bird families, as well as the partnership of Colleton and Campa.

African Americans

During the summer months, the average temperature on the South Carolina coast is similar to that in Barbados. Thus the Barbadian settlers believed that they had relocated in the tropics, and since most believed that the hot, humid climate and low coastal lands were too oppressive for white laborers, they concluded that slavery was unavoidable. This initial belief, as well as the Barbadian's long dependency on slave labor in the West Indies resulted in the early implantation of the slave system in Goose Creek. Slavery was firmly established from the first settlement and as the plantations developed staple crops, the demand for inexpensive labor increased until the economy depended upon bound servants. A social order based on slave labor and landed gentry, persisted in Goose Creek for nearly two hundred years. It dominated the colonial economy, survived the American Revolution and remained an influential political force in South Carolina until the emancipation of the slaves and the end of the Civil War in 1865.

The names of the newly arrived Africans are far more difficult to determine than the Europeans because the African identities, both tribal and individual, were lost. Many of the slaves were brought from the West Indian islands where their island masters gave them new world names. Many fresh arrivals from Africa lost their identities by the abrupt departure from Africa, the long voyage and their implantation into the New World. Shipping records are of little help in identifying the individual Africans. Generally, cargoes of slaves were merely advertised in such terms as "very prime Congo slaves," "prime Mandingo Africans," "choice Gold Coast Negroes" or "prime Windward Coast Africans."[67] Truth in advertising was questionable at that time, and if a slave was brought from the Congo or similar location, their tribal identity was lost as soon as an American identity was bestowed. There are few records of the actual origin of the newly arrived black Americans and sales records gave only the name of the buyer. Once purchased and taken to Goose Creek, as in most plantation communities, the slave's identity was that of his owner. A slave would be known as "the property of Mr. Porcher or Mr. Izard." At best, the slave was given a first name or a nickname such as "Ben" or "Toby," and Roman classical monikers such as "Pompey," "Cato," "Caesar" and "Jupiter" were popular.[68]

The Africans quickly outnumbered the Europeans in Goose Creek, as well as in South Carolina. In 1720, there were approximately eighteen hundred slaves in Goose Creek with approximately eighty white families.[69] The population figures reveal the important role played by the African work force. One historian aptly noted, "America was saved by Africa."[70] White men, who were unable to interpret the multitude of African languages and cultures, made incomplete written records of the Goose Creek Negroes. Nevertheless, early reports showed the high intelligence of many of the African slaves who quickly learned to read and write English. Unfortunately, most of the rich African culture was lost in the process of Americanization, and records of the lineage of the Americanized African families in the New World were seldom, if ever archived.

Native Americans

As with the Africans, it is difficult to identify the Native American individuals who resided in Goose Creek during the frontier period. Like the Africans, few identifying records survived.

There is much evidence that bands of Native Americans hunted, planted and lived along the rivers and creeks of coastal Carolina long before the arrival of Europeans. Archaeological studies in recent years uncovered remains of Native American culture at sites on property that is the Mt. Holly Alcoa Plant and Industrial Park today. Remnants of native culture have also been unearthed along the banks of Back River, Cooper River and Goose Creek. The archaeological firm of Brockington and Associates Inc. investigated a native site near Foster Creek in 1998. This and more archaeological findings indicate that the natural resources of Goose Creek supported a Native American culture since at least 8000 BC. Brockington concluded that the cultural evolution in Goose Creek spanned from ancient hunting and gathering societies to post Columbian pottery and corn production.

At the time of the first English settlements, the Cusabo were a small group of less than a dozen native tribes that occupied the Carolina Lowcountry from the Savannah to the Wando Rivers. They were part of a wider group of Native Americans of the southeast who based their culture on the planting and harvesting of corn.[71] They were the first to greet the English settlers at Charles Towne, the original location of the Charleston settlement. They assisted the newly arrived English colonists and were important to the survival of the infant colony, but they were much smaller and weaker than other tribes farther inland such as the Catawba and Cherokee. When the English arrived, they found that prior Spanish and French explorers had altered the native culture by the introduction of horses, Christianity, European languages and other cultural features. They also found that earlier Spanish and French contacts introduced small pox and other European diseases that resulted in the reduction of the Cusabo to small, scattered bands. Fortunately, prior European influence did not appear to discourage the native's friendly reception of the English. The coastal natives were hospitable, peaceful and friendly.[72] They welcomed the English colonists as protectors against the more powerful inland tribes, especially the much-dreaded Westos who were reported to be ferocious warriors and cannibals.[73] Thus, the mutual reliance on defense against powerful enemies merged the coastal tribes and European settlers.

As the English settlers followed the rivers and creeks inland from the seacoast, they found the Etiwan and the Sewee tribes dwelling along the banks of the Cooper River and its tributaries in the area that is today Berkeley County.[74] The Sewees inhabited the lands near the headwaters of the Cooper River extending to the Santee River. The Sewees were Siouan, related to western tribes, with a language and culture that differed from the Etiwan.[75] In contrast, the Etiwan were Muskogean, one of the Cusabo group and occupying what is today southern Berkeley County. Map 2.2 shows the location of the coastal tribes and Map 2.3 shows Goose C(reek), Midway R(iver) (Back River), Cooper R(iver) and a Sewee Settlement in "Barkley (Berkeley) County."

Hunting, fishing, and gathering gave both tribes a nomadic character, but the dependence on corn production required that the planted fields be protected until the grain was harvested. This resulted in territoriality and the emergence of village life, even though the villages were moved often in the pursuit of fertile fields and more plentiful game. Consequently, the Etiwans traveled widely throughout Goose Creek and the neighboring parishes. The Sewees traveled farther east and later, north of the parish. Francis LeJau, an early Goose Creek missionary, reported the Etiwan tribe occasionally resided near his abode but he noted that they were, "perpetually changing places to get food, having no provisions laid up."[76]

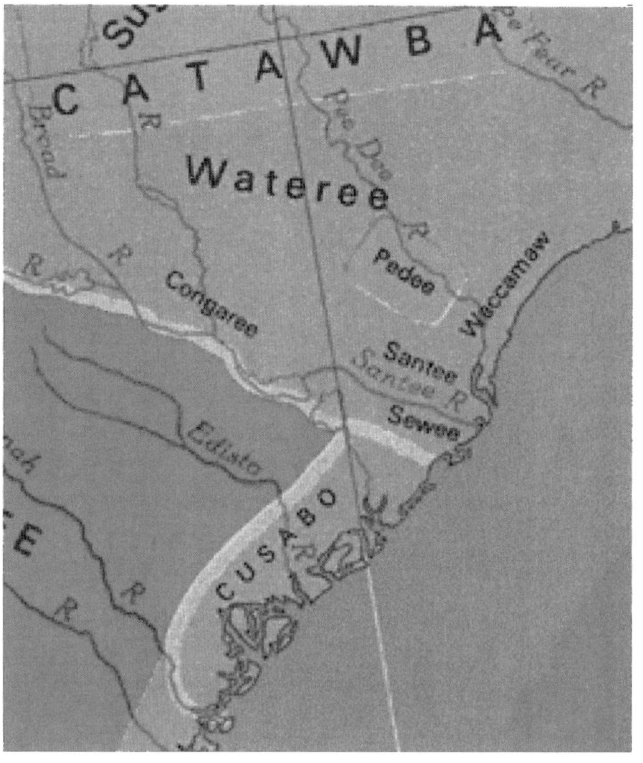

Map 2.2 This partial map shows the Native American tribes occupying a section of the coast of South Carolina. *Courtesy of the South Carolina Skyway.*

Recorded descriptions of Cusabo towns indicate that the Etiwan village in Goose Creek featured fields of Indian corn near numerous family huts. The huts were small, warm, tight and well suited to protect against the weather. They were made of branches and bark and were simple, easy to construct and well adapted to the needs of the semi-nomadic tribes. Family vegetable gardens with several varieties of beans, peas, melons and squashes, as well as roasting corn, were cultivated near the huts. The numerous family gardens were private, but communal fields supplied the corn crop. The tribal corn culture required a cooperative effort to ensure success and LeJau reported that he witnessed "war-chieftains working in common with the people..."[77]

A field in front of the central "state house" or meeting place was used for assemblies, religious ceremonies and games of sport. "Chunkey," was a native game in which a stone was bowled onto the field while contestants threw long thin poles. The objective was to spear the pole close to the final resting place of the stone. Many accounts of the game tell of its popularity among the Cusabo. In addition to gaming, the Etiwan activity field was used for ceremonial purposes. LeJau described an Etiwan ceremony in one of his accounts stating that, "Three young men holding one another under the arms began a dance followed by the rest in a long train..."[78]

LeJau's accounts offer Christian interpretations of Etiwan ceremonies. One such ceremony was centered on a symbol of a ship and three native participants. LeJau interpreted the ceremony as a reenactment of Noah, his three sons and the ark.[79] Another interpretation involved the origin of man, Adam and Eve and animal sacrifice to a divine spirit.[80] Such interpretations indicate the possibility of Christian influence from the Spanish or French prior to the arrival of the English, but

Map 2.3 This map shows a "Sewee Settlement" near some of the earliest land grants on a map entitled, *A New Map of the Country of Carolina*, Drawn by Joel Gascoyne, circa 1700.

it is also likely that the interpretation offered by LeJau may merely reveal the Christian perspective of the missionary.

Francis LeJau admired the Etiwans. He commended his Native American neighbors as a "good sort of people & would be better if they were not spoiled by our badd [sic] examples." Interestingly he commented, "I admire the sense of justice," but later complained about "their constant murdering one another which some of them cannot conceive to be evil."

The Etiwan women were assigned the duty of guarding the unfenced corn crop against wild birds, animals and their own domestic stock.[81] This allowed the men to return to the hunt after cultivation and planting. A democratic use of labor that included the work of war chiefs and women was common among many Carolina tribes. The fact that democracy extended to women refutes the popular idea that native women were reduced to roles of inferior servitude. A certain equality of the sexes is also evident among the other Cusabo tribes. An ancient treaty between the Cusabo Indians and the early settlers at Charleston contained the marks of fourteen "women captains" who held positions of authority within the tribe.[82] The Etiwan women were also responsible for burial rites.

LeJau pointed out that, "when any of them dies they anoint them all over with Oyl, either of bear or Ikkerry nuts…that's a constant practice and Women's employment."[83] In contrast, the position of native women among the Siouan river tribes was greatly inferior to the men. The Sewee men excelled at hunting and were famed for their endurance on the warpath. Their women were held as distinctly inferior to men, and a Sewee woman could be sold by her husband or traded for another wife at his will. Polygamy was also a common practice among this tribe.[84]

The Goose Creek area was the meeting place of two divergent native cultures, which were threatened from the outset by the European settlement. By 1715, merely thirty-eight years after the first settlement on Goose Creek, there remained one Etiwan village of 240 inhabitants and one village of 57 Sewees.[85] Though their numbers dwindled rapidly, the Goose Creek natives made important contributions toward the survival of the Europeans.

In addition to pressures put upon the Native American culture by the dominant Europeans, the virtual annihilation of the Sewee tribe resulted from an ill-fated commercial expedition. According to a story told by an Indian trader, the Sewee were not content with the rate of barter current among the Carolinians, and they decided to deal directly with England. Having observed that all ships came from one direction and that so many ships made the journey, they assumed that they knew the way to England and that it must not be too far away. The Sewees then assembled a fleet of large canoes filled with skins. "The affair was carried out with a great deal of Secrecy and Expedition, so as in a small time they had gotten a Navy, Loading, Provisions and hands ready to set sail, leaving only the old impotent and minors at Home, 'till their successful return…"[86] The canoes with mat sails were tossed by a storm until all but a few drowned. The survivors were picked up at sea by commercial ships and sold into slavery. A report from Governor Robert Johnson of South Carolina, dated August 1716, claimed the complete elimination of the Sewees along with some other tribes.[87] Although the accuracy of Governor Johnson's report has since been challenged, the fact remains that the Sewees disappeared as an identifiable tribe soon after his account and the Etiwans existed only a few more decades. One reason the numbers steadily declined was disease. The English weakened the natives with small pox contamination. As reported by the missionary, Reverend LeJau, "small pox always had a devastating effect on the Indian population."[88]

Before the natives disappeared, the settlers adopted native survival techniques and methods of travel, hunting and farming. There are accounts of the adoption by the settlers of native canoes and other shallow boats for local travel. Indian corn became an important food crop in Goose Creek and according to an early chronicle the white settlers acquired beans, pumpkins, squash, melons, peas, peaches, figs and even tobacco through trade.[89] The Goose Creek settlers later grew these crops, discovered how to find natural untended fruits and learned how to preserve the harvest for winter. Berries and nuts were a welcome variety to the limited diet of the Goose Creek colonists.

To some extent, the natives prepared the land for the Europeans. They cleared the thick forest cover by burning the vegetation and trees, which facilitated the hunting of deer and other wild game. If not prepared for cultivation, burned forestlands quickly cover with grasses and become natural grazing areas for game animals where they could easily be stalked. Interestingly, many of these fields were taken over by the Europeans and tilled as their first cornfields. It is very likely that the Goose Creek settlers also adopted Indian hunting and fishing techniques including methods to attract, trap, kill and preserve fish and game. In an era with limited gun range and accuracy, it was necessary to hunt deer and other plentiful game as skillfully as local natives. The important interaction extended into a significant business relationship. Barter with the natives constituted the first commerce in the province and the single most important business for many years.[90]

Most of the Goose Creek planters in the early days were also merchants because the Native American trade was too lucrative to ignore. Early correspondence from Maurice Mathews to the lord proprietors tells of a robust trade with the Etiwan (Ituan) and Sewee tribes less than a year after the first English arrival at Charles Towne. Goose Creek was situated on the principal Native American trading path and early maps illustrating the principal native trails show a route leaving Charleston and crossing through Goose Creek to Moncks Corner. The path proceeded across land that is today covered by the waters of Lakes Moultrie and Marion and continued west through the Carolina foothills. That principal trail, which became known as the Cherokee Path, caused trade to quickly expand. "Charles Town trades for one thousand miles into the continent," observed one writer, and Goose Creek, situated on the beginning leg of that trail, soon became an important trading extension of Charleston.

The most profitable products of the Native American trade were native slaves, deerskins and fur. These were almost the only exports and source of money for the young colony for several years which helped to improve the standard of living for the early settlers. Trade with the natives, though mutually beneficial and eagerly sought by the settlers, as well as the natives, worked mainly to the advantage of the Europeans. Small amounts of European goods could be exchanged for valuable skins and furs. Native trade underwent several stages of development through the years. The earliest trade involved simple swapping of European goods for needed food to survive the first months at Charleston. But constant skirmishes with natives resulting from disputes over land rights, destruction of crops or theft of cattle provided excuses for the European Americans to capture the Native Americans and sell them into slavery.[91] From an early date, the exportation of natives, usually to the West Indies, was favored as sound public policy. The natives made poor slaves in Carolina because they could easily run off into familiar environs. Moreover, in the frontier settlements there was always a fear of conspiracies by natives allied with rival European nations. Also, a native slave brought barely eighteen pounds in South Carolina currency compared to twice that much for an African slave.

The inequitable relations between the natives and Europeans were preserved by legislation. An act was passed in 1695 during Governor Archdale's administration that provided specifically for the offense of stealing or setting a boat or canoe adrift. Whereas Europeans violating the law were only fined, natives received thirty-nine lashes on their bare backs for the first offense and suffered amputation of an ear for the second.[92] The same year, the colonial legislature reduced the local natives to a state of serfdom. The Goose Creek Etiwans and Sewees were included in a list of nations required to pay tribute. The law rationalized that the natives "freely volunteered and consented to be obligated" to kill and bring animal tribute levied by the colonial assembly. Each year the Indians were obligated to bring in one wolf's skin, one tiger's (panther's) skin, one bearskin or two cat skins.[93] The law required that every native bowman capable of killing deer deliver the required number of skins to the Indian traders. Natives failing to meet this obligation were severely whipped on their bare backs in sight of the inhabitants of the town. Any native nation refusing to obey the law would, in addition to the punishment of their hunters, be denied protection and benefits of the English government, but it was further enacted that an Indian would be paid one pound of good powder and thirty bullets for each skin delivered in addition to the requirement.[94] The inequities continued when eight years later additional legislation encouraged the killing of predatory animals such as wolves and foxes. In accordance with the new law, every white person bringing in the skin of a bear, wolf or tiger (panther) received a bounty of ten shillings, but a native received half that award.

Abuse of the natives, including unscrupulous native slave trading, induced some to call for reform. Although natives were enslaved in many parts of the province, it does not appear that the Goose Creek planters commonly used native slaves. Nevertheless, slaves were awarded to the Etiwan tribe because they helped during a native uprising. In 1717, the Commons House of Assembly ordered that the Santee and Congaree native prisoners be given to the Etiwans. The report further stated that the Etiwans were "very well satisfied with having only the women and children of those nations to be their slaves…" The native trade eventually became formalized, regulated and conducted almost exclusively by professional traders who ventured into the backcountry as representatives of Charleston merchants.[95] Regulation resulted because the unregulated Indian trade deteriorated to a grossly unfair business. Some of the traders were accused of abusing, cheating and enslaving friendly natives. The lord proprietors appointed a commission consisting of Joseph West, Andrew Percival, Maurice Mathews, William Fuller, John Smith, Jonathon Fitch and John Boone.[96] The purpose of the commission was to intervene in disputes between "Christians and the Indians." In appointing this commission in 1680, the proprietors cited instances of injustice and declared that it was the responsibility of the commission to protect the natives from being "wronged or oppressed."

The commissioners appointed official native traders in various parts of the colony. George Chicken, planter and militia leader, was an assigned Native American trader in Goose Creek. His plantation was situated on the Cherokee Path and he had long been involved in the trade. After his appointment the commission supplied his plantation with rum and various dry goods to

Trade Item	Number of Skins	Trade Item	Number of Skins
A Gun	16	A Ditto Not Laced	12
A Pound Powder	1	A Yard Strouds	4
Four Pounds Bullet or Shot	1	A Yard Plains or Half Thicks	2
A Pound Red Lead	2	A Laced Hat	3
Fifty Flints	1	A Plain Hat	2
Two Knives	1	A White Duffield Blanket	8
One Pound Beads	3	A White or Red Ditto, Two Yards	7
Twenty-four Pipes	1	A Coarse Linen Shirt	3
A Broad Hoe	3	A Gallon Rum	4
A Hatchet	2	A Pound Vermillion, and two Red Lead Mixed	20
A Pound Vermillion	16	Brass Kettles Per Pound	2 ½
A Yard Double Striped Yard Wide	3	A Yard Coarse Flowered Calicoe	4
A Double Striped Cloth Coat Tinsey Laced	16	Three Yards Broad Scarlet Caddice	1
A Half Thicks or Plain Coat Gartering Laced	14		

Table 2.1 The table lists the bartering rates with the quantity and quality of goods equated to pounds of heavy dressed deerskins.

be used as trade items.[97] Eventually a table of rates (table 2.1) was published on April 25, 1718 in the Indian Trade Commission Journal that set guiding exchange criteria for the traders. The commissioners were required to settle differences arising from the enslavement of natives, though slavery was not halted. At first, the friendly Cusabo and several neighboring Siouan tribes brought in slaves, supposedly captured from tribes hostile to the English. Eventually, stronger tribes became involved in the trade. The natives began preying upon each other for the purpose of capturing and selling slaves for profit. A fixed price was placed on every imprisoned native the settlers brought to Charleston for sale. The captives were sold to traders, who in turn would ship them to the West Indies as slaves. The English rationalized this arrangement by claiming a humanitarian motive. Natives, they claimed, were in the habit of torturing captives of warfare. They reasoned that the life of a slave in the tropical West Indies was better than death by torture. Interestingly, the captives' consent had to be legally obtained before they were transported to the islands and there is at least one recorded example of consenting slaves. The Sewees, on one occasion, captured and delivered slaves to the English. According to the Shaftesbury Papers, the captured natives were enemies of the Sewees and the English, and gave consent to work in the colony or be taken elsewhere.[98]

The lord proprietors honestly tried to suppress the slave traffic but without success. Greedy slave dealers, eager for more merchandise, were instrumental in bringing on Native American wars. The proprietors upbraided the settlers for buying friendly natives, inciting wars and for doing "all these horrid wicked things to get slaves." After two years, the proprietors declared the powers of the commission null and void. They believed that the commission was "Rather...obtained for the oppression than the protection of ye Indians..."[99]

Overall, the Goose Creek Etiwans and Sewees and the nearby Cusabo tribes received little harassment from the colonial government, as long as they brought in the required tribute of skins and obeyed the governor's orders. Many natives were employed as canoe men and as hunters for plantations. Governor Archdale commented on the advantage of "keeping an Indian" and noted that those who "live in the Country Plantations procure of them the whole Deer's flesh and will bring it many miles for the value of about six pence..."[100] Understandably, "keeping an Indian," became a common practice that continued until the American Revolution and in some cases longer.[101]

Some effort was made to insure justice, punish native crimes and investigate transgressions involving natives in Goose Creek. A letter to a native chief from James Glen, Indian commissioner, stated his approval that the chief had not murdered and kidnapped as some suspected.[102] Additionally, Lewis Jones, the Pee Dee's chief, went to Goose Creek to investigate the murder and kidnapping of his people in Goose Creek. A free native named Prince who lived in Goose Creek told the Pee Dee's chief that five Cherokee and one Notchee did the mischief. [103] It appears that the Europeans and natives were cooperatively seeking justice with regard to at least this one instance and in some cases, men of conscience expressed sensitivity to unfairness. Reverend LeJau lamented that the natives had forgotten most of their traditions, and he was sad because many were maltreated. He once recounted that, "one of those traders caused a poor Indian woman, a slave of his, to be scalped." The incident occurred within two miles of the missionary's house where the poor woman lived two or three days in a miserable condition and was later found dead in the woods.[104]

According to the journals of South Carolina Commissioners of Indian Trade from September of 1710 to April of 1715, two-dozen complaints were officially made against traders.[105] Such abuse finally led to an outbreak of hostilities. Reverend Francis LeJau chronicled the impending trouble with hostile natives as early as 1708, when he cautioned that the natives were cruel to each other but that some of the traders encouraged the native hostility to procure slaves.[106] Three years later he wrote: "I hear that our Confederate Indians are now sent to war by our traders to get slaves."[107] On February 20, 1711, he wrote: "It is evident that our traders have promoted Bloody Wars this last year to get slaves and one of them bought lately one hundred of these poor souls." Soon after he wrote those comments, he reported that the natives were murdering their traders.[108] The abuses were reported to missionaries, as far away as New York. William Andrews was an Anglican missionary to the Mohawks in New York. In 1715 he wrote to his missionary society about the native hostilities in South Carolina explaining that the colonists had brought the war on to themselves by cheating the natives and kidnapping their children.[109] Andrews said that he learned of the situation from a French minister in New York who received the information from a French minister in South Carolina.[110] The South Carolina minister may well have been Reverend LeJau, who was a perceptive observer of the racial conflicts of his day.

In 1724 the journal of the Commons House of Assembly reported that the Etiwans wanted their own land. By then the Etiwans were scattered in small groups in the St. Thomas, St. Johns, St. Andrews and St. James, Goose Creek Parishes. Some natives wanted a single settlement area to bring the tribe members together and provide a means of support for their dwindling number. The Commons House of Assembly granted the request and issued land on the western side of Wassamasaw. There were about sixty adults remaining in the tribe at that time, but no records indicate that the tribe assembled on the granted land and no records mention the Etiwan tribe after 1751.[111]

The location of Goose Creek near an important native trade route where two native cultures converged gave those settlers many opportunities to witness the native struggle and the destruction of the culture. Disease, alcohol and war finally eliminated the Native Americans in Goose Creek, but prior to the demise of the natives, the blending of cultures greatly improved the likelihood of white survival. This cultural borrowing improved the European settlers' lifestyle and provided important business and agricultural opportunities during the first several decades of European settlement.

The Frontier

Land was the prize for which settlers endured hardships, and it was the scarcity of land in Europe and Barbados that was the single most important force luring the settlers to Carolina. Aside from the great distance to South Carolina and the grave hardships that met the frontiersmen, it was not difficult for a European to acquire property. The proprietors of Carolina issued their first instructions for granting land in 1669, one year before the first settlement at Charleston. This land-granting process was relatively simple, and thus for most Goose Creek settlers the land was easily acquired. If the initial "starving period" was successfully endured the settler could realize the profits from their land, and the lord proprietors back in England could reap fortunes from their vast holdings in Carolina.

The Goose Creek colonists enjoyed advantages over other colonies, as well as Charleston. The majority of the Goose Creek settlers possessed farming experience, most having recently arrived from their Barbadian plantations. In 1682, Thomas Newe, a Goose Creek landowner, wrote that the first Charleston settlers were "tradesmen, poor and wholly ignorant of husbandry…so that their whole business was to clear a little ground to get bread for their families…"[112] The husbandry experience brought from Barbados to Goose Creek put these planters at a great advantage over their "tradesmen" neighbors in Charleston. The Barbadians were surprised by the weather. They expected the same tropical climate they were accustomed to in Barbados. Although the weather was not tropical, the winters were not nearly as dangerous as the killing winters suffered by the English at the Plymouth, Massachusetts's settlement fifty years earlier. Contrary to the desires of the lord proprietors, the local soil and climate were not suitable for many European grains and a staple crop for export was not immediately found.

The search for a staple crop for export continued while the settlers expanded their herds of cattle running free and foraging on natural vegetation. Indian maize was cultivated on all Goose Creek farms. The kernels provided food for the household and the leaves and stocks were fodder for livestock. Cattle were not susceptible to disease and because of the mild winters, they thrived and multiplied with little attention. The herds grew so rapidly that in 1695, an act was passed for the destruction of wild cattle, which were over-foraging and eating valuable crops and fodder. In an effort to control the herds and manage the stocks, the animals were branded or the animals' ears were notched for identification. One example was the fleur-de-lis brand used by Goose Creek planter Isaac Mazyck and recorded as public record.[113] A 1716 drawing of Goose Creek land shown as plat 2.1 depicts deer, cattle and a horseman on the grounds indicating the importance of livestock to the early frontiersmen.

The frontiersmen used every advantage of the countryside including the turns of the creeks and the shapes of the marshlands to form livestock corrals. Some marshes were used as grazing pastures, and natural bends in the winding creeks sometimes formed peninsulas or islands that could be easily fenced. Big Island, shown as plat 2.2, was more than fifty acres of high ground surrounded by tidal influenced marsh, near the confluence of Foster Creek and Back River. This island was conveniently used as livestock pasture, since tidal influenced waters that made fencing and salt licks unnecessary surrounded it. A causeway was constructed to connect the island to the mainland, and a landing provided access to Foster Creek. Cattle were fattened on the island and transported to market via Foster Creek, Back River and the Cooper River. By the end of the seventeenth century, some colonists were prospering from a brisk trade of salted beef to the West Indies.

In addition to cattle, hogs ranged freely and were fattened with little effort. Barrels of salted pork were loaded with the beef shipments to the Caribbean Islands. In addition to a rich environment to fatten livestock, the forest abounded in deer and other fur-bearing animals. Trade in deerskins and other peltries became a lucrative business. Deer skin hats and fur accessories became increasingly popular in Europe resulting in a growing demand for these items from South Carolina forests.[114]

The forest provided other natural resources for export. Early in the settlement, soft and hardwoods were important building materials for domestic use and export, but pine trees were not common in Western Europe and at first were a strange sight to the Goose Creek immigrant. The resourceful pioneer, however, eventually found ways to profit from the pines. In addition to the lumber, the pine forests provided tar, pitch, turpentine and resin (naval stores) for the British naval and mercantile fleets. But due to the initial lack of tools and equipment, it was difficult to extract the naval store

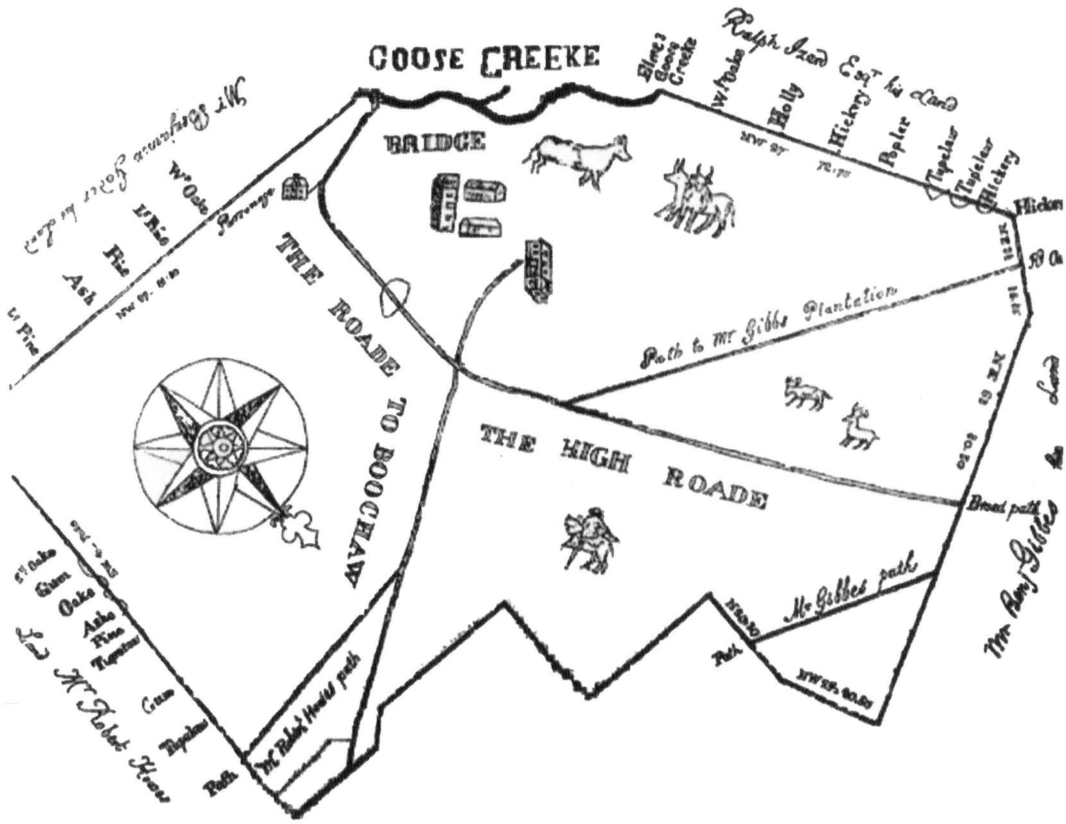

Plat 2.1 This plat shows 1,630 acres of land on Goose Creek granted to Edward Middleton in 1680. The plat was drawn from a survey made by John Herbert, Deputy Surveyor in 1716. The plat is among the collections of the South Carolina Historical Society.

products or cut and transport the lumber. Consequently, profits from the export of naval stores and lumber were elusive at first.[115] Toward the end of the seventeenth century, a staple export was not yet found and so the proprietors continued to bemoan their colony of stock raisers and deer skin traders instead of planters.

Even though a staple crop was not yet found, there was a noticeable change in the standard of living for some toward the end of the seventeenth century. As trade and commerce developed through Charleston, sugar, wine, rum and foods were imported in greater quantities. Regardless of the improvements, Francis LeJau complained of continuing food shortages during the first decade of the eighteenth century and once lamented that Indian corn bread and water was the "common food and drink for my children with a little milk."[116]

After the initial "starving period," the living conditions for the average Goose Creek colonist were in most respects superior to those in Europe. Land was cheaper and more abundant, food became plentiful after the lands were cultivated, and the people were generally self-sufficient. Unfortunately, this relatively better life did not protect them from the ravages of deadly diseases such as malaria, scarlet fever, diphtheria, smallpox, measles, typhoid, tuberculosis and perhaps typhus.[117] Sickness

Plat 2.2 This plat shows Big Island near the confluence of Foster Creek and Back River. It depicts the island connected to the mainland by an earthen causeway. Another causeway connected the island to the navigable waters of Foster Creek. The fifty-six-acre island is noted with the words "Island 56 A." John Diamond drew the plat from a resurvey made in 1803. The plat was traced by H.A.M. Smith and is among the collections of the South Carolina Historical Society.

was common in Goose Creek, and at first, because of the lack of knowledge of the cause of disease, it was often blamed on the water and mud from the creek and swamps. Records show that Samuel Thomas lived for thirty-four years in Goose Creek before he died from "pestilential fever." It appears quite likely that he was a victim of malaria.[118] Malaria was a serious problem in Goose Creek and gravely affected the development of the community. An authority that traced the early history of malaria in South Carolina concluded that the disease persisted as a problem because of the "oak lands," which were the best lands along the rivers and creeks and were also the areas heavily infested with disease-carrying mosquitoes.[119]

Dysentery affected nearly everyone at one time or another. Commonly called "the flux," it was not always fatal but frequently caused disability for months or years, leaving the victim weak and susceptible to other diseases. Epidemics were common. The Reverend Francis LeJau reported that "distemper" killed many Goose Creek people, and large numbers of settlers and four hundred of their slaves died during another four-month period of sickness.[120]

Throughout the seventeenth and eighteenth centuries, medical science was still a primitive art in Europe and America. Only a few trained physicians came to America and even fewer possessed medical degrees. A number of "country" doctors served the Goose Creek community beginning as early as 1678. Dr. Peter Bodett, who settled in Goose Creek by 1678, supplemented his income with Indian trade. Dr. Robert Adams arrived in Charleston in 1680 with four servants and occupied a plantation near the head of Goose Creek.[121] James Williams, a surgeon, received an eight hundred acre grant in 1683 next to Thorogood Plantation. Dr. Isaac Porcher, a Huguenot refugee came to Carolina in 1696 and settled on the Santee River. He later moved to property at Goose Creek and became a prominent citizen.[122] Dr. Nathaniel Snow, another surgeon owned property in Goose Creek as early as 1694.[123] Dr. Barnard Christian Cooper practiced medicine at Goose Creek. Thomas Rose of Thames in Oxfordshire, England practiced medicine in Charleston and Goose Creek. In 1716, he was one of a few who recovered from being scalped by the Yemassees, surviving until 1733.[124] Although there were doctors in Goose Creek, the evidence shows that they could do little to lessen the effects of most illnesses. The Reverend Robert Stone wrote on March 6, 1750, that: "in Goose Creek...health was so bad that forty-five was considered the common age of man."[125] By the time he wrote this, Goose Creek was already a well-established community. It is highly probable that disease, illness and early death during the first decades of the frontier settlement were even more common due to shortages of food and proper shelter.[126]

In addition to the primitive cures offered by frontier doctors, the settlers relied on any available resource to restore health after illness or injury. In one instance, an old settler in Goose Creek was bitten on the thumb by a rattlesnake. He mustered enough courage to pull the snake from a hole and took it to a nearby house. There he reportedly survived the bite by eating the boiled liver of the snake and sipping a broth made with the snake's flesh.[127] Such home remedies and superstitious cures were believed to be effective by many during this period, and some people were convinced that the weather was somehow related to illness. Francis LeJau once wrote that, "We had nothing but storms for four months, many persons are ill of strange distempers..."[128] In addition to the storms common to coastal Carolina, the summer heat brought its toll of hardships. Another report recorded, "the great heat has thrown many into fevers."[129] Yet there remained ironic optimism as revealed in a letter from LeJau when he wrote that, "This is truly a charming country when we are blessed with health." The same letter reported that, "rumors of death has kept our neighbors of supplying us with necessities as flower, wine, sugar."[130]

The activities of the Society for the Propagation of the Gospel in Foreign Parts (the SPG) were important to the people of frontier Goose Creek. The mission of the SPG was to Christianize the "pagan Indians" and African slaves, but the SPG missionaries were appalled by the ignorance of the European settlers as well. They immediately attempted to improve the situation by providing religious guidance to the planters and their slaves. The missionaries instructed the natives and the slaves in Christianity and prepared them for baptism. They taught some to read and write and encouraged enculturation of the natives to facilitate the spread of Christianity. Reverend LeJau commented that the native children began speaking English and adopting European culture soon after the arrival of the settlers, and he was impressed with their rate of learning English and the European "fair sense of justice."[131]

The early missionaries were confronted not only with ethnic complexities, but also with non-religious or dissenting groups such as the atheists and Anabaptists (Baptists). Anglican missionaries despised the latter and reported as early as 1705, that there were "considerable" numbers of Anabaptists in Goose Creek. Samuel Thomas found two families of Anabaptists living in Goose

Creek and thirty families on the western side of the Cooper River. In 1715 and 1716, the Anglican priest, Dr. Francis LeJau of St. James, Goose Creek Church was remarrying people who had been married by dissenting ministers on the grounds that the marriages were not legitimate. The struggle against the work of the devil and nonbelievers consumed much of the missionary and priest's time and attention. LeJau lamented the power of the devil in Goose Creek:

> *I must observe that the last sedition was begun while the Judge was examining evidences relating to the accused witch that is still in our prison. It don't belong to me to judge but she had many friends here. It is a dismal sight to perceive how powerful the spirit of the Devil contrary to that of Christ is here.*[132]

The SPG in London received several letters concerning Mr. Atkins Williamson who was supposed to have christened a bear in Goose Creek.[133] Though not a common occurrence, this was not as bizarre as it might at first appear. Some ministers of modern Christian congregations bless family pets, and today in Charleston, the shrimp fleet is blessed annually. Nevertheless, Rev. LeJau was asked to investigate.

It appears that the most notable achievement of the SPG missionaries in Goose Creek was their work among the white inhabitants. The church, the church school and the predominance of Anglicanism in Goose Creek were substantially the result of the SPG activities in the area. The early missionaries started a long history of Christian leadership that did more to unite the community than any other institution. Regardless of the SPG's good work, a conflict developed between its plans and those of the Goose Creek planters. The conflict centered on the fear of slave rebellion because the slaves greatly outnumbered the whites and lived and worked in close proximity to them.

During the frontier years, the slaves and their masters lived close together and subsisted on similarly coarse and limited diets. Slave quarters were usually near the main house and consisted of huts with cabbage palm leaves, or other thatch woven thickly overhead to reduce the effects of the sun and rain. Archaeological studies conducted in Goose Creek in recent years indicate that many of the early slave quarters were "wall-trench structures" about 9x13 feet with some as large as 14x21 feet. These huts were built by standing upright poles in a trench of packed clay. Loosely woven branches connected the poles and the spaces between were filled with clay. The floor was also made of clay. One or two windows were sometimes shuttered. The huts were not insulated and offered little respite from the elements. Thus, most activities were conducted outside at communal fire pits. Some of these fire pits have been unearthed in recent years and revealed crude clay pottery. Slaves, working in these open pits, fired the hand fashioned clay pots, bowls and other implements called colono ware.

The early huts used by the Europeans were not much different from the African's huts at first, and years later the typical plantation house remained little more than a simple, rough cut wood structure. During the early frontier years, the slave huts and the owner's house were situated on the same high ground, but as the years passed the thatched huts evolved into rough-hewn wooden cabins or barracks that were constructed farther from the main house and nearer to the cleared fields.

During the early years, it is likely that the slaves ate the same type of food as the European Americans except that quality and variety were limited. The provision-ground system encouraged slaves to grow much of their own food, which was usually supplemented with staples such as the broken rice remnants of the winnowing and threshing process. Interestingly, evidence condensed from the remains of colono pottery at the Crowfield Plantation slave settlement indicates that the plant called "rape" was part of slave diets.[134] Rape is a member of the greens vegetable family along with turnips, kale and rutabaga. It is a high-protein food that could also be used for cooking and lamp oil. Rape does not appear to have been eaten by the European Americans and may have been one of a few diet items exclusively eaten by the African Americans. The evidence indicates that the European and African Americans homes, utensils, diets and general living conditions were similar during the frontier period.

The similarity of living conditions and the close proximity of their lives probably contributed to the fear of the outnumbered European settlers of the insurrection of their African slaves. The masters feared that the missionaries might cause rebellions by educating and Christianizing the African slaves and consequently initiating thoughts of freedom. This fear never materialized in Goose Creek, but occasionally slaves revolted elsewhere prompting all but a few Goose Creek masters to oppose religious instruction. Reverend Samuel Thomas began teaching the slaves at Goose Creek in 1695, and worries of the planters intensified as he and other missionaries broadened their efforts to educate the slaves. The SPG position was that Christianizing did not preclude emancipation and that a Christian slave who could read and write would be a better slave. This position did not ease the planters' fears. The first rector of St. James, Goose Creek Church reported to the missionary society that he was reassuring the Goose Creek planters by making the slaves swear allegiance to their master before he would baptize them.[135] Shortly after this correspondence, Reverend LeJau recorded a rumor about an intended Negro conspiracy. He was told that a plot had been formed in Goose Creek, where there were many faithful slaves. LeJau reported to London that twelve to fifteen Negroes living on the north side of the Cooper River had been apprehended. It appeared that a Negro from Martinique had been found to be of "stubborn temper." He enticed some slaves to join him and use force to acquire liberty. He was caught and eventually put to death. Two more conspirators were severely punished for following him but their lives were spared. The remaining apprehended slaves denied the crime and were acquitted. Reverend LeJau reported that no Goose Creek Negroes were accused of having knowledge of the plot. He also reported that one of the "most sensible" of the slaves promised that if he ever heard of any ill designs of the slaves, he would report it to the Reverend.[136] LeJau also doubted whether all slaves should be taught to read. Once he wrote:

> *I fear that those men have not judgment enough to make good use of their learning and I have thought most convenient not to urge too far that Indians and Negroes should be indifferently admitted to learn to read, but I leave it to the discretion of the masters...*[137]

The early slave code was brutal, and the corresponding criminal law was typically harsh. In 1690, the law in South Carolina for the trial of slaves provided special courts. Trials were without jury, and punishment consisted of whipping, branding, amputating of the ears or death depending on the offense. According to one law, if a runaway slave was a man he was castrated. If the runaway was a woman, her ears were cut off. LeJau reported that the majority of the planters were "good natured" and treated their slaves well, but many planters used cruelty to rule those who many believed were merely "savages" from Africa. LeJau reported that some would "hamstring, mame, unlimb those poor creatures for small faults." Even burning the offender alive and branding were legal and in accordance with slave codes. In one case, Reverend LeJau reported that a slave woman was barbarously burnt alive near the priest's home.[138] Another report by LeJau referred to a man who punished his slaves by crushing them. The guilty slave was laid in a coffin where he was crushed with a weighted lid. His feet were chained and he was left in that state for twenty-four hours. One Negro man who was baptized by LeJau was punished for spilling a parcel of rice. The master locked the slave in a "coffin like" box for several days, during which he was scourged twice a day and not allowed to eat. After much punishment, the slave asked one of his children for a knife. While manacled, he stabbed himself to death. This was the fifth slave the master destroyed through cruelty within several years.[139]

Hunger, disease, injury, slave insurrections and the many personal trials confronted by the early settlers were paled by a single event that almost quelled any hope of success in the New World. This event was the Yemassee Indian War of 1715. The war left South Carolina impoverished, with the parishes of St. Helena, St. Bartholomew, St. John and St. Andrew almost totally desolated. The destruction wrought upon the Goose Creek settlers took years of recovery. According to the colonial assembly, the struggle involved as many as fifteen Indian nations extending from the South Carolina coast to Alabama. There was never a native uprising in the Carolinas, which exceeded this war in geographic scope or number of natives involved.[140]

In 1712, Captain Cantey of Goose Creek and forty-one Catawba Native American allies journeyed with other Carolinians to help colonists fight against hostile tribes in North Carolina. Soon after his return to Goose Creek, hostilities emerged in South Carolina involving the powerful Yemassee tribe, which in the 1680s moved from Georgia to South Carolina and located between the Combahee and Savannah Rivers. One cause of the Yemassee War was native resentment of the abuse suffered for many years at the hands of traders, but it is likely that the multiple uprisings at that time resulted from more than trader abuse. The Spanish in Florida and the English in Carolina incited native wars against each other to advance their footholds in North America and to undermine the colonial gains of the other.

The war strategy of the Yemassee was to first kill the traders and then attack the settlements. In response to reports that some agents were attacked and killed, Indian agents Thomas Nairne and John Cockran accompanied by Goose Creek planter John Wright acted as an advance team to meet with the Yemassee Chief, avert the war and arrange for a subsequent meeting with the chief and the Governor's representatives. Unfortunately the plan went awry. In April 1715, Wright and the agents were attacked in the council house where they were lodged and all were massacred. The Yemassee Tribe then moved quickly to gain as much advantage as they could. Within thirty days, about ninety of the approximately one hundred traders in the province were killed and plantation settlements in Pocotaligo near the Georgia border were attacked. More than ninety whites were killed there.[141] Fear, panic and rumors spread quickly causing South Carolina Governor Craven to hurriedly engage a native war party near the Combahee River. There the governor's forces temporarily halted the native advance, but it was obvious that the entire province was in peril.[142] Martial law was imposed on the colony and all available troops were mobilized.

Thomas Smith of Yeamans Hall sent his family to Charleston and took command of the Goose Creek Company. Part of his company consisted of William Bull, James Alford, William June, William Scott, John Woorams, John Moore, John Dickson, Charles Hastings, Maurice Moore, George Chicken and John Herbert.[143] This company was a formidable force for that day, but it was assembled too late to prevent approximately four hundred natives from successfully crossing the Santee River. That native force hurried toward Goose Creek unopposed except from resistance by scattered plantation settlements. At one settlement, thirty miles north of Goose Creek, Mr. John Herne (Hyrne) confronted a party of seventy Cherokee. When the natives asked for dinner and inferred that they wanted to make peace, a truce was called. After the Indians ate, they attacked and killed their host and destroyed his plantation.[144] Upon hearing the news of the Herne massacre, Captain Thomas Barker of Goose Creek collected a force of ninety mounted men from the immediate area and rode north to meet the advance party of natives. Unfortunately, his force was betrayed by a native guide and ambushed which resulted in the death of Barker and twenty-six of his men.[145] After the ambush, the natives were virtually unopposed and could have easily taken all of the plantations of the parish, but for the bravery of a small group of seventy European and forty African American defenders who dug in behind fortifications and delayed the native offense. The natives were not able to overcome the small stubborn Goose Creek stronghold; instead they sent proposals of peace. When the defenders foolishly accepted, the natives rushed inside and killed nearly all.[146]

As a result of the series of defeats, Goose Creek was exposed to the native advance with no formidable defense between them and the invaders. People fled from Goose Creek to Charleston, depopulating the entire countryside. Men, women and children with cartloads of goods hurried down the road to the safety of the city.[147] The situation remained dreadful until the Goose Creek militia, under the command of Captain George Chicken, marched from a well-fortified position at the Ponds, west of Goose Creek with 120 men. He divided his force into three parties and attempted to surround the invading natives about eight miles north of the St. James, Goose Creek Church. Before he could carry out his plan, he was forced to shoot two enemy scouts. The gunshots revealed his position, dashed the element of surprise and forced Chicken to attack immediately. In spite of the quick turn of events, the Goose Creek militia killed about forty natives, wounded more, captured two and released four European American prisoners. This battle stopped the Native American march on Charleston and precipitated the ebb of the native advance.

It appears as if the Goose Creek militia was well accommodated for that battle. An inventory of the fortifications at the Ponds, conducted sixteen years after the war in 1732, listed thirty old muskets and five carriage guns, which were likely left over from the Yemassee War.[148] If Captain Chicken's militia was armed with carriage guns, the firepower of the Goose Creek militia was formidable for defense or surprise attack. The militia was also fortunate that some of the local native tribes provided assistance during the crisis. In 1715, when the war began, the 240 Etiwans in Goose Creek was no small number, considering that the European population was not more than a few hundred during the same year, but the local Goose Creek natives were not perceived as a threat or as a formidable ally. LeJau wrote: "the poor Itwans [sic] settled among us are few in number and bad soldiers."[149] Nevertheless, they were helpful during those dangerous months. Numerous instances are recorded of friendly local natives taking Yemassee scalps for bounty. After the war, the clonial assembly ordered two coats for King Robin and Crowley, two Goose Creek Etiwans, who lent their service during the struggle and continued to assist after the hostilities.[150] In 1716, the Goose Creek natives helped defend the province against the Santee and Congaree natives, who remained dangerous for many years.

The Yemassee War caused far-reaching destruction and was one of many grievances that prompted the South Carolinians to oust the lord proprietors. Soon after the Yemassee War began, the South Carolina governor requested aid from the lord proprietors and from the governors of North Carolina and Virginia. Help arrived from the neighboring colonies, but not from the proprietors. During the fall and winter of 1716, the North Carolina and Virginia troops and the Goose Creek militia remained stationed at Wassamasaw to protect the frontier. Captain John Herbert of Goose Creek was well experienced in Indian affairs and reportedly lent a great deal of aid to the commanders of the North Carolina and Virginia troops.[151] The colonial troops enjoyed early successes, but there was still so much fear that most of the Goose Creek inhabitants remained in Charleston. Finally, near the end of 1716, the assembled troops at Wassamasaw drove the remaining natives across the Savannah River and out of South Carolina.[152] The fear abated and the people returned to their homes in the country parishes, but the lack of help from the proprietors during those trying times was not forgotten. The fear and resentment unified the colonists against the proprietors and in favor of a royal government that would be directly responsible to the king of England.

During the frontier era, many Goose Creekers became leaders in the development of South Carolina. Their previous experience as planters in Barbados, coupled with the fortitude acquired in the wilderness, influenced their political thinking and, in turn, the policies of South Carolina. Frederick Jackson Turner, trained at Johns Hopkins University, produced a brilliant thesis entitled, *The Significance of the Frontier in American History* (1893). He read his paper at the 1893 meeting of the American Historical Association in Chicago, three years after the superintendent of the 1890 census announced that the West had been sufficiently settled and there was no longer an American frontier. The conquest of the American frontier, in Turner's opinion, was more than an important chronological passage in American history. He believed that the conquest of the frontier was an evolutionary process that Americanized the settlers and gave rise to American democracy. His essay closely relates to the Goose Creek pioneers as it does to others in America. The European settlers in Goose Creek eventually conquered the wilderness and, during their long struggle, were transformed into uniquely American individuals. Turner believed that advances into the frontier meant a steady movement away from European influences, a steady growth of independence, and the steady emergence of original American institutions. He wrote:

> *Behind institutions, behind constitutional forms and modifications, lie the vital forces that call these organs into life and shape them to meet changing conditions. The peculiarity of American institutions is, the fact that they have been compelled to adapt themselves to the changes of an expanding people.*[153]

The Barbadians, the English, the French and the Africans who settled in the Goose Creek wilderness experienced the Americanization process, were altered by it and became unique European and African Americans with a Carolina frontier lineage that affected them and their heritage forever.

The failure of the lord proprietors to reap the anticipated profits from Carolina was due largely to their ignorance of the frontier influence on the colonists. The Goose Creek frontiersmen not only settled a considerable distance from England, but also beyond the relative safety of Charleston. At first, they merely struggled with a hand-to-mouth existence, but as they exported the products of the forest for livelihood and later the rice and indigo from their successful plantations, they emerged as a unified Goose Creek political force that consistently defied the proprietors. There is no doubt that the years of frontier experience honed the defiant spirit of the Goose Creek people and shaped their destiny.

Adverse economic conditions in Barbados, religious intolerance in France, scarcity of available land in Europe and the grand designs of the lord proprietors resulted in an unusual wave of immigration to a small corner of North America. The English, the French and their African slaves arrived in Goose Creek during the last decades of the seventeenth century and the first decades of the eighteenth and composed an unusual demography that left durable impressions. The heterogeneity of the earliest immigrants subtly shaped the social, economic and political philosophies that impacted all of South Carolina for centuries. The Goose Creek people faced the starving period, disease, slave revolts, native wars and many trials of fear and personal tragedy, but prosperous plantations finally arose from the rich soil, deep creeks and dense swamps. South Carolina became a royal colony, and as the fear and memories of the Yemassee War faded, a prosperous plantation system replaced the frontier. The records and chronicles of those years shifted from fear to optimism as the dreams of many were realized. One letter written by Francis LeJau showed his optimism when he wrote:

> *The climate and soil are admirable, produces asparagus, roses, and woods full of flowers very fine and unknown in Europe. Green peas and beans, greens all year, fish and fowls. We have all manners of grains, fruits, herbs and flowers. Fruitful soil where anything grows without much trouble.*[154]

As the frontier period waned, an optimistic attitude prevailed among those who recognized the beauty and bounty of the land they traveled so far to settle.

Chapter III
The Goose Creek Men
1670–1719

beware of the Goose Creek men…[155]

MANY OF THE ORIGINAL GOOSE Creek settlers sailed from the West Indies island of Barbados. These comparatively homogeneous immigrants were experienced planters and well educated members of the Church of England (Anglicans), who brought investment capital from the sale of their Barbadian lands. Soon after their arrival, they unified to become the dominating political force in South Carolina during the first fifty years of settlement. The Barbadians were the largest group of immigrants who settled in the colony during its first decade. A year after the first immigrants landed at Charleston in 1670, Sir John Yeamans arrived with fifty Barbadian immigrants. He and many of those immigrants settled in Goose Creek. Yeamans organized and became the leader of the "Barbados Party." These Barbadians, soon known as the "Goose Creek Men," forged their planter community into a dynamic political force with the help of the Goose Creek women who likewise developed an interest in political events during this time. One Goose Creek chronicler observed "the women of the town (Goose Creek) are turned politicians also and have a club where they meet weekly."[156] Apparently the women were activists, which was highly unusual and progressive for the era.

The Barbadians were Anglicans opposed to the religious dissenters who came to Carolina for religious freedom. During the fifty year period of proprietary rule from 1670 to 1719, government policy changed dramatically, but the political animosity between the people of Goose Creek and the dissenters remained constant. Additionally, the angst of the Goose Creek Men extended beyond mere antipathy toward non-Anglicans. Throughout the entire period of proprietary rule, the people of Goose Creek opposed a wide range of governmental policies and regulations. They disagreed with the constitutional provision allowing religious toleration and they refused to settle in contiguous settlements as the constitution designed and the proprietors directed. These Goose Creek Men also engaged in illegal business activities including the native slave trade and business with pirates. Later they opposed the arrival of indentured servants, as well as French Huguenots, and they complained about unfair representation, the shortage of currency, land-granting policies, quit-rents and a long list of what they perceived were injustices. At the same time, the Goose Creek planters became wealthy, independent and influential, eventually replacing proprietary rule with a Royal Charter controlled by the king of England. M. Eugene Sirmans, author of *Colonial South Carolina, 1663–1763,* labels the opening section of his book, spanning the years 1670 to 1712, as the "Age of the Goose Creek Men," concluding that the Goose Creekers were primarily interested in dominating the affairs of South Carolina so they could build fortunes in any way possible. Apparently, the political history of Goose Creek during this period was one of protest, dissent and chicanery.

When Anthony Cooper assumed the leadership of the Carolina proprietors, he and his friend, the distinguished philosopher John Locke, formulated a new political design for the colony known as the Fundamental Constitution.[157] During the era of monarchs, this constitution was progressive in many ways and became noted for its liberal expression with regard to society and government in the frontier. The design proposed by Locke provided for an aristocratic society based on land ownership. He believed that land ownership was the best foundation for a social order because, in his words, "all power and dominion is most naturally founded on property."[158] The constitution assigned two-fifths of the land of the colony to the nobility and three-fifths to the manorial lords and commoners. The highest level in this governmental and social hierarchy consisted of the eight Carolina proprietors who owned Carolina as their personal property. The constitution divided the province into counties and each county into forty squares. To own and develop these squares, Locke's constitution provided landed gentry with the title and rank of "landgrave" and "cacique." (Landgrave Thomas Smith of Goose Creek for example held such a title.) The original charter required one landgrave for each county and entitled each landgrave to four squares. There were two caciques assigned to each county with the entitlement to one square. The proprietors retained whatever remained as long as they wished. The squares were called "baronies" if owned by a landgrave or a cacique and "seigniories" if owned by a proprietor.

Power and authority was founded on the ownership of the land, but the ruling of the vast acreages was shared. A governor, appointed by the proprietors, oversaw the affairs of the colony and a legislative house called the Assembly and Grand Council of Fifty assisted the governor. The constitution was liberal for the times, especially in relation to suffrage and religion. It only required that the people believe in God and own a certain amount of land or wealth to vote and hold various offices. The governing assembly was composed of the governor, eight deputies of the proprietors, all the landgraves and caciques of the province, and the elected deputies of the freemen. The Fundamental Constitution was an elaborate plan considered by most to be well conceived, but it was never initiated as designed, and the parts of it that were implemented were never popular or effective in South Carolina.

The lord proprietors of Carolina issued instructions for granting land in 1669. For forty years these instructions were revised and reformed but remained basically the same. The settlers appeared before the governor and council to request land. The governor issued a warrant to the settlers for the land and the surveyor general made a plat. When the warrant was properly certified, signed and recorded, the settler became a landowner.[159] Thus, by becoming a landowner a new form of nobility was established in Carolina through the Carolina land grants.

Political problems emerged soon after the arrival of the first settlers. Faced with starvation and the fear of death by slaughter at the hands of hostile natives or the dreaded Spaniards in Florida, the people looked for strong leadership and found it lacking. At first the Goose Creek Party did little but complain about incompetent colonial leadership, and in response, Governor William Sayle

(1670–1671) enacted laws to discourage colonists from deserting the colony and to gain control over an increasingly unruly population. Attempts by the governor to garner more control over the people generated more resistance and complaints from the Goose Creek Men. As a result the lord proprietors, from their distant places in England, appointed the Goose Creeker, John Yeamans to replace the first governor. The proprietors expected that the replacement of the governor by a Goose Creeker would effectively quell dissent, but this strategy failed because Yeamans became unpopular too. In 1674 Yeamans summoned the people to assemble, had the Fundamental Constitution read into law and without submitting it to the people for a vote, declared it the law of the land.[160] This autocratic style of leadership caused an uproar and began decades of political dispute about the progressive constitution.

The Goose Creek planters were ardently opposed to the constitution and rejected any regulations that interfered with their freedom to make money. In their view, religious freedom allowed too many to vote and shared representation diluted their clout. It appeared that the Goose Creekers were to rule, at least for a while, and although the political and economic situations were grave, trade with the natives and the use of slave labor provided some relief, allowing the colony to grow slowly. By 1683, thirteen years after the first arrivals, there were one thousand immigrants in the colony.[161]

Complaints from the colonists continued and dissatisfaction with Governor Yeamans's administration prompted the proprietors to replace him with Joseph West (1674–1682). The next eight years were relatively harmonious in Carolina because the governor and the Goose Creekers worked cooperatively. More and more of the Barbadians settled in Goose Creek during this period and increased their domination of the council and assembly. The governor simply succumbed to the Barbadians; however, the close working relations between the governor and the Barbadians did not work well for the proprietors. The proprietors sought profits but received few during the first decade. They did not even receive enough legal tender to pay the governor's salary. The legislature agreed to pay the salary in commodities, not currency, which irked the proprietors. Furthermore, the governor and the people could not agree on the market value of the commodities. Another area of proprietary dissatisfaction was the inefficiency in land distribution. The proprietors expected the simple land granting process to return perpetual rents from the millions of acres of land they owned, but the distribution of land was inconsistent with proprietary instructions and resulted in both the proprietors and the settlers becoming dissatisfied. The land-granting process was slow, many settlers could not get clear title to their land and the proprietors were collecting far less rent than they expected. The whole situation was unsettling. During the first decade, the proprietors invested almost £10,000 in Carolina, but after twelve years they received no return on any of it.[162]

Confronted with the problem of an unprofitable colony and the obstinacy of the unruly Barbadians, the proprietors initiated new strategies in the 1680s to correct the situation. One tactic was to dilute the power of the Goose Creek Men by recruiting hundreds of new families to Carolina. The proprietors advertised throughout Europe and attracted diverse groups to the colony including Huguenots, English Baptists, English and Scot Presbyterians and Quakers. Most of these families were dissenters of the Anglican Church who came as indentured servants and doubled the population to more than two thousand by the year 1685.[163]

As expected, the Goose Creek people greatly resented the immigrants, partly because the indentured servants posed another problem to the Goose Creek Men. One unrelenting problem perceived by the Goose Creek planters was an unsafe economic relationship between the African slaves and the indentured servants. The vast amount of land in South Carolina and the very large holdings in Goose Creek lent to the common practice of allocating a small amount of provisional lands to slaves and allowing time for the slave to work his lands. This typical practice in Barbados was transplanted to Goose Creek. The slave grew his own food, including livestock, and would sell the excess to the master, who in turn resold it at the market for a profit. This "provision ground system," as it was known, resulted in the production of more food, as well as, provided some social control by giving the slave a vested interest in the success of the plantation. Consequently the slaves were less likely to run away. The provision ground system was an integral part of the Goose Creek economy, but the indentured servants threatened the system by trading directly with the slaves. The Goose Creek Men believed this trade was a dangerous relationship that could cause slave escapes or rebellion. Consequently, soon after the arrival of indentured servants, laws were enacted to correct the economic relationship. One law passed during these difficult years was an "Act Inhibiting the Trading Between Servants and Slaves." The law was not effective in curbing the trade because it lapsed in 1683, was re-enacted in 1686 but, like most laws during that time, was never well enforced. The passage of that law does indicate that the Goose Creek political faction feared losing control over the "lower classes."[164]

Governor West, appointed by the proprietors to replace the unpopular Yeamans, soon succumbed to the influence of the Goose Creekers, joining some of them in the lucrative business of illegal native slave trade.[165] Because of his unscrupulous behaviors, he was dismissed in 1682 and replaced by Governor Joseph Morton (1682–1684), a leader among the newly arrived English dissenters. The lord proprietors hoped that careful directives to the new governor could successfully install the fundamental constitution and make the colony profitable. Consequently, a series of directives were issued during the 1680s and 1690s, one of which required settlers to live in adjoining settlements for the purpose of advancing commerce and facilitating defense. The Goose Creek people defied this directive by settling miles from Charleston. Other directives resulted from the large amount of discretion left to local officials when they granted land. Some settlers complained of favoritism or undue delays, and others complained that they never received the deed to the land they occupied. The shortage of currency added to the land problems. The laws required settlers to pay an annual rent of one penny (or the value thereof) per acre. Another directive was issued in 1682 that struck the words "or the value thereof" from the law, meaning that only cash could be used as rent payment. The following year, a provision was added empowering the proprietors to confiscate land if rent became six months in arrears and the settlers were required to sign an indenture contracting them to quit-rent provisions. Coins and other currency were so scarce in the province that it was unreasonable to ask for payment in currency. The colonists preferred paying in commodities or country produce. The Goose Creek people regarded the quit-rents as a burdensome obligation but paid grudgingly. To the proprietors quit-rents were a permanent endowment of considerable worth, considering the millions of acres held.[166] This difference of opinion persisted until the proprietors relented, but not until after the issue became severe. Some settlers refused to sign the new indentures that bound them to pay the rents and some refused to pay any rent at all on the grounds that the deeds were not signed or sealed by all the proprietors. The lord proprietors responded by refusing to issue warrants for land until the indenture was signed by the grantee and ordered that grantees sign or leave the colony.

The impasse finally broke when the proprietors agreed to accept commodities to quell the continued unrest. The Receiver of Rents was empowered by the proprietors to accept various currencies or county produce including cotton, silk or indigo.[167]

Governor Joseph Morton was well aware of the bitter factionalism between the proprietary and anti-proprietary parties. During his term, the leaders of the Goose Creek Men were Maurice Mathews and James Moore. These men were not Barbadians but were fully committed to the Goose Creek style of politics. Mathews was one of the leading dealers in illegal native slave trade. He profited from a lucrative business with pirates and he later became governor with support from the Goose Creek Men. James Moore was touted as the son of Roger Moore, one of the leaders of the Irish Rebellion in 1641. He supposedly inherited his father's rebellious nature.[168] James Moore married the daughter of John Yeamans and became one of the most influential and notorious Goose Creek Men. The proprietary supporters, mostly religious dissenters, despised them. John Stewart, a dissenter, called Maurice Mathews "Mine Heer Mauritius" and his "Welch Highness." He claimed that Mathews was "Hel itself for malice, a Jesuit for Designe politick." He labeled Colonel James Moore "the heating Moore" and "the next Jehu of the party."[169] Other influential "Goose Creek Men" were Thomas Smith, Peter St. Julien, Thomas Smith, Jr., Captain George Chicken, Benjamin Schenckingh, John Newe, Benjamin Godin, Henroyda Inglish, Major Robert Daniel (deputy governor 1716–1717), Arthur Middleton, Ralph Izard, Robert Gibbes (chosen as governor by the council 1710–1711), Edward Hyrne and Benjamin Mazyck.[170] Nathaniel Johnson later joined the group and became one of the most influential leaders. The Goose Creek Men controlled the assembly and Governor Morton was powerless at their hands. The proprietors attempted to regain control by removing the Goose Creek Men from office and replacing them with their supporters. They declared that Maurice Mathews and James Moore were outlaws and ousted them, but the strategy failed. The population largely resented the new replacements appointed to high positions and rallied more support for the Goose Creekers.

The pirate issue permeated the administrations of the next several governors. Currency shortage persisted as a problem but a temporary solution was found by doing business with the coastal pirates. The Goose Creekers were involved in the lucrative pirate trade. Long before Charleston was settled, pirates used the bay and the coastal islands as a safe retreat and were familiar with the rivers and coves. After the English settlement, the pirates recognized Charleston as a favorite resting place. Henry Morgan, Richard Worley, Captain Kidd, Stede Bonnet, Captain Flood and others frequented the protected bay waters and purchased goods from the colonists with silver coin. The trade provided a quick and easy market and a steady source of currency.[171] The Barbadians in Goose Creek saw little harm in such trade because the practice was common in Barbados and the English encouraged the pirate plundering of Spanish ships and outposts. Pirates were not much of a bother to the colonists at first. The colonists were just a struggling lot, hardly worth the pirates' bother. As long as the hostilities were directed against the Spanish, the colonists were tolerant of the swaggering pirates on Charleston's streets who spent their stolen silver freely. This mutually beneficial arrangement, however, was short-lived because the proprietors declared the trade illegal. After short terms of office by Governors Richard Kyrle (1684) and Joseph West (1685), Robert Quary (chosen by the council 1684–1685) was appointed as governor. His term was short as well. The proprietors quickly dismissed him because he joined the ranks of the Goose Creek Men and openly traded with the pirates.[172] During this period of transient governorships, the ranks of the Goose Creek Party swelled with new additions such as Benjamin Waring, Job Howe, James Stanyarne and many of the newly arrived French Huguenots.

When Joseph Morton (1685–1686) returned as governor, he was again confronted with an assembly dominated by the Goose Creek Men. They had such a strong hold on the assembly that the returning governor stopped enforcing the laws against native slave and pirate trade and openly traded with the pirates. This situation made Charleston a welcome port for buccaneers, which resulted in occasional protests from some Charlestonians, but provided a source of silver coins and commodities such as silk.

James Colleton (1686–1690) who followed Joseph Morton as governor, conscientiously followed proprietary instructions and attempted to end the outlawed trade. He enjoyed short-lived success controlling the native slave and pirate trade but, like his predecessors, was out-maneuvered by the chicanery of the Goose Creek politicians. The Goose Creek Men who controlled the assembly magnanimously offered to increase the governor's salary by levying a tax on liquor and sugar. Governor Colleton, as was expected, supported the proposal and even convinced some proprietary supporters to vote for it. When the bill passed the grand council, the Goose Creekers made their attack. They accused the governor of being a tyrant and opposed the proposal in the assembly. They argued that the tax bill would place such a high price on commodities that the governor would get rich at the people's expense.[173] The maneuver placed the governor in an embarrassing position. The tax levy bill was defeated and the Goose Creek Men were further empowered at the governor's expense.

Colleton conscientiously continued with his earnest efforts to execute the directives from the proprietors and went to work to resolve some of the long-standing problems with the Fundamental Constitution. Goose Creeker Ralph Izard supported the adoption of the innovative instrument written by the renowned John Locke, as did many of the Goose Creek people, but there were many proprietary men who were opposed to it. Thus the governor was in the precarious position of having his proposal opposed by a minority on both sides of the issue but being unable to gain a clear majority of support from either side. The Goose Creek faction characteristically went into action. They challenged the legality of the governor's authority and laid the groundwork for revolution when Goose Creeker Maurice Mathews issued a resolution declaring that the only legal constitution was a Royal Charter and all laws passed under the new Fundamental Constitution were null and void.[174] Another Goose Creek planter, Job Howe, had the Royal Charter resolution passed through the assembly but the council rejected it. The attempt to pass the bill by the Goose Creek Men and the subsequent rejection by the governor and the council caused many colonists to conclude that the proprietors were continuing to force an illegal government upon them. Opposition to this enforcement was strong causing Governor Colleton to refuse to reconvene the assembly. By doing so, he lost more popular support, which lead to his ultimate ouster.

Year by year, the Goose Creek Men steadily strengthened their political ranks and successfully forged a firm alliance with former Governor Morton and a number of other dissenters such as Sir Nathaniel Johnson, a man of wealth and prestige. Johnson was an especially powerful addition to the Goose Creek faction.

Despite his weakening political position, Morton returned to the governorship for a short time and enforced proprietary directives to the best of his ability. Additional restrictions were placed on native trade, and landowners were reordered to pay their land rents. It appeared that compromise was beyond political possibility when Goose Creek leaders James Moore and Maurice Mathews defied the new orders and openly sent an expedition to trade with the Cherokee.[175] Political tensions mounted. Governor Colleton assumed authority from Morton and declared martial law to quell the local uprising. During a brief reprieve, the Goose Creek Men petitioned the proprietors with five hundred signatures to have Seth Sothel (1690–1692) appointed as governor. Sothel allied with the Goose Creek Men, dominated the assembly and successfully ousted Colleton from office. He and his compatriots moved quickly to consolidate the political victory. They imprisoned Paul Grimball for refusing to relinquish the Great Seal of the colony, dismissed many proprietary supporters, barred Governor Colleton and four proprietary supporters from ever holding political office and banished them from Carolina. They also hurried Maurice Mathews to England to present Goose Creek grievances to the proprietors.

It was at this time that many Goose Creekers spread an unrealistic fear of French Huguenot settlers. News of the "Glorious Revolution" reached the colony bringing with it threats of a war with France. The colonial legislature reacted to pressure from the Goose Creek faction and disenfranchised the Frenchmen. This political prowess eliminated French influence in the legislature and provided Goose Creek total control over the legislature and clear dominance of the colony. This dominance along with their open alliance with Governor Sothel permitted the return of the illicit native slave and pirate trade, which made some Goose Creekers, such as Nathaniel Johnson, the richest men in Carolina.[176]

Sothel's administration was highly irregular, which alarmed the proprietors in distant England. In response they ignored Maurice Mathew's appeal, suspended Sothel from office and appointed Governor Philip Ludwell (1692–1693) in Sothel's place. The proprietors also recognized that they were losing control of the colony and attempted to save what was left of their investment by compromising. The first compromise was their directive to Governor Ludwell to pardon all offenses committed against the proprietors or the Fundamental Constitution prior to Ludwell's administration. Not included on the pardon list were Colonel James Moore, Maurice Mathews, Arthur Middleton, Major Robert Daniel and a few other Goose Creekers.

The proprietors were cautious and deliberate in their instructions to the newly appointed governor and warned Ludwell in a written directive to keep a watchful eye upon Sir Nathaniel Johnson.[177] In 1693 they warned:

> *beware of the Goose Creek men, reconcile yourself to our deputies, don't expect to carry on the government with all parties.*[178]

Despite the pardons and the warnings, Governor Ludwell had no success with Goose Creek and consequently little success with the colony. The problems with currency, pirates and quit-rents were not yet solved, and heated arguments about fair representation erupted during his term of office. When the colony was established, it was ordered that representatives from each county comprise a parliament. The Goose Creek planters protested this arrangement so adamantly that the proprietors sent a written response in 1685 challenging the governor to garner control of the situation. The proprietors asked Governor Ludwell, "Pray are you to govern the people or the people you?"[179]

Governor Ludwell was directed to establish a parliament of twenty comprised of five members from each of the four counties of Albemarle, Craven, Berkeley and Colleton. Because Albemarle was hundreds of miles from Charleston, the proprietors directed that none be sent from Albemarle but instead that seven delegates be sent from Berkeley and Colleton and six from Craven. The governor called for an election in accordance with these directives. Berkeley County sent Major Benjamin Waring, Colonel James Moore, Ralph Izard, John Ladson, Jonathan Amory, John Powis and Joseph Pendarvis, but the people of Goose Creek resented having equal representation with Colleton County and protested the six representatives from Craven because that county was sparsely populated and mostly occupied by French Huguenots. They argued, "Shall the Frenchmen who cannot speak our language make our laws?"[180] This ethnic controversy continued for many years resulting in the French appealing to the proprietors for assistance. This hostility finally subsided near the turn of the century and Governor Joseph Blake assured the proprietors that the French, "have a long time lived together as if they were one nation, their former animosities being quite forgotten."[181]

Landgrave Thomas Smith (1693–1694), a wealthy Goose Creeker who replaced Ludwell as governor, had some successes. James Moore, who had refused to pay his land rents, came forth with payment, and the governor successfully suppressed the illicit pirate and native slave trade. Shortly before Smith's death in 1694, he reported to the proprietors that the colony was finally progressing in the right direction. He was correct to be optimistic. During the reign of Smith's successor, Governor John Archdale, Carolina enjoyed unprecedented prosperity based on rice culture and expanded legal trade with Cherokee, Creeks, Choctaws and Chickasaws.[182] By this time, the Goose Creek planters successfully used slave labor to build beautiful creek-side plantations and were a distinct class of landed gentry.

Much of the progress was credited to the leadership of Governor John Archdale, who began his duties in 1695. Archdale was given full authority to "do anything that can reasonably be thought to advance peace and prosperity."[183] Archdale's leadership was effective, and he worked relatively well with the colonial government. At the end of the seventeenth century, the colonial government was clearly in the hands of the Goose Creekers. Nineteen men representing all religious and political factions were identified as legislative leaders during the last decade of the century, but most of the leaders were Anglicans associated with the Goose Creekers. Goose Creekers like Job Howe, Ralph Izard and Robert Stevens dominated the assembly.[184]

Under pressure from the Goose Creek faction, Governor Archdale reformed the land grant process. He initiated new laws that liberalized quit-rent regulations and simplified land grant and conveyance procedures. The new quit-rent law remitted rents for three years for all who held land by grant and for four years for those who held land by survey. All former grants or purchases from authorized agents were confirmed and new settlers were exempt from rent for five years.[185] The land granting process was simplified to convey lands with less delay and the long and bitter controversy over quit-rents finally ended.

Still the Fundamental Constitution remained a heated point of contention. Major Robert Daniel, one of the Goose Creek Men not included in the general pardon of 1693, went to England in 1698 to work with the lord proprietors in revising the often-rejected Fundamental Constitution. It was at this time that the "nobility of Carolina" was put on the market. The title of landgrave could be purchased for one hundred pounds and the title of cacique for fifty pounds. Major Daniel was granted a landgrave without cost and was authorized to sell six titles of landgrave and eight of cacique.[186] Daniel brought this plan and a revised constitution back to Carolina for approval, where the people again promptly rejected it. This was the final attempt, as the constitution was never again brought before the people for adoption. Ironically, it was a Goose Creek man who brought the final revision back to the colony, and it was the Goose Creek people who most adamantly opposed it.

The Fundamental Constitution did not prohibit the purchase of land, but encouraged the distribution of land on a rental basis that ensured perpetual proprietary control. This was a boon for landless immigrants and promised a perpetual source of revenue for the proprietors. Additionally, by 1695 many Goose Creek people were purchasing large quantities of land outright with the proceeds going directly to the proprietors. The income from land sales along with the income from quit-rents was used to pay the salaries of appointed officials. This was sufficient enough for the proprietors to finally realize an actual return on their colonial investment.[187] Near the end of the seventeenth century, Governor Archdale was successful in compromising many long-standing political differences. The proprietors were making money and by the time Governor Joseph Blake (1696–1700) succeeded Archdale, South Carolina was peacefully enjoying a period of prosperity.

Governor Blake continued with the successes of his predecessor, but interestingly during his term, the British parliament created the Board of Trade to oversee the enforcement of the shipping and trade laws of the empire. The colonies were also guilty of flagrant violation of these laws and continued to disregard them for three quarters of a century, resulting in the grievances that led to the American Revolution.

Although the Goose Creek Men were staunch Anglicans who resented the various religious dissenters, religious rivalry simmered but seldom surfaced during the first thirty years of settlement. During this period, religious rivalry took second place to more pressing issues, but by the beginning of the eighteenth century many immediate problems were solved, allowing religious conflicts to emerge. Upon the death of Governor Blake in 1700, James Moore (chosen by council, 1700–1702), a member of the Church of England, was appointed governor instead of the leading dissenter, Joseph Morton. Moore was a fierce Goose Creek activist and was supported for governor by the leading proprietor, an aggressive Anglican. His elevation over the dissenter was the catalyst for a bitter religious rivalry between the Anglicans and the dissenters. Also, at this time the Anglican missionary society known as the Society for the Propagation of the Gospel in Foreign Parts (SPG) was activated in South Carolina. The impetus of the missionary society, along with the Goose Creek Men, other Anglicans and the governor, acted to establish the Anglican Church as the official state church of South Carolina.

Robert Stevens, a former leader of the Commons House of Assembly and an Anglican communicant at St. James, Goose Creek Church, became spokesman for the Anglicans and worked for the establishment of the Anglican Church as the state church.[188] Through his efforts, the support of the Goose Creek faction, and Governor Johnson, the Church of England was established as the official church in 1706.[189] That same year, the colony was divided into parishes named after parishes in Barbados. These events caused bitterness among the non-Anglican dissenters in South

Carolina who felt deceived and disappointed by the actions of the government but apparently Francis LeJau, the Goose Creek Church minister did not share their sense of injustice. Once he opined in a letter to his missionary society that the "meanest sort of people seem to be better disposed than the dissenters."[190]

The dissenters were just as indignant and bitter toward the Anglicans. Joseph Boone was sent to England by the Carolina dissenters to appeal for the disallowance of the Church Act. In his appeal, he accused the Anglicans of securing sufficient votes to pass the Act by gathering "all the scum they could rake together" and then complained that the Anglicans "scoured to Goose Creek and Silk Hope [Plantation], and their creatures echoed out, that there was an Assembly chosen."[191]

The issue of native trade re-emerged at the same time the church establishment issue was battled. The magnitude of the unfair native trade practices and the strong possibilities of native uprisings caused the Goose Creek Men to find common cause with the French Huguenots and to unify in opposition to the dissenters, in an attempt to gain control of the native trade and to reform trade practices. The Goose Creek leaders including James Moore, the Governor; Sir Nathaniel Johnson, a wealthy slave owner; Ralph Izard, planter; Job Howe, planter and Robert Daniel were, as Anglicans, the center of the native trade reform movement.

Moore was the first governor to regulate native trade with agents. He was in debt when he took office and sought a bill to give him a monopoly on the trade. When the bill failed to pass, he ordered the assembly dissolved and called for new elections, but was replaced before he could shore up his position. In 1702, Nathaniel Johnson (1702–1710), an ally of the Goose Creek Men, replaced him. At this time, Colonel James Moore simultaneously held the offices of receiver general, attorney general and judge of the admiralty, as well as member of the grand council. The Goose Creek Men maintained their political stronghold, but bitterness among the factions persisted and carried over to the regulation of the native trade.

The controversies resulting from the acts to establish the church and regulate native trade caused a series of events to follow that led to the replacement of the proprietors with royal rule. The possibility of hostilities from natives, pirates and the European rivals, France and Spain, created fear that caused panic among the colonists and stirred them to generate additional taxes for self defense under the new church establishment laws. When the proprietors rejected the church establishment laws, they unintentionally voided the taxes enacted for self-defense. The fear of attack felt by the colonists transferred to resentment and anger at the incompetent and neglectful behaviors of the proprietors. These fears and resentments were the last of many issues that separated the colonists from the proprietors.

The abuse by the Indian traders caused colonists to fear a native war, which eventually came in 1715 causing more than four hundred deaths. While the colonial assembly was struggling with the aftermath of the war, a revival of the old pirate grievances returned to the political arena. The proprietors declared pirate trade illegal but never invested in protection of the colony from piracy. As soon as the colony became wealthy, the pirates moved their base of operations from the rich Caribbean Sea to the Cape Fear River in North Carolina, to be closer to the lucrative Carolina coastal shipping lanes. Without proprietary protection, a large number of colonial ships were attacked along the coast making it impossible to take a safe voyage. Increasingly, rich cargoes of imports, coupled with weak defenses, made South Carolina a prime target for piracy. The notorious pirate Blackbeard, as well as pirate Stede Bonnet, terrorized Charleston harbor and paralyzed the city. The colonists appealed to the proprietors for help but received no response. The colonists then attacked the problem themselves. A Virginia fleet killed Blackbeard, while a South Carolina fleet, led by William Rhett, captured Stede Bonnet and his crew.[192] Also, under the personal command of Governor Nathaniel Johnson, the colonists broke up a pirate blockade of the port of Charleston. The colonists were flushed with confidence. Goose Creeker, George Chicken served as special judge for the trial of Stede Bonnet and sentenced him to hang.[193] Other pirates were driven off and a sense of relief was felt in Goose Creek, but the colonists could not forget the failure of the proprietors to help at a grave time of peril.

According to directives from the proprietors, the people from each county chose the representatives to the assembly and thus the colony was to have elections from time to time. It was customary to choose the members of the assembly with elections in Charleston, but the Church Act of 1706 established the parish electoral system and decentralized the elections by establishing and appropriating duties to the wardens of each parish. St. James, Goose Creek Parish was allocated three representatives. The people were pleased with the first election under the new law in 1717, since there was greater convenience in voting closer to home and the process was much more orderly with no drunken riots for the first time in memory.[194] However, the proprietors objected and ordered the governor to void the new parish election law and dissolve the assembly. They called for a new election in accordance with the old election law and declared all laws passed by the assembly repealed. This repeal was dangerous to the colony because the repealed laws had regulated trade and raised the taxes for defense. After the election, the new members protested the orders of the proprietors and formed themselves into a convention. The infuriated conventioneers announced their intention to reject the proprietors and seek the protection of the king of England. The resolve of the conventioneers translated into action on the part of the assembly. The fear and resentment resulting from the Yemassee War, the battles with the pirates and the resulting convention of protest prompted the assembly to bypass the proprietors and appeal directly to the British government for protection.

The rising tide of dissent was unstoppable. Governor Robert Johnson was popular among the Goose Creek Men, but even though he was asked to continue as governor in the king's name, he refused, declaring his loyalty to those who appointed him. The political turmoil was further complicated by the threat of Spanish invasion, giving the governor an excuse to mobilize the militia. He hoped that the Spanish threat would keep the colonists' minds off political issues but this maneuver failed. The militia, once mobilized, became a formidable force, and it almost unanimously supported the move to reject proprietary rule. The colonial assembly refused to recognize the proprietary vetoes and when Governor Johnson refused to align with the assembly, the convention chose James Moore II as governor (1719–1721), the son of former governor James Moore, a Goose Creek man. Governor Robert Johnson (1717–1719) continued to try to restore proprietary rule, but because of the threat of militia violence he succumbed to the revolution. James Moore II was then installed as governor and served in that capacity until the king sent the first royal governor in 1721. Upon the completion of this first revolution, South Carolina became a royal colony.

During the first fifty years of the Carolina colony, the Goose Creek settlers were remarkable people. They were energetic, ambitious, resourceful, independent-minded and instrumental in effecting twenty-two changes in the governorship. With each passing year they, as products of the frontier, became more apt and able to resist overseas authority. The Goose Creek people developed rich lands, and battled aggressively to survive in the Carolina frontier and to impose their political philosophy on the British colony. The political arena was harsh during the years of proprietary rule. It was a rough frontier society where violence was commonplace and where a man's worth was measured by his strength and cunningness.

The transition from proprietary rule to royal government did not alleviate all of the problems that troubled the Goose Creek Men. There remained the heated issues of currency, political representation and taxation. These issues were argued, debated and finally led to an even more significant and broader revolution for independence. Fifty years after the rejection of the proprietors, the sons of the same men who praised the king as the new ruler were rejecting the king's ministers in the Revolution of 1776.

Chapter IV
A Plantation Society
1719–1790

The revolution that freed the settlers from the negligent rule of the proprietors is much easier to place in historical chronology than the passing of the Goose Creek frontier. The frontier had a dynamic impact upon the lives of the people, but its influences waned and it was replaced by a plantation society sometime during the early years of the eighteenth century. In 1719, South Carolina became a royal colony and by then, plantations in Goose Creek were well established and the beautiful parish church was filled to capacity with worshipers. The frontier times passed and Goose Creek became a prosperous corner of South Carolina.

Mrs. St. Julien Ravenel provided a good description of the frontiersmen who became the Goose Creek landed gentry in her book, *Charleston, The Place and The People*. She wrote:

> *Many rich planters from Barbados and other West Indian islands came to the province, bringing their Negroes with them. They settled themselves chiefly on a small affluent branch of the Cooper, called, from the fancied resemblance of its winding course to the curving neck of the goose, "Goosecreek..." Thus began—and not from the fanciful nobility—that untitled class of landed gentry.*[195]

These frontiersmen tamed the wilderness and paved the way for subsequent settling of professionals, such as were encouraged in a 1732 advertisement in the *South Carolina Gazette*. The advertisement enticed craftsmen and tradesmen to settle in Goose Creek by offering leases on eight-acre tracts of property fronting the "Broad Path." The advertisement described cleared land suitable for agriculture or pasturage and ideally situated for craftsmen near the Goose Creek Bridge. The notice continued, "Trades thought most proper to settle on it are, a Smith, Carpenter, Wheelwright, Bricklayer, Butcher, Taylor, shoemaker and a Tanner."[196] By the time this article appeared in the Charleston newspaper, the pirates had been cleared from the waters and the hostile Yemassees were only memories in the minds of aging militiamen. Now the plantation owners needed craftsmen and tradesmen to support their improved lifestyles.

The lives of the European Americans in Goose Creek during the years of the plantation society were far advanced from frontier time. The carriage ride from the plantation to the church was safe and pleasant. The rice and indigo economy of colonial Goose Creek produced prosperity. Plantations hosted fairs, horse races, religious celebrations and weddings. A typical wedding cake recipe of this period began with twenty pounds of butter and two hundred eggs.[197]

Tidewater, Virginia; Maryland; and northeastern North Carolina were colonies of English extraction. In these areas, the economy was based on tobacco. Under the political leadership of an elite group of landed proprietors, these planters kept close ties with their mother country and adopted the manners of the English aristocracy. Powerful families, especially the Carters, Lees, Byrds and Randolphs of Virginia, and the Carrolls, Dulaneys and Galloways of Maryland, became politically and financially dominant in their respective areas. The Carolina Lowcountry was settled later than Virginia, Maryland and North Carolina and differed from those colonies in its ethnic composition, its economy and its culture. The Fundamental Constitution provided the foundation from which the Carolina landed gentry emerged. Grants of land were awarded to settlers in accordance with the provisions of the Constitution and upon these grants was founded the aristocracy of the Lowcountry.[198] The size of Goose Creek land grants was largely due to the nature of the terrain and the methods of agriculture. Hardwood trees and cypress were highly desired and increased the value of the land. Thus, Goose Creek lands were prized because they were flush with oak, cypress and hickory forests, but soil exhaustion frequently resulted from the lack of proper fertilization. Rotating crops and using manure for fertilization were not practiced during the colonial period. As one field was exhausted, another was prepared for planting. The large amount of swamplands and the need for vast amounts of fertile ground accounted for the desire for large Goose Creek estates. A partial listing of landholdings in Goose Creek in 1745 indicated that the median land holding was more than nine hundred acres and that 75 percent of the owners possessed plantations larger than five hundred acres.[199] Throughout the colonial period, the mean size of the landholdings remained nearly unchanged. The average Goose Creek plantation in 1790 was about the same size as the 1745 median. Table 4.1 is derived from a partial tax record of landholdings for forty-four residents in Goose Creek and shows the percent of holdings of varying acreage.

The main house was the central feature of the plantation and was usually located on the highest ground near the center of the property. Main houses on the Goose Creek plantations were spacious for the times but usually not elaborate. Only a small number of Goose Creek main houses featured columns and intricate woodwork. Most were simply well-constructed, practical buildings designed to provide comfort and shelter for the household. Most owners of the properous plantations kept homes in Charleston. Daniel and Solomon Legare owned houses on Broad Street. John Deas built an elaborate house on Bedon's Alley. George Chicken lived most of his later years on Tradd Street.

Table 4.1

Number of Acres Per Holding	**Percent of residents in St. James, Goose Creek Parish**
0	23
1–99	2
100–200	4
201–300	2
301–500	11
501–1,000	27
1,001–2,000	16
2,001–3,000	9
3,001+	11
Median Acreage 908	

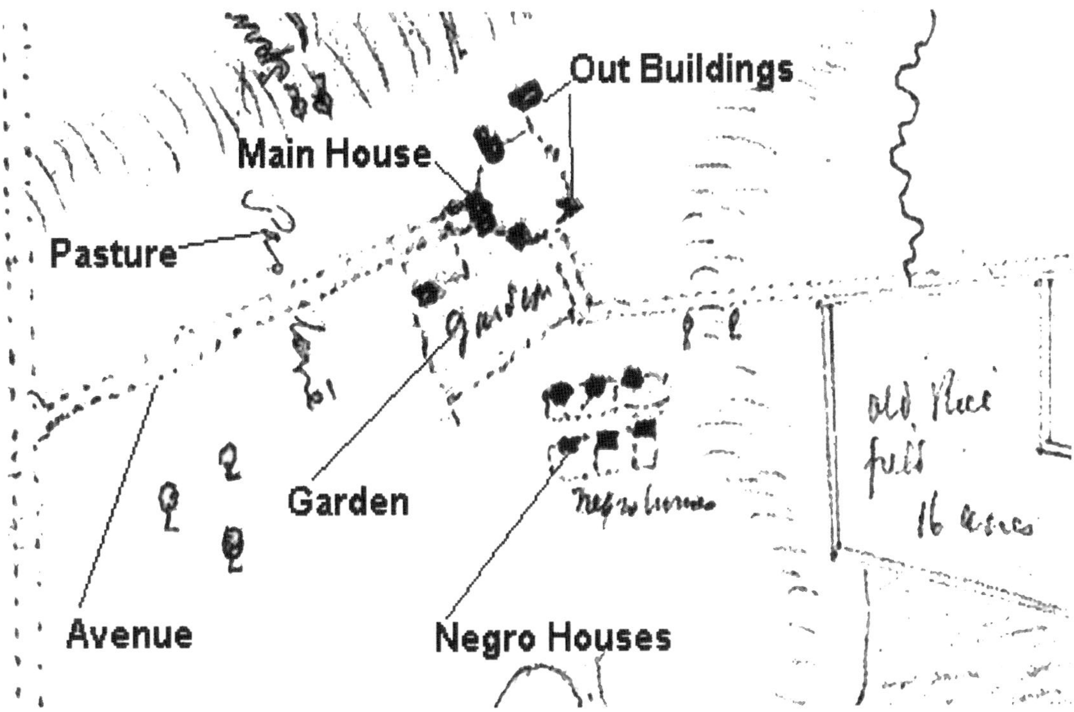

Plat 4.1 This partial plat shows the avenue and main house of Fountainbleau Plantation as surveyed in 1786. H.A.M. Smith traced the plat. The manuscript labels are included for this publication. The tracing is among the collections of the South Carolina Historical Society.

Peter Hume enjoyed a home downtown. Thomas Loughton Smith kept a home on Church Street, and Mathurin Guerin on Broad. The Charleston homes showed off the wealth of the larger Goose Creek planters, but the wealth of some of the owners was evident in the countryseats as well. Avenues from the nearest road to the house were sometimes elaborately developed and shaded with a double row of trees. Often the avenue ended in a "pleasure garden" planted with ornamentals. Outbuildings often included an overseer's quarters, kitchen, carriage house and barns. Plat 4.1 of Fountainbleau Plantation shows the avenue passing through a pasture to a garden and main house. Outbuildings, including two rows of "Negro houses" are apparent on the plat. The entrance avenue at Fountainbleau intersected the main road from Charleston to Goose Creek.

Plat 4.2 shows the avenue leading from the Dorchester/Goose Creek Road to the main house at De La Plaine's Plantation. It passed between a double-row of twelve small buildings that may have been slave quarters. Outbuildings flanked the main house and an orchard or forested lawn served as a backdrop. The shaded avenues leading to the front door of the main houses in Goose Creek connected to public or private roads. Some private avenues such as "Gibbes Path" and "Back River Upper Road" and "Back River Lower Road" extended for several miles tying numerous plantation main avenues to public right-of-ways.

Springfield Plantation was accessible by way of Gibbes Path. Plat 4.3 shows the Springfield avenue, main house, flanking structures, "Negro Houses" and an elaborate pleasure garden with an

Plat 4.2 This partial plat shows De La Plaine's Plantation as surveyed by Joseph Purcell in 1791 and traced by H.A.M. Smith. The manuscript labels, "Avenue," "Garden," "Main House" and "Slave Quarters?" were added for this publication. The plat is among the collections of the South Carolina Historical Society.

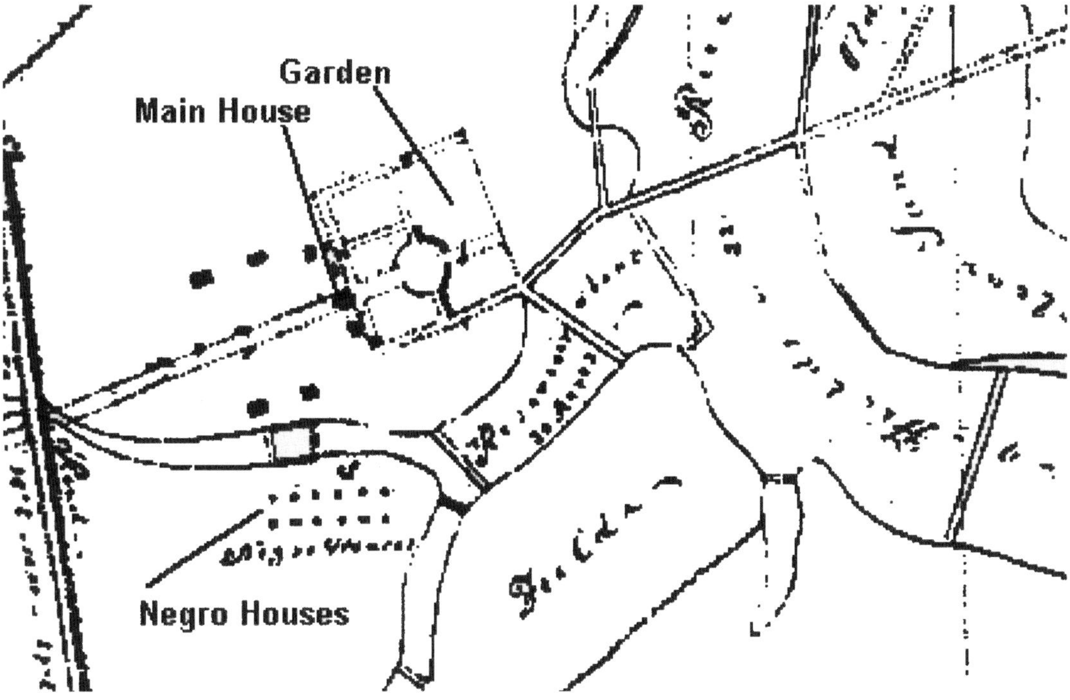

Plat 4.3 This plat was drawn from a 1791 survey of Springfield Plantation. The manuscript labels, "Main House," "Garden" and "Negro Houses" were added for this publication for clarity. The McCrady Plat, number 1646 is on microfilm at the Charleston County Library.

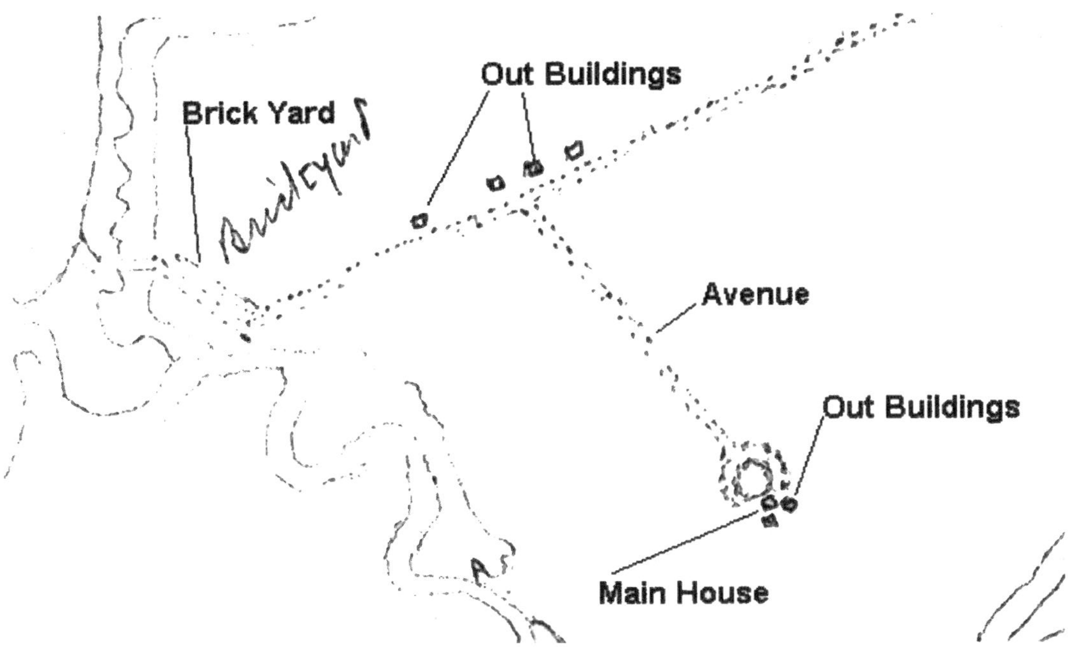

Plat 4.4 This partial plat of Ararat Plantation was drawn from a survey made by Joseph Purcell in 1799 and traced by H.A.M. Smith. The manuscript labels were added for this publication. The plat is among the collections of the South Carolina Historical Society.

off-center circular feature and radiating walkways. Back River Upper Road tied the main avenue of Medway and Back River Plantations to the State Road. The Back River Lower Road was an extension of a private mile long tree-lined avenue leading from Parnassus Plantation on Back River to the State Road at the 17-Mile House near the Goose Creek Church. Ararat and Howe Hall also used this private right-of-way.

Plat 4.4 shows Ararat Plantation owned by Harriet Horry. A single avenue ran parallel to Foster Creek and terminated in a circular drive at the front door of the main house. Outbuildings were located behind the main house and opposite to an entrance road some distance from the principal dwelling. The main house at Howe Hall plantation is shown in partial plat 4.5. The house was approached by a frontal avenue and supported by two access roads. Outbuildings lined one side of the entrance drive and the principal dwelling. A "Fish Pond" is noted near the house.

Out of necessity, successful Goose Creek planters were multi-talented who managed vast acreage and large numbers of slave labor. They were farmers, lumbermen, cattlemen and merchants because successful plantations were not merely large farms, but agricultural factories that boarded laborers and specialized in growing and marketing single cash crops. Thus, plantations were usually multi-faceted settlements with varying numbers of specialized buildings and different kinds of skilled and unskilled people. Often the larger plantations were self-contained with carpenters, brickmakers and bricklayers, cow and swine tenders, poultry and dairywomen, nurses for the slave sick house, blacksmiths and house servants. All used provision fields to provide food stores and in a few cases, Goose Creek plantations featured a schoolhouse for the children of the owners and white overseers.

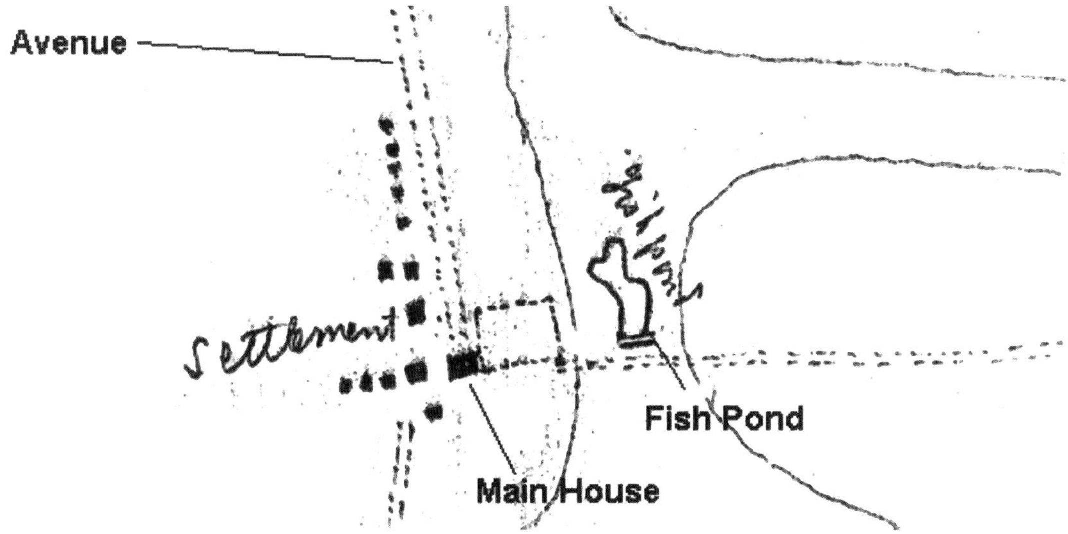

Plat 4.5 This partial plat shows Howe Hall as drawn from a survey by Joseph Purcell in 1775 and traced by H.A.M. Smith. The labels, "Main House" and "Fish Pond" were added for clarity. The plat is among the collections of the South Carolina Historical Society.

An interesting list of the basics needed to start a plantation and a summary of the costs associated with starting a Carolina plantation is shown in table 4.2. It cost more than £2,000 to start a typical Carolina plantation in 1775.

Successful Goose Creekers such as William Johnson of White House, John Ball of Back River and Alexander Mazyck of Springfield Plantation were multi-talented planters who used every advantage of the forests and fields. Their plantation journals, letters and other private papers give detailed accounts of the operation of their estates. They recorded their observations of the climate, made weather predictions for the days ahead and based daily decisions on temperature and rainfall. The health of their slaves was a constant concern because each was an expensive asset. They kept their slaves clothed, sheltered, fed and productive and consistently directed the labor force to move from task to task based upon the availability of labor, the season, the stage of development of crops and available opportunities in the marketplace. They relied heavily on the waterways for inexpensive transportation, and along with the neighboring planters, transported country produce and staple crops that made the waters of the Cooper River and its tributaries the life-blood of Charleston.

A great highway of trade along the Ashley and Cooper Rivers made Charleston the cultural and trading center of the colony. The Cooper was navigable for twenty miles from Charleston, and its many tributaries, including Goose Creek, reached into the pinewoods and forests of the Lowcountry. The water of the Cooper was busy with traffic. Governor James Glen wrote in 1751 that the "Cooper River appears sometimes a kind of floating market and we have numbers of Canoes, Boats, and Pettygues that ply incessantly, bringing down the Country Produce to Town and returning with necessaries the Planters want..."[200] By this time, life for the Goose Creek people on their plantations was not the lonely and isolated existence of their frontier forefathers. As the Goose Creek community matured, craftsmen and professionals found opportunities for

Items	Pounds	Shillings
1,000 acres of land (1/3 good swamp and remainder upland)	575	15
Buildings	142	15
Two good Negro mechanics	142	15
Two old Negroes to care for stock	57	0
26 field slaves (1/3 Women)	927	10
Two house servants	69	5
Stock (including 80 oxen and cows, and eight horses)	88	16
Plantation tools, carts and plows	21	8
Total	2,024	9

Table 4.2 The table is entitled, "Some Typical Costs of Establishing a Plantation in Carolina, 1775."

livelihood. During the frontier period most, if not all, homesteads were virtually isolated and self-contained and the larger plantations kept many craftsmen fully employed. During the plantation era service centers emerged. Taverns capitalized on their locations near busy crossroads to become general purpose centers offering lodging, food, livery and mercantile conveniences. Although the taverns were initially constructed to serve travelers, they also provided a place for locals to gather to socialize, conduct business, eat, gamble and drink. Bishop Bowen was a frequent visitor to the 10-Mile Tavern on the southern section of the Goose Creek Road. As a resident of the Neck, he was required to serve patrol duty, but preferring to spend his evenings at the tavern he frequently paid a substitute to serve in his stead. One evening when Bishop Bowen's name was called out in the tavern to serve patrol, someone loudly announced that he was, "Drunk under the table!"[201] There were inns throughout Goose Creek. The Goose Creek Friendly or River Club met monthly at Edward Keating's place. For many years, he operated a social hall at the 23-Mile House on the Moncks Corner Road. Benjamin Mazyck, the organization's secretary listed eighteen members of the club. All were wealthy young planters who resided in the general vicinity. They are listed here:

> *The honorable James Kinloch, William Middleton, Isaac Childs, Zacher.* [sic] *Villeponteaux, Benjamin Mazyck, James McKelphin, Peter Taylor Thomas Wright, Thomas Middleton, John Morton, Richard Shingleton, William Allen, Nathaniel Broughton, Andrew Broughton, Richard Gough, John Gough, Peter Hume and Robert Boddin.*[202]

Taverns were often busy and ribald places of commerce, but these social centers in Goose Creek never expanded into towns, as they did in many other communities. Nonetheless, some became important to the development of skilled services such as blacksmith and livery businesses. The 10-Mile Tavern was one such place, as was Vance's Tavern at the divergence of the Goose Creek and Dorchester Roads. There was another tavern at the 17-mile marker near the Goose Creek Bridge, which was a convergence point for land traffic and where, in addition to the tavern, a church and school brought people together. About two miles northwest of the bridge was the intersection of the road to Wassamasaw and the road to Moncks Corner. This was a busy place where taverns were situated at both the 18 and 19-mile markers. The 22-Mile House Tavern was located near the intersection of the Moncks Corner Road and the road to Strawberry Ferry. Here, as well as on larger plantations, the craftsmen and professionals found customers. Many types of craftsmen and professionals lived and worked in Goose Creek during the flourishing plantation era.

Most Goose Creekers who bought and sold land were identified as "planters"; others were "gentlemen" or carried a landed title such as landgrave or cassique. One Goose Creeker, Sir Hovenden Walker, was a knight, a high honor granted only by the king. "Esquire" was an ancient title one step below a knight. A squire was a knight in training, but by the colonial period it was usually abbreviated as Esq. appearing after the family name and used as an honorary title, often associated with attorneys, barristers or elected officials. Isaac Godin was an esquire, as well as John Sommers, Joseph Glover, Maurice Simmons and several others. Civil titles were also listed such as "Francis Lejau, Justice of the Peace." Justices of the peace, notaries and attorneys were much in demand to prepare and certify various suits, mortgages and other agreements needed in trade and commerce. Sometimes titles were mixed with responsibilities such as "Peter Hume, gentleman, of St. James, Goose Creek, as attorney for..." [203] The "Clerk" or "Clark" was usually a church minister such as Elias Prioleau. A "servant" was a person with an indenture to provide service for a defined period of time in exchange for shelter, lodging and other promises.[204] In addition, military titles appeared such as Colonel Benjamin Singleton and Captain George Chicken. A variety of other occupations were noted in the land transactions. Conrad Smisser, John Creighton and Conrad Keckley were innkeepers. Joseph Griffin was a weaver; John Filbin, a tailor; Abraham Dupont, a brazier and William Gickie, a mariner. Joseph Griffin, John Bayley and John Fraser were Indian traders. Edward Shrewsbury and his wife made brick while James Withers and David Skinner were bricklayers. Edward Smith was a "plasterer;" James Rochford, Henry Rigby and James Lewis were carpenters. John Hutchinson was a chairmaker, John Fisher was a cabinetmaker and Peter Guerin made shoes. He was titled "cordwainer" as one who worked with cordovan leather. John Filbin was a saddler, Gideon Faucheraud a gunsmith and Daniel Legare a gold and silversmith. Interestingly, blacksmith as an occupation title did not appear among the many deeds and mortgages, perhaps indicating that the profession was not lucrative enough in Goose Creek for the craftsman to purchase land. There were also tanners, coopers, rope makers, masons, sawyers and joiners, but like blacksmiths, none of these occupations appeared among the land transfers and deeds of Goose Creek properties of this period.

Some Goose Creekers were small farmers with few or no slaves. Those small farmers who owned land such as Mathurin Guerin were referred to as yeomen.[205] Surveyors were very important during this agricultural period when land ownership was the basis for social and political status. Thus, Goose Creek surveyors such as John Diamond and James Cook were esteemed and in demand. Women's names appearing on deeds did not carry titles other than wife, widow, minor, spinster or relict to note their status, relative to their state of marriage. As an older lady who never married, Elizabeth Clifford was a spinster.[206] Another land transaction in 1774 described the wife of William Haggett, owner of Crowfield, as a "wife," "spinster," "widow" and "relict" in the same document.[207]

During this era, Goose Creek was a mosaic of service centers with a wide variety of occupations and expendable wealth, but the typical central town never developed because the creeks and rivers served as the main streets, and the proximity of Charleston and the convenience of the waterways made a central business area unnecessary. Nevertheless, the main houses were close enough for easy

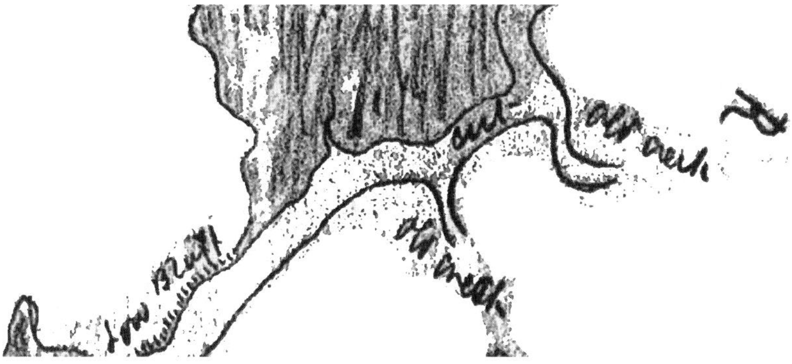

Plat 4.6 This plat is a tracing of a section of a plat of Yeamans Hall drawn by John Purcell from a 1786 survey. Henry A.M. Smith traced the original plat. The tracing is among the collections of the South Carolina Historical Society.

social intercourse, and although water was a common means of business transport, various designs of fine carriages and superb riding horses were also widely used to carry planters and their families along roadways and paths that connected plantations to each other and to Charleston.

Canals (Cuts), Roads, Bridges and Ferries

Petitions to the Commons House of Assembly for canals or "cuts" through marshes were not uncommon in South Carolina and cuts on Goose Creek were requested from time to time. One request resulted in a debate, which weighed the benefits of the canal against the loss of marsh grazing land. John Deas and eight others requested that a cut be made on Goose Creek. They appealed to the House of Representatives in 1785 to make "a few short cuts through the marshes that…thirteen miles and a quarter may be shortened to a distance of…one and one quarter mile."[208] Counter petitions from John Bowen, a plantation owner on the north side of Goose Creek and Thomas Smith, a landowner on the south side, pleaded with the Commons House of Assembly to deny the request, because a cut through the marsh would deprive them of the use of six hundred acres of "hard marsh," which was land used to graze cattle and the only pasture they owned.[209] This request for a cut was denied, but on another occasion a cut was made on Goose Creek near Yeamans Hall. Plat 4.6 shows two sections of "old creek," which was an obsolete oxbow span of the waterway. The water route was abridged when a "cut" shown on the plat, was dug through the marsh to shorten the travel distance.

The ownership of ferries or toll roads afforded opportunities for profit. The toll itself was not a significant source of income, but the ferry location enhanced the nearby property values and offered an advantageous place for a store or tavern. Providing assistance to the passage of people and produce through Goose Creek was an important function of government from the earliest period. Much of the country trade moved through this area and benefited greatly from the construction of bridges and the establishment of the ferry at Strawberry, near the colonial town of Childsbury on the western branch of the Cooper River.[210] The franchise to the ferry was granted for seven years to

James Child, but after his death, Mrs. Lydia Chicken, whose family members were early settlers in that section of the parish, assumed management of the ferry and charged a new fee commensurate to what she thought the service was worth. Complaints were lodged at the Commons House of Assembly stating that the previous ferry operator once had "a good boat and hands to ferry people across the river for one shilling and three pence for man and horse and seven pence and half penny for a single man."[211] The law that established the fare expired and "now Mrs. Lydia Chicken oblige travelers to pay twice that amount." The petitioners asked that a set rate be enacted for "horsemen, Chairs, Chaises..."

The many lowlands, creeks and river inlets made roads, causeways, bridges and ferries necessary for travel and commerce. The rivers and creeks were important transport routes, but the road system was increasingly used to carry commerce from the ever more distant hinterlands to the consumers and shippers of Charleston. Thus the maintenance of the roads became an important responsibility of the colonial and later the state governments. Map 4.1 shows the interconnected wet areas that caused land travel to be difficult and made expensive bridges and raised roadways necessary. Thus, commissioners were appointed in each parish to carry out the responsibilities of road and bridge construction and maintenance. Road commissioners from St. James, Goose Creek named in the 1721 Road Act were Thomas Smith, Captain Benjamin Schenekingh, Captain Roger Moore, Captain William Dry, Captain Edward Hyrne, John Stone and John Parker.[212] The low lying condition, especially in the eastern part of the parish, and the scarcity of rock and stone made it necessary to use timber as a road surface to traverse shallow water. These "corduroy" roads were built by laying logs side-by-side perpendicular to the direction of travel and covering the logs with a mixture of sand and clay. This design raised the road surface above the water and mud, but made

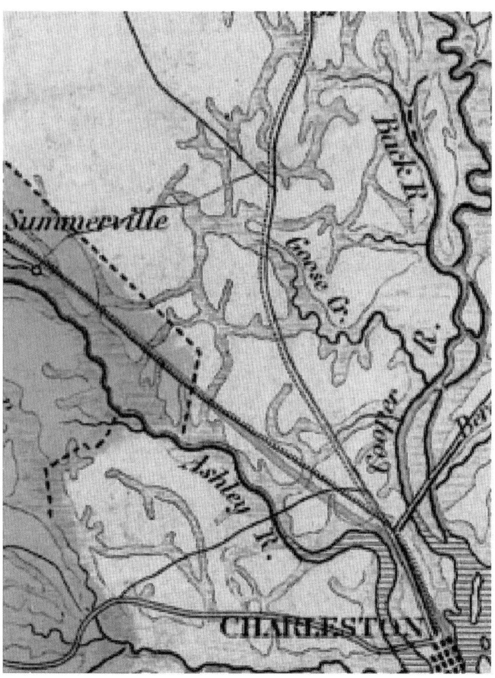

Map 4.1 The 1839 *Burr Map* shows the waterways and wetlands in the eastern part of the St. James Goose Creek Parish. The headwaters of the creeks and rivers interconnect allowing no dry land passage.

travel bumpy and uncomfortable. Property owners along the route were assessed timber for these projects, a practice that began during the colonial period and continued into the nineteenth century. According to the proceedings of the Commons House of Assembly, that body was sometimes called upon to reimburse landowners for timber used in road construction.[213] In addition, because of the shortage of stone for gravel, less durable clay was used as a road surface, which made frequent repair necessary. The journals of the Commons House of Assembly contain frequent petitions from Goose Creek planters desiring bridge, road or ferry work. An act approved in 1737 authorized a road from Dorchester to Captain Izard's Cowpens Plantation on Cypress Swamp.[214] A petition from Alexander Wood asked the general assembly to establish a road and ferry that would be of great advantage to "all persons traveling to and from the northern parts of this province."[215]

The journal further recorded that Goose Creeker Robert Brown requested that the Commons House of Assembly repair the bridges and roads at public expense. In 1752 Doctor Robert Brown, whose Goose Creek plantation was on the Moncks Corner Road near the 22-Mile House, petitioned for payment from the Commons House of Assembly for timber taken from his property to repair two bridges.[216]

Clearly, a reliable funding and maintenance system was needed to keep the roads and bridges passable. Slaves, supervised by road commissioners, built and maintained the roads and bridges, but valuable slaves, needed on the plantation, were not easily spared for roadwork. Consequently, a law was passed that required all male slaves from sixteen to sixty years of age to perform road duty when called by the commissioners. Thus, slaves built the Goose Creek Bridge and repaired it many times, but the required maintenance became increasingly onerous. A petition from the Commission for the Highways brought to the Commons House of Assembly as early as 1757, explained that the Goose Creek Bridge was typically repaired only once every five or six years, but due to the increased passage of heavy wagons with iron-rimmed wheels traveling from the back settlements and North Carolina, it was necessary to repair the bridge twice a year. The petitioners requested that a toll be initiated at the bridge on all wagons and carts to alleviate the expense caused by the expense caused by the scarcity of slave labor.[217]

Slaves

The institution of slavery was clearly the most dynamic and important element of the era due to its effect on so many human lives, its influences on the economy of Goose Creek and the lasting impact on society. From early on, the number of Negro slaves in Goose Creek outnumbered the Caucasians. In 1709, eighty families owned 450 slaves.[218] By the end of proprietary rule, South Carolina showed a clear African majority and the St. James, Goose Creek Parish kept the greatest percentage of their population in bondage. In 1720, St. James, Goose Creek was the fourth largest by area and the fourth greatest by population of the twelve parishes, but with 535 Caucasians and 2,027 enslaved Africans, the Goose Creek Parish kept 79 percent of its people enslaved.[219]

In 1737, Lieutenant Governor Broughton warned that "our Negroes are very numerous and more dreadful to our safety than any Spanish invasion."[220] Yet, despite the constant fear of rebellion, the planters in Goose Creek became increasingly dependent on large numbers of Africans. New immigrants to Carolina were encouraged to bring as many slaves as they could afford. One of

Governor Johnson's directives stated that, "No man should own more than fifty acres of land for each member of his family." The family defined in Governor Johnson's instructions included slaves, and the directive pertained to new grants and ignored any previous ownership. Thus, the new plan allowed large land grants to be added to previous acquisitions if the family was sufficiently large. Consequently, more slaves were imported. Slaves were sometimes leased temporarily to acquire land according to this law. Charles Lowndes purchased one thousand acres of land on Goose Creek shortly after his arrival from St. Kitts. Several years later, he acquired a grant for twenty-two hundred acres. In compliance with the law, his household amounted to forty-four members. To accomplish this he secured temporary ownership of slaves to enlarge his "family" and qualify for more acreage. On April 15, 1732, he paid Henry Gibbes £300 for a mortgage of five slaves and six days later, he paid James Kinloch £600 for the mortgage of seven additional slaves.[221]

Table 4.3

County or Area	**Mean Aggregate Wealth per Inventoried Estate in Pounds Sterling (£)**
Charleston District	2,337.7
Anne Arundel County, Maryland	660.4
Charlotte/Halifax Counties, Virginia	564.4
Philadelphia, Pennsylvania	396.7
Suffolk County, Maryland	321.3
New York	278.0

From 1720 to 1745, the population of the Goose Creek Parish experienced a net increase of 789 people, but most of the increase was a result of the growing slave population. While the Caucasian population dropped 25 percent due to planters leaving marginal and exhausted lands for fertile fields elsewhere, the slave numbers increased by 924 (45 percent) during that twenty-five year year span.[222] By 1745, almost 90 percent of the population in the Goose Creek Parish was in bondage with 70 percent of the slaves residing on large plantations with more than fifty slaves each.[223] The 1745 tax return for the Goose Creek Parish provided a unique look at the wealth of the households during a time when the parish was approaching its apogee of prosperity. At mid-century, South Carolina was the most prosperous of the British colonies in North America, and Goose Creek appears to be the wealthiest parish in Carolina. Table 4.3 shows the comparative private wealth of districts and counties in North America in 1774.

The Charleston District, which included the Goose Creek Parish, was exceedingly wealthy and no other area in North America could compare to the personal affluence. The second wealthiest area, Anne Arundel County, Maryland, boasted a mean wealth that was only 28 percent of the mean private wealth of inventoried estates in Charleston. Appendix 5 lists most of the residents of Goose Creek in 1745, as well as their slaves, land and financial worth. By comparison to the mean given in table 4.3, Goose Creek planters as a whole were the wealthiest in the Charleston District.

Peter Manigault of Goose Creek was the richest man in North America, amassing a net worth of £32,737.8 sterling, which is almost $3,000,000 in today's currency. A painting of Peter Manigault by George Roupell entitled *Mr. Peter Manigault and His Friends* depicts Manigault and dinner guests at his Goose Creek home sometime in the 1750s. The painting is on display in the Winterhur Museum. After Peter Manigault, the next richest man in North America was a New Englander with less than half the wealth of the Goose Creeker.[224] Manigault does not appear in appendix 5 nor do three other of the wealthiest Goose Creek planters, Henry Izard, James Kinloch and Sarah Wilkinson Middleton. These three wealthy planters lent an average of £3,500 sterling amounting to more than $450,000 in today's money, at 6 percent interest. The incomplete records reported only approximately 70 percent of the taxpayers because some of the records were lost or destroyed. But, regardless of the incomplete report, the immense wealth of many Goose Creekers is obvious, and there appears to have been an abundance of money in Goose Creek for investment. The money was primarily invested in land and slaves, a combination that returned large dividends. By 1750, St. James, Goose Creek boasted a larger proportion of rich households than any other locality in British North America.[225]

What is surprising from the incomplete tax records of 1745 is the percentage of households that did not own land. About one-third of the households owned more than a thousand acres and two-thirds owned more than five hundred acres, but 23 percent of the households owned no land. One such resident was Robert Brown, a physician who owned thirty-five slaves and was obviously wealthy but possessed no acreage. He and others like him were professionals or artisans who did not rely upon land management for sustenance and thereby evaded the tax burdens. A smaller percentage of Goose Creekers were landless when compared to neighboring parishes, and the statistical comparisons remained constant until after the American Revolution, when Goose Creek prosperity dwindled.

Number of Slaves	Percent of Owners in 1745*	Percent of Owners in 1790**	Differences of Percents Between the Years 1745 and 1790
0	3%	17%	+14
1–10	27%	36%	+9
11–20	14%	13%	-1
21–50	29%	23%	-6
51–100	19%	5%	-14
100+	23%	3%	-20

Table 4.4 * The numbers were taken from Waterhouse, p. 217 and rounded up to the nearest whole number.

** The numbers were taken from the U.S. enumeration census and rounded up to the nearest whole number.

Records in subsequent decades show declines in acreage and slave counts. In 1790, the year of the first federal census, slaves represented 84 percent of the Parish population, but fewer people owned large numbers of slaves. Table 4.4 gives the comparative slave holdings in Goose Creek spanning four decades of the eighteenth century. The notable difference in slave holdings is the percent of owners with no slaves and the percent of owners with one hundred or more slaves. Almost all Goose Creekers owned slaves in 1745 with nearly a quarter of the owners possessing more than one hundred slaves. By 1790, these numbers shifted when only 3 percent of the owners kept one hundred or more slaves and 17 percent kept no slaves.

During this period, an African male slave sold for £250 or close to $5,000 in today's currency. Because slave numbers are an indication of wealth, Goose Creek appears to have become economically more stratified during the second half of the eighteenth century with fewer people possessing more of the wealth. Just 116 families owned all of the 2,333 slaves in Goose Creek in 1790. The total number of slaves was probably less than the period prior to the Revolutionary War because many slaves were taken from Goose Creek by British troops.[226] There were twenty families who owned no slaves and there were five families in Goose Creek that owned nearly one third of all the slaves. John Deas, Sr., owned 208 slaves; John Deas, Jr., possessed 170; Joseph Glover had 123 and Ralph Izard worked 105 slaves on his Goose Creek estate. In 1790, Izard owned 594 slaves on his eight plantations in three parishes making him the second largest slave owner in South Carolina.[227] Despite the widespread use of water culture after the American Revolution for irrigation and the elimination of the rice weeds, the demand for slaves remained to produce rice, indigo, foodstuffs, naval stores, livestock, bricks and to serve the plantation family. By the 1790s, tidal rice fields dominated the ranks of the most profitable plantations, and the estates of the wealthiest planters were along the banks of the Goose Creek, Cooper, Combahee, Santee and Waccamaw Rivers. Along those waters, slaves could produce twelve hundred to fifteen hundred pounds of rice per acre, which was five times more than the typical production of an inland swamp rice field.[228]

Slaves were important collateral and very expensive. Susannah St. John, widow of Stephen St. John of Back River Plantation, requested that the value of one of her slaves who was executed by the state be used as payment on a bond posted for the purchase of that slave.[229] In 1722, Edward Keating sold "5 negro men, 6 negro women, 1 indian boy, 1 negro boy and 2 negro girls" for £1,000.[230] In perspective, those slaves worth £1,000 equaled the value of a large one thousand acre plantation of good farmland. As valuable as the slaves were, all household members did not easily fit into measurable arrangements of ownership and servitude. One example is the Goose Creek family of Alexander Wood, which included slaves, freemen and children of mixed lineage. The records in the Charleston County inventories accounted for his wealth as of June 3, 1757. His estate included a Native American slave family, unrelated American natives, an "Indian" hunter, an African slave craftsman, an African slave hunter and an African field hand. His inventory included:

> *10 slaves: Ophella, his wife Jenny an Indian woman with two children, a 7 yr. old girl Phillis & 5 yr. old boy Frank; York an Indian fellow one of the hunters, old Moll almost past labor an Indian woman; Pompey black a carpenter; Hannibal black a field slave; Nero black a boy & a hunter; Peter black.*[231]

The records further account that Alexander Wood freed three "halfbreed" children: Dukey Cox and George Cox, whose mother was an Indian named Jenny and Mineva Watson, whose mother was "Indian Moll." [232] Free Native and African Americans lived on other Goose Creek plantations as well. "Free Harry" lived at George Parker's Plantation and the mother of Peter Holmes, a free black woman, lived on Mr. Coachman's estate.

There were many examples of non-standard family members and dubious lineage, but nevertheless a successful plantation depended on the productivity of healthy slaves. The slaves needed consistent and cost effective care for the plantation to succeed. Thus, as the area became wealthier, the care and maintenance of slaves generally improved. Slave quarters were better constructed, replacing the thatched huts of the frontier period, and moved farther from the main house and closer to the ever-expanding fields.[233] By the 1730s, some plantations boasted slave barracks. Charles Lowndes owned one thousand acres on Goose Creek with his plantation home, a sixty foot long cypress barn and slave barracks. His advertisement to sell the plantation appeared in the *South Carolina Gazette* January 18, 1735 and described some outbuildings as, "Negro houses to hold 50 Negroes." [234]

Some Goose Creekers purchased insurance policies to hedge against the loss of expensive slaves. Elizabeth Poyas insured her slave Julius through an Illinois insurance company,[235] and some planters purchased expensive professional medical treatment for their slaves. Dr. Samuel McCormick made several visits to Back River Plantation to give varying treatments to ailing or injured slaves. Dr. Alexander Garden of Otranto Plantation was employed by planters to use the new small pox vaccine to treat slaves. The treatment was expensive but a small pox epidemic could kill an entire slave village and bankrupt a plantation.[236]

In Goose Creek, the number of required slaves depended on the amount of swampland on the plantations. Swampland required great amounts of human toil in unhealthy environs before they were useable for rice cultivation. The thick growth of tupelos, cypress, willows, water oaks and others trees abounding in the swamps needed to be cleared away. Also planters needed to dig ditches and construct embankments and water reservoirs for irrigation. Fortunately, the imported slaves from western Africa were knowledgeable of rice culture, having grown rice in their African fields for generations, and were familiar with tools that had remained unchanged for centuries. The hoe was the principal implement for the cultivation of rice, indigo, corn and other crops, and harvesting was done with sickle and scythe.

The Reverend Richard Ludlam, who officiated at St. James, Goose Creek Church from 1723 to 1728, was a keen observer of local social and economic conditions during the early years of the plantation society. His travels through the parish brought him into contact with great plantations and small farms. In his letters to England, he repeatedly commented on the importance of rice as the staple crop in Goose Creek and its dependence upon slavery. The warm climate, the low Goose Creek swamps, the port at Charleston and the proximity to the West Indian slave trade were all factors contributing to the success of rice production. Consequently, some believe that rice became more of an "institution than a cereal."[237]

In his Fundamental Constitution, John Locke stated, "every freeman of Carolina shall have absolute power and authority over his Negro slaves, of what opinion or religion soever." Slavery was sanctioned and its existence was protected against any presumed jeopardy. In no other colony did slavery begin more auspiciously nor was there any greater prospect for its success than in South Carolina.[238] Regardless of the "auspicious" beginning, many South Carolinians were greatly concerned about the large importations of Africans, and as early as 1686, the colonial legislature passed laws to insure the domination of the Caucasian master over the slave as promised by the Fundamental Constitution.

Slaves were not allowed to engage in business or trade nor leave their plantation at night without written permission, but there are some indications that the wealth in Goose Creek lent itself to a more liberal treatment of slaves. For example, Goose Creek slaves seemed to fare better than those in other parts of the colony. Despite the slave codes, some Goose Creek slaves traded their own goods with neighboring plantations and at markets in Charleston. Goose Creeker Gabriel Manigault directed his slave, Cudgo, to "go to town with vegetables once a week as usual."[239] Sometimes a planter would send a slave with a note to the neighboring planter explaining that the slave had some of his own produce to sell. In Goose Creek, a traveler saw slaves collecting spanish moss. The assumption was that some masters allowed slaves to collect moss and sell it as mattress fillers to upholsterers in Charleston. Also, it was a general practice for Goose Creek slaves to grow rice and other produce on their own time for sale in Charleston. The practice became so common that planters near the Goose Creek Road to Charleston complained of "the great number of Negroes who are continually passing and repassing [sic] selling vegetables, etc. without tickets." The "tickets" were required by local ordinance, which prohibited slaves from holding money at the market and thus required shoppers to purchase tickets (script) with which they traded to the slave for the country produce. Receiving money in lieu of tickets, not only violated the ordinance but also encouraged a sense of independence and self-determination for some Goose Creek slaves. The governor complained in 1782 about the steady supply of foodstuffs from Goose Creek into British occupied Charleston when the patriots surrounded the city during the Revolutionary War. Governor John Mathews wrote to patriot General Francis Marion that a dozen to twenty slaves traveled from Charleston each night to "Goose Creek and up the Cooper River" and returned with supplies.[240] He stated, "The Chs Town markets are now daily supplied with the greatest plenty of everything they want." After the Revolutionary War, the governor attempted to limit the Sunday visits of "Country Negroes" who sold their "truck" on the town wharves on the Sabbath. His efforts failed and the common practice of slaves from the countryside coming to town on the Sabbath to sell on South-Bay Street continued. The *City Gazette* reported a complaint in 1798 of two fugitive slaves, a father and son from Goose Creek, supporting themselves by plundering plantations and "going backwards and forward to town by land and water" to sell in Charleston.[241] Yet, there were exceptions to the liberal treatment of Goose Creek slaves. One group of fifteen slaves escaped their Goose Creek plantation, complaining that they were mistreated and almost starved and threatening to hang themselves or cut their throats if they were sent back.[242] Such complaints were rare because it was imprudent to mistreat slaves to the point of desperation. Nonetheless, these desperate men resided on a leased plantation with an incompetent overseer and beyond the careful eye of their owner. Early in the eighteenth century, the slave code was strengthened to forbid possession of weapons by slaves and to provide severe penalties for offenses. Murder, burglary, robbery, arson and running away were capital offenses. Lesser crimes such as stealing hogs and chickens were treated by branding the slave with a letter that indicated the crime, such as "R" for runaway. Chronic offenders were put to death. Runaway slaves and slave rebellions were not uncommon, and some slaves were branded for general identification. On March 8, 1742, the journal of the Commons House of Assembly authorized payment for "beef killed" and used by the Goose Creek Company during the "time of the Negro insurrection..." The return of runaway slaves was frequently advertised. Thomas Monck owned a Goose Creek plantation during the eighteenth century. In September of 1736, Monck offered a reward of forty shillings each for the return of three Gambia Negroes.[243] He was one of the few slave owners who branded his slaves. In an advertisement in the *South Carolina Gazette* of March 12, 1737, he offered a reward of five pounds local currency for the return of an Angola Negro named Cudja. He described him as being "branded on his right breast 'T Monck'." In January of that year, he advertised for the return of a slave named Sampson "to me at my plantation in Goose Creek." A slave was a costly investment and a steady return was expected.

No idleness was permitted and the slaves' work year included few holidays. From spring until fall, the slaves cultivated rice, indigo and other crops. In the fall, the slaves beat out rice, cleared land, sawed lumber, coopered barrels and split rails, staves and shingles. Peter Smith of Broom Hall plantation owned a number of highly skilled and costly slaves. Among his slaves were valuable craftsmen including Tommy, who was a cooper. He and his wife Jenny were valued at £650. Peter, a carpenter, was valued at £600; and a second carpenter, Tom was valued at £400. Other plantations were the home of skilled slaves. After the death of Mr. William Holliday, owner of Richmond Plantation, "on Cooper River in Goose Creek," the executors of his estate advertised the property in the *Royal Gazette* in 1781. The advertisement stated that the sale included "about twenty valuable Negroes, among whom are a complete waiter, a very good carpenter, a cooper, bricklayer and some boatmen; also, plain cooks, washers and ironers, mostly all young slaves."[244] Edmund Fitzgerald sold two slaves in 1789 named Jacob and Tom who were tanners by trade.[245] John Coming Ball of Back River made specific orders about selected slaves in his will dated December 3, 1792.

> *...I give my Negro man Nat his freedom and all my wearing apparel. I give my Negro woman, Hagar and her child Charlotte their freedom and, desire my executors will have the latter educated & when she shall be old enough placed out as an Apprentice to a Milliner or Mantua Maker. I give my Negro Man, Jackey (Son of Lucy) who is at present my driver his freedom, I give and bequeath to my sister, Mrs. Wilson, any Negro Girl among my female Slaves she may prefer...*[246]

Stephen Mazyck wrote to his brother from Springfield plantation in Goose Creek about, "That faithful old servant Sylvia...Both he and Mrs. Mazyck are so kind to her that she says she lives far happier."[247] Sylvia was a slave who was freed by the will of Isaac Mazyck II, who also devised that £300 be kept and the interest used for Sylvia's support.[248]

Not all were as fortunate as Sylvia. A typical slave's working day was monotonous and demanding. A British officer described the working day as lasting from daybreak to late in the evening. At night he said, "They sleep on a bench, or on the ground, with an old scanty blanket, which serves them at once for bed and covering." Attempts have been made to glorify the singing Negro as he toiled in the fields and to portray him as a content, "happy-go-lucky" carefree inhabitant of semi-tropical Carolina, but his singing was not always indicative of a jovial mood. In fact, the endless hours in the fields were made less monotonous with song. The rhythm maintained a steady working motion and commands or orders could be relayed. Songs were a conspicuous characteristic of the African slave. As the plantations varied so did these characteristics. Their songs, their stories, even their spirituals changed from plantation to plantation. It was noted that a more singing speech and a lifting tone on the last syllable was common on the plantations settled by the Huguenots.[249]

Not all slaves toiled endless hours in the fields. Some were house servants who performed the majority of the household chores. One "domestic" was a slave named Bob who was a member of that respectable class of gray-headed family servants and who was also "a native and to the manor born, never passes without involuntarily removing his hat." Bob began his career as a postillion "boy" and later drove a four-horse carriage to carry his "old maussa" to the parish church or to drive his "old Misses" to sales at the 10-Mile Hill House. Bob remained at his home at Goose Creek Plantation (now Yeamans Hall) until his death.[250] Other slaves worked on public roads and bridges or other public work projects. When the Commons House of Assembly convened in 1740, St. James, Goose Creek and other parishes were ordered to send 20 percent of their slaves to work on fortifications. The order stated that "the owner of slaves...be obliged to employ every 5th able male slave to work for a week together in erecting forts on the frontiers."[251]

Some Goose Creek planters cooperated with the missionaries and were zealous in encouraging the instruction of their slaves. Lady Moore, Captain David Deas, Mrs. Sarah Barker and several others encouraged slave instruction.[252] As during the frontier period, the missionaries worked to earn the confidence of the slave masters so the slaves could be educated and baptized. In spite of the noble efforts of the missionaries, great skepticism prevailed among the planters and, regardless of some good intentions, slavery remained a hideous institution until the Civil War.

All plantations worked slaves because the definition of a plantation required the boarding of at least ten laborers. Records indicated that large numbers of African slaves and much fewer free people boarded on Goose Creek plantations.

The number of slaves on a plantation was determined by an assessment by the landowner that balanced the return from slave labor with the cost of purchase and care. Slavery brought extraordinary wealth to many Goose Creekers. One historian wrote, "On the eve of the American Revolution, the white population of the Lowcountry was by far the richest single group in British North America." He continued to colorfully explain that the Lowcountry prosperity was based upon "the expropriation by whites of the golden rice and blue dye produced by black slaves..." [253] Slavery was a dynamic institution throughout the colonial period because it was a serious economic consideration for the landowner and a lifelong commitment for the slave.

Rice

The colonists borrowed the production of maize (corn) from the natives and by 1739 it was a valuable product of export. However, by the end of the seventeenth century, rice became a more important cash crop. Rice was first cultivated on dry lands but by the early decades of the eighteenth century, swamplands that were beyond the reach of the salty high tide were planted in rice. The abundance of natural water reserves such as shown in photograph 4.1 allowed rice to become the most important product and brought immense wealth to some landowners. English investors recognized that the climate and soil of Carolina was suited to rice culture, so early settlers experimented with the grain. Some historians credit Goose Creeker Thomas Smith, who arrived in 1684, with growing the first plants and sharing the second generation of seed with his colleagues. Other historians offer conflicting theories, but the record is clear that by 1690 rice was so abundant that planters asked to have it as one of the commodities with which to pay quit-rents. By 1700, according to the collector of customs, there were not enough ships at Charleston to export the milled grain. In some cases rice was used as legal tender. In 1724, John Moore and his wife, Rachel, conveyed to Edward Keating two plantations of 500 acres and 850 acres in Goose Creek. The purchase price was Keating's promise to pay 137,000 pounds of rice in two installments of 68,500 pounds each.[254]

Rice remained an important cash crop in Goose Creek until after the Civil War and was cultivated on most farms as late as 1880.[255] John F. Poppenheim was the last Goose Creek farmer to plant rice

Photograph 4.1 This photograph shows "Lower Tennent Pond" a water reserve pond near the banks of Goose Creek. The photograph was made March 7, 2005, and is in the private collection of the author.

as a cash crop. He grew rice on Marrington Plantation until the early years of the twentieth century. Aerial photographs of the Marrington Plantation grounds at the Naval Weapons Station show a series of ponds used for irrigation from colonial times until the early twentieth century. The remains of rice field dikes, ditches and drains are also visible in the shallow sections of the Goose Creek waterway, as well as Back River Plantations such as Spring Grove.

The development of rice fields required arduous and exact work. First, a large earthen dike with a gate was built across the lowest section of an inland swamp. The gate called a "trunk" was closed to cause the water to flood the land. The trunks were large boxes with a door that could be raised and lowered to allow water to pass through. The flooded land was drained after the grasses, bushes and small trees were killed by the high water. The drained land was cleared of debris and the larger trees were cut and removed. A smaller dam was then built across the lower expanse of the upstream swamp area to create a reserve pond. A trunk gate to control the flow of irrigation waters was installed in that dam as well. Dams were also built across the future rice fields to control the water depths and side ditches were dug to release overflow around the lower fields if necessary. After all the dikes, dams and ditches were built, the entire area downstream from the water reserve was drained as thoroughly as possible. Then the exact work of leveling the drained field commenced to prepare the ground for final cultivation. The elaborate system worked well in Goose Creek, as long as the water levels were monitored and adjusted as needed. A proper depth of water at the appropriate time killed weeds. At other times, water was released from the reserve pond to irrigate. Too much water would kill everything including rice, and an uneven field affected water levels and greatly reduced the yield per acre. If insufficient rain caused low water levels, the fields could not be flooded for weed control but instead were hoed and raked.

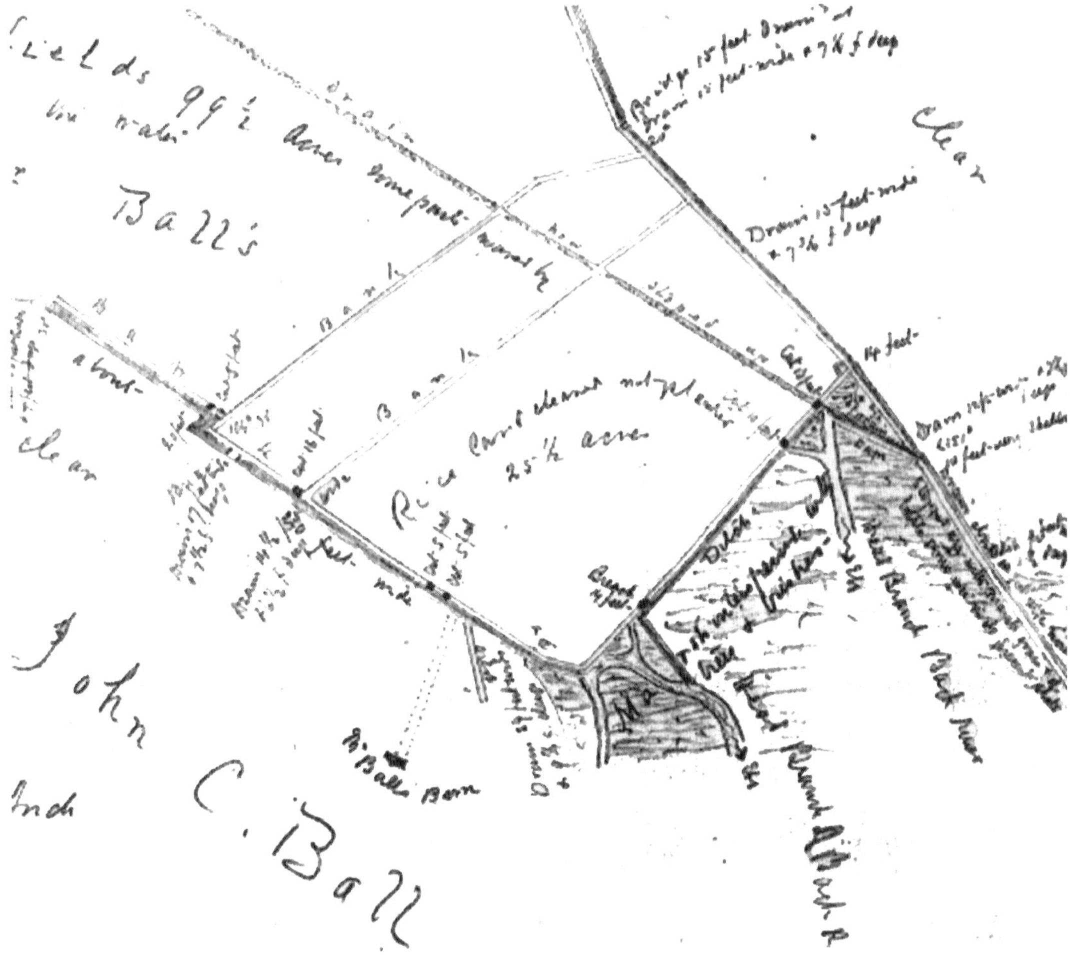

Plat 4.7 This plat shows John C. Ball's White Hall Plantation on the headwaters of Back River as surveyed by Joseph Purcell in 1789 and traced by H.A.M. Smith. The plat is among the collections of the South Carolina Historical Society.

Plat 4.7 depicts John Ball's plantation on the headwaters of Back River, and shows the large scale and intricate work required for a plantation to be successful. By one estimate, a five hundred acre rice field required sixty miles of dikes and ditches.[256] John Ball's plantation used canals as large as thirty-three feet wide and seven feet deep to channel water. Floodgates were as large as nine feet wide and eight feet tall. His fields ranged from eight and a half acres to ninety-nine and a half acres. The plat indicates the care needed to properly build straight and sloped banks. The plat also shows the outfall to the creeks leading to Back River.

Inventive Goose Creek planters advanced improvements in rice production. The simplest way of cleaning rice was by pouring it into a dug out hollow in a tree trunk. The rice could then be "beat out" with a wooden pestle. This action removed the straw like husk from the hard kernel. Winnowing further separated the light chaff from the rice and finally, sifting separated the whole grain from broken pieces and fine flour. The whole grain was usually sold and the broken grain was consumed locally. The flour was mixed with husks and fed to livestock. Because this simple process was time consuming, Peter Villeponteaux, a Goose Creek planter, invented an animal powered machine to clean rice efficiently. His advertisement in the *South Carolina Gazette* lists the lumber required to construct the apparatus, but it did not explain how the machine worked. The purchaser was required to provide the listed items and to have all parts available when Mr. Villeponteaux and his partner, Samuel Holmes, arrived to construct the machine:

> *Oak plank, 100 feet, 5 inches thick / 4 pieces pine, 12 feet long, 6 inches square / 12 pieces pine 7 feet long, 22 x 18 inches / 2 pieces pine 30 feet long 7 X 5 inches / middle post 8 feet long and 18 inches in diameter.*[257]

Villeponteaux provided the required iron pieces and the knowledge. His partner did most of the construction. He charged £60 and promised that his invention, powered by four horses, could clean two thousand pounds of rice a day. His machine never sold well, even though he continued to improve it until in 1734. That year, the machine powered by four horses could process one thousand pounds of rice an hour without breaking the kernels. One reason for the low sales was competition from two other Goose Creek planters who also appealed to the legislature for patents. Charles Lowndes claimed the rights to the invention, as did Samuel Knight.[258] Because the three requests appeared so close in time, the legislature granted no patents but encouraged each to build and sell competitively.[259]

In 1783, Gideon Dupont, Jr. of Goose Creek sought compensation from the state for inventing a method of water cultivation.[260] With the probable guidance of his West African slaves, he developed a system of flooding the fields by tidal influenced creek water at Otranto. Open trunk gates would allow flooding of fields with fresh waters lifted by the rising tide. The fields would drain when the ebb tide lowered the fresh water. This manner of water cultivation provided a more abundant and reliable source of irrigation than reserve ponds and abundant floodwaters to kill weeds. Grasses and weeds were formerly often removed by hand and hoe. Slaves stood bent over for endless hours removing weeds prior to the invention of Dupont's water method.

Until long after the American Revolution, much slave labor was used to clear fields and erect networks of dikes and sluice gates for the production of water-cultivated rice. This method became widely used on Goose Creek and Cooper River plantations resulting in rice becoming an even more important money crop. This was especially important to Goose Creek during the difficult economic period after the American Revolution. During the eighteenth century, the profits made from rice were enormous, netting from 12 percent to near 28 percent annual return. These numbers were greatly diminished by the beginning of the 1800s. The rate of return was reduced to 2 percent at best and then later dropped to negative 3 percent and then to negative 7 percent. In 1859, the return on the investment of rice production dropped to negative 28 percent.[261]

Indigo

Indigo was a highly prized dark blue dye, which was especially effective on expensive linens and silks and was ideal for army and navy blue woolen uniforms. However, so much attention was given to rice cultivation in Goose Creek that the production of indigo was at first neglected and almost abandoned after production of the dye was introduced in the early 1700s. Demand for the dye revived indigo production by the 1740s and offered a way for Goose Creek planters to diversify their staple crop production. Indigo became an important cash crop when war with France (1754–1763) caused the halt of dye import and the British parliament enacted a protective tariff, which encouraged the production of indigo and decreased the British Empire's dependence on imported French and Spanish dyes. In addition, parliament paid a subsidy to indigo growers until the American Revolution. Consequently, along with rice production, indigo became an important crop in Goose Creek and was intensely cultivated on some plantations until 1776.

Accounts of the equipment used in indigo processing included wooden or masonry vats of various sizes. The process usually required at least two vats, one higher than the other. The broad leaves of the plant were harvested and laid in the highest vat to be treated with urine and water (urine was later replaced by potash). Fermentation then occurred for ten to fourteen hours depending on the temperature and humidity. At the appropriate time, the valuable liquid was drained into the lower vat leaving the mash behind. Single level operations required the use of wooden suction pumps to draw off the liquid. The drained liquid was stirred, beaten and cleaned of stems and other debris. A lime mixture was added which caused the liquid to turn blue and reduce to a paste. This paste was referred to as "indigo mud." The mud was pressed into cakes and moved to storage barns to dry and cure. Some accounts testify that proper timing was essential for success. The cakes were ready after a fine mold began to grow. At this time the mold was cleaned away, the cakes were cut into two-inch squares and graded into four categories: fine blue, ordinary blue, fine purple or ordinary copper. The graded squares were then packed for shipping.

Designs of indigo vats varied. The remains of the vat at William Johnson's White House estate features an arched roof made of brick. The remains of the large, two level vats at Alexander Garden's Otranto Plantation featured no masonry cover although a cover of some sort was probably used to keep rainwater from diluting the fermenting stew. It is likely that a wooden roof or shed was used at Otranto. Vats were usually located near the banks of waterways because a large amount of water was needed to treat the leaves, and moving water provided a convenient sewer for the foul smelling runoff. The vats were also located away from the main house because of the obnoxious odors emitted during the fermentation process. Few ruins of vats have survived since it is likely most vats were made of wood and have not been preserved.

Brick

Clay mining and brick and tile making were common practices in Goose Creek since the earliest settlement. Below the topsoil throughout Goose Creek is a thick layer of clay. Natives used this resource for pottery long before the Europeans, and plantation slaves used it to make crude earthenware for domestic use. Clay was also a useful caulking material for waddle-constructed walls and linings and insulation for wooden chimneys. Later, as more permanent homes were built, plantations typically used clay to bake their own brick. Brick is an extremely durable building material used on the plantations as building foundations, footings, walls, gates and garden walls.

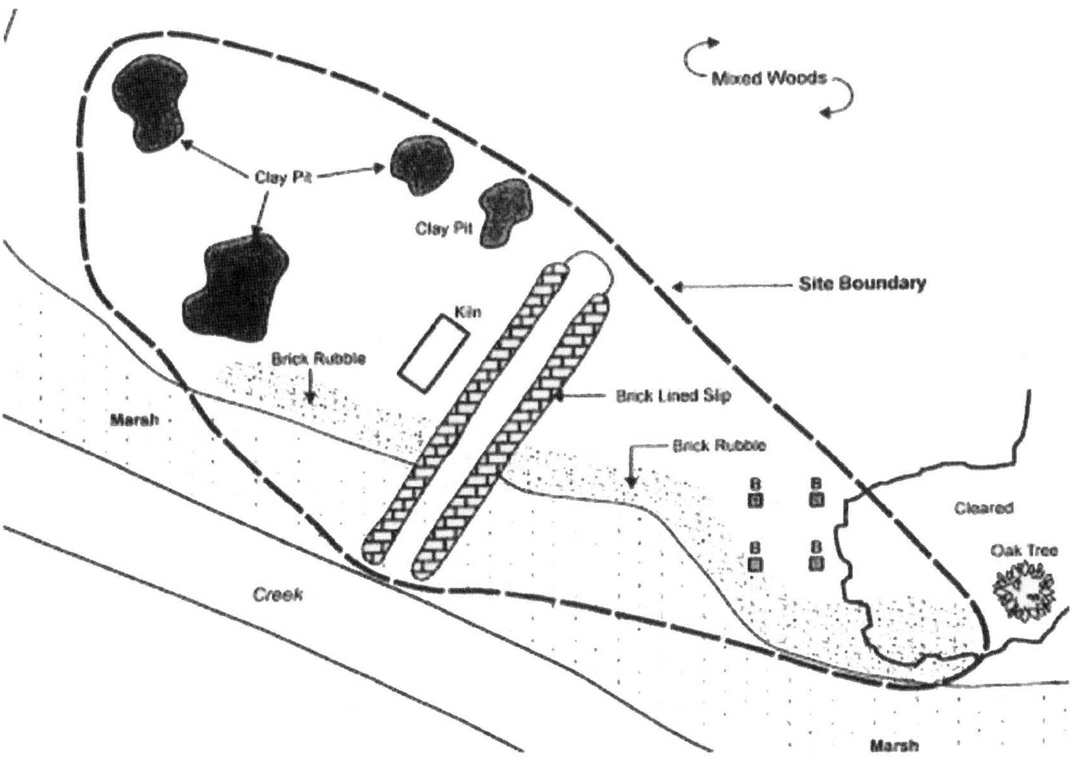

Plat 4.8 This plat was drawn from the archaeological study conducted by Brockington and Associates Inc. in 1998 and 1999. The location of the site is not disclosed due to the lack of site preparation for public viewing and preservation.

Brick construction was prized as the preferred building material. The January 25, 1739 edition of the *South Carolina Gazette* advertised the sale of James Moore's "very good brick two-story house" at his plantation in Goose Creek. Bricks were first produced in Goose Creek merely for domestic use, but a market was created in 1713 when the assembly responded to a series of large fires in Charleston by requiring all new buildings within Charleston proper to be constructed of brick. This act received many complaints because of the scarcity of bricks and was repealed, but it was reinstated in 1740 as the result of another serious fire. Consequently, during the next century, brick making became an important industry in Goose Creek.

The industry required clay for material wood for fuel, inexpensive labor and market availability. Plantations without access to deep water could not inexpensively transport the heavy product to market, but those who could, took advantage of access to deep water and entered into the brick production business during the fall and winter months. The O'Hear family at Medway and the Villeponteaux family at Parnassus, both on Back River, were two of three Lowcountry families who dominated the brick business.[262] Evidence of the wide use of brick manufacturing is replete along both sides of Foster Creek and the lower sections of Goose Creek, Cooper River and Back River. Brick Hope Plantation, the one time home of Charles Graves, featured frontage on Foster Creek between Liberty Hall and Parnassus Plantations. Plats show brickyards on the north and south sides of Foster Creek, as well as several places such as "Gray's Landing" where brick can be transferred to water craft.[263] When Henry Gray advertised his Foster Creek Plantation for sale in 1773, he described his tract as located "on a bold deep creek called Foster's…" and that a "very advantageous brickyard may be established on it."

The Ararat Plantation featured a brick kiln and maintained a landing on Foster Creek. Other planters known to have manufactured brick on Foster Creek were Samuel Elliot, as well as Benjamin and Stephen Mazyck.[264] Archaeologists found remains of a tile-manufacturing site near Red Bank Landing, and plats 7.20 and 7.21 show sections of Parnassus Plantation with an "old brick kiln" near Big Island and "brick yards" on Back River. Remains of a brick kiln were found at Crowfield Plantation, but there is no record of the bricks being sold. All of the Crowfield bricks were probably used on-site because the nearby water was too shallow to float bricks to market.

Bricks were made entirely by hand. Clay was dug from pits of differing shapes, sizes and depths according to the run of the clay. The clay was then chopped into small sticky pieces. The pieces were mixed with the correct amount of water, plied until well blended then forced into wooden molds. The plying of the clay was arduous labor and was probably augmented by the treading of horses or cattle through the clay pits to break the clumps and mix water into a thick paste. The raw brick was dried in the sun for days, removed from the molds and stacked in wood-fired kilns. The finished item measured approximately eight and a half inches long, four inches wide and three inches high and weighed about five pounds each. The dimensions differed from site to site with up to a three-quarters inch variance in the length, width and depth and a half pound difference in weight. The baked bricks appeared as various shades of brown, but were marketed as gray, brown or red brick according to varying tinctures. The mortar was a careful mixture of clay, water and crushed shell. Lime was sometimes added to improve the durability of the mortar, which was sometimes used as masonry to waterproof the semi-porous bricks. Remains of brick kilns are visible today on old plantation sites at Foster Creek, Back River and Goose Creek as indicated by numerous plats of Goose Creek plantations. Brick scatters are easily found today at landings where the product was loaded and shipped, and place names such as Red Bank Road and Brick Bound Swamp indicate the importance of the industry.

Even though English and French settlers brought brick making skills to Carolina during the early years and brick manufacturing survived in Goose Creek until the Civil War, it appears that the skill of mining, mixing and baking was passed on almost entirely to the African slave. Skilled slave labor was essential to the process and after the manufacture was established, it is likely that white overseers and owners had little direct experience with the brick-baking craft. After the emancipation of the slaves, the brick industry disappeared in Goose Creek, leaving the knowledge and skills almost solely in the hands of the freed Africans. As evidenced in the Lowcountry today, the masonry trade is disproportionately an African American craft, and many successful masonry businesses continue to be passed from one African American generation to the next.

Cotton

The lord proprietors also encouraged the production of cotton. However, though some cotton was planted at an early date, the process of removing the seeds from the cotton bolls made it unprofitable.

Cotton became a leading industry in South Carolina after 1794 when the cotton gin was invented. Even though cotton grew on almost every Goose Creek farm after the Civil War and some farmers even hired cotton pickers to supplement the family labor force, cotton never became a staple crop in Goose Creek as it was on many South Carolina farms.[265]

Livestock

Livestock was brought to the colony at an early date and cattle and swine were soon raised on every plantation. Horses were also imported and bred successfully. Eventually many plantation owners, such as John Ball, bred horses for racing, as well as general use. Several racecourses were established in Goose Creek including at Medway and Otranto where many fine racehorses were bred on the plantations. Many of these were descendants of imported English thoroughbreds. Horsemanship was one of the necessities of the gentleman planter and was expected for plantation management, deer and fox hunting and competitive tournaments.[266] Goose Creek planters owned two of the best racehorses in the colony. Colonel Richard Singleton's plantation was the home of "Shadow," winner of the first great race in South Carolina between a native and an imported horse. "Shadow" remained at Singleton's until 1771.[267] "Tartar," an imported horse belonging to Robert Hume, ran several seasons at his popular Goose Creek racecourse and lived until 1767.[268]

Silk/Grapes/Citrus/Olives

Silk, grapes, citrus and olives were experimental crops planted with the hopes that semi-tropical Carolina could produce items that were imported from competing nations. England imported silk from the Far East and wine, olive oil and citrus from France and other Mediterranean countries. Many entries in the journals of the Commons House of Assembly record Lowcountry interests in silk production. On January 19, 1738, Captain Morris offered one hundred acres in Goose Creek, twelve miles from town, free for the experimentation with silk. He also requested that the assembly appeal to the Parliament of Great Britain to reduce the duty on silk. Despite much effort, the experiment in Carolina failed. Silk production disappeared about the same time as native trade, but not before hundreds of mulberry bushes were planted on Goose Creek plantations to provide food for silk worms. Also, orange trees were planted in Goose Creek on the sunny south side of protective walls. Although some survived mild winters, none could be kept for more than a few years. Olive and grape production met the same fate as citrus.

Naval Stores

Naval stores production became an important Goose Creek industry during the colonial period. Naval stores consisted of pitch, tar and turpentine derived from pine and fir trees that were abundant in Goose Creek and throughout the southeast. The sprawling English Empire depended upon a large naval and merchant marine force for trade and protection and encouraged the production of naval stores. The common process to extract pitch and tar is ancient. Pitch and tar are similar products and the terms are sometimes used interchangeably, but both were used to caulk ship planking and deck boards and to coat rope, canvas and other maritime articles susceptible to wear and tear by the wind and sea. In addition to the pitch and tar, cooking the wood produced rosin, which was distilled to separate the turpentine. The separated turpentine was collected and used for the production of paints and varnishes.

Large quantities of naval stores were needed and the production was supported with a British bounty that made it profitable. Each ton of pitch and tar was worth £4 in bounty, which was equivalent to more than $300 in today's currency. A ton of turpentine was worth almost $250 in today's money.[269] The abundance of tar pits recorded on plats and discovered by archaeological studies indicated the spread of the industry in Goose Creek. The easiest process involved simply slashing pine trees and collecting the sap that oozed from the under bark. Trees were cut with notches shaped like cat ears similar to cuts made in maple trees when the syrup is extracted. The sap, called rosin, was distilled by cooking in a kiln then stored in wooden barrels for export. "Every once in a while we still find a tree with what people call cat faces," observed Olga Caballero, a U.S. Forest Service archeologist in the Francis Marion Forest.[270] This naval store process continued in the upper Sandridge section of the Goose Creek Parish until well after the Civil War. Some sap trees were reportedly larger than three feet in diameter.[271] The slashing eventually killed the trees, but the dead trees were piled on bigger kilns and burned for tar and pitch.

The Plantation Economy

Table 4.5 lists the most valued exports during the mid-eighteenth century. It is not surprising that rice was the most valued commodity but the importance of deerskins as the second most valued export is interesting. Seventy years after the first settlement and long after the end of the frontier period, native trade reached far into the interior and the popularity of leather hats, vests, purses and other accessories in Europe kept the export of deerskins profitable.

Table 4.5

Commodity Exported	Amount of Value in Pounds	Percentage of Total Export Value Rounded to Nearest Whole Number
Rice	618,750	55
Deer Skins	252,000	22
Indigo	117,353	10
Pork	31,140	3
Naval Stores	24,548	2
Lumber Products	23,490	2
Indian Corn	19,654	2
Leather, Tanned	18,123	2
Beef	11,466	1
Peas	3,053	>1

The colonial planters in Goose Creek profited from lumber, rice, naval stores, indigo, bricks, cattle and hogs, as well as deer and other skins. These items formed the economic foundation of the Lowcountry, but ironically the Goose Creek economy waned in the midst of a flourishing culture. The process of retaining and restoring fertility by using manure did not reach South Carolina from England until long after the Revolution. Consequently, the loose, light soil on top of the Lowcountry clay began to show signs of exhaustion early in the eighteenth century. As early as 1736, the SPG reported a migration from the eastern to the western section of the parish with some leaving the parish entirely.[272] Reverend Robert Stone wrote in 1750 that the lands in Goose Creek Parish were "worn out" and many people were planters "running away" to new settlements.

Lands were granted to twelve settlers in the central and western parish from 1722 to 1749,[273] and the wills of some landowners such as Thomas Smith in 1723, Charles Colleton in 1727 and Benjamin Marion in 1734, document that they owned lands in the central section of the parish. Records also show that John Wright, Soloman Legare and Abraham Dupont, as well as the Seaman, Deas and Broughton families owned large tracts of land in the central and western sections. There was also movement out of the parish to lands farther west. In 1741, nine families and 202 slaves moved from the Goose Creek Parish but this outflow was temporarily halted as a result of the war with the Cherokee. Reverend Harrison of St. James, Goose Creek Church wrote in 1759 that his congregation had increased and the SPG reported that people were returning from the frontier because of that war.[274] This halt, however was short-lived because soil exhaustion caused migration to resume and continued for many decades.

Medicine, Science and Society

The plantation society that characterized Goose Creek during the colonial period produced a number of natural and medical scientific endeavors. The frontier doctor, who earlier risked being scalped while supplementing his medical practice with Indian trade, was inclined to take advantage of the prosperous plantation era and devote his full energies to the practice of medicine. One of the early physicians in Berkeley County was Lewis Mottet, a well-educated and talented French physician. For a while he lived at Stoney Landing and attended some of the plantations in St. James, Goose Creek but in the spring of 1761, he moved to Goose Creek and continued his medical practice.[275] Joseph Johnson recorded some humorous stories about Dr. Mottet in his book entitled *Traditions and Reminiscences, Chiefly of the American Revolution in the South*, published in 1851, including the time he was sued for malpractice by one of his patients. At one point Dr. Mottet took control of the court hearing for "assault and battery" by exaggerating his French accent, pretending to not understand the charges and feigning indignation by declaring that the charges of "salt and batter" were matters for a baker and were altogether unfounded. The courtroom convulsed in laughter and the judge dismissed the charges.[276] Doctor Mottet was a comical addition to the Goose Creek physicians during the days of plantation life.

As indicated by table 4.6, it appears as if there were always a number of physicians in Goose Creek during the plantation era. The most noteworthy Goose Creek practitioner was Dr. Alexander Garden, who resided at Otranto Plantation and was the most important scientific figure in colonial Carolina. His eminence was in botany and natural science, but he was also a renowned personality in Charleston medical circles from 1752 until the American Revolution.[277] Dr. Garden did not make major contributions to worldwide medical science but he was an esteemed practitioner. His only published writings related to medicine were *An Account of the Medical Properties of the Virginia Pinkroot* and *The Effects of Ashes of Tobacco in the Cure of Dropsy*.[278] His contributions to natural science were far more numerous and noteworthy, but in spite of his work, there were few advancements in treating illnesses and diseases during that time.

Table 4.6

Name	Date of Record	Note
Robert Brown	1714–1757	A surgeon. Owned property in Goose Creek by 1741 (Langley, V.2: p. 18). Tombstone inscription at the Chapel of Ease.
Peter Hurne (Hyrne)	1740	Resided in Goose Creek (Waring, 1964, p. 386).
Richard Boddin	1742	Resided in Goose Creek (Waring, 1964, p. 386).
A. Brown [Broun?]	1742	Resided in Goose Creek (Waring, 1964, p. 386).
George Smith	1751	Resided in Goose Creek (Waring 1964, p. 386).
Lewis Mottet	1761	Moved to Goose Creek from Stoney Landing (Johnson, 1851)
John Hendrick Swint	1763	Resided in Goose Creek (Waring, 1964, p. 386).
Ernest Hahnbaum	1780	"Practitioner of Physic" on Foster Creek (C-5. p. 214–18).
[Ernest?] Poyas	1790	Recorded in 1790 Census (Waring, 1964, p. 386).
Stephen St. John	1805	Death notice was published (Waring, 1964, p. 386).
John Wilson Jr.	1805	Representative (Waring, 1964, p. 386).

There were many cases of yellow fever, malaria and pleurisies (chest and lung disorders), "quinsis" (throat problems), "fluxes" (fluid discharges) and whooping cough during the mid-1700s.[279] Measles, smallpox and other life threatening diseases frequently caused death because they were virtually incurable by the medical science of those days.

Although always close to illness and injury, most landowners of colonial Goose Creek successfully ruled over vast estates with dozens and sometimes hundreds of laboring subjects. They made fortunes with family and business alignments in Charleston that lasted a hundred years, but the era of the grand estates did not persist far beyond the colonial era. During the colonial period, Goose Creek was a mosaic of agriculture, business and society, but shortly after the Revolutionary War, many planters abandoned their Goose Creek lands due to soil exhaustion and malaria. Some planters built summer homes in the pinewoods in and near Berkeley County and others traveled to nearby sea islands to escape illness that became so prevalent. The high, well-drained pinelands in the inland areas did not foster the spread of mosquitoes and the malaria that caused illness in the lower and wetter areas. The sandy soil of inland retreats and the sea breezes on the islands slowed, but did not prevent the exodus from the soil exhaustion and disease in the eastern parish. Although some planters continued to successfully work their plantations from afar by using land managers, the era of the grand estates soon ended. The Goose Creek plantations that were the agricultural and industrial giants of the colonial South Carolina Lowcountry steadily declined during the nineteenth century, and were finally divided into many small farms or relegated to hunting clubs for a privileged few.

Chapter V
Planters, Politicians and Patriots, 1719–1783

Goose Creek lifestyles changed dramatically throughout the fifty years of proprietary rule. During that time, the Goose Creek frontiersmen elevated their positions from struggling farmers to gentlemen planters. By the end of the period, the cunning "Goose Creek Men" of an earlier era were a special group of planter-merchants who, with large grants of waterfront property, developed their plantations and native trading businesses into lucrative Charleston mercantile enterprises. Dr. George C. Rogers likened the Goose Creek planters to London merchants in his book, *Charleston In The Age of The Pinckneys*:

> *Since the eighteenth-century ideal was the landed gentleman, there was a tendency for retiring merchants to become gentlemen-planters. A principal settlement of such was at Goose Creek, eighteen miles up the Neck from the city, rather reminiscent of clusters of London merchants at Hampstead or at Newington Green.*[280]

According to historian M. Eugene Sirmans the "Age of the Goose Creek Men" ended early in the eighteenth century but their influence persisted. The gentlemen planters of Goose Creek contributed more than just wealthy life styles to the Carolina Lowcountry during the decades leading to the American Revolution. Some played important political roles, and many were patriots who lent vital leadership needed to steer the colonists through the turbulent years of revolution.

During the sixty-four years from the beginning of royal rule in 1719 to the Peace of Paris that ended the Revolutionary War, Americans came into their own. The colonial settlers rejected their mother country, established a home government and entered the international world as an independent nation. These world-shaking events were marked in Goose Creek by unrest that occasionally erupted in hostilities. British lawmen sailed by warship up Goose Creek to kidnap a protest leader from his bed, Goose Creek militia threatened open rebellion against the governor, and a large cadre of armed backwoodsmen stormed the Goose Creek polls. The finale to this period of unrest was total war that divided Goose Creekers, as well as all South Carolinians into two camps: one loyal to Britain and the other loyal to the patriot revolutionaries. Goose Creek came of age through tests of war and rebellion and earned its place among the communities that made up the new American Republic.

The Church Act of 1706 established the parish electoral system that was the basis for the political decision-making in the decades leading to the American Revolution. The parishes were political, as well as ecclesiastical subdivisions and the parish of St. James, Goose Creek, like the other South Carolina parishes, conducted elections to send representatives to the House of Assembly. The churchwarden, appointed by the governor and council, acted as the election manager who posted the public notice of the election on the door of the parish church two Sundays before, and notified the persons elected by attaching their names to the same door.[281] Goose Creek churchwardens during these years were Benjamin Coachman, Robert Hume, Gideon Dupont, Charles Faucheraud, William Wood, Zachariah Villeponteaux and Richard Gough.

The elected representative was required to appear before the assembly and announce whether or not the office was accepted or refused. The new assembly consisted of thirty-six members, four of whom were from St. James, Goose Creek.[282] Appendix 6 lists the names of the representatives from Goose Creek during the period of 1736–1754 according to the records in the *Journal of the Common House*. The parish was aptly served during this period by some of the wealthiest and most influential representatives in the Province.

A voter in South Carolina was a free white man of twenty-one years or older. He was a resident of the province for at least one year prior to voting, and owned at least fifty acres of land or paid at least 20 shillings of annual tax. A representative was at least twenty-one years of age, resided at least one year in the parish, and owned five hundred acres of land and ten slaves or possessed personal property valued at £1,000 or more.

The Goose Creek representatives during this period often brought grievances to the full body. For example, many resented the need to travel the distance to Charleston for court service or to vote. The passage of an act in 1721 proposed a remedy by directing that a court be established at Wassamasaw for the parishes of St. James, Goose Creek, St. John Berkeley and St. George Dorchester. The act required that the courts hear criminal cases not extending to life or limb, and civil cases not involving more than one hundred pounds sterling. A year later, another act authorized judges to purchase land, build courthouses and schools, and levy taxes for such, but both laws were ineffectual because most people continued to journey to Charleston for legal services. Courthouses were never built in St. James, Goose Creek Parish, the justices remained untrained and revenue from taxes was never collected.[283] Nevertheless, the Election Act of 1721 apportioned the representation as shown on table 5.1 and listed the number of acres, slaves and taxpayers in each parish.[284]

The problem with the courts and the currency shortage almost caused a rebellion. For ten years after the Royal Government was established in 1719, a continual debate over the issuance of currency ensued. The Goose Creek people wanted either more paper currency or a law that would make country produce legal tender. Governor Francis Nicholson (1721–1725) failed to adequately address this problem, and to make matters worse, he failed to appoint an acting governor when he returned to England in 1725. Instead he let the council elect a successor. They chose Arthur Middleton (1724–1729), president of the council to serve as acting governor. The currency issue was now left in Middleton's hands. He was an advocate of the people during the last years of proprietary government but, as acting governor, he worked to uphold the Crown and the Crown objected to the issuance of paper money. That unpopular position, upheld by Middleton, dominated his administration.

With the ever-decreasing amount of paper money and the spread of counterfeiting, a popular movement for more paper money gained momentum. When the Council refused to budge from

Table 5.1

Parishes	Acres	Average Acres per Taxpayer	Slaves	Taxpayers	Representation allowed	Representation according to population
St. Philips/ Charles Town	64,265	220	1,390	283	4	6
Christ Church	57,580	538	637	107	2	3
St. Thomas and St. Dennis	74,580	661	942	113	3	3
St. John	181,375	1,885	1,439	97	3	2
St. James, Goose Creek	153,537.5	1,432	2,027	107	3	3
St. Andrews	197,168	938	2,493	210	4	5
St. George	47,457	679	536	68	2	1
Colleton County						
St. Paul	187,976	935	1,634	201	4	5
St. Bartholomew	30,559	650	44	47	3	1
Granville County						
St. Helena	51,817	1,727	42	30	3	1
Craven County						
St. James, Santee	117,274	2,792	548	42	1	1
Total	1,163,319	NA	11,868	1,305	30	30

the king's orders, a group of protesters took matters into their own hands. Thomas Smith, a Goose Creek planter and a member of the assembly, became the leader in opposition to the president and the council's currency policy. Thomas Smith was prominent in the Commons House of Assembly and popular with the people. He declared "now there was necessity for a bold stroke" and that "some men must be put in bodily fear."[285] These words were followed by a series of protest meetings wherein the protesters bound themselves to defend each other in refusing to pay their taxes and to work toward a liberal currency law. Thomas Smith wrote and presented a memorial to the president. In it the people complained that they traveled far to Charleston to plead cases before unjust judges and were forced to pay legal fees with scarce currency. The memorial called for a law making country produce legal tender or a law producing sufficient amounts of paper money for provincial trade. The Goose Creek planters needed currency to pay debts and taxes. Table 5.2 shows land and slaves owned during Middleton's term of office. Taxes were required for both land and slaves, occasionally resulting in estates sold at a fraction of their worth to pay taxes.[286]

President Middleton, angered by the petitioners, denounced their activities as riotous and ordered them not to meet under threat of arrest. In retaliation, two hundred men with arms rode into town and delivered a petition to the president.[287] They were determined to evade arrest and they succeeded. As the protests grew in intensity, Thomas Smith became more and more adamant and

Table 5.2

Berkeley County	Acres	Slaves 7–60 Years Old
St. Philip's and Charles Town Neck	68,975	1,113
Christ Church	65,091	557
St. Thomas' and St. Dennis	91,420	775
St. John's and English Santee	182,659	1,271
St. James, Goose Creek	163,871	1,650
St. Andrew's	188,862	1,831
St. George's	52,710	469
Total	813,588	7,666

rumors spread that the country, including Goose Creek, might rise in revolution. President Middleton was concerned about the fearful events and acted decisively. He ordered warrants issued and sent constables up Goose Creek on a man-of-war to Thomas Smith's home at Yeamans Hall. There, at three in the morning, the constables burst into the home and pulled Smith and his son from their beds. The arrest at Yeamans Hall traumatically affected Smith's pregnant wife and the assault reportedly caused his daughter to fall ill for six weeks.[288] News of the event spread quickly. When the Smiths were imprisoned, the countryside erupted in fury. As protest meetings intensified, President Middleton failed to quell the unrest and lost more and more of his popularity. The president and assembly unintentionally elevated the crisis when they decided to force the countryside to order by calling out the militia. This strategy spelled disaster for Middleton. Several militia companies organized and immediately sided with the reformers. The militia loudly denounced the arrest of Landgrave Thomas Smith and his son and threatened the president.

Captain William Dry commanded the Goose Creek militia. He was firmly in support of Landgrave Smith and extremely slow to rally the militia to President Middleton's defense. Middleton became alarmed at the non-responsive Goose Creek militia and ordered it completely discharged from service. Immediately upon discharge, the Goose Creek militia reorganized itself into an independent company, much to the applause of the Goose Creek people and the chagrin of the president.[289] The situation became so serious that Charleston merchants reacted and persuaded President Middleton to reconvene the assembly, and thus induce the people to return to their homes. Once reconvened, the tensions quickly subsided and the dispute was moved from the streets to the assembly hall. There the membership considered a memorial from Smith requesting relief from his imprisonment. While debating the question of what to do with the imprisoned Smith and his son, word of the Creek Indian uprising diverted the attention of the assembly. Thomas Smith and his son soon returned to their plantation upon a security bond of £10,000, but their case never came to trial.[290]

The paper money controversy, one of the causes of Goose Creek rebelliousness, was partially resolved in 1730, when all old bills were recalled and £100,000 in new bills were issued. In this way, the currency controversy was quieted for a while and threat of open rebellion subsided for several decades. In 1728 the assembly elected Captain William Dry as speaker. He took a prominent role in the recent disturbances, but his political activism decreased as the situation consistently improved. Soon after, the Goose Creek militia reassembled and normalcy returned.[291]

The practice of keeping active militias continued throughout the colonial period. This practice ended at the commencement of the Revolutionary War when they were absorbed into provincial units. The Goose Creek Parish kept a local militia composed of four muster rolls. The Council Journal for May 4, 1757, lists the Goose Creek muster roll of the regiment of foot under the command of Colonel Walter Izard, Lieutenant Colonel Robert Rivers and Major Benjamin Singleton. Captain Peter Faure and Lieutenant Ludovic Linder led the Four Hole Company. This company counted forty-eight private men and three alarm men (scouts and couriers). The Wassamasaw Company under the command of Captain William Parker included fifty-one private men. The Lower St. James, Goose Creek Parish militia was under the command of Captain Richard Singleton and Ensign Robert Hume and listed fifty-six private men and eleven alarm men on roll. The place of rendezvous for the militia in 1757 was at Peronneaus (near Ladson), Goose Creek.[292]

The people depended on the militia for self-defense and safety, but such security was increasingly lacking in the backcountry sections of South Carolina, where demands for law enforcement and other services merged with demands for appropriate representation in the government. Representation in the provincial government remained controversial in Goose Creek, and by mid-century there were twenty parishes and fifty members of the assembly. A writer in 1766 observed, "The reason why no more parishes were laid out arises from political motives, as it would increase the number of assemblymen…" The assembly preferred to manage affairs from the older sections where the established church was a fixture and the people were more homogeneous. Thus the Lowcountry continued as a powerful faction, but the ever-increasing population in the backcountry threatened the dominance. The burgeoning population in the backcountry resulted in demands for public service. Backcountry residents of the colony complained of a need for law and order, and resented the lack of help from the Charleston-dominated government. The culmination of this dissatisfaction was the formation of a backcountry group called the Regulators. The purpose of the Regulators was to provide law enforcement and justice in an area where there were few courts and sheriffs and a high rate of crime.[293] Outlaws roamed the backcountry freely for many years, but in the summer of 1767, the situation became so severe that a crisis ensued with many deaths and injuries and vigilantes acting on both sides of the conflict. A Charleston newspaper reported that summer of the possibility of the backcountry being depopulated if law and order was not reinstated. The Regulators emerged at this juncture with wide popular appeal. They restored order and assembled as a type of local government that replaced corrupt constables and judges with their own brand of justice. According to author Richard M. Brown, "the people were governed by their officers who decided all disputes over the drumhead in the muster field." This direct assault on crime purged the backcountry of "all villains."[294]

The following summer Charlestonians read news reports of Regulator meetings. The Regulators demanded backcountry representation in the upcoming elections and they generated rumors of marches on Charleston and other parts of the Lowcountry. The Regulators never marched on Charleston, but they did in Goose Creek, where they elected representatives to the assembly in that parish.[295] The churchwardens in charge of the voting became so startled by the appearance of a large number of armed backcountry men, that they did not know what to do. The Regulators insisted that they had the right to vote as freeholders within the parish because recently drawn parish boundaries had excluded them from the newly established parish of St. Matthews. The Regulators therefore came to Goose Creek to vote. The wardens later reported that they "favored the liberty of the subject and the right of voting." The Regulators voted and the wardens wisely left the validity of the election to the judgment of the assembly.

The Regulators dominated the Goose Creek poll and elected their choices: Moses Kirkland, Aaron Loocock and Tacitus Gaillard, but representation still remained a serious problem. By the mid-1700s, more than half of the Caucasian population lived in the western parts of the colony, but royal policy prevented increasing membership in the South Carolina Commons House of Assembly. The backcountry repeatedly petitioned for representation during the 1760s, resulting in the establishment of additional parishes. It was possible to increase the number of parishes by decreasing the number of assemblymen. This was affected in 1768. The representation of three parishes was reduced for the purpose of granting representation to new backcountry parishes. Representation in the

St. James, Goose Creek Parish was reduced from four to three assemblymen. Residents of Goose Creek complained bitterly about the loss of a parish seat, but the complaints were directed against the Crown's restriction of the size of the assembly, and not against backcountry representation.[296] The majority in the assembly believed that they possessed the authority to grant representation. Conversely, they believed that they possessed the authority to reduce representation of a parish. All of this was based on the principle that the power that gives can also take away. A freeholder in Goose Creek published an article at that time on this question of representation. The Goose Creek writer contended that representation rested on the English constitution, and the right of community representation he contended could never be taken away.[297]

These additional parishes provided some relief for the backcountry, but the Regulators remained dissatisfied and became some of the most ardent patriots in the struggle for independence. They continued to protest the lack of local government, adequate representation and a school system.[298] Interestingly, as the war years approached, the Regulators found strong allies in Goose Creek against what they perceived as the increasingly tyrannical rule of Great Britain. By this time, the Goose Creek Men were credited with one revolution by ousting the proprietors. Now many joined with the backwoodsmen in armed rebellion for independence from royal rule.

Royal rule was increasingly unpopular in the northern colonies. During the decade preceding the American Revolution, the northern colonies suffered considerably from attempts by the British to enforce the principles of the mercantile system. The Navigation Acts, the Stamp and Sugar Acts and the Townshend Acts were all measures taken by the British to maintain the economic system. These agitations were not acutely felt in Goose Creek or South Carolina, but a small group of patriotic dissenters emerged in Charleston to keep the issues of protest in public view. A leader of this group was Christopher Gadsden of Charleston. William Johnson of Goose Creek was a staunch supporter. These two men kept political issues in the limelight and led the opposition to the British Crown. They enjoyed the support of many influential people in the backcountry parishes. An embargo on the port of Charleston during the Stamp Act was largely the result of Christopher Gadsden and his Sons of Liberty.[299] Political activist groups during that time were divided along merchant, mechanic and planter lines. The merchants and planters were divided, with many planters supporting law and order and royal rule, while many patriots came from the ranks of mechanics. There were of course exceptions in both groups. Rawlins Lowndes was a popular merchant and also a renowned patriot. He later owned Crowfield plantation in Goose Creek and served out the term of President John Rutledge after his resignation. Still, even with the protest of patriots in the years leading to war, the people of Goose Creek and the rest of Carolina were not nearly as incensed as the rebels in the northern colonies.

One issue that was taken as a protest cry in South Carolina was the Crown's practice of appointing salaried British civil servants to political office in the colony. These appointees were often referred to as "strangers" and were greatly resented by the local talent. Some Berkeley County planters refused to hold voluntary offices along with the salaried appointees. The appointment of Governor Thomas Boone in 1762 led to bitter controversy over what many thought was the governor's obstinate and dictatorial behavior. It became impossible to achieve a quorum in the 1763 Assembly because many members protested by refusing to attend. The colonial government came close to paralysis, but quickly improved when Boone departed in 1764. Goose Creek representatives in the 1763 general assembly were Peter Taylor, Thomas Wright, John McKenzie and John Parker.[300] William Bull (1764–1766) replaced Governor Boone (1761–1764) and was a popular and able local governor but he was never able to atone for Boone's mismanagement. Boone's placement of men from England in positions of honor, which the people felt should be filled by Carolinians, was not easily forgiven.

South Carolina was not as greatly affected by the Navigation Acts as the northern colonies, and for some time they did well despite the trade regulations. Thus, South Carolina remained unconcerned about Parliamentary Acts that did not directly interfere with their own prosperity. Consequently, South Carolina entered the political struggle later than the New England colonies. More people in South Carolina eventually voiced complaints against the British Government and supported the Charleston patriots. The controversy over the salaried appointments made by Governor Boone helped solidify resentment toward the Royal government and Gadsden and his followers used the resentment to garner support for rebellion. The Stamp Act and the poor conduct of some English officials added to the ire. Finally, when Gadsden and his followers sought support for an American Assembly composed only of Americans, the people of Goose Creek became more sympathetic and entered the fray.

One amusing story about St. James, Goose Creek Church reflects the local spirit of the days just prior to the Revolution. The Reverend Edward Ellington was a staunch loyalist. Once while he was conducting the church litany in an appropriate manner, he read, "That it may please thee to bless and preserve our sovereign lord, King George." The congregational response was supposed to be, "we beseech thee to hear us, Good Lord." There was silence instead and moments later a loud response came from one pew, "Good Lord deliver us."[301] Evidently, patriotism had clearly infiltrated the Church of England sanctuary in the 1770s.

After the repeal of the Stamp Act, a new Royal governor was well received in Charleston but the patriotic work of Christopher Gadsden continued. In 1774, a series of meetings in Charleston and the distribution of circulating letters resulted in a July assembly. This first committee appointed a delegation of five to meet and discuss the situation between the colonists and the British parliament at a general congress to take place in Philadelphia. In the meantime, a General Committee of fifteen mechanics and merchants, as well as sixty-nine planters was appointed to oversee matters at home. This committee called for an election of six representatives from each parish. Charleston was the site of the first meeting of these representatives when the body assembled in 1775, one year before the Declaration of Independence. Representing Goose Creek in the first assembly were Thomas Smith Sr., Benjamin Singleton, John Parker, Benjamin Smith, John Izard and John Wright. These men and the delegates from the other parishes resolved themselves into a Provincial Congress and pledged to defend South Carolina. The body elected Colonel Charles C. Pinckney as president.[302]

Shortly after, news arrived that men died at the battle of Lexington, Massachusetts. That was the first engagement of the war and the famed "shots heard round the world" caused strong reaction in Charleston. The general assembly reacted by calling for the assembly of a state congress. At that congress, Henry Laurens was chosen to succeed Pinckney as president and plans were made immediately to raise two regiments of infantry with which to oppose the British. Plans were also made to assign a Council of Safety to manage military affairs and act as the executive branch of the government of the province. All members were required to profess obedience to the new provincial congress and were subjected to the justice of parochial and district committees.

The colony divided. Some Carolinians remained loyal to England (Loyalists) and some opposed the mother country in support of the new provincial government (Patriots). To put pressure on the citizenry to oppose Britain, the patriots threatened to banish and confiscate the property of any who would not show overt support for the new state.[303] Committees were formed to execute the directives of the rebellious government. The *South Carolina Gazette*, on January 30, 1775, reported that Benjamin Coachmen, Henry Smith, John Davies, James Streater, Alexander Mazyck, Benjamin Mazyck and Thomas Walter composed the committee from St. James, Goose Creek. One year later, Thomas Smith, Colonel Benjamin Singleton, John Parker, Benjamin Smith, John Izard and John Wright served as the rebellious committee. In 1776, Thomas Smith died and was replaced by Thomas Middleton. James Akin, a planter, was appointed Justice of the Peace for Goose Creek at this time, and a year later, John Parker was listed in the *Journal of the General Assembly* with "persons proper to put into the Commission of the Peace." William Parker of Goose Creek served as Commissioner of the Treasury.

The Provincial Congress adopted the South Carolina Constitution in 1776 and resolved itself into the General Assembly of South Carolina. The constitution provided that the members of the general assembly elect a president and commander-in-chief, as well as a vice president. John Rutledge was elected president and Henry Laurens vice president. The executive authority was vested in the president and legislative council composed of thirteen members to be elected by the general assembly from its own membership. The new constitution gave St. James, Goose Creek, a total of 6 of the 202 seats of the assembly.[304] The president was the commander-in-chief and was responsible for defense of South Carolina. The militia of South Carolina numbered about fourteen thousand. It consisted of twelve regiments of foot soldiers with one regiment in each district and county. There was one regiment of horse commanded by Colonel William Moultrie of Goose Creek and one artillery company. The provincial congress also raised three additional regiments as an independent force.

Word was received that the British troops were expected to arrive in September. In mid-summer, the Council of Safety appointed a committee to make the village of Dorchester an armed post. Powder and weapons were rushed to the magazines at the fort for safekeeping. Soon after, Captain Francis Marion was ordered to take command of two companies of the 2nd Regiment and Captain Benjamin Smith was ordered to take the command of the Goose Creek Company of the Berkeley Regiment of militia. Smith was sent to Dorchester to support Marion.[305]

During this period, the British blasted into Charleston harbor and attempted an invasion of the city, but were repulsed by resistance from General William Moultrie's command at the little palmetto fort on Sullivan's Island. The British made no additional attempts to invade Charleston for several years, but they remained a threat and thus prevented the town from returning to normal. Business suffered greatly, the people were suspicious of each other's loyalties and many abandoned the city for the safety of the countryside. Stephen Mazyck left his Charleston townhouse to reside with his cousin, Alexander Mazyck, at Springfield Plantation in Goose Creek. He wrote his brother in Ireland in February 1776 to report upon the trials of the war and complained that Charleston had, "the most melancholy appearance," because the bulk of the population had retreated into the countryside. He further lamented that the, "whole province is in such a melancholy disturbed situation that there is no peace, satisfaction or happiness to be enjoyed in it..."[306]

In December, a new assembly re-elected the president and vice president and designed a new constitution. The second constitution was adopted in March of 1778. It provided for a governor, a lieutenant governor and a senate consisting of twenty-eight members to be elected by the people in their respective parishes. The legislative council that served as an executive branch was dissolved. The next year, a revenue act was passed by the general assembly. In accordance with this act, inquirers and collectors named for Goose Creek were Peter Smith, John Withers and William Eckles. The *South Carolina Gazette* reported that Goose Creek elected Senator John Parker and Representatives John Deas, Peter Bacot, Aaron Loocock, William Price, Benjamin Smith, and Peter Smith that year.

In 1778, the British landed in Georgia and captured Savannah. The next year they began a series of probing attacks into South Carolina, and by early summer, the British army was at the gates of Charleston. Fierce land resistance in the Charleston vicinity, as well as the appearance of a French navy, which supported the Americans, caused the British to withdraw, but a second attempt by the British to occupy Charleston occurred a year later. Sir Henry Clinton commanded a British army of eleven thousand well-supplied soldiers. His force landed thirty miles south of Charleston and marched north through the sea islands to set siege to the city at the Charleston neck. This maneuver trapped the American commander Benjamin Lincoln with his fifty-five hundred Continentals on the Charleston peninsula between the Ashley and Cooper Rivers. Later that year, as the siege mounted, the British successfully moved inland from the Charleston neck, when Britain's Lieutenant Colonel Banastre Tarleton and Major Thomas Ferguson established a strategically located base of operations at the Oaks Plantation in Goose Creek, within easy striking distance of both Moncks Corner and Charleston. Sir Henry Clinton endeavored to sever Charleston from communication with the interior and to halt the flow of desperately needed supplies into the patriot held city.

At this time, American General Isaac Huger with his 379 patriot cavalrymen controlled Bacon's Bridge on the headwaters of the Ashley River. He moved with his cavalry, Colonel Peter Horry's patriot dragoons and a small infantry unit to Moncks Corner in an effort to harass the British Army that had partially encircled Charleston. To contravene these moves, Sir Henry Clinton sent Lieutenant Colonel Webster to re-enforce Tarleton's and Ferguson's troops in Goose Creek and with these reinforcements the British moved north along the Moncks Corner Road, past the 22-Mile House on a cautious march to Moncks Corner. There they engaged the American forces and soundly defeated them. This defeat was a serious blow to the patriots, because the British now controlled the countryside around Charleston and could prevent supplies and reinforcements from reaching the Continentals trapped on the Charleston peninsula. As a result and in spite of the resourcefulness of Francis Marion's guerilla tactics, Sir Henry Clinton's British Army, supported by a naval convoy, succeeded in assailing the breastworks at the neck and forcing the American surrender of Charleston.

By 1781, both Goose Creek and Charleston were in the hands of the British, but the American General Nathaniel Greene had already agreed with General Thomas Sumter's plan to send an expedition into the Lowcountry to free it from British possession. The military campaign that resulted that year was commemorated with a plaque displayed in the Upper Goose Creek Parish on the Four Hole Swamp Bridge in 1930. The plaque records the dates of some of the battles that led to the British evacuation of Charleston. The text of the plaque is given here:

Four Hole Swamp

The first causeway and bridge here was built under terms of an act passed April 21, 1753. Col. Henry Hampton of State Troops of S.C. Seized the bridge July 14, 1781, and established a post here to check Lord Rawdon on his retreat from Orangeburg. Several actions took place here later in 1781 and 1782. The causeway and road were paved in 1928.

In the campaign to retake Charleston and the surrounding Lowcountry, General Thomas Sumter, General Francis Marion and Colonel Henry Lee were detached to move through St. James, Goose Creek Parish along the Wassamasaw Road toward the Goose Creek Bridge. The mission was to secure Goose Creek and cut it off from British-controlled Charleston. Colonel Lee moved his regiment toward Dorchester as the other units continued east. Patriot Colonel Wade Hampton arrived at the Goose Creek Parish church on Sunday morning, July 15, 1781, while service was in progress. He captured some horses and made prisoners of a number of attendants. He then paroled the prisoners on their oath not to take up arms against the Americans. Colonel Hampton stayed a short time in Goose Creek but soon continued his march along the public road toward Charleston. The word quickly spread that the patriots had returned to Goose Creek and commanded the bridge. Upon receiving this news, the British became concerned that they may lose control of their eastern flank and quickly withdrew from Fort Dorchester and hurried toward Charleston. Their hasty retreat enabled Colonel Lee to capture a large amount of desperately needed livestock, supplies and ammunition left behind at the fort.

Berkeley County was the scene of many revolutionary encounters with the British. Patriot General Thomas Sumter's penetration into Berkeley and General Francis Marion's guerrilla tactics in his home county kept the countryside active. Virtually every plantation participated in the struggle on one side or another and many neighbors were pitted against each other. Some Goose Creekers were patriot stalwarts from the beginning, like Elizabeth Ball Smith of Goose Creek Plantation (Yeamans hall). Her husband died soon after the British first attacked Charleston, and she was left responsible for the estate. For years following her husband's death, she kept her storehouse open for any patriot in need of supplies.[307] However, a relative of hers, John Ball of Back River, was a loyalist in support of the king. When Francis Marion captured one of Ball's thoroughbred horses, he kept it as his own and renamed it "Ball" in dubious honor to the previous owner. Marion trained this horse to swim rivers with the general on its back, and when the other horses in the command learned to follow, Marion and his daring cavalry were able to move rapidly through the countryside by crossing streams and rivers without boats or bridges.[308]

The Goose Creek Bridge was a strategic passage that conveniently connected all land travel to and from Charlestown to the eastern part of the state. Consequently, the British occupied Goose Creek to protect the bridge and keep it out of patriot control. The British used the bridge to effect foraging raids into the countryside but they were countered by patriot ambushes and by patriot efforts to remove or destroy available supplies. Marion wrote Colonel Peter Horry ordering "no boats or persons should pass from or to Charles Town without your or my pass-port." He also ordered that no plantations should "thrash or beat out any rice but what may be necessary for home use." [309] When the British retreated to Charleston, Goose Creek fell under the control of Francis Marion who recognized the strategic value of the Goose Creek plantations and bridge and stayed concerned over both for the remainder of the war. Marion's commander, General Nathaniel Greene was especially worried about the flow of supplies going from Goose Creek into British occupied Charleston. He complained to Marion about the large numbers of cattle that were sent to Charleston and he suggested that Marion keep consistent patrols on the Goose Creek Road to prevent the passage of cattle and other supplies.[310] Nevertheless, men, such as Leonard Askew were employed by the British Army to drive cattle from Goose Creek to Charleston and supplies continued to flow.[311] Governor Mathews chided Marion to get control of the smuggling operations that were not improving and were reflecting badly on him and his patriot cavalry.[312]

Shutting off the flow of supplies over the Goose Creek Bridge into Charleston was a daunting task for Marion. He wrote Governor Mathews in September of 1782 expressing his frustration with the persistent smuggling, and suggesting that any action short of imprisoning every person near Charleston and keeping them away from their plantations would be fruitless to stop the illegal trade.[313] Later General Marion acted on his frustration, short of imprisoning Goose Creekers. He ordered his small band of men at Goose Creek to prevent "women and others" from going to town by confiscating their horses and sending them back home on foot, but even these stern measures did little to halt or slow the illicit trade.[314]

Although the Goose Creek Bridge was strategically important, it was never the scene of a major engagement while the countryside remained embroiled in conflict and the problem of shifting loyalty persisted throughout the struggle even as the tide of war turned in favor of the patriots. Consequently, the lucrative smuggling activities in Goose Creek continued until the British returned to their ships and evacuated the Lowcountry.

Charleston remained occupied by the British in 1782, making it necessary for the state legislature to meet in Jacksonboro about twenty miles south of Charleston. General Greene moved his army to a position between Jacksonboro and Charleston to provide armed protection. The elected officials to the Jacksonboro Assembly from Goose Creek were Senator William Logan and Representatives John Braddley, Alexander Broughton, George Flagg, William Johnson and Thomas Elliott of Wappoo. These men met January 18, 1782.[315] Governor Rutledge's term had expired, but the countryside was in such turmoil that no election could be arranged. Consequently, the assembly chose their own executive officers. John Mathews and Richard Hutson served as governor and lieutenant governor, repectively.

By the time of the Jacksonboro Assembly, the die was cast for the British withdrawal and no major battles remained to be fought. General Cornwallis had surrendered to General Washington at York Town the previous year, and all that remained of the conflict was proper peace arrangements and the withdrawal of the invading army. The people of Goose Creek, the rest of Berkeley County and all of South Carolina soon celebrated victory.

In Goose Creek the victory celebrations were quickly replaced by the hard work of rebuilding a destroyed countryside. The people of Goose Creek were impoverished because both the "Red Coats" and patriots had damaged their properties during the conflict. The invading armies foraged at any patriot plantation they came upon, and the Americans did the same at the properties owned by the loyalists. Slaves and stock were stolen and crops were destroyed, but most of the damage was due simply to neglect. Many Goose Creekers entered into the patriot service and served as officials or militiamen and both groups left their properties untended and at the mercy of nature for months or even years. Consequently, there were few Goose Creek properties not adversely affected by the war. For example, Colonel John Boddely (Baddeley) owned 760 acres on Foster Creek, fifty-five slaves and two schooners.[316] He was an adjutant in the Charleston militia in 1776, but after his capture was confined to the prison ship *Torbay* in Charleston Harbor.[317] He also served as a member of the general assembly. Lieutenant Alexander Fraser from Goose Creek was a member of the House of Representatives in 1766 and 1778, and was a senator from St. James, Goose Creek Parish in 1785. Major Alexander Garden from Otranto Plantation was a cornet in General Lee's Legion in 1780. Peter Gray was a Goose Creeker who was commissioned as a captain in 1778, and also served as a member of the State Convention of 1790. Captain James Graham was from Goose Creek. Lieutenant John Izard, whose father owned the Elms Plantation in Goose Creek, was an aide-de-camp of General Isaac Huger. He was also a member of the 1775 Provincial Congress. Ralph Izard, owner of the Elms Plantation, was a representative at the Jacksonboro Assembly, served as a delegate to the Continental Congress and as senator in the First Congress. He was safe in England prior to hostilities but returned to Goose Creek to serve the cause as one of the most renowned patriots. He wrote in 1774 from England to a friend who was managing his "Elms" plantation, lamenting, "Nothing gives me so much concern as the thought that my people may want for clothes and blankets." In the same letter he suggested the possibility that cotton production might provide an eventual solution to the shortages of materials for clothes.[318]

Lieutenant William Johnson was a Goose Creeker who joined hands with other patriots around an ancient oak tree on the outskirts of Charleston and pledged loyalty to the patriot cause. Two other Goose Creekers, Robert Howard and Daniel Cannon, both carpenters, joined with William Johnson at the tree.[319] Upon his return to Goose Creek, William Johnson and his family remained a brief period at Thorogood Plantation, then owned by John Deas on the Moncks Corner Road. He went ahead to his White House Plantation on the Goose Creek neck to check on his slaves and the condition of the estate. He found that during his absence his slaves had continued to work the land and had concealed provisions in the woods so that the British would not take them. He also discovered that the British had removed most of the livestock including horses, cattle, sheep, hogs and poultry.[320]

Colonel William Mallard was active in the Revolution. In 1816, after the war, he served as treasurer of the road commissioners of the parish. He was a member of the general assembly in 1826–27 and was an active opponent of the federal tariff laws in 1828. Lieutenant Stephen Mazyck was commissioned as first lieutenant of Captain Ravenel's company of the Berkeley Regiment and was also one of General Marion's men. Captain James Mitchell was a patriot soldier from the parish. Lieutenant John Parker from the Hayes Plantation was a patriot who served as a senator from the parish in 1778. Captain Benjamin Singleton was a Goose Creeker. Lieutenant Richard Singleton lived at Wassamasaw and served in the First Regiment under Colonel Gadsden.

Major Benjamin Smith was a captain in the Berkeley Regiment in 1777. He served as a Goose Creek member of the general assembly in 1780 and as a delegate to the Constitutional Convention in 1788. Lieutenant James Smith was another Goose Creeker who served as a member of the Constitutional Convention. Captain James Stevenson lived at Wassamasaw and Lieutenant Peter Taylor served with General Francis Marion. Other Goose Creek patriots included Captain Hugh Strain Winter, Major William Vance, Captain William Withers and Captain Richard Withers. The

British seized Richard Withers's plantation in Goose Creek in 1780 and did much damage. Captain John Wright resided at Wassamasaw and served as a member of the Provincial Congress in 1775.

Goose Creek Men who served with General Francis Marion included: John Brown, John Burbridge, George Cannon, John Deas, Andrew DeHay, John DeHay, Alexander Douglas, John Downing, Jones Douglas, Peter Dubose, William Logan, Robert Martin, John May, George Morris, Robert McCants and Thomas Owens. Major Robert Thornley also served with Marion. Upon his death in 1805, the *City Gazette* published a glowing memorial calling him "an old, respected and useful citizen of this state," and conveying that he "served as an officer in the militia, from the beginning of the Revolutionary War to its termination…"[321] Other Goose Creekers, who fought, though not with Francis Marion, were John Cooper, Charles Johnson, William Michaer and William Parker.

Marauding parties of British soldiers did unwarranted damage in Goose Creek during the period that Charleston was occupied. On one occasion, two men went to John Parker's Hayes Plantation home but were refused entry. When the men moved to Parker's storehouse and attempted to break in, Parker shot. One soldier died and the other intruder ran off. Parker sent a letter to the commandant of Charleston to inform him of the fatality. The commander sent a return note saying he approved of the actions by Parker and sent another soldier to the plantation to bury the marauder.[322] Another party of marauders went by water to the old brick mansion of the Smiths near the mouth of Goose Creek. The house was tightly locked against the approach of the intruders. When they refused to leave, Mrs. Smith shot and killed one of them. The other carried the body to the boat and left. Such incidents were not uncommon during the war.

There are stories that tell of humane relations between the Goose Creek people and the British soldiers. John Deas of Thoroughgood Plantation directly confronted the British. A British officer called Deas to the front door and pleaded for help for his sick comrade. The Deas family welcomed both of them and provided hospitality until the next morning. About a year later, when the British were withdrawing from the countryside to the city, two officers paid a visit to the Deas's home. They politely inquired as to the welfare of the family and, not being recognized as the sick and weary travelers of a year prior, they stayed for friendly conversation for a number of hours. The officers then left, saying that the British Army was passing nearby and they were aware of the mischief such a retreating army could cause. They remained those hours to protect the Deas home. Then, having accomplished their mission, they thanked the family for their assistance a year before and rode off.[323]

The new American government was too weak to provide much assistance to the war torn and neglected regions of the young nation, but the records indicate that compensation was granted to the extent possible. Thomas Harris and Samuel Adams both appear as Goose Creek residents in the 1790 census. Both men appealed to the state and received compensation for losses during the war. Samuel Adams was paid for food and horses supplied by him to the militia, as well as payment for his days of service as a horseman under the command of Colonel Edward Lacey.[324] Thomas Harris was given compensation for supplying beef to the Continental Army, as well as his service in the militia as a wagon driver and sergeant of horse and foot under the command of Captain Joseph Pickens. This compensation was given seven years after the war.[325] Daniel Horry's Regiment of Light Dragoons camped on Benjamin Mazyck's Howe Hall Plantation in April 1780. Horry requisitioned "12,000 weight of corn blades" for animal fodder. Mazyck also claimed that he sent "14 head of large full grown sheep" to Charleston for the use of the Continental Army, as well as hay and corn blades to American troops at Fort Dorchester. He also claimed to have periodically supplied rice to American troops. Lt. John Garden testified that in 1782 Mazyck sent "500 bushels of clean rice for the use of the guard under my command at Goose Creek."[326] Benjamin Mazyck's claim totaled more than £428 for food, wood, leaden balls and the labor and loss of some slaves.[327] Alexander Mazyck, owner of Springfield Plantation contributed to the American war effort. Alexander Mazyck's executor received more than twenty-four pounds on behalf of the Springfield estate for providing three oxen, 383 sheaves of rough rice and half of a bushel of clean rice for the State Legion encamped near the Goose Creek Road.[328]

The Goose Creek patriots rebuilt their war torn plantations, while the Goose Creek loyalists were either banished from the colony, suffered property confiscation or fined. During the Jacksonboro Assembly in 1782, the assembly established categories of loyalty that were dealt with by the Councils of Safety. Some of the people in Goose Creek suffered at the hands of these patriot councils and in some instances forfeited the ownership to their properties. Commissioners were empowered to take control of confiscated lands, manage it and supply slaves for public work and food for the patriot army.[329] A list of names accompanying the confiscation acts resulting from the Jacksonboro Assembly appeared March 20, 1782 in the Charleston's *Royal Gazette*. Twelve Goose Creek landowners were included on the Jacksonboro list including: Peter Taylor, William Ancrum, Gideon Dupont Jr., Aaron Loocock, Dr. Robert Wilson, John Wragg, John Tunno, John Glen, Dr. Alexander Garden, Moses Kirkland, as well as the heirs of John Hume and James Mitchie. These Goose Creekers were listed in one of six categories that delineated various degrees of culpability.[330]

The landowners appearing on the Jacksonboro list and others faced punishment at the hands of the victorious Americans. The most serious offenses resulted in banishment and confiscation of the estate. Those guilty of lesser offenses were pardoned with a penalty of 12 percent of the assessed value of their properties. The least offensive acts resulted in a 10 percent penalty.[331] Immediately after the war, efforts were made to get individuals removed from the list or at least the penalty reduced, and some Goose Creekers appealed to the House in 1783 for the return of confiscated properties.[332] Goose Creek sent eight representatives to the general assembly in 1783 including Ralph Izard, Sr., George Flagg, John Braddeley, William Johnson, Alexander Moultrie, Captain James Stevenson, Thomas Middleton and Peter Smith. Benjamin Smith served as a South Carolina justice.

During the 1783 session of the House of Representatives, William Clarkson petitioned on behalf of Goose Creeker, Aaron Loocock. He asked for relief from the Confiscation Act, citing Loocock's aid to prisoners of war in England and asking that his property and citizenship be returned to him.[333] Others appeared before the assembly on behalf of Archibald Brown "praying that he be relieved of the Confiscation Act."[334] His wife made an appeal to the record that explained some of the confusion and mixed feelings at the time. After Charleston fell to the British, patriots, such as Brown believed that the country was "irrecoverably lost,"[335] and the journal records dated February 15, 1783 state that he accepted the protection of the British and assumed command of the Goose Creek Company "...chiefly to prevent its being given to a black man." The report further explained that his action kept peace in Goose Creek.[336]

Others, as patriotic as Archibald Brown, accepted the protection of the British after the fall of Charleston. Rawlins Lowndes accepted British protection after he protested from his confinement in Charleston that his Crowfield home was plundered by maurading British cavalry and his wife and family members were subjected to "outrageous and indecent behaviour," and Henry Middleton, who earlier served as President of the Continental Congress, took the oath of allegiance to the king.[337] Many relied on family ties and friendships to protect their property from confiscation. Some even swapped loyalty at opportune times to protect their estates. Alexander Garden Jr., whose famous father was a firm loyalist, was at school in England when the Revolution began. He took the oath to the king when he returned to South Carolina in 1780, but later switched to the patriot side. Garden was successful in getting the sale of his father's Goose Creek property postponed at the Jacksonboro Assembly. Edward Rutledge distrusted Garden and commented:

> *Young Garden I suppose you know is with us, he is full of trouble, not on account of our taking of his Father's Estate, but lest we should touch his Plantation at Goose Creek.*[338]

Alexander Garden asked the House of Representatives to transfer his father's confiscated property to him, which he accomplished the following year.[339] Gabriel Manigault, Jr., was able to save his property. Although he had signed the address congratulating the British victory at Camden, he reaffirmed his support for the patriots in time to save his property from confiscation. He recorded in his diary in November 1781, that he departed British occupied Charleston with his family and relocated to his country home in Goose Creek. Soon after, he defected from the British and found his way to "General Marion's Camps." This action, late in the war, saved his property from confiscation but Edward Rutledge was outspoken in his condemnation of such fickle loyalty.[340]

Other requests from Goose Creekers to the House of Representatives in 1783 came from:

- Benjamin Villeponteaux, requesting that an investigation into his past behaviors be made, so that he may be allowed to return to his family.[341]
- Benjamin Villeponteaux, on behalf of Charles Johnson concerning his actions during the British occupation and asking that Johnson be restored to his family.[342]
- William Price, concerning his actions during the British occupation and asking that the amercement levied against him be removed.[343] St. James, Goose Creek elected him to the Third General Assembly 1779–1780, but the 12 percent amercement was not removed.[344]
- John Deas, concerning his actions during the war asking that he be relieved from the amercement levied upon him.[345]
- Richard Wayne, asking that his citizenship and property be restored to him and explaining his actions during the war.[346]

The legislators at the Jacksonboro Assembly valued the confiscated estates as a source of ready cash and "as a means of establishing a capital to build a present credit upon." The preamble to the Confiscation Act stated that it was "just and reasonable" to use the property of loyalists toward alleviating and lessening the burdens and expenses of the war, which must otherwise fall very heavy on the distressed inhabitants of the state.[347] Confiscated properties could be used to repay debts. The St. James, Goose Creek Parish made ten loans to the patriot government between 1778 and 1779, amounting to £40,492 and assessed at £60,463 by May 1780.[348] This was a formidable amount of money to loan and to pay back, but in most cases, all or most of the money was repaid. The records also show that the bulk of the Goose Creek properties were returned to the original owners.

The British seized some Goose Creek properties because the owners supported the American patriots. Some Goose Creekers whose property was sequestered included Ralph Izard, William Moultrie, William Parker and Richard Withers.[349] The land was easily returned to the rightful owners after the British departed, but other property, particularly slaves, was not easily retrieved. A slave mulatto girl, who was greatly favored by the Rawlins Lowndes family, was sought but never found after the conflict.[350] She may have been one of many Goose Creek slaves who boarded British ships and relocated to other parts of the British Empire. Recorded in the British "Book of Negroes" is the name of Andrew Izzard (Izard), a South Carolina Negro who boarded the British ship Nisbet in New York on November 19, 1783 and sailed to Nova Scotia.[351]

Not all damage was done at the hands of the British. Some Goose Creekers appealed to the British after the war to compensate them for losses to the Americans. John Deas complained that both the American and British armies "made use of every article of stock and provisions they had a mind to."[352] Dr. Hugh Rose hid three horses at Dr. Garden's plantation, but lost them to the patriots. Another complained to the British that Americans confiscated two casks of his indigo dye when they seized a ship, and Gabriel Manigault asked the British to compensate him for the use of his property while he was a prisoner. No requests for compensation were granted.[353]

The rehabilitation of the Goose Creek property was much more difficult than reassignment to appropriate ownership. Many years of recovery ensued and despite great efforts, the grand Goose Creek plantations never regained the prosperity enjoyed during the mid-colonial era. Lingering bitterness between one-time friends, family members and neighbors took many years to abate. One year after the final peace, Ralph Izard wrote Thomas Jefferson from his Goose Creek estate. He commented that the "animosity and hatred" of the days of British conquest was the most baneful social effect of the Revolution in South Carolina. Izard further commented that the deprivation caused by the loss of property to the British and the destruction of crops and structures was not as serious a loss as the "animosity and hatred planted by them in the breasts of our citizens against each other."[354] In addition to the physical and emotional damage caused by the war, soil exhaustion had an irreversible effect. In Goose Creek, soil exhaustion slowed a struggling recovery for eighty years after the war, at which time the community suffered the Civil War and the debilitating economic and cultural collapse resulting from it.

From the Goose Creek perspective, problems with the British government, be it proprietary or royal rule, were present from the first settlement of the colony. Thus in a broad sense, the American Revolution was not the same as the American War of Independence. For Goose Creek, the revolution began in 1670 and lasted more than 150 years, finally culminating in a relatively brief war. The problems that the Goose Creek Men blamed on the Fundamental Constitution, proprietary directives, regulators or despotic governments were not unlike problems faced by other Americans in other places. Immigrants, who were discontented for any number of reasons in the old world, found that all of their grievances did not vanish upon the shores of America. Whether in Goose Creek or in any other lonely frontier in Virginia, Pennsylvania or New York, they had settled a great distance from home and they possessed the assertiveness, bravery and independent spirit that drove them from the old world to the new. In hindsight, the personal characteristics that motivated the immigrant to suffer the voyage to America and the great distances that diminished authority, made independence inevitable.

Chapter VI
The Neighborhoods
1790

The United States Constitution required all citizens to be counted every ten years for the purpose of apportioning representation in the national congress. The first census count was taken in 1790. This census reported 118 families, 454 free persons and 2,333 slaves residing in the St. James, Goose Creek Parish. By the year of the first census, Goose Creek was a mature community that provided political leadership during the eighteenth century, survived the front lines of the American Revolution, sent representatives to vote in favor of the new South Carolina State Constitution and was well occupied with families residing in eight neighborhoods. The neighborhoods were:

The Neck

The Neck was the home of some of Charleston's oldest families. In 1790, it was the place of pleasant residences and working fields but, not grand agricultural factories. Today, the neck is a busy industrial and commercial part of the city of North Charleston. It includes all lands on both sides of Rivers Avenue from Meeting Street extension to Durant Avenue.

South of Goose Creek

These agricultural lands were reasonably successful plantations, but by 1790 the neighborhood was becoming increasingly more important as a transport and commercial area. Today, the land on both sides of Rivers Avenue from Remount Road to Highway 78 and west to Ladson comprise this neighborhood.

North of Goose Creek

This neighborhood featured a small community center with the parish church, school and inns, but in 1790 it was primarily an area of diversified estates. Today, the neighborhood is occupied by the Crowfield section of the City of Goose Creek, the land on both sides of Red Bank Road and a section of the Charleston Naval Weapons Station.

Cooper River

This neighborhood served as the transfer center for goods moving by land and water. Today, the United States Naval Weapons Station, Charleston, occupies this neighborhood.

FOSTER CREEK

This was the brick-baking neighborhood that is partly occupied today by Department of Defense properties, including the Men Riv residential subdivisions of the United States Naval Weapons Station. The upper waters of the old neighborhood are occupied today by the land on both sides of Liberty Hall Road and the commercial center of the City of Goose Creek.

BACK RIVER

These plantations were grand agricultural giants that had survived decades of soil exhaustion, malaria and war, and in 1790 still made fortunes. Some of this neighborhood today is within the bounds of the Department of Defense properties that include the U.S. Border Patrol School. Other sections are included in Medway Plantation and its environs, as well as the Strawberry Community, Alcoa, the Mt. Holly Industrial Park and the vicinity.

WASSAMASAW

This was a place of many moderately sized and diversified holdings with yeoman farmers, growing families and a small trading center. Today the neighborhood can be found west of Carnes Crossroads on Highway 176 (Old State Road).

UPPER PARISH

In 1790, this neighborhood was the newest frontier in the Goose Creek Parish with unclaimed lands and opportunities for small farmers. Today many of these lands are planted with timber and remain sparsely populated. This neighborhood includes a western section of Berkeley County on both sides of Highway 176 (Old State Road) west of Wassamasaw to the Orangeburg County line.

The census taker traveled to the homes of more than one hundred families scattered throughout each of the eight Goose Creek neighborhoods to record the name of the head of the household, and to count the members of the immediate family and all others residing in the settlement. The census taker did not record the name of the plantation or account for the location of the family, resulting in a census report that failed to connect the families to specific land or identify the family locations in any way, except by order of visitation. The names on the census report appear in the order of visitation and thereby partially tracked the route traveled by the census taker as he sought the identity of each family head.

The ordered track indicates the location of the families relative to each other, and when the family census information is combined with a description of the family land, much can be learned about the neighborhoods. Matching the households to their land is essential to understanding the characteristics of each neighborhood because the land was the basis of political and social order and was the single most valued commodity. The head of each household was explicably tied to the property and unquestionably responsible for the care of the land and all who lived on it, which could include more than a hundred people. The household included the spouse and children, the related and unrelated free persons and any bound servants. Thus, most households resided not in a single structure, but in a settlement that consisted of an assemblage of buildings that likely included a main house, an overseer's house, slave quarters and a number of barns and sheds. Thus, the family resided in the settlement, and a number of settlements composed each neighborhood that was located along a road, near a road intersection or lined a waterway. These neighborhoods were indistinguishable as a traveler moved from one to another, but each as a whole was unique with discernable differences from the others.

The census taker first visited the households at the Neck, and then counted most of the people along the south side of Goose Creek. He crossed the Goose Creek Bridge and counted some families on the north side of Goose Creek before visiting Foster Creek. He then traveled north to the settlements along Back River and its headwaters before he departed the eastern section of the parish and traveled to Wassamasaw and the Upper Parish. He returned to the eastern section to visit remaining homes not counted earlier, including households on the south side of Goose Creek and a few tracts on the Cooper River. Table 6.1 lists the heads of households visited by the census taker in the order of visitation, as well as the number of family members and slaves reported on the 1790 census.

The parish was home to 2,787 people, but 84 percent were in bondage and there were only 158 free white males over the age of sixteen, and 79 younger free white males. There were more than 200 free white females and 15 other free persons, but almost all family heads were white males. Albeit, a few heads of households were white females and one was a free black female who claimed no family members other than her two slaves. Most families included three to five people and ten or fewer slaves, but there were many exceptions. For example, Ann Wilson lived alone but was the wealthy owner of 17 slaves. Robert Thornley resided with seven immediate family members, one freedman, and seven slaves. J. and M. Lehaffe reported a family of 12 with two slaves. In all, less than 20 percent of the population was white but the average white family owned 20 slaves albeit, 20 families (17 percent) owned no slaves at all and were among the poorest residents. Some of the wealthiest heads of households were John Deas Senior and Junior, Benjamin Maryck (Mazyck), Ralph Izard, Samuel Prioleau and John C. Ball. They owned the most slaves, and along with others on the report were among the richest men in South Carolina.

The Neck

While an anonymous traveler spent the night in Goose Creek, he recorded in his journal that he passed near "several beautiful plantations on each side of the road, and mostly brick houses…"[355] That anonymous reporter was traveling on the Goose Creek Road. The Goose Creek community was accessible from Charleston by a road first named "The New Broad Path." Later it was referred to as "The Path," and still later it was known as the "Goose Creek Road." Today it is Rivers Avenue. Proceeding along this road from Charleston, a traveler entered the St. James, Goose Creek Parish at the Neck. The Neck was a land passage slightly more narrow than the Charleston peninsula between the Ashley and the Cooper Rivers where the Charleston peninsula abuts the mainland. The southern-most line for the St. James, Goose Creek Parish was drawn along the Neck from St. George Parish to the Cooper River.

Upon the Neck were some of the earliest proprietary land grants, and by 1790 these estates represented several of South Carolina's "old money" households such as the Wragg family. Some of these estates were developed along the deep waters of the Cooper River and were well accommodated with fine furnishings and expensive carriages. In 1790, the main houses in the Neck neighborhood

Table 6.1

Head of Household	Free White Males 16+ Years	Free White Males Under 16 Years	Free White Females	All Other Free Persons	Slaves
Harris, Thom	2	0	3	0	5
Curtis, Francis	1	0	1	0	8
Adams, Sam	1	0	2	0	4
Prioleau, Sam	1	0	0	1	80
Simpson, John & Wm	1	0	0	0	18
Martin, John C.	1	0	0	0	22
Philbin, Chas	1	0	1	0	7
Bosman, Ralph	2	2	2	0	0
Glenn, John	2	1	2	0	33
Glenn, Dan	1	0	2	0	26
Cannon, Dan	1	1	1	0	22
Poyas, Dr	1	0	1	0	26
Singletary	1	0	0	0	2
Smith, Geo. (esta.)	1	1	2	0	28
Howard, Rob	1	0	0	0	24
Tims, Thom.	1	1	2	3	10
Philhower, Geo.	1	0	1	0	8
Segler, Geo.	1	0	3	0	3
Micheau,Wm.	2	0	1	0	24
Dillon, Robt.	1	0	1	0	13
Manigault, Gab.	1	0	0	0	38
Kekeley, Jane	0	2	1	0	3
Fraser, Alex (esta.)	0	0	0	0	29
Manigault, Jos.	1	0	1	0	2
Ellington, Rev.	2	0	0	3	10
Smith, Rebecca	1	0	6	0	42
Bowen, John	3	0	1	0	25
Smith, B. (esta.)	1	0	0	1	16
Maryck, Ben.	3	0	1	0	100
Graham, Capt.	1	0	0	0	47
Maryck, Alex (esta.)	2	1	3	0	54
Ball, John C.	2	1	1	1	82
Oillepontoux, Zacho.	3	1	0	1	44
Cholette, Alex	3	0	1	0	53
Parker, Geo.	2	0	0	0	48
Swinton, Hugh	2	1	2	0	22
Deas, J. Sen. (esta.)	1	2	1	2	208
Deas J. Jr. (esta.)	1	0	0	0	170
Wilson, Ann	0	0	1	0	17
Redhimer, Peter	1	0	1	0	3
Taylor, Ann	0	0	3	0	3
McBride, Ja.	1	0	2	0	1
Bacot, Thos.	1	1	1	0	8
Hoff, Sam	3	0	3	0	1
Brown, Chris	2	0	1	0	4
Rast, Thos.	2	1	3	0	2
Snyder, Wm.	1	1	2	0	0
Smith, Peter	0	0	0	0	64
Danelly, Amhert	1	2	2	0	3
Ounielt, John	1	2	0	0	16
Glover, Chas.	2	1	3	0	44
Simmons, Robt.	1	0	0	0	10
Platt, John	2	2	4	0	1
Falling, Willm.	1	2	2	0	1
Stevenson, Ja.	2	0	1	0	23
Dangerfield Wm.	1	1	3	0	1
Burbridge, John	1	0	4	0	0
Burbridge, Tho.	1	1	2	0	0

Table 6.1 cont.

Head of Household	Free White Males 16+ Years	Free White Males Under 16 Years	Free White Females	All Other Free Persons	Slaves
Theus, Simeon	3	1	3	0	21
Cannon, Wm.	1	2	2	0	16
Ringer, Jacob	1	2	5	0	8
Jennings, Robt.	1	0	2	0	0
Braker, Geo.	1	3	2	0	0
Legare's, Dan (esta.)	2	0	3	0	15
Huxford, Herely	1	2	5	0	0
Gibson, John	1	0	3	0	0
Douglas, Ja.	3	0	3	0	0
Doram	1	0	4	0	0
Ballard, Mrs.	0	4	2	0	0
Blewer, John	2	1	2	0	0
Blewer, Peter	2	1	4	0	0
Hurst, Robt.	2	0	3	0	7
Legare, Sol.	1	0	3	0	30
Ayrs, Peggy	2	0	1	0	1
Miland, Toney	1	3	1	0	0
Stevenson, Thos.	1	0	0	0	2
Vere, Mr.	4	2	4	0	3
Jackson	1	0	2	0	2
Lyons, Isaac	2	2	6	0	1
Dubois, Peter	1	1	1	0	0
Fitzpatrick	1	0	2	0	1
Martin, Robt.	1	3	1	0	2
Lindsay	2	0	6	0	14
Winter, Hugh	1	2	4	0	13
McCants, Nath.	2	2	3	0	12
Blackman, Sarah	1	0	1	0	18
Dehay, Zach.	1	1	1	0	1
Blackman, Thom.	1	3	1	0	9
Grumes, Mary	2	1	2	0	0
Bachelor, John	1	0	1	0	0
Cree, James	1	1	3	0	1
Thornley, Rob	2	2	3	1	7
Dehay, John	5	0	4	0	6
Platt, Tilman	1	2	1	0	0
Getringer, Adam	1	2	1	0	0
Leitz, Bernard	1	1	4	0	4
Williams, B.P.	1	0	0	0	21
Loocock, Aaron	1	0	1	0	45
Izard, Ralph	1	0	0	0	105
Lehaffe, J. & M.	4	4	4	0	2
Dupont, John	2	0	4	1	47
May, Peter	1	0	1	0	2
Tamplet, Peter	2	0	2	0	28
Gray, Peter	1	0	2	0	6
McDowell, Arch.	1	0	1	0	10
Johnson, Wm.	0	0	0	0	16
Withers, John	1	1	3	0	14
Withers, Rebecca	0	0	1	0	12
Lavall, Jacinth	1	2	1	0	6
Gray, Henry	3	0	1	0	32
Castell, Benj.	1	0	0	0	14
Eucleigh, Thom.	0	0	0	0	0
Glover, Joseph	0	0	1	0	32
Gough, Richard	2	0	1	0	123
Parker, John	1	0	0	0	45
(free woman)	0	0	0	1	2
Total/Mean	158/1.3	79/ .7	202/1.7	15/ .13	2,333/20

were working plantations and although they were comfortable and well furnished, they were not similar to the elegant townhouses of Charleston. These tracts kept high property values per acre due to the proximity of the land to the public road, the navigable waters of the Cooper River, and the city markets and merchants just seven miles to the south. Consequently, these expensive plantations on the Neck were much smaller in size (419 mean acres) than the agricultural spreads further from town. Oak Grove Plantation owned by Samuel Prioleau was an exception. Prioleau purchased two neck plantations that he combined into a tract of 1,036 acres. In addition, he owned Parnassus, a

Plantation Name or Location	Name of Head of Household	Number Whites in Family	Number Freemen in Family	Number Slaves	Number Acres	Parish of Residence
NA (note 1)	Thomas Harris	5	0	5	250	St. James
Filbins	Francis Curtis	1	1	8	344	St. James
Near Dorchester Road (note 2)	Sam Adams	3	0	4	110	St. James
Marsh Lands	John Wragg	1	0	6	349	St. Phillips/St. Michaels
The Retreat	Samuel Prioleau	1	1	13	(note 3)	St. James
Oak Grove	Samuel Prioleau	1	1	13	1,036	St. James
Hurst's/Simpson's	Jonathan and William Simpson	1	0	18	452	St. James
Hickory Hill	John C. Martin	1	0	22	365	St. James
Baldrick's	Charles Philben	3	0	7	445	St. James
NA	Ralph Bosman	6	0	0	NA	St. James
Totals/Mean (note 4)		23/2	3	96/10	3,351/419 (note 5)	

Table 6.2

Note 1: Thomas Harris was also part owner of a thousand acres at Four Hole Swamp.

Note 2: Samuel Adams was a Charleston merchant who owned more than one Goose Creek tract. He owned the 10-Mile House for a short time. In 1780 he purchased 600 acres from Daniel Tharin. That land was located at Button Hall. A 1791 plat states that he owned 110 acres about seven miles north of Charleston near the Dorchester Road. He probably owned more than 1,000 acres at more than two sites at the time of the census. He also owned property on Back River near the time of the census.

Note 3: Samuel Prioleau owned two plantations on the Neck and one on Back River in 1790. He owned a total of 2,687 acres with 1,651 or 48 percent of the land on Back River and 32 percent on the Neck. For this study his slaves are divided proportionately between his three sites. He owned two Neck estates with a combined 1,036 acres or 32 percent of his total land. He is shown in Table 6.2 with thirteen slaves at each of his Neck plantations. These twenty-six slaves on the Neck represent 32 percent of his slaves.

Note 4: Dividing the sum by the number of addends derives the mean.

Note 5: The average number of acres is determined by counting Samuel Prioleau's estate one time with his combined number of acres.

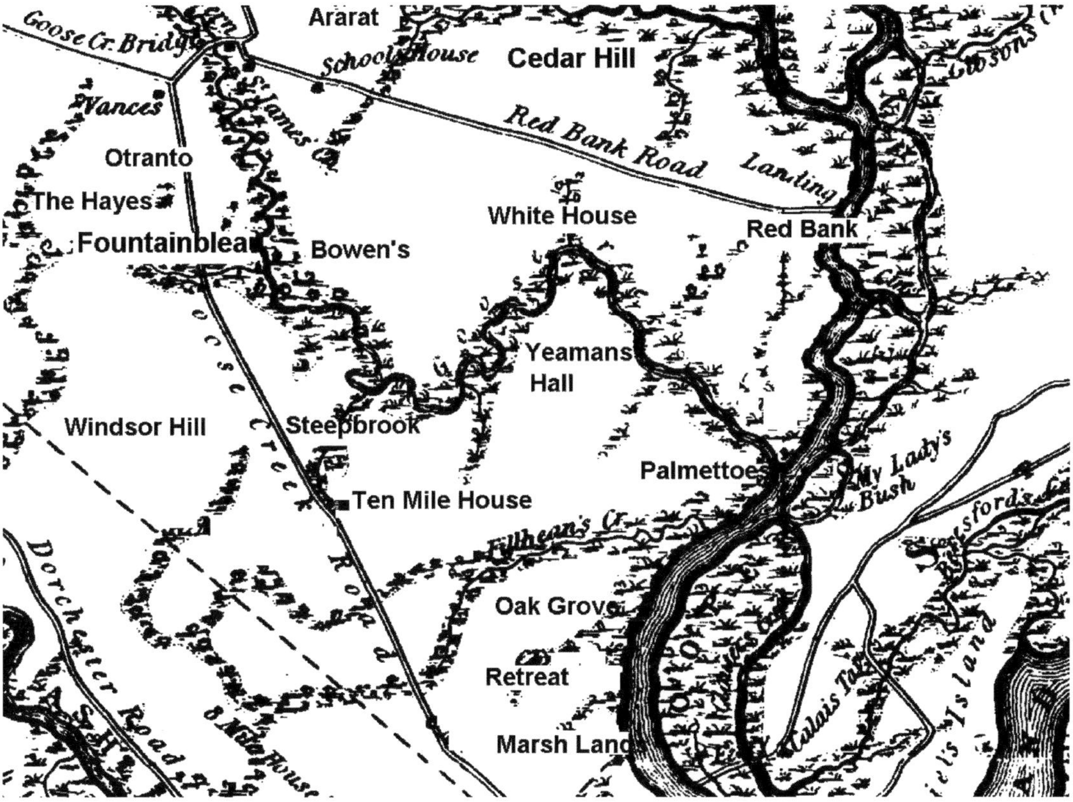

Map 6.1 This map is an enhanced version of Mills' Atlas of 1825. The Goose Creek Road is shown as it continued northwest from Charleston. Names of selected plantations as they were situated in 1790 were added for this publication.

working plantation on Back River where most of his eighty slaves lived and labored. Only about ten slaves per family worked the smaller Neck plantations. Table 6.2 lists the heads of households on the Neck visited by the census taker. The census data is supplemented with information from property deeds, surveys and plats and show that Ralph Bosman was the only head of household on the Neck who did not own land in Goose Creek. He owned land in Georgetown District and Cheraw but he and his family probably leased property in the Neck neighborhood at the time of the census.[356] Many of these leased and owned lands, 140 years later, became the Charleston Naval Base and Ship Yard. The other properties are residential and commercial sections in the city of North Charleston east of Remount Road. Map 6.1 shows the location of Marsh Land, Retreat and Oak Grove, three of the nine plantation homes on the Neck at the time of the census.

South Side of Goose Creek

Traveling inland from the Charleston neck, the census taker passed through another neighborhood with the homes of rich planters on both sides of the road. He also came upon taverns, some named in accordance with their distance from Charleston. Thus, ten miles from Charleston was the 10-Mile

House Tavern owned by Thomas Tims in 1790. Today, the section of Rivers Avenue near the public train depot is still referred to as 10-Mile Hill. The tavern was a popular drinking and trading place, as well as an inn that remained in operation until after the Civil War. Located next to the 10-Mile House Tavern was Andre Michaux's French Garden. Michaux was sent by the Royal French Government to study American flora and conduct botanical experiments. Adjoining French Garden was Cyprian Bigelow's plantation. This land was once the home of Dr. John Moultrie, patriarch of the famous Moultrie family. John Fisher, a cabinetmaker, acquired the southern half of Bigelow's tract near the time of the census and resided there adjacent to Gabriel Manigault's country home at Steepbrook. The waters of Goose Creek provided the east boundary for Manigault's Steepbrook Plantation. This

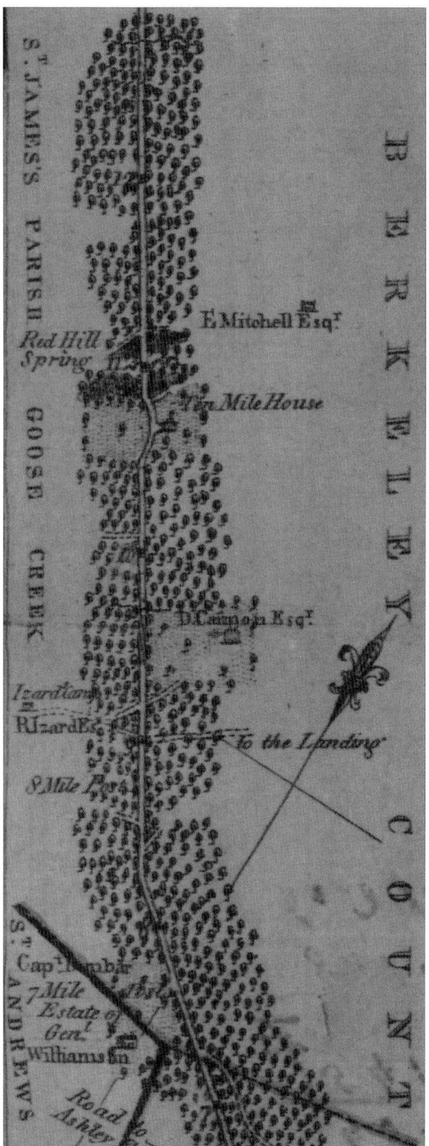

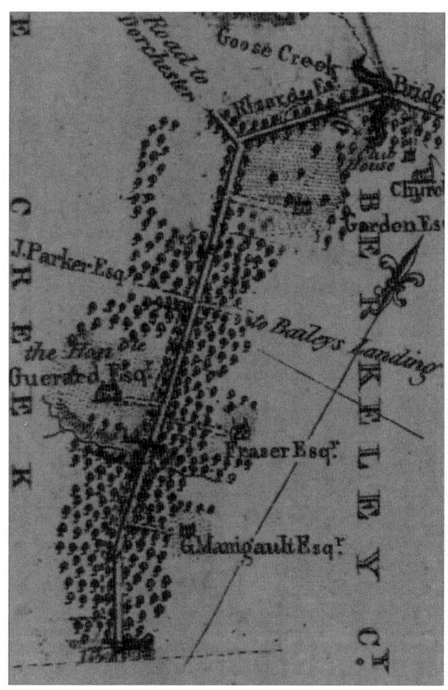

Map 6.2 The partial map shows the section of the Walker and Abernethie, 1787 map that describes the road from Charleston to the Goose Creek Bridge. *Courtesy of the Library of Congress.*

extremely valuable country estate was the one time home of Peter Managault, the wealthiest man in North America. North of Manigualt's land was the large estate that belonged to Benjamin Godin, a wealthy Charleston merchant. His Fountainbleau Plantation contained 3,847 acres with a large frontage on Goose Creek. Benjamin Guerard owned this tract while he served as Governor of South Carolina from 1783 to 1785. At one time these lands supported some of the wealthiest families in America, and their large brick homes remained in 1790 as reminders of the opulent past. Map 6.2 shows the road through this neighborhood as it was in 1787, three years before the first census. The map describes the road as it entered St. James, Goose Creek Parish from St. Phillips Parish at a place close to the St. Andrews Parish line. The road proceeded north to the Goose Creek Bridge.

The Goose Creek Road proceeded past Fontainbleau and along the estate called The Hayes, owned by John Parker. North of The Hayes and Fontainebleau was the renowned Otranto estate. This early Middleton property was later the home of the renowned botanist, Alexander Garden. The Goose Creek Road forked near the northwestern boundary of Otranto. The western branch served The Hayes, and Woodstock Plantations and ran parallel to the Elms for several miles before it continued to Dorchester Village in St. George, Dorchester Parish. The Elms was the country home of the Honorable Ralph Izard, renowned statesman. The eastern branch later became part of the State Road. It crossed the Goose Creek Bridge before it turned northwest toward Wassamasaw.

After visiting Joseph Manigault's settlement, the census taker failed to find the property owners at the next several estates, but likely found the families of overseers and land managers. Consequently, the names of some absentee property owners do not appear on the census report. Some, such as Alexander Garden of Otranto, resided in England at that time and his family and slave information were omitted, while others appear on census rolls of nearby parishes. Two such landowners were John Splatt Cripps, and William Moultrie. John Splatt Cripps owned two plantations, in addition to his Goose Creek property and resided on the Ashley River. William Moultrie, the owner of Windsor Hill in 1790 was residing in Charleston. His name appeared on the St. Phillips and St. Michaels Parish census. Thus, it is likely that an overseer or managing family resided at Cripps and Moultrie's country estates, but the records do not indicate whether the overseer families were counted on the first census. In other cases, such as Woodstock and Fountainbleau Plantations, the land titles were in transition due to the death of the owner, and in some cases, the executor of the estate was listed instead of the head of the household. Additionally, some names appear on plats without additional information, such as the number of acres. Thus, heads of households such as Thomas Young and Robert Howard are accurately assigned to the neighborhood, but their number of acres is unavailable. Lastly, the census taker, upon a return trip, visited some more settlements in the neighborhood. Ralph Izard at the Elms, J. and M. Lehaffe at the 8-mile stone and John Parker at The Hayes were visited later and included on the list of the South of Goose Creek Neighborhood.

The listing given in table 6.3 shows that the size of holdings on the south side of Goose Creek ranged from approximately one hundred acres at French Garden and the 10-Mile House to as large as fifteen hundred and sixteen hundred acre tracts at Otranto and the Elms. The average size of the tracts on the south side of Goose Creek was almost eight hundred acres with approximately twenty-three slaves per household.

The lands along the Goose Creek Road were near Charleston and consequently kept a higher value per acre than the lands further inland, but most were not among the prodigious rice-producers

Plantation Name	Name of Head of Household	Number Whites in Family	Number Freemen in Family	Number Slaves	Number Acres	Parish of Residence
Live Oak	John Glen	5	0	33	360	St. James
NA	Dan Glen	3	0	26	NA	St. James
Oak Land	Daniel Cannon	3	0	22	571	St. James
Poya's	Dr. Poyas	2	0	0	207	St. James
Yeamans Hall	George Smith, Esta.	2	2	28	1,371	St. James
NA	Robert Howard	1	0	24	NA	St. James
Ten-Mile	Thomas Tims	4	3	10	180	St. James
NA	George Philhower	2	0	8	200	St. James
NA	George Segler	4	0	3	NA	St. James
French Garden	William Michau	3	0	24	111	St. James
NA	Robert Dillon	2	0	13	NA	St. James
Steepbrook	Gabriel Manigault	1	0	38	1,105	St. James
NA	Jane Keckley	3	0	3	350	St. James
Wigton	Alexander Fraser, Esta.	0	0	29	605	St. James
Wilson's (note 1)	Joseph Manigault	2	0	2	523	St. James
The Elms	Ralph Izard	1	0	105	1,500	St. James
Lehaffe's at 8-Mile - stone	John & M. Lehaffe	12	0	0	NA	St. James
De La Plaine's	George Parker	2	0	48	797	St. James
The Hayes	John Parker	1	0	45	1,382	St. James
Woodstock	Susannah Bee	NA	NA	NA	932	Not on Census in S.C.
Windsor Hill	William Moultrie	9	0	0	800	St. Phillips/St. Michaels
Otranto	Alexander Garden	NA	NA	NA	1,689	Not in S.C.
Spring Grove/Barker's	Thomas Young	NA	NA	NA	1,494	NA
Fountainbleau	Charles Lining (Executor)	NA	NA	NA	1,474	Not Applicable
NA	John Splatt Cripps	7	0	18	64	St. Phillips/St. Michaels
Totals/Mean		69/3	5	479/23	15,715/786	

Table 6.3

Note 1: After counting Joseph Manigault's family at Wiilson's, the census taker apparently crossed the bridge to the north side of Goose Creek. On the north side, he traveled to households along the northern shore of Goose Creek and proceeded along Red Bank Road visiting Foster Creek families.

Photograph 6.1 This photograph shows a family fishing the water reserve at Ingleside (The Hayes). This reserve is on the headwaters of Goose Creek in North Charleston. The photograph was taken May 16, 2003, and is in the possession of the author.

of colonial times. Regardless, these were valuable tracts because the creek was navigable for miles, and estates not on the navigable waters benefited from the natural reserves in the fresh water swamps that could be banked, ditched and channeled. This was an important agricultural area near an essential commercial route to Charleston and because by 1790, the western lands of South Carolina were well occupied, the residents on the south side of Goose Creek became accustomed to the sights and sounds of back country horsemen driving herds of cattle, and pedestrians, wagons and carriages of varied designs moving east and west along the road. Toward the end of the eighteenth century, larger and heavier transport wagons, loaded with stacks and barrels of products from the western lands and pulled by two or more horses or mules were common sights along the route at all hours of the day.

North Side of Goose Creek

Vance's Tavern was situated near the point where South Carolina Highways 52 and 78 interchange today. At that intersection, the road forked west toward Ladson and east toward the center of Goose Creek. The road proceeded east over the Goose Creek Bridge and past another tavern at the 17-mile stone where Back River Road intersects with Red Bank Road today. The Goose Creek Bridge was an important front door to this neighborhood and its construction and maintenance was the earliest public works project in the Parish, because the location of the bridge allowed the shortest and easiest land travel from the eastern half of South Carolina to Charleston. The Lowcountry is noted for the many creeks, swamps and rivers that allowed for profitable agriculture and convenient water transport, but these bodies of water were obstacles to land travel. During periods when the bridge was impassable, disappointed wagon drivers and horsemen were forced to travel thirty-five additional miles above the headwaters of Goose Creek to Bacons Bridge near Dorchester before reaching Charleston. Thus, the bridge was a defining feature of this neighborhood and by 1790, this section was a busy transport area where many travelers and transporters converged in the vicinity of

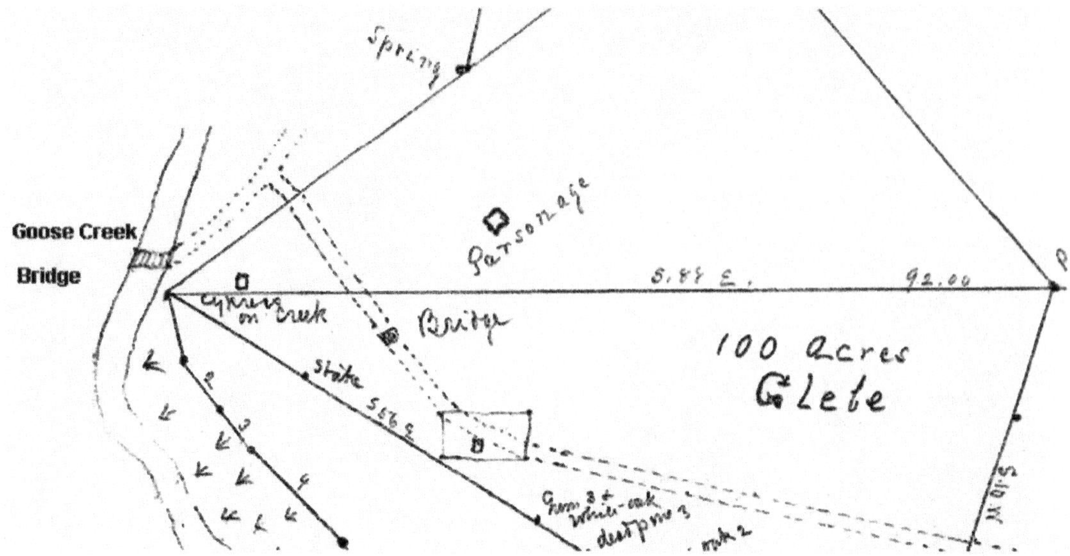

Plat 6.1 This partial plat shows the St. James Goose, Creek Church, Parsonage and Glebe. The partial plat is a tracing of the original in the possession of S. Lewis Simmons, 1906. The words "Goose Creek Bridge" were added for this publication. The original plat was not dated. The tracing was made by H.A.M. Smith and is in the possession of the South Carolina Historical Society.

the bridge creating a semblance of a town center that featured a church, parsonage, school, tavern and busy homes. Here, the census taker made stops at the parsonage and three plantations before proceeding along Red Bank Road to settlements on Foster Creek.

Plat 6.1 shows a road approaching the church, parsonage and glebe, and two bridges near the Goose Creek Church. One bridge crossed Goose Creek, the second smaller bridge carried travelers over a narrow branch emptying into the waterway. The plat is not dated, but Thomas Middleton's name appears on the full plat. He owned the nearby Oaks Plantation shortly after the American Revolution and at the time of the 1790 census. Therefore, it is likely that the plat was made prior to and near the year of the census and near the time that map 6.3 was drawn, which shows Middleton's Plantatiom, the Goose Creek Bridge, the Parsonage and 17-mile marker.

Across the road from the parsonage was the beautiful avenue of live oaks that led to the front door of the Middleton mainhouse. The Oaks Plantation was a working farm situated on navigable Goose Creek waters that became too shallow to navigate near the northern boundaries of the estate. The Middletons used the shallow waters to produce bounties of rice, and the deeper waters to float the products to market, but the census taker found no Middletons to count. The Thomas Middleton family was recorded as residents of the Charleston Parishes that year, and the census taker probably found only an overseeing family and the Middleton slaves.

Red Bank Road branched east from the State Road near the Oaks Avenue and proceeded past the schoolhouse and Howe Hall and on to Ararat Plantation on Foster Creek. Howe Hall, where Sedgefield residential area is today, was the original home of Job Howe, the speaker of the Commons House of Assembly, but Benjamin Mazyck owned it at the time of the census.

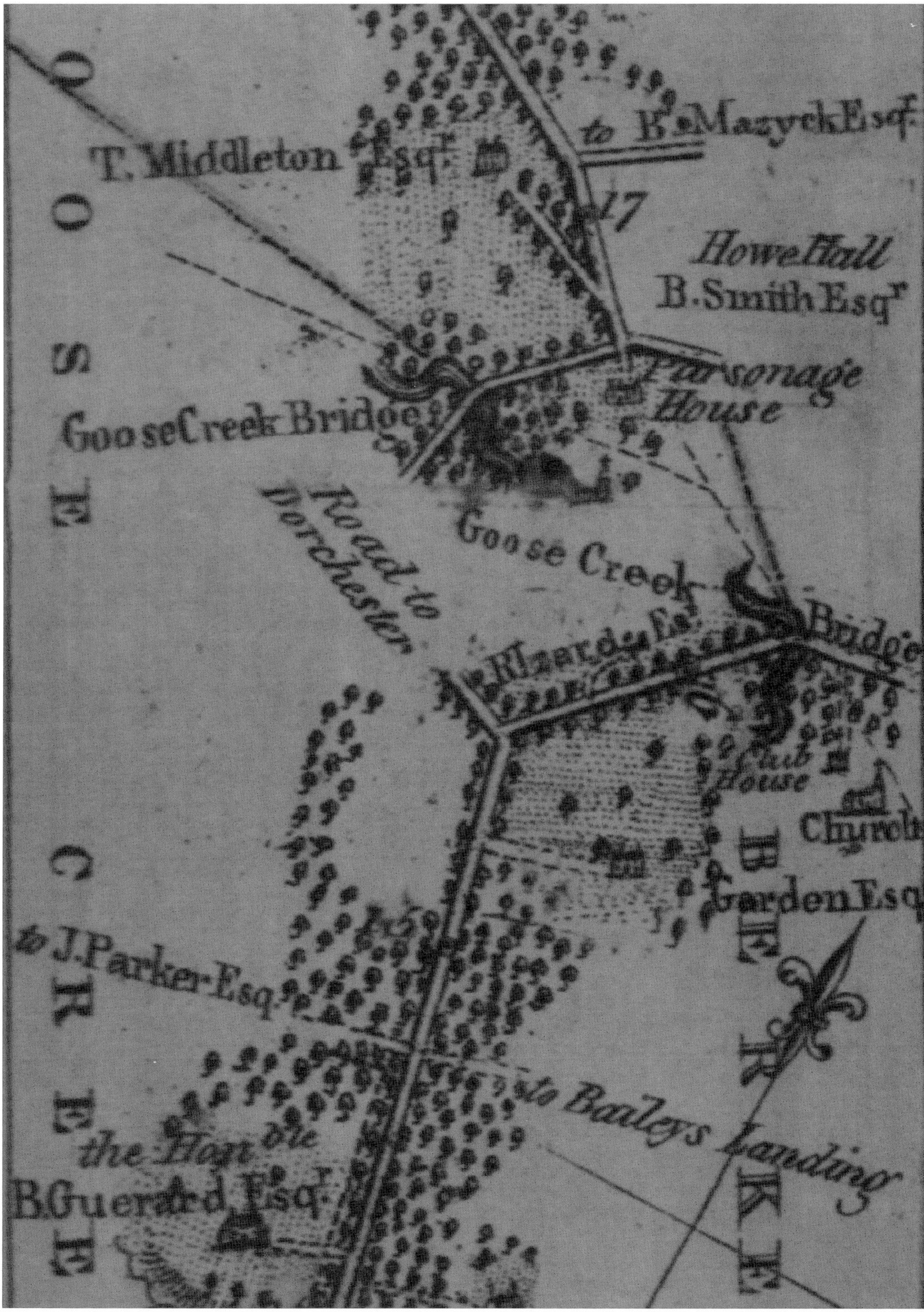

Map 6.3 This partial map shows the section of the Walker and Abernethie map that describes the road to the Goose Creek Bridge and from the bridge to Red Bank Road. *Courtesy of the Library of Congress.*

Ararat, where Men Riv Housing is situated today, was the home of Harriet Horry, who named the plantation after Noah's Mt. Ararat, when disastrous floods drove her from her lands on the Santee River. The road continued eastward past Ararat and four miles further to Red Bank Landing on the Cooper River.

The publicly supported State Road and Goose Creek Bridge provided access to the plantations on the north side of Goose Creek, but private paths and roadways in all neighborhoods connected the land and people to each other. A well-kept private road called "Gibbes Path" connected the main avenues of Crowfield, Bloomfield, Fredericks, Mt. Holly and Springfield Plantations. From Springfield, the path connected to Back River Upper Road, another privately maintained road that reached four miles to Back River. The census taker probably used Gibbes's Path to visit the plantations along its way.

The plantations on the north side of Goose Creek contained an average of more than one thousand acres and worked about twenty-seven slaves per household, and thus were larger than those on the south side of Goose Creek and on the Neck. Most were working estates that survived the soil exhaustion of the colonial period and the destruction of the Revolutionary War, but some large estates, such as Crowfield and Bloomfield were no longer the main residences of the landowner. By 1790, these plantations were merely country retreats showing early signs of neglect and the Oaks estate was soon sold outside the Middleton family and later reduced in size, as individual parcels were sold. Bowen's Plantation and two others, Mt. Pleasant and White House were still successful agricultural plantations that used the navigable waters of Goose Creek to bring bountiful harvests of rice, as well as other grains and foodstuffs to market, and some plantations in this neighborhood sent timber and brick to markets as well.

Plantation Name/Location	Name of Head of Household	Number Whites in Family	Number Freemen in Family	Number Slaves	Number Acres	Parish of Residence
St. James Church	Rev. Ellington	2	3	10	548	St. James
The Oaks	Thomas Middleton	9	0	10	1,800	St. Phillips/St. Michaels
NA	Rebecca Smith	7	0	42	NA	St. James
Bowen's (21)	John Bowen	4	0	25	1,370	St. James
Mt. Pleasant	John/Rebecca Withers	6	0	26	1,880	St. James
White House	William Johnson	0	0	16	800	St. James
Red Bank	Peter Gray	3	0	6	314	St. James
Crowfield	John Middleton	5	0	1	1,464	Prince George
Cherry Hill	Thomas Bacot	3	0	8	478	St. James
Bloomfield	Peter Smith	0	0	64	840	St. James
Frederick's (note 1)	Ralph Izard	1	0	105	584	St. James
Totals/Mean		40/4	3	313/28	10,078/1,008	

Table 6.4

Note 1: Ralph Izard owned Fredericks at the time of the 1790 census. An overseer's house was probably on the site as well as slave quarters. The records do not show who resided at Frederick's in 1790.

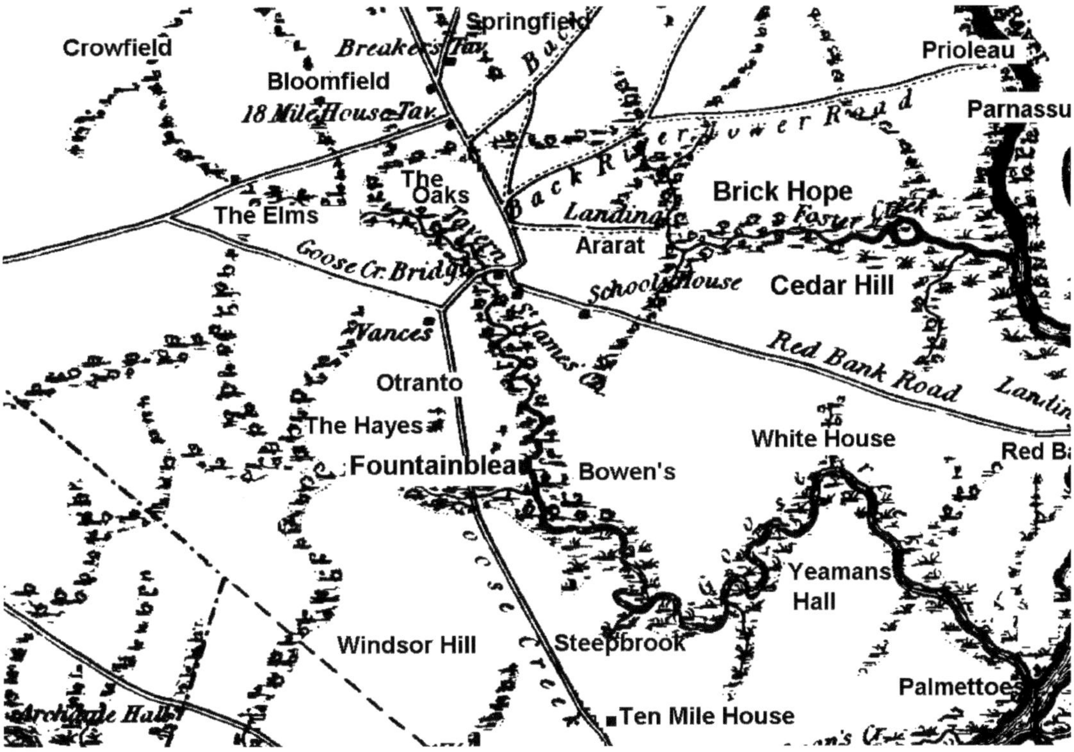

Map 6.4 This map is an enhanced section of Mills' Atlas, 1825 showing the road system and selected plantations on the north side of Goose Creek, on Foster Creek and the Cooper River.

Cooper River

Located at Red Bank Plantation was Red Bank Landing, an important transfer point on the Cooper River and the site of an extensive pottery for the manufacture of tile and brick. Also at Red Bank Landing was the "cut." Near Red Bank, the Cooper River coursed an oxbow turn that added considerable labor and travel time to watermen. To improve the travel conditions, a canal was opened through the marsh that connected both ends of the oxbow. This canal, referred to as the "cut," allowed the ebb and flow of the tides to scour a passage through the marsh, which bypassed the oxbow and shortened the travel distance.

Red Bank Landing and the properties north and south of it were highly valued because they were contiguous to the deep navigable river. A landing at Archer Smith's Palmetto Plantation and near Robert Hurst and Thomas Harris's estates was situated on the Cooper River south of the confluence of Goose Creek with the Cooper, but plantations north of the confluence benefited from the convenient access to the Red Bank Landing. Here the landing to navigable waters made brick making and transport cost effective. Jacinth Lavall owned the 6-acre tract at Red Bank Landing at the time of the census and Henry Gray and the Tamplet family owned productive plantations nearby. Interestingly, Benjamin Castell appears on the census with one person in his family and fourteen slaves. He owned 440 acres on a branch of the Cooper River, but sufficient information to locate his property on the north or south side of Goose Creek is not available.[357] Table 6.5 shows the heads of households residing on the Cooper River. These plantations averaged 548 acres and were worked by an average of fifteen slaves.

Plantation Name	Name of Head of Household	Number Whites in Family	Number Freemen in Family	Number Slaves	Number Acres	Parish of Residence
NA	Thomas Harris	5	0	5	250	St. James
NA	Robert Hurst	5	0	7	294	St. James
NA	Peggy Ayers	3	0	1	NA	St. James
Palmetto	Archer Smith	1	0	28	1644	St.Phillips/St. Michaels
Red Bank	Henry Gray (Note 2)	4	0	32	540	St. James
Red Bank Landing	Jacinth Lavall	4	0	6	6	St. James
NA	Mary/Peter Tamplet	4	0	28	662	St. James
NA	Benjamin Castell	1	0	14	440	St. James
Total/Mean		27/3	0	121/15	3,836/548	

Table 6.5

Note 1: Thomas Harris property and Robert Hurst lands were on the Neck and bordered by the Cooper River and are therefore listed in both neighborhoods.

Note 2: Aaron Loocock and Henry Gray shared ownership of Redbank Plantation at this time.

Foster Creek

Foster Creek was navigable for nearly four miles inland from Back River and was the water highway for a brick-making neighborhood. All plantations on the north and south sides of the navigable section of the creek engaged in baking and shipping brick to Charleston. The headwaters of Foster Creek reached for more miles into swamps where the owners of large estates, such as Thorogood and Mt. Holly dammed and channeled the fresh water for irrigation. The inland tracts were large plantations that averaged more than eleven hundred acres and worked more than fifty slaves. These plantations included Glover's two-thousand-acre tract, but there were also small landholdings of about one hundred acres that supported taverns, inns and trading centers. The headwaters of Foster Creek drained the lands as far inland as the 18-Mile House where the modern center of the City of Goose Creek is busy with traffic and commerce today. Plat 6.2 shows the 18-Mile House Tract in the center of this busy area. William Laughton Smith owned it at the time of the census.

Properties near intersections of public roads were eventually sold as several smaller tracts when commerce and demand increased the value of the land. Such was the case when William Laughton Smith sold 109 acres of Button Hall Plantation to Lewis Breaker, who operated the 18-Mile House Tavern for many years. Interestingly, plat 6.2 shows Smith's tract at the time of the sale with two main houses and two parallel avenues. No explanation is available for the two structures and redundant avenues that approximate the location of today's Brandywine Boulevard. This tract remains today

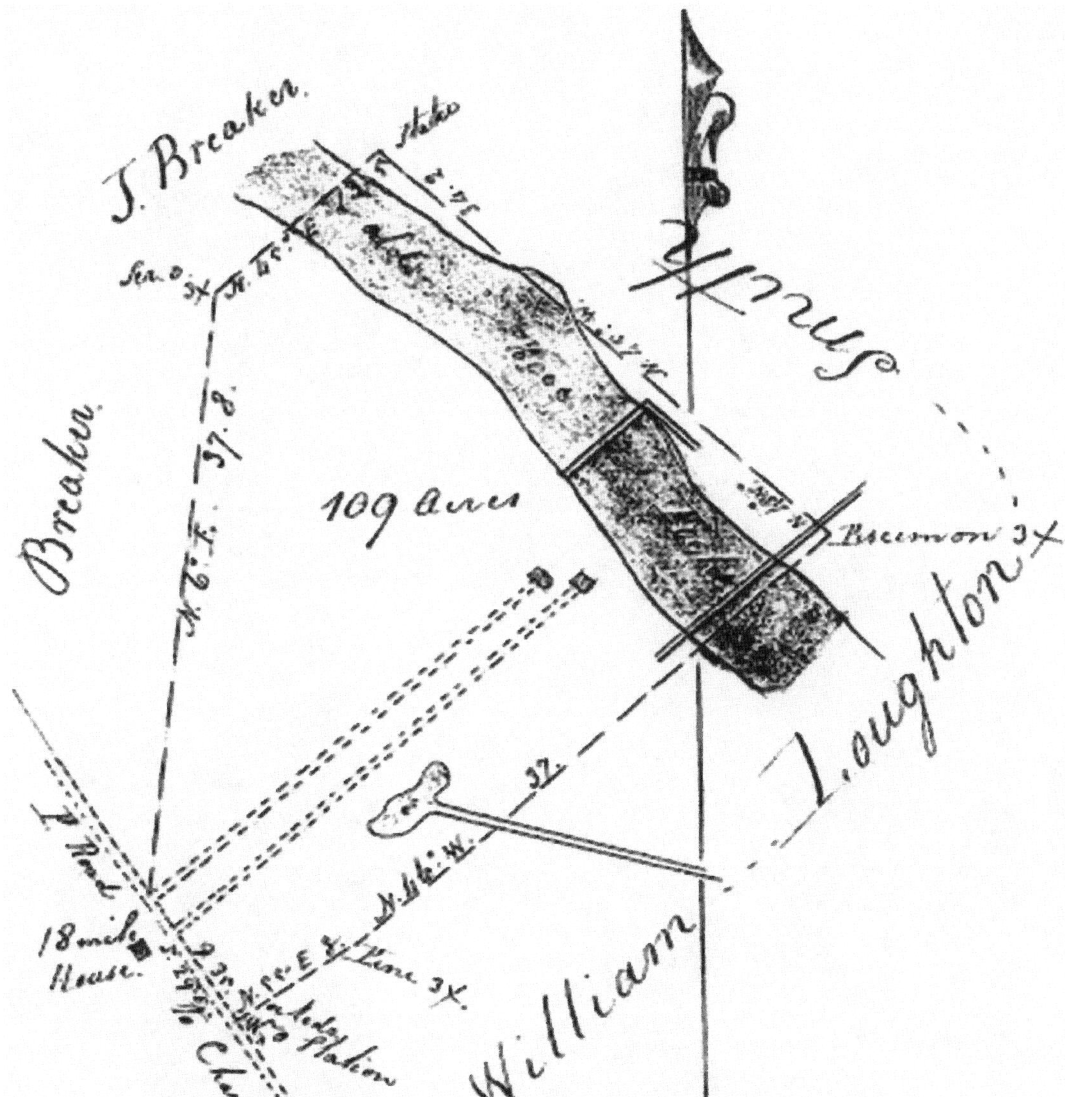

Plat 6.2 This plat represents 109 acres of land conveyed by William Laughton Smith to Lewis Breaker at the 18-Mile House in February 1810. John Diamond made the survey and plat. This plat is among the Wragg family papers on deposit at the South Carolina Historical Society.

the center of commerce as it was in 1790 when the 17-Mile House, 18-Mile House, and 19-Mile House taverns were situated within a two mile stretch of road.

The 18-Mile House Tavern is shown on the 1825 Mills Atlas near "Breaker's Tavern." Interestingly, the map shows two taverns, named "Breaker" in the same vicinity and it is likely that George Breaker, whose name appeared, as "Braker" on the 1790 census, owned both inns. George

Braker (Breaker) is listed with six slaves on table 6.6 with the other heads of households residing in the Foster Creek neighborhood.

Plantation Name/Location	Name of Head of Household	Number Whites in Family	Number Freemen in Family	Number Slaves	Number Acres	Parish of Residence
Grove Hall	Charles Glover	6	0	44	1,432	St. James
Foxhunt (?) (note 1)	Singletary (Richard Singleton?)	1	0	2	NA	St. James
Laurel Swamp (note 2)	Joseph Glover	1	0	32	NA	St. James
Laurel Swamp	Sam Huff	6	0	1	NA	St. James
NA	John Onsitt (Ounielt, Cunsall)	3	0	16	666	St. James
Thorogood	John Deas Sr.	4	2	208	1,100	St. James
Mt. Holly	John Deas Jr.	1	0	170	1,050	St. James
Brown's Field	Aaron Loocock	2	0	45	900	St. James
18-Mile House	George Br(e)aker	6	0	0	105	St. James
Springfield	Alexander Mazyck	4	0	100	1,007	St. James
Button Hall	William Smith	3	0	3	970	St. Phillips/St Michaels
Howe Hall/Boochowee (note 3)	Benjamin Smith Esta.	1	1	16	1,110	St. James
Howe Hall/Boochowee (note 3)	Benjamin Mazyck	4	0	100	1,079	St. James
Liberty Hall	Stephen Mazyck	3	0	100	2,744	St. James
NA	Peter May	2	0	2	NA	St. James
Cedar Hill	John Dupont	6	1	47	1,026	St. James
Cow Jig (note 4)	John Sommers	NA	NA	26	760	NA
Total/Mean		53/3	4	912/54	13,949/1,073	

Table 6.6

Note 1: The name Singletary on the census may be Richard Singleton who owned Foxhunt Plantation in the Black Tom/Foster Creek area.

Note 2: Joseph Glover's household contained one female and thirty-two slaves. This estate was near land owned by Richard Gough. Joseph Glover's household was counted after Richard Gough, who owned lands west of the Glover Family Estate on Laurel Swamp. He added 222 acres in 1787 when he bought lands next to John Deas at Thorogood (Thoroughgood).

Note 3: Mazyck (spelled as "Maryck" on the census) owned the bulk of the Howe Hall/ Boochowee Plantation but Smith representatives owned some of the lands.

Note 4: John Sommers mortgaged Cow Jig for £5,300 in 1784.

Back River

At Breaker's (Braker's) Tavern, the Moncks Corner Road branched north from the State Road toward Moncks Corner. The road proceeded past Reidhemer's (sometimes Redheimer's) Tavern and through the headwaters of Back River until it entered the Parish of St. Johns, Berkeley. Map 6.5 shows the Road to Moncks Corner as it crossed the lands that drain into the headwaters of Back River. Another route to Back River was by way of the Back River Upper Road, which intersected the State Road east of the 18-Mile House Tavern near today's intersection of Highways 52 and 176. This road connected the State Road with landings on Back River at Medway Plantation. No section of the Back River Upper Road is accessible to the public today, but a part of it is barely passable for nearly one mile at the western boundary of the Liberty Hall Plantation and a section of it will soon be developed into a useable road to serve the new housing development.

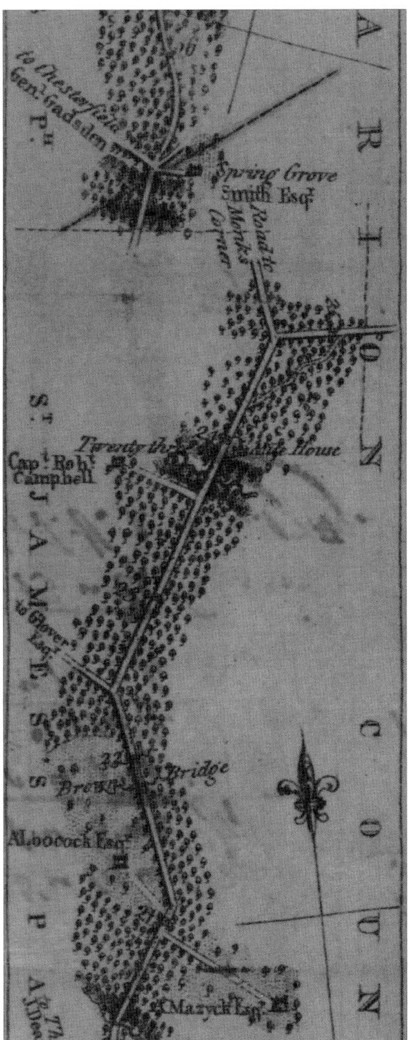

Map 6.5 This map depicts the road from Goose Creek toward Moncks Corner in 1787.

The remaining sections have flooded, grown up or have been built upon. A third road to Back River was the Back River Lower Road, which intersected Red Bank Road at the 17-Mile-House and where the modern Back River Road intersects Red Bank Road today. The Back River Lower Road connected the State Road with a landing on Back River. Here on Back River were Samuel Prioleau's versatile and profitable estate, and the elegant gardens of Zachariah Villeponteaux's Parnassus Plantation. Also here was a bustling waterfront with well-constructed brick lined landings and brick baking and storing facilities. Watercraft of varying sizes from small skiffs to large schooners used these landings, and from here plied the Back and Cooper Rivers to and from Charleston Harbor and beyond. Neither of the Back River roads were constructed or supported with public money but contiguous landowners maintained them. Both roads provided important transit for products and people until they fell out of general use toward the end of the nineteenth century and closed entirely in the early twentieth century.[358]

Plantation Name/Location	Name of Head of Household	Number Whites in Family	Number Freemen in Family	Number Slaves	Number Acres	Parish of Residence
Richmond (note 1)	Alexander Moultrie	8	0	19	951	St. Phillips/St Michaels
NA	Hugh Swinton	5	0	22	666	St. James
NA	Keating Simmons	NA	NA	NA	901	St. Johns Berkeley
NA	Anne Wilson	1	0	17	NA	St. James
22-Mile House/Sociable Hill	Peter Reidhemer	2	0	3	630	St. James
NA	Ann Taylor	3	0	3	NA	St. James
NA	James McBride	3	0	1	NA	St. James
Cedar Grove (note 2)	Benjamin P. Williams	1	0	21	982	St. James
NA	Tilman Plat	4	0	0	NA	St. James
NA	Samuel Adams	3	0	4	620	St. James
Cyprus Grove	Isaac Parker	8	0	8	1,406	St. Phillips/St. Michaels
White Hall/Back River	John Ball	4	1	82	1,676	St. James
Medway	John Bee Holmes	12	0	13	1,301	St.Phillips/Michaels
Prioleau's (note 3)	*Samuel Prioleau	1	1	70	1,651	St. James
Parnassus	Zachariah Villeponteaux (note 4)	4	1	44	1,792	St. James
Total/Mean		46/4	3	266/21	10,959/996	

Table 6.7

Note 1: Alexander Moultrie also owned 661 acres on Foster Creek.

Note 2: B.P. Williams is recorded with an additional 380 acres in 1794.

Note 3: Samuel Prioleau also owned Oak Grove and The Retreat Plantations on the neck. He probably employed some of his eighty slaves at those places. Thus only seventy of his servants are counted at the Back River plantation.

Note 4: Zachariah Villeponteaux appears on the census as Zacho Ollieponteaux.

Table 6.7 lists the heads of households in the Back River Neighborhood. These estates lined the deep waters of Back River and dotted its headwater swamps. They averaged more than 990 acres and an average of twenty-one slaves per household worked the lands. The estates varied from large tracts, such as Medway and Cyprus Grove, to smaller parcels with taverns and inns. Reidhemer's Tavern was situated on a small tract at the 23-Mile House. Peter Reidhemer appeared on the 1790 census with one freedman and one slave and his tavern also appeared on Mills' Atlas, shown as map 6.6, along with the 22-Mile House, and Reardon's taverns nearby. Reardon's tavern was situated on a 539.5-acre tract "on Chapel Swamp.[359] These three inns were within a mile of each other and served this busy section of the Parish for many years. This section is shown on partial plat 6.3 as it was in 1788. The plat shows "Public Road Moncks Corner," a bridge, a chapel, the 23-Mile House tract and some of the access roads to the main houses of nearby plantations. This area began as an early commercial center for the Indian trade, carried people and products to and from a nearby ferry, and eventually became so heavily traveled that a "chapel of ease" was erected for the St. James, Goose Creek Church. Two service roads intersected with the Moncks Corner Road to access the chapel and the "Chapel Road" reached west toward Cyprus Grove Plantation. A path leading east from the chapel skirted Cedar Grove Plantataion to John Ball's estate. John Ball bred highly prized racehorses and trained them at his Back River Plantation. He used a horse-exercising ring, as well as a horse landing for loading the animals onto boats. Many of Ball's

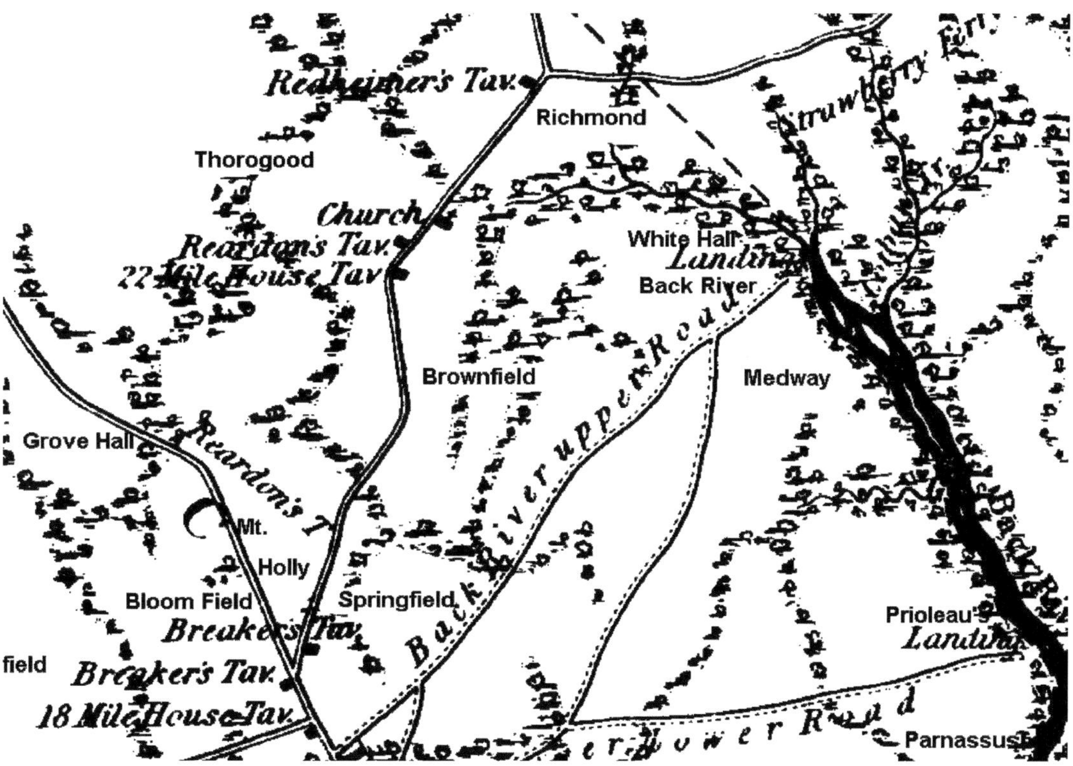

Map 6.6 The Mills' 1825 Atlas has been enhanced for this publication to show the location of selected plantations on Back River and its headwaters.

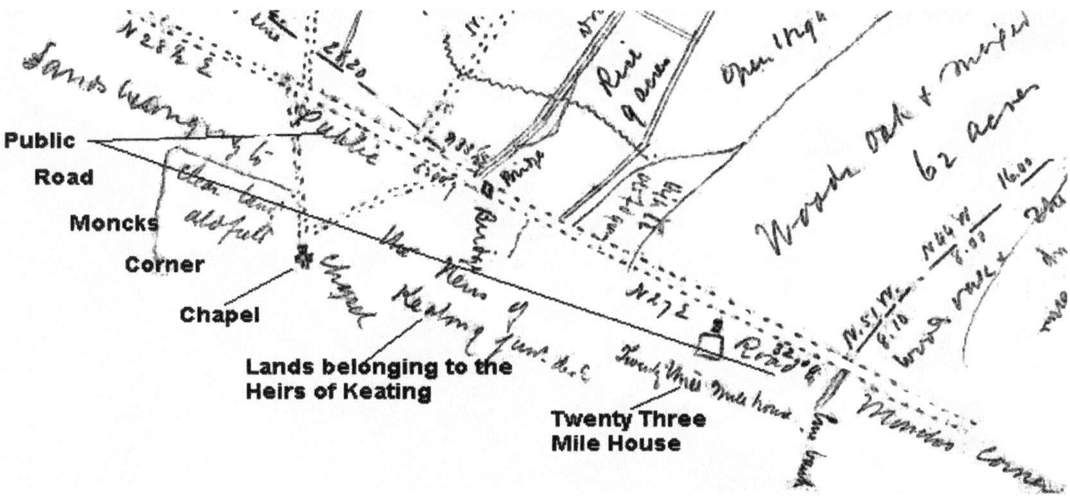

Plat 6.3 This partial plat shows the Moncks Corner Road near the chapel and the 23-Mile House. The manuscript labels were added to this publication for clarity. This partial plat is a tracing of the original. The tracing was made by H.A.M. Smith and is in the possession of the South Carolina Historical Society.

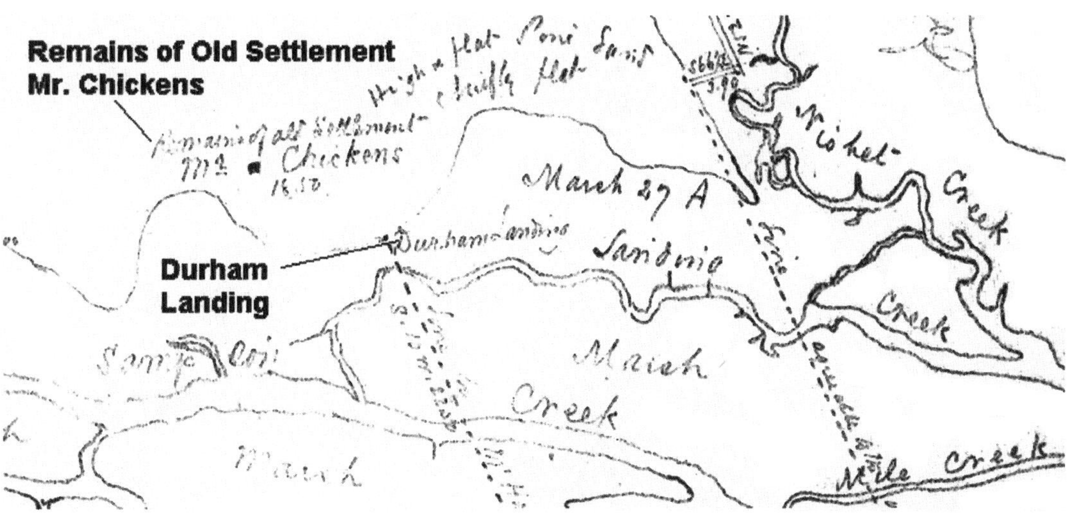

Plat 6.4 This partial plat shows lands in the upper Back River section of the Goose Creek Parish. The plat shows the Chicken Settlement and some of the many nearby waterways. The manuscript labels were added to this publication for clarity. The plat was drawn from a survey made in 1796 of White Hall Plantation. The plat was traced by H.A.M. Smith and is among the collections of the South Carolina Historical Society.

fine thoroughbreds ran at the Strawberry Jockey Club track that operated until 1822 at nearby Childsbury. Also near the chapel was the main avenue to Richmond Plantation that intersected the western side of the Moncks Corner Road. On the chapel side was another tract noted on the plat as "Heirs of Keating." Thomas Keating was an early proprietor of the 23-Mile House Tavern where wealthy members of the Goose Creek Friendly Club met monthly to enjoy food, drinks and share the latest news, but by the time of the census the tavern had passed to new hands.

The road to Strawberry Ferry is not shown on partial plat 6.3, but that road intersected the Moncks Corner Road north of the 23-Mile House, and the surrounding vicinity was called "Strawberry" from an early date because it was on the route to the nearby ferry landing. Less than two miles east of the intersection, the headwaters of Back River were navigable and reached almost to deep Cooper River waters at Childsbury. At this point, the two rivers were separated by little more than half a mile of shallow swamplands. Consequently, the navigable waters of both rivers were almost within sight of each other, but not easily portaged requiring the support of public roads, bridges and a ferry. The ferry was established at Strawberry Landing near the colonial town of Childsbury on the western branch of the Cooper River to facilitate the movement of people and products in these low, soft and wet sections of the St. James, Goose Creek and St. Johns Berkeley Parishes.[360] Plat 6.4 shows some of the land on the St. James, Goose Creek Parish side of the river including the land that once belonged to Captain George Chicken, the Indian trader. Chicken's tract, labeled "Remains of old Settlement Mr. Chicken[']s," was situated near Durham Landing, where the ferry operated. The plat shows many branches and creeks that made land travel difficult and prompted the construction of the public road and ferry. John Ball owned the Chicken Plantation at the time of the census, and his, as well as a few other plantations were situated near the main waters of the Back and Cooper Rivers and were among the most successful in the Parish.

Wassamasaw

At Breaker's Tavern, near the 19-mile stone, the main road through Goose Creek continued west toward Wassamasaw. The road was originally known as the "Wassamasaw Road" but it later became part of the "Mountain to the Sea Highway" built with state funding in 1818 and was renamed "State Road," and later "Old State Road." Today, a section of that important byway is known as "St. James Avenue" and "State Highway 176." The taverns along the highways were used for rest and recreation, and became important livestock trading centers as that industry grew into the most important source of capital in the vicinity of Wassamasaw and the Upper Parish. As the State Road proceeded west, it passed Reardon's 25-Mile House, and Willson's estates and then crossed the Wassamasaw Causeway. This causeway traversed the shallow waters that flowed from Black Tom Bay through Wassamasaw and Cypress Swamps to the upper reaches of the Ashley River. The State Road continued west to Four Hole Swamp, and eventually to Greenville.

Few plantations were given names in Wassamasaw or the Upper Parish, as was the custom in the eastern section where such plantations as Steepbrook and Windsor Hill were named. Instead place names of various locales in the central and upper parts of the Parish were usually referenced in official records. Some lands were merely associated with nearby water sources such as Black Tom Bay, Cypress Swamp and Wassamasaw in the central section and Dean's Swamp, Caton's Bay, Four Hole Swamp, Tupelo Bay,

Pigeon Bay or Mosquito Bay in the upper part. Other places, such as Sandridge and Sandy Run were named because of the soil type. Places associated with sandy soil were considered to be healthy because the lands drained well and were less likely to support swarms of disease carrying mosquitoes.

Wassamasaw was a settlement in St. James, Goose Creek Parish since the earliest years and was well inhabited by the time of the first census. Reverend Timothy Millechamp of St. James Church reported as early as 1736, that he administered the sacraments at the Wassamasaw Chapel because the village was too distant for the people to attend the Goose Creek Church and twenty-three years later, Reverend James Harrison reported that eight families were settled near that chapel at Wassamasaw. By the time of the first census, two of the leading families at Wassamasaw were the Blackmans and Fallings. Sarah and Thomas Blackman resided at Wassamasaw near the 29-mile marker and were quite wealthy with twenty-one slaves. William Falling (Faulling) also resided at Wassamasaw at a place called Sandy Run and in 1796, he was the owner of the 28-Mile House Tavern on the State Road. He also received three small state land grants amounting to 243 acres and worked as a planter, as well as a tavern keeper.[361] In additionm to Falling, there were many more families working on land granted to them by the State of South Carolina.

The young state of South Carolina granted land as early as 1784 and evidence suggests that many Wassamasaw landowners were overlooked by the first census count. Several reasons may explain why some were omitted. Families may have never taken-up their new land, or may have vacated their Wassamasaw properties prior to the arrival of the census taker, but it is also likely that some were simply overlooked by the census taker in the thinly populated backcountry. For example, John Dawson purchased Izard's Cowpen Plantation, a 3,870-acre estate in 1788. There is no explanation why his name did not appear on the 1790 census two years after he purchased the land. It is possible however, that he did not reside on the land but left the on-sight management to an overseer. Other landowners not counted on the census are listed in table 6.8.

Table 6.8

Name of Land Owner	Year	Number Acres	Place
Thomas Harper	1775	464	Wassamasaw
Samuel Wescott	1785	461/500	Wassamasaw
John Switzer	1785	640	Wassamasaw
William Lee	1785	245	Wassamasaw
Samuel Timmons	1785	97	Wassamasaw
Arnold Harvey	1785	247	Wassamasaw
John Diamond	1785	570	West Side of Wassamasaw
Keating Simmons	1785	440	Wassamasaw
John Thompson	1786	640	Wassamasaw
Robert Hurst	1786/88	236.5/47/87.5	Wassamasaw
James Nicholson	1786	640	Wassamasaw
Blake Leay White	1786	75/900	Cypress Swamp
Shadrack Easterling	1786	100	Wassamasaw
John Hutchinson	1786	212/322	East Side of Wassamasaw
James Nicholson	1786	500	Wassamasaw
Sarah Taylor	1786	100	East Side of Wassamasaw
Andrew Broughton	1786	1000	West Side of Wassamasaw
Thomas Page	1786	846	Cypress Bottom Bay
Benjamin Singleton	1786	1,611	Wassamasaw
Patrick Duncan	1786	250	Wassamasaw
Benjamin Walker	1787	16,000	Wassamasaw/Four Hole
James Heyward	1789	214	Wassamasaw

The order of the census taker's visitation indicates the location of the family, relative to neighbors, but more evidence is needed to identify a family with a specific neighborhood. Land records can clearly identify households with specific locations and other records can reasonably associate names with varying degrees of reliability. For example, court records often give information about disputes between neighbors, which can associate a family with a neighborhood. Furthermore, witnesses to renunciations of dowers or a last will and testament can suggest who one's neighbors might have been. This type of evidence is required in conjunction with the order of visitation to justify assigning the name to the Wassamasaw list. Consequently, some names that the census taker recorded in succession with known Wassamasaw residents were not assigned to the Wassamasaw list for the purpose of this study. As a result, table 6.9 is an incomplete list of the names of heads of households residing within the Wassamasaw section of the parish in 1790, but map 6.7 further describes the Wassamasaw section of the parish and notes a few of the prominent families.

Large families inhabited Wassamasaw and although the average number of slaves was only thirteen per family, all but five families owned slaves indicating that the farms were successful and the landowners relatively wealthy. Two men, Dan and Sol Legare were very wealthy. They were descendants of an old French Huguenot family of which patriarch Sol Legare, Sr. supplemented income from his land holdings by working as a gold and silversmith in the Charleston Neck. At the time of the census, his sons, Dan and Sol owned property in Wassamasaw, tracts on the Chareston Neck and three lots in downtown on Gadsden and Pinckney Streets.[362]

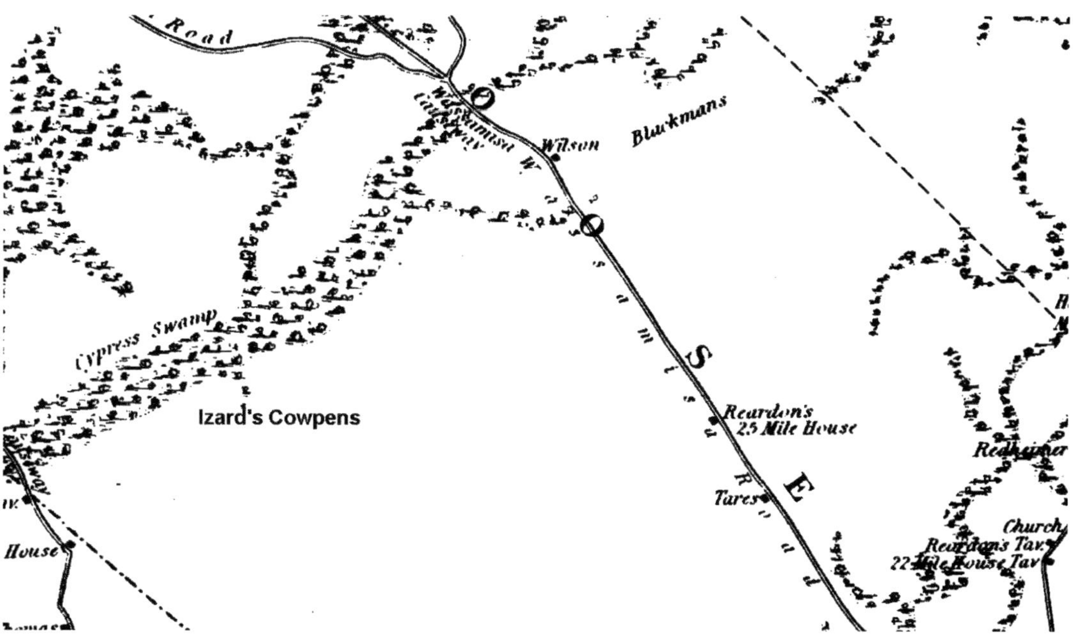

Map 6.7 This map shows a section of the Mills' 1825 Atlas of the central part of The St. James, Goose Creek Parish. The State Road then referred to as the "Wassamasaw Road," continued northwest from Goose Creek. The atlas noted some prominent family names. The location of "Izard's Cowpen" was added for this publication.

Plantation Name/Location	Name of Head of Household	Number Whites in Family	Number Freemen in Family	Number Slaves	Number Acres	Parish of Residence
Wassamasaw	John Plat	8	0	1	300	St. James
Wassamasaw/Sandy Run	William Falling	5	0	1	243	St. James
Wassamasaw	James Stevenson	3	0	23	905	St. James
Wassamasaw (Captain 32)	William Dangerfield	5	0	1	232	St. James
NA	John Burbage	5	0	0	NA	St. James
Wassamasaw (26)	Thomas Burbage (Burbridge)	4	0	0	100	St. James
Wassamasaw (note 1)	Simeon Theus	7	0	21	1,233	St. James
NA	William Cannon	5	0	16	NA	St. James
NA	Jacob Ringer	8	0	8	NA	St. James
NA	Robert Jennings	3	0	0	NA	St. James
Wassamasaw	Sol Legare (Souleggre)	4	0	30	360/540	St. James
Wassamasaw	Daniel Legare Esta.	5	0	15	1250	St. James
Wassamasaw	Sarah Blackman	2	0	18	NA	St. James
Wassamasaw (29)	Thom. Blackman	5	0	9	150/200	St. James
West Wassamasaw	Mary Grumes (Grooms)	5	0	0	100	St. James
Wassamasaw	Hugh Winter	7	0	13	392	St. James
Wassamasaw (40)	James Cree (note 2)	5	0	1	200	St. James
Cypress Swamp	Peggy Ayers (note 3)	3	0	1	100	St. James
Wassamasaw	Robert Thornley	7	1	7	840	St. James
Wassamasaw	John Dehay	9	0	6	640	St. James
Wassamasaw	George Flagg	NA	NA	NA	1,642	St. James
Wassamasaw	John Ounielt (Cunsall)	3	0	16	1,233 (note 1)	St. James
(note 5)	Robert Simmon	1	0	10	523	St. James
Wassamasaw/Black Tom Bay	Isaac Lyons (Lynes) (note 6)	10	0	1	234 (note 6)	St. James
Wassamasaw	John Gibson	4	0	0	440	St. James
Black Tom Bay (note 7)	Richard Gough	3	0	123	500	St. James
Izard's Cowpen/Cypress Swamp	John Dawson (note 4)				(note 4)	
Wassamasaw	Nathan McCants	8	0	12	476	St. James
Total/Mean		134/5	1	333/13	12,833/583	

Table 6.9

Note 1: Simeon Theus shared ownership with George Flagg, Vincent Guerin, John Diamond and John Ounielt. He also owned 333 acres on the headwaters of Foster Creek contiguous to Grove Hall. He is counted in the Foster Creek neighborhood where he had full ownership of the land and probably resided.

Note 2: James Cree owned 200 acres in 1790, 400 acres in 1797, 993 acres in 1809 and an 1825 tax return shows 2,295 acres.

Note 3: Thomas Ayers owned 100 acres at Cypress Swamp in 1785.

Note 4: John Dawson purchased 3,870 acres in 1788. A 1791 plan on record shows that John Dawson owned 810 acres at "Izard's Neck." Because the amount of acreage is unclear, the numbers were not used to tabulate the totals or the means.

Note 5: Robert Simmons was counted after John Ounielt in the order of visitation.

Note 6: Isaac Lyons (Lynes) owned 183 acres in 1785, 234 acres in 1794, 400 acres on Lynes Creek and 329 acres on Black Tom Bay in 1816. Moses Lynes owned 174 acres in 1785 but does not appear on the census in 1790. Lynes family members are buried in the Bethlehem Baptist Church cemetery at Strawberry.

Note 7: Richard Gough owned more than 3,000 acres in Berkeley County.

The Wassamasaw neighborhood featured a small community core with a chapel, school, and a popular livestock watering hole situated a short distance from the busy State Road. Travelers stopped here for many years and by 1790, it had evolved into an important livestock-trading corral. This trading center was convenient to Richard Gough, one of the more prosperous cattlemen, who owned land south and east of the Wassamasaw center.

Partial plat 6.5 shows five hundred acres of property owned by cattleman, Richard Gough. The full plat shows that the land was situated at the southernmost reaches of Black Tom Bay, near the Wassamasaw waterway and that it was contiguous to property owned by James Glover on the south. Glover's expansive Grove Hall tract reached to the western boundary of Thorogood Plantation. Gough's five-hundred-acre tract was a typical grant size in this part of the parish, and he used the available fresh water reserves to produce corn, rice and livestock. Today, this land is traversed by Highway 17-Alternate and reaches north of Carnes Crossroads.

Upper Parish

Few of the names that appeared on the 1790 census were matched to land records in the Upper Parish Neighborhood. Consequently little is known about the distribution of land and the status of

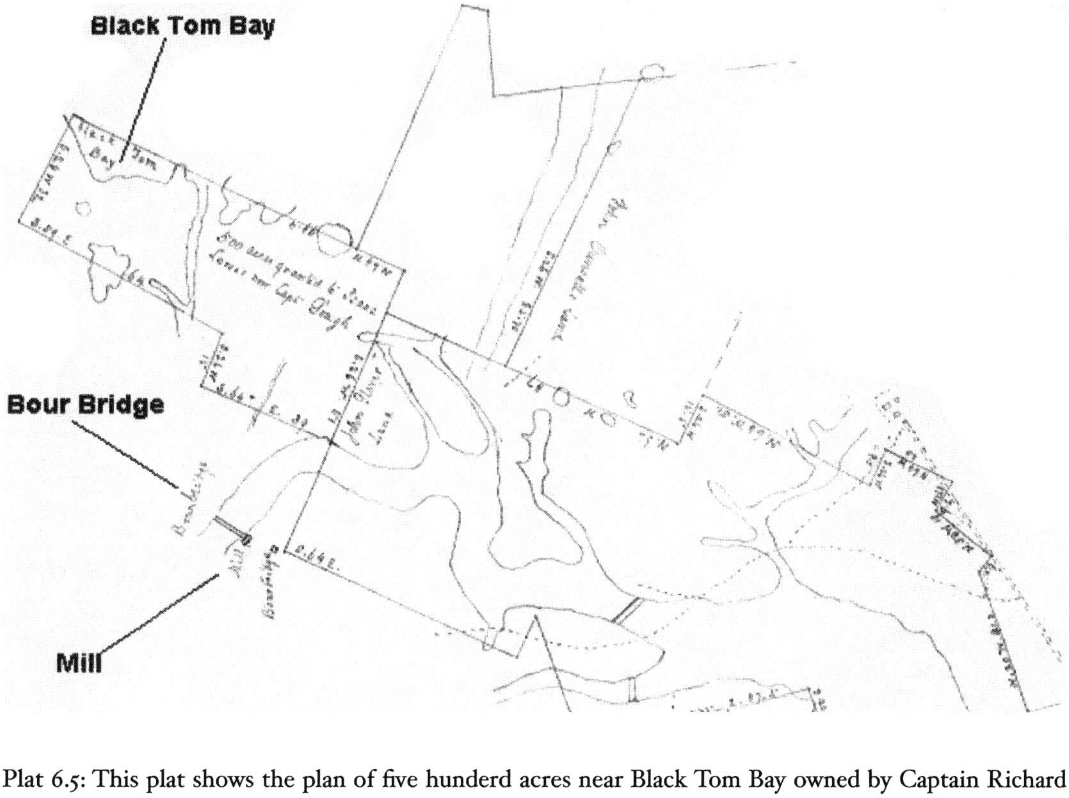

Plat 6.5: This plat shows the plan of five hunderd acres near Black Tom Bay owned by Captain Richard Gough. The plat notes a "mill" and "bour bridge" in the lower left quadrant. The plat is in the possession of the South Carolina Department of Archives and History, L10005 Reel 8 Plat 4251.

the families at that time. Some of the tracts were settled in the early 1700s, and except for a few large parcels, the majority of the grants were less than five hundred acres. Isaac Porcher, John McGee, Stephen Monk, John Gibbes, Tobias Fitch, and Abraham Brunson acquired land in the Upper Parish between 1707 and 1732. John Lloyd received a large grant of two thousand acres in 1732.[363] Daniel Dean received land in 1735, as well as Gideon and Abraham Dupont, Cornelius Duprie, William Smith, and Hugh Grange. Peter Manigault and others received land in the 1730s. Although the census report indicates that the Upper Parish was sparsely occupied, it is possible that the census taker merely failed to identify most of the families residing on the small, isolated farms. Table 6.10 shows twenty-five landowners in the Upper Parish near the time of the first census but none of these landowners appeared on the 1790 census report.

Table 6.10

Name	Number of Acres/Location	Year of Land Record
Joseph Purcell	400 Sandy Run at Four Hole Swamp	1775
Meraday Elsey	100/200 Four Hole /Dean Swamp	1775
William Blake	200 Four Hole Swamp	1775
John Howard	450 /500 Four Hole Swamp	1775
Joseph Dunklin	457 Four Hole Swamp	1775
Ezekial Backler (Bachelor?)	450 Four Hole Swamp	1775
James McIntosh	50 Four Hole Swamp	1775
Melchior Garner	600 Four Hole Swamp	1775
Robert Mills	500 Four Hole Swamp	1775
Jacob Ott	50 Four Hole Swamp	1775
Thomas Young	688 Four Hole Swamp	1775
William Nesbitt	400 Four Hole Swamp	1775
George Thompson	1,000 Four Hole Swamp	1775
Mary McQuillon	200 Four Hole Swamp	1775
William Johnson	500 Four Hole Swamp	1775
Martha McQuillon	100 Four Hole Swamp	1775
Felix Brunner	200 Four Hole Swamp	1775
Thomas Young	250 Four Hole Swamp	1775
Jacob Stroman	250 Four Hole Swamp	1775
Patrick Hinds	1,150 Four Hole Swamp	1775
John Brotherer	100 North Side Four Hole Swamp	1778
James Dounan	100 Four Hole Swamp	1785
Hans Carr	385 Four Hole Swamp	1787
James Askew/Thomas Harris/James Carpenter	1,000 Four Hole Swamp	1788
John Lochmann	200 Four Hole Swamp	1788

Some of the early landowners were associated with old colonial families, but the great majority of the planters and farmers in the upper section were newcomers, without the advantage of large land grants and apparently without the desire to name their land or mark their place in the South Carolina landscape. Thus, map 6.8 depicts the upper section of the parish without named plantations but with a few of the prominent landmarks. Most planters in this part of the Parish kept few or no slaves and not many claimed tracts larger than two or three hundred acres. Although the majority of the people in the upper part of the parish owned their lands, they were relative newcomers and left fewer land records than those in the eastern parish. These were predominately yeoman farmers who raised corn, upland rice, pigs and cattle. Some rice was grown using water reserves, but such opportunities were not available to all and the sale of cattle provided the common source of cash. Away from the swampy areas, the farmers relied entirely upon the weather to irrigate the fields. Neither windmills

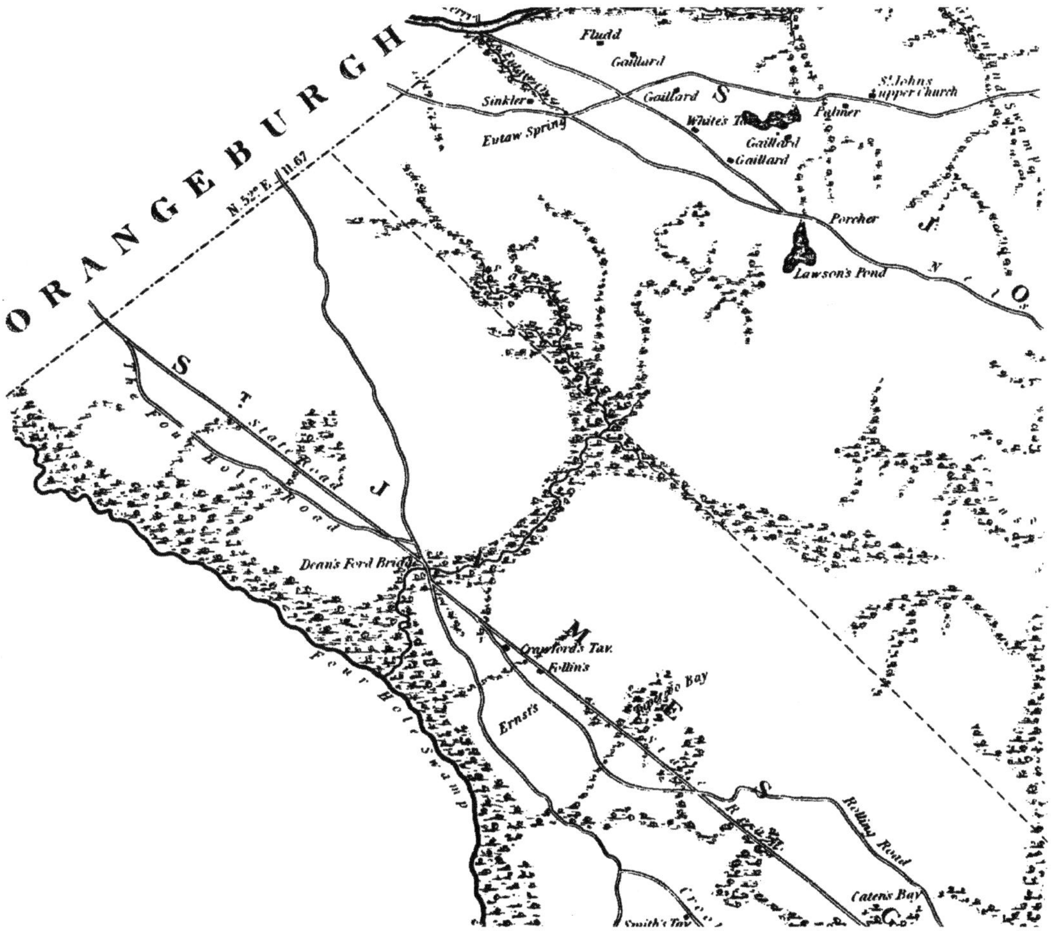

Map 6.8 This map shows a section of the Mills' 1825 Atlas of the upper part of The St. James, Goose Creek Parish. The State Road (Highway 176) proceeds northwest from Goose Creek. The atlas noted the taverns on the road as well as Dean's Ford Bridge. The map has been enhanced for this publication.

nor other mechanical pump devices were used for irrigation while the farmer relied entirely upon mule and manpower. The farmer built his notched log cabin walls similar to the *Hilton House* built in 1823 in Sandridge and shown in photograph 6.2. He used clay to caulk the log walls and fashioned a clay and wattle chimney and hearth to use for cooking and warmth. Cedar shingles were commonly used for roof material and kept the occupants reasonably dry.

Table 6.11 lists only seven names representing households in the Upper Parish that appeared on the 1790 census, although land records indicate that many more families resided in the Upper Parish at that time. The number of landowners increased soon after the first census, when the steady stream of new families continued to move into the upper section to build farms on small land grants. The state of South Carolina continued to issue grants in the Upper Parish well into the nineteenth century with some land in that neighborhood remaining unclaimed as late as the 1880s.

Photograph 6.2 This photograph shows the Hilton House in Sandridge. Nathaniel Hilton built the house circa 1823. The log house now features a metal roof but probably used cedar shingles when it was first erected. His estate consisted of 297 acres in 1790. The photograph was taken March 7, 2005, and is in the private collection of the author.

Plantation Name	Name of Head of Household	Number Whites in Family	Number Freemen in Family	Number Slaves	Number Acres	Parish of Residence
NA	Peter Dubois	3	0	0	NA	St. James
Four Hole Swamp	Garrett (note 1) Fitzpatrick	3	0	1	200	St. James
NA	Robert Martin	5	0	2	NA	St. James
Four Hole Swamp	James (?) Lindsay	8	0	14	NA	St. James
Caton's Bay	Zach. Dehay	3	0	1	345	St. James
Four Hole Swamp	Alex Cholette	4	0	53	2,350 (note 2)	St. James
Four Hole Swamp	Arch McDowell	2	0	10	NA	St. James
Total/Mean		28/4	0	81/14	2,895/965	

Table 6.11

Note 1: Garret Fitzpatrick owned 200 acres at Four Hole Swamp in 1774. No first name appears on the census.

Note 2: Samuel Cholette is on record owning four tracts totaling 2,350 acres in Berkeley and Craven Counties in 1775. This is probably the same family as Alex Cholette appearing on the census. For this purpose one half of the acreage is included in the tabulations for this table.

Conclusion

Because historical research is an imperfect science, additional investigation into the names of the heads of households in the 1790 census is needed to fill omissions of those names not assigned to a neighborhood. Assumptions that required interpretations of misspelled names on the census report, such as Mazrck for Mazyck or Oilleponteaux for Villeponteaux were made with confidence, but in the absence of supporting documentation, assigning a name to a neighborhood based merely on the order of visitation of the census taker was inconclusive. Consequently, some names are not assigned to any of the eight neighborhoods and are listed on table 6.12.

Table 6.12

Name of Head of Household	Number Whites in Family	Number Freemen in Family	Number Slaves
Adam Getsinger	4	0	0
Bernard Leitz	6	0	4
Thomas Eucleigh	0	0	0
Tonie Miland	5	0	0
Mr. Vere	10	0	3
Jackson	3	0	2
Peter Dubois	3	0	0
John Bachelor	2	0	0
Thomas Stevenson	1	0	2
Herely Huxford	8	0	0
James Douglas	0	0	0
Doram	5	0	0
Mrs. Ballard	6	0	0
John Blewer	5	0	0
Chris Brown	3	0	4
Thomas Rast	6	0	2
William Snyder	4	0	0
Binah (free woman)	0	1	2

Two of the unassigned names, Adam Getsinger and Bernard Leitz, probably owned parish property. There is a record of both wives of these men renouncing their dower rights.[364] Dower rights were usually forfeited when a married couple obtained land but no land records were found for these two men. Two other names on the unassigned list, Thomas Eucleigh and James Douglas, were recorded with no family members. The head of the household was included in all of the family counts, except in these two cases and no explanation was given for the omission. The greatest number of the remaining heads of households on the unidentified list resided with medium to large families and with no slaves. These families may have rented farms, managed someone else's farm, or worked at inns or landings. Interestingly, the *Directory of the White Inhabitants of the Charleston District in 1808* recorded the names of nineteen overseers in the Goose Creek Parish eighteen years after the census.[365] It is likely that some of the names not associated with land in 1790 were overseers; but because they owned no land and were not associated with land records, it is not possible to confidently assign them to a neighborhood. Binah (free woman) was the last name entered on the census. The addition of her name on the census roll may have been an afterthought with no relevancy to the order of visitation. Also, no records connect her to a neighborhood or illuminate her status. Thus, her name and position remain a mystery.

By 1790, Goose Creek was a well-established community with eight distinct neighborhoods. The findings from each neighborhood, condensed in table 6.13, show that the range of land acreage was as few as 419 mean acres in the Neck Neighborhood to a high of 1,218 acres on Back River. The range of the mean number of slaves was much greater. A Foster Creek Plantation was likely to work eight to eleven times more slaves than a Neck or Upper Parish estate. There were large families north of Goose Creek and in the western section of the parish where new farms abounded. These large families contrasted with the notably smaller ones on the Neck. The "old money" neighborhood on the Neck appeared to be an uncommon place for large, growing families near the end of the eighteenth century. No other statistical findings appear to be remarkable.

Table 6.13

Neighborhood	Number of Whites	Mean Number of Whites Per Family	Number of Free Non-Whites	Number Slaves	Mean Number of Acres	Mean Number of Slaves
The Neck	23	2	3	96	419	10
South Side of Goose Creek	69	3	5	479	786	23
North Side of Goose Creek	40	4	3	313	1,008	28
Cooper River	27	3	0	121	548	15
Foster Creek	53	3	4	912	1,073	54
Back River	46	4	3	266	1,218	22
Wassamasaw	134	5	1	333	583	13
Upper Parish	28	4	0	81	965	14

This chapter provides a snapshot of the people and lands of Goose Creek during an early year of the republic. Each of the neighborhoods supported plantations or smaller tracts at varying levels of development, and all of these lands were home or business sites where people lived increasingly diversified lifestyles. The estates ranged from small, specialized tracts, such as landings, taverns and little isolated farms at Four Hole Swamp, to vast agricultural spreads and brick factories on Foster Creek and Back River. By 1790, some lands had developed to opulence, others to marginal efficiency and many were beginning to decline. Thus the lands in Goose Creek in 1790 differed widely along with the lifestyles of the people.

In the year of the first census, it was obvious that the parish was changing. The fortunes of the old landed aristocracy were shifting and the aging plantations in the eastern parish neighborhoods were showing signs of failure. Overuse sapped the nutrients from the land causing soil exhaustion, and persistent illness weakened the people. Consequently, during the decades leading to the first census, the white population in the eastern neighborhoods declined significantly, as new families sought fertile fields farther west and the older families habitually departed from their estates during much of the year.

The decrease in population continued partly as a consequence of the predictable summer fevers that caused more and more planters to spend summers in Charleston, and return to their plantations after the first frost. Hired managers and renters increasingly occupied more of the plantation lands during this period, while the slaves remained in Goose Creek all year around with their overseers. The practice of landlord absenteeism and the neglect that often accompanied it increased until the Civil War.

The Neighborhoods, 1790

By 1790, some of the grand estates such as Crowfield and Bloomfield were no longer working plantations, and the Middleton's Oaks was soon sold out of that well-known family as fewer dollars were invested in Goose Creek properties. Diversification of some plantations, such as William Johnson's on Goose Creek and John B. Holmes's on Back River, kept some lands marginally profitable, but the great fortunes were never made again. In some cases, reserves of family resources kept facades of wealth at places such as Manigault's Steepbrook and the Elms owned by Ralph Izard. In addition, the use of some lands as country retreats kept the old Charleston names connected to neighborhoods in the eastern parish for more decades, but successful entrepreneurs found better places than Goose Creek to invest their fortunes.

This chapter uses census information and supporting records to describe eight Goose Creek neighborhoods when the parish was a small corner of the new and upcoming republic. By 1790, it was obvious that the eastern parish population (white and black) was leaving for opportunities elsewhere. Near the time of the first census, many young families with state land grants moved west with some going to the untouched tracts in the upper part of the Parish. At the same time, cohorts of slaves were marched much farther west to the fresh cotton fields in Georgia, Alabama, Mississippi and Louisiana. Thus, in the last decade of the eighteenth century, Goose Creekers in each of eight neighborhoods witnessed the continuation of westward movement that began when the first shipload of settlers arrived at Charles Towne Landing 120 years earlier. Within the scope of the parish history, the movement involved a few dozen families who traveled a few dozen miles from Charleston along the State or Gailliard Road toward the Upper Parish. In the broader perspective, this movement was an insignificant aside to a grand migration sweeping the nation. Along the entire Atlantic seaboard thousands of strong and hopeful families, with nothing more than what they could carry in their wagons, were moving farther toward the distant setting sun. This westward movement would continue until the manifest destiny spirit of the nation carried some families all the way to the Pacific Coast. In perspective, the small movement of people in the St. James, Goose Creek Parish, around the year 1790, was hardly consequential in the state or nation. Nevertheless, the westward movement in the Goose Creek Parish was part of a national demographic tectonic shift that continued for the next 100 years and shaped the character of the American people to this day.

CHAPTER VII
THE ESTATES
1670–2003

THE FUNDAMENTAL CONSTITUTION WRITTEN BY John Locke was progressive in many ways and was noted for its liberal expression with regard to society and government, but the design was simple in that it provided for an aristocratic society based on land ownership. The belief that land ownership was the best foundation for efficient order was the genesis of South Carolina culture from which enduring social, economic and political systems evolved. The 330-year history of land ownership in Goose Creek partially explains these systems and partly interprets the values and lifestyles of this South Carolina community.

Judge Henry A.M. Smith, a past president of the South Carolina Historical Society in Charleston, South Carolina was keenly interested in Goose Creek lands and people. He and his ancestors owned property in Goose Creek from the earliest settlements until well into the twentieth century. He wrote articles for the *South Carolina Historical and Genealogical Magazine* describing Lowcountry lands, and he collected vast amounts of information on the Goose Creek estates. After his death, some of his work was published in the *South Carolina Historical and Genealogical Magazine*, but much of his unfinished work was too rudimentary to print. His published works, plus his unprinted notes and papers are used in this chapter to provide a model upon which to track the evolution of the Goose Creek properties. Henry Smith's work, as well as notes and records of many other Goose Creek landowners provide abundant information toward the understanding of the transcient ownerships of the properties. Published abstracts of deeds, warrants and memorials, as well as wills provide additional documentation and descriptions. Professional title searches of properties and the interpretive findings of archaeological studies from more than sixty examined sites fill in many details. These sources and many others are used in this chapter to trace the history of prominent land holdings in Goose Creek.

The tracings begin with the lands at the Neck, the neighborhood nearest Charleston. Next, the estates on the south side of Goose Creek are examined followed by an examination of those on the north side of Goose Creek and along Cooper River, Foster Creek and Back River. Finally, the significant landowners at Wassamasaw and in the Upper Parish are reviewed.

The Lands at the Neck

Marsh Lands/Marshlands

In 1682–83 a warrant was issued for a tract of land for Paul Grimball on the west side of the Cooper River. The grant that followed the warrant allocated only thirty acres, but that 30-acre parcel was the nucleus of an estate that increased in small increments over the next hundred years until it encompassed 349 acres of prime real estate.[366] Soon after the original grant, some of the neighboring lands were awarded to Christopher Linckney. Linckney's land was located northeast of Paul Grimball's tract and on "a great marsh in Cooper River and southeast and northwest on two marshes."[367] Linckney married Paul Grimball's daughter and probably because of this marriage, Grimball acquired Linckley's land and significantly expanded his holdings. Grimball eventually sold his larger estate to Joseph Wragg in 1728. Joseph Wragg added four additional tracts contiguous to his neck lands so that by the time of his death in 1796, John Wragg, son of Joseph, owned 349 acres of high ground with a large amount of marsh. The high ground and marsh together amounted to more than 800 acres. An 1806 plat shows that John Wragg owned 822 acres of marsh on Charleston Neck next to the Cooper River[368] and Map 7.1 shows the relationship of Marsh Lands to other properties.

John Ball, a rich Back River planter, acquired the lands and immediately began to build an impressive main house, shown in photograph 7.1, which he enriched with lavish gouge work. At Ball's death, his executors sold the tract to Nathaniel Heyward.[369] According to John B. Irving, author of *A Day on Cooper River*, Heyward was the wealthiest rice planter in the Carolinas. Dr. Irving

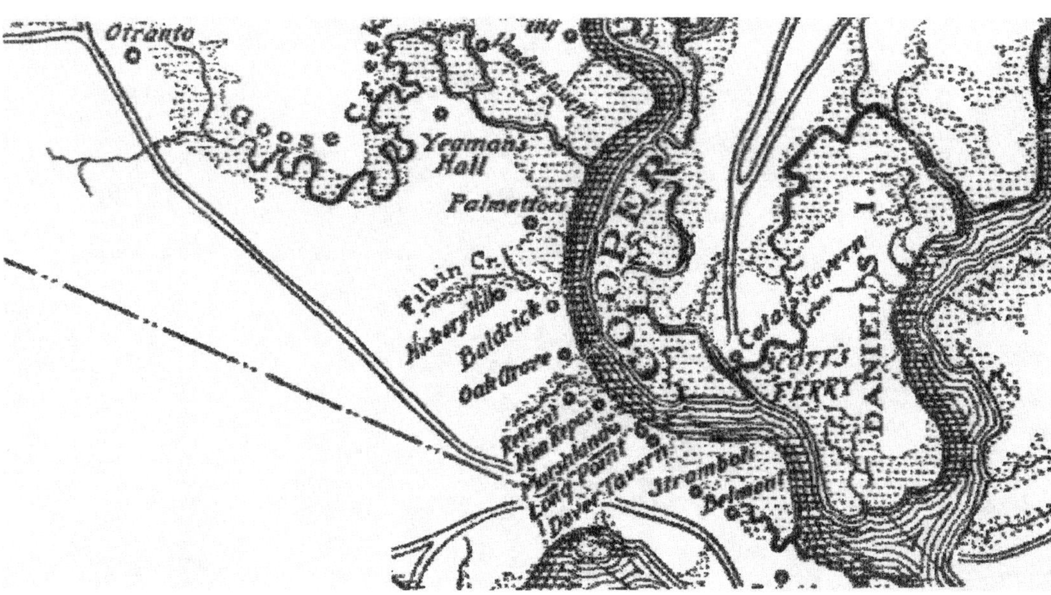

Map 7.1 This is a segment of a *Map Showing the Plantations along the Cooper River as they were in the year 1842*. This segment of the map is borrowed from *A Day on Cooper River* by J.B. Irving, enlarged and edited by Louisa Cheves Stoney. *Courtesy of the R.L. Bryan Company*.

Photograph 7.1
This photograph shows the main house at the Marsh Land Plantation. John Ball, a wealthy rice planter, built it in 1810. The photograph was taken from page 17 of *Charleston's Navy Yard*, by Jim McNeil, published by The R.L. Bryan Company, 1985. The source of the photograph is not noted in the publication.

described the plantation noting, "it contains a large quantity of very valuable rice land and annually sends good crops to market." At his death, Heyward devised this rich rice plantation to his daughter, Elizabeth Manigault, who had married Charles Manigault. This rice land was known as Manigault's Farm or Marsh Land. In 1880, Elizabeth and Charles Manigault's son sold the tract to Mrs. Cecilia Lawton. The entire tract eventually became part of the United States Government Navy Yard and Reservation in the City of North Charleston. The Marsh Lands house was included in the Navy Yard until 1961 when the College of Charleston moved the structure to its property at Fort Johnson where it was restored. The structure is noted for its well-crafted woodwork on the interior. Photographs were taken of the interior in 1925 to be used in remodeling the White House, in Washington, D.C.

Mons Repose/The Retreat

On the northern border of the Marsh Lands Plantation was "The Retreat." A initial warrant for this land was awarded to Thomas Hurt in 1672. Two awards of 370 and 128 acres were subsequently granted in accordance with the procedures of awarding acreage based on the number of family members and servants. The combined grant amounted to 498 acres.[370] Thomas Hurt held the property briefly before selling a section of it to Thomas Stanyarne and a larger parcel to Edmund Gibbon. Edmund Gibbon died ten years later, leaving his Carolina lands to his brother, Francis Gibbon. In 1693, the Gibbon land was conveyed to William Hawett. This parcel consisted of 370 acres.[371] By 1721, Arthur Foster and his wife, Mary owned the tract described as "bounding east on a river formerly called Itawan River now Cooper River..." The land passed to Charles Burnham,

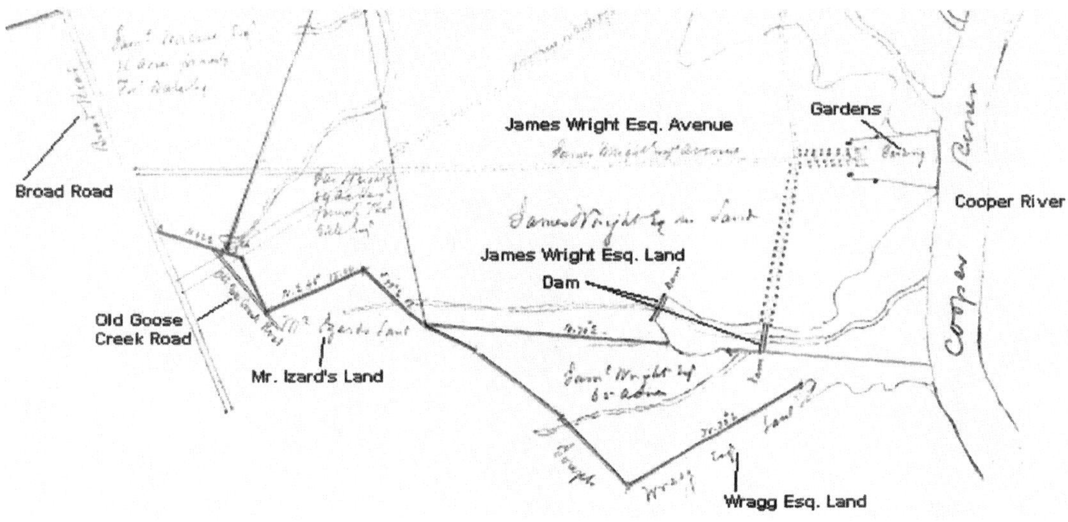

Plat 7.1 This plat shows the Retreat Plantation when James Wright owned it in 1758. The 508 acres tract reached from the Cooper River to the Broad Path. This plat is a tracing done of the original by H.A.M. Smith but the manuscript labels were added for this publication. The tracing is among the collections of the South Carolina Historical Society.

and then to James Wright. Wright later became the governor of the province of Georgia under the royal government. Wright increased this holding to 508 acres when he recombined the original two parcels and added ten acres of marshlands in the new survey.

A plat of neighboring Oak Grove Plantation owned by James Mitchie, and shown in part in plat 7.1, showed Wright's tract with its relationship to the river and road. Wright's property was bordered by the Broad Path on the west and by the Cooper River on the east. Mitchie's estate was situated to the north and Wraggs's property was on the south. One avenue approached the plantation's main house from the Broad Path. Avenues proceeded north and south from the main house. A garden between the main house and the river is indicated on the plat at the terminus of the central avenue.

James Wright conveyed the estate to Samuel Brailsford and seven years later, Brailsford sold it to Henry Middleton. Middleton held the land for two years, added a few acres of marsh and sold it in 1765 to Edgerton Leigh.[372] Edgerton Leigh was the son of Peter Leigh, the chief justice of the province. Edgerton served in prominent offices and once served as baronet. In his book *Day on Cooper River,* Dr. Irving notes that the property belonged to Sir Edgerton Leigh.[373]

Leigh sold the property to Thomas Laughton Smith, who in 1778 sold it to Samuel Prioleau. A 1784 plat drawn by Joseph Purcell shows a well-developed estate.[374] The plantation featured neatly arranged gardens and ponds and a brick main house that overlooked the river. Samuel Prioleau owned both the Retreat and Oak Grove, and is credited with developing both to a large extent. Edward Hare owned the site for a short time before he sold it to James Strachan and James McKenzie in 1796. At that sale the plantation was called "The Retreat," and contained 389 acres. By 1798, James Lee owned the land and soon divided and sold sections of it. Theodore Gaillard bought a southern piece and called it "Mons Repos." Thomas Hunt bought a parcel and Wilson Glover purchased the remainder.

Charles Wilson Glover (1756–1819) was the son of Joseph Glover and Anne Wilson. The 1790 census recorded that he owned 44 slaves in Goose Creek. He owned and resided at Grove Hall on the upper waters of Back River, but by 1803 he purchased "Happy Retreat," a 263-acre estate on the Neck. Charles Glover was a militia major during the revolution and was part of the skirmish that resulted in the capture of Isaac Haynes. The British hanged Isaac Haynes and his name became a rally cry for the patriots. Glover also provided rice provisions to the militia, the continental army, and the Jacksonboro Assembly. After the war, he was elected to represent Goose Creek in the Eighteenth and Nineteenth Assembly and finished the Nineteenth Assembly (1811–1812) as senator from Goose Creek. He married Anne Coachman and together they reared four children.[375]

In 1851, Andrew Turnbull purchased the "Retreat" as his residence. He built a beautiful home and resided there for several decades. The city of Charleston bought the land in 1895 and developed Chicora Park. This park was especially popular among young couples who rode the streetcar there for afternoon picnics and evening dances. Before the completion of Chicora Park, the city of Charleston sold it along with neighboring plantation lands to the United States Government for the development of a navy yard that was greatly needed for employment opportunities. That land is described on plat 7.2.

Oak Grove

Oak Grove was a large tract contiguous to Noisette's Creek. The earliest conveyance was a 960-acre grant in 1680 to Robert Drye. His son, William inherited the land and added to it through his own small

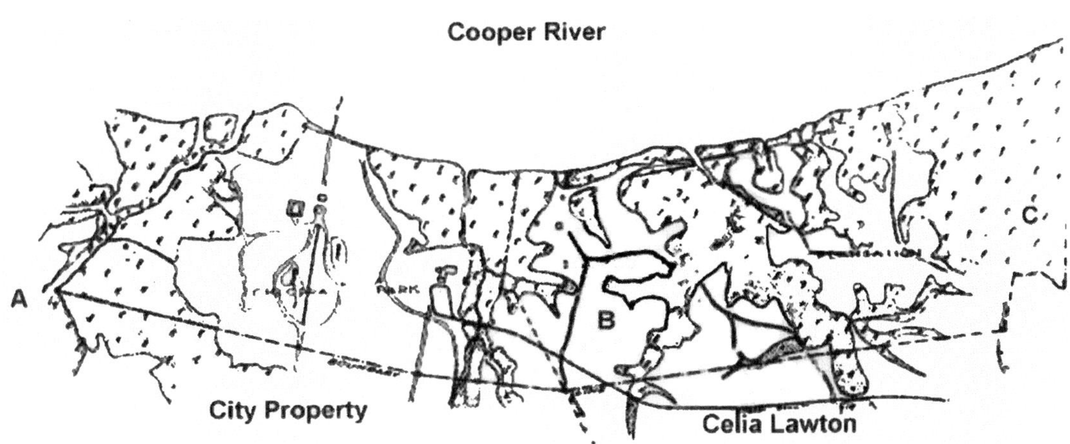

Plat 7.2 This plat shows land sold to the U.S. government for the Charleston Navy Yard. The letter "A" indicates the location of Noisette Creek near the northern boundary of the tract. Chicora Park is indicated on the left third segment of the plat. Chicora Park was built on the Retreat Plantation lands. Lawton Plantation is noted on the central segment of the plat noted with a "B." The Lawton estate was once called Marsh Lands. The property purchased for the navy included 171 acres of Chicora Park, 258 acres of the Lawton Place and 760 acres of marshlands to the south indicated with a "C." The great amount of marsh noted in the shaded sections of the plat is a good indication of why Celia Lawton's estate was once called Marsh Lands. *The map was taken from* Charleston's Navy Yard, *by Jim McNeil, page 39, and is used here courtesy of the R.L. Bryan Company.*

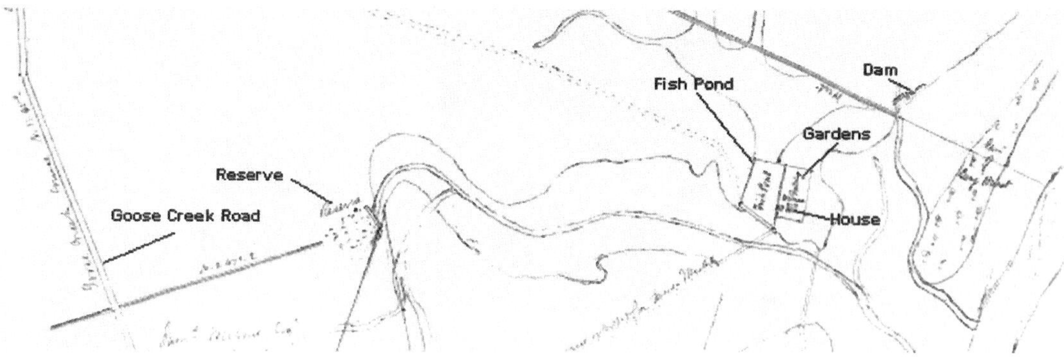

Plat 7.3 This partial plat is not dated but the number of acres in each parcel of Oak Grove Plantation amounted to 1,079 acres. The manuscript labels were added for this publication for clarity. The plat is a tracing of the original by H.A.M. Smith and is among the collections of the South Carolina Historical Society.

grants, until he accumulated 1,127 acres. A section of the estate was sold to Stephen Clifford and later to Robert Elliott and his son Artemus.[376] The remaining 827 acres passed to Kenneth Mitchie, a Charleston merchant. The plantation was touted in its sales advertisement as containing a "good dwelling and several other convenient buildings," as well as apple and pear orchards and gardens.[377] Another valuable feature was a dam across a creek that created a water reserve to irrigate downstream rice lands.

Kenneth Mitchie resided there until his death when he devised it to his brother, James. James Mitchie was a prominent attorney who served as Chief Justice of the Province. He added to his estate until it amounted to 1,079 acres.[378] He renamed his plantation, Oak Grove. Plat 7.3 shows an avenue leading from the Broad Path to the main house. One flanking outbuilding next to the main house is indicated along with a fishpond and garden. A water reserve and dam is indicated near the left margin and a large reserve of trees with the name "Benj Hurst" is shown near the right margin. The tract owned by Benjamin Hurst, as well as the Palmettos Plantation, bordered the property on the north. James Wright's estate was situated on the southern boundary. Mitchie's tract featured a large Cooper River frontage and an avenue leading to the Broad Path. A main house, four outbuildings, and a garden overlooking the Cooper River are indicated on another plat of that property. The Broad Path and the Cooper River provided the east and west boundaries. After the death of James Mitchie, the property was conveyed to James Hutchins, and then to Samuel Prioleau. Prioleau consolidated the lands on the east side of the public road and sold all the parcels lying west of the public road. The bulk of the tract was conveyed to Thomas Screven after Prioleau's death in 1794.[379] Later, part of the land was devised to his son, Thomas Screven II but the remaining acreage was passed to Robert E. Cochran in 1835. Eventually George Chisolm acquired the tract and held it for many years.[380]

Hurst's/Simpson's

A warrant was issued to Benjamin Hurst in 1698 for 200 acres on the Cooper River and south of Oak Grove Plantation.[381] Hurst added seventy-five acres, which included an island in the river.[382] Joseph

Hurst inherited the land from his father, added to it and subsequently mortgaged his accumulated property, which amounted to 575 acres, to Charles Filbin, in 1737.[383] The Hurst tract was a long and narrow piece of land reaching from an island in the Cooper River to the public road to Goose Creek. Joseph Hurst held the land until his death in 1758. His will devised the tract to his son, Robert who sold a small section adjacent to the road to Daniel Cannon and another part to James Streator. Twenty years later, the remaining parcel, consisting of 452 acres, was sold to William Holliday.

The *Royal Gazette* carried a descriptive advertisement for the sale of this property when William Holliday died in 1781. According to the advertisement, the estate was referred to as "Richmond" and consisted of 470 acres. The plantation featured almost a mile of frontage on the Cooper, and was situated about eight miles by land and six miles by water from Charleston. Ships in the harbor were visible from the mainhouse and the water at Richmond was deep enough "that any vessel that comes over the bar can ride safely within ten or twelve yards of the hard marsh," The plantation included two dwelling houses, kitchen, wash house, overseer's house, stable, coach-house, barn, fowl-houses and slaves cabins.[384]

Thomas Bourke purchased the tract, which later passed to Jonathan and William Simpson and then to Thomas McMillan.[385] Henry A.M. Smith stated in the late 1800s that the Burton Lumber Mill was situated on the part of the tract that was the seventy-five acre marsh island in the Cooper River.

Baldrick's/Hickory Hill

Contiguous to the Simpson's Estate were plantations called "Baldrick's" and "Hickory Hill." These combined tracts amounted to 800 acres and bordered on the Cooper River and Filbin's Creek. Henry A.M. Smith found an early reference to these tracts in a grant awarded to John Collins in 1700, and he found a clear reference to a place called "Baldrick's" in a memorial by Richard Baker setting out his ownership of land that he purchased on the west side of the Cooper from John Filbin in 1714.[386] The land passed from Richard Baker to his grandson and then his great grandson, William Logan (1727–1802). The records show that William Logan owned a 76-acre plantation on the Cooper. That tract may have been the 75-acre island mentioned in the vignette describing the "Hurst/Simpson" property.[387] Logan named his small tract "Broad Axe." Logan was a Charleston merchant who owned seven trading vessels and partnerships in many other ships. He brought in six cargoes of slaves and owned considerable other properties including 446 acres of Wadboo Barony, an upper section of the Cooper River. He was elected by Goose Creek to the state senate, but declined to serve. He did represent the city parishes in the Commons House during the Fifth General Assembly.[388]

John Christopher Martin bought the Baldrick's/Hickory Hill Plantation in 1784, which consisted of 365 acres at that time. A 1786 mortgage record states that this tract was formerly the property of James Atkins, and was bought by Martin at a sheriff's sale.[389] The land passed first to John Sabb, then to John Baldrick and later to William Johnson. The land passed from Johnson to Charles Filbin. Charles Filbin's will in 1799 refers to his property as "Hickory Hill." In his will, Filbin devised the estate to his "Negro woman Flora" whom he freed along with her three children. In 1820, Flora Filbin, a free black woman, along with executor James Gantt, conveyed the land containing 365 acres to James Streator Glenn. Seven years later, Jervis Stevens, guardian for Flora Filbin, brought

Drawing 7.1 This picture shows Yeamans Hall Plantation main house that was built about 1693. ***Courtesy of the South Carolina Historical Society.***

court action against James Streator Glenn for non-payment.[390] As a result of the court action, the land was sold to Charles T. Brown, and later to William Johnson, son of the Revolutionary War patriot. Johnson combined Baldrick's 441 acres and Hickory Hill's 365 acres into one 806-acre tract and conveyed it as a whole to Rudolph C. Geyer Trustee in 1835.

Estates on the South Side of Goose Creek

Yeamans Hall

Yeamans Hall lies on a high sandy section overlooking the waters of Goose Creek. A warrant was issued in 1674 for 1,070 acres to Lady Margaret Yeamans and her servants.[391] The grant for this warrant was issued for land upon "Yeamans his Creeke in Ittawan River." Yeamans Creek is known today as Goose Creek, and the old main house was known for many years as "Old Goose Creek." Sir John Yeamans, Lady Margaret's husband, died prior to the date of the land grant and probably never resided on the property.

In 1677, James Moore was the proprietor of Yeamans's tract. James Moore married Margaret Berringer, the daughter of Lady Yeamans by a former husband. Moore later became the governor of the province. Mrs. Poyas, author of *Olden Times in Carolina* published in 1855, stated that Thomas Smith took possession of the estate in 1694.[392] He was the son of the first Landgrave Smith of Medway and added to the acreage with a subsequent grant that increased the area to 1,869 acres. When Smith died, he devised some of his property to his eldest son, Henry. His will stated that he bequeathed to Henry, "My brick house or family mansion at Goose Creek together with 500 acres of land joining on my brother, Dr. George Smith."[393]

The brick house referred to in the will was a large brick house built about 1693, known as the mansion on Goose Creek. It was constructed for defense against the natives. The house had portholes for muskets and a well underneath for a water supply during sieges. It supposedly featured a subterranean passage from the cellar to the graveyard and on to the creek where boats were tied. The tunnel was to be used as an escape passage in case of prolonged native attacks, but historian, Henry A.M. Smith doubted the existence of such an egress route. He believed the land was situated in such a way that a passage was not practical.

Edward McCrady recorded the existence of a secret chamber in the old Yeaman house, consisting of a small space between two walls accessible through a sliding panel. The space was used to hide valuables during the turbulent Proprietary rule, as well as during the American Revolution. A one hundred foot deep well was situated near the house. It featured a chain and bucket and remained in use until 1842. The spring that flowed into the well also filled a spacious pond below the hill, which was generally well stocked with fish.[394]

When Henry Smith (1727–1780), the third landgrave, inherited Yeamans Hall, he also inherited two lots in Georgetown along with lands at Wassamasaw and on Back River. During his lifetime he added more property through grants. He acquired plantations in two other parishes and owned the schooner *Wambaw*. By the time of his death in 1780, he owned 105 slaves. As the third landgrave, Smith was elected to represent Goose Creek in the Twentieth, Twenty-fourth and Twenty-fifth Royal Assemblies. He married Ann Filbin and fathered four children and after her death, he married Elizabeth Ball, and fathered at least nine more children.[395]

Partial plat 7.4 shows Yeamans Hall as it was after the death of the third Landgrave Henry Smith. The 1784 plat shows the large main house and fourteen out-buildings accessed by two avenues and a lesser path. A "Park" is drawn behind the main house. This park was probably an ornamental

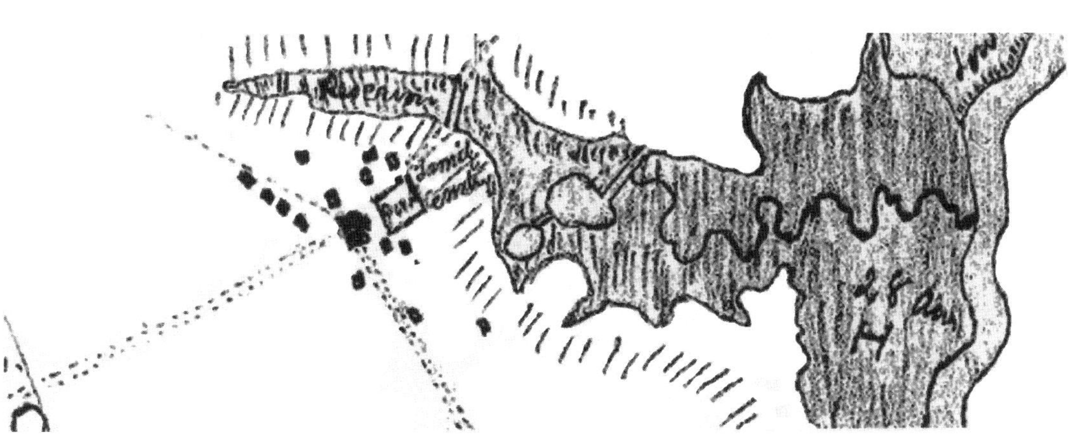

Plat 7.4 This partial plat shows a section of Yeamans Hall Plantation. The plat was drawn from a survey made by "J.P." who was probably Joseph Purcell, in 1786. H.A.M. Smith traced the original plat. The tracing is among the collections of the South Carolina Historical Society. The original McCrady plat # 4263 from which the tracing was made is on microfilm at the Charleston County Library.

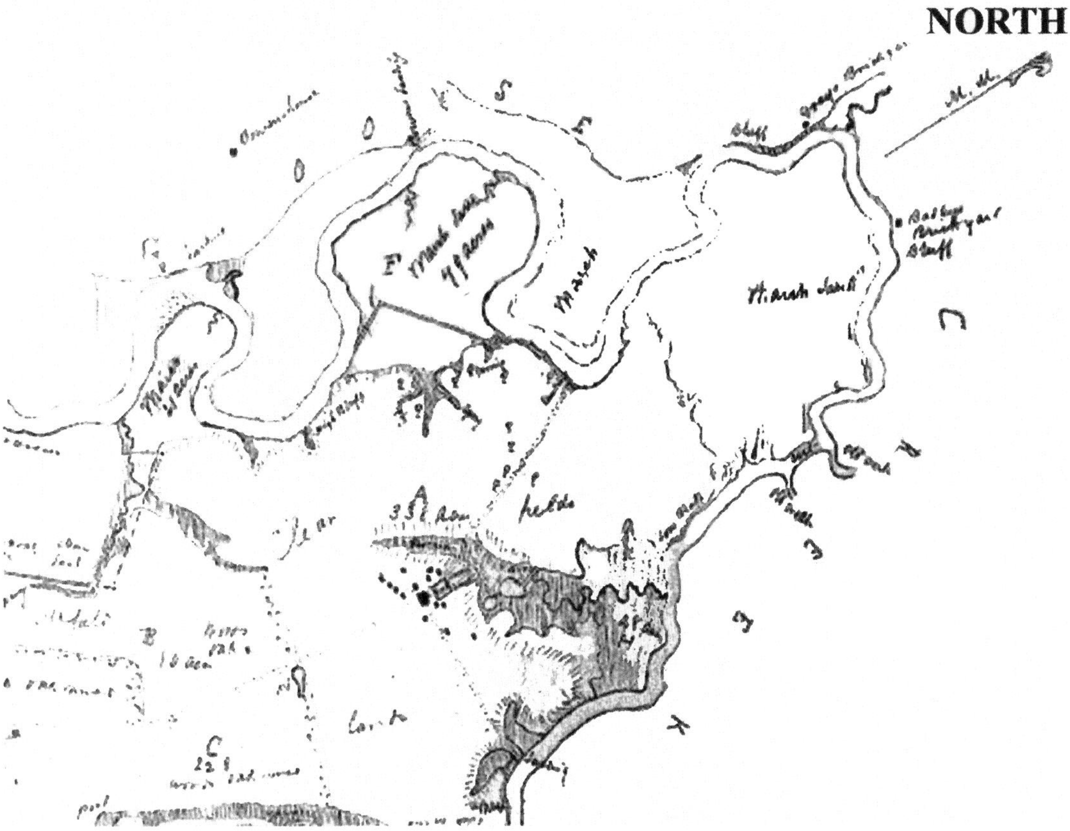

Plat 7.5 This plat shows Yeamans Hall Plantation as surveyed by "J.P.," probably Joseph Purcell, in 1786. The plat is shown as traced by H.A.M. Smith. The tracing is among the collections of the South Carolina Historical Society. The original McCrady plat # 4263 from which the tracing was made is on microfilm at the Charleston County Library.

garden that was popular during the colonial era on most large estates. Behind the "Park" is an area marked "Family Cemetery." Past the cemetery, the land falls away into an area labeled "Reservoir." A land bridge crosses the low lands to higher ground and in the center of the plat two short causeways appear to connect small islands to high ground. Plat 7.5 is a wider view of partial plat 7.4. It shows the buildings in relation to the remaining property.

Henry devised Yeamans Hall to his son, Thomas Smith. Thomas served as magistrate for St. James, Goose Creek and was elected to represent Goose Creek in the Twenty-sixth General Assembly in 1824–25. He owned twenty slaves.[396] The land descended to Thomas's son, George Henry Smith. From George Henry Smith the land was passed to his son, Thomas Henry Smith. A 1908 plat shows that Thomas Smith owned 1,371 acres at Yeamans Hall.[397]

Leize F.B. Lockwood gives credit for the name of "Yeamans Hall" to her grandmother Eliza F. Lockwood, who married George Henry Smith in 1850. She was supposed to have had the old portholes cut into windows and renamed it "Yeamans Hall."[398] The house is two stories high with stucco walls and old-fashioned panels. The piazza or gallery on the front face was reportedly a

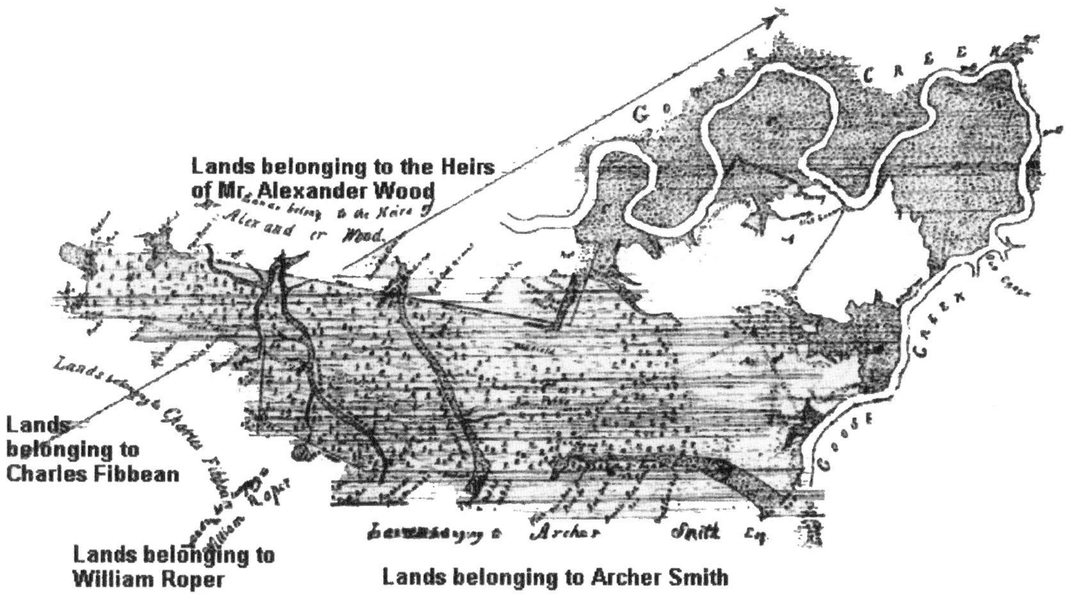

Plat 7.6 This plat shows lands south of Goose Creek and near the Neck. The "Lands belonging to the Heirs of Alexander Wood," "Lands belonging to Charles Fibbean," "Lands belonging to William Roper" and "Lands belonging to Archer Smith." are noted on the plat. The plat was drawn from a survey made by Joseph Purcell describing the 1,371-acre estate of Thomas Smith called Yeamans Hall.

late addition. Piazzas, so common in the South, were not generally introduced until the end of the nineteenth century.[399]

The Yeamans Hall Club was created as a winter retreat in the early 1920s. The clubhouse was completed in 1927, with groups of corporation-owned cottages and private homes situated around the white brick clubhouse. Clare Booth Luce and her husband Henry Luce, the *Time-LIFE-Fortune* magazine mogul, owned a "cottage" at Yeamans Hall and the club was frequented by celebrities such as John F. Kennedy. The grounds extended to the Cooper River where boat landings provided for members' yachts and boats. There is also an eighteen-hole golf course. Buried on the grounds are Thomas Smith, second Landgrave, and his Dutch wife, Anna Cornelie Myddagh. Other inscribed monuments mark the burial places of members of the Smith, Poyas, Adams, Lockwood, and Waring families.

Live Oak

West of Yeamans Hall was a four hundred acre tract granted in 1671 to William Murrell. Apparently this early grant was never claimed because that same land was granted again in the early 1700s in smaller amounts to James Kennedy, Thomas Ferguson and Edward Curzon for one hundred acres, two hundred acres and one hundred acres respectively. Thomas Ferguson was an ancestor of another Thomas Ferguson who was an active participant in the Goose Creek Council of Safety during the American Revolution.

Alexander Wood eventually owned Thomas Ferguson's 200-acre tract and later mortgaged it to Alexander Garden.[400] Wood owned a shop at or next to the Ten-Mile House that remained in Wood's and his heir's ownership until it passed to John Glen in 1785. Plat 7.6 and map 7.2 show the relationship of some of the lands in that vicinity to Yeamans Hall and each other.

John Glen was a successful merchant and Indian Commissioner during the colonial period. He acquired Wood's tract and other contiguous parcels until his estate totaled 360 acres.[401] He also acquired the plantation known as "Streators" on Charleston Neck and upon his death the land passed under the name of "Live Oak Hill" to his son, John Glen Jr. Live Oak Hill stayed in the Glen family until 1845, when a section was sold to P. D. Torre and the remaining to George Henry Smith, owner of Yeamans Hall. The next year, Torre sold his section to Smith. The executors for George Henry Smith later sold this tract to William Brown in 1868, who conveyed it to Isaac F. Hunt two years later.[402]

Filbins/Fibbeans

A small tract consisting of 344 acres lay south of Yeamans Hall. This was commonly called "Filbin's" and was owned by John Filbin as early as 1727. John Filbin, the son took ownership after the death of his father and kept it throughout his life. The land passed through several hands, including Francis Curtis's in 1821, and William Johnson in 1835.[403]

The Camp

A large one thousand acre tract conveyed by grant to Christopher Smith in 1705, was first called "Cow Pen." Ralph Izard acquired the tract when he married.

Smith's widow in 1709. The second Ralph Izard became the owner after the death of his father, and added lands until the estate amounted to 1,180 acres. The Izards called the tract "The Camp" possibly because Governor Charles Craven used it as a bivouac area when he assembled his colonial forces to march against the natives in the Yemassee War of 1715. The mansion at "The Camp" survived the Revolutionary War, but was thoroughly destroyed by fire before 1789.[404] This inland rice plantation passed to the second Ralph Izard's son, Henry and later to his only son, Ralph Izard III. The third Ralph Izard was Commissioner to Tuscany, Italy during the Revolution and one of the first two United States Senators from South Carolina after the adoption of the Constitution.[405] The land stayed in the Izard family for 122 years but was sold out of the family in 1831 to settle the estate of Ralph Izard III's son, Henry.

Cripps's/Langstaffe's

West of Live Oak Hill was the estate known as "Cripps'" or "Langstaffe's." William Perryman was the first owner. He received a warrant in 1677 but Benjamin Perryman, probably the grandson of William, owned the land in the early eighteenth century and sold it to Barnard Christian Cooper, "Surgeon."[406] This five hundred acre tract passed through two more owners before Richard Splatt, a Charleston merchant, purchased it.[407] Another one hundred acres of adjoining lands were added so that upon his death in 1728, Splatt devised six hundred acres to his son, John. It appears as if John

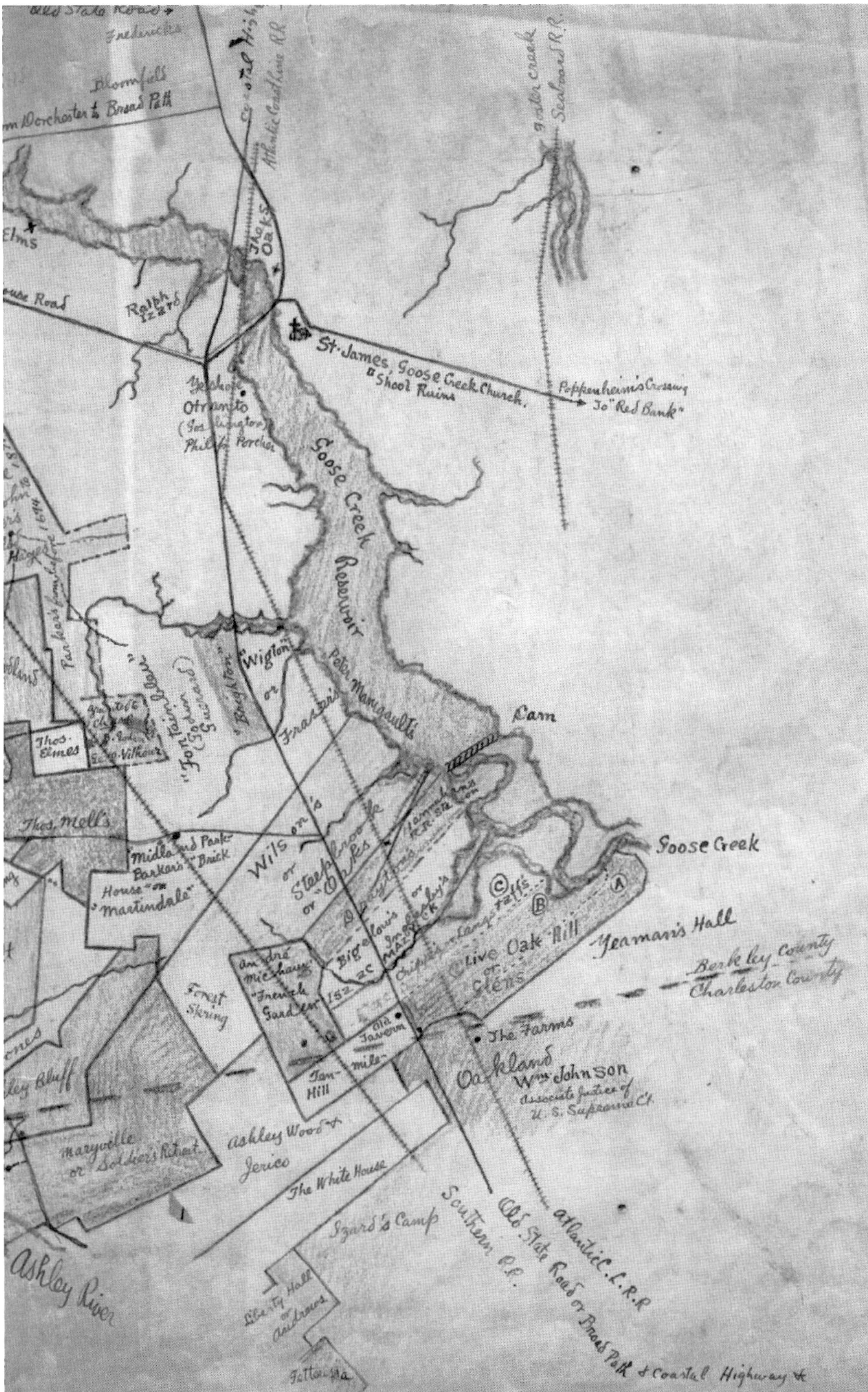

Map 7.2 William Henry Johnson drew a map from his collection of plats. A section of the map shown here describes some of the estates on the Neck and on the south side of Goose Creek. This map is in *Johnson Scrapbook, Volume 1. Courtesy of the South Carolina Historical Society.*

Splatt died young, because the property was transferred to his only sister, Mary. Through Mary's marriage to William Cripps, the property passed to the Cripps family and later to their son, John Splatt Cripps. A Joseph Purcell plat of the tract in 1785 cited John Splatt Cripps as the owner. He was a Charleston merchant and owned two other plantations on the Ashley River. The 1790 census listed his residence in Charleston.

He sold the Cripps tract to Robert Howard in 1792.[408] On an 1826 map, the land was labeled as Langstaffe's, and in 1835, Ann Langstaffe, widow, conveyed the land to Charles J. Steedman, Sheriff of the Charleston District. The land passed through several ownerships during the next fifty years, until it was sold along with Live Oak Hill to D. Watts and Company. Henry A. M. Smith visited the estate in the early years of the twentieth century and reported that remnants of the house foundation and family graveyard could still be seen.[409]

Cannon's/Oakland

Daniel Cannon owned 566 acres at the head of Onsaw Creek next to the 10-Mile tract. He acquired this tract in several steps and finally amassed more than 598 acres. As early as 1755, he purchased 303.75 acres from Joseph Hurst, who inherited the land from his father, Benjamin Hurst.[410] In 1762, he added 189 acres through purchase of this tract from Benjamin Smith, heir and son of Mary and Landgrave Thomas Smith. In 1772, an additional 88 acres were purchased from Robert Hurst. A note on an 1800 plat stated that Mr. John Glen gave 18 acres of land to William Cannon making the estate total, 598.75 acres. The plat made from a survey shows that this land was bound to the north, west and east by land owned by John Glen. Situated to the west was the 10-Mile House tract owned by Thomas Tims. Henry Izard's "Camp" was south of Cannon's property. Part

Plat 7.7 This partial plat shows Cannon's "Settlement" near the public road to Goose Creek. This plat is a tracing from the original. The tracing was made by H.A.M. Smith and is among the collections of the South Carolina Historical Society. The manuscript words "9 Mile Stone" were added to the tracing for this publication to improve orientation.

of the 1800 plat is shown as plat 7.7. That partial plat shows a "Settlement" with a main house, seven outbuildings and six slave quarters. A large garden behind the main house is also indicated.

Contiguous to Cannon's were several smaller tracts. John Poyas owned 207 acres on the "Old Goose Creek Road" and Benjamin Hursts owned 304 acres. Some business arrangement between Cannon and his neighbor, John Glen at "Streators" reduced the estate to 566 acres and the tract was sold in 1800 to Mrs. Hanna Heyward who passed it to Hannah Roper. At Hannah Roper's death, her will directed the sale of Oakland.[411]

10-Mile Hill

Located ten miles from Charleston on the public road to Goose Creek, 10-Mile Hill was the site of a well-known tavern. The name was given early in the 1700s and still remains today. The earliest grant for this tract was issued to Thomas Perryman prior to 1717. A section of the original tract passed to Edward Weekly, and became part of the Oakland plantation. The 10-Mile Hill tract remained intact as it was conveyed through several hands until Robert Flud purchased it in 1763. At that transfer, it was known as the "Ten-Mile House."[412] Thomas Tims was the owner and proprietor of the inn in 1790, the year of the first federal census. Tims and his family kept the tract, inn and store for many years until it finally conveyed out of the family and through the hands of many owners. This tract appears to have supported a tavern or inn until the mid-nineteenth century. Henry A.M. Smith

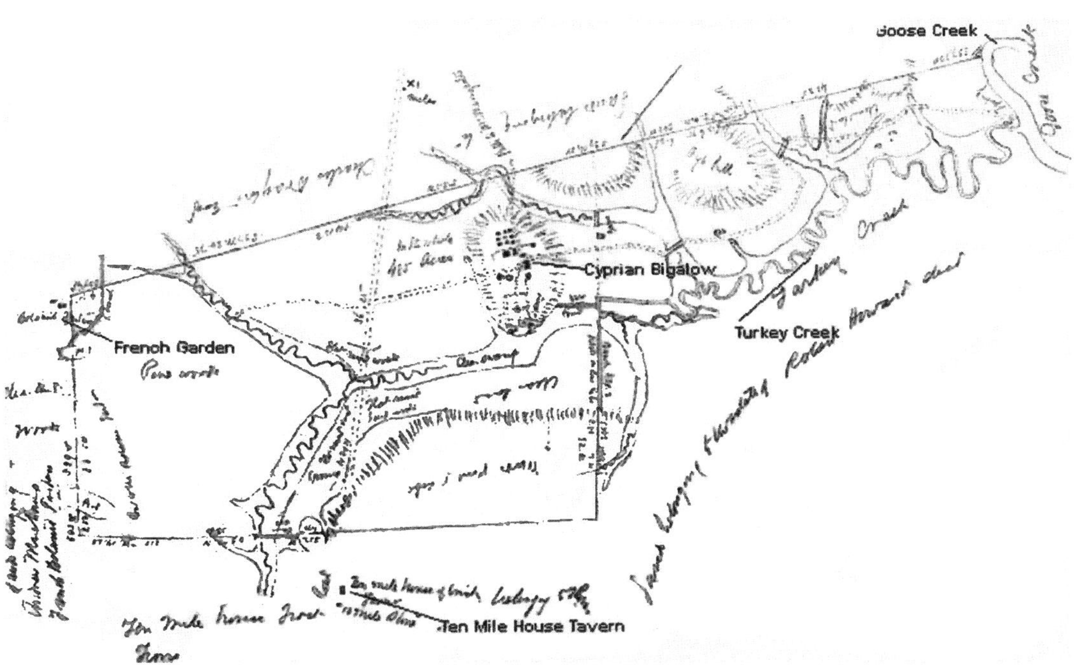

Plat 7.8 This partial plat drawn from a survey made in 1805 describes the estate of Cyprian Bigelow. The plat shows the Ten-Mile-House and French Garden. The manuscript labels were added for this publication for clarity. The plat was traced by H.A.M. Smith and is among the collections of the South Carolina Historical Society.

reported that he saw the ruins of the inn and store when he was a boy during the 1850s. When the state railroads were constructed in 1833, the rail lines originated approximately half a mile from the old 10-Mile Tavern. Today that rail station is known as the "10-Mile Hill Station."

Plat 7.8 was drawn from the survey made in 1805. It shows 10-Mile Hill and its proximity to French Garden and Cyprian Bigelow's estate. The public road is shown dividing the plat from bottom to top. The plat shows the words "Ten Mile House of Brick," "Tavern," "Ten Mile Stone" and "Ten Mile Tract" near the public road at the lower center of the plat. At the lower left of the plat, the words "Lands Belonging to Andre Michaux French Botanic Garden" appears in the margin. A "Road to Botanical Garden" is drawn from bottom left to upper left and terminates at the upper left at two buildings. There the words "settlement" and "Botanical Garden" appear. A road is shown from the botanical garden at upper left corner to an obvious settlement at the upper right. This collection of structures is Bigelow's main house and outbuildings discussed under the Bigelow/Inglesby heading. The Bigelow settlement and the 10-Mile House Tavern were approximately three quarters of a mile apart. Charles Drayton's land was north of these tracts, and Robert Howard's tract lay east of it. This land drained into Goose Creek by way of Turkey Creek.

French Gardens

French Garden plantation is remembered because of the extensive botanical nursery developed there. The French Garden tract was originally a grant to Robert Wood in 1716–17.[413] It originally consisted of 220 acres located southwest of Live Oak Hill, which adjoined Yeamans Hall. The 111-acre tract passed by conveyance to Andre' Michaux in 1786.[414] Michaux was the celebrated botanist who was sent to the United States by the Royal Government of France to explore trees, shrubs and other plants for possible use in his homeland. Michaux, accompanied by his son, left France in 1785 and took up residence in Goose Creek. There he established a nursery for his seeds and plants and sent the seeds and seedlings back to France. Andre' Michaux called his new residence "la plantation" and "L'habitation" but it was generally known as "French Garden." He probably lived in the old house built by Robert Wood and used it as his headquarters while he made botanical and collecting expeditions. His treks stretched throughout the eastern states from Florida to Canada, including the Appalachian and Allegheny mountain regions, and as far west as the Mississippi River. His journals are a careful record of his explorations and his successful botanical experimentation. The American Philosophical Society published his journals in 1888.

Michaux is credited with the introduction of many plants to Carolina. He probably introduced the beautiful Camellia japonica, ginkgo tree, and candleberry tree. Upon his return to France in 1796, he was shipwrecked off the coast of Holland. He fastened himself to a plank and washed ashore unconscious but alive. He lost his baggage and some of his journals, but most of his packages of plants and seeds were salvaged. In 1800, he sailed to Madagascar on a new botanical expedition. While preparing his nursery there, he was taken ill with fever and died in 1802.

The French Garden Plantation, although conveyed to Michaux, had been purchased with government funds and was the property of the French Government. In 1802, Michaux's son, F. Andre, sold the property on behalf of the French government to John James Himley.[415] This property was later conveyed from Himley to the Agricultural Society of South Carolina, who held it until

1820 when it was conveyed to John Carwile. Subsequently it changed hands many times, including ownership by Thomas Malone and Jeremiah Rhame. In 1857, Charles Lee purchased the 111 acres "commonly known as French Garden." [416]

Bigelow's

Dr. John Moultrie, an immigrant to Carolina, was the ancestor of the famous Moultrie family. He came prior to 1729 and made his home in Goose Creek. The original grant for the land was made in 1694–95 to Samuel Hartley for four hundred acres on the south side of Goose Creek but was the home of Dr. John Moultrie by 1729.[417] Dr. Moultrie married Lucretia Cooper from the neighboring "Cripps" or "Langstaffes" Plantation, which also lay on Goose Creek and with her fathered four sons. All of Dr. Moultrie's sons attained prominent positions in public service. His son, John became Lieutenant Governor of East Florida under the Royal Government, and supported the British government during the Revolution. The second son, William became a Major General in the Continental Army during the Revolution, and afterwards, the governor of the new state of South Carolina. James became Chief Justice of East Florida, and Thomas became a captain in the regiment of his brother, William. Thomas was killed in 1780, at the siege of Charleston.

Dr. Moultrie later married Elizabeth Mathews, by whom he had one son, Alexander Moultrie who resided at Richmond Plantation in Goose Creek. In 1776, Alexander became the Attorney General for South Carolina. Dr. John Moultrie died in 1771 leaving his estate to his sons. The sons conveyed the land to William Gickie, "late mariner but now of St. James, Goose Creek, Gentleman." Gickie held the property about seven years, and eventually divided it into halves,

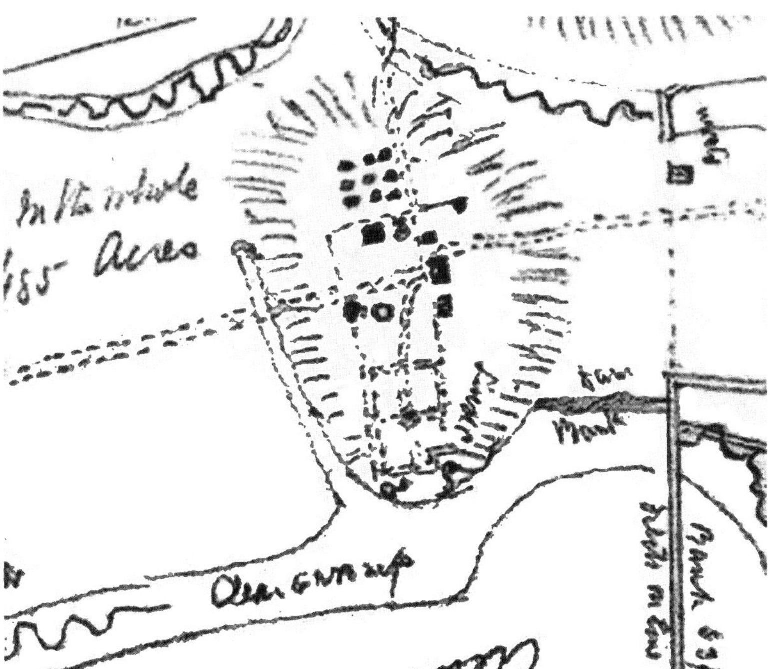

Plat 7.9 This partial plat was made from a survey conducted in 1805 for the estate of Cyprian Bigelow. The plantation was at that time owned by William Inglesby. The original plat was traced by H.A.M. Smith and is among the collections of the South Carolina Historical Society.

selling the northern half to Dr. Charles Drayton and the southern half to John Fisher, "cabinet maker." The land was situated next to the Broad Path between the 10-Mile House and the 11-mile marker. Some maps refer to this plantation as "Bigelow's," after Cyprian Bigelow, the owner in 1793. It is called "Inglesby's" in other references.

The plantation was bordered by French Garden on the west. An 1805 plat of Inglesby's, presented as partial plat 7.9, shows five large structures, nine small structures, and square areas, which are probably formal gardens. William Inglesby held the property for twenty-nine years until he gave it to his grandson, William H. Inglesby, who conveyed it out of the family shortly thereafter.

Dr. Charles Drayton's

William Gickie devised the southern section of the old Moultrie estate to John Fisher for more than £978.[418] He sold the northern half to Dr. Charles Drayton "Doctor of Physics." Charles Drayton was the son of John Drayton of Drayton Hall. He inherited Drayton Hall when his father died in 1777 and resided there probably using the Goose Creek property for investment purposes. He held the Goose Creek tract for thirty-eight years then sold it to Rebecca Gadsden, the daughter of Benjamin Coachman. She held this land for many years, as well as the property on the north side of Goose Creek that she inherited from her father. She eventually sold the land on the south side of Goose Creek in 1838 to William J. Sineath.[419]

Sineath's

William J. Sineath began amassing acreage near the Goose Creek public road in 1833, when he purchased the southern section of Peter Manigault's Steepbrook estate.[420] Peter Manigault had devised part of the tract to his son Gabriel who later conveyed the 650-acre tract to William Allen Deas. In 1833, the tract was referred to as "Oaks." Court action in the case of Deas vs. Deas required that the 650-acre tract called Oaks be conveyed to William J. Sineath to settle debts.[421] Three years later, Sineath bought the Brick House and Fieldhour (Villhower, Vilhour) tracts with a combined total of 634 acres.[422] This tract is now referred to as Midland Park and the Brickhouse residence stood near the Southern Railway line.[423] In 1838, Sineath bought the 446 acres from Rebecca Gadsden, who was noted in the vignette of Dr. Drayton's land. Another Steepbrook tract was called "Wilson's" and was inherited by Joseph Manigault at the time of his father's death. William J. Sineath purchased Manigault's 585-acre "Wilson's" tract in 1844.

The Sineath family history entitled, *The Sineath's Family* records that the family lived at the 12-Mile House on the public road from 1829 until 1865. Today Trident Technical College is situated on the Sineath home site.[424] Also, nineteenth century maps locate Sineath Station on the Southern Railway near today's Ashley Phosphate Road. Thus, it appears that several tracts of land, purchased at different times, were probably contiguous to each other. These tracts consisted of at least 2,315 acres, and reached from the public road to the Southern Railway line and beyond.

Map 7.3 labels "Sineath" as a railroad station on the South Carolina Railroad and map 7.4 show its location on the State Road. The stylized rendering of map 7.3 indicates four structures at the Sineath rail stop and is likely an effort on the part of the cartographer to signify a cluster of buildings

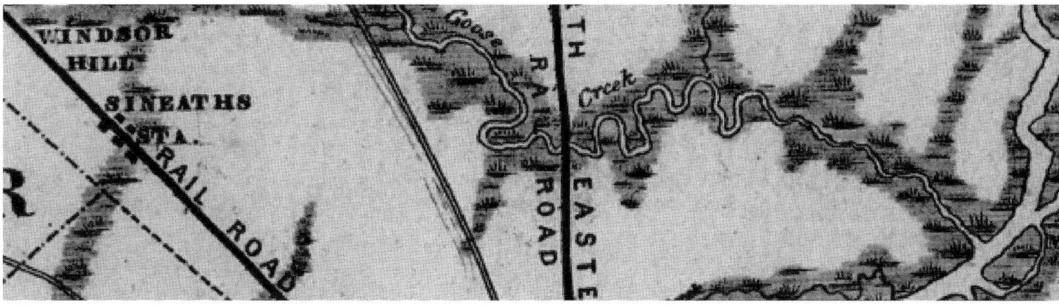

Map 7.3 This partial map shows Sineath Station on the South Carolina Railroad near Windsor Hill. The map is part of the E. and G.W. Blunt's Map of Charleston and Vicinity, 1862.

and activities. The Windsor Hill home of the Moultries is noted north of Sineath Station. Ashley Phosphate Road did not appear on this early map, but today it lies between the old sites of Windsor Hill Plantation and Sineath Station and intersects with the public road to Goose Creek (Highway 52) near the old 12-Mile House site. A tollhouse station was situated on the Goose Creek Road near the 12-Mile House, and was assigned to Lavinia Sineath. She operated the toll station until 1849.[425] Willaim J. Sineath II was born at the 12-Mile House in 1834, as well as his son, William Sineath III. William Sineath II served as a second lieutenant in the South Carolina Infantry during the Civil War and managed a phosphate mine in Goose Creek after the war.

The Sineath ancestors appear in Goose Creek at a time when the fortunes of the grand colonial estates had greatly declined. Most of the old plantations were subdivided and sold to enterprising yeoman during the early decades of the nineteenth century. The break-up of most Goose Creek estates continued throughout the 1800s, with only a few properties remaining intact into the twentieth century. Regardless of the large size of some of the holdings, no colonial style plantations remained. William Sineath owned only eleven slaves at the time of his death in 1847 and according to the 1860 census, William J. Sineath II owned only seven slaves. The large agricultural factories, which once produced grand homes and country gentry, were not represented in the Sineath estate.

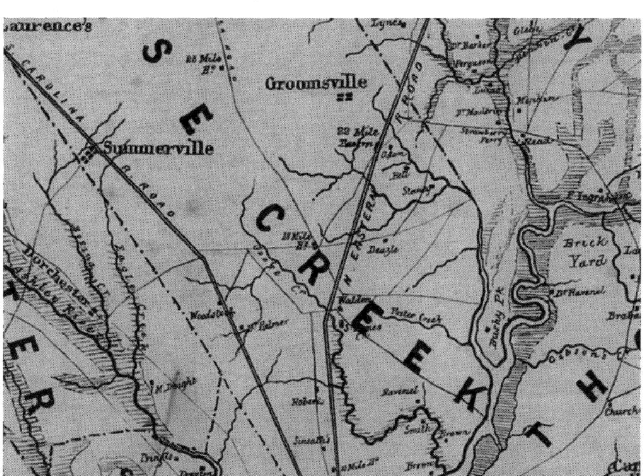

Map 7.4 This partial map shows "Sineath's" on the public road. The map is a section of one produced in 1861 by Evan's and Cogswell, Charleston, South Carolina.

The interesting and extensive Sineath family made lasting contributions to Goose Creek and the South Carolina Lowcountry. Several generations were born in the 12-Mile House and many stayed in the South Carolina Lowcountry to share their name in marriages with the Wannamakers, Rhames, Orvins and others. The James Sineath family resides in the old parish today. James is a businessman, his wife, Linda, is a retired Goose Creek schoolteacher, and their son, Drew, is a realtor with a family in the City of Goose Creek.

Steepbrook

The Honorable Peter Manigault, Esquire, a Speaker of the Commons House of Assembly, owned 1,300 acres of land with a large frontage on Goose Creek. Peter was the son of Gabriel Manigault who purchased the land as a country home for rest and recreation. This land was originally a 600-acre site on the south side of Goose Creek next to Bigelow's plantation. The tract was passed down through conveyances and wills until John Wilson conveyed all his part northeast of the road to Peter Manigault in 1757. In addition, Moses Wilson conveyed his land southwest of the road to Peter Manigault. The property amounted to 633 acres at that time. Manigault also acquired the adjoining plantation when the owner, Isaac Godin, conveyed to Peter Manigault, "Barrister at Law," the land on the east side of the public road between the road and the waters of Goose Creek in 1757. Isaac Godin conveyed additional land to Peter Manigault until the Manigault estate amounted to 1,300 acres.

Peter Manigault referred to his Goose Creek residence as "Steepbrook." This name was probably derived from the fact that a stream, leading to Goose Creek, cut through highland near the bank where a dam was used to reserve the waters for irrigation. At that point the water flowed down a steep brook to Goose Creek. The main house was built near the brook and thus the name. The property was bound on the west by the "Broad Road to Charleston" and on the east by Dr. John Moultrie's estate. William Wilkins drew a plat of the estate from a survey made in 1759 that described the dam and brook.[426]

Steepbrook was one of the many estates owned by the Manigaults.[427] Anne Manigault's diary frequently notes visits of her family to Goose Creek in the 1760s and 1770s and Peter Manigault entertained there. The following notice appeared in the *South Carolina Gazette* on November 10, 1766:

> *Wednesday last being the Anniversary of the Glorious Revolution, by the landing of King William and the Nation's happy deliverance from the horrid Popist Plot, the same was observed here with suitable demonstration of joy. The hon. Peter Manigault, Esq., speaker of the Common House of Assembly, gave upon this occasion, an elegant entertainment of the Light Infantry Company, at his seat at Goose Creek, 14 miles from Charles Town where the Company arrived at 7 o'clock in the morning, Spent the day most agreeably, and returned before 9 at night.*[428]

Allen Ramsey of London, renowned painter, created a portrait of Peter Manigault that is now in a London collection. Also, George Roupel sketched Peter Manigault in ink depicting him at a Steepbrook dinner party with his guests and a servant.[429]

Gabriel Manigault, son of Peter, inherited 24,719 acres on a number of estates including Steepbrook. The 1790 census lists him with 265 slaves on his properties in Goose Creek, St. Phillips, St. Michaels and St. Dennis Parish. The records show only 38 slaves in St. James, Goose Creek. He studied law in Europe during the Revolutionary War, but was compelled to return to defend his properties in 1780. At that time, he enrolled in the Charleston Battalion of Artillery to defend the city but when the city fell to the British, his Charleston home was confiscated. In response he took an oath of allegiance to the British, was paroled and successfully petitioned for the return of his house. He then accepted a position as magistrate for the Charleston District. A year later, in 1781 he left Charleston, briefly resided at his Goose Creek home and then reported to Francis Marion's patriot camp. From there he traveled to the headquarters of Governor John Rutledge where he repented for his disloyalties.

After the war, he pursued the life of a wealthy planter. He owned several estates, but resided at Steepbrook, which at that time was referred to as "Oaks." He controlled over half of the shares in the Catawba Canal Company, and in addition to these interests he pursued architecture. He designed many Charleston buildings including his home at the corner of Meeting and George Street, the Orphan House Chapel, Charleston City Hall, and the South Carolina Society Hall.[430] He represented Goose Creek during five sessions of the general assembly and voted in favor of the Federal Constitution at the State Convention. He married the daughter of Ralph Izard and became politically aligned with Izard and William Laughton Smith. These three men formed a powerful Federalist faction in the new republic during the 1790s.[431]

Wigton/Fraser's

John Fraser emigrated from Wigton County, Galloway, Scotland to a plantation on the southern bank of Goose Creek that he named "Wigton" after his Scotish home.[432] He was a native trader during the early frontier period and fortunately garnered the trust of Sanute, one of the Yemassee chiefs. Fraser took refuge in Charleston and survived the Yemassee War because Sanute warned him of the pending Yemassee hostilities.[433] Alexander Fraser, son of John, inherited Wigton in 1754. He divided his time between his 793-acre estate and his Charleston house on Tradd Street. He staffed his town house with 12 servants and worked 139 more on his lands in four parishes. Additionally, he received grants for 5,000 acres of land in the backcountry. He was elected five times to represent Goose Creek in the general assembly and one time to represent St. Philips and St. Michaels. He served his community as a tax collector, justice of the peace, and commissioner to improve navigation on Goose Creek. He was wealthy and loaned the State of South Carolina £92,225.[434] Alexander and his second wife, Mary Grimke, reared fourteen children. Charles Fraser, the celebrated portrait painter and author of ***Reminiscences of Charleston,*** was the youngest child of Alexander and Mary Grimke Fraser.

After Alexander died in 1791, the Wigton property remained in the Fraser family more than forty years until 1834 when the lands were sold to Robert Y. Hayne, onetime governor and senator from South Carolina. Hayne fervently debated Daniel Webster in the United States Senate during the nullification crisis.

Fontainbleau/Fountainbleu

Benjamin Godin was a wealthy Charleston merchant who owned Fontainebleau, a 2,158-acre estate adjoining Otranto Plantation.[435] At one time Godin owned both Otranto and Fontainbleau, which included 3,847 acres and a large water frontage on Goose Creek. This excellent location made him one of the wealthiest Lowcountry landowners. A conveyance by William Sanders and his wife to Benjamin Godin in 1707, consisting of 500 acres on the southwest side of Goose Creek, was the first of a series of conveyances that became Fontainbleau.[436] Godin added to his estate until his death when he left the plantation to his son, Isaac Godin.[437] According to the February 12, 1737 issue of the *South Carolina Gazette*, Benjamin Godin was a Charleston merchant who retired to his Goose Creek estate prior to 1748. On April 27, 1748, the *South Carolina Gazette* paid a memorial tribute to Benjamin Godin as "A gentleman of unblemished character for Integrity, Benevolence and every Moral Virtue."

The plantation passed to Isaac's wife who conveyed it to Benjamin Guerard in 1784. Guerard was governor of South Carolina during the early years of the republic from 1783 to 1785, and died in 1787. One of his executors was his cousin, Major Charles Fining who became owner of Fountainbleau until his death in 1813, after which the property was sold in tracts.

David Godin, son of Benjamin Godin and Marianne Mazyck, and brother of Isaac also inherited lands from his father. He resided on his inherited property in St. Bartholomew, but owned 1,689 acres in Goose Creek and a pew in The St. James, Goose Creek Church. He represented St. Bartholomew Parish in the general assembly. The beautiful old brick house at Fontainbleau crumbled during the nineteenth century. Henry A.M. Smith investigated the property near the close of the nineteenth century and described the remains as evidence of a good size house with a number of outbuildings. Smith found little of the garden, but he believed that it was likely that the wealthy Godin and his well-to-do successors maintained a well-built and ornamented plantation as a typical countryseat of the period. A brick wall enclosed the old family cemetery near the main house.

Otranto

Arthur and Edward Middleton were granted a 1,780-acre tract at the head of Yeamans Creek in 1678.[438] Edward conveyed his share of the original grant to his brother Arthur two years later in 1680. Arthur Middleton's estate was referred to as "Yeshoe" during the early years, as well as in his marriage settlement to Mary Smith. "Yeshoe" is probably a Native American name but it has not been definitely translated. It may have referred to the land or to the creek on which the tract was situated.

Under the terms of his deed and will, the property passed to Arthur's widow, Mary Middleton. Mary Middleton married Ralph Izard, the immigrant ancestor of the South Carolina Izard family. Upon Mary's death, Ralph Izard acquired all of the Goose Creek holdings including Otranto. Izard subsequently sold 1,649 acres to Jacob Allen in 1696, but he retained 131 acres adjacent to the Oaks Plantation.[439] The land obtained by Allen was passed to his son, and later conveyed to Benjamin Godin. Benjamin Godin sold 548 acres on the east side of Goose Creek to Charles Pinckney in 1735.[440] He apparently retained the remaining properties until it devised to his son, David. Benjamin

Godin owned this land but resided on his adjoining Fountainbleau property. The original Arthur Middleton grant, excluding the 131 acres, passed to his wife's second husband, Ralph Izard, was conveyed to Jacob Allen, to Benjamin Godin, to Godin's son and grandson and in 1758 to the Honorable John Moultrie. When John Moultrie purchased the tract it consisted of 1,689 acres.

John Moultrie, the son of Dr. John Moultrie mentioned in the account of "Bigelow's" Plantation, was Lieutenant Governor of East Florida under the Royal Government. He probably resided on the Goose Creek tract until 1771when he moved to East Florida and conveyed the land to Dr. Alexander Garden. Alexander Garden was a renowned medical practitioner in Charleston for many years, and was well known as an excellent botanist. He corresponded in Latin with the internationally renowned botanist Carl Von Linne (Linnaeus).[441] Linnaeus named the genus of plants, gardenia after Alexander Garden, which includes the *Gardenia florida*, commonly called the "cape of jessamine." [442] In Dr. Johnson's book, *Tradition and Reminiscences, Chiefly of the American Revolution in the South,* he told a delightful story of another Goose Creek doctor who named a flower. According to Johnson, Dr. Lewis Mottet was jealous of the well-merited celebrity of Dr. Alexander Garden. Thus, when he was told that Linnaeus complimented Garden when he named the beautiful plant "*Gardenia*," Mottet pretended to be unimpressed. Mottet professed that such an event was common and that he too had discovered a very beautiful native plant, and had named it "Lucia,"after his cook "Lucy."[443]

Dr. Garden was an outstanding Carolina naturalist who, in addition to writing Linne, recorded his work in correspondence with John Ellis of England, and John Bartram in Philadelphia and other famed naturalists. His discoveries included the Congo snake and the mud eel. In 1764, Dr. Garden published a botanical account of the Virginia Pink-Root or *Spegelia merilondecia*, an herb indigenous to South Carolina.[444] As a Doctor of Medicine, he introduced the method of isolation and vaccination for small pox and was interested in raising experimental plants for healing. He also published and read a paper on "The Electric Eel" to the Royal Society of London. His accounts of selected insects and animals were also read before the Society in 1762, 1766 and in 1771. He was elected a member of the Royal Society in 1773 and its vice president 1782.[445]

Dr. Garden was concerned with the dependence on slave labor for the cultivation and threshing of rice. He wrote, "Our Staple Commodity for some years has been Rice and tilling, planting, hoeing, reaping, threshing, pounding have all been done by the poor slaves…" He was most concerned that the greed of many slave owners caused the unprofitable death of valuable slaves through exhausting work in miserable conditions in the rice fields. He explained that the work was "tedious, laborious, and slow..." but the process of planting and reaping was merely the first of several labor-intensive steps. According to Garden, "the worse comes last for after the rice is threshed, they beat it all in the hand in large wooden mortars to clean it from the husk, which is a very hard and severe operation as each slave is tasked at seven mortars for one day, and each mortar contains three pecks of rice." The more severe masters tasked their slaves more than seven mortars a day, which Garden believed caused the premature deaths of many slaves because, "they often overheat themselves then exposing themselves to the bad air, or drinking cold water, are immediately…seized with dangerous pleurisies and peripneumonies of which soon rid them of cruel masters, or more cruel overseers, and end their wretched being here."[446] To relieve this hard labor, Dr. Garden advocated the improvement of horse-powered threshing machines and continually sought ways to improve the living conditions of the slave and landowner in the Lowcountry.

Dr. Garden became ill and returned with his wife, Elizabeth Perronneau, to Europe where he died. Before departing Goose Creek, he conveyed the 1,689-acre plantation to his only son, Alexander II, who was born in 1757 and was educated in England. Alexander II was admitted to Lincoln's Inn as a barrister at law, and earned a Masters of Arts degree from the University of Glasgow in 1777. A year later, against his father's wishes he returned to South Carolina to assist in the struggle for independence. He served in Light Horse Harry Lee's Legion of Cavalry as a cornet and later as aide-de-camp on the staff of General Nathaniel Greene with the rank of major.[447] Major Alexander Garden remained in active service until the evacuation of Charleston by the British in 1782.

It appears that Major Garden's father, Dr. Alexander Garden, was an ardent loyalist who never forgave his son for supporting the American cause. The new South Carolina government confiscated Otranto after the war because of the loyalty of Dr. Alexander Garden to the King, but the estate eventually conveyed to the son after Major Garden appealed to the House of Representatives for its return.[448] The son married Mary Anna Gibbes after the Revolutionary War and later penned *Anecdotes of the Revolutionary War in America,* published in 1822 and *Anecdotes of the American Revolution*, published in 1828. He represented Goose Creek in the Sixth General Assembly and Prince William Parish in the Tenth and Eleventh General Assemblies.

Near the end of the eighteenth century, Otranto passed through a series of owners and was divided into smaller holdings, beginning when Garden sold the plantation in two separate transactions. In 1785, he conveyed 339 acres between the public road and the road to Goose Creek Bridge to Ralph Izard, Jr. This land was incorporated into the larger Elms estate. It was in this deed that the plantation was first referred to as "Otranto." When the name "Yeshoe" was changed to "Otranto" is not certain, but Major Garden also conveyed the remainder of the plantation to Robert Reeve Gibbes under the name "Otranto" in 1798.[449] Major Alexander Garden lived his remaining years in Charleston where he died without children in 1829 leaving an estate of household items, 480 books and pamphlets along with fourteen slaves.[450]

Reverend Milward Pogson of St. James, Goose Creek Church resided on the Otranto property for a few years because the original parsonage nearer the church had deteriorated. Pogson purchased the northern tract then sold it to Thomas Gadsden in 1796.[451] Captain Thomas Gadsden was a member of the first regiment of South Carolina infantry commanded by Charles Cotesworth Pinckney during the Revolutionary War.[452] Soon after Pogson sold the northern half, he purchased the southern section from the estate of Thomas R. Waring, but both halves of Otranto were recombined when John Stanyarne Brisbane purchased both and held the tract from 1801 to 1804. It was reported that when John Brisbane's father was banished from Charleston after the Revolution, John hid under the seat of a small passenger boat and returned to shore instead of boarding the ship bound for England.

The four hundred acre parcel with the dwelling and the outbuildings passed through several hands until 1851, when it was conveyed to Philip Porcher who called his home "Goslington." [453] Goslington, meaning "little goose," was the name bestowed upon the location by the Honorable James L. Perigee during a dinner party in the main house. Porcher's daughter, Marion watched Brigadier General R.B. Potter's troops ransack the family home during the Civil War. She later married Arthur Peronneau Ford and moved to Aiken. When asked to visit some new members of the Episcopal Church in Aiken, she refused to visit one of the officers who had ravaged the Otranto home. She said, "I will...with pleasure when they return my silver!"

Photograph 7.2 This photograph shows the Otranto clubhouse c. 1924. The photograph is included in *Johnson's Scrapbook Volume 1*. Today the Otranto clubhouse is surrounded by a residential subdivision. *Courtesy the South Carolina Historical Society.*

After Mr. Porcher's death in 1872, the property was sold to trustees of a hunting club, which was formed that year. The club restored the name "Otranto," a name originally derived from Horace Walpole's gothic novel, *The Castle of Otranto,* published in 1764.[454] The Otranto club held the property longer than any previous owner and used the old dwelling as a clubhouse. During the last decade of the nineteenth century the place was known as "Crovatts" and featured a private racetrack, which started in front of the house and ran in a circle for one mile, in order that guests could sit on the piazza and have a full view of the course and races.[455]

It is not certain when the dwelling was built, but it was probably constructed prior to the American Revolution. According to some historians, Arthur Middleton built the original edifice in the 1670s.[456] The Garden family later made additions in medieval style. The 1672 Culpepper map of Charleston shows remarkable similarities to the basic structure as proof of the earlier origin. Within the house there is a three-sided fireplace that heats the living room, study and kitchen. A colonnade characterizes the home. The slave-built columns are of Italian design. A wide veranda extends on three sides of the house to provide shade during the hot Carolina summers. The structure is probably located on the site of Arthur Middleton's original home. In 1977 the house was named to the National Register of Historic Places.

The charming little house is now surrounded by private homes and condominiums. The ancient live oaks, the avenue of which tradition says was planted by Captain John Cantey, remind contemporary visitors of the grandeur of the place.[457] Brick pillars and an iron gate once marked the entrance to six acres of the old Otranto property that remained undeveloped in twentieth century style until the twenty-first century. This undeveloped section of old Otranto abounded in natural beauty reminiscent of the expansive landscaped gardens of bygone days. Magnolia, dogwood, and

Photograph 7.3 This photograph shows the double tub indigo vat located at the entrance to Mobay Industry at Bushy Park. The vat was disassembled at Otranto and reassembled here in the 1970s. This vat and the remains of one at White House Plantation on Goose Creek are the only known brick vats in South Carolina. The photograph was taken March 7, 2005, and is in the possession of the author.

numerous hardwood trees provided a dense covering for the old site. In the copse of foliage were the remains of a double basin brick indigo vat. This large brick vat was moved to the entrance park of Mobay Industry for preservation and public viewing and is shown in photograph 7.3. Each basin is approximately six feet square. One section is higher in elevation than the other to allow the fluids to flow from the upper basin to the lower.

Plats of the Otranto estate are in the possession of the Charleston Museum and a tracing of a plat is among the collections of the South Carolina Historical Society. The plats show that the public road from Charleston to Goose Creek ran through the eastern quarter of the estate. At the northern border of the estate the road forked. To the west, the road served as a boundary between Otranto's western sections and Ralph Izard's "the Elms," after which the road continued west to Dorchester. To the east, the road served as a boundary between Otranto and the Elms until it crossed the Goose Creek Bridge. Otranto was bordered on the west and south by John Parker's "The Hayes" Plantation. Part of the western property line bordered Woodstock plantation. Near the public road entrance to the Otranto property was what appears to be a circular entrance drive with a central fountain. The drive continued to a collection of buildings known as the "Otranto settlement." A plat of the property shows sections for producing rice, cleared lands for raising provisions, various sections of hard and soft wood forest. A 1784 plat traced by Henry A.M. Smith shows the remains of a tar kiln.[458]

De La Plaines's/Parker's

Two brothers by the name of "Fleury" were French Huguenot immigrants to Goose Creek. One of the brothers, Abraham Fleury de la Plaine arrived in the Province in 1680.[459] By 1704 he received a number of warrants for land totaling 1,390 acres. A large section was situated west of Crowfield and spanned what is today's Interstate Highway 26 to include part of Ladson. Later Isaac Parker acquired this westen section. The plantation consisted of 797 acres when John Purcell surveyed it in 1791. Plat 7.10 shows an avenue leading from the "Road to Dorchester" to the main house and twelve structures, probably for slaves, are noted along the main avenue, as well as a garden and three buildings. A second collection of eight buildings is noted near the Road to Dorchester. The early French Protestants built their church on Abraham Fleury de la Plaine's plantation in the 1680s. The church served a small congregation of Huguenots but records of the church members have not been found. The "Remains of the French Church" is noted in section E of the plat providing the only record of its location.

Although it is not included on partial plat 7.10, the land of John Harleston is shown at the northern boundary of the full plat. The "Harleston house ruins" are indicated on the original plat. John Middleton's Crowfield is noted on the northern boundary, and the "Road to Dorchester" provides the southern boundary. The plantation passed through family ownership until Isaac Parker, acting as executor for William Parker's estate, released the property to George Parker in 1791.[460] These Parkers were not descendants of Abraham Fleury and were not related to the Parkers of "The

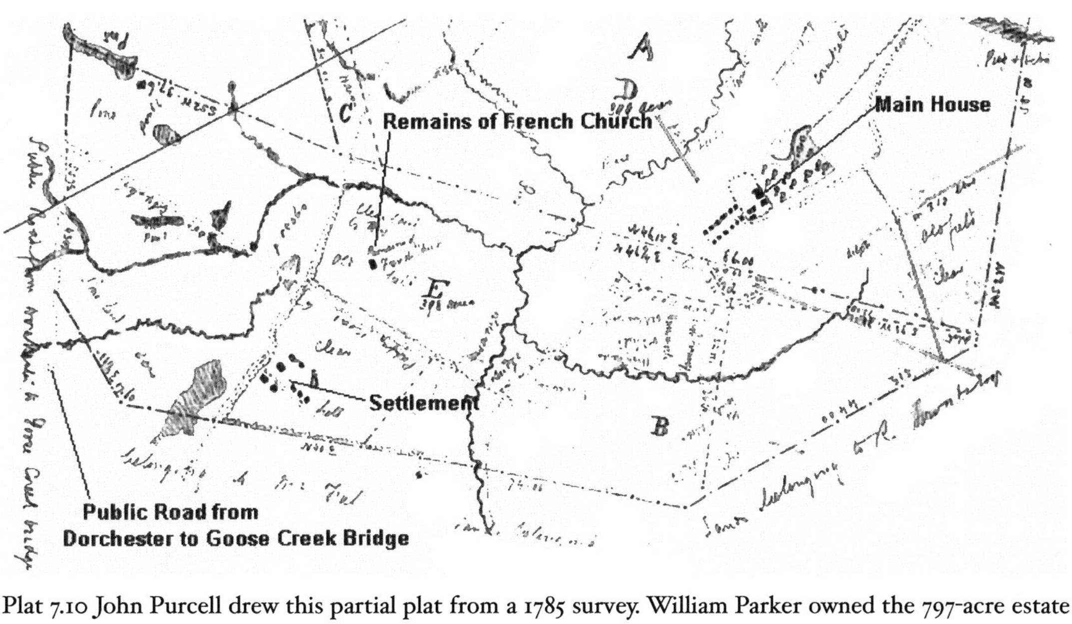

Plat 7.10 John Purcell drew this partial plat from a 1785 survey. William Parker owned the 797-acre estate in 1791 when the land was divided into two tracts. The manuscript labels were added for this publication. H.A.M. Smith traced the original plat. The tracing is among the collections of the South Carolina Historical Society.

Hayes" Plantation. They were Charleston merchants who kept the plantation in the Parker family until 1837 when it was sold to William Washington Ancrum. It changed hands in 1849, and again in 1858 when Lamb Stevens, a freedman, purchased it. Stevens was described as being "nearly coal black," and having unusual capacity and integrity.[461] He purchased his freedom from his master and became owner of the old Parker estate and the adjoining Bacot's "Cherry Hill" estate. He was a successful planter who amassed considerable personal property, which included slaves. As early as 1845, he purchased a slave named Judy and her two children Rachel and Robert.[462] The 1860 census slave schedule reported that he owned seventeen slaves. He was said to have the respect and consideration of his neighbors but like all of the land-holding class in South Carolina, he lost all but his land as a result of the Civil War. Upon his death, he left his property to his children and was buried on the site.

Lamb Stevens appears in the 1860 census as a ninety-seven year old man with a sixty-five year old wife, Elizabeth and a thirteen year old son, Lamb Jr. Historian Henry A.M. Smith visited the site in the early years of the twentieth century, and reported that only a few remaining broken bricks marked the prior location of the old house once occupied by Abraham Fleury and the Parkers. The old French church site was surrounded by land owned by the Orphan Aid Society at the beginning of the twentieth century. The one-acre site upon which the old church rested was conveyed from the Orphan Aid Society to the Huguenot Society, which owns it today.[463]

Photograph 7.4 This 1930 photograph shows the gravestone of Lamb Stevens. The inscription reads: "In Memory of LAMB STEVENS Died 23rd Sept. 1868 Aged 102 Years." The photograph is in *Johnson's Scrapbook Volume 1. Courtesy of the South Carolina Historical Society.*

Boisseau's

Jean Boisseau received a small grant of 210 acres at the head of Yeamans Creek next to Abraham de la Plaine in 1696. In 1705, he received a much larger grant of 2,700 acres near today's town of Summerville.[464] After the death of Boisseau, his widow, Marie, married James Gignilliat. James Gignilliat was titled "clerk" and was probably the minister of the French church situated on De La Plaine's neighboring estate. After their marriage, Mary and James Gignilliat sold half of the tract to Isaac Porcher in 1711, and the remaining half to Jonathan Fitch. Isaac Porcher was the father of Peter Porcher. Peter inherited this land from his father and resided there. Peter served Goose Creek as a tax inquirer and as representative in the Sixteenth Royal Assembly in 1747.[465] He and his wife, Charlotte Marianne, reared five children.

Tobias Fitch, brother of Jonathan, purchased his brother's half of Boisseau's lands in 1716. His wife, Marianne DuGue inherited an 830-acre estate from her father Jacques DuGue and Marianne Fleury. This Goose Creek property, plus inherited land in St. Andrews Parish and 3,323-acres of Proprietary granted land in the Cypress Swamp, made him a wealthy man.[466] Fitch worked to reform the native trade and served Goose Creek as a militia captain. He lived in Goose Creek, represented his home parish seven times and was elected three times to serve other parishes. He died after 1748.[467] Fitch's Goose Creek tract passed to Sir Hoverden Walker, a Knight. The land was then known as "Malling Barony."[468] Map 7.5 shows part of the tract owned by John Boisseau and its

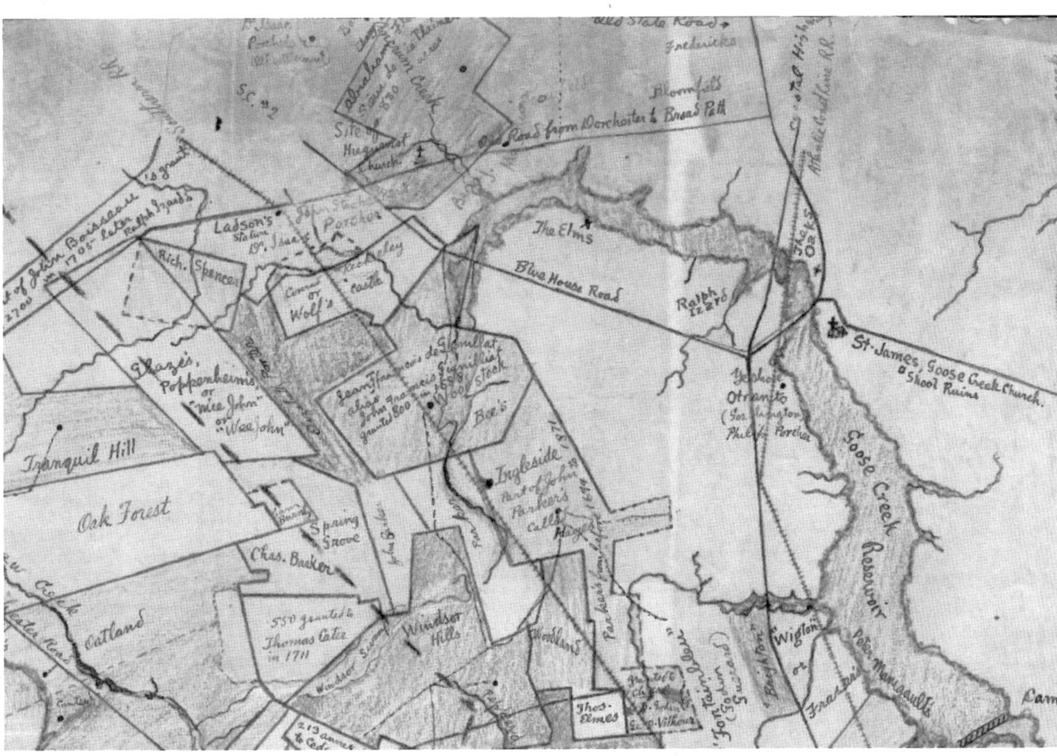

Map 7.5 William Henry Johnson drew this map from his collection of plats. The map is in the *Johnson Scrapbook, Volume 1. Courtesy of the South Carolina Historical Society.*

proximity to other lands. Some of the property in the vicinity was acquired by Ralph Izard to enlarge his Elms Plantation. Ralph Izard annexed 400 acres of Boisseau's tract and the section of Boisseau's tract acquired by Dr. Isaac Porcher was also conveyed to Ralph Izard. These 1,350 acres owned by Izard were named "Spenser's" and is situated today in the Ladson community.

Bacot's/Cherry Hill

Peter Bacot, son of the French immigrant of the same name, acquired property in Goose Creek near Abraham de la Plaine's estate prior to 1720.[469] His earliest acquisition was part of the old Boisseau tract that had already passed through several hands. He also purchased land from Charles Franchomme, elder of the French Church in Charleston. Upon his death, he divided the tract between his two sons from his second wife, Marie Perronneau, with whom he reared four children.

Peter Bacot, the grandson of the immigrant with the same name, lived on his half of the estate and added to it until his death in 1781. Peter Bacot was born in Goose Creek, the son of Peter Bacot and Marie Peronneau. He acquired more than five hundred acres of the original Boisseau tract through inheritance and purchase. The tract became known as "Cherry Hill" or "Bacot's." [470] Bacot kept a house at Cherry Hill but preferred the mercantile business in Charleston to planting.[471] He and his brother-in-law, Charles Dewar, formed a partnership and participated in the fur trade and African slave trade and he was part owner of a sea going ship, *Pallaton.* He served as a paymaster during the Cherokee War and supported the patriots during the Revolutionary War by serving on opposition committees and by loaning £8,000 to the young South Carolina Government. He was banished from Charleston by the British during their occupancy but returned after the war to be elected to the Provincial Congress twice representing St. Philip and St. Michael. He was also elected to represent Goose Creek in the general assembly three times and served on several commissions. His wife, Elizabeth Harramond, bore eleven children, but only six survived childhood.

Peter Bacot died in 1787 leaving an estate that included twenty-two slaves.[472] He devised the use of his house to his widow and divided the land between his two sons, Thomas and Henry Bacot. The 478-acre tract was conveyed to William Gist soon after the death of Peter Bacot III. An 1802 plat refers to the tract as "Cherry Hill" and records the size as larger than 533 acres. Dr. William Smith purchased the property in 1802, and resided there until 1823. Later, the land passed to Lamb Stevens, a free black landowner. Lamb Stevens held the property and the neighboring De La Plaine estate until his death. Henry A.M. Smith visited the property in 1890, but found little of the Cherry Hill main house except the remains of a chimney.

Woodstock

Northwest of the Hayes Plantation was a large estate known as "Woodstock." In 1685, the lord proprietors directed Governor Joseph West to allocate to a Swiss settler, "Mr. Jean Francois (ffrancois) De Ginellat…three thousand Acres of land…"[473] The property passed to John Moore in 1692, then to Edward Rawlins and later to Thomas Bee.[474] Thomas Bee was a member of the South Carolina State House of Representatives, 1778–79, 1786–88; Lieutenant Governor of South Carolina, 1779–80; Delegate to the Continental Congress, 1780–81; member of the South Carolina State Senate,

1788–90; and the first Judge of the United States Court for South Carolina in 1790. Thomas Bee died in 1812, and was buried in the family cemetery on the property. Upon his death, Woodstock estate was devised, with all the household furniture and stock, to his son, Bernard E. Bee. Bernard E. Bee departed his Woodstock estate in 1836 and became a resident of Texas. Later the St. James, Goose Creek Church Vestry acquired his Texas land, sold it and used the proceeds to fund the education of Goose Creek children.[475] "Bee School" appears on some maps of the early nineteenth century. The school was located on Red Bank Road near the St. James Church on the lands purchased much earlier for educational purposes.

Bernard E. Bee's son, Bernard E. Bee Jr. was a graduate of West Point and an officer in the United States Army. He served as a Brigadier General in the army of the Confederate States of America and was killed at the first battle of Manassas in 1861. In 1886, Judge Henry A.M. Smith visited the plantation site and found little of the structures remaining. The old family mansion house was situated near the South Carolina Railway line. A number of oaks shaded the main house, which was a large wooden structure in colonial style, with tall brick pillars on the front portico. In the 1880s, there remained large gardens on the grounds where rice was produced and there was a drainage canal from the rice field to Goose Creek. The 1886 earthquake destroyed most of the house, and by the twentieth century the structure, as well as the gardens were barely discernable.

Keckley's

Next to Woodstock was "Keckley's" plantation, once the original home of John Bulline. The small tract of 350 acres was the composite of three sections of 200, 100 and 50 acres.[476] John Bulline's nephew acquired the property and held it until he died in 1762. Upon his death, the tract was sold to Paul Smizer who conveyed the land to Conrad Keckley in 1771. Conrad Keckley kept the land until he died in 1789, at which time the property transferred to his three sons. His will stated that he resided on this tract, and the 1790 census, taken one year after his death, lists his widow, Jane Keckley as a Goose Creek resident. The three sons were not included in the 1790 census and thus apparently resided outside the parish at that time. Michael Keckley, a son of Conrad and Jane received all interests in the plantation in 1803, which had expanded to 420 acres. Upon Michael's death in 1830, the land passed to his four children. The main house stood near the old Ladson train station, where Ladson Road intersects the railroad tracks today. The Keckely family burial site markers stood within a graveyard protected by a brick wall near the end of the nineteenth century.[477]

Charles Barker's/Spring Grove

Southwest of Woodstock, on the St. James/St. George Parish line was a large tract of land once known as "Barker's" and later known as "Spring Grove." In 1704, a warrant was arranged for Thomas Barker.[478] In 1711, two grants totaling 1,245 acres were awarded to Sarah Barker, the widow of Thomas. Fourteen years later, Sarah Barker gave the tract to her son, Charles Barker who resided on the land until he died in 1755. An unclear title chain resulted when the land was divided among siblings, and a series of unrecorded transfers and deeds followed. The title was reestablished when the entire tract was sold to John Glaze in 1776. More owners held and transferred the land until Thomas Young bought it in 1784. He added 302 acres, which increased his large holding to 1,494 acres. He and his wife sold the northern section to Martha Godin, the widow of Isaac Godin of Fountainbleau. This land passed from Martha Godin to her daughter, Martha Godin Stewart. Martha Stewart sold the tract to Mary Legge and Elizabeth Porter in 1793. The Keckley family acquired the Spring Grove section prior to 1790. Jane Keckley appears on the 1790 census as a head of a three-member household with two her daughters, both of who were under 16 years of age. Jane was the widow of Conrad Keckley. Her two daughters married and transferred the property through their extended families including Margaret Egan Solan who bequeathed the tract to her two daughters in 1802. In her will, the property was referred to as "Spring Grove." The Solan sisters kept Spring Grove for fifty years, but the site remained associated with the Keckley family and held the Keckley family burial grounds. [479]

When Thomas Young sold the northern section of the plantation to Martha Godin, he retained the southern section, which consisted of 694 acres. Although he does not appear on the St. James, Goose Creek census in 1790, he reportedly resided on the St. James section of the old Barker's estate until his death in 1797. At that time, the land was conveyed to Archibald McKewn. The 1824 tax return shows that Archibald McKewn resided on 694 acres and owned 13 slaves in Goose Creek.[480] He was buried at the St. James, Goose Creek Church.

Glaze's/Poppenheim's/Wee John's/Strohecker's

Next to the Barker's estate was Glaze's Plantation. The original 500-acre grant was made to Samuel Sumner in 1705. Malachi Glaze purchased the tract in 1723 and lived on the plantation until he died in 1740. He devised the land to his four living sons. One son, John Glaze acquired the entire estate: his quarter portion as well as his brothers' three-quarters portion.[481] He eventually amassed 693 acres and devised all of it to his son, John Glaze. The son and his wife, Margaret, sold the tract to John Benfield and later Lewis Poppenheim purchased the tract in 1794.

Lewis Poppenheim was a Bavarian "soldier of fortune." He fought with the British army during the American Revolution, but when the British army evacuated Charleston in 1780, he remained and eventually purchased property on Cooper River and in the city of Charleston. His only son was a thirteen-year-old named John who sailed to Charleston from England upon his father's request. This young John Poppenheim remained in Goose Creek to become a successful planter and the father of Dr. John Frederick Poppenheim. Dr. John F. Poppenheim lived and died at his plantation known as "Gallant Hill," on the nearby headwaters of Goose Creek, south of the Elms but the family called the original Poppenheim Plantation "Wee John," so named after the thirteen-year-old son of the Bavarian soldier.[482]

The plantation lands were later purchased by John Strohecker and was known by his name for many years. "Wee John" or "Strohecker's" eventually consisted of 4,004 acres located about a quarter mile from Ladson Station.

Faucheraud

According to the February 12, 1737 issue of the *South Carolina Gazette*, Gideon Faucheraud settled in Goose Creek in 1707 and accumulated property for twenty years until the many tracts amounted to more than three thousand acres. He lived on his estate from 1707 until 1753.[483] In his will, he bequeathed some wealth to the French Church in Charleston for poor French people and he left all of his lands to his wife, Mary, and at her death, to their only son, Charles Faucheraud. Charles could have been the wealthiest planter in the province, but his mother survived him and he never inherited the large estate.[484] Regardless, he was a wealthy man. He married Jane Smith, daughter of George Smith of Goose Creek and resided with his bride in the large framed dwelling on the one hundred fifty acre Bacot's plantation section of Faucheraud. Later he moved into the large brick mansion that was the main house for the estate. He owned one thousand acres at Wassamasaw, and in 1760 acquired another four hundred undeveloped acres by way of a grant.[485]

Charles Faucheraud served Goose Creek as a churchwarden, tax collector, and supporter of the Ludlam School fund. He also served in the Royal Assembly in 1757–1760. When he died in 1766, he freed two of his eighty-one slaves and bequeathed to each ten acres, a house and an annual income. One of the freed slaves, a mulatto woman, received an annual payment eighty pounds for the duration of her life.[486] His land was divided between his two daughters, Mary Allston and Elizabeth Faucheraud. The land was owned by their extended families and divided and shared, but Cashwell Mims reconstituted it when he acquired all of the original lands of Gideon Faucheraud through several purchases in 1848. Henry A.M. Smith visited the ruins in 1890 and found brick remnants of the house and chimney, but the gardens were overgrown and not discernable.[487]

The Hayes / Inglesides

West of and adjoining Otranto and Fountainbleau lay "The Hayes," (sometimes "Hayes") the beautiful plantation home of the Parker family. John Parker immigrated to Carolina in the early 1700s from Jamaica. He received a land grant in 1702 for the land that he resided upon and named "The Hayes." Upon his death he left his estate to his widow, Sarah Parker, and their son, John Parker. The Hayes became a successful inland rice plantation of 1,166 acres on the headwaters of Goose Creek. John Parker Jr. acquired thirty-four slaves along with the land and purchased an additional 216 contiguous acres. He resided there until his death in 1802.[488]

John Parker (1735–1802), the son, enjoyed a long political career. He represented Goose Creek in the Royal Assembly, Provincial Congress and general assembly from 1761 to 1776. He represented the parish of St. John Colleton in 1767. Parker actively supported the patriot's cause during the years leading to the American Revolution, as well as during the war. He loaned £100,000 to the state, as well as supplies to the state militia and continental troops.[489] He married Susannah Middleton and at the time of the Revolution, British marauders fired upon Susannah as she stood in her doorway, but the musket ball missed and struck the wall, where its mark could be seen for many years thereafter.[490] After the war he held a number of commissions, contributed to the Ludlam School, and was active with the St. James, Goose Creek Church. He and his wife reared eight children. Prior to his death, he requested that he be buried simply, "all pomp and ostentation [to] be carefully avoided..."[491]

John Parker (1759–1832) the grandson of the immigrant also resided at the Hayes after the death of his father. He was a member of congress from 1774 to 1787. After his death, the property remained in the family for many years until it was conveyed to Professor Francis S. Holmes.[492] Although an advertisement for its sale appeared June 6, 1771 in the *Gazette,* the Hayes Estate from the first property

Photograph 7.5 This photograph shows the Hayes Plantation situated on the headwaters of Goose Creek. The photograph is in the *Johnson Scrapbook, Volume 1. Courtesy of the South Carolina Historical Society.*

Photograph 7.6 This photograph shows Francis Holmes in his study at the Inglesides' (The Hayes) main house. The photograph is in the *Johnson Scrapbook, Volume 1. Courtesy of the South Carolina Historical Society.*

grants in 1702 until its sale to Francis Holmes in 1871, remained in the Parker family for 169 years. A marble memorial of John Parker, the immigrant, John Parker, the son and John Parker, the grandson, is displayed in the St. James, Goose Creek Church.

Francis Simmons Holmes is shown in photograph 7.6. He served as a professor at the College of Charleston until the Civil War. During the Civil War, he was appointed as officer in connection with coastal defense, and served as Chief of the Nitre and Mining Bureau in South Carolina and Georgia. After the war, he used his knowledge and experience gained in the defense industry to develop the fertilizer industry so that the commercial success of Charleston's fertilizer industry is credited to the work and achievements of Professor Holmes.

The Hayes Plantation was renamed "Ingleside" during Professor Holmes's occupation and it acquired a reputation for its beautiful lake and gardens. Professor Holmes provided information for the December issue of the *Harper's Magazine* in 1875, wherein descriptions of ornamental plants were given, especially the "Sacred Lily of the East" that "grows in profusion" on the seventy-five acre lake. Twenty-three years later (1898) Ann Simons Deas described the main house at Ingleside Plantation about half a mile from the marlpits near the South Carolina Railroad. She described the entrance road as a "mere cart-track through the old field...over a causeway skirting the reserve-or 'lake' as they grandly style it..."[493]

The front door opened directly from the large front porch into a spacious parlor, which was adorned with ornamental hand-carved woodwork. Each floor had four rooms that were wainscoted halfway to the ceiling and featured deep, low window seats. The shutters were solid wood and painted white. The cellar was a slightly excavated basement with an entrance under the back porch, and was apparently used as a kitchen pantry.[494] According to tradition, the extremely thick and heavy back door was built to resist native attacks during the colonial days. A wide expanse of lawn extended from the front door to the Parker burial plot where a marble shaft once marked the final resting site, but has since been moved to the cemetery at St. James, Goose Creek Church.

Photograph 7.7 This photograph shows the monument that marked the burial location of John Parker in the family burial grounds at the Hayes Plantation. The monument is located today in the yard of the St. James, Goose Creek Church. The photograph was taken March 7, 2005, and is in the possession of the author.

From the back of the house, the land sloped to a lake, which served as a reservoir for irrigating the rice field. A large tree, near the lake is called, "Marion's Oak." Tradition claims it was a meeting place for Francis Marion and his patriots during the revolutionary war.[495] Today, large cypress trees, cypress knees and mature moss-draped oaks surround the lake and large oaks remain scattered on the spacious well-kept grounds. Photograph 7.7 shows the ruins of the house in 1920. Today the outline of the house remains recognizable, but the walls are crumbled to a height of only two or three feet. A brick basement floor is still in place, and part of an arched fireplace in the cellar is intact (see photograph 7.8). The remaining brick walls indicate that the house was forty-five feet long and forty feet wide. The plantation property is protected by gates, which feature decorative, leaping horse figures. "No Trespassing" signs appear at the end of the state maintained frontage road near the Ashley Phosphate exit on Interstate Highway I-26.

Woodlands

John Parker of the Hayes Plantation and son of John Parker, the immigrant conveyed the 932-acre estate and dwelling house to his eldest son, also named John Parker. He devised 234 acres of the original Hayes Estate along with other tracts he acquired to Thomas Parker, his second son. This 451-acre tract was named "Woodlands." Thomas Parker was an attorney, and for some years served as U.S. District Attorney for South Carolina. He added 202 contiguous acres to his tract. He married

Photograph 7.8 This photograph shows the Hayes ruins in April 2003. The photograph is in the possession of the author.

Mary Drayton, daughter of William Henry Drayton and she acquired Woodlands when Thomas died. The widow conveyed the 653-acre tract to Edward H. Edwards in 1824. The land depreciated as did most Goose Creek estates during the 1800s and was bought and sold several times before it was subdivided and absorbed by neighboring farms.[496]

Brick House / Martindale's

A Parker/Barker relationship resulted when John Parker Sr. emigrated from Jamaica and died soon after arriving in South Carolina. His widow Sarah and first son, also named John Parker, survived him. Sarah remarried Thomas Barker, a neighboring planter. Thomas Barker's estate began as a 1,200-acre Proprietary grant in 1704 and was acquired by Sarah Barker when he died. Upon Sarah's death in 1729, the Barker land passed to her son, John Parker Jr. of the Hayes Plantation. Thus at that time, John Parker Jr. owned both Parker and Barker lands. Soon after inheriting his mother's plantation, he sold the main house where she lived and 412.5 acres of the Barker tract to Benjamin Wood.[497] John Parker Jr. appears to have retained ownership of the remaining section of the Barker Plantation until his death, when it passed to his son and upon the son's death to Benjamin Wood's daughter.

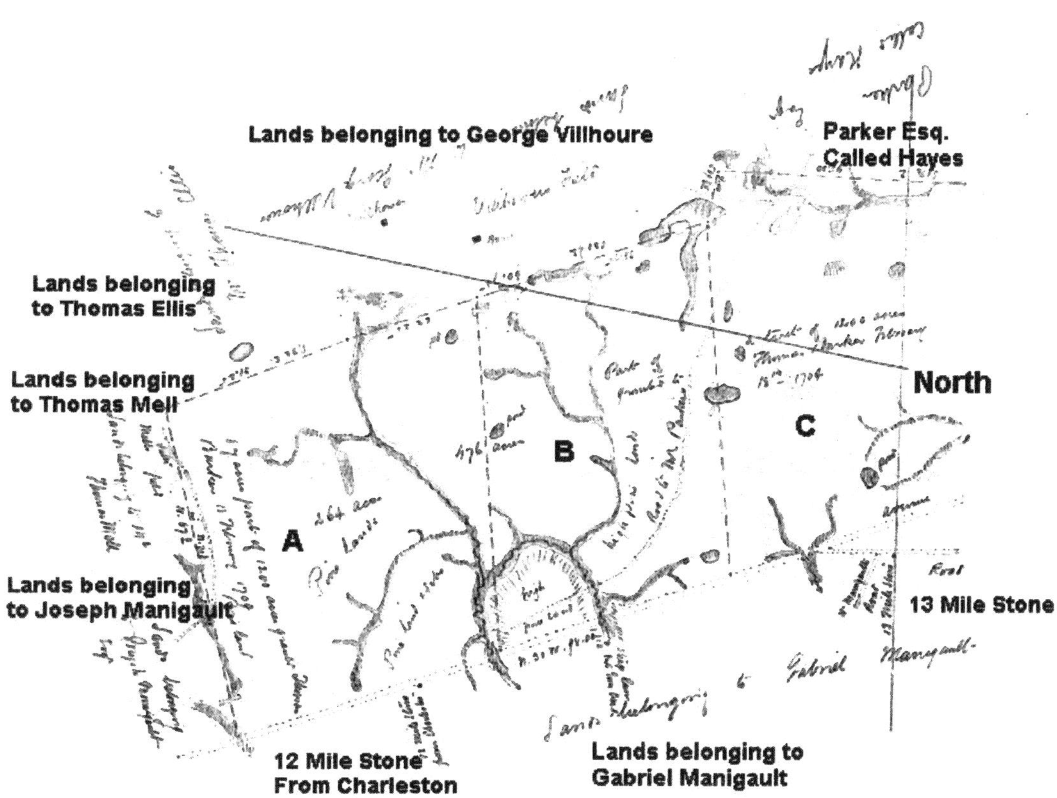

Plat 7.11 H.A.M. Smith traced this plat from the original. The tracing is among the collections of the South Carolina Historical Society. No date or name of the surveyor appears on the map.

In 1789, the records indicate that Thomas Ellis owned the old Barker Plantation but later, the land passed through several hands until James Moore purchased the 634-acre section in 1813. At the time of that purchase, the old Barker lands were known as "Brick House." In 1819, James Moore sold the tract to James C. Martindale, and in 1836, Brick House was sold to William J. Sineath, discussed earlier in this chapter. Henry A.M. Smith visited the Brick House home site near the end of the nineteenth century. He described the location at the Midland Park Southern Railway Station, but reported that only brick scatters remained of the old settlement. Plat 7.11 describes the land along 1.5 mile length of the Broad Path. The 12-mile and 13-mile stones, as well as the north orientation, and the manuscript labels of land ownership were added to this publication because the handwriting on the original plat is small and difficult to read. This plat notes, "Lands belonging to Gabriel Manigault" near the right margin. Manigault's Steepbrook tract was situated to the east of Brick House and the main avenue of Steepbrook intersected the public road near the 13-mile stone. The avenue is noted on the plat as "Mr. Manigault's Road." "Lands belonging to Joseph Manigault," "Lands belonging to Thomas Mell" and "Lands belonging to Thomas Ellis" are noted near the left margin.

"Villhouer," "Villhouer's Field" and "Barn" adjacent to one structure appears near the upper margin. The words "Parker Esq. called Hayes" appear at the upper right corner. The accumulation of lands and transactions between the Barker and Parker families and their neighbors is clarified with the descriptive notations on the plat. Notations describe the three divisions of the land, and each tract is notated as it relates to the original Barker grants in 1704 and is labeled "A," "B," and "C" in this publication for clarity. The tract labeled as "A" contained lands that were part of the original 1,200 acres granted to Thomas Barker in 1704. Tract "B" contains 476 acres of the original Barker grant of 1704 and section "C" contains 218 acres of the Barker lands granted in 1703. The plat also shows a path from the public road that crosses the Barker property in tracts "B" and "C" from center left to upper right, and is noted as "Road to Mr. Parkers." This road intersects with the public road at the "high ground." This high ground was probably the location of the 12-Mile House.

Thomas Mell's

Contiguous to Brick House and Fountainbleau was an estate composed of a number of tracts, called "Thomas Mell's." Records of small grants of land to Mell on the north and south sides of Goose Creek, and on the Ashley River appear as early as 1677. Mell finally amassed approximately 600 acres on the south side of Goose Creek, near the public road. He died in 1759, devising less than 300 acres to each of his two sons. The land was increased by the sons and remained in the Mell family throughout the eighteenth century. Some old maps show a considerable number of buildings on the property. William Mell, acting as executor for Thomas Mell, sold a 940 acre tract to Reverend Thomas Frost in 1799.[498] The estate passed through many more hands during the 1800s and was eventually sold in small parcels.

Thomas Elmes

South of the Barker estate was once part of Thomas Elmes's tract. Elmes received this land from George Cantey through marriage to his daughter, Elizabeth in 1692. Cantey was one of the earliest

Goose Creek settlers. When Thomas Elmes died in 1724, he left his estate to his widow and children, and according to a 1764 plat, the tract contained 523 acres and remained in the name of "Thomas Elmes." At that time, John Parker's Hayes Estate bounded the Elmes tract on the north and east, and Captain Ainslei's Windsor Hill Plantation and Mell's estate bounded the tract on the west. A 1786 plat shows the tract belonging to Robert Simmons, who is listed in the 1790 census with ten slaves.

Windsor Hill

Windsor Hill is a prominent land rising fifty feet over freshwater swamps at the headwaters of Goose Creek. The hill is easy to find today. It stands 1.2 miles west of Ashley Phosphate Road and 2.5 miles from the intersection of Ashley Phosphate Road with Interstate Highway 26. This interesting hill is bordered on three sides by a freshwater swamp and was well suited for inland rice production, but the hill is best remembered as the burial ground of Major General and Governor William Moultrie. The original five hundred acre grant was awarded to James Child in 1701. He increased his lands by three hundred acres and upon his death; Child devised eight hundred acres with a house and outbuildings to his son Benjamin. The ownership passed to John Ainslie when he married Mary Child, daughter of Benjamin.[499]

Hannah Ainslie inherited the plantation in 1776 from her father.[500] When William Moutrie, son of the general married Hannah he became joint owner of Windsor Hill. William, like his father, earned an impressive public service record. He was a Second Lieutenant in the 2nd Regiment in 1775, and was promoted to Captain. His grave marker indicates that he rose to the rank of Major. In 1781, he was elected to the House of Representatives for the new State of South Carolina. He died prior to his father in 1796, and was buried at Windsor Hill.

William Moultrie, the father of William was born in Charleston in 1730, and was notable for his political and military career. Major General and Governor William Moultrie, is best remembered for his heroic defense of Sullivan's Island when the American forces repelled the British. He fought in numerous battles until the British captured him when they occupied Charleston. He was later released as part of a prisoner exchange and promoted to Major General. Prior to the war, he served in The Commons House of Assembly, and as a captain, he fought in the Cherokee War. He was elected to the Commons House of Assembly several times and was a member of the first General Assembly of the State of South Carolina. William Moultrie was a member of the Legislative Council, and in 1778, was elected as the first Senator from St. Johns Parish. In 1785 and 1794, he was elected governor of South Carolina and served two, two-year terms. He died in 1805, while under investigation for impeachment.[501] He was buried next to his son on Windsor Hill. The Moultrie family Bible states, "General William Moultrie was buried at Windsor Hill, next to his son at his earnest request."

The Moultrie family occupied the plantation from approximately 1790 to 1830.[502] The general's granddaughter, Eliza Charlotte Moultrie, married Edward Brailsford and the Brailsford family sold the plantation in 1837. Near the end of the nineteenth century, Joseph Ioor Waring explored the grounds and recorded the cemetery markers for publication in the *South Carolina Historic and Genealogical Magazine.*

The Institute of Anthropology and Archaeology at the University of South Carolina conducted a study at Windsor Hill in 1976. The house had burned in 1850, leaving an archaeological time capsule of that period. Consequently, the archaeological team found the foundation of the main house, as well as the remains of a kitchen and a chimney. Also remains of dikes, ditches and drains were identified in the old rice fields. Additionally, the cemetery with a number of marked graves was uncovered in thick brush and the family bodies and possibly the bodies of slaves were identified. General Moultrie's remains were moved to Fort Moultrie on Sullivan's Island, so that they could be properly protected. A marker identifies the burial site today near the Museum parking lot. The remains of the other family members were re-interred in the St. James, Goose Creek Church grounds where their markers may be read.

The Elms

The Elms was the original settlement of the Izard family. This plantation was situated northwest of Otranto and northeast of Hayes and Woodstock. Ralph Izard immigrated to Carolina in 1682, and twenty-two years later, purchased 250 acres from John Francis Gignilliat. This was the beginning of the Izard Plantation.[503] He increased his holdings to 581 acres before he devised it to his eldest son, Ralph. Ralph Izard II was also a successful planter and increased the Elms Plantation to 2,736-acres by the time of his death in 1743. In addition to the Elms, he owned nine other plantations and 171 slaves. He was elected twice to represent Goose Creek in the assembly and four times to serve neighboring districts. During his tenure in the assembly, he supported the movement to make South Carolina a Royal Province and was eventually appointed to the Royal Council. He also served in a number of commissioner posts. He and his wife, Magdalene Chastaigner reared eight children.[504]

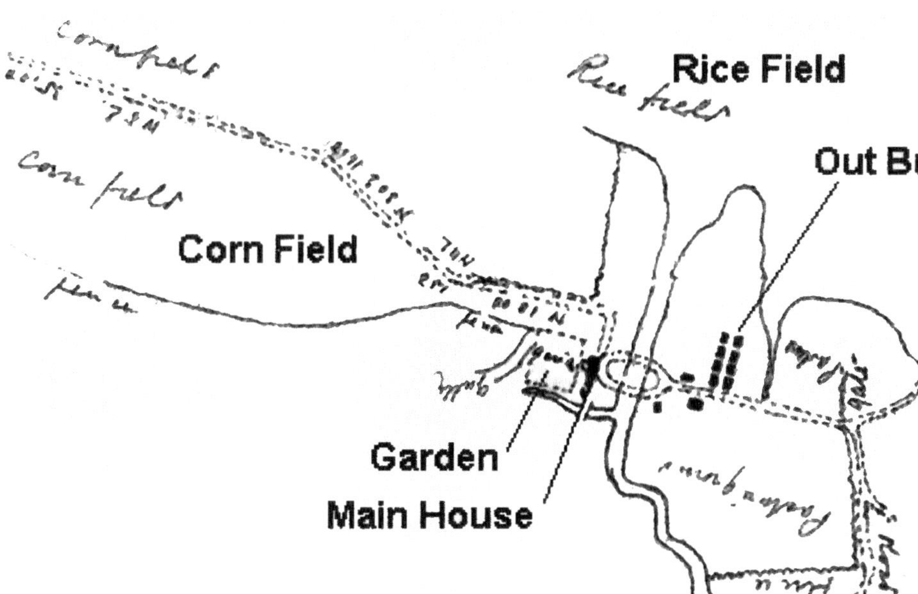

Plat 7.12 This partial plat of the Elms was drawn from a survey of 925 acres in 1796. The manuscript labels were added for this publication. The original plat was traced by H.A.M. Smith and is among the collections of the South Carolina Historical Society.

Ralph Izard's son, Henry Izard, was born at the Elms, and inherited that estate, as well as five other plantations, including The Camp on the Charleston neck. He worked 239 slaves on his lands and lived at The Camp until his father died, when he relocated to the main house at the Elms. He contributed to the Ludlam school fund, served as churchwarden at the St. James, Goose Creek Church, and was elected six times to represent Goose Creek in the Royal Assemblies. He and his first wife, Margaret Johnson had two children, Ralph and Margaret. He and his second wife, Charlotte Broughton had two children, Nathaniel and Charlotte, both of whom died young.[505]

Henry Izard died in 1747. His only living son, Ralph III, was formally educated in England and attended Christ Church Cambridge University before returning to Goose Creek in 1764. He inherited the Elms and Fredericks Plantations in Goose Creek, as well as The Camp, but he resided at the Elms, which he improved and expanded. He also owned over two thousand additional acres on Goose Creek, part of which were once Otranto lands, as well as additional lands from the neighboring estate of the late Benjamin Marion, father of the famous patriot, Francis Marion.[506] He was a "gentleman of great property" who owned five large tracts in other parishes and was listed in the 1790 census with 602 slaves. [507]

Plat 7.12 shows the Elms, as surveyed in 1796. The plat shows an avenue terminating with a circular drive at the main house. A garden is indicated behind the main house. The avenue skirted a double row of eight outbuildings, which may have been a slave settlement. A single outbuilding flanked the main house and three more buildings were situated along the avenue. A "Road to the Dorchester Road" intersected the avenue on the original plat. The Elms was bordered to the east by Otranto Plantation, to the south by the Hayes Plantation, to the west by Conrad Keckley's land and to the north by Crowfield. Another plat drawn during this period describes 172 acres of rice fields and five acres set aside for the "Garden." This plat also described land with rye, oats, corn, and pasture.

Ralph Izard III was one of the outstanding men of Goose Creek who served his parish and country in many ways. He lived for a short time in London where he became the friend of Edmund Burke, the great English statesman, who had advocated conciliation in the dispute with the American colonies. Ralph Izard, Benjamin Franklin and Arthur Lee met in London for the purpose of presenting petitions to the parliament and the king, opposing unfavorable British laws in America.[508] While Izard was in London, the Continental Congress appointed him Commissioner to the Grand Duke of Tuscany. The government of Tuscany would not receive him, so Izard stayed in Paris where he became unofficially involved in negotiations for an American alliance with France. Upon his return to the United States, he arrived in Philadelphia and used his influence to persuade George Washington to appoint Nathaniel Green as commander of the southern army. He loaned the government £152,500 to help with the war effort. He was selected to serve as a representative in the Fourth General Assembly for Goose Creek, and that body selected him as a delegate to the Confederation Congress. Thus he remained involved with the national government until the end of the Revolutionary War. Upon his return to South Carolina in 1783, he again resided at his Goose Creek home, the Elms. A letter to Thomas Jefferson dated April 27, 1784, indicates that he was content in Goose Creek. He wrote, "I am settled upon an agreeable spot about 18 miles from Charles Town. A plantation long neglected but pleasantly situated and capable of improvement." He continued in the same letter to inform Thomas Jefferson that he never again intended to "enter into public life."[509] He did however return to public life when he was elected to represent Goose Creek in the Fifth, Sixth, Seventh, and Eighth General Assemblies. He was twice elected to the Privy Council, and to the United States Senate in 1789 where he served for one session as President *pro tempore.*

Working in alliance with his sons-in-law and fellow Goose Creekers Gabriel Manigault and William Laughton Smith, he wielded a great amount of political power while in the Senate. He stayed a firm ally of the Federalist political faction and remained influential nationally until Thomas Jefferson and his Democrats ascended to power. After his six-year Senate tour, he retired to Goose Creek. In 1795, the Duke de la Rochefoucault-Liancourt visited him in Goose Creek. At the time of the visit Izard owned about five hundred slaves, but kept only twenty-five to thirty to work three hundred or four hundred of the fourteen hundred acres at the Elms. According to the Count, Izard's "mansion" (drawing 7.2) was merely "a country house" but the home was pleasantly designed and charmly set among "a fine plantation of Elm trees" from which the name was derived.[510]

The Elms was a working plantation. Ralph Izard planted about one hundred acres of rice and three hundred acres of Indian corn, potatoes and barley, but the Izards also lived in lavish style. While Izard and his wife, Anne DeLancey of New York, were in Rome, Italy in 1775, John Singleton Copley, the celebrated American artist, painted their portrait.[511] Mr. Izard entertained the French General La Fayette very lavishly during his tour of the country. One of the octagonal wings of the Elms house was renovated into an elegant entertainment hall, where La Fayette spent the night. Afterwards that room of the house was known as "La Fayette Lodge." Ralph Izard died in 1804 at the age of sixty-two, and was buried in the St. James Church yard. His eldest son, Henry (1771–1826) inherited the 1,717 acres at the Elms. He was elected to the house and served Goose Creek in the Thirteenth and Fourteenth General Assemblies. As a senator, he represented Goose Creek in the Sixteenth and Seventeenth General Assemblies. He later represented the Charleston parishes. He married Emma Philadelphia Middleton and had nine children.[512] Henry Izard resided at the Elms until his death in December 1826, after which the Elms was sold to Jacob Barrett in 1831.[513]

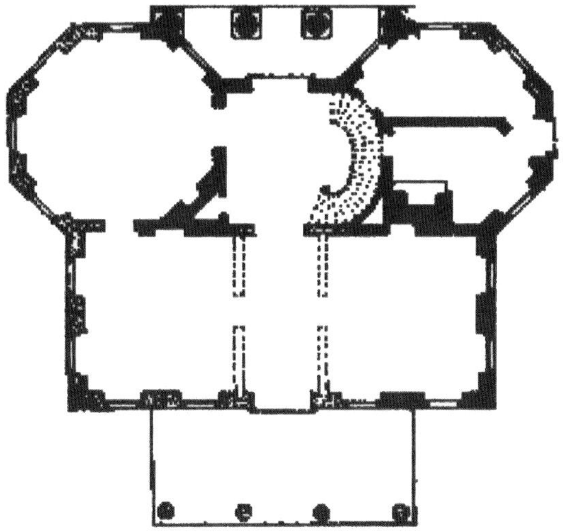

Drawing 7.2 This drawing shows the ground floor plan of the Elms in 1810. The two octagon wings and four front columns are apparent. The drawing was taken from, *Plantations of the Lowcountry* by Samuel Gaillard Stoney.

Photograph 7.9 This photograph shows the ruins of the Elms Plantation circa 1930. The photograph is in the *Johnson Scrapbook, Volume I. Courtesy of the South Carolina Historical Society*.

George Izard, the second son after Henry, acquired a portion of the Elms after his father's death. George was an officer in the United States Army and earned the rank of Major General during the war of 1812. Afterward he was Governor of the Territory of Arkansas. George Izard's section of the original Elms passed in 1858 to Lewis Cannon.

The Izard family enjoyed a number of country homes, living in good houses with fine gardens and grounds of taste and beauty.[514] The 1824 tax return for Henry Izard showed that he owned 3,042 acres and ninety slaves in the Goose Creek Parish.[515] When Henry inherited the Elms he also inherited the 1,200 acres at The Camp. The house called "The Camp" was built in 1718 near the Broad Path and the 10-Mile House. The family arms were embossed in plaster on various parts of the exterior. It was the one time home of General George Izard who recorded in his autobiographical sketch that the house at the camp, "Which I remember when I was a boy was burned before the year 1789, it had been some years the residence of the overseer." [516] "The venerable edifice at the

Elms underwent the same tale about twenty years afterwards and has been replaced by one of more modern construction by my brother Henry within a few years."[517]

The Izard family was able to maintain the prosperous appearance of the Goose Creek estate longer than most of the neighbors, but the grand structures declined during the nineteenth century and almost all the evidence of the beauty and luxury of the Elms had disappeared by the dawn of the twentieth century.[518] Dr. Joseph Ioor Waring recorded that all that remained of the old house near the end of the nineteenth century was "a single, tall column of the lofty porch, standing like a monument over its departed glory." [519] Dr. Waring noted that the site was overgrown and found it difficult to locate a path to the mainhouse, but he noted that the overgrown forest near the ruins of the house sprung forth in the spring of the year with bulbs and garden plants that marked the site of the old flower gardens.[520] Also nearby was an adobe fort. The remains of the peculiar structure indicated that it was designed for defense against Native Americans. Blocks composed of clay mixed with straw were stacked to make walls about ten feet high. The clay, when hardened by the sun, formed a remarkably solid wall. Loopholes for aiming and firing muskets were cut through the walls on all sides of the fort.[521]

The house finally crumbled into a mass of brick amidst a tangle of trees and vines (photograph 7.9). Today, part of the foundation, with the bases of some columns and the hexagonal design is still discernable. A few shrubs and ornamental trees remained on the garden terraces when Henry A.M. Smith visited during close of the nineteenth century. He found a nutmeg hickory tree that Andre Michaux may have noted in his journal many years earlier. Michaux recorded that he had learned about a Nutmeg Hickory only by a handful of nuts given to him in 1802, by the gardener of Henry Izard at the Elms.[522] This species of hickory, according to Smith, was not found anywhere else. Judge Smith wondered, during his investigation of the site, if the tree was the same sampled by the botanist, Michaux, or a lone survivor of the one time extravagant Elms shrubbery. Today, a botanist at the nearby Charleston Southern University continues to find varieties of rare plants in the forest that is the remnants of the ancient Izard gardens. [523]

Like the Elms, the Izard family has nearly vanished, but in the Museum of Fine Arts in Boston hangs a large double portrait of Mr. and Mrs. Ralph Izard, painted by John Singleton Copley. The Izards intermarried with a number of families, including the family of the last Royal Governor but the Izard name disappeared from the Lowcountry. A memorial tablet, and Ralph Izard's hatchment may be seen on the balcony face in the St. James, Goose Creek Church. Part of the northern portion of the Elms estate came into the possession of Dr. Eli Geddings, a well-respected Charleston physician. Later the Charleston Commission of Public Works, Charleston Southern University and numerous commercial and residential developers purchased the various tracts.

Estates on the North Side of Goose Creek

Crowfield

The beautiful Crowfield Plantation was one of the most extensive plantations of colonial Carolina. It was built on the headwaters of Goose Creek and was second only to Middleton Place on the Ashley River in its beauty and expansiveness. Crowfield was a Middleton estate that featured elegant landscaped gardens, ponds, and a fine brick mansion long before Middleton Place was built on the Ashley River. The original eighteen acre tract of property later known as "Crowfield" was granted to John Berringer in 1701. The land belonging to Abraham de la Plaine was situated to the south, the lands owned by Benjamin Marion was to the west, Robert Metlock owned the property on the southeast and James Beard owned the property to the north.

It appears that Berringer emigrated from Barbados, but lived on his Goose Creek estate for only a short time, because in 1703–04 he accompanied his relative, Colonel James Moore, on a military expedition against the Appalachia natives as a captain and was killed.[524] Berringer's sister, Mary, received the estate. Mary Berringer and her husband resided in Barbados and conveyed the South Carolina property to Col. John Gibbes.[525]

Colonel John Gibbes was a man of some prestige in Barbados where he was elected a member of the Assembly several times. He moved to South Carolina, and may have resided on his newly acquired Goose Creek estate before he died in 1711, and was buried in St. James, Goose Creek Church. A tablet was placed in the church in his memory, along with his coat of arms. Unfortunately, the 1886 earthquake destroyed the coat of arms.[526] After the death of Col. John Gibbes, his son John inherited the property. The second John Gibbes married Anne Broughton, the daughter of Thomas Broughton of Mulberry Plantation on the Cooper River. He held the property until 1722, when he divided and conveyed it in sections. Arthur Middleton purchased 1,440 acres for £4,000.[527] This land passed from Arthur Middleton to his eldest son, William in 1727 who resided at Crowfield.

The avenue to the Crowfield main house connected it to Ladson Road, a public road that carried traffic from the State Road (State Highway 176) to the Elms Plantation and on to Ladson. Today, a power line easement follows the old Ladson roadway and parallels Westview Boulevard for a short distance. Early records indicate that there was an expansive lawn and garden area (drawing 7.5). Eliza Lucas visited the Crowfield gardens in 1740, and provided an elaborate description of the property. She recorded that the house stood a mile from, but in sight of the road, and made, "a very handsome appearance." She found brick walls that lined elaborate gardens and a large pond "situated in the midst of a spacious green." A wide walk reached a thousand feet from the back door of the elegantly furnished house onto wide expanses of lawn and live oaks.[528] William Middleton, the builder of the Crowfield mansion, was the son of Arthur Middleton of "The Oaks," and the older brother of Henry Middleton of Middleton Place. It was Arthur Middleton or his son, William, who gave the name "Crowfield" to the property. This name comes from Crowfield Hall, a property in County Suffolk, England, which was owned by the aunt of Arthur Middleton. William Middleton married after he received Crowfield, and although the records do not state the fact, it is likely that William soon began construction of the main house that he described as the, "Capital mansion… with twelve good rooms with fire places in each, besides four in the basement with fire places." [529] Drawings 7.3 and 7.4 show the first floor house plan and elevation. The elevation drawing shows the first floor from the north. The plan of the first floor shows the great hall, three smaller rooms and a stairway next to the foyer, which led upstairs to sleeping chambers. The house featured a frontage of fifty-four feet and was forty feet wide.

During his tenure at Crowfield, William Middleton amassed great wealth. His 1745 tax return recorded that he owned 2,433 acres and one hundred slaves. He worked extensive rice fields, which produced a fortune during his time at Crowfield. It is likely that on-site brick kilns supplied building materials for the large house, outbuildings and extensive gardens. There is no indication that bricks were made to sell at the marketplace, since Crowfield was situated on the headwaters of Goose Creek, and the waters were too shallow to float bricks to market. Archaeological studies conducted in recent years indicate that indigo was grown at Crowfield, but there is no evidence of indigo vats or other industry.

The dependence on rice production may have caused the early decline of Crowfield. During the first half of the eighteenth century, the profits from rice production were enormous, sometimes returning 28 percent on the investment. During the second half of the century, the rate of return became negative, and other enterprises, such as brick manufacture, were employed as substitutes for rice production. The rebellion against England, and the lost markets and subsidies resulting from the separation from the British Empire, doomed the economy of non-diversified plantations. It was during these difficult years that Crowfield gradually stagnated from the neglect of its absentee owners. Interestingly, it was noted in the *South Carolina Gazette* June 3, 1753, "tis reported that 17 northern Natives were seen on Mr. Middleton's place on Goose Creek." This report may indicate that the estate was not occupied at that time.

In August 1753, William Middleton advertised that he and his family would sail for England, and wished to dispose of his Goose Creek plantation. He defined his plantation as eighteen hundred acres of land on which rice, corn or indigo would flourish. Another advertisement appeared in the *South Carolina Gazette*, in January 1754, for the sale of his large brick house with many convenient outhouses and a "near regular garden." Middleton sold "furniture, china, plate and three hundred books," as well as the house and land to William Walter.[530] Walter owned the estate from 1754 until his death in 1766. He devised the estate to his daughter, Elizabeth Walter when he died.

Some documents indicate that the Goose Creek estate was neglected after William Walter's ownership. One such document is the diary of William Dillwyn of New England who visited Crowfield in 1772. He wrote in his diary that Crowfield was in decline and described his visit:

> *... and myself with a Negro boy for our guide went to the next plantation at which has been as much money expended in improvements as I believe has been the case anywhere in America tho now much in decay...The Gardens, Fishponds and walks occupy about 20 acres, which has been well planned.*[531]

It appears that the estate was unoccupied when the diarist visited. The "much in decay" note indicates that the estate may have been abandoned for some time. The visitor also noted that William Haggatt "politely shewed" the estate, and the visitors never stopped at the door of the main house. It was probably unoccupied.

Elizabeth Walter married William Haggatt of London and the land passed to Haggatt's second wife after his death. She sold it to Samuel Carne of London who conveyed Crowfield Plantation to Rawlins Lowndes of Charleston, for £2,000 sterling in 1776.[532] Lowndes may have leased the property during this period because records indicate that William Middleton resided at "Crowfield" at the time of Lowndes's ownership. It is not clear on which Crowfield estate he lived. Thomas Middleton, William's father, also owned an estate called "Crowfield" in Beaufort County.

Rawlins Lowndes played a significant role in the history of Carolina prior to and during the Revolutionary War, as well as during the early years of statehood. A temporary constitution was

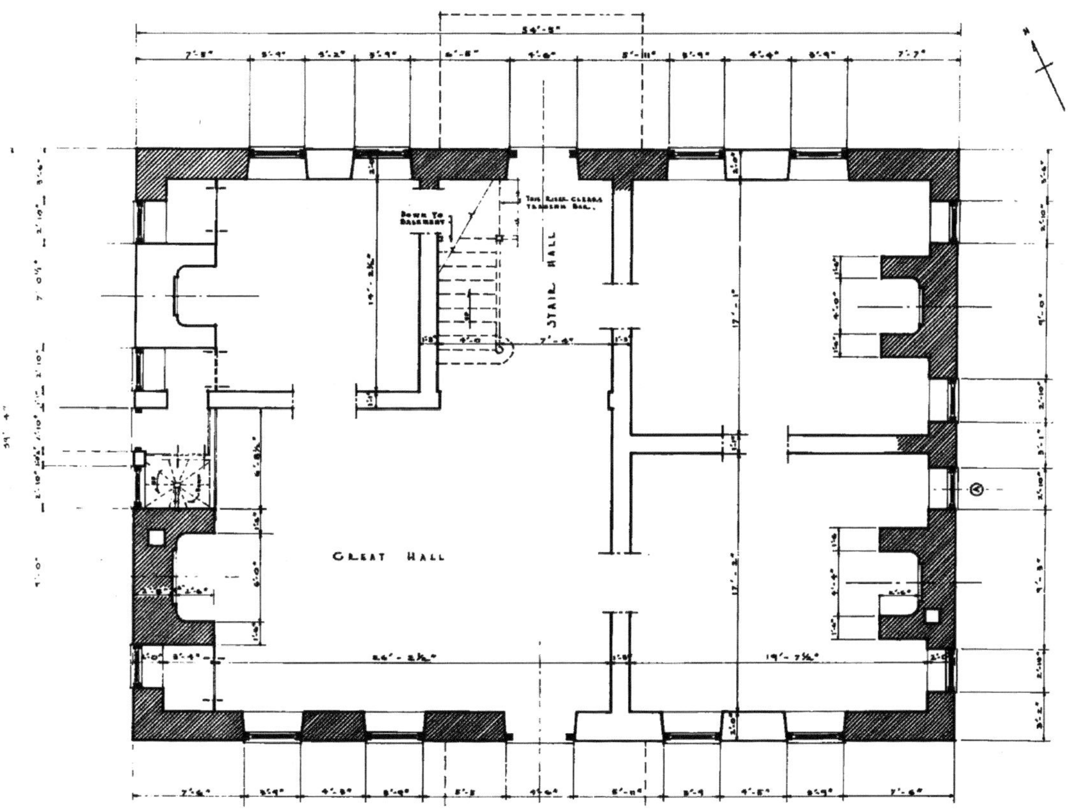

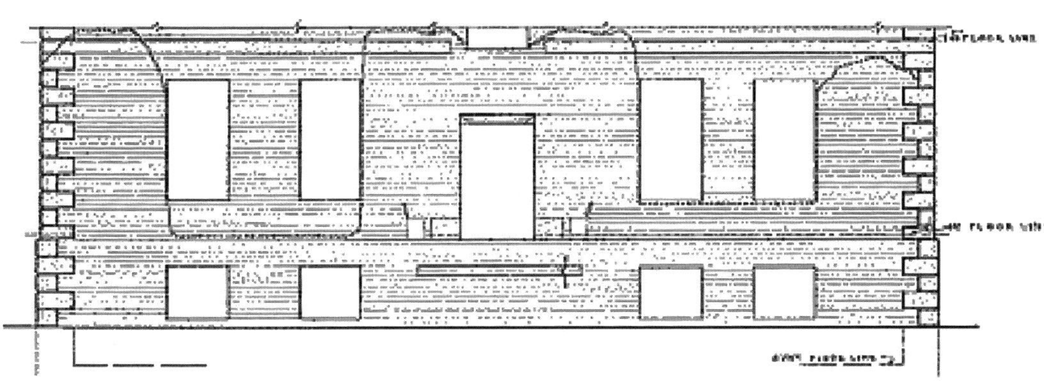

Drawings 7.3 and 7.4 These drawings show the first floor plan and elevation of the Crowfield House. The Historic American Building Survey made the drawings in 1940. ***Courtesy of the Library of Congress.***

adopted in March of 1776, and John Rutledge was elected president of South Carolina. Under the same constitution, Rawlins Lowndes was elected to succeed Rutledge in 1778. It is not certain how long, if at all, Rawlins Lowndes lived at Crowfield, but during the Revolutionary War when Charleston was under siege by the British, he sent his family to Crowfield for their safety. Sarah, his wife acknowledged being, "often alarmed & sometimes a good deal frightened," by marauding British cavalry who plundered the estates of those whose husbands and sons were elsewhere fighting the

British. Her letters tell of the perils of those days. She wrote, "There are vast numbers of plunderers up this way, a large party came here yesterday." The remarkable woman told the raiders that they would receive nothing except what she willingly gave. She provided breakfast, "plenty of drink" and dismissed them a short time later.[533] It appears that after the war, the Lowndes family stayed most of the time in Charleston and later on their plantation in Beaufort. They used Crowfield as a retreat, but by 1781–1782, it appears that Crowfield was abandoned and within two years it was sold. The advertisement in the Charleston *Gazette* described the estate as "that elegant most admired seat called Crowfield in the Parish of St. James, Goose Creek..." The plantation contained fourteen acres at the time of the sale and the advertisement claimed that the "commodious dwelling house of excellent brick work...wants very little repair." The advertisement also described the extensive gardens and claimed that the fishponds and canals were "superior to anything of the kind in the State and abound with excellent fish." Crowfield was touted as "a most desirable abode where profit and pleasure may be as well combined as at any place in the State at the same distance from Charleston."[534]

John Middleton, the youngest son of William Middleton who was the former owner of Crowfield, purchased the estate. John Middleton served in the Revolutionary War in Lee's Legion, died shortly after his purchase of Crowfield in 1784, and passed the estate to his only child, John Middleton III. It may be that John Middleton occasionally lived at Crowfield, but evidence indicates that the house was not fully used. He retained the ownership until 1826, when it was devised after his death to Henry A. Middleton, Esquire, and remained in the hands of his descendants for many years. It is clear that by 1840, the building had been long abandoned. Recently, archeologists examined the grounds and found few nineteenth century artifacts, reinforcing the belief that the estate was not consistently occupied during the 1800s.[535]

The property was in the possession of Henry A. Middleton at the time of his death, and in March 1876, the *Washington Chronicle* reported that Henry Middleton died at the age of 79. The death notice cited that he was a graduate of West Point, resided a long time in England and France, and was the author of several works of political character. The notice commented that his father was the Honorable Henry Middleton, Governor of South Carolina and member of Congress and his grandfather was Arthur Middleton, one of the signers of the Declaration of Independence. His great-grandfather, Henry Middleton was one of the presidents of the first Congress in 1774 and Arthur Middleton, was one of the first Royal Governors of the colony.[536]

Langdon Cheves acquired the property and rented tracts of five to ten acres of land to small farmers from the closing decades of the nineteenth century until it was purchased for timberland. Judge Henry A.M. Smith, a business partner of Cheves, recorded his visit to the plantation in the 1880s. He found that the walls of the "Capital Brick Mansion" were still standing intact to the eaves of the old roof. The roof, floors and all the staircases were gone, but the walls, both exterior and interior were in such condition that the beams and floors and roof could have been replaced. He also found that he could outline many of the old gardens.[537]

Judge Smith found extensive remains of the mounds and earthwork enclosing the pond and a small island in the center of the pond. On the island he found the remnants of the "Grotto" or summerhouse. He accused the local people of cutting the pond's dam to "get at" the fish.[538] More damage to the remains occurred as a result of the earthquake of 1886, afterwhich only portions of the first story of the main house walls remained intact. T.S. Stoney drew the plan of Crowfield

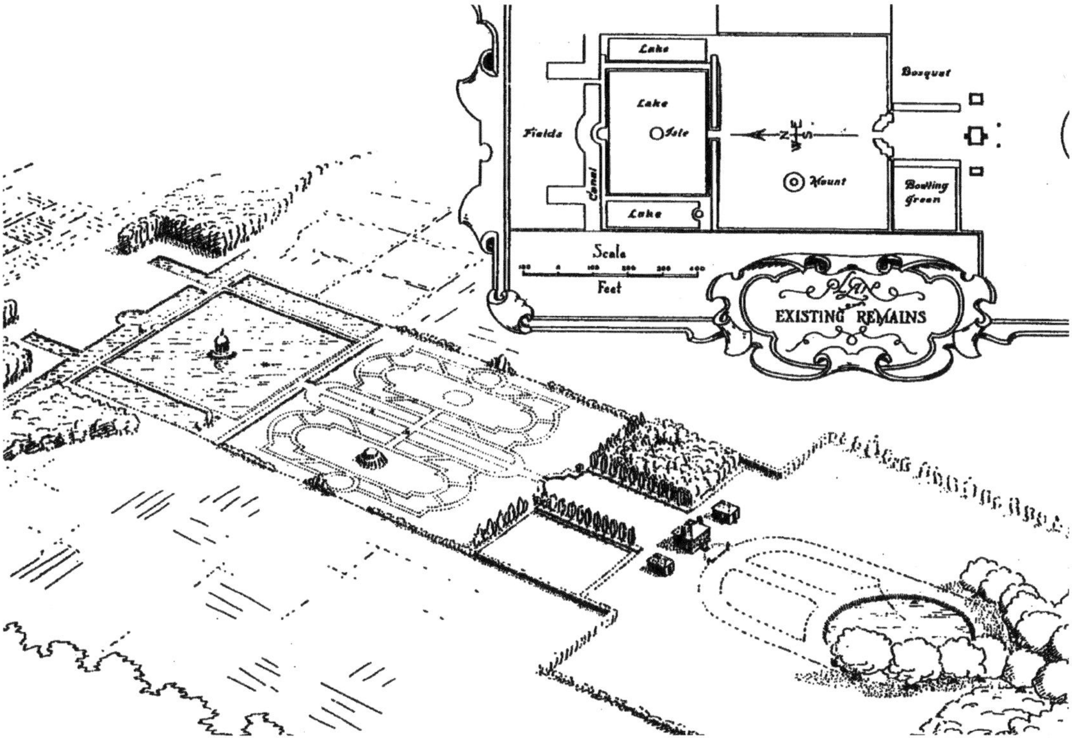

Drawing 7.5 This drawing shows the Crowfield house and gardens. *Courtesy of the South Carolina Art Association.*

Photograph 7.10 This photograph shows the ruins of "The Capital Brick Mansion" at Crowfied as it appeared in the 1930s. *Courtesy of the Library of Congress, HABS SC, 8-GOOCR.V, 1-6.*

gardens in 1938, and skillfully described the rectangular landscaped gardens and the outbuildings near the main house.

The West Virginia Pulp and Paper Company purchased Crowfield for the valuable stand of pine trees in the early 1930s. As demands for housing increased in the 1970s, Crowfield forests were subdivided and developed as residential, commercial and industrial tracts. Today, a golf course owned by the City of Goose Creek covers and surrounds the ornamental gardens. Most of the ponds have been filled, the upper lake has been dredged and used for recreation, and the lower rice fields have reverted to natural cyprus swamp. The ruins of the main house are marked and protected in a small park owned by the Crowfield Homeowners Association. The house site is located in the Hamlets residential area in the City of Goose Creek, and is accessible from The Crowfield Golf and Country Club.

Broom Hall, Broomville, Broomfield, Bloomville, Bloomfield

The land that would one day be known as Broom Hall was first granted to Arthur Middleton. This grant is probably the only document that records a native name for Goose Creek. The journal of the Grand Council in 1678 records that at that meeting, it was resolved that Mr. Arthur Middleton would acquire "his greate Lotte of Land" on "the upper part of Adthan (Anchaw/Anchau) Creek. [539] This property at the head of Goose Creek was granted to Middleton in 1680. Arthur Middleton kept the Goose Creek property only four years before he conveyed it to Robert Mallock, a Charleston merchant. The land descended to Robert Mallock's son and through the son's lawyer to Moses Medina in 1708 for £200. Finally, Colonel Thomas Broughton acquired the one thousand acre tract.

Thomas Broughton made a fortune from the deerskin trade, but gained an unscrupulous reputation. He plied native slave hunters with rum and cheap goods to encourage the slave trade, and stayed in frequent controversy with the Colonial Council and the native nations; but when he failed to acquire a monopoly on the native deerskin trade he turned his attention to rice planting. He purchased the tract as a rice plantation situated near the water reserve east of Crowfield. For some reason he soon became disillusioned with his Goose Creek

Photograph 7.11 This photograph shows the memorial tablet to Jane and Benjamin Gibbes that is displayed in the St. James Church. The photograph was taken March 14, 2005, and is in the possession of the author.

investment and sold it to Benjamin Gibbes. This sale marked a turning point in the history of the plantation.

Gibbes made Broom Hall his home either in 1710 or 1711. He greatly improved the plantation and was probably the first owner to reside on the land. The Gibbes family genealogy states that a Gibbes ancestor came from Brome or Broom house in the parish of Backham, Kent in England. This is probably the origin of the name of the Goose Creek estate.[540] Benjamin Gibbes married Jane Elliott of Barbados who died in 1717. The Gibbes's family was important to the development of the Goose Creek plantation community and was much involved with the construction of the St. James, Goose Creek brick and masonry church that replaced the earlier wooden structure. Benjamin Gibbes was a member of the church vestry and made many contributions toward the upkeep of the church in the early years. A tablet to the memory of Benjamin and Jane Gibbes can be found today at St. James, Goose Creek Church. Benjamin Gibbes married Amarinthia Smith after the death of his first wife, Jane, and fathered one daughter by Amarinthia. He died in 1722, leaving the estate to his second wife and daughter.[541] He appears to have been a successful planter who left a net worth of £400, twenty slaves and livestock. His total estate, which included furnishings and farm tools, was valued at £5,339.

The widow, Amarinthia married Captain Peter Taylor, an Irish immigrant who arrived in South Carolina in 1715. He was granted 500 acres in St. Paul's Parish, but moved to Broom Hall after his marriage to Amarinthia. Through the marriage, he acquired 930 acres at Broomhall and seventy slaves.[542] He remained at his plantation for forty years and was a well-respected member of the Goose Creek planter society. He was a church vestryman, a militia captain, and held several commissions of parish affairs. He was elected eight times to represent Goose Creek in the colonial Commons House of Assembly, but when he was invited to serve on the Governor's Privy Council, he declined the office.

Peter Taylor was a founding member of The Goose Creek Friendly Society and was much involved in literary pursuits through the prestigious Charleston Library Society. He, along with other church members, subscribed funds for the construction of the church school. He promised £75 to the church's Ludlam fund to educate the poor. Upon his death in 1765, his estate was valued at £3,000, well above the average devised estate of £400. The inventory of his property indicates that he produced rice, indigo and corn and owned eighty-one head of cattle and seventeen head of oxen. He took great interest in the condition of his slaves and left several bequeaths to faithful servants. He stipulated that £1,000 be used for the instruction of slaves, because he believed that a great debt was owed to the labor of the slaves and that all should do something toward promoting the Eternal Felicity of so useful a Body of reasonable creatures... [543] There is a tablet to the memory of Peter Taylor in St. James, Goose Creek Church. Buried with him are his wife, Amarinthia, and their son, Joseph. Peter Taylor gave the vestry of St. James, Goose Creek Church £100 sterling to be paid after his death for the building of a schoolhouse for the Goose Creek children.[544]

None of his children survived him. In the will of Peter Taylor, dated July 1, 1765, his Broom Hall Plantation was devised to his close friend and business associate, Thomas Smith. Smith, a merchant and planter, had a multitude of business and civic interests. He was active in the native trade as a junior partner with William Hopton in the firm Hopton and Smith. Later he was a successful merchant with his own company, and was part owner of five trading vessels. He was twice appointed director of native trade and was elected to represent Goose Creek in the Thirtieth, Thirty-first and Thirty-third Royal Assemblies and the First Provincial Congress in 1775. When he inherited Broom Hall, it consisted of 840 acres with thirty slaves. He then retired from trading, and took up residence at his Goose Creek plantation as a retreat and kept a house in town on Broad Street. He served in the local government as a commissioner and churchwarden. He followed what was becoming the typical habit of rich Charleston merchants of using Goose Creek plantations for recreation and retreat. He enjoyed Bloomfield as his country home from May through July, staying there regularly during the 1760s and 1770s. In a letter to a relative in Boston, he wrote that Taylor had left him a pleasant seat...in a good neighborhood.[545] He continued to explain that he employed about thirty hands, which will afford me some employment and amusement. He used Broom Hall as his country manor to produce food for his family and workforce, but did not take up the profitable rice and indigo production that had made his predecessor rich. Taylor also left Smith a brick house built sometime in the 1730s or 1740s. On Smith's invitation, William Dillwyn visited Broom Hall and described the grounds. He wrote in his diary that he arrived at Broom Hall at dusk after "passing a very long Avenue of wood and a part of it stately live Oaks." He described the mainhouse as having a great outside appearance, being comfortable and neatly furnished, "having all of the conveniences."[546]

Some evidence indicates that Smith supported the patriot cause prior to the revolution, but was not an eager participant after the fighting erupted. Josiah Quincy noted in his diary that he dined with Smith and enjoyed a pleasant evening with excellent wines and no politics.[547] When the fighting erupted, Smith retired to Broom Hall. After the war, he wrote his cousin that he "was truly in the way of both parties" causing distress and trouble for both himself and his family. He hinted that his estate suffered at the hands of marauders and one chronicler wrote that black dragoons came through Goose Creek destroying some property.[548]

One patriot reported that Smith provided funds for a loyalist regiment during the British occupation of Charleston. He must have successfully defended himself against this accusation because his name did not appear on the Jacksonborough confiscation list. The only Thomas Smith on the list left the state prior to the British invasion.

Thomas Smith of Broom Hall married Sarah Moore and fathered twelve children with her. The weak, post war economy forced Thomas Smith to leave Broom Hall in 1783 and turn it over to his son, Peter. Peter worked to bring the estate back to its previous standard with some success. He changed the name to Bloomville and exchanged 131 acres of the land for the 585-acre Fredericks tract, thus increasing the acreage to 1,293 acres.[549] According to the 1800 census, Peter Smith owned fifty slaves on his Goose Creek property and owned property in Charleston as well. He was elected to the general assembly four times to represent St. James, Goose Creek. As a delegate to the state convention, he voted to ratify the Federal Constitution in 1788.

Broom Hall appears to have been one of the few Goose Creek plantations that returned to its pre-Revolutionary War splendor, despite a weak economy and exhausted soils. Ariel Abbot traveled to Broom Hall in 1818, and described neatly apportioned gardens and impeccable grounds. He wrote, "The glory of this extensive garden are the walks. They are perfectly embowered with wild oranges & other ornamental trees." [550] Peter Smith married Mary Middleton, of The Oaks, and with her had six children. Upon his death in 1821, he directed in his will that his plantation, called Bloomville, be sold and the proceeds divided between his sons and daughters.[551]

Apparently the instructions in the will were not literally followed, because Peter Smith's son Henry Middleton Smith seems to have resided on the estate until his death. Henry married Elizabeth Sully, a sister of the noted portrait painter. She survived her husband and in 1853, conveyed the estate to four neighbors for a lifetime annuity of $600. The 1830s, 40s and 50s witnessed the abandonment of many plantations in Goose Creek due to soil exhaustion and maintenance costs. It may be that Mrs. Smith was too old, or financially troubled to keep the property. A visitor to Goose Creek in 1843 recorded that he, "passed two abodes of former magnificence …as appeared from the still beautiful remains of live oaks." It is probable that he was referring to the Bloomfield and Crowfield houses. He continued to report that, "One plantation, which had been profitable, had neither a resident or foreman and had been sold for $3,000 to be used as a resource for timber for another place."[552]

When it was sold, the property was described as Bloom, Bloom Hall, Bloomville, and Fredericks. Three years later, the four neighbors who purchased the property from Mrs. Smith sold their interest in "Bloomfield" to Henry Arthur Smith for $5,250.

Henry Arthur Smith never lived in Goose Creek but he acquired Crowfield, the 18-Mile House and Bloomfield as well as other properties. He hired overseers to manage the lands. His watchman in Goose Creek was John Driggers, who had a difficult time preventing post Civil War freedmen from squatting on the property and cutting the wood. It was during these troubled post Civil War

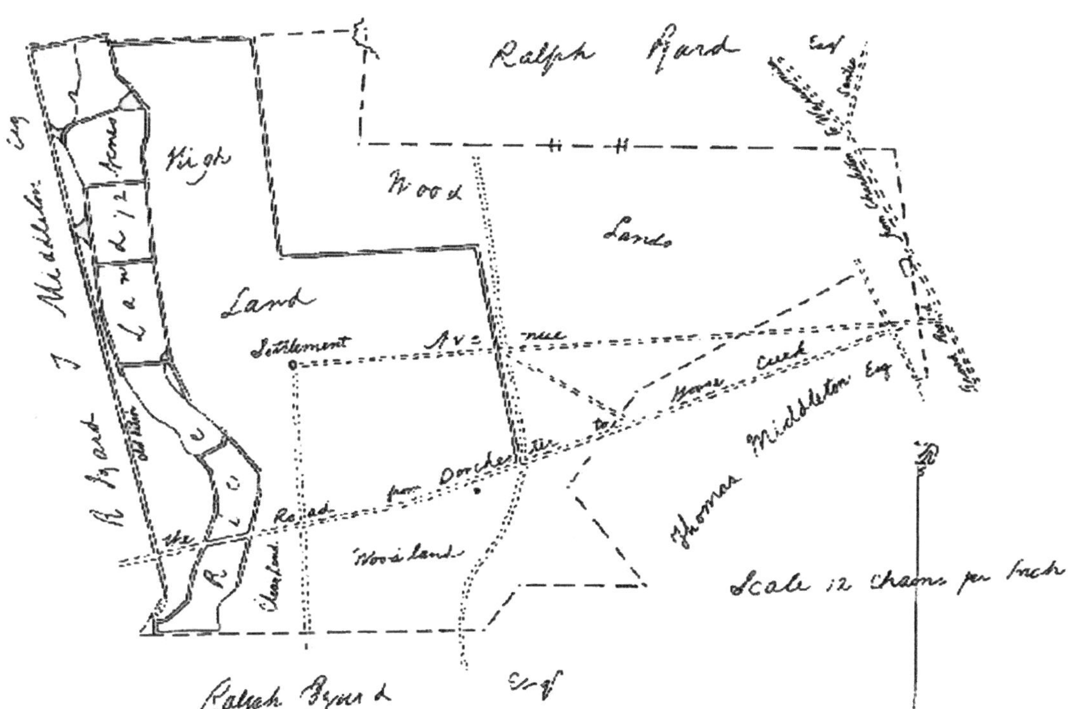

Plat 7.13 This plat of Bloomfield Plantation was surveyed and drawn in 1784 by John Fenwick. H.A.M. Smith traced the plat. The tracing is among the collections of the South Carolina Historical Society.

years that much of the brick was taken from the manor houses at Crowfield and Bloom Hall. When Middleton signed with a new watchman in 1874, the new man, Jacob Minott, was given the right to all Middleton lands to live, till the soil, cut timber for the market, as well as make turpentine. He was even given the right to use or sell any brick except those at the Crowfield and Bloomfield house sites. During these decades, tenant farmers rented small plots of this land until West Virginia Pulp and Paper (Westvaco) purchased it for timber in the 1920s.

The plats show that the settlement home was accessible by two avenues. One avenue intersected Ladson Road and the other traversed the plantation to the State Road (Highway 176/St. James Ave.) near the 18-Mile House. The Berkeley Electric Cooperative Office and the Westview Schools now occupy part of the avenue way. Bloomfield was contiguous to the Oaks Plantation and today Camelot and Pineview residential subdivisions occupy that section of the Oaks.

It appears that the name of the plantation was originally Broom Hall, which in the process of time was corrupted to Bloom Hall, Bloom and Bloomville. It was finally known as Bloomfield. Broom Hall had a large brick house with several brick outbuildings, a dairy and stable. The house was well preserved until after 1865, when a fire, caused by some careless deer hunters who occupied the house for a night, destroyed it. Judge Henry A.M. Smith visited the site in 1883 and found considerable evidence of gardens and ornamental grounds. He also reported "one of the finest springs for furnishing water."[553]

A plat drawn from a survey made in 1916 shows that "Bloomville" consisted of 588 acres at that time.[554] Near the time of the 1916 survey, Joseph Ioor Waring visited the site and found an avenue of "fire scarred oaks a half mile long" leading to the house. He noted that the house rested on a hill overlooking broad terraces, which led down to a large pond. He noted that a small "artificial pond" was situated near the house and that the bottom of the pond was lined with a "course of bricks."[555]

Photograph 7.12
This photograph shows the ruins of the Bloomfield main house near the turn of the twentieth century. *Courtesy of the South Carolina Historical Society.*

When Langdon Cheves visited the site in 1923 he left a description of the last vestiges of the house. He believed that the house was standing intact after the Civil War including the roof, and he recorded that the walls and chimney were standing until the earthquake of 1886, when all but the first and part of the second story were destroyed. Cheves accused brick thieves of removing the last remnants of the once elegant home.[556]

Recent archaeological studies indicate that a "tile lined" pool graced the extensive gardens. The study conducted in 1995, found evidence of this pond, remains of the original house foundation and a portion of an approach avenue. A passive roadside park noted for the large fallen and burned oak trunks protects the Bloomfield home site today contiguous to Westview Boulevard. The park overlooks the old water reserve and rice fields that produced fortunes during the heady decades of the early 1700s.

A tall tree on the northern edge of the upper water reserve, north of today's Crowfield Boulevard, held the nest of an eagle family for several years during the late 1990s. The high, flat nest perched on the very top branches of the tree, hearkened back to an interesting story told by the daughter of Benjamin and Amarinthia Gibbes in the early eighteenth century. The story tells of a dead pine tree in the reserve. The bark had fallen off, as well as all of the branches except two or three at the top of the tree. A fishhawk (osprey) made a nest in the crotch of the uppermost branches. The nest remained for many years and no one had ever been able to climb up to it. An old African claimed that a white stone rested in the nest, and anyone who could climb up and retrieve the stone would be free.[557] The osprey's nest has been gone for centuries and the eagle family recently departed, at least for now, but the intriguing story remains to remind us of how much and how little things have changed.

Fredericks

Thomas Moore was awarded a land grant for 460 acres in 1714. The tract bounded on Thorogood (Thurgood), Berringer, Moore, Stevens and Mallock.[558] These boundaries place the acreage on lands north of Bloom Hall and Crowfield, in the general area referred today as Plantation North. Charles Moore acquired the ownership from the original grantee, and was able to add 148 acres from the contiguous Bloom Hall tract to the south. In 1723, these two tracts, containing 608 acres, were conveyed to Ralph Izard after which the land remained in the Izard family for three generations. The 1784 plat, by John Fenwick, showed the tract north of Bloomfield, and indicated that the second Ralph Izard owned the land at the time of that survey. Later Peter Smith, one time owner of neighboring Bloomfield, acquired the whole tract from Ralph Izard in a land trade and made it a part of Bloomfield.[559] The property changed hands again in the mid 1800s, when Arthur S. Gibbes sold Bloomfield (770 acres) and Fredericks (613 acres) to Henry A. Middleton for $5,250.[560] This transaction described the combined tracts of Bloomfield together with Fredericks, as bounding Crowfield on the west, the road to Dorchester on the south (old Ladson Road), the property of C. Vose (the Oaks) and M.J. Keith (Mt. Holly) to the east, and Lewis Cannon and J.F. Droze to the north.

The Izard family owned the acreage for nearly eighty years and probably built a working settlement on the tract, but Henry A.M. Smith investigated the land in the late nineteenth century and found no indication of buildings or gardens. It is likely that the Izards never lived at Fredericks, because they already owned the beautiful home nearby at the Elms. The Izards may have merely kept an overseer house and slave quarters at Fredericks, as long as the land was profitable. Evidence of a settlement is indicated today by a partial avenue of mature oaks, immediately west of the Walmart Department Store on St. James Avenue (Highway 176) in Goose Creek.

The Oaks

A beautiful and stately avenue of Oaks led to the Oaks Plantation main house near the St. James, Goose Creek Church. This plantation was one of the homes of the Middleton family. The Proprietors granted the plantation estate to Edward Middleton and his wife Sarah in 1678. The original mansion was built about 1700, and was one of five plantation homes owned by the Middleton family. The Middletons were wealthy and close to European royalty. Mary Middleton, wife of Henry, was the daughter of the Earl of Cromartie.[561] In addition to their royal connections, the Middletons served South Carolina and the nation in many esteemed offices. They served as governor, president of the Continental Congress, signer of the Declaration of Independence, foreign minister and president of the Provincial Congress. In addition, family members served as representatives in numerous assemblies and commissions. Seven members of the Middleton family represented the St. James, Goose Creek Parish, and four generations owned the Oaks Plantation.

The first owner was the immigrant, Edward Middleton. The warrant authorized Captain Maurice Matthews, Surveyor General, to apportion 1,780 acres of land for Edward Middleton and his wife, Sarah. The grant specified that, if the land should be "upon any navigable river or river capable to be made navigable you are to allow only the fifth part of the depth thereof by the water side." Mr. Middleton, himself a member of the council, presented to the council a motion that he be allowed all of his land on the creek, where he has settled because the Creek was not capable of being made navigable. This creek would later be known as "Yeamans Creek" and finally "Goose Creek."

In 1680, Edward and Sarah received a warrant for 1,630 acres of land on Yeamans Creek, which were bounded by other lands owned by Edward Middleton. The property was called "The Oaks." His combined awards of land included Bloomfield and amounted to nearly 4,000 acres. The vast estate encompassed lands on the north and south sides of Goose Creek. The property was contiguous to Crowfield, the Elms and Otranto, as well as lesser properties to the east. He was generally known as "Edward of The Oaks" and served as a justice of the peace, a lord proprietor's deputy, a member of the grand council, and an assistant justice. He employed a French landscape gardener to build ornamental gardens and terraces near the main house and supposedly planted the live oaks lining the avenue in 1680.

When Edward Middleton died in 1685 the property passed to his widow Sarah and the lord proprietors freed the 1,630 acres from the one-penny per acre-quit rent. Thus, she was a wealthy widow when she married Job Howe soon after. She also survived Job Howe at which time she conveyed the large estate in consideration of "love and affection" to her oldest son Arthur.[562]

Arthur was the second Middleton to own the Oaks. He inherited the Oaks with sixty slaves, a large fifteen hundred acre tract at Wassamasaw with thirty slaves and land at Wampee with twenty-five slaves. In addition, he held almost eight thousand acres of undeveloped lands. Although he kept a

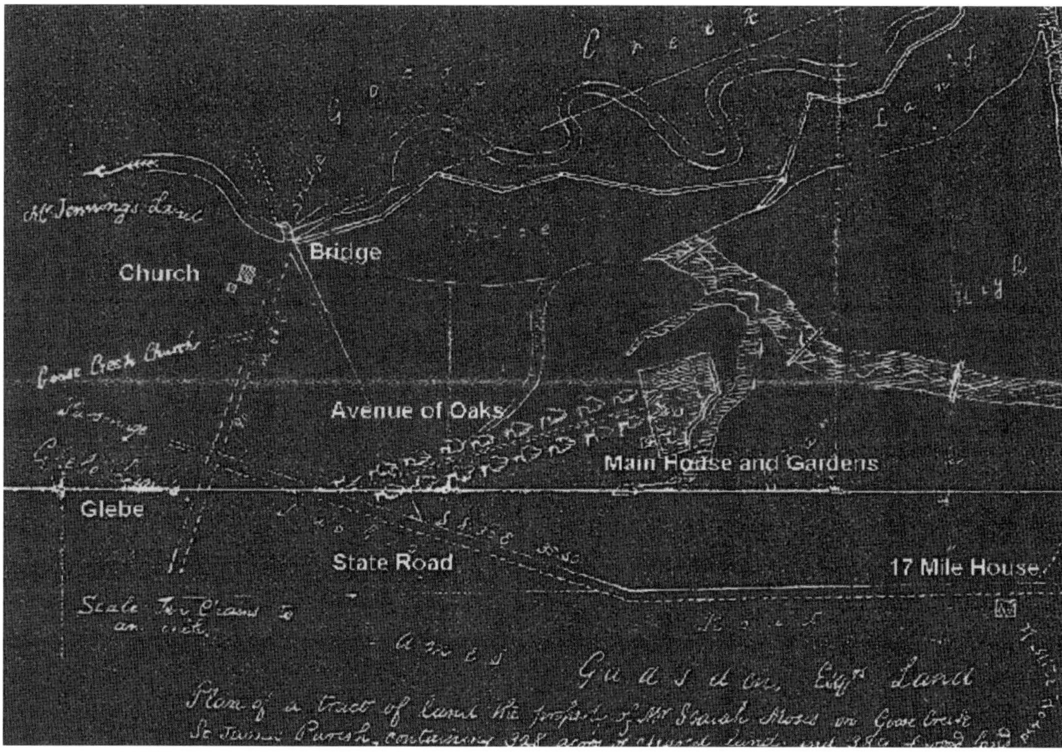

Plat 7.14 This partial plat describes the Oaks Plantation as drawn from a survey made in 1817 by William Brailsford. The plat is among the Langdon Cheves Papers in the possession of the South Carolina Historical Society. The plat has been notated for this publication to show the location of the Bridge, Church, the Avenue of Oaks, Oaks Main House and Gardens, Glebe, State Road and 17-Mile House.

house in Charleston, his principal residence was at the Oaks.[563] In 1707 Arthur married Sarah Amory, daughter of Jonathan Amory, Speaker of the Commons House of Assembly. After her death, he married Sarah Wilkinson, widow of Joseph Morton, Landgrave of Carolina. By his second marriage, he formed connections with the prominent dissenter families of Colleton County. Arthur was known as "The Honorable Arthur Middleton of the Oaks, and Crowfield in Carolina and Crowfield Hall, county of Suffolk, England." He served in several local offices and commissions including working as a vestryman, a commissioner for the free school at Charleston, and a commissioner to build a library and state house. In addition he was a tax collector, captain in the Berkeley Militia, and justice of the peace. In recognition of his work in building the St. James, Goose Creek Church, the vestry presented him an enclosed pew. He was also a commissioner under the Act of Establishment and was elected to the assembly five times, and served as a commissioner of native affairs.

From 1716 to 1719, Arthur supported the king in the struggle with the lord proprietors. He was the king's man in Carolina affairs and signed several petitions requesting the overthrow of Proprietary rule. As a member of the seventeenth assembly, he urged Governor Robert Johnson to remain in office until the royal government was installed. The new royal governor, Francis Nicholson, named Middleton to the new royal council, which then elected him as president of the council. It does not appear that he served that position well. He was accused of selling public offices for his own benefit, delaying the orders from England, and refusing to follow some of the council's directives. Under his leadership, the province came close to civil strife. When he arrested Landgrave Thomas Smith, the province almost erupted in civil war. Furthermore, Middleton remained on the council past his presidency and used his position to acquire more wealth. He and his wife Sarah Amory had four children. Arthur died in 1737.

Arthur Middleton's sons were Henry and Thomas. Henry was the third Middleton who owned the Oaks. Henry inherited 1,630 acres of the Oaks estate from his father and added more than 2,000 acres to his holdings, when he married Mary Williams. She was an heiress with property on the Ashley River. He added to his wife's inheritance and named it "Middleton Place." At his death in 1784, he owned more than 26,000 acres of property and 199 slaves. He was elected eight times to represent St. George, Dorchester and three times to represent St. Philip and St. Michael in the general assembly. Once he was elected to represent St. James, Goose Creek and St. George Dorchester together, but he declined to serve both. He also served as Speaker of the Assembly twice. He represented South Carolina in the First Continental Congress, where he once served as president. He allied with the British when Charleston fell, but was never penalized by having his estates confiscated or amerced. His immunity from any penalties probably resulted from the fact that he loaned the State over £100,000 during and after the struggle.[564] He died in 1784, and is buried in the St. James, Goose Creek Church.

Arthur, son of Henry and grandson of Arthur, was not directly connected to the Oaks. He was elected once to represent Goose Creek and St. Helena Parishes and once to serve St. Helena. He did not reside at the Oaks, but lived at Middleton Place where he was born. He was sent to England, at an early age, for his education. He served the patriot cause with distinction during the Revolution and was imprisoned with other rebels when he refused the King's protection, and was exiled to St. Augustine. The provincial congress elected him to the Continental Congress, where he signed the Declaration of Independence but illness forced him to remain close to home in South Carolina after the Continental Congress adjourned. When Charleston fell, Arthur, the grandson, went back to the Oaks in broken health and died there at his father's estate in 1787. His body was returned to Middleton Place.

When Henry died in 1784, he left a large family from three marriages. The Oaks went to his second son, Thomas Middleton, who also held offices of importance and aided the American cause. Thomas, son of Henry Middleton and Mary Williams, was born in 1753 in Charleston. He was educated in England and upon his return to South Carolina inherited the Oaks Plantation and a house in Charleston. In 1787, he owned 441 slaves and almost eight thousand acres of land in four parishes. Thomas Middleton entered public service during the Revolution when he served as a Lieutenant in the Charleston militia in 1775 and 1776. Goose Creek elected him that same year to the Second Provincial Congress and the First General Assembly. After the war, he represented Goose Creek in the Fifth General Assembly and Prince William in the Sixth General Assembly. He married Ann Manigault, daughter of Peter Manigault and Elizabeth Wragg and they had nine children. Thomas died in 1797, and was buried at the St. James, Goose Creek Church.

For more than 116 years, the Oaks Plantation remained in the Middleton family, but in 1796 Thomas Middleton and Ann, his wife, conveyed "All that plantation…containing 1,800 acres…in

Photograph 7.13 This photograph is labeled "The Oakes" and is in *Johnson's Scrapbook, Volume 1*. The photograph was taken near the beginning of the twentieth century. The scrapbook is among the collections of the South Carolina Historical Society.

St. James, Goose Creek..." to James Gairdner.[565] That sale of the Oaks ended four generations of Middleton ownership. A tablet was erected in St. James, Goose Creek Church in honor of the four Middleton generations. Arthur Middleton, the eldest son of the Honorable Henry Middleton, signer of the Declaration of Independence, is buried at Middleton Place, and is not mentioned on the tablet at St. James.

James Gairdner lived at the Oaks until he sold it to Adam Tunno, a Charleston Merchant. The next owner was Isiah Moses. The 1824 tax returns showed that Moses owned 790 acres and nineteen slaves, which indicates that he was well to do. Nevertheless, he seems to have had some financial troubles.[566] Moses sold some tracts of the large estate to satisfy debts, and tried other schemes to pay his mortgage to retain ownership. He even arranged a scheme to sell the avenue of oaks for shipbuilding timber. Fortunately, the deal failed to materialize when the selling price remained too high. One chronicler noted, "We stopped a few moments to gaze down the avenue of live oaks belonging to Mr. Moses, a son of Abraham, who in the true style of his nation offered it to the ship carpenters..."[567]

In 1841, the Charleston Jewish Congregation of Beth Elohim obtained the property in a foreclosure action. Moses was forced to surrender the remaining 795 acres for $2,000 to satisfy the mortgage. The congregation immediately sold the plantation to Charles P. Shier, who one year later conveyed it to George M. Cannon.[568] John Willson bought the estate for $1,650 in 1850. At that time, it contained only 717 acres including 50 acres of rice lands and the remaining as high ground. A few years later Carlton Vose bought the plantation, and retained ownership until 1859, when he sold it to Edward R. Miles for $2,450.00. Edward Miles devised the property to his widow, Mary Peronneau Miles, who held it until she sold it to Edwin Parsons in 1892 for $2,500.

Photograph 7.14 This photograph shows the Oaks main house built by Edwin Parsons in 1892 on the site of the original home. The photograph was taken March 7, 2005, and shows the structure without the large front portico. The photograph is in the possession of the author.

Edwin Parsons was from Kennebeck, Maine; one of the northern entrepreneurs who came south to purchase greatly undervalued property. The main house at the Oaks built by the Middleton family survived the Revolutionary War, but was destroyed by fire in 1840. Parsons was one of the first to invest in the rehabilitation of old Southern plantations, when he built upon the Middleton home site in 1892. The house stands at the head of an avenue of oaks, which runs for a quarter of a mile and shades the broad approach road. It was built around the foundation of the original house and has eighteen rooms. The first floor consists of a living room, library, billiard room, three bedrooms and baths, kitchen, pantry, servant's dining room, main dining room, powder room and bath, drawing room and lounge. The second floor consists of a master bedroom, four bathrooms, two servant's bedrooms and a bath. Ernest Flagg of New York designed the house. He was the designer of the Naval Academy at Annapolis, the Corcoran Gallery of Art in Washington, D.C. and others. His work in Goose Creek is one of the finest examples of Georgian architecture in America and is today used as the central feature of the fine country club. Sunken gardens and a well-designed rose bed grace the lawn to the side and rear of the house. Azaleas border the paths approaching the lake, resting amidst a grove of ancient live oaks. The plantation was the scene of William Gilmore Simms's novel entitled *Katherine Walton*.[569] It was also the setting of several scenes of the movie *Little Miss Rebellion*, starring Dorothy Gish.[570] The house and the avenue of giant oaks were used to depict scenes of juvenile royalty, and revived all of the colorful and stirring life of colonial Goose Creek.

In 1930, Charles Sabin, former President of the Guarantee Trust Company of New York, purchased the Oaks for $58,500 [571]and spent more than $100,000 (some reports state $300,000) making the 419-acre estate one of the finest plantations in the South. His renovation removed the elaborate Georgian woodwork and the six Corinthian columns that supported the two-story portico.[572]

During the 1940s and 1950s, the property went through a series of owners. Two of the owners were unusual–Hurst Waterman Conant in the late 1940s intended to raise three hundred head of white-faced Hereford cattle on the 680-acre tract and Sun Oil Company purchased the tract to drill for oil. Neither venture materialized. In 1956 four local businessmen formed The Oaks Co. Inc., paid $125,000 for the house and 140 acres, and began to build an exclusive residential development called The Oaks Estate. Later in 1964, Harold L. Mims purchased the 40-acre estate and revitalized the golf course and added a ballroom to the two-story house.[573] The names of two of the nineteenth century owners remain recognizable in Goose Creek today. Descendents of Carlton Vose, as well as those of the Cannon family continue to reside on old Oak Plantation acreage.

Seventeen Mile Tract or 17-Mile House Tract

The 1,093-acre parcel, known as the "Seventeen Mile Tract," (17-Mile House Tract) was once part of the Middleton's Oaks Plantation. James Gairdner purchased the 1,800-acre Oaks Plantation from Thomas and Anne Middleton in 1796. Three years later, he sold the Oaks land to Adam Tunno. Adam Tunno divided the estate along the State Road into two parcels, and sold the tract east of the road to Stephen Mazyck in 1805. The parcel on the east side of the State Road was referred to as the "Seventeen Mile Tract." It consisted of 392 acres at first, but Mazyck added 701 more acres contiguous on the south of the tract to make a 1,093-acre estate at and south of the 17-mile stone.[574] After the death of Stephen Mazyck, his widow, Mary, was forced to sell the lands to James Gadsden in 1810, for $4,350.[575] Gadsden made a profit when he sold the tract to Charles Graves eight years later for $5,000. Joel Huff purchased 260 acres of the tract with a mortgage from Graves in 1828. This smaller tract was described in the transaction as situated east of the bridge road and west of Back River Road reaching from the 17-mile stone to almost the 18-mile stone where David Breaker's 18-Mile House was situated.[576]

For some reason Huff's mortgage was assigned to Rebecca Gadsden, who conveyed the property to Joel Huff by quit claim in consideration for $500.[577] It appears that the 17-Mile Tract was made part of Bella Vista Plantation, owned by Huff at that time. Today, the 17-Mile Tract is used as mixed commercial and residential areas east of Red Bank Road, south of the intersection of Highways 176 and 52.

Mount Pleasant

Mount Pleasant Plantation was situated on the north side of Goose Creek, east of the Oaks and northeast of Nathaniel Snow's Red Bank tract. The Proprietors originally granted land here as an eight hundred acre tract to Robert Howe in 1706.[578] Robert Howe passed the land to his son, Job, who, in 1731, gave Clifford Thomas the power of attorney to sell it. Robert Hume bought Mt. Pleasant, but there is no record of him selling it. Near the time of the sale, Vanderdussen bordered the land on the southeast, Alexander Nesbitt's land was northeast, James Grange's property was to the northwest and the waters of Goose Creek was the southern border.[579] The land apparently passed to James Withers, because according to his will proved in 1756, the same year he died, he owned the tract, which he referred to as his principal residence. His will also referenced "Spring Garden," which he defined as "land at Goose Creek."[580]

James Withers was a Charleston bricklayer and founder of a successful rice-planter family, who later owned huge estates on the Sampit River near Georgetown. His Mount Pleasant Plantation on Goose Creek consisted of six hundred acres and contiguous Spring Garden was comprised of four hundred acres, but he also owned lands in Christ Church Parish and worked as many as thirty-one slaves.[581] He ran afoul with the Charleston city fathers when he contracted with them to build a powder magazine. His work appears to have been substandard because upon completion, he was ordered to disassemble the structure, clean the bricks and rebuild it under penalty of breach of contract.[582] He served a number of commissions and represented Goose Creek in the Twelfth and Twentieth Royal Assemblies. During the Twelfth Assembly, he teamed with fellow Goose Creekers Gabriel Manigault and Thomas Smith Sr. to obstruct Governor James Glenn, which eventually led to the governor's dismissal over a dispute regarding Charleston's defenses.[583]

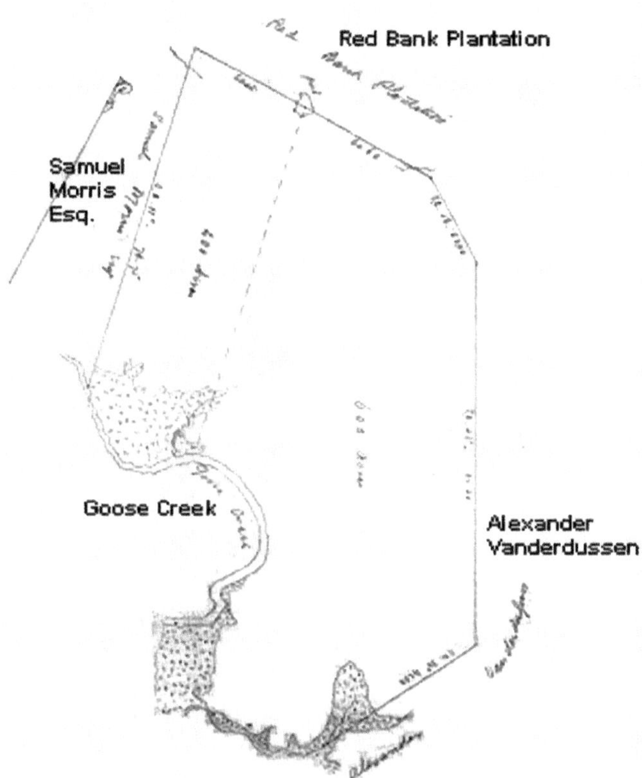

Plat 7.15 This plat describes the eight hundred-acre plantation named Mt. Pleasant as drawn by Joseph Purcell in 1790. The plantation once belonged to James Withers. The plat is a tracing of the original by H.A.M. Smith and is among the collections of the South Carolina Historical Society.

James Withers married Mary Cartwright, and with her had seven children. The widow, Mary Withers, received Mount Pleasant and William, a son, received Spring Garden. Plat 7.5 was made from a survey conducted by Joseph Purcell in 1790. It shows that Goose Creek was on the southern boundary of the Mount Pleasant Estate. John Bowen's plantation bordered on the west. Peter Tamplet's part of Red Bank and the Red Bank lands owned by Nathaniel Bordeaux were situated to the north. It appears that William eventually acquired Mt. Pleasant from his mother because it was he who sold the property, totaling 1,197 acres, to Archar Smith in 1800. William Withers apparently operated a successful brickyard on Goose Creek, evidenced by recent archaeological discoveries at that site.[584]

The Mount Pleasant Plantation was mentioned in the book, *A Day on Cooper River.* It was described as situated, "About three miles higher up Goose Creek," and "once a happy hospitable mansion of Mr. Wm. Withers."[585] Another reference was made to Mount Pleasant in 1838, when Charles Brown was sued for debts. Mount Pleasant was one of two Goose Creek plantations that he purchased.[586] Brown owed overwhelming debts and was forced to sell it, together with thirteen slaves, to John Alexander Keith and Reverend Paul Trapier Keith at auction, in trust for Charles Brown's wife, Sarah and their children. Sarah Brown kept the land until her death in 1874, when it was divided among her children. In the 1880s, the land was involved in various lawsuits and owned by members of the Brown family until John Poppenheim purchased it in a public auction in 1888.

Earlier historical accounts indicate that the grave markers of William Barnett, who died in 1917; Lavinia Watson, who died in 1939, and other unmarked graves were found, but those markers are not evident today.[587]

Marrington

Marrington Plantation appeared in the late nineteenth century, formed from the accumulation of a number of smaller tracts. Much of Marrington was comprised of the old Red Bank estate. Red Bank was mostly situated south of today's Red Bank Road, and was originally owned by the Snow, and later, by the Tennent families. North of Red Bank Road was a tract originally granted to Landgrave Thomas Smith in 1711, but the land later passed to James Coachman and then to Peter Tamplet. This upper tract was an L-shaped piece of land that reached from the junction of the Cooper and Back Rivers, and ran west and south, but within a few years of Peter Tamplet's death, his land became part of Back River Plantation, owned by Charles Graves. A copy of the L-shaped plat owned by Peter Tamplet is provided in the vignette of Red Bank Plantation.

Charles Graves accumulated several large tracts, including Brick Hope and Cow Jig until his estate contained 1,446 acres at the time of his death in 1845. Charles Graves's son Daniel DeSaussure Graves was a Charleston physician. He acquired his father's plantation in 1847 and further expanded the holding. He purchased land from Daniel Wood, including part of the Red Bank lands, and he bought more lands that reached east to the Cooper. He turned this large estate into a profitable rice plantation known as Marrington Plantation.

In 1871, Graves's heirs sold Marrington estate to John F. Poppenheim.[588] At that time, the large tract consisted of 1,859 acres contiguous to Back River, Foster Creek and Cooper River. Poppenhein held this land for several decades before it passed in succession to P.O. Mead, W.L. Stribling,

Photograph 7.15 This photograph shows Marrington Plantation House as it appeared as the residence of John Poppenheim. ***Courtesy of Terrence Larimer.***

Adolphous N. Manucy, Westvaco, and finally to the United States' Department of Defense. The Department of Defense renovated and rebuilt the elaborate series of water reserve, irrigation ponds, and rice fields that were remnants of the earlier agricultural enterprise, as part of a North American Waterfowl Project for wildlife viewing and for recreation.

White House

Alexander Vanderdussen was a merchant and planter who acquired a well-situated plantation on the north side of the Goose Creek neck, across the water from Yeamans Hall.[589] His Goose Creek plantation was noted for its dairy and large grove of mulberry trees, but his sixty-three slaves knew him for his bad temper and cruelty.

Vanderdussen was an experienced soldier when he immigrated to South Carolina and upon his arrival offered his skills to the militia. He rose quickly through the ranks. In 1740, he was a colonel in the militia that accompanied James Oglethorpe on his expedition to St. Augustine. The Crown commissioned him as brevet lieutenant colonel in the British Army and commander of three independent companies in South Carolina. He was also active politically. He was elected six times to the Royal Assembly, but represented Goose Creek in only the Twelfth and Fourteenth Royal Assemblies. He was removed from council for being "disordered in his mind," and by 1756, trustees were named to his estate. After his death in 1759, his lands on Goose Creek were deserted for a while and supposedly haunted by "Old Bandiston Ghost." It seems that "Bandiston" was a vocal derivation of "Vanderdussen."[590]

William Johnson acquired the Vanderdussen Plantation prior to the American Revolution. Johnson was a blacksmith and ironwright from New York who came to Charleston in the 1760s and entered into a partnership with another blacksmith at first, but later established himself as an independent artisan and became quite wealthy. He purchased the Vanderdussen lands and built on the site of the Vanderdussen house. He named his Goose Creek plantation "White House" and resided there, but he eventually also owned seven houses and six lots in Charleston and lands on the Edisto River. At the time of his death, he owned ninety-eight slaves and stock valued at more than $80,000.[591]

Johnson was a patriot. He supported the American cause and worked with Christopher Gadsden's Liberty Tree Party to advance revolutionary ideas. He was a member of the committee of correspondence, and represented the Charleston parishes in the Second Provincial Congress and First General Assembly. Johnson was one of the "Liberty Tree Men" taken prisoner when Charleston fell to the British. He was sent to prison in St. Augustine and his family was shipped to Philadelphia. His son, Joseph Johnson, wrote of the journey from Philadelphia to Charleston after the war and relayed that, upon arrival at Charleston, the family visited Mr. John Deas of "Thorough-good," while his father "went down on Goose Creek Neck" to inquire about his "farm on Red Bank." He found that the slaves had "faithfully kept together under their drivers and had made a good crop of provisions." [592] He returned his family to resettle on their land at White House and although the British still occupied Charleston, Johnson watched from his plantation as the flames lit up the night sky when the British burned their fortifications in preparation for evacuating the city.

After the war, William Johnson represented the parishes from Charleston five times and served as a Goose Creek representative in Fourth, Fifth and Sixth General Assemblies. He served as a delegate for the city parishes and voted to ratify the federal constitution. He held numerous commissions. He married Sarah Nightingale and with her had at least nine children named Thomas, William, Joseph, John, Benjamin, Jane, Sarah, Isaac and James. He died in 1818 at the age of seventy-seven.[593]

The records indicate that William Johnson expanded his original White House tract east toward the Cooper River. A plat was made in 1786 for him, which described 550 acres on the Cooper River and Goose Creek. The Mills Atlas Map of 1825 notes that "Johnson" occupied property at the juncture of Goose Creek and the Cooper. An 1826 deed by Henry Ravenel shows Sarah Johnson as the owner of the land bordering on Ravenel's Goose Creek estate and in 1829, Joseph Johnson, the son of William and Sarah, purchased land from the executors of the estate of Nathaniel Slawson. This action followed a lawsuit brought against the Slawson estate by three of William Johnson's sons: Joseph, Isaac and James. It is likely that Nathaniel Slawson purchased the property from the Johnson family, but failed to make the mortgage payments.

Ownership of this tract changed frequently during the 1820s and 1830s. Joseph Johnson, a son, purchased the land in 1827. He sold it in 1830 to William Doughty, who held it for a year and then sold it to James Parkinson.[594] The land reverted back to Doughty when Parkinson failed on make payments. Henry Woddrup bought the land at auction in 1838, but was forced to mortgage the tract to James Heilbron in order to buy it. Several more rapid transactions occurred before Daniel and Mary Brown bought it in 1846.[595] The Brown family held and successfully worked the lands for more than fifty years, before Colin McKay Grant bought it in 1894.[596]

Early references to the land north of Goose Creek and south of Foster Creek are few. These tracts bounded by the Cooper on the east and church lands to the west, changed hands often during the eighteenth and nineteenth century, and left a poorly defined title trail, but it is clear that near the end of the nineteenth century, John Poppenheim consolidated most of this property into a single holding called "Marrington Plantation."

The earliest legal reference is made when the Lord Proprietors granted 700 acres to Barnard Schenklingh in 1680.[597] Lands belonging to Jonah Lynch, John Null and John Maverick bordered this property, but no records of their grants have been found. Barnard Schenklingh's son, Benjamin, received a grant of 340 acres in the same vicinity as his father's and in 1703 sold this land, as well as the land granted earlier to his father, to Willoughby Gibbes, a widow from Barbados. She mortgaged 200 acres of the land in 1711 that was described as bounding on Goose Creek with the "marsh before it." Roger Moore, from Cape Fear, North Carolina, purchased the property from Mrs. Gibbes's heirs in 1743, and in turn sold it to Thomas Smith who then sold the 700 acre tract to William Coachman. This is the last mention of this particular tract until it reappears as part of a number of plantations including Melgrove Plantation. This plantation was a 730 acre tract purchased by James Withers from John Martini, a "Practitioner of Physick" in 1751. This tract was situated on the north side of Goose Creek, where the Goose Creek Reservoir dike is situated today.

James Withers, the brickmaker, sold the tract to his neighbors, John and William Coachman. John, William and James Coachman Jr. appraised Wither's estate in 1752—the year Benjamin Coachman purchased the seven hundred acres.[598] Benjamin Coachman was elected to the Twenty-second and Thirty-second Royal Assemblies and was a contributor to the Ludlam school fund. He was also a captain in the militia. He died a wealthy man and was buried at the St. James, Goose Creek Church.

William Coachman bought James's interest and sold the entire tract to Peter Manigault, who subsequently sold it five years later to John Bowen. An 1802 plat shows the John Bowen property on Goose Creek, west of the Lower Tenant Pond. The plat shows a main house, outbuildings, and a slave village.[599] This was the 730 acre tract purchased from Coachman and an additional contiguous 250 acres. Bowen's will, proved in 1812 devised two tracts of land known as Morris Hill and Sambo Hill to his daughter, Mary. Partial plat 7.16 shows the extent of the tract when Henry Ravenel owned three of the parcels contiguous to Goose Creek in the early nineteenth century.

The principal antebellum occupant of this section was Henry Ravenel. Ravenel bought the land from Nathanial Slawson in 1821.[600] The name "Ravenel" appears on Mills' 1825 Atlas, on the northern side of Goose Creek, west of the old "White House" tract. Ravenel expanded his holdings by adding 340 acres purchased from Sarah Brown[601] and some of Bowen's property to the west.[602] The 7.16 partial plat, drawn in 1857, shows that Ravenel's estate totaled 1,685 acres. The plat shows that "Mr. Gadsden" owned property to the west and "Mrs. Brown" owned property to the east. Red Bank Road touched the property on the northern boundary, and the waters of Goose Creek ran the entire length of the southern boundary.

Ravenel's tract was divided into two sections called "Melgrove" to the northeast and "Old Tom" to the southwest. Gadsden owned Cedar Grove Plantation to the north and Mrs. Brown owned the Mount Pleasant seat to the east. William Hume purchased Melgrove at a court sale from the estate of Eliza Tennent, widow of William Tennent, and sold it to Charles Tennent in 1873. Samuel Gaillard Stoney bought this tract in 1889 and sold it to John F. Poppenheim, who consolidated most of the properties in that area in the late eighteenth and early nineteenth centuries.

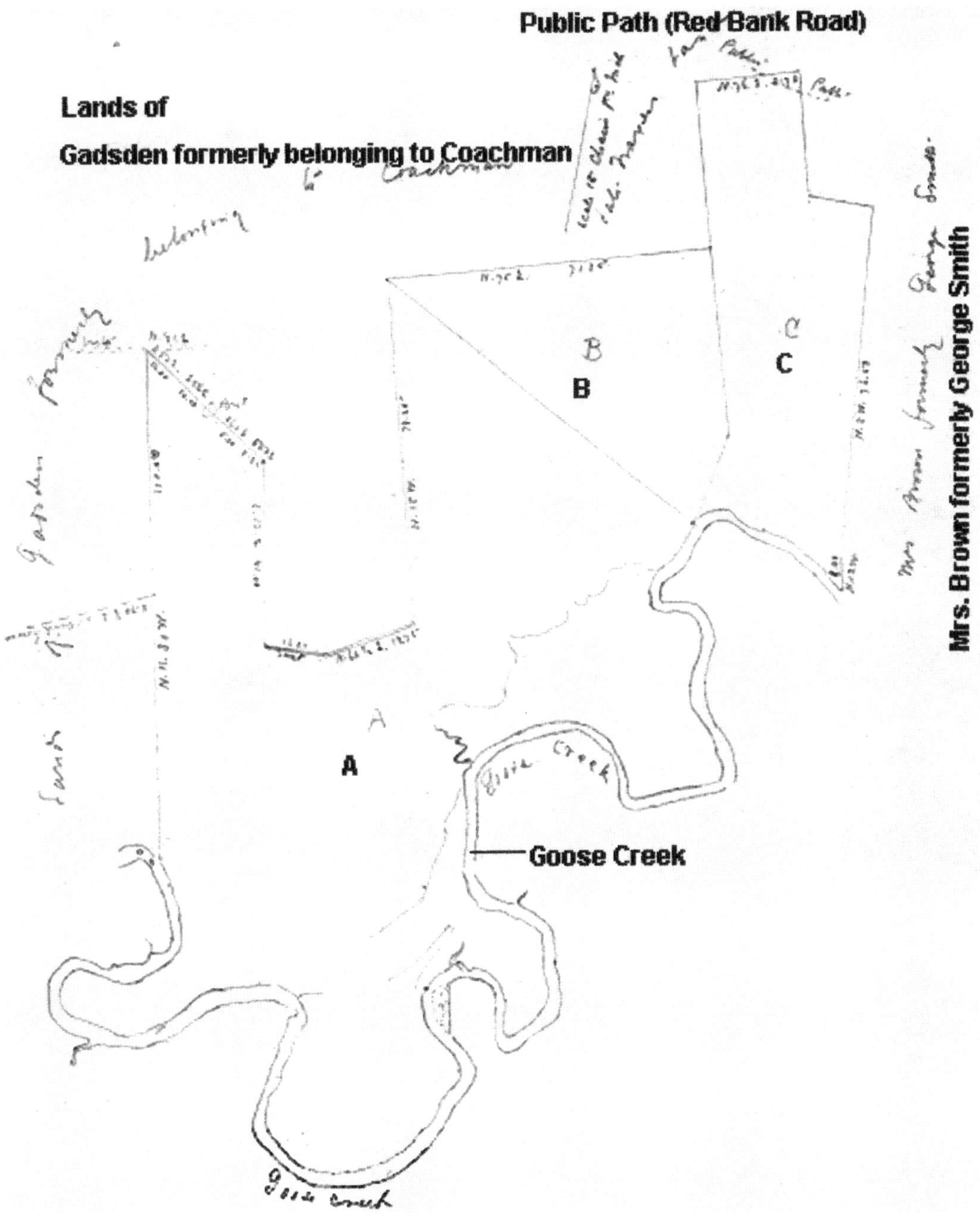

Plat 7.16 This partial plat was made from three surveys to show the accumulation of acreage that made up "Ravenel's" estate in 1857. Section A was surveyed in 1788 by John Purcell and consisted of 1,173 acres. Section B was surveyed by John Purcell in 1802 and consisted of 237 acres. Section C was surveyed by Mr. Sckrine in 1800 and consisted of 275 acres. The total plantation was 1,685 acres. The tracing of this survey was made by H.A.M. Smith and is among the collections of the South Carolina Historical Society. The manuscript words were added for this publication.

The Brockington archaeological study indicates that the Ravenel Plantation overlaid land that was once part of William Johnson's White House Estate. The archaeological team investigated a settlement found on an 1857 plat. This settlement featured one building, a main house and at least four lesser structures lining both sides of the entrance road. An old chimney is marked on the plat, indicating an earlier occupancy. This may be the remains of White House. Contemporary aerial photographs of the lands show water reserves and outlines of abandoned rice fields on Goose Creek.

The Johnson house at White House was destroyed by fire and temporary structures were erected on the site from time to time that were occupied by tenant farmers. A small cemetery is located on a high bank on a restricted portion of the national defense property. Two markers are present, but only one was legible in the twentieth century. It read: "In Memory of Julia Giles Died Jan. 24, 1885 Aged 84 Years May Her Soul Rest in Peace." Near the Vanderdussen/Johnson settlement is another small cemetery. Two of the grave stone inscriptions read "Abraham Loney December 31, 1890 to February 3, 1911," and "Charles Carey March 4, 1864 to April, 1916." The third marker is merely a few bricks and bears no inscription. Also nearby and overlooking the waters of Goose Creek are the remains of an indigo vat. This unusual vat is constructed of bricks and features an arched brick roof. Most indigo vats were made of wood with wooden or thatch roofs and have not survived. The brick vaulted roof served to protect the mixture from dilution from rain while fermenting. This rare find has been recommended to the National Register of Historic Places.

Estates on the Cooper River

Palmettos

Palmettos Plantation was located where Goose Creek flows into the Cooper River. The Proprietors issued a grant to John Coming in 1672, just two years after the earliest English settlement in Charleston. The deed to the property was transferred to Landgrave Robert Daniel in 1698 and then passed to James Risbie.[603] It contained 638 acres when it later conveyed to George Smith.[604] An early narrative described the tract as the site of an "old brick dwelling house." The home was destroyed by fire, but had been one of a few, "where the basement or ground floor was loopholed through the brick wall so as to use musketry for defense against attack by Indians…"[605] It is likely that the house was constructed prior to the Yemassee Indian War of 1715. George Smith (1674–1753) was the son of the First Landgrave Thomas Smith and Barbara Atkins. He was born in England, immigrated with his parents to South Carolina, and then returned to Great Britain for his education. He studied medicine and was again in South Carolina by late 1697. He inherited the brick house at Yeamans Hall and his father's medical instruments.[606]

Archar (1702–1760) was the son of Dr. George Smith and Dorothy Archar Smith. He inherited all of the 810 acres at Palmettos from his father. While Archar owned Palmettos, he worked approximately nineteen slaves and was the co-owner of the schooner *Trial,* which he used to bring one cargo of slaves to Charleston. He was elected to represent Goose Creek in the Eleventh, Thirteenth and Fifteenth Royal Assemblies, but declined to serve in all except the Thirteenth Assembly. He and his wife, Edith Waring, had eight children. The land remained in the family after Archar's death eventually passing to a grandson who was also named Archar. Archar the grandson lived on the estate where he mortgaged the property in 1786 and with the money made many improvements.[607] He owned the Plantation during the Revolutionary War when a party of British landed their boat at Palmettos and approached the mainhouse. Archar Smith defended the place by shooting the officer in command. Smith's portrait hung in the hall of the old house for many years.[608]

A large tract of marshlands was added to the estate early in the 1800s when another descendent, George A.Z. Smith, was the owner, but the plantation was transfered out of the Smith family to Charles T. Brown in 1826. At that time, the tract consisted of 1,644 acres, which was bounded on the south by Filbin Creek, east by the Cooper and west by Yeamans Hall. The United States Government purchased the tract during World War I. Today, the South Carolina State Ports Authority occupies the waterfront and a section of the Naval Weapons Station is situated on the remaining section.

Red Bank

Red Bank Plantation is located on the Cooper River south of the confluence of Back River and is bordered by Goose Creek on the south. A title search conducted in the late 1800s for John Poppenheim, traced the division and recombination of the property during the late eighteenth and nineteenth centuries. Confusion of land ownership resulted when various intermarriages divided the land among extended family members and transfers of titles and deeds were made in an effort to keep the property within the ownership of the two extended families during a two hundred year period.

The lord proprietors issued the original Red Bank grant in 1710 to Nathaniel Snow. This small grant of four hundred acres was strategically situated on the deep waters of the Cooper River at the "cut." The importance of water travel for trade was demonstrated in 1705, when a cut was made through tidal marshes to circumvent an oxbow in the river. The cut made the water journey to Charleston considerably shorter. Nathaniel Snow, a surgeon, added to his holdings with a second four hundred acre grant that doubled the size of his estate. He and his wife, Frances, gave a deed of land to two friends, Edward and Mary Shrewsbury. The agreement stated that the land was awarded for "love and affection." The land included the property next to the cut, along with the use of the woodland, in partnership with Snow, for making bricks. For five shillings annually the couple could also use the woodlands to support their "island plantation." [609] The "cleared land next to the Cutt [sic]" as set aside for this gift may have been the origin of the small lot, later known as Red Bank Landing. Dr. Snow lived at Red Bank until his death in 1728.[610] The inventory of Snow's estate revealed the standard household items and also listed "some brick layer tools & brick molds."[611] It appears that Snow was one of the earliest brick makers in Goose Creek and a forerunner to the important brick industry in that area.

Snow's last will and testament ordered that his son, William, sell the combined eight hundred acre tract. Accordingly, William sold the land to Alexander Nisbett in 1729.[612] The sale included a seventy-five acre island in the marshes on the northern bank of Goose Creek called Snow's Island.[613] Nisbett worked the land for four years before he sold both tracts to John Walker for £350. John Walker worked the land for more than thirty years before he, by way of his attorney, sold Red Bank, minus the seventy-five acres on Snow Island, to William Withers in 1765.[614] This sale also excluded

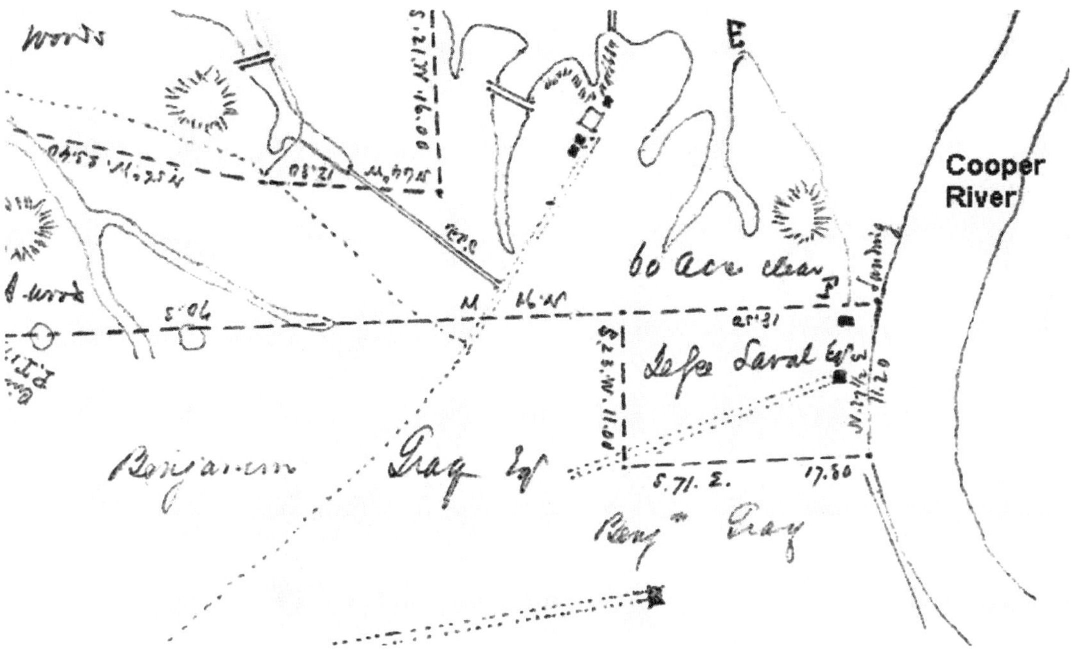

Plat 7.17 This partial plat shows the eight- to ten-acre tract on the Cooper River called Red Bank Landing. The plat is part of a larger plat made from a 1797 survey by John Diamond that was traced by H.A.M. Smith and is among the collections of the South Carolina Historical. The words "Cooper River" were added for this publication to improve orientation.

an eight to ten acre parcel at the deep water landing on the river. This small parcel, called "Red Bank Landing," remained a separately owned transfer area for goods moving from land transport to barge, or boats bound for Charleston and beyond. Partial plat 7.17 indicates that by 1797, the lands near the cut were well occupied with roads, paths and structures.

The 1797 plat (plat 7.18) noted that Mary and Peter Tamplett owned the tract consisting of 662 acres on the Back and Cooper Rivers, called Red Bank, prior to 1797.[615] The exact period of ownership is not documented on the plat, but the notation indicates that at least two hundred of the acres were once part of Landgrave Thomas Smith's early grant, and five hundred acres were part of the original grant to Nathaniel Snow made in 1739.[616] The lands of Hugh Swinton, Benjamin Gray, Benjamin Bordeaux and the heirs of John Withers bound the Red Bank property in 1797. Nathaniel Bordeaux bordered the lands to the west. The 1797 plat also shows the small rectangular property consisting of eight to ten acres at the Cooper River landing, and a building at the landing with a road leading to it. The plat indicates that Jesse Laval (Colonel Laval) owned the parcel. John Irving visited the site and stated that there was "an extensive pottery for the manufacture of tile."[617] Archaeological investigation at the water's edge of Red Bank Landing found brick scatters below the water surface and three wooden piles, which were probably the remains of a dock. The plat also shows a building and three smaller structures situated near an inlet north of the Red Bank Landing. An earlier 1789 plat showed a main building with six smaller structures lining the approach road.

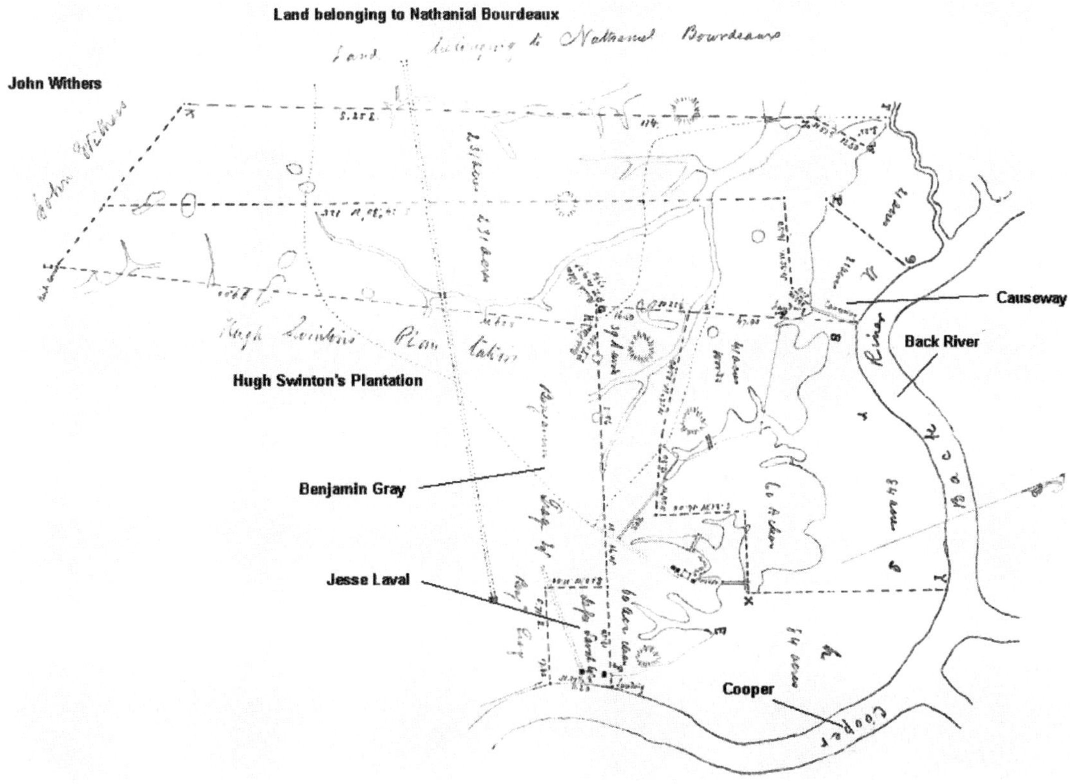

Plat 7.18 This partial plat was drawn from a survey made in 1797 by John Diamond. The plat shows 662 acres of land called Red Bank at the confluence of the Cooper and Back Rivers. The plat was traced by H.A.M. Smith and is among the collections of the South Carolina Historical Society.

Aaron Loocock acquired Red Bank, excluding Snow Island and the landing. He was a prominent landowner, buying, leasing and selling a number of plantations in Goose Creek. He and his wife, Mary, leased half of Red Bank Landing to Peter Gray in 1789 and three years later, sold 314 acres to Gray. Peter Gray was the son of Henry Gray and Anne Villeponteaux. They resided nearby on a 570-acre tract, mortgaged from Anne's father, Peter Villeponteaux.[618] Henry was a tax collector for the Goose Creek Parish with 32 slaves.[619] His son, Peter Gray, appears on the 1790 census as the owner of six slaves. Peter served as a Lieutenant in the Second Regiment of Foot for the Americans during the Revolution and fought at Fort Moultrie. He was promoted to Captain, but taken prisoner of war after the fall of Charleston. After the war, he was elected to represent Goose Creek in the Eighth General Assembly. He also served as a delegate to the state constitutional convention in 1790. He and his wife, Hannah, reared one son, Benjamin Francis Gray.[620]

Peter and Hanna Gray conveyed their 314-acre site to their son Benjamin Gray in 1795. Later this tract passed from Gray to John Bowen, and then to Joseph H. Ramsey and William Tennent. The Loococks, who owned the other half of Red Bank, sold their tract to Hugh Swinton in 1792. Snow Island nearby had stayed in the Snow family for three generations, but James Snow, the grandson of Nathaniel, sold it to Edward Tanner and he in turn sold the island to Hugh Swinton. With the

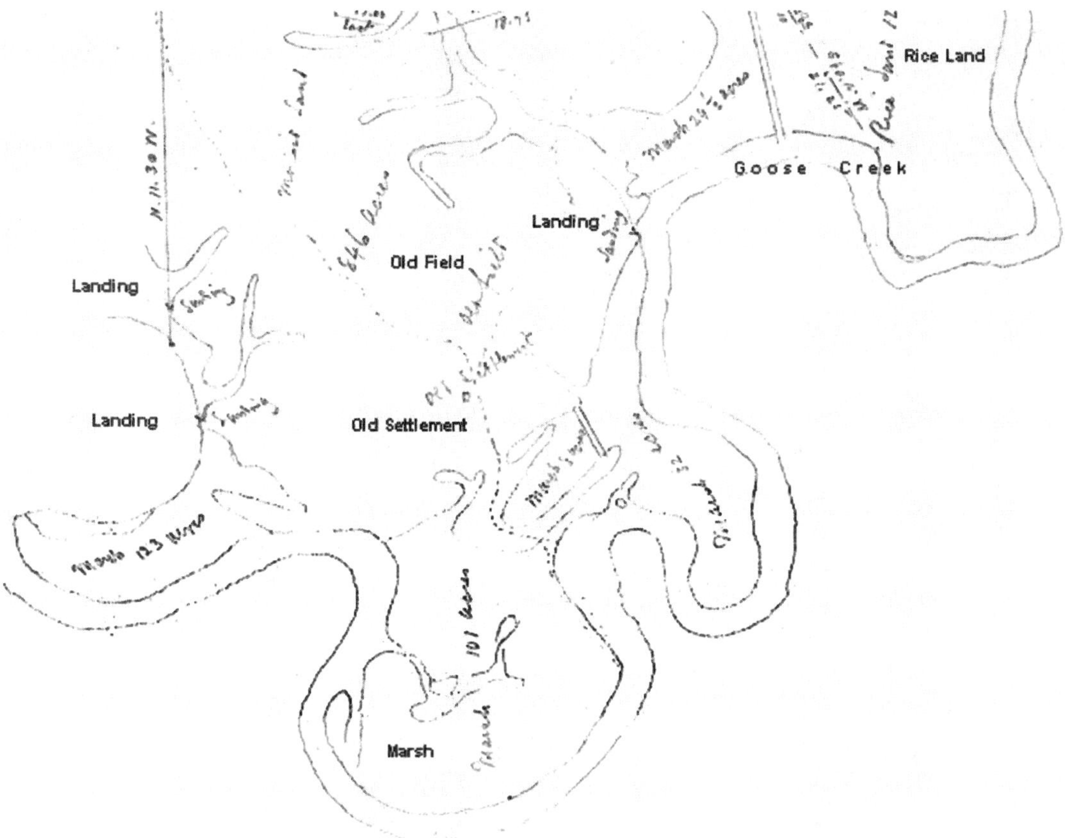

Plat 7.19 This partial plat shows the southern lands owned by the Tennents. The manuscript was added for this publication. The plat was traced by H.A.M. Smith and is among the collections of the South Carolina Historical Society.

purchase of Snow Island, Hugh Swinton's holdings consisting of 666 acres of the original 800-acre of Red Bank estate.

Joseph H. Ramsey and William Tennent, in partnership, managed to consolidate all of the old Red Bank estate and more. They purchased the original Red Bank tract along with additional lands on Goose Creek contiguous to the west and south so that by 1803, Ramsey and Tennent owned an estate larger than the original grant. Their property consisted of 966 acres for a short time, but it was soon divided between two Tennents in 1805. Charles Tennent acquired a U shaped, 656-acre section with both ends bounding on the Cooper. William Tennent kept the central section with three sides bounded by William's land, and one side bordering the Cooper River.[621] William Tennent was wealthy. The records show that he purchased twenty-three slaves from his neighbor, Antoine Delajonchere, in 1804.[622]

It appears as if the Tennent/Ramsey families intermarried and parts of the original estate were devised to subsequent generations of Ramseys and Tennents until Mary Ramsey Tennent received the lands in 1856. Mary acquired the tract, "for consideration of natural love for our daughter…wife of J.S. Tennent."[623] At that time, only the northern half of Red Bank passed to Mary Ramsey Tennent. Charles Tennent conveyed the southern section consisting of 356 acres to his son, William in 1805. Eight years later, Alexander Kirk acquired these 356 acres.

Plat 7.19 shows the southern Red Bank tract on Goose Creek. Dikes and ditches that regulated the water reserve are shown in the upper right quadrant. A long causeway through the marsh to the deep waters of Goose Creek is shown right of center, and a smaller causeway is shown at the bottom left. Also at bottom left is a structure indicated with the words "old Settlement" which probably indicates the location of Johnson's earlier White House Plantation main house and slave quarters.

A Methodist-meeting campsite was located near Red Bank Landing close to the mouth of Goose Creek. It featured a convenient landing on a small bluff on Tucker's land.[624] John Tucker held the deed to the southern tract until 1856, and apparently allowed the camp to occupy his property until the camp burned some years later. Charles Graves held the title in 1862 and used the property as a landing. There were challenges and exceptions to the title, but in spite of some irregularities Mr. John F. Poppenheim purchased the tract with a clear title in 1880.[625]

Near the end of the nineteenth century, John Frederick Poppenheim owned farmland in Berkeley County. The 1880 Agricultural Census shows that John F. Poppenheim owned and farmed 47 cleared acres and owned an additional 853 acres of wooded land. He raised fifty thousand pounds of rice in 1879. John Frederick was the son of Dr. John Lewis Poppenheim. Dr. Poppenheim, the father, owned and farmed 90 acres where he produced one hundred thousand pounds of rice in 1879. Both raised corn and cattle, as well as the large rice crops on properties south and contiguous to the Elms Estate.

John Frederick Poppenheim and Ann, his wife, reared nine children on properties that eventually included most of the land between Foster Creek and Goose Creek, east of the Seaboard Coastline Railroad and west to the Cooper River. Early in the century, the whistle stop at Red Bank Road was named "Innis Station," (sometimes "Inn Nest") but the area was often referred to as "Poppenheim's Crossing." John F. Poppenheim married Victoria Caroline Cummings near 1887 and they occupied two houses on their Red Bank estate. In the winter, they remained at their home located where the Marrington outdoor recreation center is located today. In the summer, they sought the river breezes, and stayed at their Red Bank Landing home on a high bank overlooking the Cooper River. Today the home of the commanding officer of the Naval Weapons Station is situated on that spot. Remaining at that site is a small cemetery with two inscribed markers and one brick tomb.

It appears as if Poppenheim was a careful steward of his large estate. He practiced selective cutting of trees and used control burns to keep his pine forests open, with unrestricted views for hundreds of yards. He raised cattle and hogs in the forests and pasture, grew cotton and almost every produce imaginable. He hired local "cotton pickers" and paid them fifteen cents per pound. He kept a small sawmill for his building needs and used his tugboat named "Willie" to push his floating rafts of timber downstream to the Halsey Lumber Mill on the Ashley River. Roper Hospital stands at the lumber mill location today.

An important family residing at the Red Bank/Marrington Estate was of Japanese ancestry. At the urging of U.S. Christian missionaries and counter to the wishes of their parents, twenty-four-year-old Hisa Aona (1885–1968) and twenty-five-year-old Takai Kodama (1885–1941) emigrated from Japan to the United States on their wedding day in 1906. The Kodamas arrived in South Carolina to work

Photograph 7.16 This photograph shows Mr. John F. Poppenheim at his home at Marrington Plantation. The photograph is among the private papers of Terrence Larimer.

on the Back River rice fields owned by the Stoney family at Medway, but devastating hurricanes in 1910 and 1911 damaged the dikes so severely that rice agriculture was no longer profitable. Fortunately the Kodamas were introduced to John F. Poppenheim. Poppenheim rice fields were still workable, he needed assistance and the Kodamas understood rice culture. Consequently, the Kodamas began sharecropping on Poppenheim's land beginning a long relationship between the two families.[626] Poppenheim was one of the last rice farmers in the state. Tobacco was fast replacing rice as a cash crop and a series of seven devastating hurricanes in twenty years destroyed dikes and put an end to competitive production. It was also becoming increasingly more difficult to find experienced rice farmers such as the Kodamas.

The Kodamas first lived in a small house near Poppenheim's winter home at Marrington. When Poppenheim retired from farming in the early 1920s, the Kodamas moved into his Red Bank house overlooking the Cooper River. Eight children were born at Marrington, including: Ida, John, Tokeo, Henry, William, Mack, Caroline and Jack.[627] The 1920 census recorded one other Japanese family residing near the Kodamas, but no other information about this family is available. The Kadoma children attended the one-room, Red Bank School, funded by the Berkeley School District. Later they walked to Cannon's General Store near the Oaks Country Club to catch a ride to Mt. Holly, where they transferred to a bus for a fourteen mile ride to Berkeley High School.[628]

The Poppenheims had no children of their own and welcomed Kodama's oldest child, Ida into their home and reared her as their own. Ida used the Poppenheim name when she attended school and married, but she was never legally adopted. John F. Poppenheim died in 1934 at the age of seventy-seven and devised to Ida 542 acres of Cooper River waterfront. He also left Takai Kodama 62 acres on the river where the Naval Weapon's Station commanding officer's house stands today. One hundred and six acres were left to four of the Kodama boys: John, Tokeo, Henry and William.[629]

In 1926, Percy Orian Mead, Sr. moved with his family to Berkeley County from Savannah, Georgia and began purchasing property. He bought the Red Bank tract from the Orangeburg Hunt Club (lands between Red Bank Road and Goose Creek). Later he bought the Marrington Tract (lands between Red Bank and Foster Creek) from Poppenheim. He added the Sunnyside Property at the confluence of Goose Creek to the Cooper and the Dute property (a small tract at Dute's Pond). He also bought Cedar Hill (now Menriv Housing). These acquisitions included most of the lands owned by Poppenheim and the Kodamas except one tract overlooking the Cooper. Eventually, Mead controlled all the lands between Foster Creek and Goose Creek, east of the Seaboard Coastline Railroad line.

P.O. Mead built a large thirty-two room home at the site of the old Vanderdussen/Johnson house with a dock on Goose Creek, and thus enjoyed access to a deep waterway to Charleston. The Yeamans Hall Estate was visible directly across the marsh and creek water.[630] W.L. Stribling bought Marrington from Mead to harvest timber and held it only a couple of years before selling it to Adolfus N. Manucy.

Adolphus N. Manucy (1895–1981) was the last private owner of Marrington. He was a self-made Italian immigrant, who in spite of a mere fourth grade education became a well-to-do entrepreneur and businessman. He was a business partner with P.O. Mead who worked with him until 1932. At that time Manucy returned to Savannah, Georgia. He later returned at the encouragement of Mead to buy the Marrington Property. It was either Stribling or Manucy who built the Marrington house on Poppenheim's home site. Westvaco used the house as a hunting lodge, and later the navy used it as the Rod and Gun Club House. It burned in 1977.

P.O. Mead harvested timber and used mules to drag the logs to Mary's Landing on Foster Creek or to Snow Point on the Cooper. There he used a tugboat to tow the log rafts to the Charleston Lumber Mills.[631] During the 1940s, West Virginia Pulp and Paper Company (Westvaco) bought most of Marrington and during the same period Ida Kadoma and Westvaco agreed on a price for her Red Bank land. The paper company first wanted the Red Bank site to house a proposed Cooper River paper plant, but these plans were thwarted when the Federal Government expanded the nearby military holdings. The United States Navy desired the proposed paper mill site because of the deep water and the inland security. Thus, the navy acquired the properties and added more lands for housing, schools, and recreation areas in 1970. Congressman L. Mendel Rivers facilitated the purchase of the land and was honored by having his name attached to the "Menriv" housing subdivision.

When the navy began expanding their holdings and buying lands from the paper company, the Kodamas sold their farms and moved to nearby Mt. Holly. There they opened a general store and continued as well-respected members of the tight knit Mt. Holly community. A death and funeral notice, which appeared in the February 16, 1953 edition of the *Berkeley Democrat,* tells much about the Japanese family. The notice explained that William Kodama of Mt. Holly was found drowned in the Cooper and buried at Smyrna Methodist Church in Groomsville. The notice explained that a married sister resided on the Naval base and another sister lived at Mt. Holly. Two brothers were at Mt. Holly, one at Bonneau and one stationed with the U.S. Army in California. Members of the Poppenheim and Kodama families are buried at Smyrna United Methodist Church on Cyprus Garden Road in the old Groomsville community a few miles north west of Mt. Holly.

Estates on Back River

Parnassus

Parnassus (once "Mount Parnassus") was the home of Zachariah Villeponteaux, a French Huguenot. As a young man, Villeponteaux settled upon the 543-acre land grant on Back River in 1733. He increased his land holding to 748 acres, worked as many as forty-six slaves and became a wealthy and prominent South Carolinian.[632] He was probably the most important brickmaker in the Charleston area during the mid-eighteenth century.[633] Villeponteaux's bricks were cited as the standard when St. Stephens Parish ordered bricks for construction of a new chapel in 1759, and he supplied the brick for Charleston's city fortifications, St. Michael's Church, Pompion Chapel and Charles Pinckney's downtown residence.[634]

Plat 7.20 describes sections of Parnassus near the main house that shows that Villeponteaux manufactured brick at that site. The plat indicates "Old Brick Works," "Brick Yard," and the "Landing" on Back River. Wooden brick molds were likely built and packed with wet clay at the brick works site and the area probably featured kilns for brick baking. Cords of firewood were kept on hand along with a supply of unbaked brick stacked nearby. The brickyard was likely a series of sheds or barns where the unbaked brick (sometimes called green brick) was stacked and dried. The "landing" consisted of a built-up causeway that traversed the marsh to the deep water of Foster Creek. Here the bricks were loaded onto barges and sent downstream to Charleston. Brick scatters and clay pits are evident at these sites today.

It is likely that this brick industry evolved into a lucrative roofing tile manufacturing industry. The Brockington archaeological team examined a tile factory site in 1995. The team found evidence of a brick lined cistern. This cistern was bell shaped with dimensions of about two meters in diameter and two meters deep. A wide scatter of tile was found near the cistern. The tiles were manufactured with red ware clay and glazing techniques and each featured a curved shape for overlaying as roofing material. The underside of each tile was also treated with black glazing, as well as a notch to secure one tile to another during and after installation.

The site described by plat 7.20 is probably the "Tile Manufactory" advertised in the Charleston paper in 1786. The advertisement enthusiastically described the benefits of building with Goose Creek brick.

> *It is with pleasure we inform you that the Tile Manufactory established in Goose Creek, about sixteen miles from this city, is brought to great perfection. A correspondent hopes the citizens will encourage so good an undertaking, to prevent the dreadful calamity of fire, as they can be sold at a very cheap rate; a cargo of them has already been brought to market, and esteemed by judges to be no inferior to those from Europe, Carolinians encourage your own manufacture!*[635]

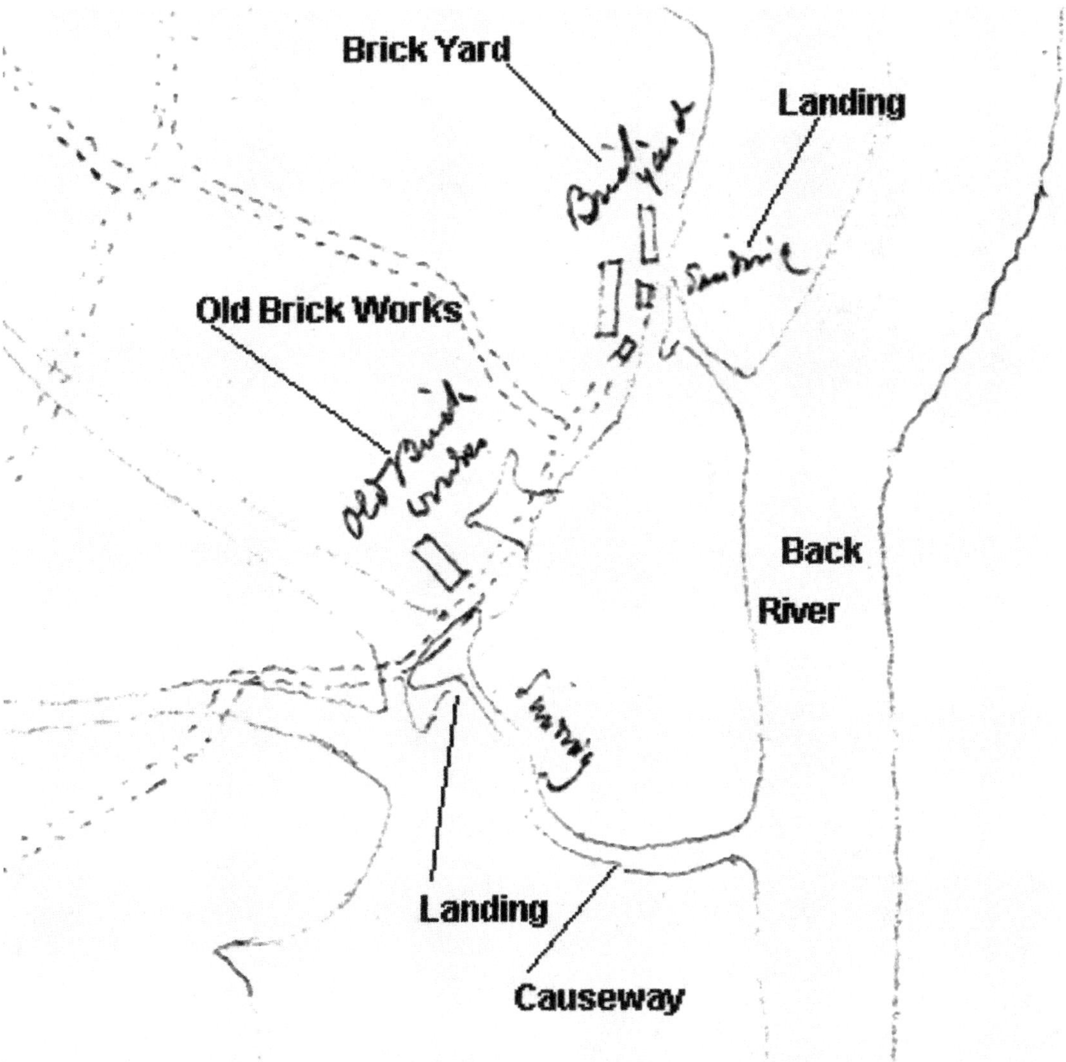

Plat 7.20 The partial plat shows an "Old Brick Works," "Brick Yard" and "Landing" at Parnassus on Back River. The plat was drawn from a resurvey done in 1803 by John Diamond. The plat was traced by H.A.M. Smith and is among the collections of the South Carolina Historical Society. The manuscript labels were added to this publication for clarity.

Plat 7.21 shows a southern section of Parnassus near the confluence of Foster Creek and Back River. This plat shows six structures labeled "Old Brick Kiln." Nearby, on the southern side of Foster Creek was Mary's Landing. A wide scatter of broken bricks and borrow pits define the landing site today. This was probably an important processing and shipping point. Also there are fifteen clay pits evident today. The pits are round, oval, square or rectangular and are as long as thirty feet and as deep as six to eight feet. Mary's landing is approximately a quarter mile from Back River. Plat 7.21 shows a section of Parnassus with four structures labled as "Old Indigo Vat" on the marsh banks near Big Island. Four

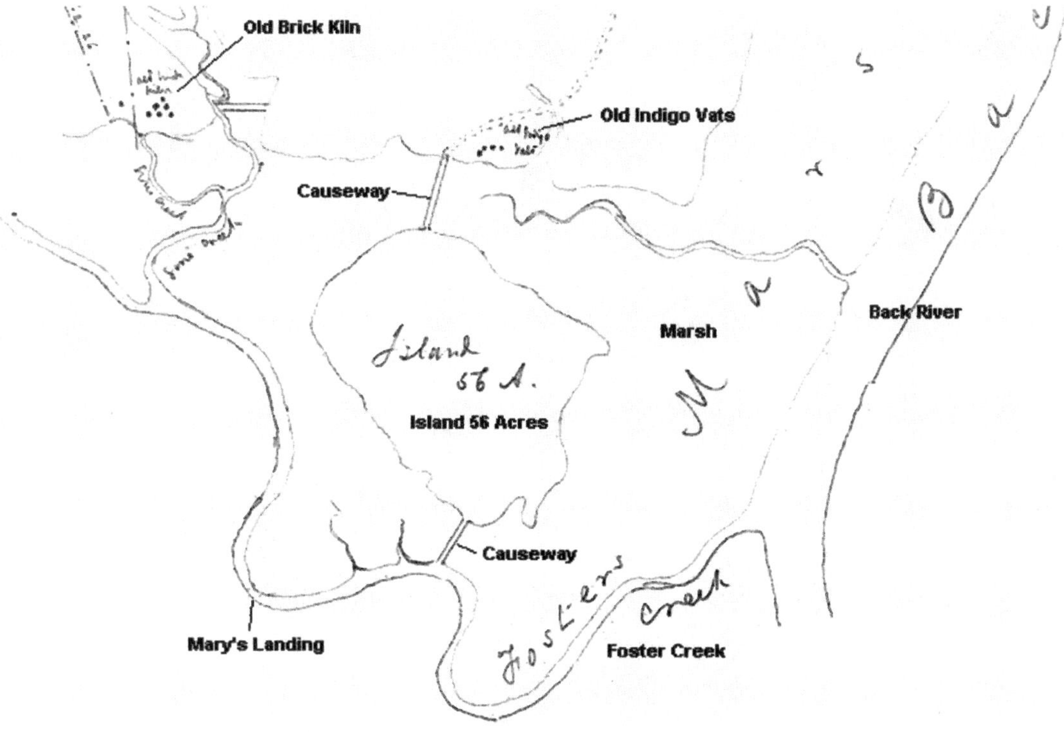

Plat 7.21 This partial plat shows an "Old Brick Kiln" and an "Old Indigo Vat" on the marsh banks near Big Island at the confluence of Foster Creek with Back River. The plat was drawn from a resurvey conducted in 1803 by John Diamond. The plat was traced by H.A.M. Smith and is among the collections of the South Carolina Historical Society. The manuscript labels were added to this publication for clarity.

vats at this location indicate an unusually large industrial site for the colonial era. As a brick baker and indigo processer Villeponteaux was one of the first significant industrialists in South Carolina.

It appears that Villeponteaux resided at Parnassus until his death at eighty to eighty-two years of age and was a long time, active member of the parish. He began his public service in 1731, at the age of thirty-three, when he was named tax inquirer and collector for Goose Creek. Thirteen years later his name appeared on a list of subscribers for a free school in Goose Creek. He promised to pay £59 annually for three years. His pledge was the second largest among the subscribers on the list. Other evidence indicates his importance as a long-term vestryman. On April 7, 1755, he testified under oath that no public register had been kept for eighteen of the twenty years he had served on the church vestry. He also appears to have entered into a business partnership with a neighboring landowner, Henry Gray. Henry Gray and Zachariah Villeponteaux kept a joint account with Thomas Elfe of Charleston for £500.[636] Villeponteaux was also a founding member of the Goose Creek Friendly Society and served several commissions, including commissioner for cleansing the Red Bank Cut and commissioner of the free school at Childsbury. He represented Goose Creek four times in the Royal Assembly and during the American Revolution. He was the father of three children.

After Villeponteaux, the ownership of Parnassus passed to Antoine Francois Michel Delajonchere.[637] Antoine Delajonchere sold the plantation, including 1,355 acres of high ground and 437 acres of marsh in 1803 to Samuel Smith and Dr. Charles Tennent. The Smith/Tennent partners quickly turned the land over to Josiah Smith and others as trustees for Ann Martha Tennent, wife of Charles Tennent.[638] The land was sold at auction due to Smith's debts and changed hands again when it became the property of Dr. Charles Tennent in 1843. Tennent held the land until after the Civil War, and the 1860 census shows that he owned 3,000 acres including the Red Bank land. He was a member of the Tennent family who were leading Presbyterians related to William Tennent, the founder of the famous "Log Cabin" college in New Jersey in 1726. It later became New Jersey College and in 1896, Princeton University.

John B. Irving visited Parnassus a few years after the Civil War. He found little except giant oaks and the remains of a tree lined avenue that led for nearly a mile toward Goose Creek. Numerous large oaks and magnolias remained, as well as roses and other garden flowers. He reported, "In the tangle of vines you find oddly shaped pieces of brick: hemispheres and rounded bases, parts of finials that some ingenious plantation artesan baked."[639] The full 1803 plat partially shown as plat 7.22 describes the principal buildings, outbuildings and worked lands that were probably pleasure gardens. Brockington and Associates, Inc., an archaeological company, studied Parnassus in 1995 and discovered remains of the main house, a formal garden and a slave row. An ornamental surface feature was discovered on the south side of the entrance avenue near the remains of the main house. A small "water feature" about ten

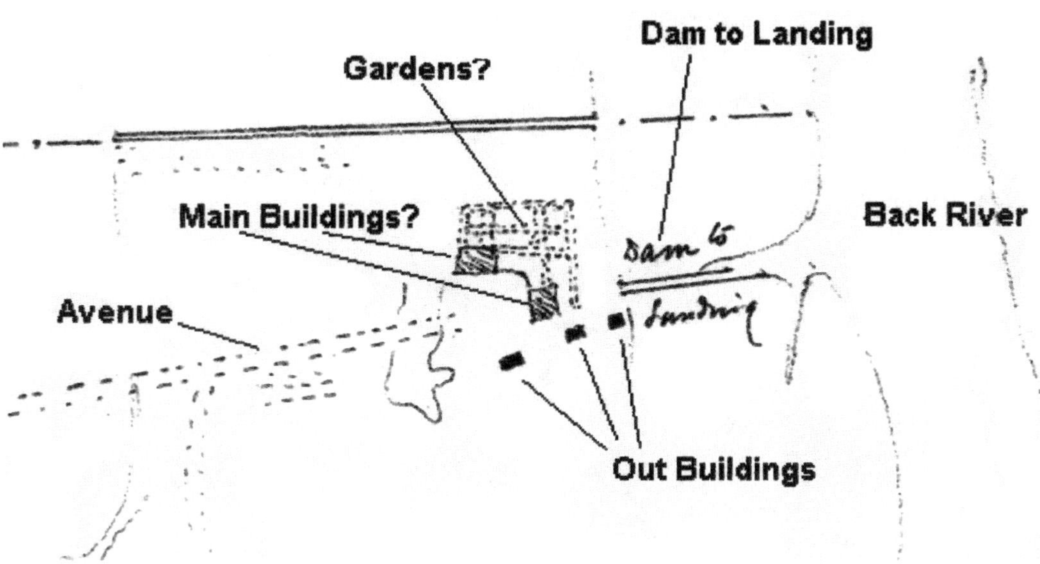

Plat 7.22 This partial plat shows the settlement with the main house and outbuildings. Walls or walkways may indicate a "pleasure garden." The "Dam to Landing" is shown crossing the marsh to Back River. John Diamond made this drawing from a resurvey in 1803. The plat was traced by H.A.M. Smith and is among the collections of the South Carolina Historical Society. The manuscript labels were added to this publication for clarity.

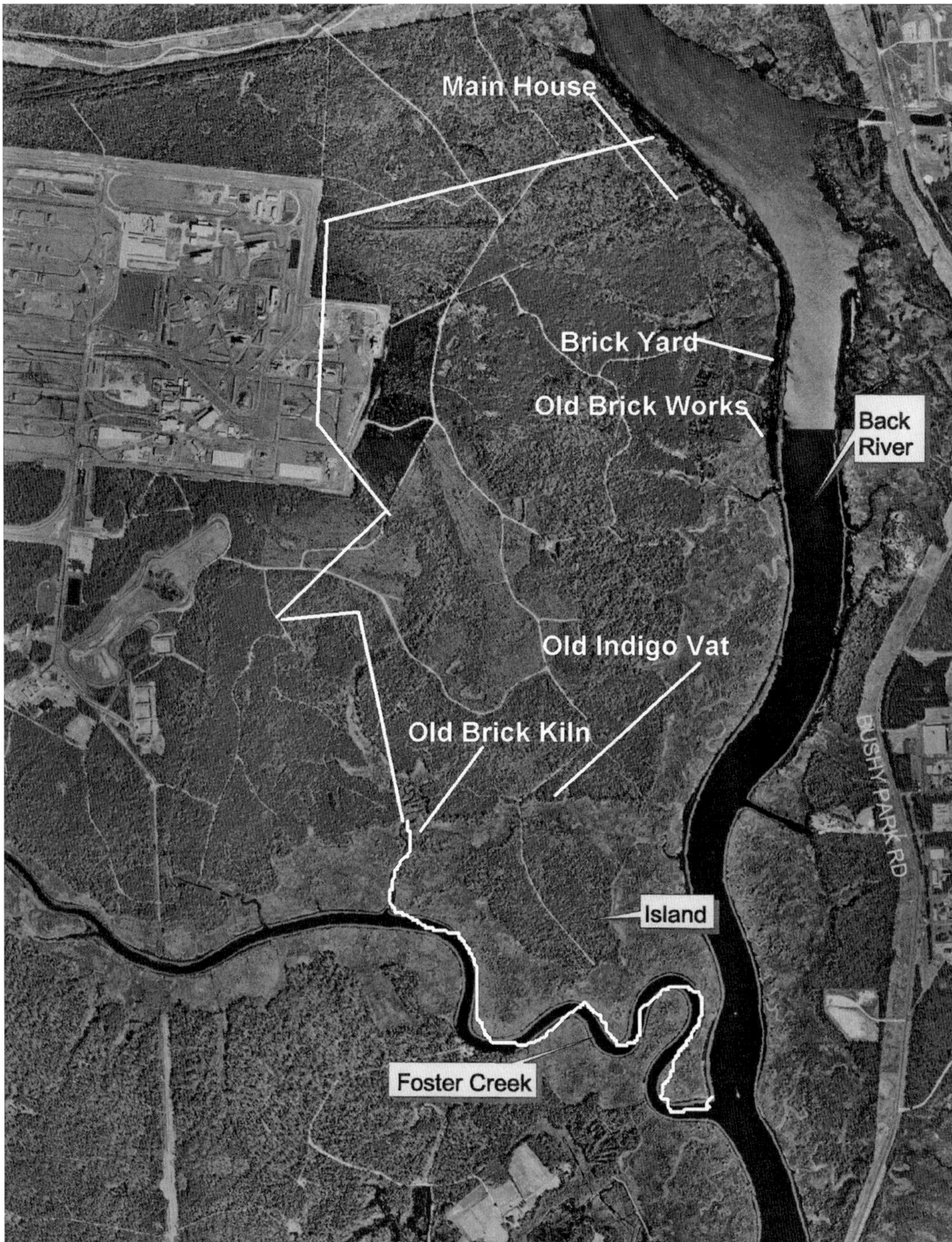

Photograph 7.17 This photograph shows the Parnassus Plantation overlay on an aerial photograph. The approximate locations of the important historic sites are noted. The photograph is in the possession of the author.

feet in diameter, a dike and brick piles nearby appears to have been a support such as a wall or gate pillar. This probably was part of a large "pleasure garden." Remains of another brick building were found south of the road represented by the rubble of a chimney base. Thus, there appears to have been two general residential areas—one included the main house, the other included the slave residential area. The slave residential area revealed a high percentage of colono ware and few ceramics. The formal garden probably served as a division between the two living areas.

Parnassus was not affected by the Civil War until late 1865, when all except Mrs. Tennent and her daughters were forced to abandon the plantation. A band of foraging Negro troops invaded the house and demanded dinner, which caused the remaining Tennent family members to leave the next day. Shortly thereafter, smallpox drove the marauders from the plantations, but not before the home was vandalized and ransacked. In *A Day on Cooper River,* Louisa Stoney wrote of recollections of one of the sons of the Tennent family. She wrote, "He rode up to find no living soul in the line of Negro houses that flanked the avenue…" The following year, the house was caught in a forest fire and burned to the ground.

William Tennent, trustee of the property for Mrs. Tennent, sold Parnassus to Edwin H. Schirmer in 1876.[640] Schirmir probably did not farm the land, but leased it to various tenant farmers and others. He rented it for three years to J.H. Parker and Company for production of turpentine and another tenant was accused of damaging the grounds. He cut the walk of cedar trees and looted the brick from the house and graveyard. In 1888, William E. Stoney, Samuel Gaillard Stoney and John Taylor bought the seventeen hundred acre Parnassus Plantation from the South Carolina Loan and Trust Company.[641] The Stoneys owned Medway Plantation at that time and joined Parnassus to that property. A 1906 plat of Stoney's Back River plantations included Parnassus, Back River, the Cottage, and the Prioleau and Donnelly tracts totaling 5,492 acres.[642]

Some grave markers remain at Parnassus. On the Negro burying ground, approximately sixty yards north of the entrance road, is a lone headstone that marks the grave of a Tennent family nurse. The inscription reads, "Bella, a faithful servant." A footstone is located nine feet west of the head marker. The Brockington and Associates archeologists recommended that the Parnassus Plantation be nominated to the National Register of Historic Places. Specifically, the brick kiln ruins owned by the renown Frenchman, Zachariah Villeponteaux, the slave cemetery, the main house, associated outbuildings and the earthen causeway that connects the main plantation with kilns, are important evidence of this early industrial location. Photograph 7.17 shows a current aerial view of the land and the approximate location of the important historic sites.

Prioleau

Little more than a quarter mile north of the Parnassus main house, near a high bank of Back River, was the home of the Prioleau family. Elias Prioleau was a native of Poms and Saintonge, France, and one of the Huguenot emigrants. Elias came to Carolina about 1687, two years after the revocation of the Edict of Nantes. He purchased 140 acres of land on the west bank of Back River from John Davies.[643] This was the first of five land purchases that eventually amounted to a 1,651-acre plantation. According to a plat drawn from a 1792 survey by Joseph Purcell, the estate was the combination of five tracts.[644] One tract was originally devised to John Davies in 1692. Nicholas Pettibois owned another tract as early as 1692. A third tract was the property of Captain George Smith as early as 1698, and Thomas Smith owned the fourth tract in 1716. The fourth tract was likely the property of Thomas Smith of Bay Street (1695–1769). He was a successful Charleston merchant and part owner of the ship *Charming Nancy*.[645] Alexander Parris owned the fifth tract as late as 1733. Elias Prioleau died in 1699 at the age of forty, probably from malaria after buying three of the five tracts. His grandson, Samuel, added the last two tracts when he inherited the Plantation.

Samuel, son of Elias Prioleau, was born in 1690. He married Mary Magdelon Gendron. An interesting memorial was made to her and her four sisters. The memorial resulted from the planting of five live oaks that were known for many years as the "five sisters." [646] These trees survived many fires, but in 1918 a timber company damaged them badly, and only one tree remains today. Samuel Prioleau was a member of His Majesty's Council, and in 1732 was an officer in His Majesty's Horse Guards. The Horse Guards were the military forerunner of the Charleston Light Dragoons.

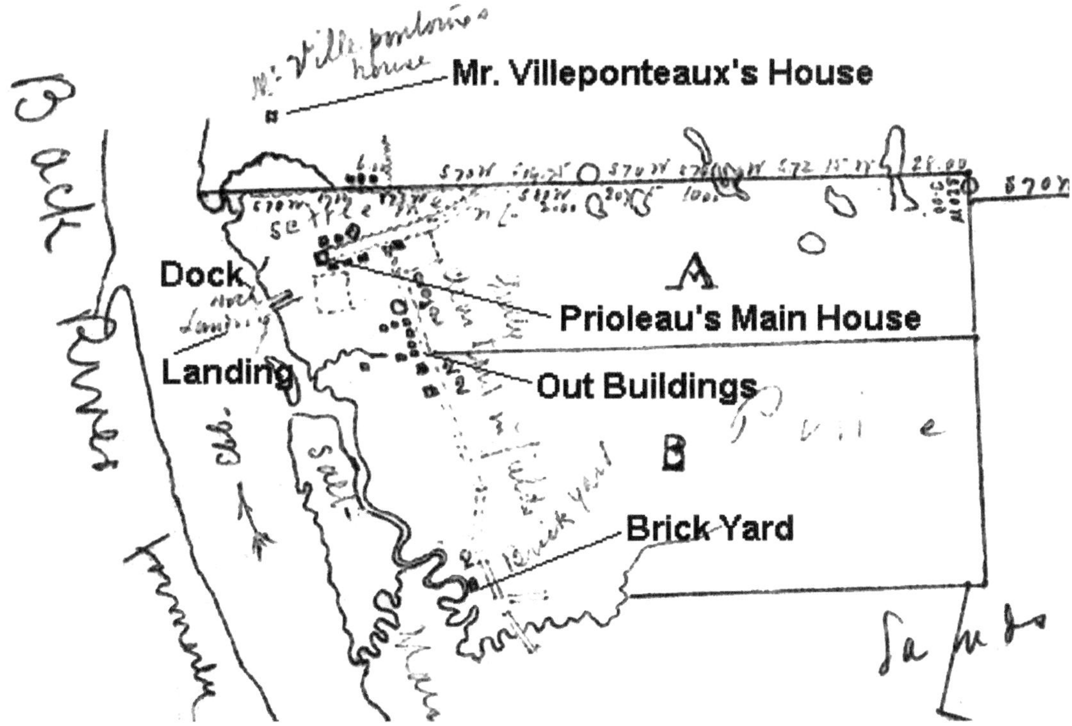

Plat 7.23 This partial plat describes the settlement part of Prioleau's Plantation. The main house belonging to Zachariah Villeponteaux is shown on the bank of Back River near the upper margin. Prioleau's main house and outbuildings are shown in the center of the plat. Joseph Purcell drew the plat from a 1792 survey. The manuscript labels were added for this publication. H.A.M. Smith traced the plat. The tracing is among the collections of the South Carolina Historical Society.

The son of Samuel Prioleau was also named Samuel. He inherited the plantation and increased the acreage by purchasing surrounding tracts. The Prioleau family continued to expand the estate until by 1796 it had increased to approximately 1,240 acres. Plat 7.23, drawn from a 1792 survey shows a clearly defined plantation complex near the banks of Back River. This complex used two approaches, one from the river and one from the land. The approach road from land appeared to intersect Villeponteaux's Avenue. This avenue proceeded to the State Road and appears on Mills' 1825 Atlas as "Back River Lower Road." A landing was located near the main house. Two rows of three buildings flanked the approach avenue. A square area north of the house indicates a formal garden and farther north are structures that were likely farm buildings or perhaps more slave quarters. The approach road continued north to the "Brick Yard" that was near a small tributary to the river. The Prioleau family was not listed among prominent brick producers, and it is likely that the bricks made at this site were used exclusively on the plantation.

Samuel Prioleau Jr. was the son of Samuel Prioleau and Providence Hext. He was a merchant planter with a thriving business in Charleston, his own private wharf and the large estate on Back River. When he died in 1813, he owned ninety-six slaves. He represented the city parishes before and after the revolution and was active in the war. He married Catherine Cordes and with her reared at least eight children. He was one of the many men who were exiled to St. Augustine when Charleston fell to the British. He died in 1813 and was buried on the plantation grounds.[647]

The land was sold to Peter Gaillard Stoney in 1834. According to the 1850 agricultural census, Stoney was a successful rice producer but he sold his plantation three years later to Mary S. Stevens, sister of Dr. Charles Tennent of Parnassus. The land was purchased for her son, Norman Stevens, Jr. He was an invalid, and a little cottage house with high, sharp gables was built on the land for him. Norman Stevens and his wife lived there, and the plantation came to be known as "The Cottage."[648] A German named Lousi, later owned the Cottage and was accused of killing his neighbor's cattle and of destroying a short avenue of oaks by "ringing" them.

Near 1880, Samuel Gaillard Stoney consolidated this tract with his Medway holdings and held it for decades, until the United States Army acquired the land in 1943 under a condemnation suit that consolidated several tracts for the proposed Charleston Ordinance Depot. The Navy's real estate acquisition files record that the land was acquired from George C. Taylor, Samuel G. Stoney and others in the Parnassus area, and Colin Mckay Grant in the Brick Hope and Liberty Hall area. The Navy then obtained more land in 1956 for the Polaris Missile facility.

A small brick-walled family cemetery stands today on a terrace approximately fifty yards from Back River. The cemetery contains four marked graves with inscribed marble ledgers. The inscriptions are weather worn and difficult to read but Samuel Gaillard Stoney was able to record the inscriptions in 1939 and confirmed that this site is the final resting place of Reverend Elias Prioleau, Samuel Prioleau Jr., his wife Catherine Cordes Prioleau, some of their children and other decedents.[649] According to the inscriptions the final internment was in 1874. Brockington and Associates Archaeologists recommended the Prioleau/Cottage Plantation complex for nomination to the National Register of Historic Places in 1997.

Painting 7.1 This painting shows the second Samuel Prioleau painted by Jeremiah Theus. The picture was taken from *Transactions of the Huguenot Society*, vol. 71: pp. 90–91.

Photograph 7.18 This photograph shows "The Cottage" near the site of the Parnassus main house. The photograph is from the *Johnson Scrapbook, Volume 1*, on deposit at the South Carolina Historical Society.

Photograph 7.19 This photograph shows the Prioleau Cemetery. The photograph was taken March 14, 2005, and is in the possession of the author.

Medway Plantation

"The peace of Medway permeates my soul."

Gertrude Sanford Legendre

Sometime near 1687, Signeur D'Arssens arrived in South Carolina. He was probably related to Franciscus Van Arssens (Aarssens, Arrssens, Arsens) who was born at the Hague and who negotiated the marriage of the Prince of Orange and Mary, daughter of Charles I of England. Signeur D'Arssens settled on a Proprietary grant of twelve hundred acres on Back River.[650] The Lord Proprietors informed South Carolina Governor Colleton that, "Mr. John D'Arsens seigneur of Wernhaut being a Person of Quality and the First of his Nation that hath undertaken to Plant in our Province of Carolina." The instructions ordered the governor to survey twelve hundred acres for Van Aarssens and if requested, to arrange that it be, "erected into a Manor with all the Priviledges of a Barony."[651] Van Arssens was in the colony for approximately two years before he died. At that time his widow, Sabina De Vignou, appealed to Governor Colleton for administration of the vast estate.

Thomas Smith soon entered Sabina's life. Thomas Smith of southwest England married Barbara Atkins and fathered two sons, Thomas and George. His family and servants boarded a ship at

Painting 7.2 This painting shows Landgrave Thomas Smith, Esq. one of the "Goose Creek Men" and a proprietary governor of the province of South Carolina. *Courtesy of the South Carolina Historical Society*.

Dartmouth in 1683 and arrived in Carolina the following year. A year after he arrived in South Carolina, Smith received a four-hundred-acre tract of land from the Lord Proprietors for twenty pounds sterling and after some bureaucratic delays and legal problems, Smith took possession of his land and settled upon it. Upon the death of his wife, he married his wealthy widow neighbor, Sabina and "Happily they settled down upon a plantation on Back River, and caused to be built the first brick house in the province, beyond the precincts of the town."[652]

Thomas Smith's marriage to Sabina made him one of the wealthiest men in Carolina and one visitor observed, "We see that drink was served to guests in goblets of pure silver."[653] Smith entertained friends who arrived by boat or carriage including "the Blakes, Boones and many other gentlemen [who] were asked into the Back river parlor to drink beer, smoke a pipe, and take a sly chew from the Landgrave's Tobacco Box."[654]

Medway's early land history was a complex series of transactions, but by 1701 the plantation consisted of three parcels of land totaling 2,550 acres. The first tract was a 400-acre parcel granted to Thomas Smith upon which Medway's present house is situated.[655] The second tract was a 2,100-acre parcel to the north of Smith's 400 acres, and was part of the 12,000 acres originally granted to Van Arssens. In 1689, Smith petitioned the Proprietors for permission to assume the Van Arssen claim to 12,000 acres. The fact that he had to petition the Proprietors for the rights to the grant suggests that the rights had reverted to the lord proprietors. No warrants, surveys or plats related to Van Arssens ownership have been located, but surviving records indicate that the Proprietors acknowledged Van Arssens's original right to the 12,000-acre grant and transferred those rights to Thomas Smith in 1693.[656] The third tract was fifty acres of unclear origin, situated on the dividing line between the two larger parcels. These 50 acres appear to be an additional grant given to account for 50 acres missing from the promised 400-acre tract. The records contain an abstract of a land grant that includes a note stating "quantity missing and 50 acres."[657] The 50-acre grant was awarded and a 350-acre award replaced the 400-acre grant in 1694.[658]

Sabina Smith died in 1689 and was buried near the Medway house in the presence of a number of Goose Creek gentlemen.[659] After her death, Thomas Smith was the sole owner of the large estate with a handsome house and outbuildings. He was appointed governor of southern Carolina in 1693 and served with distinction. During his term he was faced with controversies with regard to tenure of lands, payment of quit rents, naturalization of French Huguenots and other issues with the Proprietors, but he appears to have aptly overcome the heated disagreements. While still governor at the age of forty-six, Landgrave Thomas Smith died and his children buried him at Medway beside his wife, Sabina. A slab was laid over his grave and the inscription can be read today. Sabina received no stone. Gravestones were imported at great expense and she had no children to make that purchase for her.

Governor Archdale described Thomas Smith as "a wise sober and moderate well-living man" and the Proprietors, writing to Governor Archdale on January 10, 1695, stated in part that, "He [Smith] appears to us to have been a man not only of great parts, integrity, and honesty but of a generous temper and a nobleness of spirit as to the public good as is scarcely to be met withal in this age."[660]

In his will, Thomas Smith devised his Charleston house and medical instruments to his son, George, his landgrave's patent to his friend Joseph Blake and the rest of his extensive, valuable estate, including Medway and other lands, to his son, Thomas. By 1702, Thomas Smith II recovered his father's patent from Joseph Blake and "styled himself as Landgrave." The second Landgrave Smith was a planter and large-scale native trader whose agents roamed throughout North and South Carolina. He served several terms in the Commons House of Assembly and held many local commissions, but the younger Landgrave Smith, unlike his father, was a fighter not a negotiator, and after instigating riots in 1704 and 1727 and plotting to usurp the governorship in 1728, he was removed from his seat on the Royal Council. He eventually retired to his home at Yeamans Hall.

On February 28, 1701, Smith sold the Medway house and three parcels of land to Edward Hyrne for £800 of South Carolina currency. Edward Hyrne, an Englishman, was a merchant from Norfolk who came to Carolina in 1700. His young wife, Elizabeth (Massingbred) Hyrne joined him the next year. Hyrne's finances, as well as some questions of character, figured into his emigration. He was accused of misappropriating more than £1,300 sterling, while a port collector in England. Nevertheless, Smith granted him credit to purchase Medway.

Edward Hyrne described what he called his "brave plantation," in a letter he wrote to his brother-in-law in 1701. He wrote that his estate consisted of "2,550 Acres of land, whereof 200 clear'd & most fenc'd in, tho wants repairing; 150 Head of Cattle, 4 Horses, a native Slave almost a Man, a few Hogs, some House hold stuff, & the best Brick-House in all the Country; built about 9 years ago, & cost £700, 80 Foot long, 26 broad, cellar'd throughout."[661] Sadly, soon after writing the optimistic letter, Edward Hyrnes and his young bride suffered a series of misfortunes. Their small child died, they lost a slave to a rattlesnake bite and their home burned to the ground. She described the fire by writing, "we was burn[ed]...out of all, our house taking fire I know not how in the night and burned so fiercely that we had much to do to save the life of poor burry [Burrell, their son] and two beds just to lye on which was the chief of way we saved we also had all our rice and corn and all sorts or our provisions burned. Close and every thing nothing escaped the fire so that if it had not bin for some good people we must have perished."[662]

Undaunted, the Hyrnes rebuilt a smaller version of the original structure on the same site, but bad luck continued and culminated in the loss ownership of Medway due to failure to pay the

Photograph 7.20 This photograph shows the side of the Medway House facing Back River. This view gives a good perspective of the stages of construction beginning with the small central section with stepped gables. The non-symmetrical wings are also shown. ***Courtesy of the Library of Congress.***

mortgage. The estate reverted to Thomas Smith II in 1711. Remarkably, the Hyrnes left an indelible mark on their home when they imprinted their family seal in the wet clay bricks used in the front doorway of the small home built after the fire. The impressed bricks were not discovered until 1984, when a sticking interior door required renovation. The repair work exposed the hidden bricks with the indented seal of the Hyrne family.

The plantation house was altered several times during the past three hundred years. The original structure was built of handmade bricks, and styled by Van Arssens as typical one-story stucco Dutch house. The second home was a smaller replica of the first with evidence indicating that the Hyrnes built onto the undamaged floor joists and foundation of the original house.

After the death of Landgrave Smith, the house and plantation had many owners including James Hasell,[663] James Wathen, Thomas Wright,[664] Aaron Loocock and Thomas Drayton. Thomas Drayton sold it to John Bee Holmes.[665] Holmes appears to have owned Medway for more than twenty years. A 1775 plat made by Joseph Purcell lists him as the owner, and his name appeared as the owner of Medway on plats made from surveys of neighboring properties in 1792 and 1796. His name also appears on a plat of Medway drawn in 1792. This plat may be the only surviving drawing of the property lines prior to the twentieth century.[666] John Bee Holmes possibly managed the estate as an absentee landowner because he is listed as a resident of St. Michaels/St. Phillips Parish on the 1790 census.

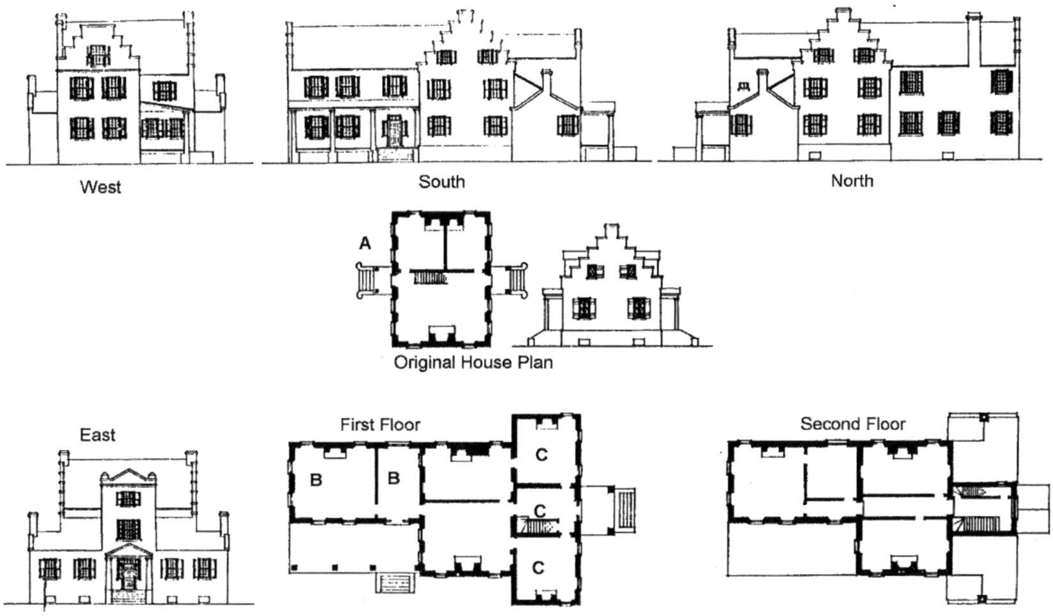

Drawing 7.6 This drawing shows the elevations and floor plans of Medway Plantation's main house. The Medway floor plans and elevations were measured by Albert Simons and drawn by Frank E. Seef. *Courtesy of the South Carolina Arts Association*.

Holmes lost the estate due to his failure to pay the taxes and it was purchased in 1797 by Theodore Samuel Marion, son of Job Marion and the nephew of General Francis Marion.[667] Theodore Marion died in 1827 leaving the land to his grandson, Theodore Samuel Dubose. Dubose married Jane Porcher. She planted large oaks and ornamental trees in a pattern near the house. During that period, a second story to the house was added that retained the stepped gable style.

Peter Gaillard Stoney and his wife Anna Maria Porcher bought Medway in 1833. He added an unsymmetrical wing in 1855, but blended the new with the older Dutch style. Additional rooms were added some time before 1875. Records do not indicate who built this last section or when it was constructed.

"A" Front door location where the Hyrne seals were found.
"B" Addition built in 1855 by Peter Gaillard Stoney.
"C" Addition built prior to 1875 by an unknown builder.

Medway was a versatile and profitable plantation that endured longer than most. Timber products and livestock were produced at first. Later rice was an important commodity evidenced by the ruins of a rice mill, as well as storage and drying barns. Rice drains and dikes at Medway are visible on a survey made in 1796 of White Hall Plantation, the neighbor on its north boundary. The survey also shows dammed water reserves that remain evident today. The deep water at Medway made water transport possible, so when rice production no longer brought sufficient returns, clay deposits near

Back River were extracted for profitable brick manufacture. Brick was produced on Medway from an early date, but Peter Gaillard Stoney is credited with greatly improving the quality. The high quality "Carolina gray" brick produced at Medway was used to build Fort Sumter.[668]

Peter Gaillard Stoney was also a successful planter and developed profitable water reserves and rice fields, and he and his sons raised thoroughbred horses. He and his six sons are also renowned for their public service, and all fought for the Confederacy with distinction. Grandson, Thomas Porcher Stoney was born at Medway and served two terms as mayor of Charleston. Two other of Peter Gaillard Stoney's grandsons, Arthur Jervey Stoney and Pierre Gaillard Stoney were with the old Charleston Light Dragoons, with the 30th Division when it broke the Hindenburg Line in World War I.[669]

In 1906, Medway plantation was sold to Samuel Gaillard Stoney, the nephew of Peter Gaillard Stoney.[670] At the time of the purchase Samuel G. Stoney surveyed the five tracts that combined as Medway with a total of 5,492 acres. In 1906 at the time of the survey, Medway consisted of Parnassus Plantation with 1910 acres, the Cottage tract with 60 acres, Prioleau's Plantation with 1,651 acres, Back River Plantation with 1,671 acres and Donnelly's Plantation with 200 acres.[671] Samuel's wife, Louisa Cheves Stoney, restored the old gardens and planted additional ones, but the old plantation fell into disuse and became part of a large hunting club. Medway was the largest of several Back River plantations. Pine Grove, Parnassus, Brick Hope, Back River, White Hall and

Photograph 7.21 This photograph shows a statue gracing the grand lawn at Medway. The photograph was taken March 14, 2005, and is in the possession of the author.

Liberty Hall are all neighboring plantations of Medway. For some time, all the lands were fenced in as a hunting park, and deer were hunted twice a week when in season.

Five Stoney generations of ownership ended in 1930 when Medway was sold to Mr. and Mrs. Sidney Legendre of New Orleans. The Legendres revived the plantation, added extensively to the outbuildings and improved the interior of the old home. Their work at Medway received some worldwide notoriety following World War II, when the celebrated "Medway Plan" was employed for the rehabilitation of Europe. American cities adopted French cities and sponsored rehabilitation after the devastating war. The "Medway Plan" adopted the name of the Goose Creek plantation to reinforce the idea of rehabilitating worn but worthy structures.

Today much of the old splendor of Medway remains. Rice is no longer planted but water reserve ponds and fields are still evident. One of the old tracts is still referred to as "Smithfield," after the landgrave. Thoroughbreds are no longer raised, but the old racetrack can be traced. When the Legendres acquired Medway in 1930, they also acquired two adjoining properties, Spring Grove and Pine Grove and portions of several other plantations that brought the estate total to 7,600 acres. Mrs. Legendre lamented that almost all of the adjoining plantations have fallen victim to strip malls and industrial development, and as a result, Medway has become a vital refuge for many creatures, some of them endangered, whose habitats have been consumed by the relentless expansion of urban sprawl.[672]

The beautiful gardens and timeless pride of the ancient gray brick house are memorials to the Goose Creek plantation society. Mrs. Gertrude Legendre owned and loved Medway from the time she and her husband, Sidney, purchased the land and home in 1930, until her death in 2000. Mr. and Mrs. Legendre are buried on the grounds just a few dozen yards from Landgrave Thomas Smith

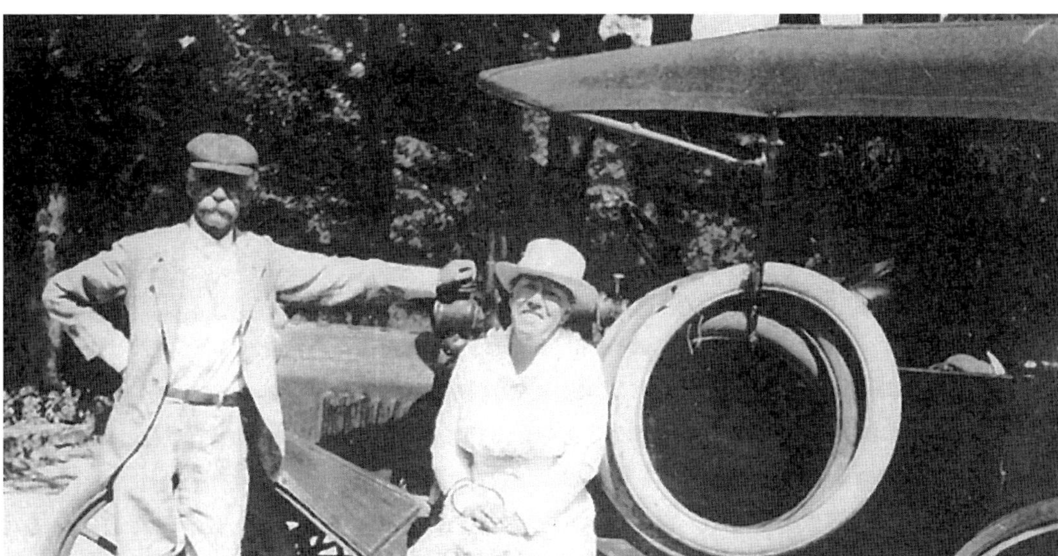

Photograph 7.22 This photograph shows Captain Samuel G. Stoney and his wife Louisa. He was an avid sportsman and hunter at Medway in the early twentieth century. The Stoneys spent twenty years reclaiming the ancient gardens and planting new ones.

Photograph 7.23 This photograph shows Medway House as viewed from the south. The picture was taken in April 2003, and is in the private collection of the author.

Photograph 7.24 This photograph shows Medway House as viewed from the east. The picture was taken in April 2003, and is in the private collection of the author.

Photograph 7.25 This photograph shows Medway House as viewed from the west. The picture was taken in April 2003, and is in the private collection of the author.

and his wife, Sabina. Mrs. Legendre wanted to place the holding into trust for perpetuity to forever protect the wildlife that thrives there. After several failed efforts, the Medway Environmental Trust was established and easements were placed on the property for its future protection.

Back River/White Hall

John Coming Ball was a successful planter who, at the age of twenty-seven, worked approximately eighty slaves to develop an extensive and prosperous plantation.[673] A plat drawn from a 1775 survey and redrawn in 1790 shows Back River Plantation consisting of 1,159.75 acres, where John Ball made fortunes growing rice.

Plat 7.24 shows a single structure with two paths. On the full 1775 plat, one path is labeled "path to the world's end." The property was bounded by White Hall Plantation to the north, as well as the lands of Miss Judith Wragg. Robert Hume owned the property on the west, and Aaron Loocock owned lands to the south and east. Another plat drawn from a survey conducted by Charles Hatley in 1792 shows a well-developed estate much improved from the land described by the survey of seventeen years earlier.

The 1792 plat shows a plantation with 1,196.5 acres, an elaborate system of dikes, drains, roads and paths and a series of structures that indicate a well-developed settlement. The drawing also shows that

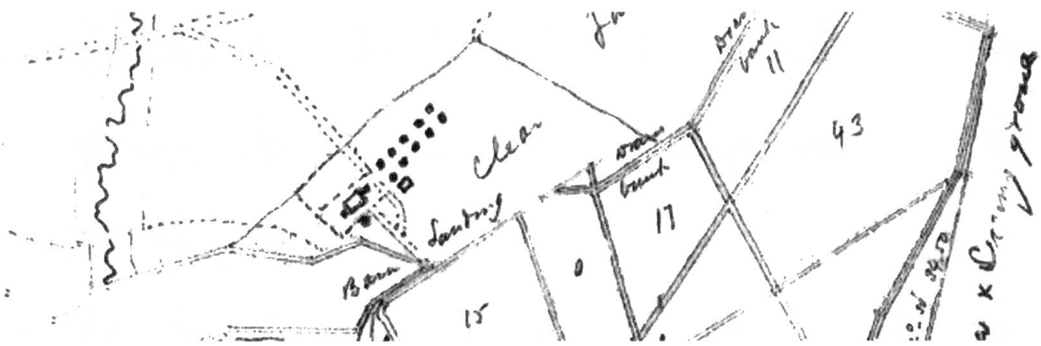

Plat 7.24 This partial plat describes a section of John Coming Ball's Back River Plantation in 1775. H.A.M. Smith traced the original plat. The tracing is among the collections of the South Carolina Historical Society.

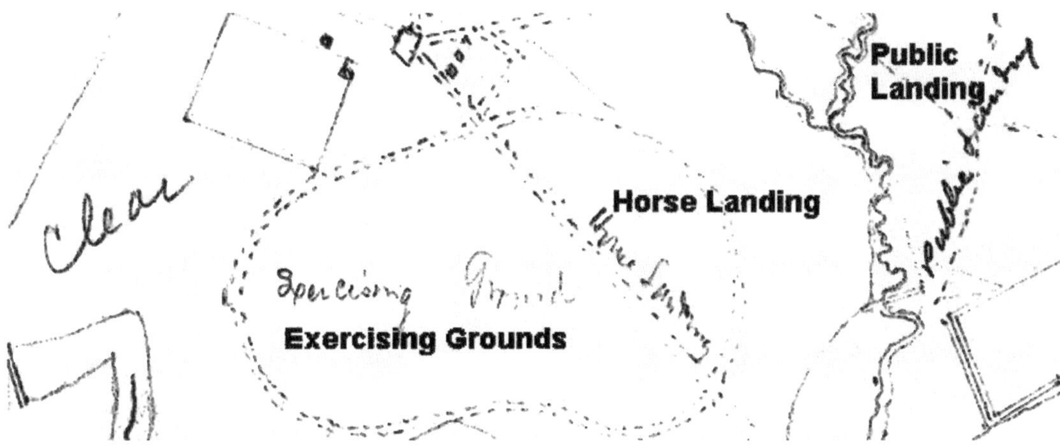

Plat 7.25 This partial plat describes part of Back River Plantation in 1792 owned by John Coming Ball. H.A.M. Smith traced the plat. The tracing is among the collections of the South Carolina Historical Society. The manuscript labels were added to this publication for clarity.

the estate was divided into two distinct settlements. Plat 7.24 describes the settlement on the northern section of the estate, a large structure that may be the main house, another large structure and a double row of ten smaller structures. This may represent the living area for the owner and slaves.

Plat 7.25 shows the southern settlement on Back River Plantation. The plat shows "Plantation Road" that connected the two settlements. It also shows a number of structures, a square area with a structure within that may represent a corral and barn and a large round area labeled "Exercise Ground." A road running through the exercise grounds is labeled "Horse Landing." This probably indicated that a special landing was arranged on the nearby river to bring horses in and out by water. In 1792 Back River contained 831 acres of high ground, 127 acres of cultivated rice lands, 83 acres of undeveloped land and 155.5 acres of unused swamplands. This large estate was bounded on the west by Cyprus Grove Plantation owned by B.P. Williams. John B. Holmes's

Medway was to the south and Back River provided the eastern boundary.[674]

Several Back River planters asked the South Carolina General Assembly in 1796, to "cut a canal from the Chapel Bridge to Back River," but Ball successfully opposed the project.[675] A canal was dug in this vicinity in the 1950s, not to carry products or people, but to flow fresh water from the Cooper River to Back River and to provide fresh water for the residents of the City of Charleston and the industry above the Back River dike at Bushy Park. An aerial photograph describes the property today. Photograph 7.26 shows Back River Plantation survey lines drawn over an aerial photograph taken in 2001. The location of the slave quarters and main house is indicated on the recent photograph.

The Ball family held these lands until William Bell purchased it. He was a successful rice producer in the decades leading to the Civil War and was renowned "as a furious driver of a pair of fast trotters."[676] The 1860 Agricultural Census reports an estate containing 6,000 acres. He owned 160 slaves at that time.[677] A plat drawn from a survey made thirteen years later, in 1873, shows that his acreage was reduced by a quarter to 4,572 acres, but even after emancipation of the slaves, he

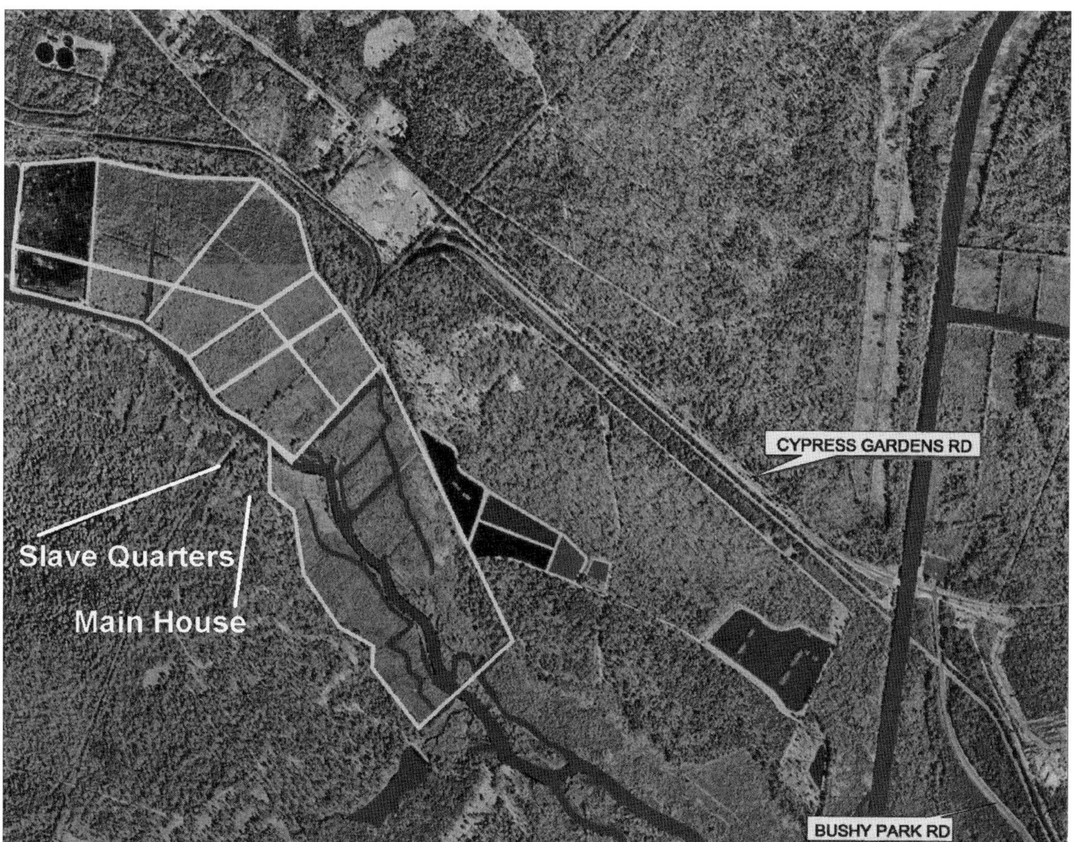

Photograph 7.26 This aerial photograph is overlaid with the 1775 survey lines of John Cumming Ball's Back River Plantation as drawn for plat 7.24. The locations of the main house and slave quarters are provided. *Courtesy of the City of Goose Creek.*

appears to have continued successful rice production.

The plat shows an extensive dike and drainage system and indicates that Bell cultivated 541 acres of rice and 200 acres had been recently planted. His large tract straddled the St. Johns Berkeley and St. James, Goose Creek Parish lines and incorporated Back River and White Hall Plantations. His land was bound on the east by Back River, on the north by Strawberry Ferry Road, on the west by the road to Moncks Corner, as well as the lands of "Huff" and "Theurin," and on the southwest by lands owned by John Cannon. His southern neighbor was P.G. Stoney of Medway.[678]

A hunting and retreat club purchased these lands, as well as the Pine Grove and Spring Grove tracts in 1905. E.W. Durant led the hunting enterprise and was responsible for refurbishing the old house as a lodge.[679] The tracts were sold again in 1929 to four neighboring plantation owners including Clarence Chapman of Mulberry, G.D.B. Bonbright of Pimplico on the Cooper and two other landowners.[680]

Pine Grove/Spring Grove

Pinegrove and Spring Grove Plantations were contiguous properties located on the headwaters of Back River west of Back River Plantation and Medway. These plantations were developed on lands that earlier supported the estate of the Chicken family. The lord proprietors first granted a parcel of

Photograph 7.27 This photograph shows the road and gate at White Hall Plantation in March 7, 2005. The photo is in the private collection of the author.

this land in 1705 to Thomas Bellamy. The initial grant was small, but it was followed with a 1,050-acre grant the next year to Catharine Bellamy, widow of Thomas.[681] This large grant encompassed most of the property that composed all or parts of the four tracts and some of which was originally part of Henry Smith's large grant.

George Chicken acquired the land when he immigrated to South Carolina, married Catharine Bellamy and settled on that large tract consisting of 1,150 combined acres. Colonel George Chicken was influential in native affairs and served in a number of civic capacities, which included representing St. James, Goose Creek in the Second Royal Assembly in 1724–1727.[682] George and Catharine Chicken reared five children, one of which was also named "George" who inherited the plantation. George II resided on the plantation with his wife Lydia and their daughter Catharine. An interesting little book entitled, *Little Mistress Chicken,* tells the tragic story of Catharine Chicken who was sent to board and attend school at Childsbury across the Cooper from her plantation home. Catharine, the daughter of George II and Lydia, was tied to a tombstone in Childsbury Cemetery, now Strawberry Chapel graveyard, as a punishment by her schoolmaster.[683] The schoolmaster forgot Catharine and she was found after remaining bound for many hours in the dark. The fright and exposure was believed to have brought on a paralysis that affected her facial nerves and caused her mouth to be drawn permanently. Catharine became the wife of Mr. Simons at Middleburg Plantation. There her portrait was displayed for many years in the formal front room. Evidence of her childhood trial was displayed in the painting. The portrait showed her "with her mouth awry."[684]

Photograph 7.28 This photograph shows the Pine Grove main house. This photograph was taken in 1924 and is among the collection in *Johnson's Scrapbook, Volume 1*, on deposit at the South Carolina Historical Society.

Interestingly, the Childsbury School was located less than four miles from the Chicken Plantation. Nonetheless, according to the story, Catharine was obliged to board with the schoolmaster and his wife. The need to board so close to home validates the extent that travel conditions in that corner of the Goose Creek Parish were exceedingly difficult, due to the two converging deep waters of the Cooper and Back Rivers and the interconnecting swamps. Strawberry Ferry afforded some convenience because it carried people and products across the Cooper, and connected the lands north of the Cooper with the lands at Back River by way of the road that traversed the nearby swamp. An interesting description of the ferry is provided by an account of Catharine Chicken:

> *Below her lay the ferry, with the lumbering ferry-boat, freighted with passengers, heavily lurching across the river. That ferry belonged to her mother, Catherine knew; and she knew too, that every passenger had to pay a royal or riall, to cross except on Sunday, or in times of alarm, when they might cross free of charge.*[685]

The ferry services continued throughout the nineteenth century and some nearby planters, such as John Ball, used the transport regularly. He rented the ferry for $200 a year.[686]

Noah Serre, George Chicken's brother-in-law purchased the plantation in 1743 for £3,100.[687] He was the husband of Catharine Chicken, daughter of George Sr. and Catherine Bellamy. Upon Noah's death, Catharine married David Caw and together they reared three children. David Caw was a wealthy apothecary and physician in Charleston, where he kept a well-apportioned town house. After the death of his wife, Catharine, he married Rachel Keating, the widow of Richard Gough. Rachel possessed considerable property, which made David Caw even wealthier. He eventually accumulated three plantations.[688] He kept thirty-seven slaves on his Goose Creek Plantation, thirty-nine on his plantation in St. James Santee and staffed his town house with twelve servants. He represented Goose Creek in the Commons House of Assembly in 1755–1757 and St. James Santee during one earlier session.[689] A plat drawn from a 1796 survey of White Hall Plantation shows "Remains of Settlement Mr. Chicken." That same plat also shows "Remains of White Hall House," "old chimney," "Remains of Mr. Durham's Settlement," and eight "Negro Houses."

The Chicken estate succumbed to the common perils of soil exhaustion and malaria and by the time of the American Revolution other smaller tracts displaced it, but during this period lands with tidal influenced fresh water lowlands regained much value due to the introduction of a new method of growing rice. Gideon Dupont, a Goose Creek planter at Otranto Plantation, popularized a new agricultural method of rice production that employed the lifting and lowering of fresh water resulting from coastal tides. Thus some inland plantations with tidal influenced wetlands that were abandoned due to soil exhaustion were reworked as rice lands. This was the attraction for George Keckley, a South Carolina State Representative, who purchased a section of the old Chicken tract called Spring Grove Plantation.

Interestingly, the Keckley family owned two plantations in the St. James, Goose Creek Parish both of which were named "Spring Grove." One Spring Grove Plantation was located in the Ladson area and extant records indicate that the Spring Grove Plantation in the Back River neighborhood was surveyed later but prior to 1790.[690] A 1788 plat of Sociable Hill shows neighboring Spring Grove in the ownership of a "Mr. Smith." Another plat drawn two years later, in 1790, shows the boundaries of Spring Grove but indicates no structures on the tract and the Keckley family was not counted in

St. James, Goose Creek Parish that year. A second plat, drawn three years later, in 1793, shows a settlement consisting of a main house and eight outbuildings that were approached by a tree-lined avenue intersecting the Road to Strawberry Ferry.[691] It appears that the plantation was occupied and significantly improved during the early 1790s.

George Keckley purchased 1,406 acres to comprise his Spring Grove Plantation from the estate of Judith Wragg who was the deceased widow of John Wragg, owner of a large contiguous tract. At the time of the purchase, the Keckley tract was bounded by Chapel Swamp and Benjamin Paul Williams's Cedar Grove Plantation to the south, the lands of Mary Broughton to the southwest, the Chesterfield Plantation, owned by Christopher Gadsden to the north and west and properties owned by John Louis Gervais to the east.

George Keckley married Ann Dorathea Kelly and resided with her at Spring Grove. He was a successful rice planter who also produced corn, potatoes, peas, livestock and wood for the Charleston market.[692] He was elected as a vestryman for the St. James, Goose Creek Church and as a South Carolina State Representative. He accomplished the one-hundred-mile journey to the Columbia

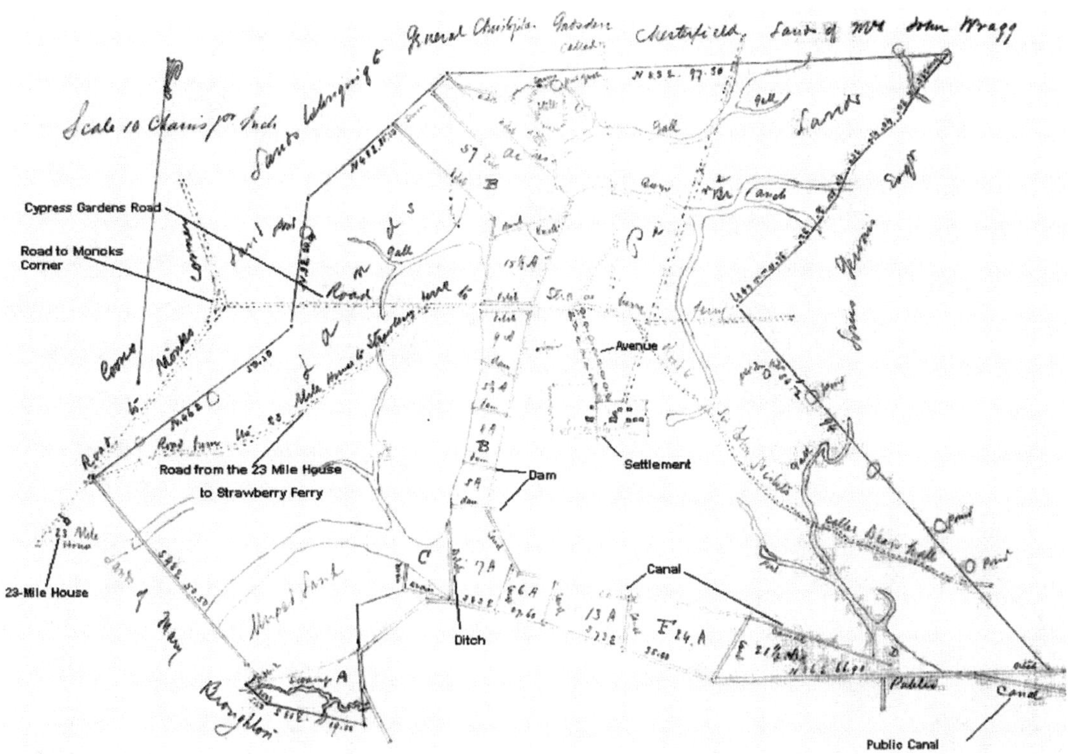

Plat 7.26 This plat shows Spring Grove Plantation in 1793. The settlement featured a main house and eight other structures. The main avenue was lined by trees and led to the "Road to Strawberry Ferry." A second avenue led beyond the "Road to Strawberry Ferry" toward Chesterfield Plantation. A "public canal" is noted in the bottom right corner of the plat. The 23-Mile House was located on the Road to Moncks Corner and is shown in the bottom left corner of the plat. The plat was traced by Henry A.M. Smith and is among the collections of the South Carolina Historical Society.

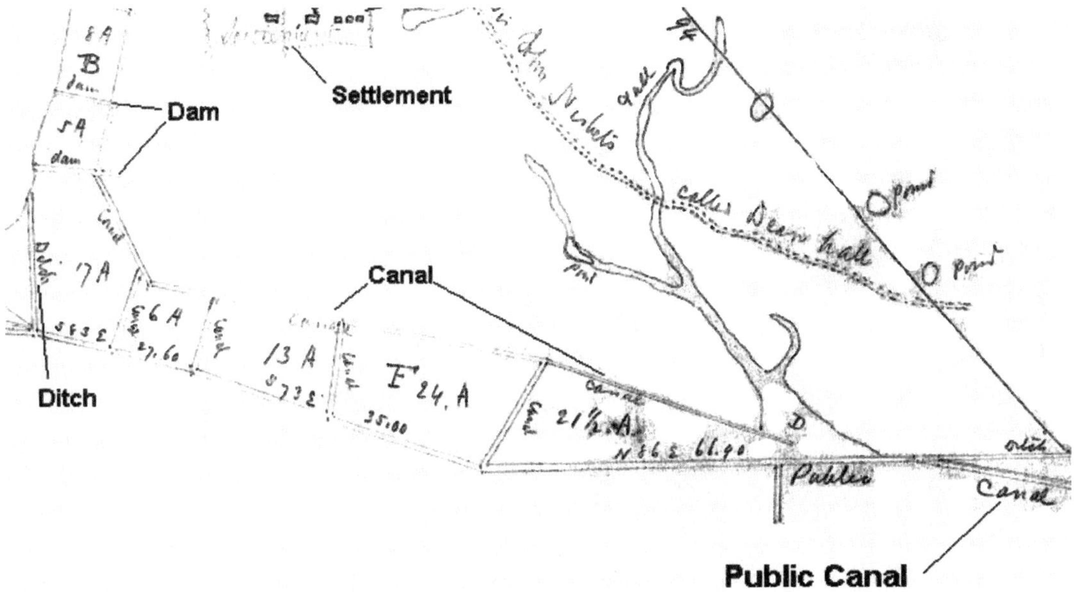

Plat 7.27 This partial plat shows some of the dams, canals and ditches that comprised Keckley's "agricultural machine." The 1793 plat was traced by Henry A.M. Smith and is among the collections of the South Carolina Historical Society.

Statehouse by riding his private horse-drawn coach. [693] While he was a representative he, two of his neighbors, Benjamin Paul Williams, and John Cumming Ball and others, asked the South Carolina General Assembly in 1796, to "cut a canal from the Chapel Bridge to Back River." This proposed three-mile canal would have linked the lands of the upper Back River headwaters with the deep waters of Back River and would have eased transport of goods to market. John Ball, (not John Cumming Ball) owner of neighboring Back River Plantation presented a counter-petition to this request claiming that he would be damaged by such a waterway.[694] The general assembly organized a committee to rectify the conflicting claims but the project was never undertaken.[695]

Although a canal was not authorized by the state, two canals are shown on the 1793 Spring Grove plat. Apparently, a fifteen-foot-wide private canal was dug to float Keckley's market-bound produce along his twelve diked fields to a public canal that flowed into the deeper waters of nearby Back River. Rice was a heavy staple, as well as most market commodities of the forest and fields and little profit returned unless large quantities could be transported cost effectively. Thus, horses pulled small barges by attached ropes or men poled narrow watercraft along the canal from the headwater swamps to Back River. At Back River, the watercrafts were steered south approximately five miles to the fast flowing Cooper River that carried the boats, sloops, and barges into Charleston Harbor.

Keckley's rice fields were the preferred "agricultural machine" of the day. The water that was trapped and drained by the dikes and ditches was powered by the Atlantic tides that lifted the fresh river water into the fields approximately three hours behind the Charleston Harbor high tide and drained the fields three hours after the tidal ebb in the harbor. The slowly rising and falling fresh waters were controlled by a series of open and shut "trunk" gates that employed the waters to carry rich alluvial silt to the fields, to irrigate and at appropriate intervals, to drown the invading weeds.

The Keckley family held the property for most of the nineteenth century but resided in Charleston and elsewhere after the Civil War. Some emancipated African Americans became neighboring landowners and tenant farmers as the nineteenth century waned. The emergence of the African American community occurred as the European American families slowly retreated from that corner of the old parish and resettled near the rail stops at Strawberry, Groomsville and Mt. Holly in the vicinity.

By the twentieth century the Spring Grove tract and much of the adjacent lands were acquired by the E.P. Burton Lumber Company. [696] The Burton Lumber Company purchased great swaths of Goose Creek forestlands during this era. When the wood was harvested the company sold Spring Grove to the Cooper River Mining and Manufacture Company for phosphate and clay mining. That company held it for a short period before selling to Wilmost L. Harris who kept it for only two years.[697]

Afterwards, the land converted to a hunting club. [698] A hunting and retreat club purchased Spring Grove along with other neighboring tracts, and effected some improvements but it soon passed from a hunting club, to the Pine Grove Livestock Company, and in 1929 to George Bonbright, a New York land speculator. He and three additional plantation owners acquired Spring Grove along with several surrounding tracts. [699]

Soon after, Sidney and Gertrude Legendre annexed the tract to their 6,500-acre neighboring Medway Plantation and kept it until the Celanese Corporation acquired Spring Grove in 1980 to construct a plastic production facility. When their plan failed, Steve Pendley, an upscale Goose Creek developer purchased a large section of the old estate in 2003 for residential and commercial properties to accommodate the residential demands of a burgeoning population in southern Berkeley County.

Sociable Hill

The 23-Mile-House Tavern was situated at Sociable Hill on the headwaters of Back River. The tavern was located at the intersection of the Moncks Corner Road and the road to Strawberry Ferry. An Indian trader, William Hatton and his wife Margaret owned the 80-acre tract during the frontier era. William and Margaret Hatton sold the tract to a planter Jonathan Skrine in 1726. It was named "Sociable Hill" at that time. Edward Keating purchased and consolidated land in that vicinity beginning in 1724. In that year he bought two plantations, totaling 1,370 acres, from John and Rachel Moore for the sum of one hundred thirty-seven pounds of rice.[700] He must have sold some properties because the records indicate that he only owned 1,000 acres in 1742.[701] The Keating family continued to amass acrerage when Edward Keating's son received land grants in the same vicinity amounting to 901 acres in 1785 and 1786.[702]

The Keating and Simmon families intermarried and joined in business. A generation later, a descendent named Keating Simmons who was a wealthy businessman, inherited the Keating Simmons and Sons mercantile/counting house in Charleston. He also owned Lewisfield Plantation in St. Johns Berkeley Parish, houses on Sullivan's Island and in Charleston, and more than 3,000 acres of land in several Parishes. At the time of the 1790 census, he owned Sociable Hill in the

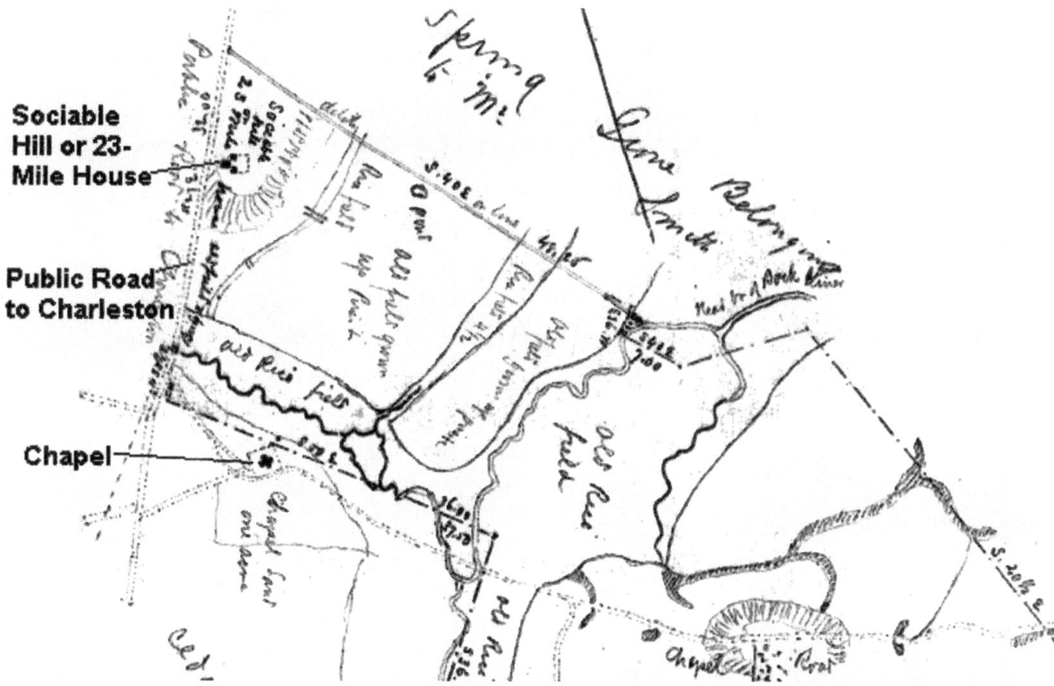

Plat 7.28 This partial plat describes Sociable Hill Plantation according to a survey taken in 1788 by Joseph Purcell. H.A.M. Smith traced the original plat. The tracing is among the collections of the South Carolina Historical Society.

Goose Creek Parish, but he probably did not reside there. The Sociable Hill plantation consisted of 630 acres when Joseph Purcell surveyed it in 1788. Plat 7.28 shows a cluster of three buildings in the upper left corner. The notation near these buildings states "Sociable Hill or 23-Mile House." At the bottom left is a structure shaped like a cross and the words "Chapel Lands one acre." This is the Chapel of Ease for the St. James, Goose Creek Church. The main church was situated near the 17-mile stone, approximately five miles south of the chapel. The path labeled "Chapel Road" leads to Isaac Parker's Cyprus Grove Plantation.

Keating Simmons was active in the Revolutionary War. When Charleston fell, he was taken prisoner and swore an oath to the Crown. Upon his oath he was paroled to his estate at Lewisfield Plantation, but following a skirmish at his plantation, he renigged his oath and joined Francis Marion's Brigade to serve as a brigade major during the remainder of the conflict. He represented St. James, Goose Creek in the First General Assembly in 1776, and later represented St. Johns Berkeley in the Third and Sixth General Assemblies. Keating Simmons married twice. By his first wife, Ann Lewis, he fathered nine children. He survived his second wife, Eleanor Ball and died in 1834. At the time of Keating Simmons death, he owned 178 slaves at Lewisfield Planation on the Cooper and 22 slaves in Charleston.[703] He is buried at Lewisfield Plantation.[704]

Before the death of Keating Simmons, the Sociable Hill or 23-Mile House Plantation tract was purchased by John James Reardon and held for several decades. The Mills 1815 Atlas shows Reardon's Tavern located near the chapel on the Moncks Corner Road and a plat shows that Reardon owned

Plat 7.29 This partial plat is a tracing of the original by H.A.M. Smith and is among the collections of the South Carolina Historical Society. The original plat was drawn from a survey made by Joseph Purcell in 1788 showing Richmond Plantation. An original McCrady plat #1474 of Richmond Plantation is on microfilm at the Charleston County Library.

537.5 acres on "Chapel Swamp" in 1822.[705] It seems as if the Sociable Hill Tavern was sometimes referred to as the "23-Mile-House." This area appears to have been a busy corner of the parish. The Mills Atlas shows Redheimer's (Reidheimer) tavern located nearby at the 22-mile marker.

Reardon owned more than the one tavern at Sociable Hill. Two other taverns named "Reardon's" are also cited on Mills' Atlas. One is situated on the Moncks Corner Road near the intersection of Old Moncks Corner and Old Mt. Holly Roads, the other is at the 25-mile marker on the State Road between Goose Creek and Wassamasaw. Reardon was a Goose Creek planter who appears on the 1810 census with nine slaves and the 1820 census with twenty slaves. The inventory of his estate in 1825, the year of his death, shows that he owned 1,620 acres and twenty-four slaves.[706] He represented Goose Creek in the House of Representatives during the Twenty-second and Twenty-third General Assemblies. His son was also named John James Reardon.[707]

Richmond

Alexander Moultrie owned land on the western boundary of Sociable Hill, contiguous to the Moncks Corner Road. His 951-acre tract was named Richmond Plantation (plat 7.29). Alexander Moultrie studied law in England and was admitted to the South Carolina Bar. He owned a great deal of property in four sections of the state and was elected to represent the Charleston city parishes six times and the Goose Creek Parish one time in 1783. He was active in the revolution, rose to the rank of Colonel in the militia, and was among those arrested by the British and exiled to St. Augustine. He served as South Carolina's attorney general from 1776 to 1792 and was convicted by the Senate and found guilty for embezzling £60,000. This crime disqualified him from holding office for seven years. He died in 1807.

Two years after Moultrie's death, Jacob Belser (1781–1833) acquired Richmond Plantation. He also bought lands in other districts and moved out of the Goose Creek Parish near 1816. While in Goose Creek, he served in the senate for the Twentieth and Twenty-first General Assemblies (1812–1816). He and his wife, Martha Clark Belser, had seven children. He sold 358 acres of his estate to Thomas Scriven in 1810, and retained the balance of the property.[708] Peter and John Redheimer purchased the 787-acre Richmond tract prior to the Civil War. A plat from an 1857 survey noted that the Redheimers were owners at that time and the Mills Atlas shows Redheimer's Tavern at this location as early as 1815. Thus it appears that the land stayed in the Redheimer family for more than forty years. A later plat, dated 1869, shows Richmond Plantation with 790 acres.[709]

Cyprus Grove and Cedar Grove

Cyprus Grove and Cedar Grove were contiguous to the 23-Mile House, near the St. James Chapel of Ease. Some of this land was probably the early estate of John Bayley. Records show that John Bayley (Bailey, Baily, Bayly) resided in Goose Creek and died there in 1733. He was from Ballinaclough, County of Tipperary, Ireland. He sold 270 acres of property to Edward Thomas for sixty-five pounds in 1730. That small tract bounded on property owned by Thomas Smith and Mrs. Durham in the vicinity of the land that later became Cedar Grove Plantation.[710] The lease and release record states that John, Earl of Bath and the Lord Proprietors, by letters in 1698, created John Bayley, the father, Landgrave and Cassique, granting him 48,000 acres. The son and heir employed an attorney to reserve 8,000 acres for "John Bayle's [sic] use" and to dispose of the rest of the land. John Bayley, the son, was a surveyor who was elected to represent the Goose Creek Parish in the Fifth, Sixth, Seventh and Eighth Royal Assemblies. He was elected clerk of the House in 1730, but political problems caused him to resign from that post. He owned properties in other parishes, but identified himself in his will as being "of Goose Creek." [711] Records indicate that James Bagby owned a Goose Creek tract around 1755.[712] There is a lease and release record on file that shows John Bagby owning 640 acres in Goose Creek in 1762.[713] Both of these men may be heirs of John Bayley from Ireland.

A later plat of this property taken from a survey by Joseph Purcell shows slave houses, rice fields, and an old settlement. The plat shows a structure, three stately trees and the words "old chimney," "Remains of old Settlement," and a word that may be "Bagleys." By the later 1700s, these lands comprised two successful estates. Cyprus Grove Plantation, owned by Isaac Parker, and Cedar Grove Plantation, owned by Benjamin Paul Williams, were situated to the west of Sociable Hill.[714]

Estates on Foster Creek

Thorogood (Thoroughgood, Thurgood)/Mount Holly

Thorogood was one of the first plantations in Berkeley County. Today it is the site of Alcoa Aluminum Plant and the Mount Holly Commerce Park on Highway 52, north of the Goose Creek City limits. Joseph Thorogood, a gentleman, received a grant of three thousand acres of land in 1682.[715] The land was identified in the Proprietary grant as being located "near the head of a branch of a creek which runneth into Medway River and called by the native name of Oola-Coll."[716] Medway (Meadway) River was an early referral to Back River. What the native name refers to specifically is not clear. It could be the native name of the creek, Medway River or the granted land. Joseph Thorogood did not retain the property very long. He sold it in 1684 to James Moore, but the tract retained the Thorogood name throughout the eighteenth century.

Andrew Allen and William Gibbon formed a partnership and purchased Thorogood from Jasper Ashworth and his wife Susanna as an investment in 1724. The purchase included Ashworth's entire inventory including "all Negro, Mulatto, Indian and other slaves; all livestock, goods and chattel; all lands, tenements, goods and slaves in St. Phillips and St. James Parishes."[717] Andrew Allen assumed full ownership of the three thousand acre tract when his partner died in 1725. Allen was the father of seven children with his first wife, Elizabeth Mackpherson. When she died in 1727, he married Sarah Lewis. He was a successful planter and merchant and upon his death left a large and prosperous estate to his son William.[718] In 1740, young William Allen and others founded the Goose Creek Friendly Society or River Club that met at Sociable Hill. He also made three yearly contributions of twenty-five pounds sterling to the Ludlam School Fund of the St. James Church and was elected to the Fourteenth and Nineteenth Royal Assembly.[719]

William Allen married Mary Keating and although he devised his plantation to his daughter Elizabeth, his wife Mary survived him and assumed ownership of the estate. When she married George Seaman, he became the owner of Thorogood. He was one of the wealthiest merchants in Charleston who owned two other plantations in addition to the Goose Creek tract. In his will, Seaman claims that he worked 81 slaves at his Goose Creek plantation and 32 at his Charleston house. George Seaman and Mary Keating had no children together so when he died in 1769, most of his estate went to his wife's daughter, Elizabeth including William Allen's plantation and 141 slaves.[720]

Elizabeth Allen had married John Deas, ten years before Seaman's death. John Deas, along with his brother David, had immigrated to Charleston in 1749 and established a mercantile partnership with James and William Lennox. The Deas brothers eventually formed their own company and profited from the slave trade. Consequently, John was already a wealthy man when he inherited Thorogood through his marriage to Elizabeth. The Ship Registers in the South Carolina Archives show that John Deas and his minor son, Seaman Deas owned the thirty ton schooner *Thorogood,* which was docked at Charleston Harbor. The 1790 census reports that Deas owned 208 slaves at Thorogood. His slaves worked extensive rice fields, processed indigo and harvested vast acreage of woodlands. A tar kiln, usually used for making naval stores, is shown on a Lewis Simons plat.[721]

John Deas and Elizabeth reared eleven children and kept an expansive and beautiful country home. Dr. Alexander Garden of Otranto and John Bartram, a renowned botanist, visited Thorogood to inspect the gardens and agricultural methods. The men found that Deas planted rows of corn spaced ten feet apart and grew indigo between the rows and successfully harvested two indigo crops annually. Deas kept a "kitchen" garden" where he grew grapes along with a plethora of produce and he converted a worn-out rice field into a reflection pond, which attracted various birds such as white herons.[722]

This pleasant country estate featured a main house and several substantial outbuildings. The archaeological studies conducted in 1978 discovered the remains of the main house and revealed more about the plantation settlement. Investigations exposed an intact foundation, a brick floor and piles of brick rubble that appears to represent the remains of associated outbuildings or slave residences. The location of this archaeological site matches the location of the main house on a plat drawn by surveyor Lewis Simons in the early 1800s. The home site is located near the center of the property on high ground. Part of the main avenue is still named Thorogood Avenue today and intersects with Old Moncks Corner Road near the Goose Creek Recreation Center.

The early survey also shows a proposed avenue to the State Road (Highway 176) in the same vicinity of the front drive to today's Alcoa Manufacturing Plant. The plat indicates that the main house was east of the parking lots of today's Alcoa Plant.[723] Partial plat 7.30 shows "Goose Creek Road," "Old Moncks Corner Road," and "Wassamasaw Road." At the time of the survey, Thorogood Plantation was bound on the east by Alexander Mazyck's Springfield Plantation. "Mr. A. Mazyck" is written next to a drawn structure that was certainly representing his main house at Springfield. Also east of Thorogood was Aaron Loocock's Brownfield Plantation. On the South was William Smith's Button Hall and the Wassamasaw Road was the western boundary. Although no other descriptions of the property have been found, the archaeological study conducted in 1997 gives some description of the Deas's settlement. The investigators found a brick linedwell along with bits and pieces of ceramics indicating a mean year of 1795.[724] The investigation also found that the soil consisted of a heavy clay composition that slowed the absorption of ground water, which was certainly a factor in the success of rice cultivation.

John Deas served as a private in a Charleston militia company in defense of Charles Town in 1778. He loaned the South Carolina State Government £17,800 in 1779, long before the outcome of the Revolutionary War could be predicted. He also provided supplies to the militia and the Continental Line.[725] He was indeed a patriot early in the struggle, but when Charleston fell to the British, he accepted the protection of the British government. His capitulation to the British resulted in a fine of 12 percent of his estate by the prevailing American government. He served as justice of the peace (1774, 1776), vestryman and churchwarden of St. Phillips Parish, commissioner of the road from Santee to Goose Creek, and in other social and cultural positions such as a member of the library society.[726] Deas also possessed a humorous personality. One day a gentleman entered into a conversation with Deas and commented that he scarcely traveled the Goose Creek Road without encountering a member of the

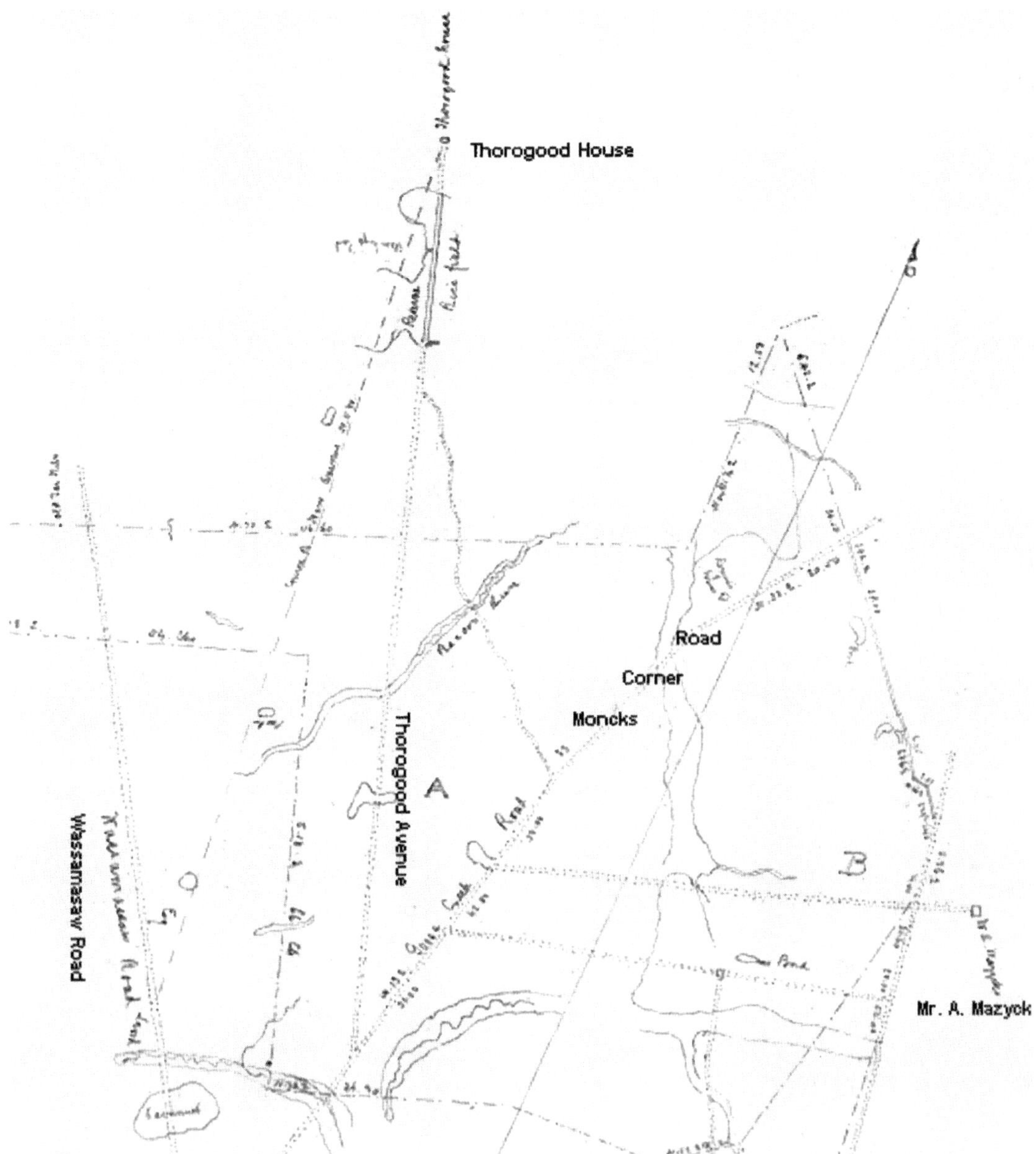

Plat 7.30 Lewis Simons made this partial plat from a survey. H.A.M. Smith traced the plat. The tracing is among the collections of the South Carolina Historical Society. The words, "Thorogood House," "Wassamasaw Road," "Moncks Corner Road" and "Mr. A. Mazyck" were added to the plat for this publication for clarity and orientation.

Deas family. Deas explained that he had nine sons, and each son had a sister. The gentleman did not appreciate the play on words and was astonished when he supposed that there were eighteen children in the Deas family, but in actuality Deas's only daughter, was a cherished sister to each of his sons.[727] An image of Deas is preserved in a fine miniature painted by Pierre Henri.[728]

John Deas Jr., was twenty-seven years old when he inherited his father's estates, which included Thorogood, Cyprus Plantation and Mt. Holly Plantations in Goose Creek along with several more plantations and tracts throughout the Lowcountry.[729] Thus John Deas Jr. was a wealthy landowner and he married Maria Smith, the daughter of wealthy Goose Creek landowners William Laughton Smith and Elizabeth Inglis. According to the 1790 census, he worked 170 slaves at his Mt. Holly Plantation, but he owned both Mt. Holly Plantation and Thorogood in 1790 and lived in his father's house at Thorogood.[730] He served as tax inquirer and collector, as well as a representative for the Seventh and Eighth General Assemblies for St. James, Goose Creek. He attended the state convention in 1788 and voted in favor of the new constitution.

John Deas Jr. died in 1790, the same year he inherited his father's estate. Upon his death, the properties passed to his brother, William Allen Deas and by 1806 to another brother, David Deas. William Allen Deas owned a Charleston house in addition to his Goose Creek properties and in 1807 acquired the 650-acre Oaks Plantation on Goose Creek. This Oaks Plantation was located near the 12-Mile House on the Goose Creek Road and should not be confused with the Oaks owned by the Middleton family near the Creek Bridge. In 1790, William Allen Deas was a delegate to the constitution convention in Philadelphia. He was then elected to represent Goose Creek in the House during the Ninth General Assembly. Soon after, he accompanied Thomas Pinckney, minister to the court of St. James, to England where he served as Pinckney's private secretary.[731] Again in the House, he represented Goose Creek in the Twelfth and Thirteenth General Assemblies. St. James, Goose Creek elected him to the senate for the Fourteenth and Fifteenth General Assemblies (1800–1804). He and Anne Izard reared five children.

The brothers, William Allen Deas and David Deas, owned several contiguous plantations. All of these tracts were sections from the original Thorogood estate. Toms Hill Plantation, owned by David Deas, was on the northern portion of the estate. It contained 573 acres and was sectioned off from the main tract to be mortgaged in 1806. Mt. Holly was a southern contiguous tract owned by William Allen Deas. Contiguous on the western boundary was "Old Barn" owned in 1806 by another brother, Henry Deas.[732] In 1821 David Deas conveyed to Henry Charles and Thomas Deas, grandsons and trustees, the 1,200-acre Thorogood tract.[733] The extant Thorogood estate contained only 1,100 acres three years later, when Mary Deas conveyed the Thorogood Plantation to the State Bank. In that year, David Deas still owned Toms Hill, but Mt. Holly was no longer in the family. Mt. Holly was sold to Dr. Matthew Irvine in 1809 for $2,142.75.[734] "Old Barn" was the property of the estate of Vance, owner of Vance's Tavern. Still later, Edward Simmons purchased 359 acres of Thorogood in 1858.[735]

Mt. Holly remained in the Irvine family for many years. It was conveyed a number of times within the family by bequests and marriages until a grandson on the mother's side, Matthew Irvine Keith, sold his interest to Benjamin D. Heriot in 1831. The plantation contained only five hundred acres at that time. Later, part of Mt. Holly was sold to Lewis Cannon, who sold a parcel to Benjamin Donnelly in 1853, but held the larger part of the tract until 1868.[736] In 1868 Cannon sold two hundred acres to John R. Pinckney for $700. A portion of that tract is today's Woodland Lakes Subdivision and the Goose Creek Municipal Center. At the same time, Cannon sold twenty-five acres to T.W. Lewis, trustee for the Cayce Methodist Episcopal Church for $125.[737] Benjamin Donnelly sold and bequeathed his section of Mt. Holly to small farmers in the years following the Civil War.

Tenant farming and share cropping after the Civil War dominated southern agriculture. Rice production was abandoned by most, and subsistence farming with some cotton took its place. By the turn of the twentieth century, most rice fields had been abandoned for more than thirty years and had returned to cyprus swamps, while most large estates were subdivided into small tenant farms. This seems to have been the case at Thorogood. An archaeological study found remains of nineteenth-century tenant houses.[738]

The subdivided tracts of Thorogood Plantation were reconstituted when the land was incorporated into the holdings of H. Smith Richardson in 1920. Richardson, a New Yorker, recognized the investment opportunity in purchasing large undervalued tracts in the south. He eventually purchased 7,910 acres, including all of Thorogood and Mt. Holly. It appears as if Richardson was well respected by the black tenant farmers who worked his lands in the first half of the twentieth century. Loretta Parsons and C.J. Bryant, who lived and farmed the lands during the 1930s and 1940s, warmly and respectfully, spoke of him. Alumax and later Alcoa industries purchased the property in the late 1970s and have since operated a successful aluminum industry.

Persimmon Hill and Old Barn

The Persimmon Hill property was long associated with Thorogood and Mt. Holly Plantations. This tract was situated at the apex of three drainage sytems: Goose Creek through Huckhole Swamp, Back River through Daisey Swamp and Foster Creek through Mt. Holly and Liberty Hall. Henry Deas of the Thorogood Plantation family gained ownership of this 1,748-acre tract when he married Margaret Horry, the daughter of Elias Horry. In some references, this property is referred to as the "Old Barn" tract. Old Barn was contiguous to Mt. Holly on the east, and Persimmon Hill and Fredericks to the south. William Vance, owner of Vance's Tavern, purchased all the acreage in 1820 for $8,500.[739] The land remained in the Vance family for thirty years, until George P. Whaley bought it in 1850.

Pursuant to the request of George P. Whaley, a survey and plat were made in 1850. Plat 7.31 shows 1,725 acres at Old Barns that bordered the land of "Mr. Baxter" and the State Road on the south. The 20-mile and 21-mile posts are indicated on the plat along the State Road. Jeremiah Martin owned property to the west and Theodore Thairen owned the land to the north. Thorogood Plantation lands are shown to the east.

As indicated on the plat, Baxter's house is situated on the State Road near the 22-mile marker. Plat 7.32 shows Baxter's House and land on the State Road that ran an east–west route. The plat identifies the State Road and lands to the south and contiguous to the road as property owned by Dr. John Poppenheim. Thus, it appears that the residential site known today as "Persimmon Hill" is situated on property owned by Dr. John Poppenheim in 1853.

Whaley only paid $1,700 for the entire tract of land, but although a small amount of money was involved, the lands passed out of and then back into the hands of Whaley in 1857.[740] These prewar years were economically difficult times and lands typically passed through frequent conveyances.

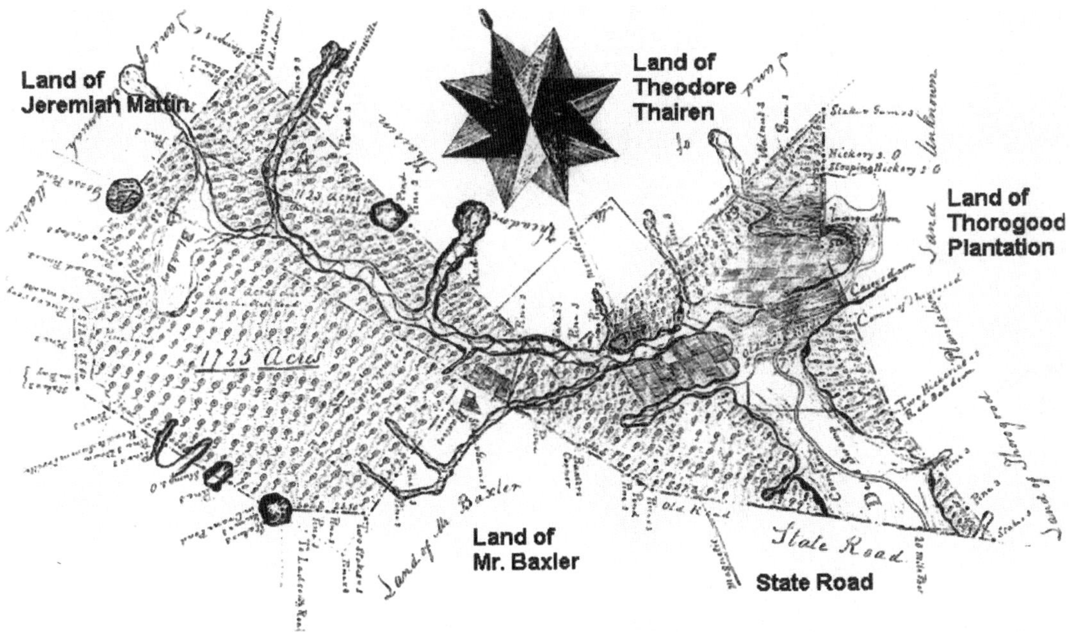

Plat 7.31 This plat shows Old Barn Plantation consisting of 1,725 acres. The plat was drawn from a survey made in 1850 by Sam W. Joyner. The plat indicates that the original grant was made in 1696 to William Haweth. The plat is deposited with the *Hutchinson Papers* among the collections of the South Carolina Historical Society. The manuscript words were added to this publication for clarity.

That tract also moved in and out of the ownership of John Poppenheim and was eventually sold to Rufus Knight and G.L. Corn, whose ownership is shown on the 1936 Gaillard map. Also farms owned by W.C. Whaley, T.J. Whaley, and C.M. Whaley are noted on the map, indicating family ties with George P. Whaley who owned the entire tract eighty years earlier.

H. Smith Richardson consolidated all of the Persimmon Hill and Old Barn lands and many more in the 1950s. He sold some tracts for residential use where the Boulder Bluff and Beverly Hills subdivisions were constructed. Soon after, he sold 660 acres to John H. White for $1,123,020 in 1969, but White could not pay the mortgage and sold the land back to Richards for $5, ten years later.[741] Today these properties are highly valued commercial, industrial and residential lands. An interesting avenue of mature oaks remains visible at the Persimmon Hill condominium community. It is likely that these old oaks shaded an earlier residential settlement, but neither land records nor recent archaeological studies identified any significant structures associated with the oak alee.

Grove Hall

The earliest reference to the Grove Hall property is a 500-acre Proprietary grant to Francis Noble in 1684. This land was located north and west of Thorogood Plantation. Another grant of 1,070 acres was given in 1705, contiguous to Noble's land. James McCall acquired both tracts and named the plantation "Grove Hall." [742] More contiguous land was granted to George Chicken in 1706 and 1707,

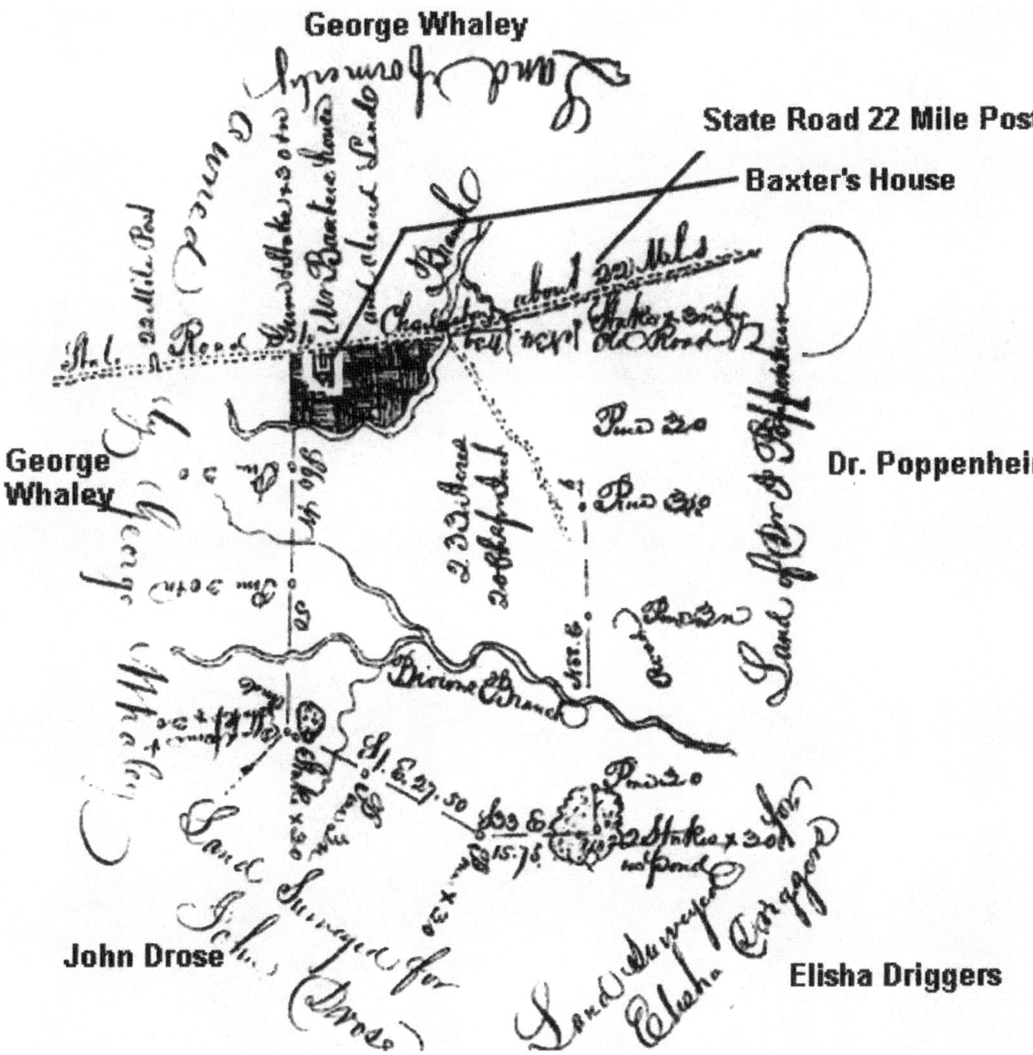

Plat 7.32 This plat shows a tract of land owned by Daniel Baxter containing 233 acres at the 22-mile post on the State Road. The plat was drawn from a survey made by Thomas Joiner, Deputy Surveyor.

and in 1711 to John Wood. Therefore, when William Branford Jr. acquired and consolidated all five tracts, Grove Hall Plantation consisted of 3,015 acres in 1769 and reached from Laurel Swamp west to Black Tom Bay.[743] Branford built a home on the tract and made many improvements by the time he gave the estate as a wedding gift to his daughter. She married Elias Horry Jr., a Santee River rice planter and a man of considerable wealth, but he showed little interest in Grove Hall while both he and his bride lived on the Santee. Colonel Joseph Glover acquired 4,474 acres of property in Goose Creek including 3,015 acres at Grove Hall Plantation, which he purchased in 1778.[744] The *South Carolina Gazette and Public Advertiser* carried the death notice for Joseph Glover in its August 9, 1783 edition and noted that he died at the age of sixty-five and was buried "at his seat, in Goose Creek." The land passed to his son, Sanders. He and his wife Lydia resided there for several decades as indicated by birth, death

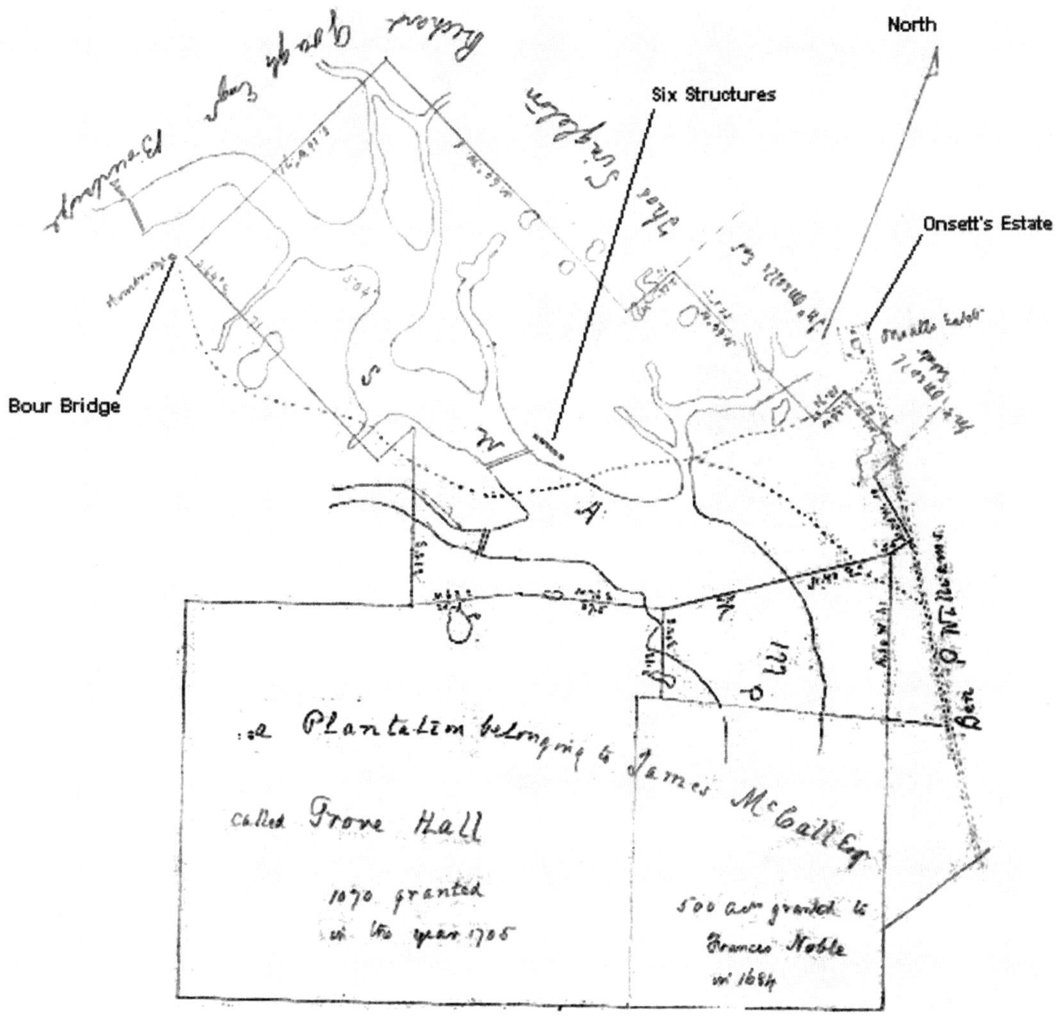

Plat 7.33 According to this 1795 plat by John Diamond, Grove Hall was owned by Sanders Glover and consisted of 1,432 acres. The plat shown below is a tracing by H.A.M. Smith of the original. The manuscript labels were added for this publication. The tracing is among the collections of the South Carolina Historical Society.

and marriage notations in their family bible.[745] Plat 7.33 made from a 1795 survey indicates that Grove Hall, consisting of 1,432 acres and featured a "mill" and "Bour Bridge." The design and purpose of the Bour Bridge is unknown, but it may have been designed to lift and close as needed to prevent livestock from crossing the water or it may have featured a covered walkway of some sort. The plat also shows six structures near a dike or causeway but no main house is indicated on the Grove Hall plat. "Onsetts Estate" is indicated on the north boundary with a central structure and three flanking structures. Benjamin Snipes purchased the land in 1797 for £1,310 sterling and made a profit when he sold Grove Hall to Matthew Irvine for £1,500 a few years later. Irvine held the land until his death when he bequeathed the estate to his widow. The 1795 plat shows Richard Gough as owner of the property to the west. Gough's estate consisted of 500 acres that touched the southern most waters of Black Tom Bay. John Onsett's property bordered on the north and Deas's Thorogood Plantation was to the south. The Grove Hall tract was bordered by land owned by James McCall who appears to have lent his name to that location. The Ford map shows "McCollie" near the 23-Mile House in 1844, and a 1909 plat made from an earlier survey mentions "McCalls Swamp.[746] Another plat, dated 1907–04 shows 400 acres at McCall's Swamp near Strawberry then owned by Professor C.M. Furman.[747]

Pawley's

Richard Gough purchased Pawley's Plantation on the western branch of the Cooper and on the northern line of the Goose Creek Parish. He was a very wealthy planter with seventy-three slaves. He and his wife Rachel Keating reared one son, Richard Jr., who served as a churchwarden and was elected to the Nineteenth Royal Assembly. He and eighteen other young and rich planters in the neighborhood established the Goose Creek Friendly Society.[748] His son, Richard, was also a planter in the vicinity. He purchased five hundred acres of land west of Pawley's on the southernmost section of Black Tom Bay.[749]

Brounfield/Brownefield

George Broun, born in 1680 in Scotland, and his wife, Lady Mary Broun, arrived in South Carolina in 1735. Their son, Dr. Robert Broun accompanied them to South Carolina and remained after they continued on to Virginia. He married Elizabeth Thomas in Goose Creek in 1738 and settled on a plantation called "Brounfields," on the headwaters of Foster Creek near Thorogood. Elizabeth Thomas was the granddaughter of the SPG missionary, Reverend Samuel Thomas. Dr. Robert Broun was only twenty-one years old when he arrived in Goose Creek. The records do not indicate where he received his doctoral degree at such a young age, but he was accepted into the homes of the "best" families and thus was likely well educated. Captain Archibald Broun, son of Robert and Elizabeth, was born at Goose Creek in 1752. He married his wealthy neighbor Mary Deas, the daughter of John and Elizabeth Allen Deas of Thorogood Plantation. He became wealthy through this marriage and was able to acquire additional properties near Goose Creek on the Cooper River.

Prior to the Revolutionary War, Archibald Broun was assigned to a mission in France on behalf of the American revolutionary forces, to negotiate a loan for military supplies and equipment. He was successful negotiating the loan, but the British captured the arms-laden ship on its voyage to America. In spite of the failed mission he sailed to Boston, rode horseback to Goose Creek and continued to serve the patriot cause with the rank of Captain. He befriended the Marquis de Lafayette while he was in France, and after the war entertained the Marquis at his Blessings Plantation on the Cooper River.

At the siege of Savannah, he was stabbed by a bayonet and died years later because of complications from the wound. He was buried at the Goose Creek Chapel of Ease. Aaron Loocock acquired the nine-hundred-acre Brounfield Plantation through marriage to Mary Broun, daughter of Doctor Robert Broun and Elizabeth Thomas, and sister of Archibald. He was a typical merchant-planter who immigrated to Goose Creek in the 1750s. At first he dabbled in the fur and slave trade and through land grants, he acquired a great deal of property in the backcountry. He died in 1794 and was buried at the Goose Creek Chapel of Ease near his wife, Mary Loocock.

Springfield

Alexander Mazyck, son of Paul Mazyck and grandson of Isaac Mazyck Jr., owned the 940-acre Springfield Plantation on the headwaters of Foster Creek during the decades leading to the American Revolution.[750] He built an expansive main house with ornamental grounds and developed a versatile estate with rice as the staple crop. Partial plat 7.34 was drawn from a survey made in 1791 shortly after Alexander Mazyck died. The plat shows a tree-lined avenue leading from the west by way of Gibbes Path to the main house. The main house appears to have featured a large frontal extension that was probably a portico. Behind the house was a large and well-planned ornamental garden. A walkway led from the house to an off-center open area. It appears that walkways radiated in four directions from a circular open area behind the main house. Away from the main house and

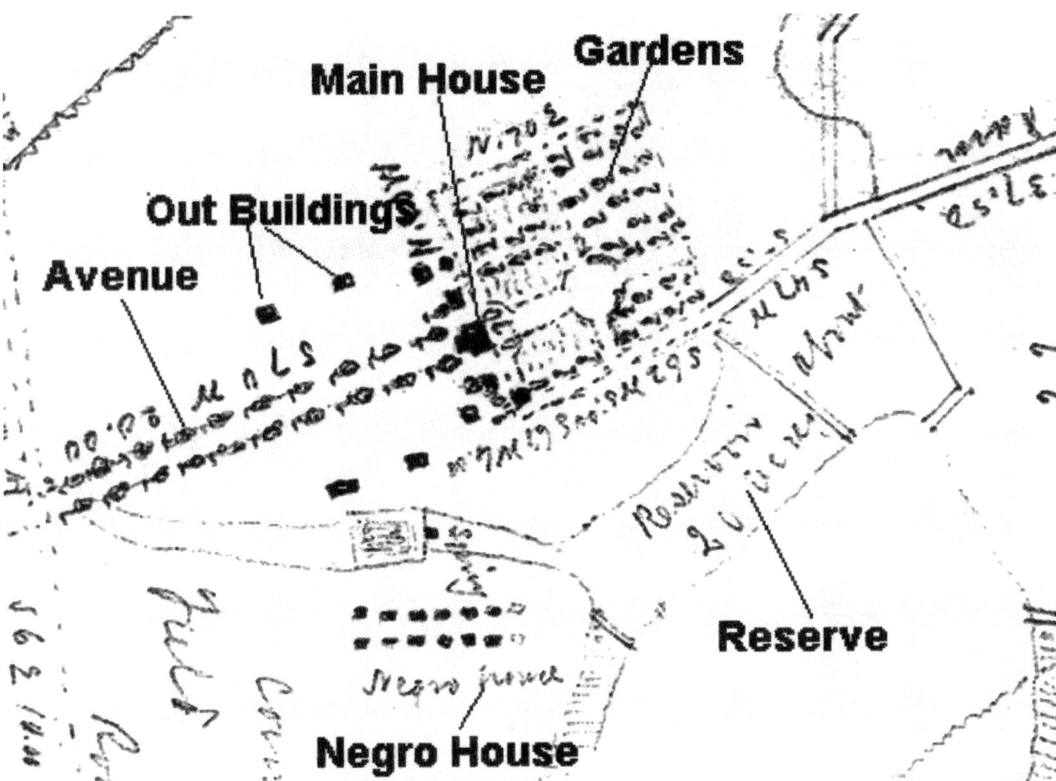

Plat 7.34 This partial plat is a tracing by H.A.M. Smith of the original drawn from a 1791 survey of Springfield Plantation. The tracing was made from the original McCrady Plat # 1327. The original McCrady plat does not include the ornamental trees. The manuscript labels were added to this publication. The tracing is among the collections of the South Carolina Historical Society.

separated from the main house by a water reserve, were fourteen structures labeled "Negro Houses." A "spring" is also noted at the waterway leading to the reserve. Diked rice fields are indicated. The plat notations state that the 940-acre estate consisted of 643 acres of forest and pastureland, 208 acres of cleared highlands for crops and pasture, 78 acres of low rice lands and an 11-acre water reserve. Mazyck's land was bounded on the west by Thorogood/Mt. Holly lands, on the north by Aaron Loocock's property, and on the east by James Graham's 200-acre tract.[751] William Smith owned Button Hall Plantation south of Springfield. A later survey made in 1858 indicates that little changes had occurred since the first survey sixty-seven years earlier. Dr. J. Keith Furman owned the 940-acre tract in 1858.[752] The site of the main house remains today on a 50-acre hill, forty-two feet above sea level, east of Woodland Heights Subdivision. The thickly forested hill remains unimproved and contains no overt ruins.

Castlebrawn/Button Hall

James Moore Esquire received a 2,400-acre grant from the Proprietors in 1683. This grant was a large inland tract of land known by the native names of "Boochowee" and "Wapensaw." This grant was the foundation from which a number of important estates later evolved. One estate was Button Hall/Castle Brawn. James Moore conveyed a portion of this frontier estate to his daughter, Rebecca in 1707. She married Captain Thomas Barker, but she sold two large tracts and resided on the remaining 515 acres after he was killed in the Yemassee War in 1715. Rebecca Moore Barker then married William Dry, who had received an early land grant in Goose Creek. With this marriage Dry amassed an even larger estate and added 130 acres when he purchased a section of contiguous Broom Hall from Benjamin Gibbes in 1719.[753] Dry greatly improved his 795-acre estate until he offered the plantation for sale in 1733. At the time of this sale, the tract was known as "Button Hall."[754] The well-developed estate boasted 400 cleared acres and many amenities. The property fronted the main Goose Creek Road and featured "a good Brick Dwelling House, several rice Mills, Mortars and winnowing house, an oven, a large Stable & Coach house, a cooper shop & a house built for a smith shop." A small house with a brick chimney stood across the road from the mainhouse, which could be used by a member of the family or an overseer. The main house was flanked with gardens and was situated near a fishpond that was stocked with perch, roach, pike, eels and catfish. There was also a spring within "three stone throws of the house" where one could conveniently bathe and where dams created three large ponds for water reserves. The reserve irrigated a fruit orchard where apples, pears and peaches were harvested.[755]

An indenture for this property shows that William McKenzie purchased the 795-acre estate for £5,700 in 1734.[756] When he died from a fever four years later, at the age of forty-five, his widow Sara McKenzie offered the estate for sale in the *Gazette*.[757] The property was advertised for sale the same year, John McKenzie, son of William and Sara, was born. John inherited his father's wealth and eventually increased the family fortune to include 6,900 acres in several parishes, 207 slaves and an elaborately accommodated town house. He kept 38 slaves and named the Goose Creek estate that he inherited from his father, "Castle Brawn."

John McKenzie was an attorney by training, but pursued the life of a planter as one of many of his varied interests. He kept an elaborate library valued at £2,100 at Castle Brawn where he also experimented with hay production. He used his unencumbered time to pursue political interests and was elected to the Royal Assembly three times, served in various commissions and served as churchwarden at the Goose Creek Church.[758] McKenzie allied with Christopher Gadsden in publishing opposition arguments against Great Britain, but he died in 1771 before the opposition to the British erupted in warfare. He greatly increased his fortunes when he married Sarah Smith, the daughter of Thomas Smith and Sarah Moore. He died after a short illness at the early age of thirty-three, at his father-in-law's home at Broom Hall, and was buried at Castle Brawn. The *South Carolina*

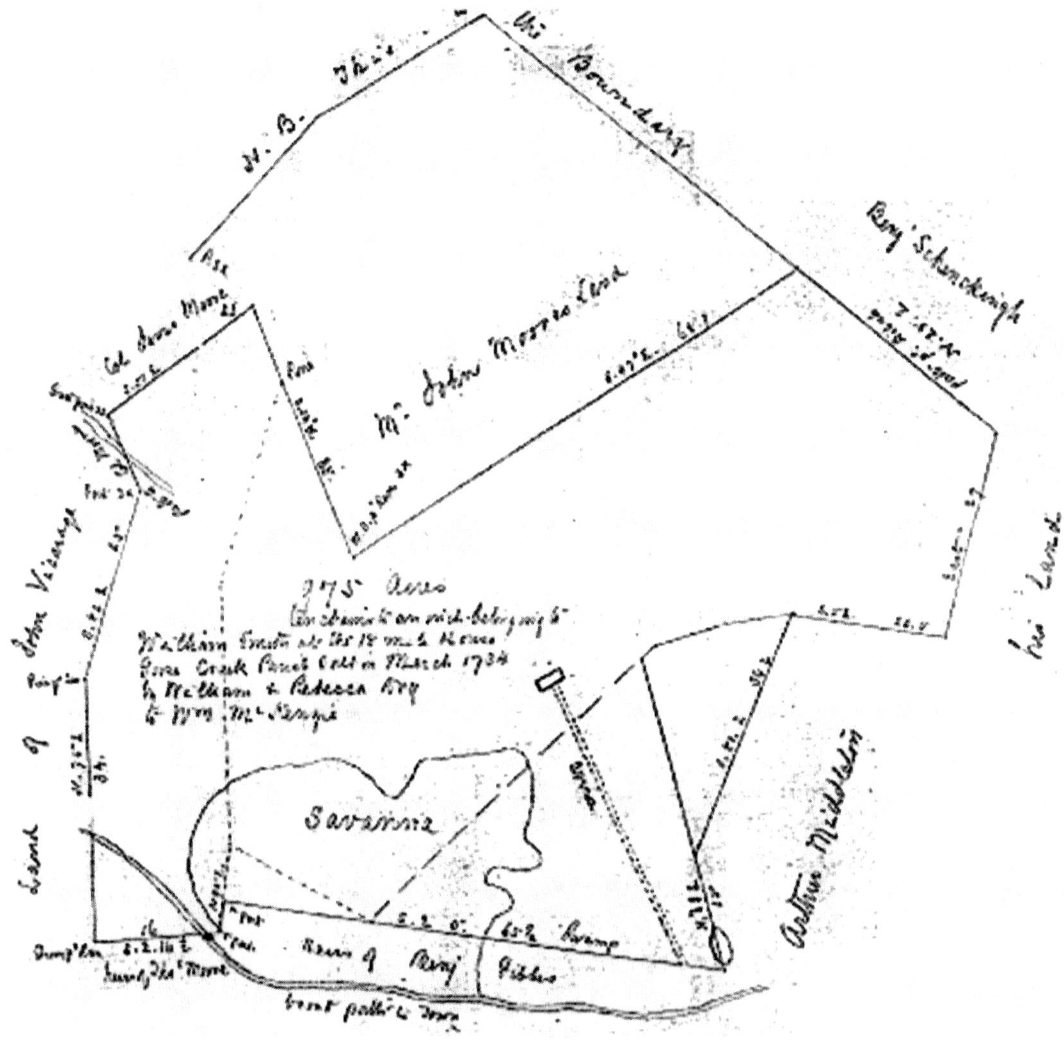

Plat 7.35 This partial plat was copied from a survey made by L. Lewis Simons in 1734 when William and Rebecca Dry sold the property to William McKenzie. This plantation is labeled "Button Hall" on this copy and cited as the property of William Smith. The handwritten notation records that this land was situated at "The 18-mile House." H.A.M. Smith traced this plat. The tracing is among the collections of the South Carolina Historical Society.

Gazette eulogized John McKenzie as "that inestimable member of the Community...that zealous, disinterested, and unshaken Patriot...that true friend to America and the English Constitution...that excellent Man in every social relation."[759] He left his widow his £12,000 estate and devised £1,000 to establish a college in Charleston. He also bequeathed an eight hundred-volume library on law, political science and history to the college whenever it was established.[760]

Governor William Bull acquired the land seven years after John McKenzie's death and resided there. The tract appears on a 1778 elaborate plat for the governor. Castle Brawn appears to be the identical lands as Button Hall with more than 200 additional acres. The 1778 plat made when the governor bought the property, shows a 976-acre tract bound partially by Arthur Middleton at the Oaks, Thomas Smith at Howe Hall, Thomas Smith at Broom Hall, Back River Upper Road and Springfield Plantation owned by Alexander Mazyck.[761] Plat 7.35 is a copy of a copy. It was traced in 1778 from a 1734 plat made from a survey completed when William and Rebecca Dry sold the property to William McKenzie. The governor may have sold the estate by an unrecorded deed to Daniel Tharin and Elizabeth because the couple was in possession of the property in 1778, as indicated by the conveyance to Lewis Lestergette of 976 acres for £40,000.[762] Another plat was made when the tract at the 18-Mile House, transferred to William Laughton Smith in 1785. The plantation was referred to as "Button Hall" in that transaction.

William Smith purchased the tract in 1785 from Lewis Lestergette.[763] A 1805 plat shows Button Hall bound by Deas's Thorogood/Mt. Holly lands, Springfield Plantation, owned by Alexander Mazyck, The Oaks, owned by Thomas Middleton, the High Road (sited as "broad path to Town" on the 1734 plat), Peter Smith's Broom Hall and Back River Road. William Laughton Smith sold a 109-acre section of Button Hall in 1810 to Lewis Breaker, owner of the 18-Mile House.

William Laughton Smith (1758–1812) was the son of Benjamin Smith and Anne Laughton. He studied in England and returned to South Carolina in 1783 following the Revolution. He pursued a career as an attorney and by 1789 had amassed a fortune of £19,000 sterling. He married Charlotte Izard, daughter of Ralph Izard and Alice Delancey, and became allied with a powerful Goose Creek Izard family.[764] With his father-in-law, Ralph Izard, and brother-in-law, Gabriel Manigault, he formed one of the most powerful political factions of the day. The Izard-Manigault-Smith camp provided strong support for the Federalist Party on all political levels.

William Laughton Smith represented Goose Creek in the Sixth, Seventh and Eighth General Assemblies before being elected to the United States House of Representatives in 1788. He represented Charleston District in the First, Second, Third, Fourth and Fifth Congresses. He favored a strong central government and judicial system and was a staunch supporter of Alexander Hamilton. As a supporter of a strong central government he wanted the federal government to assume all state debts and to establish a national bank. His ardent espousal of his views on a strong central government, as well as his views on the Federal Constitution and foreign affairs made him controversial and widely known. His treatises on the Constitution became required reading at the College of New Jersey (Princeton). President John Adams nominated him as Minister Plenipotentiary of the United States to the Court of Portugal in 1797. Upon his appointment, he resigned from the House of Representatives and sailed to Europe. It was through his office in Portugal that the tribute to the Barbary pirates was sent. The pirates were threatening the Mediterranean and demanding bribes to spare American shipping. He opposed the American policy of paying bribes and advocated a strong navy instead. In 1799, he was appointed ambassador to Turkey, but Napoleon's advances in Italy delayed and finally suspended his mission, and the election of Thomas Jefferson terminated his appointment. After a tour of Europe, he returned home to his law practice and through his second marriage to Charlotte Wragg accumulated a fortune in Charleston. He invested well and bequeathed his wife an estate worth $140,000 including the Goose Creek lands.[765] By two marriages Smith was the father of four. He died in 1812 and was buried at St. Philip's Church.

Charlotte Wragg Smith, widow of Charles Laughton Smith, sold Button Hall to Thomas J. Smith in 1821 for $2,710. Button Hall consisted of slightly more than 387 acres at that time, but Smith owned the neighboring lands and wanted to consolidate the acreage.[766] In 1855, the land passed by sale to David Traxler and C.P. Shier. Both lost Button Hall three years later due to mortgage foreclosure and the property reverted to J.J. Screven Smith and Thomas Smith, who were the grandchildren of Charlotte Wragg Smith and Charles Laughton Smith. These two Smiths owned a larger tract into which Button Hall was absorbed in 1871. That newly created larger tract was situated on the headwaters of Foster Creek and bordered to the west on land belonging to Carlton Vose, on the north by lands owned by M.J. Keith, and on the east by lands owned by Charles Desel. The tract was situated on the State Road and was formed by the combination of several adjoining tracts including: part of the 17-Mile House tract containing about 210 acres, the 18-mile tract with about 70 acres, the 19-Mile House tract containing 467 acres and a part of the Oaks plantation with 364 acres. Altogether the combined tract encompassed 1,111 acres in 1871.[767]

This tract was generally referred to as "The 18-Mile House" for the next one hundred years and encompassed lands that eventually became the "Downtown" section of the modern City of Goose Creek.

Boocho(a)wee

James Moore, Esquire, received a grant of land from the Proprietors that was known by the native names of "Boochowee" and "Wapensaw" and was the same grant of land sited in the vignette of Castle Brawn and Buttonhall from which several estates evolved. The foundation grant was a large twenty-four hundred acre tract located between Bloomfield, the Oaks Plantation and Foster Creek. It had an auspicious occupancy from its start. Governor James Moore resided at the original Boochowee settlement, and after his death Colonel James Moore, the son, inherited and resided on the land. James Moore Jr. commanded the Provincial forces of South Carolina against the Tuscarora Natives admirably, and in 1704 received a warrant for land next to his Boochowee tract and contiguous to lands owned by Captain Benjamin Schenckingh. These two tracts were the origin of several important estates including Button Hall, Howe Hall and Liberty Hall. Colonel James Moore sold one thousand acres to David Davis in 1709, and mortgaged more to three Charleston merchants, Thomas Broughton, Lewis Pasquereau and John Guerard. He retained the remaining sections until his death.

Colonel James Moore was a well-respected churchwarden for Goose Creek and upon his death he left three hundred of the acres, as well as the house, kitchen, hen house, stable, garden, and orchard to his wife until his eldest son, James, came of age. To his second son John he left the remaining properties, including two hundred acres he had purchased from Thomas Smith.[768]

James, the oldest son, represented Goose Creek in the Tenth Royal Assembly.[769] He married Sarah Waring and with her reared three children. They sold Boochowee in 1739, which contained nine hundred acres at that time and relocated to St. George, Dorchester. Along with the "land convenient for damming…and good corn land," he sold fifteen "choice" slaves, a "very good brick two story house" and outbuildings in 1739.[770] After the Moore ownership, the extant plantation was divided and added to other working plantations, but retained its native name and general identity for many years.

Benjamin Schenckingh purchased almost half of the granted land and mortgaged what he owned to Richard Miles of Madeira. The debt was not paid and the eight hundred acre section of Boochowee reverted to Miles for some time before Schenckingh re-acquired it. At that time, the tract was referred to as "Bonds Bank." [771] Later, Schenckingh gave two hundred acres of Bonds Bank to his nephew, Thomas Smith.[772] This gift became known as Smith Hall. After giving the two hundred acres to his nephew, he offered eight hundred remaining acres of "Boochow" for sale in 1733. This tract contained three hundred acres of uncleared oak and hickory forest and five hundred acres of cleared land suitable for corn and rice. The sale offer included the main house, barn, stables and other outbuildings, as well as gardens and orchards.[773]

The property did not immediately sell, but upon his death, Benjamin Schenckingh's will empowered his wife to sell the estate. She sold it to Thomas Cheeseman in 1734 for £380.[774] Thomas Cheeseman held it for four years and sold it to Thomas Middleton.[775] This sale included 340 acres of Howe Hall and 305 acres of land called "Pineland." [776] Thus, Thomas Middleton came into possession of Howe Hall and Boochowee, and in that way he more than doubled the size of his Oaks Estate. Eventually, Middleton left 752 acres of this property to his son Thomas, as well as more land that he purchased contiguous to Boochowee. Thus, a single tract combined Howe Hall and Boochowee and was advertised for sale in 1752 as two plantations containing 1,397 acres and boasting a "large & commodious Brick dwelling house with convenient buildings."[777]

Joel Huff purchased these properties and renamed the combined tract "Bella Vista." He and his wife resided at Bella Vista with twelve slaves.[778] He served as a free-school commissioner.[779] Joel Huff and his wife both died without a will, passing the Bella Vista Plantation to the ownership of their daughter, Martha Behling, and her husband, Luder T. Behling.

Luder and Martha Behling sold Bella Vista to Carlton Vose in 1855. Carlton Vose became one of the largest landowners in Goose Creek when he consolidated Bella Vista with several other parcels. He eventually owned the 17, 18 and 19-Mile House tracts, as well as the remains of the Oaks estate and numerous other contiguous parcels. In 1871, he conveyed his property to his son, George, who fought in the Civil War, as well as his daughter Olivia, and his two grandchildren from his deceased daughter. These conveyances were accomplished in three separate actions that transferred 1,111 acres of property. Many of these properties eventually became valued commercial and residential tracts in the City of Goose Creek. One of Carlton Vose's descendents resides on a remaining parcel today.

Howe Hall

The origin of Howe Hall Plantation was a Proprietary grant consisting of 290 acres to Robert Howe in 1683. The size of the plantation was increased when Robert Howe received an additional 800-acre grant "near Yeomans Creek" in 1706.[780] An additional 100 acres were added the same year.[781]

Over the years, the tract increased in acreage when contiguous property was added and decreased when parcels were sold. This large estate was situated on the western side of Foster Creek and north of Goose Creek and the name "Howe Hall" remains associated with much of the land to this day.

Job Howe, son of Robert, was the Speaker of the Commons House of Assembly in 1704 and one of the notorious "Goose Creek Men." Job Howe and his wife, Sarah, raised their son on the Goose Creek plantation. As an adult, Robert Howe, the grandson of the immigrant, was a successful planter at Howe Hall and the owner of sixty-four slaves. His wife was Mary Moore, the daughter of James Moore and Margaret Berringer.[782] Thus, his father and father-in-law were leaders of the Goose Creek Men and anti-proprietary, and he by birth and marriage was closely associated with the "Goose Creek Men." Thus it is not surprising that Robert signed an address to the king, asking for a royal government and protesting the proprietary management. Robert Howe was elected twice to represent Berkeley and Craven Counties and served Goose Creek as a tax collector and church vestryman. Among Robert Howe's descendents was his grandson, General Robert Howe of the Revolutionary War fame.[783]

Robert died in 1724 and his widow, Mary Moore, wed Thomas Clifford, an attorney. Job, son of Robert and Mary, inherited Howe Hall and held the property until 1734 when he offered it for sale.[784] Job appointed Thomas Clifford, as his attorney, to sell two plantations with a total of 800 acres.[785] One tract was Howe Hall consisting of 290 acres of the original grant. A 1736 sales advertisement depicted the estate situated on Foster Creek with "about 200 acres under a very good fence for pasturage or planting and 600 acres moderately well wooded." The plantation featured a "tolerable dwelling house built indeed after the rustic order."[786] The estate did not immediately sell and the sale was advertised again in 1739. At this time the buildings were described as, "a large Brick House, a House adjoining it of two rooms on a floor, one story high, a very large store house, a Coach House and Stables, a Barn, Smoke House, and several houses for all kinds of stock, all strong and completely built...but two years ago." A "stock of cattle, horses & 32 Negroes" was also included in the sale.[787]

Thomas Clifford and his wife, Mary, reared no children and in 1735, they moved to North Carolina where Mary Moore Clifford's relatives and in-laws resided. James Irving acquired Howe Hall and held it until 1755. He then sold Boochowee and Howe Hall to Richard Dun Lawrence for £3,000. It contained 752 acres when it was sold under the name of "Howe Hall."[788]

Richard Dun Lawrence must have defaulted on the purchase arrangement, because four years later the land reverted to the ownership of Irving who soon sold it to Benjamin Smith. Smith, the son of the second landgrave, Thomas Smith and Mary Hyrne, purchased Boochowee and Howe Hall together in 1759. He also owned two houses in Charleston where he kept five slaves. He worked seventeen slaves at Howe Hall and Boochowee and also worked thousands of acres elsewhere in the province. Nevertheless, he was known as "Benjamin Smith of Goose Creek." He was elected to represent Goose Creek seven times in the Royal and General Assemblies from 1772 to 1780. He also represented Goose Creek at the state convention that ratified the constitution. His first wife was Elizabeth Ann Harleston, with whom he reared three children. After Elizabeth's death, he married Catharine Ball. Smith then wed his cousin, Sarah Smith, daughter of George Smith. With her, he fathered five children. His fourth wife was Rebecca Singleton, widow of Benjamin Coachman. No children were born of this marriage. When Benjamin Smith died in 1790 he devised the lands to his two sons—Thomas Smith received Howe Hall, the home site and part of the "Bowehoie" tract, and Benjamin received the remaining lands including the section of "Bowehoie" not devised to Thomas. The dividing line between the two devised tracts was Back River Lower Road, which proceeded to Villeponteaux's estate on Back River.[789]

Plat 7.36 was made from a survey conducted in 1775. Benjamin Smith owned both Howe Hall and Boochowee at that time. Howe Hall consisted of 620 acres and Boochowee contained only 490 acres of the original 2,400-acre grant. The drawn main house and outbuildings of the Howe Hall settlement are evident near three approach avenues. The word "Bushawee" appears on the northern section above the Lower Road to Back River that traverses the tract. Contiguous to these tracts, on the western boundary, is Henry Middleton's Oaks Estate, containing part of the original Boochowee grant. C.C. Pinckney's land is noted on the south. East is Benjamin Mazyck's Estate, which contained part of the original Boochowee grant, and northwest is part of Boochowee owned by John Davis. A section of Foster Creek appears on the southeastern corner and the Upper Road to Back River appears on the western boundary.

For eighteen years, 200 acres of the Boochowee estate remained in the Smith family. It was devised by Thomas Smith to his son Benjamin Smith in 1723, but was sold by Benjamin and his wife, Ann to Paul Mazyck, in 1741.[790] After buying this property, Paul Mazyck purchased the remaining half of Boochowee from John and Anne Davis who had inherited the property from David Davis, owner of the tract since 1707. The Boochowee tract purchased by Mazyck contained 880 acres bought from John Davis and 350 acres bought from Benjamin Smith.[791]

The February 2, 1734 issue of the *South Carolina Gazette* reported that Paul Mazyck owned a nine hundred acre Goose Creek plantation with a fine, eight-room house. In addition, there were two stables (sixty by thirty feet and sixty by twenty feet each), as well as coach houses, stock barns, sheep pens and slave quarters. This was the beginning of the large Mazyck holdings from which Liberty Hall was derived. Paul lived forty-seven years and amassed a fortune in land, town lots, houses, and slaves in his short lifetime. He was elected twice to serve Goose Creek in the Royal Assembly and contributed to the Ludlam school fund and the French Protestant Church fund for the poor. He and his wife died within a day of each other in 1749.[792] The land passed from Paul Mazyck to his son, Alexander and then to his son, Benjamin.

Benjamin Mazyck owned Liberty Hall at the time of the American Revolution and the property stayed in the Mazyck family until Stephen, the fourth generation Mazyck, lost part of the property in a forced sale for debts in 1810. After Stephen's death, Charleston District Sheriff John Steedman supervised the sale of 1,093 acres of the tract to James W. Gadsden. The Public Road, Back River Road, William Smith's property (once known as Button Hall) and the Church and Free School Property on Red Bank Road bound the estate when Gadsden bought it. This section of the property at that time was known as "Bella Vista." It was mortgaged to Charles Graves but when he defaulted on the loan, it reverted back to Rebecca Gadsden, widow of James Gadsden. She sold the estate to Joel Huff in 1828. About this same time, Mrs. Mary Mazyck, widow of Stephen Mazyck, conveyed the remaining section of the Mazyck estate to Charles Desel. This conveyance of 2,740.5 acres for $7,800 became known as Liberty Hall.[793] This tract was composed of several smaller plantations named "Brickbarn," "Rochford" and "Mulberry." These places were the original land and residence of Benjamin Mazyck.

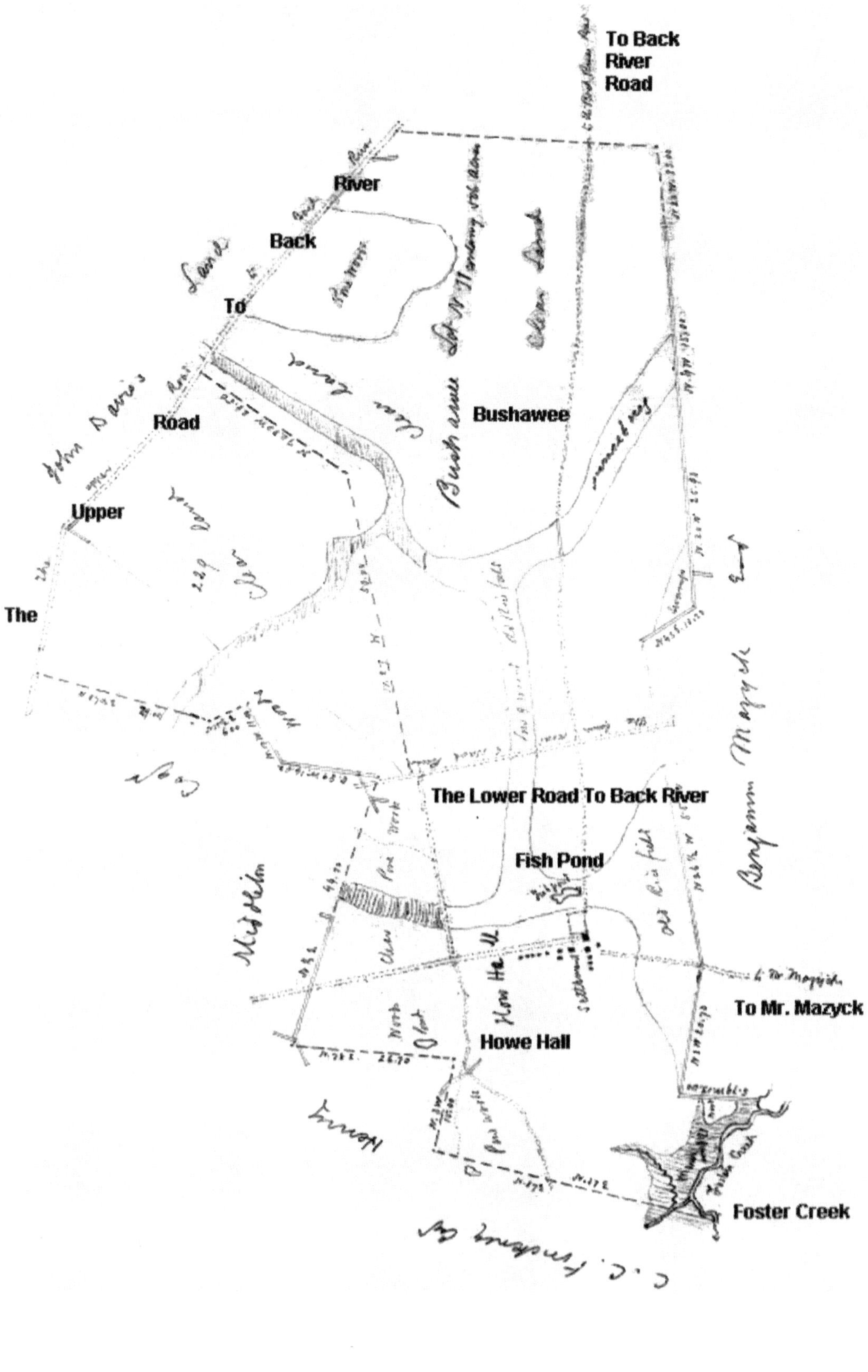
To Back
River
Road
River
Back
To
Road
Upper
The
Bushawee
The Lower Road To Back River
Fish Pond
To Mr. Mazyck
Howe Hall
Foster Creek

James Vidal purchased 1,505 acres of land between Desel's Liberty Hall, Charles Grave's lands on Goose Creek and the waters of Foster Creek in the years prior and during the Civil War. Most of these lands were at one time part of Howe Hall. His land ownership is interesting, not because of his relative success as a post Civil War farmer, but because he sold some of his property in small parcels to freed blacks after the war, and in that way provided an opportunity for black farm ownerships that have remained in extended black families on Back River and Howe Hall Roads until today.

Liberty Hall

Liberty Hall Plantation is situated on lands that were once part of a twenty-four-hundred-acre proprietary grant to James Moore Esquire in 1683. Moore called his lands "Boochowee" and upon his death in 1709, devised the entire tract to his son, James. James Moore Jr. sold almost half of Boochowee, including the Boochowee main house, to David Davis in two sales. Benjamin Schenckingh and his wife Margaret bought the Davis share of Boochowee in 1712 and later sold it to Nathaniel Moore. Nathaniel Moore and his wife sold the nine hundred acre parcel that eventually became known as "Liberty Hall" on May 31, 1726 to Isaac Mazyck of Charleston for £3,500.[794]

Isaac Mazyck was a French Huguenot immigrant, who arrived in Charleston by way of England in 1686. He was a successful Charleston merchant who, like many well-to-do businessmen of that era, acquired land in the country and lived the life of a gentleman planter. He received several grants for property, and he purchased houses in Charleston, land on the Charleston Neck, and the nine hundred acre tract in Goose Creek.[795] By the time of his death in 1736, he owned thousands of acres in several South Carolina parishes.

Isaac, son of the Huguenot immigrant, Isaac Mazyck and Marianne LeSerurier, was educated in England and served a short tour with the British Calvary before returning to South Carolina. He worked in a mercantile partnership with his successful father and eventually started his own business. He joined the ranks of the rich merchant planter class, common in Goose Creek. He and his brother, Paul, acquired their own lands and town property. He was elected twenty-three times and served five different parishes in the Royal Assembly. He was recognized as an able and astute political leader. Isaac Jr. and his brother, Paul, acting as their father's executors, sold the nine hundred acre tract on Foster Creek to their younger brother, Benjamin, for £5,200. Benjamin Mazyck amassed additional property during the next fifty years. He owned a home in Charleston and worked as a town merchant throughout his life, but his Foster Creek home was his principal residence. He grew rice at his Foster Creek plantation and he advertised in the *South Carolina Gazette* to sell brick to supplement his income.[796]

Benjamin Mazyck added 1,205 acres of land when he purchased Springfield Plantation from his nephew, Alexander Mayzck. He paid £17,955 for Springfield, which amounted to almost £15 per acre. These 1,205 acres were composed of two smaller tracts, which had been purchased by

Opposite page: Plat 7.36 This plat shows Howe Hall and Boochowee as surveyed in 1775 and traced by H.A.M. Smith. The manuscript labeling was added to this publication to improve legibility. The tracing is among the collections of the South Carolina Historical Society.

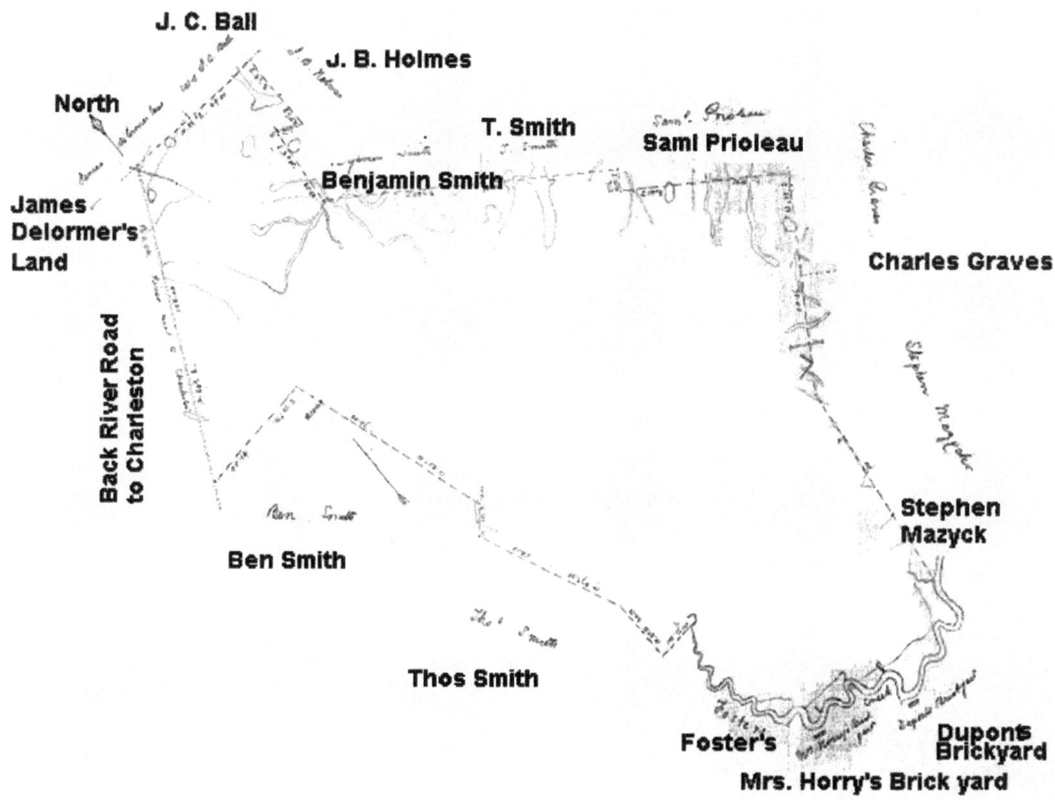

Plat 7.37 This plat describes the 2,743.5-acre tract owned by Stephen Mazyck. H.A.M. Smith traced the original plat drawn from a survey made by "Skrine" in 1802. The tracing is shown below. It is in the possession of the South Carolina Historical Society. Manuscript notations have been added due to poorly legible script.

Alexander's father, Isaac, from John Davis and Benjamin Smith. Later in 1786, he added another 183 acres purchased from James Rochford. In total Benjamin Mazyck managed to consolidate six small plantations into a single large tract.

Benjamin devised the property to his son, Stephen. The inheritance in Goose Creek included three contiguous tracts on the north side of Foster Creek: the tract he bought from his nephew consisting of 1,205 (including Spring Field and its main house), a small tract of 183 acres, he bought from James Rochford, and the original 900 acres purchased by Isaac, the immigrant. In 1808 Stephen devised these 2,288 acres to his three sons Benjamin, Stephen Jr. and Paul. Stephen Mazyck's estate is described on the 1802 plat 7.37. The property is described by the plat as bounding on Foster Creek to the south. His son, Benjamin, received the larger part of "Brick Barn" Plantation, probably including the main house. Stephen received the Rochford Tract. Paul received part of Brick Barn and the "Tunno Tract" located north of Back River Road at the old Springfield Plantation main house site.

During the early 1800s, inland rice plantations were less profitable and most investors sought tidal rice lands or sea-island cotton plantations. It appears as if the Foster Creek lands were

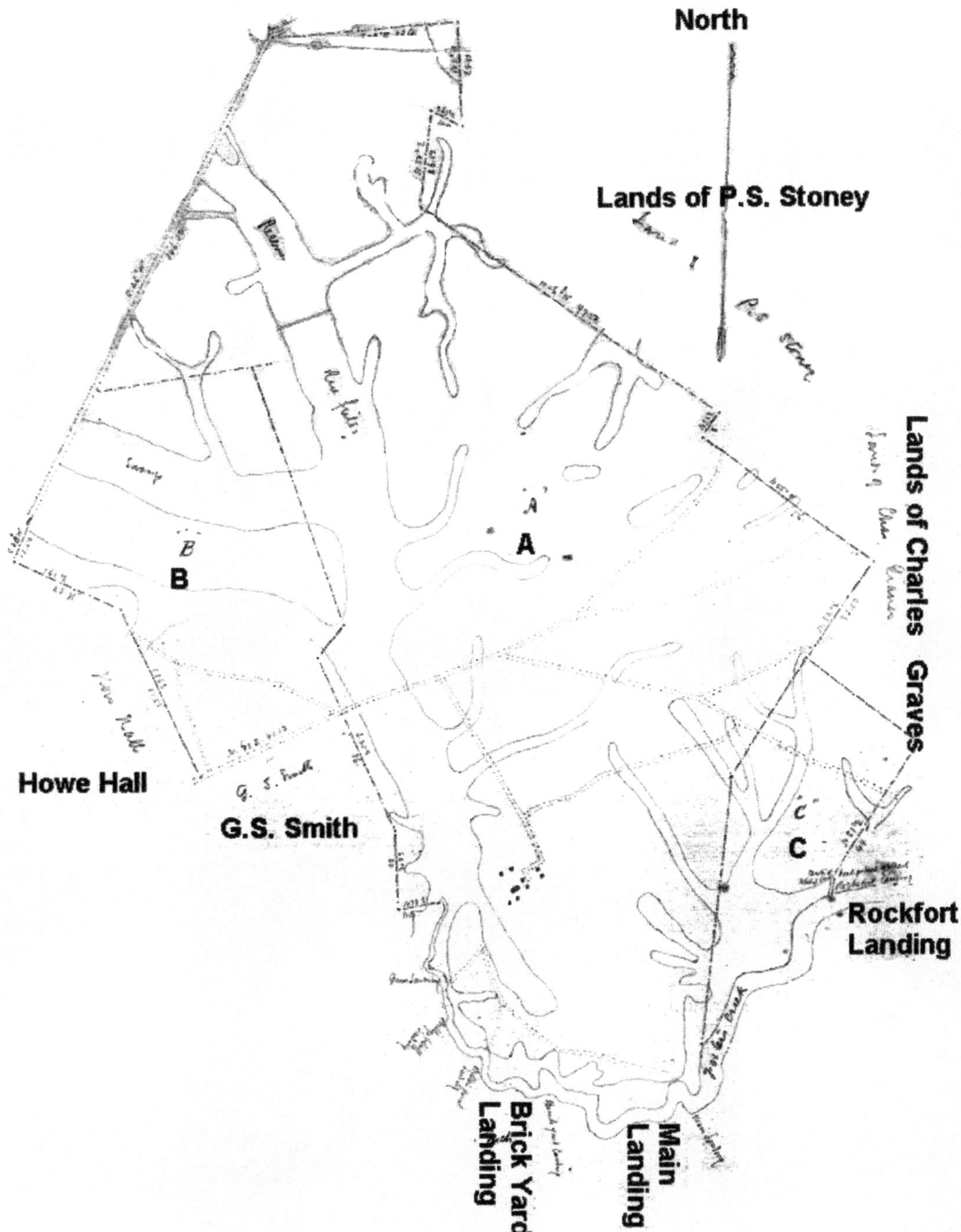

Plat 7.38 This partial plat describes Liberty Hall Plantation according to a survey made by W.N. Mellard in 1854. The survey was updated in 1870. The plat drawn from that survey shows twelve small buildings in four rows of three, a short distance from the main house. The structures may have been slave quarters. H.A.M. Smith traced the original plat. The tracing is among the collections of the South Carolina Historical Society.

marginally profitable at best during this time, and at the time of Stephen Mazyck Jr.'s death, he was heavily in debt. In spite of the debt, his personal inventory, taken in 1809, listed 47 slaves and many valuable personal possessions.[797] The Mazyck land was kept intact until two decades after Stephen Jr.'s death. In 1827 an equity case was brought, and in 1834 Mrs. Mary Mazyck, the widow of Stephen Mazyck, was ordered by the court to sell a large part of the Mazyck estate to Charles Desel at auction.[798] This conveyance of 2,740.5 acres for $7,800 included, "all that plantation on the northern side of Foster Creek…being formerly composed of several tracts commonly called Buckhorn, Rochford and Mulberry."[799]

The "Buckhorn" tract sited in the description is possibly referencing land also called "Brickbarn" and the parcel named "Mulberry" was likely the site of the main Liberty Hall house. Charles Desel added 506 acres to the tract when Jacob I. Moses sold some of the old Boochowee Plantation to Desel in 1842 for $6,050. The 1854 survey shown in part as plat 7.38 noted that 559 acres of Booshawee (shown as section "B" on the plat) and 270 acres of Rochford Plantation (section "C") were added to the 2,777-acre Liberty Hall tract (section "A"). These additions increased the size of Liberty Hall to 3,601 acres.[800] The 1850 *Agricultural Census* shows that Desel owned 3,252 acres. Nine years later the estate amounted to 3,601 acres.

Charles Desel was a good friend of Dr. John Bachman, a noted Charleston scholar and rector of St. Johns Lutheran Church. Bachman and his close acquaintance, John Audubon were frequent visitors to Liberty Hall. Audubon, a well-known naturalist and painter, gathered and created bird and animal collections at Liberty Hall. There Bachman made substantive contributions to Audubon's *Ornithological Biography*, the companion text to Audubon's landmark *Birds of America* paintings.[801] A Bachman biography, written by his youngest daughter, describes a deer hunt at Liberty Hall and the camaraderie of the two men.[802]

Partial plat 7.38 depicts Liberty Hall Plantation when it was surveyed in 1854. The plantation was bound on the north by Medway Plantation, and Charles Graves owned the land to the east. Howe Hall Plantation and land owned by George Smith bound on the south. The old Springfield Plantation was west of Liberty Hall. "Brick Bound" swamp labeled as "reserve" and "rice field" is described on the upper half of the plat, and Foster Creek is shown as the southern boundary. The main house and eight outbuildings are shown. Also "Brick Yard Landing," "Main Landing" and "Rochford Landing" are labeled on Foster Creek south of the settlement.

Desel, a physician, produced a variety of agricultural products including rice, but he did not produce huge amounts, as did some of his neighbors. Brick Bound Swamp dominates the topography of the upper half of the tract and was clearly the best rice fields on the land. Desel does not appear to have engaged in brick production, although he communicated with his brick-making neighbor, Charles Graves, at Brick Hope. In December 1854, Graves noted in his journal that he "went to hunt today with Desel, no luck."[803] Desel died about 1854 and the property passed to his wife, Catherine and then divided equally among his children.

The inventory of Desel's estate indicates that his country home was a working house, not an elegant estate home. He was a wealthy doctor with a home in Charleston. There is no inventory of his Charleston home, but it is likely that he spent most of his later years there. At the time of his death, he owned eighty-six slaves, which made him one of the larger slave holders in Goose Creek, but the inventory of his Goose Creek estate only included three horses, eight mules, fifty head of

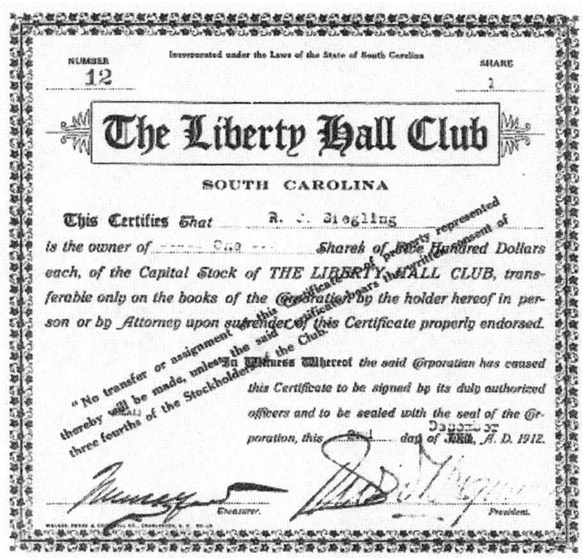

Incorporated under the Laws of the State of South Carolina

NUMBER 12 SHARE 1

The Liberty Hall Club

SOUTH CAROLINA

This Certifies That R. C. Siegling is the owner of One Shares of Five Hundred Dollars each, of the Capital Stock of THE LIBERTY HALL CLUB, transferable only on the books of the Corporation by the holder hereof in person or by Attorney upon surrender of this Certificate properly endorsed.

In Witness Whereof the said Corporation has caused this Certificate to be signed by its duly authorized officers and to be sealed with the seal of the Corporation, this 2nd day of December, A. D. 1912.

"No transfer or assignment of the property represented thereby will be made, unless the said certificate bears the written consent of three fourths of the Stockholders of the Club."

Treasurer. President.

Figure 7.1 This figure shows the stock certificate of the Liberty Hall Hunt Club dated December 2, 1912. *Courtesy of Terrence Larimer.*

cattle and thirty hogs. Such a small inventory of livestock at the time of his death may have been sufficient only to maintain his laborers. The paltry furnishings in the main house, assessed at only $250, indicate that he spent little time at Liberty Hall during his later years.

The property was sold in 1859 to Ephraim S. Mikell for $10,800. In this transfer, the land was referred to, as "Liberty Hall" for the first time on any known record, but the origin of the name is not given. The property passed through several hands because the chaos of the Civil War and the difficult economy made large land holdings workable for only a few of the most prosperous.

An 1877 plat shows that Charles Graves, owner of neighboring Brick Hope Plantation, had acquired much of Liberty Hall by that year. In 1880, the *Agricultural Census* indicates that Louis Seel owned Liberty Hall but planted only forty acres.[804] Edward G. Hanahan purchased the tract from Joseph C. Blaney in 1888, but held it for only five years.[805] It was during Hanahan's ownership that interest in the phosphate deposits at Liberty Hall surfaced. His venture was unsuccessful and he was forced to sell at auction to Colin Mackay Grant. A 1909 map shows that Colin McKay Grant still possessed the land that year, [806] and it was during this period that Colin McKay Grant gave lumber rights to the land to the E.P. Burton Lumber Company, including the right-of-way for a tram system and/or railroad. By 1912, a group of Charleston men leased the rights from Colin McKay Grant to hunt on the property. They built a hunting clubhouse on a small knoll approached by the remains of an avenue of ancient oaks.[807] The Liberty Hall Hunt Club certificate shown as figure 7.1 was produced December 2, 1912 and issued one share of stock in the club to R.C. Siegling for $500.[808]

The club was incorporated and the first hunt was held August 1, 1912.[809] The clubhouse stood on the site of Desel's house and included four bedrooms, a large dining room and a member's area with lockers for dressing. A kitchen house stood behind the clubhouse. A horse stable, corncrib, dog pens, and caretaker's house stood nearby.[810] Hunts were conducted at this site for the next thirty years. At one point, the five plantations in the vicinity, Brick Hope, Liberty Hall, Parnassus, Medway and Pine Grove were fenced into one hunting park. Two hunts a week were conducted during deer season and the starts were alternated from one of the five houses to another. Frank Ford Sr. was one of the founding members of the Liberty Hall Hunt Club. He began hunting with his father when he was a boy and raised the membership fee by collecting and selling clay tiles he found on the Brick Hope property.[811]

The club employed Sam Seel at the hunt club for many years. He is likely the son of Louis Seel who appeared as the owner on the 1880 Agricultural Census. Sam Seel was a deer driver who also cared for the hunting dogs and horses along with keeping the pantry stocked, procuring whiskey and cutting firewood. Two years later, in 1914, Colin McCay Grant released the right-of-way to the Carolina, Atlantic and Western Railway, which later became CSX.[812] This railway is the dividing line between the twentieth century Liberty Hall Tract and the Federal Department of Defense Properties. During the early decades of the twentieth century, the Burton Lumber Company retained at least one lumber settlement on the Liberty Hall property. The Chicora Foundation Archaeological study was conducted in 2002 and found evidence of eleven buildings at a junction of the main rail line and the Burton Lumber Company tramway. This settlement, referred to as "Stokes," was likely the barracks for the timber men who worked for the Burton Lumber Company.[813] That company had large land holdings and a lumber mill on the Cooper River near the Navy Ship Yard.

The property was sold by Colin McCay Grant in 1943 and passed through a number of hands, including more lumber companies until the section east of the rail line was conveyed to the Department of Defense. The western section was sold to Richard Friedburg and W.A. Moncrief in 1977.[814] Today Liberty Hall and Brick Hope are the two newest residential developments in the City of Goose Creek. The developers plan to protect the valuable archaeological sites.

Ararat

Ararat, owned by Harriet Horry of Santee, stood contiguous to Foster Creek. Harriat Horry named the estate after the Biblical Mount Ararat, when disastrous floods in the Santee River area forced her to leave. Harriet Pinckney Horry was the daughter of Chief Justice Charles Pinckney and Eliza Lucas. She was the sister of Charles Cotesworth Pinckney and Thomas Pinckney of Revolutionary fame. She married Daniel Horry and settled at her husband's home at Hampton Plantation on the Santee River, but his death and a series of damaging floods forced her to relocate to Goose Creek.[815] She was the second wife of Daniel Horry. Daniel Horry first married Judith Serre, daughter of Noah Serre and Catharine Chicken. This marriage brought him land in St. James, Goose Creek and St. James, Santee. Daniel Horry was elected seven times to represent St. James, Santee in the general assembly. He represented St. George Winyah twice and St. James, Goose Creek once. He served with distinction under Francis Marion during the Revolutionary War, but took British protection after Charleston fell. As a result of his actions, he was penalized when his property was amerced by 12 percent.

The 1799 plat shows Ararat Plantation consisting of more than 925 acres on Foster Creek.[816] The 1799 plat shows the main house with an avenue and circular drive as well as outbuildings, a slave village and a brickyard. The property was bordered by the lands of Thomas Smith and

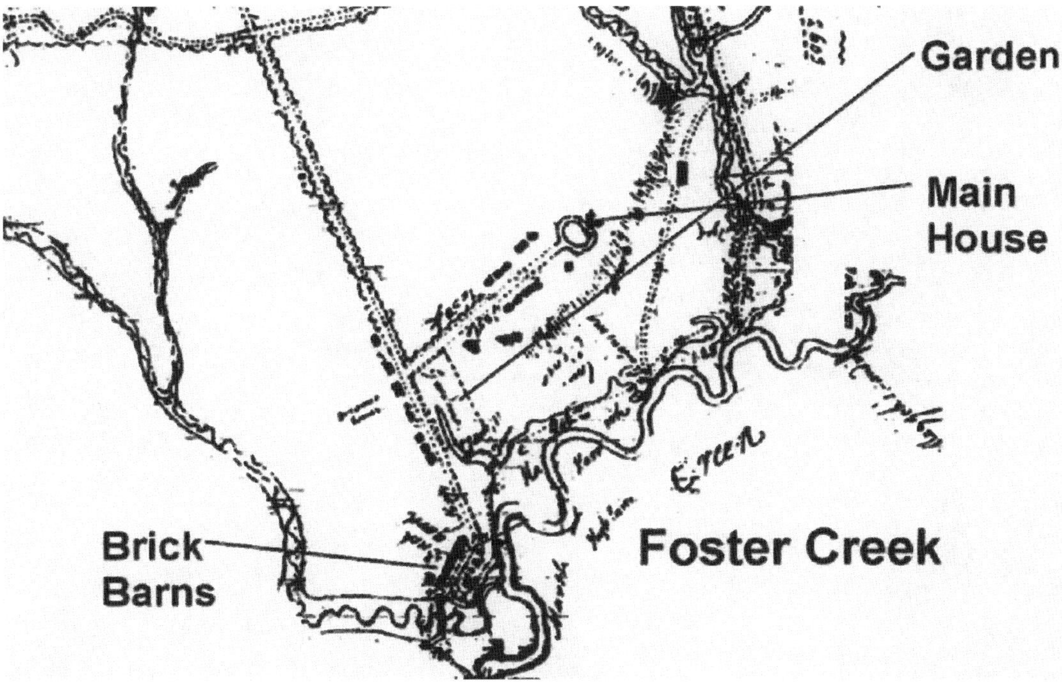

Plat 7.39 This partial plat is a section of the McCrady plat # 4202 that shows Ararat Plantation in 1799. The words "Garden," "Main House" and "Brick Barns" were added for this publication. The plat is on microfilm at the Charleston County Library.

Benjamin Smith on the south, by "Free School Lands" and Bella Vista Plantation owned by George Tunno to the west, by Howe Hall owned by Thomas Smith to the west and north, and by John Dupont's lands on the east.

Samuel Gaillard Stoney bought the property to add to his large Medway estate and in 1927, his brother, Thomas Porcher Stoney, acquired the properties. The plantation lands included all of today's Sedgefield Subdivision and part of the Department of Defense properties. A few brick mounds marked the home site in the 1940s, [817] but remnants of the main house were obliterated by the construction of the North Rhett Extension Highway and the railroad. Modern construction of Menriv housing on the Naval Weapons Station destroyed the remains of the slave village, as well as the other outbuildings. The brickyard site on Foster Creek remains evident. Many brick scatters and clay pits can be found at the brickyard location near the creek.

Brick Hope

Charles W. Graves was a principal Goose Creek brick maker. He owned Brick Hope Plantation on the north side of Foster Creek. Charles Graves purchased 661 acres of land on the northern side of Foster Creek in 1800 from William Mills.[818] This was the first of several purchases that developed into a large and successful brick industry called "Brick Hope Plantation." After his death in 1845, his will designated that his debts "be paid out of my bricks on hand." [819] The property was divided between his sons Daniel and Charles Graves Jr. Daniel's tract was named "Back River Plantation," located on the northern reach of Back River. Charles W. Graves Jr. kept the Brick Hope land situated on Foster Creek "into the water-front like a wedge between Parnassus and Liberty Hall.[820] He married Julia M. Dickson and resided on the estate. His journal gives a day-to-day record of plantation life and an extremely detailed description of the colonial brick industry on his plantation.[821] The Brockington research and title chain reported that Graves retained the property during the Civil War and sold Brick Hope to Louis Vidal.[822] The land later passed to Charles Swinton at auction in 1873.[823] The United States War Department purchased the estate in the early 1940s.

Cedar Hill

John Dupont owned Cedar Hill Plantation on the south side of Foster Creek. An 1803 "Skrine" survey and plat shows two settlements on Dupont's 1,026-acre tract. One cluster of at least four buildings is situated near the bank of Foster Creek that may have been utility buildings and barns. Another collection of seven buildings is situated toward the center of the property, and is probably the main house with two groups of three outbuildings on each flank. The "Church Road" that passed through the tract and a path to "Johnson's" is also noted on the plat. The property is bound on the north by Foster Creek, on the east by lands belonging to Charles Johnson. John Bowen and James Gadsden's lands were to the south. Horry's "Ararat," is situated to the west.

The cluster of four buildings on Foster Creek is probably "Dupont's Brick Yard," which is noted on Mazyck's 1802 plat of the north side of Foster Creek. It corresponds with the location of the four structures on Dupont's plat. Dupont's executor noted that he owned "a plantation and brickyard at Goose Creek."

Cow Jig

East of Dupont's Cedar Hill Plantation was Cow Jig Plantation, the property of Nathaniel Bordeaux on Foster Creek. It consisted of 748 acres, some of which were defined as "good rice lands" and 45 acres noted as lands for the "culture of cotton." The land was mortgaged to John Sommers for £5,300 in 1784 and was defined as consisting of 760 acres at that time.[824]

John Diamond drew plat 7.40 from an 1804 survey. It shows a "Settlement" with three structures on 26 acres of cleared land as well as "old Brick yards." [825] George Smith and John Bowen owned the property to the south. Peter Fendron's property was situated to the east, and Charles Johnson's and John Dupont's property was located to the north.

Estates in Wassamasaw and the Upper Parish

Proprietary land grants were awarded in the Wassamasaw and Upper Parish as early as the frontier period and some of these early grants evolved into working estates, but none developed into the grand plantations that characterized the other neighborhoods of the Parish. Sometimes rich planters in the eastern section used land in the Wassamasaw and Upper Parish to augment

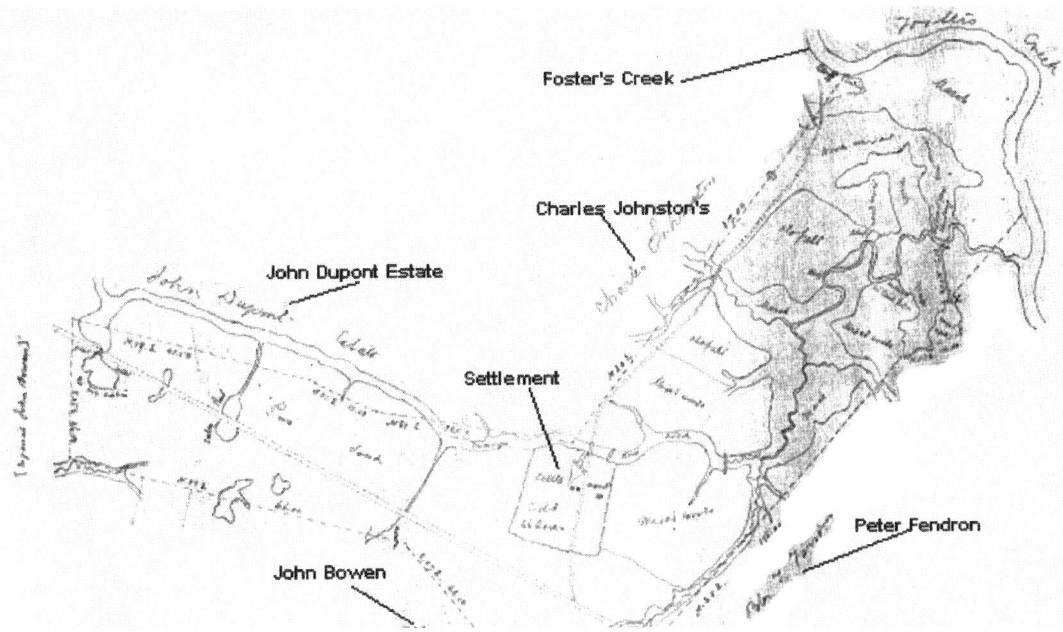

Plat 7.40 This 1804 partial plat of Cow Jig Plantation is a tracing of the original by H.A.M. Smith. The tracing is among the collections of the South Carolina Historical Society.

their fortunes. Planters such as John Deas worked forty-one slaves on his land at Tupilo and Cypress in the mid and upper sections of the Parish, but kept eighty-one slaves at his principal residence at Thorogood Plantation in the eastern part.[826] Only in a few cases did these properties become the principal estate, until after mid eighteenth century when some planters left the exhausted soils and the malarial lowlands in the eastern Parish in search of better land farther west. Also, during the early years of the republic, the State of South Carolina awarded land grants to encourage agriculture in unused sections, but remarkably some lands remained unoccuopied and unclaimed until late in the nineteenth century. Nevertheless, during this period, from approximately 1750 to 1865, this part of the parish was the home of some significant personalities who made important contributions to the St. James, Goose Creek Parish and the state.

Cordes

Francis Cordes obtained grants in Berkeley and Craven Counties. His Berkeley County grant for 927 acres was on Wassamasaw Creek, where he became a successful planter.[827] He and Peter Porcher, his brother-in-law, operated a cattle pen near Lynches Creek. Francis Cordes represented the St. James, Goose Creek Parish in the fifth Royal Assembly and the twelfth Assembly. He declined to serve in the later. His first wife was the daughter of Isaac Porcher and his second wife was Susannah Benoist. He died prior to 1743.

Davis

John Norvelle Davis attended Yale and South Carolina Colleges and read law in the office of Langdon Cheves in Charleston. He established himself as a planter when he moved to the St. James, Goose Creek Parish from St. Matthew Parish. He also owned lands elsewhere, as well as two bridges and a ferry.[828] In 1850, he owned eighty-four slaves in the Orangeburg District and ten in the Goose Creek Parish. It appears that he had some uphill political and financial battles. A petition challenging his election to the State Senate in 1832 was presented to the State Senate and several court cases between him and the State bank are on record. A report submitted by Alexander Mazyck, Chairman of the State Committee on Privileges and Elections, found that non-resident and underage voters invalidated the election of John N. Davis to the Senate in 1848.[829] Goose Creek elected him to the State Senate for the twenty-second in 1816 through the thirty-first General Assemblies in 1835. He and his wife, Julia Martha Lehre reared at least one daughter. He died in Charleston in 1851.[830]

Flagg

George Flagg (1741–1824) received four grants of property in Wassamasaw Swamp that totaled 1,642 acres.[831] Although he owned a large tract in Wassamasaw, it appears that he resided in Charleston, where at the time of his death in 1824, he owned nine lots with buildings, five slaves, 287 shares of stock valued at $18,998 in three banks, one insurance company, and over $10,000 in United States stocks. As a mechanic, he was a member of the Liberty Tree Party, with Christopher Gadsden during the Revolution. When Revolutionary War fighting began, he loaned £17,500 to the state government. He was captured during the war and the British exiled him to St. Augustine until the hostilities ended. Upon his return, he represented Goose Creek in the Fourth and Fifth General Assemblies and St. Philip/St. Michaels in the Sixth and Seventh General Assemblies. He married Mary Henderson, had two children and died in 1824 at the age of eighty-three.

Huger

Daniel Huger worked a two-thousand-acre plantation on Cypress Swamp, which his son, Benjamin Huger, inherited as well as five lots in Charleston and 113 slaves. He was a member of the Twenty-ninth Royal Assembly, representing Goose Creek. He purchased property in Prince George Winyah Parish, married Mary Golightly, a Georgetown heiress, and relocated to that parish. He served Prince George Winyah in the First and Second Provincial Congresses and the First, Second and Third General Assemblies from 1776 to 1777. Major Benjamin Huger, an officer of "great gallantry and promise" was accidentally killed while inspecting the defenses of Charleston in 1777.

Izard's Cowpens

Ralph Izard, the immigrant received a large tract of land by grant in 1705 on the Cypress Swamp in the Wassamasaw section of the Parish. These swamplands drained into the headwaters of the Ashley River and provided excellent water reserves for agriculture. This large tract was devised to his son, Walter, who combined the holdings with land of his own to amass 6,120 acres. The records do not indicate whether or not a well-established settlement emerged there. The Izards had two well-apportioned estates at the Elms and the Camp, but Ralph Izard refers to the large tract in his will as "Wassamasaw swamp upon which I am now settled." [832] Ralph Izard's son Walter probably raised livestock here. This was indicated by an act in 1737 that laid out a road "from Dorchester to Captain Izard's cowpen." [833] Walter Izard probably cultivated the property extensively in addition to stock raising because his will noted seventy-four slaves at the Wassamasaw estate. Walter Izard sold part of the land to Colonel Joseph Blake in 1724, but the remaining land was divided among his children. All of it finally passed out of the family when his granddaughters, Sarah and Rebecca, received the land and subsequently transferred the deeds after their marriages to Lord William Campbell, the last Royal Governor and Colonel Colin Campbell. John Dawson acquired these tracts one after another beginning in 1791 when he purchased 810 acres.[834] In 1812 he devised the combined properties, totaling 5,802 acres, to his three sons and one daughter.[835]

Lawrence

Nathaniel Lawrence was a substantial planter in St. James, Goose Creek by 1830. In that year he owned fifty slaves at his estate in Wassamasaw. In 1805, he was commissioned to study Wassamasaw and Cypress Swamps for channelization.[836] In 1825, he invested money in the Cypress Causeway. That year he paid taxes on seven hundred acres. Those tax records showed that he owned seventeen slaves. He represented Goose Creek in the Twenty-second General Assembly of 1822–23.[837]

Longridge

Josiah Cockfield McKewn (1823–1889) was a graduate of the Medical College of South Carolina. He settled as a physician and planter in Wassamasaw Swamp prior to the Civil War. He resided at Longridge near Wassamasaw Swamp. The 1860 census shows him with thirty slaves. He represented Goose Creek in the House during the Thirty-seventh, Thirty-eighth, Thirty-ninth and Forty-third General Assemblies. He served in the Senate during the Forty-fourth and Forty-fifth General Assemblies. He married a neighbor, Innis Elizabeth Willson, but they had no children. He died in 1889 at Long Ridge and is buried at the Wassamasaw Baptist Chapel.

Long Ridge/Sand Run/Road Place

John Willson (1805–1856), son of the Wassamasaw planter John Willson, was educated at the Medical College of South Carolina. Records show that John Willson Sr. applied for a grant to erect a toll bridge across Wassamasaw Swamp in 1818.[838] John Willson Jr. served as a medical doctor and planter at Wassamasaw. His 1824 tax return showed that he owned 5,000 acres and 86 slaves in Goose Creek.[839] At the time of his death, an accounting of his estate showed that he owned 190 slaves, three large plantations at Wassamasaw named "Longridge," "Sand Run" and "Road Place" along with a fortune in stocks and bonds.[840]

Photograph 7.29 "Cedar Grove the old John Wilson or Willson place 12 Sept. 1930" in *Johnson's Scrapbook* on deposit at the South Carolina Historical Society. This property was located at the 30-mile marker on Old State Road but has been since razed. At the time of the photograph it was the home of Mr. F.O. Rowe and was called "Cedar Grove."

John Willson represented Goose Creek in the Thirty-second and Thirty-third General Assemblies and in the senate for the Thirty-fourth and Thirty-fifth as well as the Thirty-eighth through Forty-fourth General Assemblies. He overcame a legal challenge to his election to the senate in 1848.[841] He was a free school commissioner for the parish, as well as a commissioner for roads. He married Sarah Ann Elizabeth Owens and with her had six children. He died in 1856 and is buried at Wassamasaw. Later generations of the Wil(l)son family produced Dr. John Willson, Methodist leader and past president of Lander College in Greenwood, South Carolina.[842]

Mellard's

Elisha Mellard owned a 500-acre tract on Cain Run Branch in 1797 when the land was surveyed.[843] The 1824 tax return shows that Elisha Mellard was a wealthy man with 4,633 acres and forty-six slaves. Elisha and Celia Mellard adopted William Owens. He legally changed his name to Mellard.[844] The 1824 tax return reports him with 545 acres and three slaves. This 545-acre tract was not his parent's, and a 1798 plat shows William Owens with another 500 acres on Sandy Run and Allen Branches.[845] His holdings increased when he acquired an additional 900 acres through an 1847grant. The 1860 census shows him as a wealthy man with an estate worth $26,000. That same report stated that he owned twenty-nine slaves. He represented Goose Creek in the house for the Twenty-seventh and Twenty-eighth Assemblies and the Senate for the Thirty-sixth, Thirty-seventh, Forty-second and Forty-third Assemblies. He served several commissions including the commissioner of the free schools. He had seven children with his wife Mary Elizabeth Shingler. His second wife was Mrs. C. Way. He died of pneumonia in 1860.[846]

Murray

Joseph Murray was a medical doctor who relocated to Wassamasaw from St. George Dorchester in the early 1850s. The 1860 census shows him with fifty-three slaves and an estate valued at $41,000. He represented Goose Creek in the House of Representatives during the Fortieth, Forty-first and Forty-second General Assemblies. In 1856, a petition protested his election to the State Legislature, but he overcame the challenge.[847] St. James, Goose Creek chose him for the state senate for the Forty-sixth Assembly.[848] He was married twice. By the first marriage to Mary Anne Murray, he had six children. With his second bride, Lavinia Sarah Ann Bell, he had three children.

Singleton

Richard Singleton inherited 600 acres of land from Richard, his father. He added to these properties until his estate straddled the St. James, Goose Creek and St. Johns Parish lines and sprawled from the uppermost waters of Back River to the farthest eastern reach of Black Tom Bay. The tract known as Foxbank, was in 1730, contiguous on the north to Grove Hall Plantation, and property owned by Richard Gough and west of property owned by John Onsett. Richard was wealthy and is listed in the 1745 tax roster with 40 slaves. The tax record of the same year lists his total estate with 1,145 acres and 24 slaves. He was elected to represent Goose Creek in the Eleventh Royal Assembly in 1737 and was elected again but declined to serve at that time. He also represented Goose Creek in the Nineteenth Royal Assembly. He was a churchwarden at Goose Creek and contributed twenty pounds to the St. James School construction fund. His brother, Benjamin received a 1,611-acre state grant in Wassamasaw and eventually amassed five working plantations and 225 slaves.[849] Richard was a captain and Benjamin rose to the rank of colonel in the militia. He was elected by Goose Creek to the Thirty-second Royal Assembly, but did not serve because the Revolution prevented the assembly from meeting. He subsequently served in the First and Second Provincial Congress and the First General Assembly. He and his wife Rebecca had one son, Benjamin Jr. Richard died in 1776.

Smith

William Smith owned and resided on a plantation at Wassamasaw. He was a member of the Twelfth Royal Assembly. The 1825 Mills Atlas shows Smith's Tavern in the central part of the parish.

Stevenson

James Stevenson was granted thirteen hundred acres on Wassamasaw Swamp in 1785 and 1787.[850] He served the parish as a tax collector, assessor and representative in the Fifth General Assembly in 1783–1784. He also served in the militia and appears on the 1790 census with twenty-three slaves.

Thornley

Robert Thornley received a grant for 460 acres on Wassamasaw Swamp in 1785 [851] and added to it until he amassed more than 1,000 acres.[852] He resided at Wassamasaw, but owned other properties at Lynches Creek and Brick House Plantation in Georgetown District totaling 1,300 acres. The records show that he worked twenty slaves on his Goose Creek estate in 1805, an increase from the seven slaves who he claimed on the 1790 census. He served as captain and major in the militia during the Revolution and was later elected to the State House of Representatives twice and the State Senate three times. He served his parish locally as a tax collector, justice of the quorum, commissioner for determining the parish line between St. James and St. George, Dorchester and as a road commissioner. He and his wife Mary attended the Wassamasaw Baptist Church for many years with their four children.[853]

Witherspoon

William Witherspoon (1777–1815) was a planter near Wassamasaw Swamp. He served as a commissioner to study the practicality of clearing the Wassamasaw and Cypress Swamps. He represented the Goose Creek Parish in the Seventeenth General Assembly in the house and was then elected to the State Senate for the Eighteenth and Nineteenth General Assemblies (1808–1810). He and his wife, Janet McClary, reared six children. He died in 1815 at the age of thirty-eight.[854]

Wright

John Wright owned multiple land holdings but lived on his Wassamasaw Plantation. He eventually amassed 1,413 acres from four grants he received between 1768 and 1773.[855] In addition to his Wassamasaw home plantation, he owned 400 acres nearby at Wassamasaw, as well as a lot in Charleston, and forty-nine slaves. He was elected to represent Goose Creek in the Thirty-second Royal Assembly, and the First and Second Provincial Congress, and the First and Second General Assembly. He also served as a justice of the peace for the Charleston District and was a militia captain during the Revolution. He died in a skirmish with a Royalist force of Dragoons in 1781. His wife Martha and three minor children survived him.[856]

Conclusion

This chapter examined the transcient ownerships of the major estates in six Goose Creek neighborhoods from the first owners of the frontier period to the modern era, and the significant landowners in Wassamasaw and the Upper Parish. The estates varied in size, application and bounty,

Table 7.1

The Neck	South Side of Goose Creek	North Side of Goose Creek	Cooper River	Back River	Foster Creek	Wassamasaw and Upper Parish
Marsh Lands	Yeamans Hall	Crowfield	Palmettos	Parnassus	Thoroughgood/Mt. Holly	Cordes
Mons Repose	Live Oak	Broom Hall/Bloomfield	Red Bank	Prioleau	Persimmon Hill/Old Barn	Davis
Oak Grove	Filbin's	Fredericks		Medway	Grove Hall	Flagg
Hurst's	The Camp	The Oaks		Back River/ White Hall	Pawley's	Huger
Baldrick's	Cripp's/Langstaff's	Seventeen-Mile House		Pine Grove/ Spring Grove	Brounfield/Brownfield	Izard's Cowpen
	Cannon's/Oakland	Mount Pleasant		Sociable Hill	Springfield	Lawrence
	Ten-Mile Hill	Marrington		Richmond	Castlebrawn/Button Hall	Longbridge
	French Gardens	White House		Cyprus Grove/Cedar Grove	Boocho(a)wee	Long Ridge/Sand Run/Road Place
	Bigelow's				Howe Hall	Mellard's
	Dr. Charles Drayton's				Liberty Hall	Murray
	Sineath's				Ararat	Singleton
	Steepbrook				Brick Hope	Smith
	Wigton's/Fraser's				Cedar Hill	Stevenson
	Fontainbleau				Cow Jig	Thornley
	Otranto					Wright
	De La Plaines/Parker's					Witherspoon
	Boisseau's					
	Bacot's/Cherry Hill					
	Woodstock					
	Keckley's					
	Charles Barker's/Spring Grove					
	Glaze's/Poppenheim's					
	Faucheraud					
	The Hayes/Inglesides					
	Woodlands					
	Brick House/ Martindales					
	Thomas Mell's					
	Thomas Elmes					
	Windsor Hill					
	The Elms					
5	30	8	2	8	14	16

but all directly reflected the talents and determination of the owners. The common desire of the owner in every era was to employ the property to its highest use relative to the available resources and to use whatever invention was accessible for maximizing returns from the labor pool. At first most plantations were self-sufficient and afforded modest subsistence for the extended families, but the distance between the successful landowners and those who failed, continually widened until some estates produced fortunes and others declined to be abandoned and revert to wilderness. The transcient features of these lands, whether they be the sturdy homes and outbuildings that characterized some of the larger estates or the brick walls that graced the more elegant gardens have almost entirely disappeared. Consequently, the remains of agricultural and industrial enterprises are barely discernable today, except through the work of skilled archaeologists. Notwithstanding, although the physical impressions have faded, those who built the homes, gardens and industries, and worked the forests, swamps and fields of the eighty-three estates listed in table 7.1 left durable impressions in the social, economic and political fabric of the St. James, Goose Creek Parish and state of South Carolina.

EPILOGUE

IN A LETTER WRITTEN TO his brother-in-law in 1701, Edward Hyrne described his home at Medway Plantation in Goose Creek as his "brave plantation." He and his twenty-year-old bride had survived a perilous ocean voyage from England to confront hunger and disease in the Carolina frontier, and now the young planter was feeling smug as he wrote that they lived in the "best brick house in all the country." Sadly, within a few years of that letter to his brother-in-law, the Hyrnes lost their young son to illness, their valuable slave to a rattlesnake bite and their home with all their worldly possessions to fire.[857] Yet, the Hyrnes persisted for another decade, as one of the many success stories that colored the Lowcountry landscape during the time when ambitious Europeans, with their resourceful African slaves, increasingly dominated this small section of North America. Ironically, ten years after the house fire, the tenacious Hyrne family was evicted from their plantation home because they could not pay their mortgage, and because there was no free land in Carolina.

Every acre of Carolina land—be it forest, field, or wetland—was owned by one or more of the lord proprietors who envisioned fortunes from land sales and rents. Although the proprietors' risky investment failed to return much wealth to them, their work toward implementing their grand scheme indelibly shaped Carolina. The bold initiatives of the proprietors included establishing liberal articles of John Locke's progressive constitution, flooding the landscape with an odd mixture of Europeans who brought varying backgrounds and religious faiths, installing a cruel yet prodigious slave-labor economy, and creating unique frontiersmen who were not only as brave as Edward Hyrne, but sufficiently money-wise and politically savvy to pay or evade the mortgages and other property fees. These brave and crafty frontiersmen learned how to make money and ultimately produced some of the most successful plantations in British North America. More importantly, this auspicious beginning in the Lowcountry of South Carolina spawned two great revolutions—one to rid Carolina of the proprietors and the other to rid a new republic of a king.

Volume One of *Goose Creek, South Carolina: A Definitive History* tells of the trials, tribulations, successes and failures of Goose Creekers during the perilous frontier period, the heady plantation era and the episodic decades leading to the creation of the new American Republic. Finally, the last chapter of Volume One traces the ownership of the parish lands, which were the foundation of the social, economic and political order of the seventeenth and eighteenth centuries, and that set the stage for the saga of the nineteenth and twentieth.

Volume Two of this work, ***Rebellion, Reconstruction and Beyond,*** explains the economic, social and political systems in Goose Creek that functioned as part of the new national government, and the local systems and institutions that emerged within a republic that was the most liberal experiment in governance the world had ever witnessed. Remarkably, much of the success or failures of the new systems depended upon the bounties from the farms and forests of semi-tropical Carolina. Here, the people and their emerging local governments, churches, and schools were shaken by shifting markets and racial challenges, and tested by war and reconstruction during the nineteenth century. Incredibly, they were tested again during the twentieth century by social and political revolutions imposed upon them as residents of the "New South." The people of Goose Creek lived that saga during those challenging times, and left a legacy that remains a source of pride to some and shame to others, but nevertheless continues to shape the lives of Americans, Carolinians and the people of a place named "Goose Creek."

Appendix I
A Map of St. James, Goose Creek Parish

The partial map is entitled, *An Accurate Map of North and South Carolina with their Indian Frontier...from actual surveys by Henry Mouzon and Others*, printed in London by Sayer and J. Bennett, 1775. *Courtesy of the Library of Congress*.

Appendix II The Contemporary and Nineteenth-Century Road System

The State Road proceeded north from Charleston Neck, crossed the Goose Creek Bridge and continued to Columbia and beyond. The State Road from Charleston to the intersection near the Goose Creek Church was called "The Path" or the "Goose Creek Road" during colonial times. Today Highway 52 follows the route of "The Path" to the 52/78 intersection. Highway 176 traces the route of the old State Road from the 52/176 intersection west to Columbia. Highway 52 was not constructed until 1922.

The Road to Dorchester branched from "The Path" at today's Highway 52/78 intersection in Charleston County.

Red Bank Road branched from the State Road and proceeded to a landing on the Cooper River.

Back River Lower Road (sometimes Lower Back River Road) intersected with the State Road and ended with a mile long avenue of oaks at the Parnassus Plantation house and landing on Back River.

The Back River Upper Road (sometimes Upper Back River Road) intersected with the State Road and terminated at a Back River landing. An unnamed road connected the lower and upper Back River Roads.

The Ladson Road is traced today by a power line right-of-way and runs roughly parallel with Westview Boulevard for a short distance and then continues along the power line right-of-way to Ladson.

Moncks Corner Road intersected with the State Road. Today Old Moncks Corner Road intersects with St. James Boulevard (Highway 176) and continues to Moncks Corner via Highway 52.

Gibbes Path reached from the entrance avenue at Bloomsfield Plantation to the main avenue at Springfield Plantation and beyond to Back River Upper Road.

Appendix III
Historical Markers

The Medway marker is located approximately two hundred yards north of the Goose Creek City limits on Highway 52. The marker states:

SOUTH CAROLINA/MEDWAY PLANTATION / In 1686 Medway Plantation was/ granted by the Lord Proprietors /to Jan Van Arrsen/ seigneur de Wernhoud / In 1689 the property came into / the possession of /Landgrave Thomas Smith /Governor of South Carolina /November 1693 to October 1694. / He died in November 1694/ and is buried at Medway

The Goose Creek Church marker is located on Highway 52 south of the City limits at the intersection of the Naval Ammunition Depot (NAD) Road. It states in all capital letters:

GOOSE CREEK CHURCH/THE PARISH ST. JAMES WAS FOUNDED BY/ ACT OF ASSEMBLY IN 1706. THE PRESENT/ EDIFICE WAS BEGUN IN 1714, AND COMPLETED/ IN 1719. THE ROYAL ARMS OF GREAT BRITAIN / CAN STILL BE SEEN OVER THE CHANCEL/AND HERE IS PRESERVED THE IZARD/ HATCHMENT, SAID TO BE ONE OF ONLY/ TWO IN AMERICA.

The Otranto Plantation marker is located at the entrance to Otranto Subdivision and states:

SOUTH CAROLINA/ OTRANTO PLANTATION/ Originally known as "Yeshoe" this / plantation was granted in 1679 to / Arthur Middleton great-granduncle / of the signer of the Declaration / of Independence. It was called / "Otranto" after 1771, when it was / acquired by Dr. Alexander Garden / noted physician and botanist / for whom the "Gardenia" was named / In more recent times the estate / was used as a hunt club.

The Four Hole Swamp causeway plaque was located on State Highway 176 about thirty miles west of Goose Creek at Four Hole Swamp. The plaque can no longer be located.

FOUR HOLE SWAMP/ The first causeway and bridge here /were built under terms of an act / passed April 21, 1753 / Col. Henry Hampton of State Troops / of S.C. seized the bridge / July

14, 1781, and established a post / here to check Lord Rawldon on his / retreat from Orangeburg. Several / actions took place here later / in 1781 and in 1782 / The causeway and bridge were paved in 1928.

The Spring Hill Methodist Church marker is located on Gaillard Road near the 43-mile marker in the Sandridge Community of the western section of the parish on SC Route 27.

SPRING HILL METHODIST CHURCH
According to tradition / Methodists worshipped here under /a brush arbor as early as 1800. / on august 2, 1814, Philip Keller / deeded one acre for a methodist / church and burying ground. / Eden and Rebecca Green Thrower / deeded an additional acre in 1839. / a new wooden structure replaced / the original building in 1846–47. / The present church was built in 1958.

Appendix IV
Ninety Places Named Goose Creek

National mapping information from the United States Government Services office.

Feature Name	State	Type of Feature
Goose Creek Cemetery	Alabama	Cemetery
Goose Creek School	Alabama	Historic School
Goose Creek	Alabama	Stream
Goose Creek	Alaska	Stream
Goose Creek	Arkansas	Stream
Goose Creek	California	Stream
Goose Creek	Colorado	Stream
Goose Creek Flat District Mine	Colorado	Mine
Goose Creek Spring	Colorado	Spring
Goose Creek Campground	Colorado	Locale
Goose Creek	Florida	Stream
Goose Creek Bay	Florida	Bay
Goose Creek	Georgia	Stream
Goose Creek	Idaho	Stream
Lower Goose Creek Reservoir	Idaho	Reservoir
Goose Creek Point	Idaho	Summit
Goose Creek Spring	Idaho	Spring
Goose Creek	Illinois	Stream
Goose Creek Mine	Illinois	Mine
Township of Goose Creek	Illinois	Unincorporated Township
Goose Creek	Indiana	Stream
Goose Creek	Kansas	Stream

Feature Name	State	Type of Feature
Goose Creek	Kentucky	Stream
Goose Creek School	Kentucky	School
Goose Creek	Kentucky	Populated Place
Goose Creek	Louisiana	Stream
Goose Creek	Maryland	Bay
Goose Creek	Maryland	Stream
Goose Creek Lock 25	Maryland	Dam
Goose Creek	Michigan	Stream
Goose Creek	Minnesota	Stream
Goose Creek Lake	Missouri	Reservoir
Goose Creek Lake Dam	Missouri	Dam
Goose Creek School	Missouri	School
Goose Creek	Missouri	Stream
Goose Creek	Montana	Stream
Goose Creek Island	North Carolina	Island
Goose Creek State	North Carolina	Park
Goose Creek	North Carolina	Stream
Goose Creek Airport	North Carolina	Airport
Township of Goose Creek	North Carolina	Civil Division
Goose Creek	Nebraska	Populated Place
Goose Creek Election Precinct	Nebraska	Civil Division
Goose Creek Public School	Nebraska	School
Goose Creek	New Jersey	Stream
Goose Creek	New Mexico	Stream
Goose Creek	Nevada	Stream
Goose Creek Game Preserve	Nevada	Park
Goose Creek State Recreation Ground and Game Preserve	Nevada	Park
Goose Creek	New York	Stream
Goose Creek	New York	Bay
Goose Creek Point	New York	Cape
Goose Creek	Ohio	Stream
Goose Creek	Oklahoma	Stream
Goose Creek	Oregon	Stream
Goose Creek Cemetery	Oregon	Cemetery
Goose Creek, City of	**South Carolina**	Municipality

Appendix IV

Feature Name	State	Type of Feature
Goose Creek	South Dakota	Stream
Goose Creek	South Dakota	Dam
Goose Creek Reservoir	South Dakota	Reservoir
Goose Creek	Tennessee	Stream
Goose Creek Bar	Tennessee	Bar
Goose Creek Island	Tennessee	Island
Goose Creek	Texas	Stream
Goose Creek Country Club	Texas	Locale
Goose Creek Oil Field	Texas	Oil Field
Goose Creek	Utah	Stream
Goose Creek Mountains	Utah	Range
Goose Creek Knoll	Utah	Summit
Goose Creek	Virginia	Stream
Goose Creek Valley Overlook	Virginia	Locale
Goose Creek Stone Bridge	Virginia	Bridge
Goose Creek Burying Ground	Virginia	Cemetery
Goose Creek Church	Virginia	Church
Goose Creek Country Club	Virginia	Locale
Goose Creek Dam	Virginia	Dam
Goose Creek Historic District	Virginia	Park
Goose Creek Industrial Park	Virginia	Locale
Goose Creek Reservoir	Virginia	Reservoir
Goose Creek	Vermont	Stream
Goose Creek Camp Ground	Washington	Locale
Goose Creek	Washington	Stream
Goose Creek Lookout	Washington	Locale
Goose Creek Point	Washington	Cliff
Goose Creek School	Washington	School
Goose Creek Cemetery	West Virginia	Cemetery
Goose Creek Post Office	West Virginia	Historical Site
Goose Creek	West Virginia	Stream
Goose Creek	Wyoming	Stream
Big Goose Creek	Wyoming	Stream
East Fork Big Goose Creek	Wyoming	Stream

Appendix V
Heads of Households

The table lists the names of heads of households in Goose Creek and their assets according to a partial tax report made in 1745. This partial report is among the collections of the South Carolina Department of Archives and History, Columbia, South Carolina.

Name of Head of Household	Number of Slaves in St. James, Goose Creek	Total Number of All Slaves in South Carolina	Money at Interest @ 6 Percent in Pounds	Number of Acres Owned in St. James, Goose Creek	Total Number of Acres Owned in South Carolina	Total Amount of Tax in Pounds, Shillings and Pence
William Middleton	100	123	18,223	2433	15,275	247-13-11
Henry Izard	218	218	4,887	1696	8,484	225-4-11.5
Peter Taylor	40	69	0	779	3,880	75-9-3
Mathew Beard	49	49	0	500	3,485	58-13-11
Samuel Riggs Esta	0	0	1,000	0	0	3-0-0
William Cator	9	9	0	0	0	6-6-0
William Wood	9	9	0	325	325	8-11-6
John Herbert	0	0	0	835	3,040	21-5-0
Ben	32	32	0	412.5	612.5	26-13-8
Thomas Bulline	44	44	0	890	890	37-0-7
Elizabeth Marion	3	3	0	0	0	2-2-0
Mary Auber	7	7	500	165	165	7-11-1
Richard Boddecatt	7	7	0	0	0	5-4-5.25
Richard Tookernan	35	35	0	750	750	29-15-0
James Streater	13	13	0	690	690	13-18-7
James Coachman	18	18	0	2381	2,381	29-5-4
Sarah Filbin	8	8	0	0	0	5-12-0
Thomas Bulline, Jr.	11	11	0	0	0	7-14-0

Name of Head of Household	Number of Slaves in St. James, Goose Creek	Total Number of All Slaves in South Carolina	Money at Interest @ 6 Percent in Pounds	Number of Acres Owned in St. James, Goose Creek	Total Number of Acres Owned in South Carolina	Total Amount of Tax in Pounds, Shillings and Pence
John Frederick	4	4	0	0	0	2-16-0
James Marion	23	23	0	600	600	20-6-0
Thomas Lovely	2	2	0	0	0	1-8-0
Jacob Young	1	1	0	0	0	0-14-0
Joseph Hurst	20	20	0	568	568	17-19-6
Robert Wood	9	9	0	100	100	7-14-0
E. Cooper	2	2	0	0	0	1-8-0
Gideon Gaucheraud	58	58	1,284	3484	3,484	68-16-9
Archer Smith	30	30	0	2589	2,589	39-2-5.5
William Flud	15	15	0	384	384	13-3-9
Joseph Harsford	85	85	0	246	2,693	78-10-2.5
John Haille	3	3	0	0	0	2-2-0
Hugh Grange	36	36	0	1200	1,814	NA
In Trust J. Parker Decd.	47	47	1,200	786	4,513	142-18-4
Charles Faucheraud	71	71	0	150	150	NA
The Honorable Jas Kinloch Esq.	230	230	10,000	3015	13,356	284-9-8
William Allen	150	150	0	3300	3,300	128-2-0
James Bagbey	23	23	0	720	1,109	23-17-5
Sedgwich Lewis	5	5	0	500	500	7-0-0
Zachariah Villeponteaux	74	74	0	987	8,879	113-19-3
Gideon Dupont	13	13	0	400	900	15-8-0
Maurice Keeting	76	76	0	2989	2,980	74-3-11
Hannah Goodbey	19	19	0	985	985	20-3-11
Samuel Bacor (Bacot)	15	15	0	800	800	16-2-0
Nathaniel Snow	50	50	0	1625	4,025	63-3-6
Mary Smith	43	43	1,900	4278	17,945	161-8-6
Benjamin Mazyck	40	40	0	3070	3,070	49-9-9.5
Mr. Richard Singleton	40	40	0	600	600	32-4-0

Appendix V

Name of Head of Household	Number of Slaves in St. James, Goose Creek	Total Number of All Slaves in South Carolina	Money at Interest @ 6 Percent in Pounds	Number of Acres Owned in St. James, Goose Creek	Total Number of Acres Owned in South Carolina	Total Amount of Tax in Pounds, Shillings and Pence
For the Estate of Richard Singleton	24	24	0	1145	1,145	24-16-3.5
For the Estate of John Bagbey	24	24	0	1060	1,060	24-8-5
Joseph Norman	55	55	0	1560	1,560	49-8-5
Sarah Middleton	215	215	57,348	2041	11,104	400-5-3.75
John Morton	74	74	7,117	927	1,621	84-8-11
Peter Hume	61	61	0	500	1,450	52-3-0
Thomas Middleton	64	644	0	3203	5,371	82-8-6
Paul Mazyck	79	79	11,769	1205	3,247	113-6-3.5
Richard Gough	6	6	3,500	0	0	14-4-0
Robert Brown	35	35	0	0	0	24-10-0

Appendix VI
Representatives

The table lists the representatives elected to serve in the Commons House of Assembly for St. James, Goose Creek Parish from 1736 to 1754.

Year Elected	Name	Notations
1736	Peter Taylor	Accepted
1736	John Ouldfield	Refused
1736	Archer Smith	Refused
1736	Zachariah Villeponteaux	Refused
1739	Alexander Vanderdussen	Accepted
1739	David Hext	Accepted
1742	Thomas Middleton	Accepted
1742	Peter Taylor	Accepted
1742	Henry Izard	Accepted
1742	Archer Smith	Accepted
1745	Thomas Middleton	Refused
1745	Ralph Izard	Refused
1745	Paul Mazyck	Accepted
1745	Thomas Drayton	Accepted
1746	Archer Smith	Accepted
1746	Thomas Middleton	Accepted
1746	Peter Taylor	Accepted
1746	Thomas Johnson	Accepted
1746	Henry Middleton	Replaced Paul Mazyck
1748	John Morton	Accepted
1748	Paul Mazyck	Accepted
1748	Henry Izard	Accepted

Year Elected	Name	Notations
1748	Thomas Middleton	Accepted
1748	John Morton	Accepted
1748	William Allen	Died
1749	Peter Taylor	Accepted
1749	Richard Singleton	Accepted
1749	Zachariah Villeponteaux	Accepted
1749	Richard Gough	Accepted
1750	James Withers	Accepted
1751	Alexanderv Frazier	Accepted
1751	Francis Kinloch	Accepted
1751	Henry Smith	Refused
1751	George Seaman	Refused
1751	Robert Pringle	Refused
1751	Jordan Roche	Accepted but died
1751	Isaac Mazyck	Accepted
1754	Robert Hume	Accepted
1754	Zachariah Villeponteaux	Refused
1754	Francis Kinloch	Refused
1754	Walter Izard	Replaced Villeponteaux
1754	David Caw	Replaced Kinloch
1754	Alexander Frazier	Accepted

NOTES

Chapter I

1. Michael Trinkley, PhD, *Landscape and Garden Archaeology at Crowfield Plantation: a Preliminary Examination* (Columbia, South Carolina: Chicora Foundation 1992), 55.

2. Stephen Carter and Associates, *Land Use Studies* (Prepared for the City of Goose Creek, 1976), 1–5.

3. Claude Neuffer, ed., *Names in South Carolina* (University of South Carolina, Columbia, South Carolina), vol.13: 6.

4. South Carolina Department of Archives and History (SCDAH), Columbia, South Carolina, S213192, v. 57:p. 171.

5. Elias B. Bull, *Community and Neighborhood Names in Berkeley County*, Part III, in *Names in South Carolina* (Columbia, South Carolina: Department of English, University of South Carolina), vol.13: 37.

6. Ibid., 37.

7. Ibid., 38.

8. Works Progress Administration (WPA) Federal Writers' Project, *Palmetto Place Names* (Spartanburg, South Carolina: The Reprint Company, 1975), 147.

9. *South Carolina Historical and Genealogical Magazine* (South Carolina Historical Society, Charleston, South Carolina), 29: 20–21. Hereafter cited as *SCHGM.*

10. Alexander S. Salley, Jr., ed., *Warrants for Land in South Carolina, 1672–1711* (Columbia, South Carolina: Historical Commission of South Carolina, 1910–1915. Reprinted in 1998 by The State Company, Columbia South Carolina), 590.

11. Ibid., 173.

12. *SCHGM* 29: 21.

13. Oscar M. Lieber, *Vocabulary of the Catawba Language, with some Remarks on its Grammar, Construction and Pronunciation* (Charleston, South Carolina: Collections of the South Carolina Historical Society), vol. 2: 327–42.

14. Ibid., 333.

15. Eugene Waddell, *Indians of the South Carolina Low Country, 1562–1751* (Spartanburg, South Carolina: The Reprint Company), 83.

16. Salley, *Warrants for Land*, 82.

17. John B. Irving, *A Day on Cooper River* (Charleston, South Carolina: A.E. Miller, 1869), 99.

18. Clara A. Langley, *South Carolina Deed Abstracts*, 4 vols., (Easley, South Carolina: Southern Historical Press, Inc., 1984), vol. 3: 277, 365.
19. Joseph Johnson, *Traditions and Reminiscences, Chiefly of the American Revolution in South Carolina* (Charleston, South Carolina: Walker and James, 1851), 380; Brewster and Burke Papers, *Abstract of the Title to Red Bank Plantation, 1880*, among the collections of the South Carolina Historical Society, number 43/0881.
20. *SCHGM* 55: 155.
21. Transactions of the French Huguenot Society, among the collections of the South Carolina Historical Society, vol.11: 31.
22. Thomas Cooper and David J. McCord, *The Statutes at Large of South Carolina, (1682–1838),* (Columbia, South Carolina: A.S. Johnson Inc. 1836), vol. 2: 328.
23. Ibid, vol. 8: 199.
24. South Carolina Archives S165005, General Assembly Committee Reports, Year 1786, Number 170.
25. Maxwell Clayton Orvin, *Historic Berkeley County, South Carolina, 1670–1900* (Charleston, South Carolina: Comprint, 1973), 6.
26. Cooper, *Statutes at Large*, vol. 22: 309.
27. Ibid., 595.

Chapter II
28. Max Savelle, *A History of Colonial America* (New York: 1966), 57.
29. Ibid.
30. Converse D. Clowse, *Economic Beginnings in Colonial South Carolina 1670–1730* (Columbia, South Carolina: University of South Carolina Press, 1971), 5.
31. Ibid., 4.
32. Ibid., 54.
33. Mrs. St. Julien Ravenel, *Charleston, The Place and the People* (New York: McMillan, 1912), 8.
34. Clowse, *Economic Beginnings*, 54.
35. Langdon Cheves, ed., *The Shaftesbury Papers and Other Records Relating to Carolina and the First Settlement on Ashley River prior to the year 1676*, among the collections of the South Carolina Historical Society, 1897, vol. 5: 360.
36. Ravenel, *Place and the People*, 15, 16.
37. Henry Ravenel Dwight, *Some Historic Spots in Berkeley* (Pinopolis, South Carolina: Women's Auxiliary of Trinity Church, 1921, Reprinted 1944), 21.
38. Clowse, *Economic Beginnings*, 79.
39. Salley, *Warrants for Land*, 82.
40. Ibid., 112.
41. Ibid., 206.
42. Ibid., 485.
43. *SCHGM* 29: 11.
44. Salley, *Warrants for Land*, 173.
45. Ibid., 486.

46. *SCHGM* 29: 34.
47. Salley, *Warrants for Land*, 107.
48. Ibid., 317, 318.
49. Ibid., 299.
50. Ibid, 434.
51. *SCHGM* 11: 205, 210, 211.
52. Ibid., vol.29: 11.
53. Walter B. Edgar and N. Louise Bailey, *Biographical Directory of the South Carolina House of Representatives: Volumes I–III, 1692–1775* (Columbia, South Carolina: University of South Carolina Press, 1974), 498.
54. *SCHGM* 3: 189.
55. Register of Mesne Conveyance, *Record of Deeds between Buyer and S*eller (Charleston, South Carolina: County Office Building), book W-5: 522–35.
56. *SCHGM* 18: 105.
57. Transactions of the Huguenot Society, vol. 21: 62.
58. Arthur Henry Hirsch, *The Huguenots of Colonial South Carolina* (London: Archon Books, 1962), 21.
59. *SCHGM* 29: 11.
60. Transactions of the French Huguenot Society, vol. 16: 44.
61. Ibid., vol., 81: 100.
62. *SCHGM* 16: 43, 44.
63. South Carolina Archives L.10005, Reel 9, Plat 4857.
64. Charleston County Deed Book, Charleston County Office Building, Charleston, South Carolina. Book Y–5, 360–362.
65. Samuel David Dubose and Frederick A. Porcher, *A Contribution to the History of the Huguenots of South Carolina* (New York, New York: The Knickerbocker Press, 1887. Columbia, South Carolina: Reprinted from the Original, The R.L. Bryan Company, 1972), 105.
66. E.A. Poyas, *The Olden Times of South Carolina* (Charleston, South Carolina: S.G. Courtney & Company, 1855), 36, 37.
67. Allan Nevins, *Slave Trading in the Old South* (New York: Frederick Ungar Publishing Company, 1959), 4.
68. *SCHGM* 8: 214.
69. Frank J. Klingberg, *The Carolina Chronicle of Dr. Francis LeJau, 1706–1717* (Berkeley and Los Angeles: University of California Press, 1956), 50.
70. Ibid., 2.
71. Lieber, *Vocabulary of the Catawba Language*, 327.
72. Chaplin J. Milling, *Red Carolinians* (Chapel Hill, North Carolina: University of North Carolina Press, 1940), 47.
73. Douglas Summers Brown, *The Catawba Indians: The People of the River* (Columbia, South Carolina: University of South Carolina Press, 1966), 61.
74. David Duncan Wallace, *South Carolina: A Short History* (Columbia, South Carolina: University of South Carolina Press, 1951), 5.

75. Milling, *Red Carolinians*, 34–35.
76. Waddell, *Indians*, 205.
77. Milling, *Red Carolinians*, 16.
78. Klingberg, *Dr. Francis LeJau*, 105.
79. Ibid., 105.
80. Ibid., 68.
81. Milling, *Red Carolinians*, 16.
82. Ibid., 30.
83. Waddell, *Indians*, 67.
84. Milling, *Red Carolinians*, 31.
85. Brown, *Catawba Indians*, 60.
86. Milling, *Red Carolinians*, 208.
87. Brown, *Catawba Indians*, 147.
88. Klingberg, *Dr. Francis LeJau*, 105.
89. Wallace, *Short History*, 39–44.
90. Clowse, *Economic Beginnings*, 40.
91. Ibid., 65.
92. Milling, *Red Carolinians*, 56.
93. Ibid.
94. Thomas Cooper and David J. McCord, *The Statutes at Large of South Carolina, (1682–1838)*, 10 vols. (Columbia, South Carolina: A.S. Johnson, 1838), 2:108–10.
95. Verner W. Crane, *The Southern Frontier 1670–1752* (Durham, North Carolina: Duke University Press, 1928), 113.
96. Milling, *Red Carolinians*, 55.
97. *Journal of the Indian Trade Commission, 1716–1718*, among the collections of the South Carolina Historical Society, p. 268.
98. Langdon Cheves, ed. *The Shaftesbury Papers and Other Records Relating to Carolina and the First Settlement on Ashley River prior to the year 1676*, among the collections of the South Carolina Historical Society, 1897, p. 474.
99. Milling, *Red Carolinians*, 55.
100. Ibid., 59.
101. Ravenel, *Place and the People*, 17.
102. William L. McDowell, ed., *Documents Relating to Indian Affairs, 1754–1765* (Columbia, South Carolina: University of South Carolina Press, 1970), 96.
103. Ibid., 87.
104. Klingberg, *Dr. Francis LeJau*, 78.
105. Brown, *Catawba Indians* 135.
106. Klingberg, *Dr. Francis LeJau* 39.
107. Ibid., 94.
108. Klingberg, *Dr. Francis LeJau*, 109.
109. Brown, *Catawba Indians* 135.
110. Ibid.

111. Waddell, *Indians*, 363.
112. Thomas Newe, *Letters From South Carolina in 1682*, A.S. Salley, ed., Narratives of Early Carolina (New York: 1911), 480.
113. Jon Butler, *The Huguenots in America: A Refugee People in a New World Society* (Cambridge Massachusetts: Harvard University Press, 1983), 99.
114. Crane, *Southern Frontier*, 110.
115. Clowse, *Economic Beginnings*, 86.
116. Klingberg, *Dr. Francis LeJau*, 104.
117. Clowse, *Economic Beginnings*, 35.
118. Joseph Ioor Waring, *A History of Medicine in South Carolina, 1670–1825* (Charleston, South Carolina: South Carolina Medical Association, 1964), vol. 1: 16.
119. Clowse, *Economic Beginnings*, 34.
120. Ibid.
121. St. Julien Ravenel Childs, *Malaria and Colonization in the Carolina Low Country, 1526–1969* (Baltimore: Johns Hopkins Press, 1940), 255.
122. Waring, *History of Medicine*, 15.
123. Brent H. Holcomb, *South Carolina Deed Abstracts* (Columbia, South Carolina: SCMAR, and Southern Historical Press, Easley, South Carolina, 1992, 1993, 1994, 1996): 1994, 94.
124. Waring, *History of Medicine*, 385.
125. Wallace, *Short History*, 190.
126. Clowse, *Economic Beginnings*, 100.
127. Ibid.
128. Klingberg, *Dr. Francis LeJau*, 53.
129. Ibid., 81.
130. Ibid., 113.
131. Frank J. Klingberg, *An Appraisal of the Negro in Colonial South Carolina* (Washington, D.C.: Associated Publishers, 1941), 68, 80.
132. Wallace, *Short History*, 73.
133. Klingberg, *Dr. Francis LeJau*, 73n.
134. Michael Trinkley, *Management Summary of Archaeological Data Recovery at a Portion of Crowfield Plantation and its Slave Settlement, Berkeley County, South Carolina* (Columbia, South Carolina: Chicora Foundation Inc. 1996).
135. Klingberg, *Dr. Francis LeJau*, 60.
136. Klingberg, *Dr. Francis LeJau*, 137.
137. Shirley C. Hughson, *The Carolina Pirates and Colonial Commerce, 1670–1740* (Baltimore, Maryland: Johns Hopkins Press, 1894), 37.
138. Klingberg, *Dr. Francis LeJau*, 55, 78.
139. Klingberg, *Dr. Francis LeJau*, 108.
140. Brown, *Catawba Indians*, 134.
141. Milling, *Red Carolinians*, 143.
142. Ibid.
143. Poyas, *Olden Times of South Carolina*, 111.

144. Milling, *Red Carolinians*, 184.
145. Crane, *Southern Frontier*, 172.
146. Milling, *Red Carolinians*, 145.
147. Crane, *Southern Frontier*, 169.
148. *The Post and Courier* (Charleston, South Carolina), February 10, 2003.
149. Klingberg, *Dr. Francis LeJau*, 152.
150. Milling, *Red Carolinians*, 61.
151. Orvin, *Historic Berkeley County*, 42.
152. Poyas, *Olden Times of South Carolina*, 111–12.
153. Frederick Jackson Turner, *The Frontier in American History* (New York: Henry Holt and Company, 1947, 2.
154. Klingberg, *Dr. Francis LeJau*, 27.

Chapter III
155. Edward McCrady, *History of South Carolina* 4 vols. (New York: McMillan, 1897–1901), vol. 1: 237.
156. Klingberg, *Dr. Francis LeJau*, 29.
157. Cooper and McCord, *Statutes at Large,* vol. 1: 43–56.
158. Savelle, *History of Colonial America*, 190.
159. Salley, *Warrants for Land*, 1.
160. Wallace, *Short History*, 36, 38,48.
161. M. Eugene Sirmans, *Colonial South Carolina, A Political History 1663–1763* (University of North Carolina Press, Chapel Hill, 1966), 24.
162. Ibid., 34.
163. *SCHGM* 94: 91.
164. Ibid., 91–92.
165. Sirmans, *Colonial South Carolina*, 34.
166. Clowse, *Economic Beginnings*, 46.
167. Ibid., 78.
168. McCrady, *History of South Carolina*, vol. 1: 367.
169. Sirmans, *Colonial South Carolina*, 41.
170. Poyas, *Olden Times of South Carolina*, 36.
171. Hughson, *Carolina Pirates*, 10–14.
172. Sirmans, *Colonial South Carolina*, 430.
173. Eugenia Burney, *Colonial South Carolina* (Camden, New Jersey: Thomas Nelson Inc. 1970), 62, 63.
174. Sirmans, *Colonial South Carolina*, 46.
175. Ibid., 48.
176. Ibid., 50.
177. McCrady, *History of South Carolina*, vol. 1: 689.
178. Ibid., vol. 1: 237.
179. Orvin, *Historic Berkeley County*, 30.
180. McCrady, *History of South Carolina*, vol. 1: 238.

181. Orvin, *Historic Berkeley County*, 32.
182. Sirmans, *Colonial South Carolina*, 57.
183. Orvin, *Historic Berkeley County*, 32.
184. Sirmans, *Colonial South Carolina*, 70.
185. Wallace, *Short History*, 53.
186. Orvin, *Historic Berkeley County*, 33.
187. Hughson, *Carolina Pirates*, 37.
188. Sirmans, *Colonial South Carolina*, 79.
189. Wallace, *Short History*, 72.
190. Klingberg, *Dr. Francis LeJau*, 29.
191. *SCHGM* 85: 182–83.
192. Wallace, *Short History*, 95.
193. Edgar and Bailey, *Biographical Directory*, 153.
194. William A. Schaper, *Sectionalism and Representation in South Carolina* (New York: DeCapo Press, 1968), 108.

Chapter IV
195. Ravenel, *Place and the People*, 8, 9.
196. Henriette Kershaw Leiding, *Historic Houses of South Carolina* (Philadelphia: J.P. Lippincott, 1921), 22.
197. Irving, *Day on Cooper River*, vi.
198. Savelle, *History of Colonial America*, 191.
199. Phillip Morgan, "The Development of Slave Culture on Eighteenth Century Plantation America" (PhD diss., University College, London, 1977), 42.
200. Savelle, *History of Colonial America*, 191.
201. *Deas-Alston Collection*. The papers are deposited with the South Carolina Historical Society, numbers 43/0014 and 43/0015.
202. *SCHGM* 27: 188.
203. Langley, *South Carolina Deed Abstracts*, vol. 2, 83.
204. Russell J. Cross, *Historic Ramblin's Through Berkeley*, (Columbia, South Carolina: R.L. Bryan Company, 1985), 104.
205. Charleston County Court of Ordinary, Inventories, Appraisals and Sales Books, 1839–1870. Charleston County Office Building, Charleston, South Carolina. Deed Book V-5, 383–85.
206. Charleston County Court of Ordinary, Deed Book W-5, 614–22.
207. Charleston County Court of Ordinary, Deed Book 0-4, 357–67.
208. House of Representatives Journal 1785–1786, 434; South Carolina Archives S165015 Year 1783 Item 37.
209. South Carolina Archives S165015 Year 1786 Item 36.
210. Journal of the House of Commons, January 19–June 29, 1748.
211. Ibid., January 19, 1748, 112.
212. Sirmans, *Colonial South Carolina*, 57.
213. Journal of the House of Commons, 1746–1747.
214. Cross, *Historic Ramblin's*, 27.

215. Journal of the House of Commons, December 9, 1746.
216. Ibid., March 3, 1751.
217. Ibid., March 1–April 2, 1757, 364.
218. Sirmans, *Colonial South Carolina*, 43.
219. Michael Trinkley, Debi Hacker, and Nicole Southerland, *Archaeology at an Eighteenth Century Slave Settlement in Goose Creek, South Carolina, Berkeley County, South Carolina* (Columbia, South Carolina: Chicora Foundation Inc. Research Series 57, 2003), 38.
220. Ravenel, *Place and the People*, 42.
221. *SCHGM* 70: 70.
222. Ibid., 81: 53.
223. Phillip D. Morgan, "A Profile of a Mid-Eighteenth Century South Carolina Parish: The Tax Return of St. James Goose Creek, South Carolina," *The South Carolina Historical Society and Genealogical Magazine* 81 (1980): 40.
224. Walter B. Edgar. *South Carolina, A History* (Columbia, South Carolina: University of South Carolina Press, 1999), 153.
225. Morgan, "Tax Return of St. James, Goose Creek," 51–56.
226. Burney, *Colonial South Carolina*, 62–63.
227. Sirmans, *Colonial South Carolina*, 46.
228. Trinkley, Hacker, and Southerland, *Archaeology*, 25.
229. South Carolina Archives S165015 Year 1793 Item 24.
230. Mesne Conveyance Office (MCO) Book Bb, p. 99, mortgage dated June 30, 1721. At the Charleston County Office Building, Charleston, South Carolina.
231. Theresa M. Hicks, ed., *South Carolina Indians, Indian Traders and Other Ethnic Connections Beginning 1670* (Spartanburg, South Carolina: Peppercorn Publications Inc., 1998), 271.
232. Morgan, "Tax Return of St. James, Goose Creek," 482–83.
233. Trinkley, Hacker and Southerland, *Archaeology*.
234. *SCHGM* 70: 217.
235. Slave Era Insurance Policies Registry, Illinois Department of Financial and Professional Regulations Insurance Division at www.idfpr.com.
236. Edward Ball, *Slaves in the Family* (New York: Farrar, Straus and Giroux Publishers, 1998), 246, 247.
237. Sirmans, *Colonial South Carolina*, 50.
238. McCrady, *History of South Carolina*, 689.
239. Manigault family papers, p. 1068.02.02. On deposit with the South Carolina Historical Society, Charleston, South Carolina.
240. Robert Wilson Gibbes, *Documentary History of the American Revolution* (Spartanburg, South Carolina: The Reprint Company, 1972), 2: 215–16.
241. *City Gazette*, August 21, 1798.
242. Anne Gregory, *Records of the Court of Chancery of South Carolina, 1671–1779* (Washington, D.C., 1950), 183.
243. Orvin, *Historic Berkeley County*, 30.
244. *SCHGM* 38: 63.
245. South Carolina Archives S213003, v. 2: p. 739.

246. Charleston County Will Book, Microfilm, p. 1145.
247. Mazyck Papers, p. 11/389/20. On deposit with the South Carolina Historical Society, Charleston, South Carolina.
248. Trinkley, Hacker and Southerland, *Archaeology*, 49.
249. Orvin, *Historic Berkeley County*, 32.
250. Sirmans, *Colonial South Carolina*, 70.
251. Journal of the House of Commons Journal, November 18, 1740–March 26, 1741.
252. Orvin, *Historic Berkeley County*, 53.
253. Peter Coclanis, *The Shadow of a Dream: Economic Life and Death in the South Carolina Low Country 1670–1920* (New York: Oxford University Press, 1989), 7.
254. MCO, Book E, p. 69.
255. U.S. Census Bureau, Census of Agriculture for St. James, Goose Creek Parish, South Carolina, 1880.
256. Michael Trinkley, Ph.D. *Cultural Resources Survey of the Liberty Hall Tract, Berkeley County, South Carolina* (Chicora Research Contribution 354. Chicora Foundation, Inc. Columbia, South Carolina. 2002), 17; from Victoria Reeves Gunn, *Hofwyl Plantation*, 1976. Manuscript on file with the Georgia Department of Natural Resources, Atlanta, Georgia.
257. Hirsch, *Huguenots of Colonial South Carolina*, 212.
258. South Carolina Archives S165015, Year 1788, Item 29.
259. *SCHGM* 70: 221.
260. Wallace, *Short History*, 188, 362.
261. Coclanis, *Shadow of a Dream*.
262. *The Post and Courier*, May 30, 1999.
263. P.E. Brockington Jr., M.V. Markham, C.S. Butler, and D.C. Jones, *Cultural Resources Survey of the Charleston Naval Weapons Station, Berkeley and Charleston Counties, South Carolina*. Final Report Prepared for U.S. Army Corps of Engineers, Savannah District. (Atlanta, Georgia: Brockington and Associates Inc., 1998), 41.
264. L.B. Wayne, "Burning Brick: A Study of a Lowcountry Industry" (PhD Diss., University of Florida, Gainesville, Florida, 1991), 51.
265. Census of Agriculture, 1880.
266. Herbert Ravenel Sass, *The Story of the South Carolina Low Country* (West Columbia, South Carolina: J.F. Hyer Publishing Co., 1956), 183.
267. Waring, *History of Medicine*, 36.
268. Irving, *Day on Cooper River*, 183; Waring, *History of Medicine*, 39.
269. Edgar, *South Carolina, A History*, 138.
270. *Charleston News and Courier*, October 11, 2002.
271. Interview with Harold Hilton, Berkeley County Landowner, at his residence in Sandridge, South Carolina, May 26, 2003.
272. Klingberg, *Dr. Francis LeJau*, 92.
273. On-Line Records of the state of South Carolina at the South Carolina Department of Archives and History, Columbia, South Carolina, Plats for State Land Grants, 1784–1868.
274. Klingberg, *Dr. Francis LeJau*, 93.
275. Johnson, *Traditions and Reminiscences*, 235–38.

276. Ibid., 237.
277. Edmund Berkeley and Dorothy Smith, *Dr. Alexander Garden of Charles Town*, (Chapel Hill, North Carolina: The University of North Carolina Press, 1966), 326, 327.
278. Frederick Patten Bowes, *The Culture of Early Charleston* (Greenwood, South Carolina: Greenwood Press, 1902), 20.
279. Ibid., 71.

Chapter V
280. George C. Rogers Jr., *Charleston in the Age of the Pinckneys* (Norman, Oklahoma: University of Oklahoma Press, 1969), 15.
281. Schaper, *Sectionalism and Representation*, 112.
282. Ibid., 114–15.
283. Orvin, *Historic Berkeley County*, 48.
284. Schaper, *Sectionalism and Representation*, 108.
285. Wallace, *Short History*, 138.
286. Sirmans, *Colonial South Carolina*, 151.
287. Wallace, *Short History*, 138.
288. Ibid.
289. Orvin, *Historic Berkeley County*, 54.
290. W. Roy Smith, *South Carolina as a Royal Province, 1719–1776* (New York: MacMillan, 1903), 256.
291. Ibid.
292. Cross, *Historic Ramblin's*, 256.
293. Brown, *Catawba Indians*, 62–65.
294. Ibid., 38.
295. Ibid., 52.
296. Schaper, *Sectionalism and Representation*, 347.
297. Brown, *Catawba Indians*, 62, 217.
298. Schaper, *Sectionalism and Representation*, 109.
299. Wallace, *Short History*, 231.
300. Orvin, *Historic Berkeley County*, 63.
301. Johnson, *Traditions and Reminiscences*, 383.
302. McCrady, *History of South Carolina*, 805.
303. Rogers, *Age of the Pinckneys*, 49.
304. Orvin, *Historic Berkeley County*, 78.
305. Ibid., 77.
306. *Mazyck Family Document. 1683–1807.* Papers, 11-389-20. Deposited with the South Carolina Historical Society, Charleston, South Carolina.
307. Ball, *Slaves in the Family*, 227.
308. Orvin, *Historic Berkeley County*, 91
309. *SCHGM* 57: 24.
310. Gibbes, *History of the American Revolution*, vol. 3: 225.

311. Peter Wilson Coldham, *American Loyalists Claims* (Washington, D.C.: National Geological Society, 1980), 17.
312. Gibbes, *History of the American Revolution*, vol. 2: 215, 216.
313. Ibid., 231,232.
314. Ibid., vol. 3: 228, 229.
315. McCrady, *History of South Carolina*, vol. 1: 739.
316. Holcomb *South Carolina Deed Abstracts*, 1994, 102.
317. Edgar and Bailey, *Biographical Directory*, 48.
318. Rogers, *Age of the Pinckneys*, 343.
319. Gibbes, *History of the American Revolution*, vol. 1: 10–11.
320. Johnson, *Traditions and Reminiscences*, 380.
321. *City Gazette*, August 13, 1805.
322. Orvin, *Historic Berkeley County*, 112.
323. Johnson, *Traditions and Reminiscences*, 381, 382.
324. South Carolina Archives, Accounts Growing out of the American Revolution, Samuel Adams AA36.
325. Ibid., Thomas Harris AA3372.
326. Michael Trinkley, PhD, *Liberty Hall: A Small Eighteenth Century Rice Plantation in Goose Creek, Berkeley County, South Carolina* (Chicora Research Contribution Series 62. Columbia, South Carolina: Chicora Foundation Inc., 2003), 50.
327. South Carolina Archives Accounts Audited, file number 4868.
328. Ibid., file number 4867.
329. Rogers, *Age of the Pinckneys*, 49.
330. *Royal Gazette*, March 20, 1782.
331. Edgar, *South Carolina, A History*, 239.
332. Journal of the House of Commons, 1783–84, 229, 640.
333. South Carolina Archives Series S165015, Year 1783, Item 50.
334. South Carolina House of Representatives, Report Number 108, 1783.
335. Carl P. Borick, *A Gallant Defense, The Siege of Charleston, 1780* (Columbia, South Carolina: University of South Carolina Press, 2003), 232.
336. Journal of the House of Commons, February 15, 1783; South Carolina Archives S165015, 1783 Item 220.
337. Borick, *Gallant Defense*, 232.
338. George Smith McCowen Jr., *The British Occupation of Charleston, 1780–1782* (Columbia, South Carolina: University of South Carolina Press, 1972), 77.
339. South Carolina Archives S165015, 1783, Item 342.
340. *SCHGM* 64: 11.
341. South Carolina Archives S165015, 1783 Item 102.
342. Ibid., Item 335.
343. Ibid., Item 75.
344. Edgar and Bailey, *Biographical Directory*, 584.
345. South Carolina Archives S165015, 1783, Item 179.

346. Ibid., Item 110.
347. McCowen, *British Occupation of Charleston*, 139.
348. *SCHGM* 72: 27.
349. McCowen, *British Occupation of Charleston*, 153.
350. Borick, *Gallant Defense*, 232.
351. *The Post and Courier*, February 14, 1999.
352. Coldham, *American Loyalists Claims*, 118.
353. Ibid., 329,423.
354. McCowen, *British Occupation of Charleston*, 129, 130.

Chapter VI
355. Michael Trinkley, Debi Hacker and Natalie Adams. *Broom Hall Plantation: "A Pleasant One and in a Good Neighborhood,"* (Columbia, South Carolina: Chicora Foundation Inc. 199), 51.
356. South Carolina Archives, Series S213190, v. 0007: p. 00384, Item 1.
357. Ibid., S213190 v:20: p. 87.
358. Langdon Cheves, 1848–1940: *Financial Papers, 1860–1925*; Ibid., Miscellaneous *land papers, 1735–1932*. Papers deposited with the South Carolina Historical Society, Charleston, South Carolina.
359. South Carolina Archives, S213190 v. 40: p. 46, Item 2.
360. *Journal of the Common House*, Jan.19, 1748–June 29, 1748.
361. South Carolina Archives, S213190 v. 24: p. 145 Item 1.
362. Holcomb, *South Carolina Deed Abstracts*, 1994, 90.
363. South Carolina Archives, S213184 v. 2: p. 5.
364. South Carolina Archives, S136009 v. 1775: p. 333.
365. Richard Hrabowski, *Directory for the District of Charleston Comprising the places of residence and occupation of the White Inhabitants of the Following Parishes to wit…St. James (Goose Creek)*, (Charleston, South Carolina: John Hobb, no.6 Broad Street, 1809), 17, 26, 32, 38, 52, 64, 75, 85, 112.

Chapter VII
366. South Carolina Archives, Plat S213019, v. 38, p. 245, item 1.
367. *SCHGM* 19: 54.
368. South Carolina Archives, SL10005, Reel 13, plat 6876.
369. *SCHGM* 19: 56.
370. South Carolina Archives, Plat S213019, v. 38: p. 79, item 1.
371. Ibid., p. 306, item 3.
372. Ibid., Plat S S111001, v. 9: p. 197, item 2; *SCHGM* 19: 59.
373. *SCHGM*19: 59.
374. South Carolina Archives, Plat L1005, Reel 8: plat 4225.
375. Louise N. Bailey, *Biographical Directory of the South Carolina House of Representatives: Volumes III, IV, 1775–1815* (Columbia: University of South Carolina Press, 1986), vol. 1: 578.
376. *SCHGM* 19: 61.
377. *South Carolina Gazette*, December 3, 1750.
378. South Carolina Archives, S213184, v. 6: p. 62, Item 4.

379. Ibid., Plat L10005, Reel 8, plat 4244.
380. *SCHGM* 19: 63.
381. Ibid., 63–65.
382. South Carolina Archives, Memorial S111001, v. 1: pp. 121, 118.
383. County Conveyance Office (CCO) Deed Book S, p. 321. At the Charleston County Office Building, Charleston, South Carolina.
384. *SCHGM* 38: 62.
385. Ibid., 19: 65.
386. Ibid., 66.
387. South Carolina Archives, Memorial S111001, v. 10: p. 442, Item 4.
388. Bailey, *Biographical Directory*, vol. 2: 944, 945.
389. South Carolina Archives, Mortgage S218157, v. A: p. 272.
390. South Carolina. Archives, Judgment Roll, L10018 Year 1827, Item 175A.
391. *SCHGM* 19: 69; South Carolina Archives, Series S213019, v. 38: p. 2, Item 1.
392. Poyas, *Olden Times of South Carolina*, 50.
393. *SCHGM* 19: 70.
394. Poyas, *Olden Times of South Carolina*, 52.
395. Edgar and Bailey, *Biographical Directory*, vol .2: 633.
396. U.S. Census Slave Schedules for St. James, Goose Creek Parish, South Carolina. 1820.
397. South Carolina Archives, L10005, Reel 3, Plat 1639.
398. Irving, *Day on Cooper River*, 107.
399. McCrady *History of South Carolina*, vol. 1: 705.
400. South Carolina Archives, Mortgage S372001, v. 2MO: p. 233.
401. Ibid., L10005, Reel 4, Plat 2335.
402. *SCHGM* 29: 71.
403. Ibid., 72.
404. Ibid., 19: 74.
405. Ibid., 75.
406. South Carolina Archives, S111001, v. 2: p. 162, Item 1.
407. Ibid., Lease and Release, S372001 v. A0: p. 17.
408. Ibid., Renunciation of Dower L10044, v. 1: p. 409.
409. *SCHGM* 29: 72.
410. South Carolina Archives, S136009, v. 1: Year 1757, p.191.
411. *SCHGM* 19: 73.
412. MCO, Book A, no. 3, p. 199.
413. South Carolina Archives, S213019, v. 39: p. 197, Item 3.
414. MCO, Book Y, no. 5, p.131.
415. Ibid., Book G, no. 7, p. 100.
416. Ibid., Book Z, no. 15, p. 3; H.A.M. Smith, *Rivers and Regions of Early South Carolina* (Spartanburg, South Carolina: the Reprint Press, 1988). Originally published in 1928 in the *SCHGM*.
417. *SCHGM* 29; South Carolina Archives, S213019, v. 38: p. 157, Item 1.
418. Holcomb, *South Carolina Deed Abstracts*, 1994, 133.

419. MCO, Book T, no. 10, p. 334.
420. South Carolina Archives, S213190, v. 40: p. 368, Item 18.
421. MCO, Book E, no. 10, p. 69.
422. Ibid., Book Q, no. 10, p. 21.
423. South Carolina Archives, L10005, Reel 8, Plat 4215.
424. William Rudolph Bauer, *The Sineath Family* (Columbia: The R.L. Bryan Company, 1970), 9.
425. South Carolina Archives, S165005, Year 1849, Item 53.
426. Smith, Henry A.M: *H.A.M. Smith Papers 1744–1922*; and *H.A.M. Smith Papers 1883–1924*. The papers are among the collections of the South Carolina Historical Society, Charleston, South Carolina. Plats # 105.
427. South Carolina Archives, S111001, v. 7: p. 364; *SCHGM* 29.
428. *South Carolina Gazette*, November 10, 1766.
429. Anna Wells Rutledge, *Artists in the Life of Charleston* (Philadelphia: American Philosophical Association, 1949) 172, 173.
430. Edgar and Bailey, *Biographical Directory*, vol. 3: 471.
431. Ibid., 472.
432. Charles Fraser, *A Charleston Sketchbook, 1796–1806* (Rutland, Vermont: Charles E. Tuttle Co.), 21.
433. *SCHGM* 29: 18, 19.
434. Edgar and Bailey, *Biographical Directory*, vol. 2: 254.
435. *SCHGM* 29: 71.
436. Ibid.
437. South Carolina Archives, S111001, v. 5: p. 189, Item 1.
438. Ibid., S213019, v. 38: p. 197, Item 1.
439. Rutledge, *Artists in the Life of Charleston*, 21.
440. Lease and Release, Book N, p. 287.Charleston County Office Building, Charleston, South Carolina.
441. *SCHGM* 29: 23.
442. Richard Goodman, "Dr. Garden's Flower" *Carologue* 19, no. 3 (Fall 2003): 11.
443. Johnson, *Traditions and Reminiscences*, 238.
444. Joseph Ioor Waring, *St. James' Church, Goose Creek, South Carolina: A Sketch of the Parish from 1706–1896.* (Charleston: Lucas & Richardson Co. Printers and Engravers, 1897) 227–230.
445. Bowes, *Culture of Early Charleston*, 90.
446. Berkeley and Smith, *Garden of Charles Town*, 58, 59.
447. Edgar and Bailey, *Biographical Directory*, vol. 3: 252.
448. South Carolina Archives, S165015 Year 1783, Item 342.
449. Leiding, *Historic Houses*, 27.
450. Edgar and Bailey, *Biographical Directory*, vol. 3: 253.
451. *SCHGM* 29: 25.
452. South Carolina Archives, S213089, Box 3, Folder 43.
453. Leiding, *Historic Houses*, 27.
454. *SCHGM* 29: 25.

455. Leiding, *Historic Houses*, 26.
456. John Beaufain Irving, *A Day on Cooper River*, enlarged and edited by Louisa Cheves Stoney (Columbia, South Carolina: R.L. Bryan Co., 1932) 71. This edition was published under the auspices of the St. John's Hunting Club.
457. Leiding, *Historic Houses*, 28.
458. Henry A.M. Smith, plat # 15, on microfilm at the South Carolina Historical Society, Charleston, South Carolina.
459. *SCHGM* 29: 174.
460. MCO, Book G, no. 6, p. 96.
461. *SCHGM* 29: 180.
462. South Carolina Archives, S213050. v. 6A: p. 497.
463. *SCHGM* 16: 43.
464. H.A.M. Smith, "The French Huguenot Church of the Parish of Goose Creek, South Carolina. Transactions of the Huguenot Society of South Carolina." *South Carolina Historical and Genealogical Magazine* 16 (1915): 43.
465. Edgar and Bailey, *Biographical Directory*, vol. 2: 532.
466. South Carolina Archives, Mortgage of Lease and Release, S372110, v. N0, p. 265.
467. Edgar and Bailey, *Biographical Directory*, vol. 2: 252.
468. *SCHGM* 15: 12.
469. Smith, "Transactions of Huguenot Society," 44.
470. South Carolina Archives, Plat S213184, v: 2, p. 278, Item 1.
471. Edgar and Bailey, *Biographical Directory*, vol 3: 46.
472. Edgar and Bailey, *Biographical Directory*, vol. 3: 47.
473. *SCHGM* 29: 87.
474. South Carolina Archives, Plat S213184, v: 9, p. 37.
475. South Carolina Archives, Vestry Report S165005, Year ND00, Item 2016; Waring, *St. James' Church*, 65.
476. South Carolina Archives, Memorial S111001, v: 3, p. 107, Item 1.
477. Smith, Henry A.M. *H.A.M. Smith papers 1744–1922*. The papers are among the collections of the South Carolina Historical Society, Charleston, South Carolina. File number 1102, p.265.
478. South Carolina Archives, S213019, v: 38, p. 461, Item 3.
479. Keckley family, *Keckley family papers, 1816–1977*, papers #: 43/2073. The papers are deposited with the South Carolina Historical Society, Charleston, South Carolina.
480. South Carolina Archives, S126061, Year 1824, Item 2288.
481. MCO, Book LL, p. 308; *SCHGM* 29: 96.
482. *SCHGM* 29: 339, 340.
483. Smith, *Smith Papers*, 1102, pp. 282–291.
484. Edgar and Bailey, *Biographical Directory*, vol. 2: 241.
485. Ibid.
486. Ibid., 242.
487. Smith, *Smith Papers*, 1102, pp. 282–293.
488. South Carolina Archives, S111001, v. 5: p. 48, Item 2 and Smith, 1988, p.281.

489. Edgar and Bailey, *Biographical Directory*, vol. 2: 504.
490. Johnson, *Traditions and Reminiscences*, 397.
491. *SCHGM* 29: 76.
492. Leiding, *Historic Houses*, 198–200.
493. Alston Deas Papers, 43/0014.
494. Ibid.
495. Leiding, *Historic Houses*, 200.
496. *SCHGM* 29: 287, 288.
497. South Carolina Archives, S111001, v. 5: p. 340, Item 2.
498. South Carolina Archives, S10018, Year 1809, Item 109A.
499. *SCHGM* 20: 30.
500. Ibid.
501. South Carolina Archives, Series S165029, Year ND, Item 85.
502. Report on Windsor Hill Archaeological Project, 1976. Report on Ceramics collected at the site. The University of South Carolina, Institute of Archaeology and Anthropology (SCIAA), Columbia, South Carolina.
503. Irving, *Day on Cooper River*, enlarged and edited by Stoney, 79.
504. Edgar and Bailey, *Biographical Directory*, vol. 2: 359.
505. Ibid., 355.
506. *SCHGM* 29: 168.
507. Edgar and Bailey, *Biographical Directory*, vol. 3: 371; *SCHGM* 29: 170.
508. Izard family, *Izard family papers, 1801–1861*, correspondence of Mr. Ralph Izard. On deposit with the South Carolina Historical Society, Charleston, South Carolina.
509. Dwight, *Some Historic Spots*, 24.
510. *SCHGM* 29: 173.
511. Dwight, *Some Historic Spots*, 24.
512. Bailey, *Biographical Directory*, vol. 2: 795.
513. *SCHGM* 29: 172.
514. South Carolina Archives, L10005, Reel 8, Plat 4229.
515. South Carolina Archives, S126061, Year 1824, Item 2261.
516. *SCHGM* 29: 173.
517. Ibid.
518. Rogers, *Age of the Pinckneys*, 117.
519. *SCHGM* 29: 173.
520. Leiding, *Historic Houses*, 28.
521. Joseph Ioor Waring, "Homes of Long Ago," *The Exposition*, p. 373. Among the Waring private papers on deposit at the South Carolina Historical Society, Charleston, South Carolina.
522. *SCHGM* 29: 172.
523. Interview with Steven Best, professor of biology at Charleston Southern University, Charleston, South Carolina, at the Oakes Country Club, March 12, 2004.
524. *SCHGM* 29: 81.
525. Lease and Release, Book E, p. 197.

526. *SCHGM* 29: 267.
527. Lease and Release, Book E, pp. 277–80.
528. Leiding, *Historic Houses*, 24, 25.
529. *South Carolina Gazette*, September 23, 1783.
530. *SCHGM* 29: 269.
531. Ibid., 36: 109; Dwight, *Some Historic Spots*, 23, 24.
532. MCO, Book E5, pp. 197–200.
533. Carl J. Vipperman, *The Rise of Rawlins Lowndes* (Columbia, South Carolina: University of South Carolina Press, 1976), 226.
534. *SCHGM* 29: 271.
535. Michael Trinkley, PhD., *Landscape and Garden Archaeology at Crowfield Plantation: a Preliminary Examination* (Columbia, South Carolina: Chicora Foundation, 1992), 49.
536. Leiding, *Historic Houses*, 25.
537. *SCHGM* 29: 266.
538. Ibid.
539. Ibid., 273.
540. Ibid.
541. Ibid.
542. Edgar and Bailey, *Biographical Directory*, vol. 2: 665.
543. Ibid., 66.
544. Waring, *St. James Church*, 15.
545. Langdon Cheves, 1848–1940, *Miscellaneous land papers*, 34/320; Michael Trinkley, Debi Hacker, and Natalie Adams, *Broom Hall Plantation: "A Pleasant One and in a Good Neighborhood"* (Columbia, South Carolina: Chicora Foundation Inc., 1995) 58.
546. *SCHGM* 36: 110; and Dwight, *Some Historic Spots*, 24.
547. Edgar and Bailey, *Biographical Directory*, vol. 2: 643.
548. Trinkley, Hacker, and Adams, *Broom Hall*, 58.
549. Bailey, *Biographical Directory*, vol. 3: 1505.
550. *SCHGM* 68: 244.
551. Edgar and Bailey, *Biographical Directory*, vol. 3: 670.
552. Trinkley, Hacker, and Adams, *Broom Hall*, 62.
553. *SCHGM* 19: 8.
554. South Carolina Archives, Series L10005, Reel 5, Plat 3011.
555. Waring, "Homes of Long Ago," 373.
556. Cheves, *Miscellaneous land papers*, 34/320.
557. Alston Deas Papers, 11-516-70.
558. *SCHGM* 29: 278.
559. Ibid.
560. MCO, Book P, no. 13, p. 572.
561. Leiding, *Historic Houses*, 23.
562. Cheves, *Miscellaneous land papers*, 34/320.
563. Edgar and Bailey, *Biographical Directory*, vol. 2: 454.

564. Ibid., 459.
565. South Carolina Archives, Renunciation, Series L10044, v. 1792, p. 442.
566. Ibid., Series S126061 Year 1824, Item 2305.
567. *SCHGM* 68: 244.
568. Cheves, *Miscellaneous land papers*, 34/320.
569. Dwight, *Some Historic Spots*, 21.
570. Leiding, *Historic Houses*, 23.
571. Cheves, *Miscellaneous land papers*, 34/320.
572. *Charleston News and Courier*, July 12, 1931.
573. *Charleston Post and Courier*, January 24, 1904.
574. Register of Mesne Conveyance Office (RMCO) Book E, no. 7, p. 332. Charleston County Office Building, Charleston, South Carolina.
575. Ibid., Book C, no. 7, p. 199.
576. Ibid., Book X, no. 7, p. 138.
577. Ibid., Book U, no. 7, p. 303.
578. South Carolina Archives, Series L10005, Reel 11, Plat 5697; Ibid., Series L10005, Reel 8, Plat 4217.
579. Deed Book P, p. 257,and Book of Lease and Release at the Charleston County Office Building, Charleston, South Carolina Archives, Series S111001, v. 3: p. 352, Item 1.
580. Charleston County Will Book (CCWB) v. 81, p. 592.
581. Edgar and Bailey, *Biographical Directory*, vol. 2; 722.
582. Ibid.
583. *SCHGM* 103, no. 4: 362.
584. Brockington, Markham, Butler, and Jones, *Cultural Resources*, 49.
585. Irving, *Day on Cooper River*, 75.
586. Brockington, Markham, Butler, and Jones, *Cultural Resources*, 49.
587. Michael J. Heitzler, *Historic Goose Creek, South Carolina, 1670–1980* (Easley, South Carolina: Southern Historical Press, 1983), 119.
588. Charleston County Deed Book (CCDB), X15: 98. County Office Building, Charleston, South Carolina.
589. South Carolina Archives, Series S111001, v. 5: p. 318, Item 1.
590. Edgar and Bailey, *Biographical Directory*, vol. 2: 686.
591. Ibid., vol. 3: 384.
592. Irving, *Day on Cooper River*, enlarged and edited by Stoney, 74.
593. Edgar and Bailey, *Biographical Directory*, vol. 3: 384.
594. CCDB, Z9: 509.
595. Ibid., C12: 356.
596. Brockington, Markham, Butler, and Jones, *Cultural Resources*, 50.
597. Langley, *South Carolina Deed Abstracts*, vol. 2: 291.
598. Record of Wills, 1786–1868. Charleston County Office Building, Charleston, South Carolina. Will Book 82-B: 973.
599. Brockington, Markham, Butler, and Jones, *Cultural Resources*, 41.

600. CCDB, K9: 88.
601. Ibid., C10: 317.
602. Ibid., G10: 83.
603. *SCHGM* 19: 68.
604. South Carolina Archives, Memorial S111001, v. 1: p. 99.
605. *SCHGM* 19: 68, 69.
606. Edgar and Bailey, *Biographical Directory*, vol. 2: 624.
607. South Carolina Archives, Mortgage S111001, v. 14: p. 93, Item 3.
608. Irving, *Day on Cooper River*, 15.
609. CCDB, Book S, p. 316.
610. South Carolina Archives, Series S213019, v. 38: p. 497.
611. Charleston County Will Book (CCWB) 76-B: 612.
612. South Carolina Archives, S111001, v. 5: p. 9.
613. Ibid., v. 4: p. 1l; MCO, Book G, pp. 389, 398.
614. South Carolina Archives, Series S372001, v. 3D0: p. 433.
615. Ibid., Series L10005, Reel 8, Plat 4258.
616. Ibid., Series S 372001, v. 3D0: p. 433.
617. Irving, *Day on Cooper River*, 22.
618. South Carolina Archives, Series S372001, v. 2A0: p. 449.
619. United States Census, 1790.
620. Edgar and Bailey, *Biographical Directory*, vol. 3: 286.
621. South Carolina Archives, S213190, v. 36: p. 161.
622. Ibid., S213003, v. 3T: p. 485.
623. Brewster and Burke Papers, *Abstract of title to Red Bank Plantation, 1880*. Papers deposited with the South Carolina Historical Society, Charleston, South Carolina.
624. Irving, *Day on Cooper River*, 15.
625. Brewster and Burke, *Red Bank Plantation*.
626. United States Census, 1920.
627. Private papers of Terrence Larimer, interview with Ida Kodama Browder, 1998.
628. Ibid., interview with Henry Kodama, 1998
629. Ibid., interview with Ida Kodama Browder 1998.
630. Larimer Papers.
631. Ibid.
632. South Carolina Archives, Series S111001, v. 5: p. 324, Item 1.
633. Wayne, "Burning Brick."
634. *SCHGM* 84: 251; Wayne, "Burning Brick," 53.
635. B.L. Rauschenberg, "Brick and Tile Manufacturing in the South Carolina Low Country, 1750–1800," *Journal of Southern Decorative Arts*, 1988, 105.
636. *SCHGM* 50: 349–350.
637. South Carolina Archives, Plat Series L10005, Reel 8, Plat 419.
638. CCDB, P7: p. 306.
639. Irving, *Day on Cooper River*, 19, 20.

640. CCDB, Y16: p. 238.
641. Berkeley County Deed Book (BCDB), C2: p. 178. Berkeley County Office Building, Moncks Corner, South Carolina.
642. South Carolina Archives, Series L10005, Reel 3, Plat 1570.
643. Smith, "Transactions of Huguenot Society," vol. 71: 88.
644. Smith, Henry A.M. plats on microfilm at the South Carolina Historical Society, Charleston, South Carolina. File 1102.
645. Edgar and Bailey, *Biographical Directory*, vol. 1: 641.
646. Irving, *Day on Cooper River*, 70.
647. Edgar and Bailey, *Biographical Directory*, vol. 3: 588.
648. Irving, *Day on Cooper River*, 18.
649. M.L. Webber, "Tombstone Inscriptions," *SCHGM* 40: 33–34; Irving, *Day on Cooper River*, 70.
650. *SCHGM* 33: 245, 246.
651. Ibid., 245.
652. Poyas, *Olden Times of South Carolina*, 19.
653. Leiding *Historic Houses*, 30.
654. Ibid.
655. South Carolina Archives, Abstract Series S213019 v. 38: p. 247, Item 2.
656. Ibid.: p. 76 Item 1.
657. Ibid.: p. 253 Item 1.
658. Ibid.: p. 91 Item 1.
659. Poyas, *Olden Times of South Carolina*, 32.
660. *SCHGM* 13: 16.
661. Virginia Christian Beach, *Medway* (Charleston, South Carolina: Wyrick and Company, 1996), 10.
662. Ibid., 13.
663. South Carolina Archives, Memorial S111001, v. 5: p. 217.
664. Ibid., v. 14: p. 230, Item 1.
665. Ibid., Plat Series L10005, Reel 8, Plat 4260.
666. Plat of Medway Plantation on Microfiche at The South Carolina Historical Society, 33-62-12.
667. Irving, *Day on Cooper River*, 68.
668. Irving, *Day on Cooper River*, enlarged and edited by Stoney, 48.
669. Ibid., 69.
670. Ibid.
671. Samuel G. Stoney, 1906 plat of Medway Plantation consisting of 5,492 acres combining five tracts. Survey and plat made by Simon-Mayrant Company.
672. Interview with Gertrude Legendre, owner of Medway Plantation, at Medway Plantation, March 12, 1996.
673. Ball, *Slaves in the Family*, 246.
674. South Carolina Archives, S165015, 1796, Item 66.
675. South Carolina Archives, Series S165015, Year 1796, Item 61.

676. Irving, *Day on Cooper River*, enlarged and edited by Stoney, 72.
677. United States Census, 1860 Slave Schedule.
678. South Carolina Archives, L10005 Reel 3, Plat 1546.
679. Irving, *Day on Cooper River*, enlarged and edited by Stoney, 72.
680. Ibid.
681. South Carolina Archives, Memorial, S111001, v. 3: p. 177.
682. George Chicken, *George Chicken Journal, 1715–1716.* Papers are deposited with the South Carolina Historical Society, Charleston, South Carolina, no.1134.03.03.
683. Irving, *Day on Cooper River*, enlarged and edited by Stoney, 31.
684. Alston Deas Papers, 43/0014.
685. Mrs. Arthur Gordon Rose, *Little Mistress Chicken*, (Reprinted by the Youth's Companion, n.d.), 15.
686. Ball Family Papers. *Back River Plantation Records 1812–1834*, Back River Account Book, 11/516/70. On deposit with the South Carolina Historical Society, Charleston, South Carolina.
687. South Carolina Archives, Memorial S111001, v. 7: p. 495, Item 1.
688. Langley, *South Carolina Deed Abstracts*, 73.
689. Edgar and Bailey, *Biographical Directory*, vol. 2: 150.
690. Plat of Spring Grove Plantation, circa 1790, (2) 32-3, among the Keckley Papers, 43/2073 at The South Carolina Historical Society, Charleston, SC.
691. George Keckley, Plat of Spring Grove Plantation #: 32/120/A017; and *Keckley family papers*, 43/2073 at the South Carolina Historical Society, Charleston, South Carolina.
692. *Keckley family papers*.
693. Ibid.
694. South Carolina Archives, Series S165015, Year 1796, Item 61.
695. Ibid., Item 15 and S.C. Archives S165005, 1796, Number 94.
696. Berkeley County RMC, Miscellaneous Record C-9: 109, 417. Berkeley County Office Building, Moncks Corner, South Carolina
697. Ibid., C-13: 28.
698. Ibid., C-14: 408.
699. Irving, *Day on Cooper River*, enlarged and edited by Stoney, 72.
700. CCDB, Book E, p. 69, January 21, 1724 Mortgage.
701. South Carolina Archives, Memorials v. 5: p. 395.
702. Edgar and Bailey, *Biographical Directory*, vol. 3: 651.
703. Ibid.
704. Ibid., 652.
705. South Carolina Archives, Series S213190, v. 40: p. 46, Item 2.
706. Ibid., S126061, Year 1824, Item 2323.
707. Alexander Moore, *Biographical Directory of the South Carolina House of Representatives, Columbia: Vol. V: 1816–1828.* (South Carolina Department of Archives and History, 1992), 221.
708. South Carolina Archives, L10005, Reel 8, Plat 4216.
709. Ibid., Reel 9, 5027.
710. Lease and Release, Book I, p. 92.

711. Edgar and Bailey, *Biographical Directory*, vol. 2: 60.
712. Langley, *South Carolina Deed Abstracts*, vol. 2: 358.
713. South Carolina Archives, Lease and Release S372001, v. 2Z0: p. 372.
714. Ibid., Series L10005 Reel 2 Plat 1336.
715. Ibid., Reel 8, Plat 4254.
716. Smith, *Smith Papers*, 1102, p. 379.
717. CCDB, Book B, p. 39, August 10 and 11, 1720.
718. Edgar and Bailey, *Biographical Directory*, 31–32.
719. Ibid., vol. 2: 34.
720. Ibid., 35.
721. Henry A.M. Smith, Plat # 141.
722. Berkeley and Smith, *Garden of Charles Town*, 201, 202.
723. Henry A.M. Smith, Plat # 241.
724. Brockington, Markham, Butler, and Jones, *Cultural Resources*, 23.
725. Edgar and Bailey, *Biographical Directory*, vol. 3: 179.
726. Ibid.
727. Johnson, *Traditions and Reminiscences*, 381.
728. Rutledge, *Artists in the Life of Charleston*, 178.
729. South Carolina Archives, Plat Series L10005 Reel 3, Plat 1, 547 and Reel 8, Plat 4261.
730. Bailey, *Biographical Directory*, 180.
731. Edgar and Bailey, *Biographical Directory*, vol. 3: 152.
732. Smith, *Smith Papers*, 1102, p. 381.
733. CCDB, Book K, no. 9, p. 353; Smith, *Smith Papers*, 1102, p. 381.
734. Smith, *Smith Papers*, 1102, p. 381; MCO, Book X 312, p. 79.
735. South Carolina Archives, L10005, Reel 4, Plat 2309.
736. Ibid., Reel 8, Plat 4268.
737. MCO, Book L, no.15, pp. 411, 467.
738. Brockington, Markham, Butler, and Jones, *Cultural Resources*, 15.
739. CCDB: 356 and Sipes, p. 22.
740. CCDB X13: 183.
741. Brockington 2002, p. 27.
742. South Carolina Archives, L10005 Reel 8, Plat 4182.
743. Ibid., S111001 v. 8: p. 449.
744. *SCHGM* 40: 2, 3.
745. Ibid., 106.
746. South Carolina Archives, Series L10005 Reel 3 Plat 1544.
747. Ibid., Reel 3, Plat 1517.
748. Edgar and Bailey, *Biographical Directory*, 287.
749. South Carolina Archives, L10005, Reel 8, Plat 4251.
750. Ibid., Reel 9, Plat 5025.
751. Ibid., plat 5030.
752. Ibid., SL10005, Reel 3, Plat 1646.

753. Ibid., Series S213019, v. 38: p. 363, Item 3.
754. *South Carolina Gazette*, August 4, 1733.
755. Ibid.
756. *Wragg Family Papers, 1708–1860*, 1118.00. The papers are deposited with the South Carolina Historical Society, Charleston, South Carolina.; South Carolina Archives, Series S372001, v. V0, p. 178.
757. *South Carolina Gazette*, September 28, 1738; Ibid., March 27, 1738.
758. Edgar and Bailey, *Biographical Directory*, vol. 2: 425.
759. *South Carolina Gazette*, May 30, 1771.
760. Edgar and Bailey, *Biographical Directory*, vol. 2: 426.
761. *Wragg Family Papers*, 11/467/10.
762. MCO, Book C, no. 5, p. 159.
763. *Wragg Family Papers*, 11/467/11; MCO, Book N, no. 5 p. 544.
764. Edgar and Bailey, *Biographical Directory*, vol. 3: 675.
765. CCWB p. 299.
766. MCO, Book G, no. 9, p. 335.
767. Cheves, *Miscellaneous land papers*, 34/320; MCO, Book A, no. 14, p. 103.
768. Cheves, *Miscellaneous land papers*, 34/320.
769. Edgar and Bailey, *Biographical Directory*, vol. 2: 470.
770. *South Carolina Gazette*, January 1739.
771. CCDB, Book H, p. 14, January 1 and 2, 1728.
772. Ibid., Book P, no.6, p. 296.
773. *South Carolina Gazette*, February 24, 1733.
774. South Carolina Archives, Series S1110001, v. 3: p. 164, Item 2; Lease and Release, Book M, p. 209.
775. South Carolina Archives, Series S372001, v. T: p. 438.
776. MCO, Book T, p. 438.
777. *South Carolina Gazette*, April 13, 1752.
778. South Carolina Archives, Tax Return S126061, Year 1824, Item 2257.
779. Ibid., S165018, Year 1824, Item 4.
780. Ibid., Plat Series L10005 Reel 11, Plat 5697.
781. Ibid., Reel 8, Plat 4217.
782. Edgar and Bailey, *Biographical Directory*, vol. 2: 337.
783. Ibid., 156.
784. South Carolina Archives, Memorial S111001, v. 3: p. 455, Item 1.
785. South Carolina Archives, Lease and Release S372001, v. M0: p. 218.
786. *South Carolina Gazette*, April 17–21, 1736.
787. Ibid., July 7, 1739.
788. MCO, Book QQ, p. 168.
789. CCWB (Probate Court Will Book), Book C, p. 438.
790. MCO, Book P, no. 6, p. 296.
791. Ibid., p. 304.

792. Edgar and Bailey, *Biographical Directory*, vol. 2: 448.
793. MCO, Book E, no. 10, p. 402.
794. South Carolina Archives, S111001, v. E0: p. 319; MCO, Book E, p. 319, Lease and Release.
795. South Carolina Archives, S372001, v. K0, p. 434.
796. *South Carolina Gazette*, February 15, 1749.
797. Charleston County Inventories Book (CCIB), Book E, p. 4.Charleston County Office Building, Charleston, South Carolina.
798. South Carolina Archives, Judgment Roll SL10018, Year 1833, Item 280A.
799. RMC, DB H10, p. 114.
800. MCO, Book Bb, p. 6.
801. Jay Shuler, *Had I the Wings: The Friendship of Bachman and Audubon* (Athens, Georgia: University of Georgia Press, 1993), 73.
802. Ibid., 145.
803. Charles W. Graves, ca. 1818–1870: *Papers and Plantation Journal 1846–1875*, 34/0183. Papers are among the collections of the South Carolina Historical Society, Charleston, South Carolina.
804. United States Bureau of Census. Census of Agricultural for St. James, Goose Creek Parish, South Carolina, 1880.
805. Berkeley County RMC, Deed Book A4, p. 137.
806. Terrence Larimer, Private papers in his possession at the Naval Weapons Station, Charleston, Goose Creek, South Carolina.
807. Larimer Papers, interview with E.F. Lowndes II, 1998.
808. Larimer Papers.
809. Ibid., Game Record, Liberty Hall Club 1912.
810. Ibid., interview with Frank Ford II, 1998.
811. Ibid., Tales of the Liberty Hall Club.
812. Trinkley, *Cultural Resources Survey*, 24.
813. Ibid.
814. Register of Mesne Conveyance, Deed Book A 321, p. 110.
815. *SCHGM* 60: 28.
816. South Carolina Archives, Plat Series L10005, Reel 8, Plat 4204.
817. Larimer papers, interview with William Wilson, 1997.
818. CCDB, Z6: 358.
819. CCWB, 43:871.
820. Irving, *Day on Cooper River*, enlarged and edited by Stoney, 77.
821. Graves family: *Graves Family Papers, 1853–1854, 1854–1855*, 43/530. Papers are among the collections of the South Carolina Historical Society, Charleston, South Carolina; Graves, *Plantation Journal*, 34/183.
822. Brockington, Markham, Butler, and Jones, *Cultural Resources*.
823. CCDB, H16: 380.
824. Brent H. Holcomb, *South Carolina Deed Abstracts* Book R-5, 14-24, p. 198,.
825. Brockington, Markham, Butler, and Jones, *Cultural Resources*, 97.
826. *SCHGM* 8: 216.

827. South Carolina Archives, S111001, v. 1: p. 441.
828. Ibid., Series S165005, Year 1829, Item 167.
829. Ibid., 1848, Number 101.
830. Bailey, *Biographical Directory*, vol. 1: 367.
831. South Carolina Archives, Series S111001, v. 13: p. 436; Ibid., L10005, Reel 11, Plat 5687.
832. *SCHGM* 20: 189.
833. Ibid.
834. South Carolina Archives, L10005 Reel 8, Plat 4468.
835. *SCHGM* 20: 190.
836. Moore, *Biographical Directory*, 154.
837. Ibid.
838. South Carolina Archives, S165015, Year 1818, Item 44.
839. Ibid., S126061, Year 1824, Item 2370.
840. Edgar and Bailey, *Biographical Directory*, vol. 4: 1748.
841. South Carolina Archives, S 165015, Year 1848, Item 63.
842. Cross, *Historic Ramblin's*, 29.
843. South Carolina Archives, Series L10005 Reel 4 Plat2385.
844. Ibid., 165015 Year 1811 Item 52.
845. Ibid., Series S213190 v. 35: p. 176.
846. Bailey, *Biographical Directory*, vol. 2: 1096.
847. South Carolina Archives, S165015 Year 00 Item 3986.
848. Bailey, *Biographical Directory*, vol. 2: 1182.
849. Edgar and Bailey, *Biographical Directory*, 616.
850. South Carolina Archives, S213190, v. 18: p. 143.
851. Ibid., v. 9: p. 87.
852. Ibid., S165015, Year 1805, Item 161.
853. Bailey, *Biographical Directory*, vol. 4: 563–64.
854. Ibid., 615.
855. South Carolina Archives, L10005, Reel 8, Plat 4243.
856. Edgar and Bailey, *Biographical Directory*, vol. 2: 734.

Epilogue
857. Beach, *Medway*, 13.

Selected Bibliography

Primary Sources

Interviews

Best, Stephen. Professor of biology at Charleston Southern University. Interview with the author at The Oaks, March 12, 2004.

Hilton, Harold. Berkeley County landowner. Interview with the author at his home in Sandridge, South Carolina, April 26, 2003.

Legendre, Gertrude. Owner of Medway Plantation. Interview with the author at Medway, March 12, 1996.

Private Papers

Alston Deas Papers. Alston Deas collection of property records, 1823–1895. The papers are deposited with the South Carolina Historical Society, Charleston, South Carolina.

Ball Family Papers. *John Ball Plantation Records, 1831–1841*. Papers deposited with the South Carolina Historical Society, Charleston, South Carolina.

———. *Back River Plantation Records 1812–1834*. Papers deposited with the South Carolina Historical Society, Charleston, South Carolina.

Ball, Jane Hayward. *Scrapbook, 1900–1929*. Scrapbook deposited with the South Carolina Historical Society, Charleston, South Carolina.

Brewster and Burke Papers. *Abstract of title to Red Bank Plantation, 1880*. Papers deposited with the South Carolina Historical Society, Charleston, South Carolina.

Cheves, Langdon. 1848–1940: *Miscellaneous land papers, 1735–1932*. Papers deposited with the South Carolina Historical Society, Charleston, South Carolina.

———. 1848–1939: *Abstracts of Titles, 1694–1850*. Papers deposited with the South Carolina Historical Society, Charleston, South Carolina.

———. 1848–1940: *Financial Papers, 1860–1925*. Papers deposited with the South Carolina Historical Society, Charleston, South Carolina.

Chicken, George 1727: *George Chicken Journal, 1715–1716*. Papers are deposited with the South Carolina Historical Society, Charleston, South Carolina.

DeSaussure Papers. DeSaussure family papers, 1716–1938. The papers are deposited with the South Carolina Historical Society, Charleston, South Carolina.

Donnelly Papers. Papers in the private collection of Thomas and Elizabeth Johnson, Charleston, South Carolina.

Dordal Papers. Papers in the private collection of the Dordal family, Goose Creek, South Carolina.

Fraser, Alexander. *Alexander Fraser correspondence, 1774–1791*. Papers deposited with the South Carolina Historical Society, Charleston, South Carolina.

Glover. *The Glover Family Papers 1731–1841*. Papers deposited with the South Carolina Historical Society, Charleston, South Carolina.

Graves, Charles W. ca. 1818–1870: *Papers and Plantation Journal 1846–1875*. Papers are among the collections of the South Carolina Historical Society, Charleston, South Carolina.

Graves family. *Graves Family Papers, 1853–1854, 1854–1855*. Papers are among the collections of the South Carolina Historical Society, Charleston, South Carolina.

Hilton, Nathaniel. *St. James Goose Creek Planter, Charleston District Ordinary Letter of Testament, 1858*. The testament is among the private papers of Harold Hilton, Sandridge, South Carolina.

Hutchinson Edward L. 1855. *Edward L. Hutchinson papers 1800–1855*. Papers are deposited with the South Carolina Historical Society, Charleston, South Carolina.

Izard family. *Izard family papers, 1801–1861*. The papers are deposited with the South Carolina Historical Society, Charleston, South Carolina.

Johnson, William Henry. 1871–1934. *William Henry Johnson Scrapbook, ca. 1920–1933.* The scrapbook is among the collections of the South Carolina Historical Society, Charleston, South Carolina.

Keckley family. *Keckley family papers, 1816–1977.* The papers are deposited with the South Carolina Historical Society, Charleston, South Carolina.

Larimer, Terrence. Private papers in his possession at the Naval Weapons Station Charleston, Goose Creek, South Carolina. The papers include notes from his interviews with:
Brower, Ida Kodama. Goose Creek, South Carolina. July and August 1998.
Ford II, Frank. C. Goose Creek, South Carolina. August and September 1998.
Herrin George. Goose Creek, South Carolina. June 1998
Kodama, Henry. Goose Creek, South Carolina. July 1998.
Lowndes II, E.F. Goose Creek, South Carolina. August and September 1998.
Manucy II, Orian A. Goose Creek, South Carolina. 1988.
Spell, Norman. Charleston, South Carolina. April 1996.
Wilson, William. Moncks Corner, South Carolina. March 1997.

Letters of the Society for the Propagation of the Gospel in Foreign Parts to the Ministers of St. James Church, Goose Creek, 1702–1765. The letters are among the collections of the South Carolina Historical Society, Charleston, South Carolina, and on microfilm at the South Carolina Department of Archives and History, Columbia, South Carolina.

Liberty Hall Club. *Tales of the Liberty Hall Club* as told to E.F. Lowndes II by Frank C. Ford in June 1985. The tales are among the private papers of Terrence Larimer, Naval Weapons Station Charleston, Goose Creek, South Carolina.

Liberty Hall Hunt Club Log, 1912. The log is among the private papers of Terrence Larimer, Naval Weapons Station Charleston, Goose Creek, South Carolina.

Lieber, Oscar M. *Vocabulary of the Catawba Language, with some Remarks on its Grammar, Construction and Pronunciation.* Among the collections of the South Carolina Historical Society, Charleston, South Carolina.

Loocock, Aaron. Private papers including his will in 1793 are among the collections of the South Carolina Historical Society, Charleston, South Carolina.

———.*Bond of Indemnity, 1792.* Deposited with the South Carolina Historical Society, Charleston, South Carolina.

Loyalist Claims. On microfilm among the collections of the South Carolina Department of Archives and History, Columbia, South Carolina.

Manigault, Gabriel. *Gabriel Manigault papers, 1775–1839.* Deposited with the South Carolina Historical Society, Charleston, South Carolina.

———. *Gabriel Manigault letters 1805–1808.* Deposited with the South Carolina Historical Society, Charleston, South Carolina.

———. *Gabriel Manigault papers with the Journal, 1774–1784.* Deposited with the South Carolina Historical Society, Charleston, South Carolina.

Mazyck Family Document. 1683–1807. Deposited with the South Carolina Historical Society, Charleston, South Carolina.

Mazyck, Stephen. *Stephen Mazyck Letter in 1776 at Spring Field Plantation in Goose Creek, to his brother Alexander.* Deposited with the South Carolina Historical Society, Charleston, South Carolina.

Middleton, Henry Augustus. *Henry Augustus Middleton Business and plantation papers, 1828–1887.* Deposited with the South Carolina Historical Society, Charleston, South Carolina.

Middleton, Thomas. *Thomas Middleton papers, 1787–1849.* Deposited with the South Carolina Historical Society, Charleston, South Carolina.

Ravenel, William. 1806–1888. *William Ravenel Papers, 1746–1886.* On deposit at the South Carolina Historical Society, Charleston, South Carolina.

Records of the 18th Regiment of the South Carolina Militia, South Carolina, Adjutant and Inspector General's Office, on deposit at the South Carolina Historical Society, Charleston, South Carolina.

Smith, Henry A.M. *H.A.M. Smith papers 1744–1922.* The papers are among the collections of the South Carolina Historical Society, Charleston, South Carolina.

———. *H.A.M. Smith papers 1883–1924.* The papers are among the collections of the South Carolina Historical Society, Charleston, South Carolina.

Smyth, Stoney Adger. *Stoney Adger Smyth Collection including the Medway Plantation Day Book, 1872 and the Medway Plantation Hunt Book 1875–1918.* The papers are among the collections of the South Carolina Historical Society, Charleston, South Carolina.

South Carolina Militia, 7th Brigade, 30th Regiment order book, 1793–1814 in Vanderhorst's Regiment Order Book. The book is among the collections of the South Carolina Historical Society, Charleston, South Carolina.

Stoney, Samuel Gaillard. *Samuel Gaillard Stoney Papers* and *Stoney Family Documents, 1775–1935 and the Plantation Journal of Medway 1852–1853*. The papers are among the collections of the South Carolina Historical Society, Charleston, South Carolina.

Wragg Family Papers, 1708–1860. Deposited with the South Carolina Historical Society, Charleston, South Carolina.

Plats deposited with the South Carolina Historical Society, and the Charleston County Library, Charleston, South Carolina

Braker, Susannah. Plat drawn at the request of Susannah Braker, Administrator to the Estate of Jacob Braker, deceased. "I have resurveyed the land attached to the 19-Mile House belonging to the estate of P. Jacob Braker containing 467 acres, 1821."

Ficken, John. Plat for John Ficken, McCrady plat number 1712, C3184.

Furman, C.M. Plat of a piece of land containing 400 acres. C.M. Furman. McCrady Plat 1517, C3182.

Goose Creek Dam. Plat of Goose Creek Dam, McCrady plat 2992, C 3184.

Goose Creek Church. Plat of a tract of land situated in St. James, Goose Creek, contains 270 acres belonging to the Goose Creek Church. Surveyed May 1888. Name not legible. Plat is on microfiche and among the *H.A.M. Smith Papers*. The plat shows the location of the "Old School House" at a point N50 S 11.70 and N 14.5 S 22.

Harmon. Plat of the Harmon tract of 1,044.5 acres, 1915. McCrady plat 3002, C3184.

Ingleside Mining. Plat of Ingleside Mining, 1,639 acres, McCrady plat number 3070, C3184.

Izard, Ralph. Plan of a body of land called the Elms Clubhouse and composed of Sundry Tracts, In the parish of St. James, Goose Creek and St. George, Dorchester, Charleston District.(C.141). Series L10005 Reel 8, Plat 4229.

Johnson, William. William Johnson plat for 550 acres of marshland on Cooper River and Goose Creek, Charleston District, surveyed by J. Schreiber. Series 213190,Volume 20: Page 199.

Martindale Plantation Situate on Southern Railroad in St. James, Goose Creek Parish, Charleston District survey made June 1840.

Onsitt, John. Plan of a body of land made at the request of the executors of John Onsitt and Margaret Riddle, formerly Margaret Onsitt to resurvey and divide the property containing 666 acres recorded in book H number 7, page 5. 1802. Resurvey and division made 1792.

Stoney, Samuel G. 1906 plat of Medway Plantation consisting of 5,492 acres combining five tracts. Survey and plat made by Simons-Mayrant Company.

Thornley, Robert. Plat for 460 acres on branch of Wassamasaw Swamp, Charleston District, surveyed by John Diamond. Series 2131190, Volume 9, page 87.

Von Kolnitzl George. Plat of George Von Kolnitz, McCrady plat 1644, C3182.

Photographs and Prints

Crowfield Ruins, Berkeley County South Carolina. The photograph is among the collections of the Library of Congress. HABS SC-6/HABS SC, 8-GOOCR.V, 1-3/HABS SC, 8-GOOCR.V, 1-6.

The Elms (Ruins), University Blvd. (U.S. Rt. 78), Charleston County, South Carolina. The photograph is among the collections of the Library of Congress, HABS, SC, 8-Otrat, 1-2.

The Elms Ruins, Charleston County, South Carolina. The photograph is among the collections of the Library of Congress. HABS, SC,8-OTRAT, 1-2/HABS, SC,8-OTRAT, 1-3.

Medway Plantation, Berkeley County, South Carolina. The photograph is among the collections of the Library of Congress. HABS, SC, 8-PIGRO.V, 2-4.

Medway Plantation, U.S. Rt. 52, Berkeley County, South Carolina. The photograph is among the collections of the Library of Congress. HABS, SC, 8-PIGRO.V, 2-4.

Mr. Manigault's Seat at Goose Creek, 1853, painted by Charles Fraser. Number 1938.036.0072, among the collections of the Gibbes Art Gallery, Charleston, South Carolina.

On-Line Records of the state of South Carolina at the South Carolina Department of Archives and History, Columbia, South Carolina

Criminal Journals, 1769–1776.

Index to Multiple Records Series, 1675–1929.

Plats for State Land Grants, 1784–1868.

Will Transcripts, 1782–1855.

Legislative Papers, 1782–1866.

Acts, Reports, Laws, Ordinances, Records, Regulations and Statutes

Charleston County Court of Ordinary, Inventories, Appraisements and Sales Books, 1839–1870. Charleston County Office Building, Charleston, South Carolina.

Charleston County Register of Mesne Conveyance Records for Charleston County, South Carolina (Records of deeds between buyer and seller, 1719–2003). Charleston, South Carolina.

Slave Era Insurance Policies Registry. Illinois Department of Financial and Professional Regulations at www.idfpr.com.

SCIWAY, South Carolina Information Highway, http://sciway.net.

United States Bureau of Census. Census of Agricultural for St. James, Goose Creek Parish, South Carolina 1850, 1860, 1870, 1880.

———. Census of Mortality for St. James, Goose Creek Parish, South Carolina 1850, 1860, 1870, 1880.

———. Federal Population Enumerations for St. James, Goose Creek Parish, South Carolina, for the years 1790, 1800, 1810, 1820, 1830, 1840, 1850, 1860, 1870, 1880,1890, 1900, 1910, 1920, 1930. Washington: Government Printing Office.

———. Products of Industry for St. James, Goose Creek Parish, South Carolina 1850, 1860, 1870, 1880.

———. Slave schedules for St. James, Goose Creek Parish, South Carolina, 1840,1850, 1860.

———. Social Census for St. James, Goose Creek Parish, South Carolina 1850, 1860, 1870, 1880.

———. Special Enumeration Census for the City of Goose Creek, April 14, 1979. Available at the South Carolina Department of Archives and History, Columbia, South Carolina.

United States Mapping Service at http://geography.usgs.gov/.

Record of Wills, 1786–1868. Charleston County Office Building, Charleston, South Carolina.

St. Andrew's Parish. Parish register of St. Andrew's Parish, 1728–. The register is among the collections of the South Carolina Historical Society, Charleston, South Carolina.

St. James Church, Goose Creek. *Minutes of the Vestry, 1872–1925*. The minutes are among the collections of the South Carolina Historical Society, Charleston, South Carolina.

Transcripts of Charleston County wills, estate inventories and miscellaneous records prior 1869. The records are on microfilm at the Charleston County Library, Charleston, South Carolina and at the South Carolina Department of Archives and History.

Windsor Hill Nomination Form. National Register of Historic Places Nomination Form. United States Department of Interior February 4, 1976. Records are on deposit at the Institute of Archaeology and Anthropology, University of South Carolina, Columbia, South Carolina.

Plats, Microfilm at the South Carolina Historical Society.

Bull, William. Plat of Button Hall, 1778. 33-40.

Deans Swamp, 1819. 33-68-13.

The Elms Plantation, 1785, 32-29-6.

The Elms Plantation, 1801. 32-44-9.

Goose Creek Church, 1888. 32-77.

Howe Hall, 1780. 33-82-6.

John Onsell Estate, 1792. 33-62-33.

Lands Adjoining Goose Creek Reservoir, 1917. 32-88-5.

Martindale Plantation. 33-72-23.

Medway, Back River, 1792. 33-62-12.

Oakgrove Plantation, 1784. 47-5-4.

Sociable Hill Plantation, 1788. 32-32-7.

Wassamasaw, 1786. 33-64-17.

William Parker Estate, Wassamasaw, 1790. 33-16-47.

Secondary Sources

Unpublished Sources

Papers and Reports

Cheves, Langdon, ed. *The Shaftesbury Papers and Other Records Relating to Carolina and the First Settlement on Ashley River prior to the year 1676*. Charleston, among the collections of the South Carolina Historical Society, 1897.

Coon, David L. "The Development of Market Agriculture in South Carolina." PhD diss., University of Illinois, at Urbana-Champaign, 1972.

Gunn, Victoria Reeves. *Hofwyl Plantation*. 1976. The manuscript is on file with the Georgia Department of Natural Resources, Atlanta, Georgia.

Lawson, Marian Averill. "Medway: a case study of the emergence of the plantation system in the proprietary period and the early royal colony of Carolina." Masters thesis, University of South Carolina, Columbia, South Carolina, 1993. Typescript available at Caroliniana Library, Columbia, South Carolina.

Morgan, Phillip D. "The Development of Slave Culture on Eighteenth Century Plantation America." PhD diss., University College, London. 1977.

Sambits, Nancy. *The Economic Decline of an Agricultural Community: a case study.* Unpublished and unbound manuscript, 1989. Available at Caroliniana Library, Columbia, South Carolina.

Smith, M.T. "Depopulation and Culture Change in the Early Historic Period Interior Southeast." PhD diss., Department of Anthropology, University of Florida, Gainesville, Florida.

Wayne, L.B. "Burning Brick: A Study of a Lowcountry Industry." PhD diss., University of Florida, Gainesville, Florida.1991.

Published Sources

Archaeological Studies and Reports

Adams, Natalie. *Archaeological Survey of the Santee-Cooper Moncks Corner Eastside Carnes Cross roads Transmission Line.* Berkeley County, South Carolina: Chicora Foundation Inc. Columbia, South Carolina, 1993.

———. *Archaeological Reconnaissance of the Berkeley County Landfill Extension.* Columbia, South Carolina: Chicora Foundation, Inc., 1993.

———. *Archaeological Survey* of the *Goose Creek Water Main Extension, Berkeley County, South Carolina.* Columbia, South Carolina: Chicora Foundation Inc., 1994.

———. *Archaeological Survey* of the *Santee-Cooper Moncks Corner Eastside-Carnes Cross roads Transmission Line, Berkeley County, South Carolina.* Columbia, South Carolina: Chicora Foundation Inc., 1993.

Bailey, Ralph Jr. *Cultural Resources of the Ingleside Plantation Tract, Charleston County, South Carolina.* Prepared for the Albert Weber Manufacturing Company, Summerville, South Carolina, 1997.

———. Principal investigator of the *Cultural Resources Survey and Testing of the Persimmon Hill Tract, Berkeley County South Carolina.* Atlanta, Charleston, Raleigh: Brockington and Associates Inc., 2002.

Bailey, Ralph Jr. and Bruce G. Harvey. *National Register of Historic Places Evaluation of 29 Sites at the Charleston Naval Weapon's Station, Berkeley and Charleston Counties, South Carolina.* 2000. The report is among the records of the Natural Resources Specialist Office of the Naval Weapon's Station, Charleston, 2316 Red Bank Road, Goose Creek, South Carolina.

Bridgeman, Kara. Cultural Resources Inventory of the Charleston Southern Athletic Field, Charleston County, South Carolina. Prepared for the Charleston Southern University, Charleston, South Carolina, 2000.

Brockington, P.E. Jr., M.V. Markham, C.S. Butler, and D.C. Jones. *Cultural Resources Survey of the Charleston Naval Weapons Station, Berkeley and Charleston Counties, South Carolina.* Final Report Prepared for U.S. Army Corps of Engineers, Savannah District. Atlanta, Georgia: Brockington and Associates Inc., 1995.

Selected Bibliography

Caballero, O.M. *Archaeological Investigations of the Proposed U.S. Highway 176 Widening, Goose Creek to U.S. 17A, Berkeley County, South Carolina.* Prepared for the South Carolina Department of Public Safety and Transportation, New South Associates Inc, Stone Mountain, Georgia, 1987.

Charles, Tommy. *An archaeological reconnaissance of the St. James Church properties of the diocese of South Carolina in Goose Creek, Berkeley County, South Carolina.* Columbia, South Carolina: University of South Carolina Institute of Archaeology and Anthropology, 1988.

Drucker, Lesley M. *A cultural resources overview of the Bushy Park Auxiliary Canal study area.* Columbia, South Carolina: South Carolina Archaeological Services, 1981.

Elliot, Daniel T. *Crowfield Archaeological Survey*. Manuscript on file, Chicora Foundation Inc. Columbia, South Carolina.

Garrow, Patrick H. and Daniel T. Elliot. *Crowfield Archaeological Survey.* Prepared for Westvaco Development Corporation, Summerville, South Carolina, 1987.

Poplin, Eric C. *Archaeological reconnaissance of the Mt. Holly Plantation, Berkeley County, South Carolina,* Institute of Archaeology and Anthropology. Caroliniana Library, University of South Carolina, 1978.

Sipes, Eric D., and Pat Hendrix. *Cultural Resources Survey and Testing of the Persimmon Hill Tract, Berkeley County, South Carolina.* Prepared for Hussey, Gay, Bell and Deyoung Inc., Mount Pleasant, South Carolina, 2002.

Tippet Lee and Michael Trinkley, *Archaeological Survey of the Proposed Goose Creek-Ladson Connector.* Prepared for the South Carolina Department of Safety and Public Transportation,1979.

Trinkley, Michael, PhD. *Archaeological Survey of the Proposed Devon Forest, Berkeley County, South Carolina.* Columbia, South Carolina: Chicora Foundation, August 7, 2000. Caroliniana Library, Columbia, South Carolina.

———. *Cultural Resources Survey of the Liberty Hall Tract, Berkeley County, South Carolina.* Chicora Research Contribution 354. Columbia, South Carolina: Chicora Foundation Inc., 2002.

———. *Landscape and Garden Archaeology at Crowfield Plantation: a Preliminary Examination.* Columbia, South Carolina: Chicora Foundation Inc., 1992.

———. *Liberty Hall: A Small Eighteenth Century Rice Plantation in Goose Creek, Berkeley County, South.* Chicora Research Contribution Series 62. Columbia, South Carolina: Chicora Foundation Inc., 2003.

———. *Management Summary of Archaeological Data Recovery at a Portion of Crowfield Plantation and its Slave Settlement, Berkeley County, South Carolina*. Columbia, South Carolina: Chicora Foundation Inc., 1996.

Trinkley, Michael, Debi Hacker, and Natalie Adams. *Broom Hall Plantation: "A Pleasant One and in a Good Neighborhood."* Columbia, South Carolina: Chicora Foundation Inc., 1995.

Trinkley, Michael, Debi Hacker, and Nicole Southerland. *Archaeology at an Eighteenth Century Slave Settlement in Goose Creek, South Carolina, Berkeley County, South Carolina.* Columbia, South Carolina: Chicora Foundation Inc. Research Series 57, 2003.

Webb, Robert S., and Mary E. Gantt. *Evaluative Testing at Crowfield Main House Site (38BK102) and Slave Complex (38BK1011), Berkeley County, South Carolina.* Prepared for Westvaco Development Corporation, Summerville, South Carolina, 1997.

Published Reports

Grover, J.E. *Historic and Archaeological Resources Protection Plan for Naval Weapons Station, Charleston.* Final Draft Report Prepared for U.S. Army Corps of Engineers, Savannah District. Pan-American Consultants Inc. Tuscaloosa, Alabama, 1997.

Articles Published by the South Carolina Historical and Genealogical Society

Dunlop, J.G., ed. "Letters from John Stewart to William Dunlop." *South Carolina Historical and Genealogical Magazine* 32 (1931): 25.

"Extracts From Harriott Horry's Receipt Book." *South Carolina Historical and Genealogical Magazine* 60 (1959): 28.

Goodman, Richard. "Dr. Garden's Flower." *Carologue* 19, no. 3 (Fall 2003).

Jervey, Elizabeth Heyward. "Death Notices From The State Gazette of South Carolina of Charleston, S.C." *South Carolina Historical and Genealogical Magazine* 51 (1950): 165.

Mathews, Maurice. "A Contemporary View of Carolina in 1680." *South Carolina Historical and Genealogical Magazine* 55 (1954): 153–59.

Mercantini, Jonathan. "The Great Carolina Hurricane of 1752." *South Carolina Historical and Genealogical Magazine* 103, no. 4 (2002): 351–365.

Morgan, Phillip D. "A Profile of a Mid-Eighteenth Century South Carolina Parish: The Tax Return of St. James, Goose Creek." *South Carolina South Carolina Historical and Genealogical Magazine* 81 (1980): 51–56.

"Papers of Gabriel Manigault, 1771–1784." *South Carolina Historical and Genealogical Magazine* 64 (1963): 11.

Salley, A.S. Jr., "Diary of William Dillwyn in 1722." *South Carolina Historical and Genealogical Magazine* 36 (1935): 107–110.

Smith, H.A.M. "Charleston and Charleston Neck. The Original Grantees and the Settlements Along the Ashley and Cooper Rivers." *South Carolina Historical and Genealogical Magazine* 19 (1918): 3–76.

———. "Goose Creek." *South Carolina Historical and Genealogical Magazine* 29 (1928): 1–25, 71–96, 167–92, 265–79.

———. "The French Huguenot Church of the Parish of Goose Creek, South Carolina. Transactions of the Huguenot Society of South Carolina." *South Carolina Historical and Genealogical Magazine* 16 (1915).

"The Ariel Abbot Journals." *South Carolina Historical and Genealogical Magazine* 68 (1967): 244.

"The Brief and Tragic Career of Charles Lowndes." *South Carolina Historical and Genealogical Magazine* 70 (1969): 220–223.

"The Diary of William Dillwyn in 1772." *South Carolina Historical and Genealogical Magazine* 36 (1935): 107–110.

Thomas, J.P. Jr. "The Barbadians in Early South Carolina" *South Carolina Historical and Genealogical Magazine* 31, 75–80.

Waterhouse, Richard. "Economic and Changing Patterns of Wealth Distribution in Colonial Lowcountry South Carolina." *South Carolina Historical and Genealogical Magazine* 89 (1988): 203–217.

Webber, M.L. "Tombstone Inscriptions." *South Carolina Historical and Genealogical Magazine* 40 (1939): 33–40.

Maps

"A New and Accurate Map of the Providence of South Carolina in North America." *Universal Magazine of Knowledge and Pleasure*. 1779. Originated in London 1754. Library of Congress.

Burr, David H. "Map of North and South Carolina, Exhibiting the Post Offices…1839." *The American Atlas*. London: J. Arrowsmith, 1839.

Carte Particuliere De La Caroline. Amsterdam, Chez. Pierre Martier Libraire. 1688.

Charleston District, South Carolina. Surveyed by Charles Vignoles and Henry Ravenel 1820. Approved for Mills' Atlas 1825.

Gaillard, John Palme. *Map of Berkeley and parts of Charleston and Dorchester Counties S.C.* The map depicts the land holdings from 1850 to 1900. The original is among the collections of the McClellanville Museum, McClellanville, South Carolina.

Gascoyne, Joel. *A New Map of the Country of Carolina*. Library of Congress.

Map of Game Preserves and Forest Holdings of P.O. Mead and W.L. "PA" Stribling situated in Berkeley County, S.C. Surveyed, 1933–34 by J.T. Kullock Inc. Among the private papers of Terrence Larimer, Naval Weapons Station Charleston, Goose Creek, South Carolina.

Mills, Robert. *Mills' Atlas of South Carolina*. 1825, Easley, South Carolina: Southern Historical Press, 1980.

Mouzon, Henry. *An Accurate Map of North and South Carolina, with their Indian Frontiers…* ,1775. Map collections of the Library of Congress. Washington, D.C.

Saint James, Goose Creek Parish. Historic Resources of Berkeley County, South Carolina. Moncks Corner, South Carolina: Berkeley County Historical Society, 1990.

South Carolina 1839 (Color Counties) U.S. Coast Survey, A.D. Bache, Superintendent, 1865.

South Carolina. Relative Importance of Places shown by Size and Type. Rand McNally Indexed Atlas 1910–1915.

Tanner, Henry Schenck, 1786–1858. "Tanner Map 1833." Act of Congress, "A new map of South Carolina with its canals, roads & distances from place to place along the stage & steamboat routes." *A New Universal Atlas* Philadelphia, 1836. Library of Congress.

Walker and Abernethie, *Specimen of an intended traveling map of the roads of South Carolina, from actual survey by Walker and Abernethie.* Alternate title: *Road to Watboo Bridge from Charleston, by Goose Creek Bridge and Strawberry Ferry.* Charleston, South Carolina, 1787. Library of Congress.

Periodicals

Charleston City Gazette, South Carolina Historical Society and on microfilm at the Charleston County Library, Charleston, South Carolina.

Charleston Courier, South Carolina Historical Society, Charleston, South Carolina.

Charleston Evening Post, Charleston, South Carolina.

Charleston Evening Post, North Metro Edition, Charleston, South Carolina.

Charleston Mercury, Charleston, South Carolina. On microfilm at the Charleston County Library, Charleston, South Carolina.

Charleston News and Courier, Charleston, South Carolina.

Royal Gazette, on microfilm at the Charleston County Library, Charleston, South Carolina.

South Carolina Gazette, on microfilm at the Charleston County Library, Charleston, South Carolina.

State Gazette of South Carolina, on microfilm at the Charleston County Library, Charleston, South Carolina.

Wright, John K. "The Study of Place Names: Recent Work and Some Possibilities," *Geographical Review*, 1929.

Journals

The Colonial Records of South Carolina: The Journal of the Commons House of Assembly, November 10, 1736–June 7, 1739. J.H. Easterby, ed. The South Carolina Department of Archives and History, University of South Carolina Press, Columbia, South Carolina, 1951.

The Colonial Records of South Carolina: The Journal of the Commons House of Assembly, September 12, 1739–March 26, 1741. J.H. Easterby, ed. The South Carolina Department of Archives and History, University of South Carolina Press, Columbia, South Carolina, 1952

The Colonial Records of South Carolina: The Journal of the Commons House of Assembly, May 18, 1741–July 10, 1742. J.H. Easterby, ed. The South Carolina Department of Archives and History, University of South Carolina Press, Columbia, 1953.

The Colonial Records of South Carolina: The Journal of the Commons House of Assembly, September 14, 1742–January 27, 1744. J.H. Easterby, ed. The South Carolina Department The University of South Carolina Press, Columbia, South Carolina, 1954.

The Colonial Records of South Carolina: The Journal of the Commons House of Assembly, February 20, 1744–May 25, 1745. J.H. Easterby, ed. The South Carolina Department of Archives and History, University of South Carolina Press, Columbia, South Carolina, 1955.

The Colonial Records of South Carolina: The Journal of the Commons House of Assembly, September 10, 1745–June 17, 1746. J.H. Easterby, ed. The South Carolina Department of Archives and History, University of South Carolina Press, Columbia, South Carolina, 1956

The Colonial Records of South Carolina: The Journal of the Commons House of Assembly, September 10, 1746–June 13, 1747. J.H. Easterby, ed. The South Carolina Department of Archives and History, University of South Carolina Press, Columbia, South Carolina, 1958.

The Colonial Records of South Carolina: The Journal of the Commons House of Assembly January 19, 1748–June 29, 1748. J.H. Easterby, ed. The South Carolina Department of Archives and History, University of South Carolina Press, Columbia, South Carolina, 1961.

The Colonial Records of South Carolina: The Journal of the Commons House of Assembly, March 28, 1749–March 19, 1750. J.H. Easterby, ed. The South Carolina Department of Archives and History, University of South Carolina Press, Columbia, South Carolina, 1962.

The Colonial Records of South Carolina: The Journal of the Commons House of Assembly, 23 April 1750–31 August 1751. R. Nicholas Olsberg, ed. The South Carolina Department of Archives and History, University of South Carolina Press, Columbia, South Carolina, 1974.

The Colonial Records of South Carolina: The Journal of the Commons House of Assembly. November 14, 1751–October 7, 1752. Terry W. Lipscomb and R. Nicholas Olsberg, eds. The South Carolina Department of Archives and History, University of South Carolina Press, Columbia, South Carolina, 1977.

The Colonial Records of South Carolina: The Journal of the Commons House of Assembly. November 21, 1752–September 6, 1754. Terry W. Lipscomb, ed. The South Carolina Department of Archives and History, University of South Carolina Press, Columbia, South Carolina, 1980.

The Colonial Records of South Carolina: The Journal of the Commons House of Assembly. November 12, 1754–September 23, 1755. Terry W. Lipscomb, ed. The South Carolina

Department of Archives and History, University of South Carolina Press, Columbia, South Carolina, 1986.

The Colonial Records of South Carolina: The Journal of the Commons House of Assembly. November 20, 1755–July 6, 1757. Terry W. Lipscomb, ed. The South Carolina Department of Archives and History, University of South Carolina Press, Columbia, South Carolina, 1989.

Extracts from the Journals of the Provincial Congress of South Carolina, 1775–1776, held at Charles Town February 1, 1775. William Edwin Hemphill, ed. Published by order of Congress, Charles Town. Printed by Peter Timothy.

Journals of the House of Representatives, 1783–1784. Theodora J. Thompson, ed. Columbia, South Carolina: University of South Carolina Press, 1977.

Journals of the House of Representatives 1785–1786. Lark Emerson Adams, ed. Columbia, South Carolina: University of South Carolina Press, 1979.

Journals of the House of Representatives 1787–1788. Michael E. Stevens, ed. Columbia, South Carolina: University of South Carolina Press, 1981.

Journals of the House of Representatives 1789–1790. Michael E. Stevens, ed. Columbia, South Carolina: University of South Carolina Press, 1984.

Journals of the House of Representatives 1791. Michael E. Stevens, ed. Columbia, South Carolina: University of South Carolina Press, 1985.

Journals of the House of Representatives 1792–1794. Michael E. Stevens, ed. Columbia, South Carolina: University of South Carolina Press, 1988.

Merrins, H. Roy, and George D. Terry. "Driving in Paradise: Malaria, Mortality, and Perceptual Environment in Colonial South Carolina." *Journal of Southern History* 50 (1983): 533–50.

Rauschenberg, B.L. "Brick and Tile Manufacturing in the South Carolina Low Country, 1750–1800. *Journal of Southern Decorative Arts*, 1988.

Waterhouse, Richard. "The Caribbean, and the Settlement of Carolina." *Journal of American Studies* 9: 259–81.

Pamphlets

Legendre, Gertrude and Carola Kittredge. *Medway Plantation Past, Present and Future.* Private publication given to guests and visitors at Medway, Goose Creek, South Carolina.

Waring, Joseph Ioor. "Homes of Long Ago" *The Exposition.* A copy of this article is in the Waring Private Papers on deposit at the South Carolina Historical Society, Charleston, South Carolina.

Plats traced from the originals among the Henry A.M. Smith Collection at the South Carolina Historical Society, Charleston, South Carolina.

Bee, Susannah. Plan of Mrs. Bee's land at Goose Creek, St. James. 1 plat: tracing; 46 x 61 cm. Request #: 32/120/A005 Property owner.

Beresford, John. This plat contains three thousand acres of land being formerly laid out unto Joseph Thorogood and Lyeth in Berkeley County on a branch of swamp within land that empties itself into Medway River. Request #: 32/120/A250

Black Tom Bay. General plan of a piece of land About Black Tom Bay. 1 plat: tracing; 46 x 61 cm. Request #: 32/120/A099

Broughton, John. Robert Daniel, Esq. Landgrave 527 Acres land upon Midway River or Black River [S.C.]. 1 plat: tracing; 46 x 61 cm. Request #: 32/120/A284

Button Hall, St. James, Goose Creek. 1 plat: tracing; 46 x 61 cm. Request #: 32/120/A220

Carson, William A. Plat of White Hall Plantation: the property of Col. William A. Carson situated in St. Johns Parish on the headwaters of Back River. 1 plat: tracing; 46 x 61 cm. Request #: 32/120/A131

Cow Jig Plantation on Fosters Creek belonging to the heirs of Nathaniel Bourdeaux, Dec'd. 1 plat: tracing; 46 x 61 cm. Request #: 32/120/A031B

Cripps. Plan of Cripps land at Goose Creek. 1 plat: tracing; 46 x 61 cm. Request #: 32/120/A097

Fraser, Alexander. Copy of a plan of Wigton Plantation in Goose Creek belonging to James Fraser Esq. part laid out for Mrs. Joseph Winthrop agreeable to the last will of Alexander Fraser, dec'd, the father. 1 plat: tracing; 46 x 61 cm. Request #:32/120/A097

Gadsden estate (Part of a Plat) on Goose Creek. 1 plat: tracing; 46 x 61 cm. Request #: 32/120/A107 (top) 1871 Survey by J.O. Tennent.

Garden, Alexander. A plan of a tract of land situated on the west side of Goose Creek in St. James, Goose Creek Parish Charleston District and state of South Carolina being originally part of a tract of land belonging to Alexander Garden Esq. called Otranto containing 535 acres. tracing; 46 x 61 cm. Request #: 32/120/A015

General plan of tracts at Goose Creek. 1 plat: tracing; 46 x 61 cm. Request #: 32/120/A004B

Glen, John and Daniel Cannon. Plat of a 566-acre plantation. The plat may have been commissioned to settle a boundary dispute between John Glen and Daniel Cannon.

Glover, Sanders. Plan of Sanders Glover's plantation, St. James, Goose Creek. 1 plat: tracing; 46 x 61 cm. Request #: 32/120/A004

Goose Creek Church, South Carolina. 1 plat: tracing; 46 x 61 cm. Request #: 32/120/A227

Grove Hall plantation, South Carolina. 1 plat: tracing; 46 x 61 cm. Request #: 32/120/A129

Guerard, Benjamin. Plan of Fontainbleau Plantation situated in St. James, Goose Creek Parish, the property of Benjamin Guerard, Esq. divided into three lots or tracts. 1 plat, 2 pages: tracing; 46 x 61 cm. Request #: 32/120/A038

Hoory, Harriet. This plan exhibits a body of land on the south side of Fosters Creek, St. James, Goose Creek containing in the whole 925.13 acres belonging to Mrs. Harriet Horry—whereon a brickyard is established. 1 plat: tracing; 46 x 61 cm. Request #: 32/120/A028

Ingraham, W.P. Springfield property of W.P. Ingraham. 1 plat: tracing; 46 x 61 cm. Request #: 32/120/A282

Izard, Ralph. Copy of the Elms Plantation belonging to Ralph Izard on Goose Creek. 1 plat: tracing; 46 x 61 cm. Request #: 32/120/A014

Keckley, George. Plan of Spring Grove Plantation: part in the parish of St. James, Goose Creek and part in St. Johns Charleston District belonging to George Keckeley. 1 plat: tracing; 46 x 61 cm. Request #: 32/120/A017

Keith, M.J. Plan of Springfield and Mount Holly Plantations, St. James, Goose Creek Parish, Charleston District, South Carolina 1 plat: tracing; 46 x 61 cm. Request #: 32/120/A010

Manigault, Peter. Manigault, Goose Creek: [two tracts of land on Goose Creek belonging to Peter Manigault]. 1 plat: tracing; 46 x 61 cm. Request #: 32/120/A105

Matthews, M. Copy of a plan of a body of land in Goose Creek, part now forming part of the glebe of St. James Church and part now belonging to the estate of Benjamin Coachman, dec'd. 1 plat, 2 pages: tracing; 46 x 61 cm. Request #: 32/120/A027

Mazyck, Stephen. Plan of a tract of land in Goose Creek on Fosters Creek belonging to Stephen Mazyck, containing 2,743.5 acres. 1 plat: tracing; 46 x 61 cm. Request #: 32/120/A096

Middleton, Henry A. A plan representing the shape, marks, boundaries, courses and distances of several adjoining tracts of land containing in all 3.971 acres belonging to Henry A. Middleton Esq. situated in St. James, Goose Creek Parish, Charleston County, S.C. 1 plat: tracing; 46 x 61 cm. Request #: 32/120/A237

Moultrie, Alexander. Plan of Richmond Plantation belonging to Col. Moultrie. 1 plat: tracing; 46 x 61 cm. Request #: 32/120/A003

Mt. Holly, St. James, Goose Creek. 1 plat : tracing ; 46 x 61 cm. Request #: 32/120/A235

North of the Elms—Duplicate. 1 plat: tracing; 46 x 61 cm. Request #: 32/120/A009

Parker, Isaac. A plan of a tract of land at Goose Creek belonging to the estate of William Parker Esq. dec'd, now divided into two tracts at the request of Isaac Parker, Executor in 1791. 1 plat: tracing; 46 x 61 cm. Request #: 32/120/A020

Postell, John. Plan of a tract of land in Berkeley County, S.C. belonging to John Postell. 1 plat: tracing; 46 x 61 cm. Request #: 32/120/ A200(bottom)

Prioleau, Samuel. General plan of land near Charleston now belonging to Samuel Prioleau and others. 1 plat: tracing; 46 x 61 cm. Request #: 32/120/A265

Sociable Hill plantation branches of Back River, St. James, Goose Creek Parish, South Carolina. 1 plat: tracing; 46 x 61 cm. Request #: 32/120/A021

Ravenel, Henry. The Goose Creek road from 10-Mile House to Vance's Tavern with the relative situations of the plantations, drawn to regulate the cutting of timber for the state road. 1 plat: tracing; 46 x 61 cm. Request #: 32/120/A007

Red Bank, Cooper River, Goose Creek. 1 plat: tracing; 46 x 61 cm. Request #: 32/120/ A102

Smith, Peter. Plantation in Goose Creek owned by Peter Smith. 1 plat: tracing; 46 x 61 cm. Request #: 32/120/A008

Withers, James. Plan of a plantation on Goose Creek containing 800 acres belonging to Withers—now known as Mount Pleasant, property of Josiah S. Brown. 1 plat: tracing; 46 x 61 cm. Request #: 32/120/A031

Books

Bachman, John C. *John Bachman*. Charleston, South Carolina: Walker, Evans and Cogswell Company, 1888.

Bailey, Louise N. *Biographical Directory of the South Carolina House of Representatives: Volumes III, IV, 1775–1815*. Columbia, South Carolina: University of South Carolina Press, 1986.

Ball, Edward. *Slaves in the Family*. New York: Farrar, Straus and Giroux Publishers, 1998.

Barry, John M. *Natural Vegetation of South Carolina*. Columbia, South Carolina: University of South Carolina Press, 1980.

Bauer, William Rudolph. *The Sineath Family*. Columbia, South Carolina: The R.L. Bryan Company, 1970.

Berkeley, Edmund, and Dorothy Smith. *Dr. Alexander Garden of Charles Town*. Chapel Hill, North Carolina: University of North Carolina Press, 1966.

Beach, Virginia Christian. *Medway*. Charleston, South Carolina: Wyrick and Company, 1996.

Borick, Carl P. *A Gallant Defense, The Siege of Charleston, 1780*. Columbia, South Carolina: University of South Carolina Press, 2003.

Bowes, Frederick Patten. *The Culture of Early Charleston*. Greenwood, South Carolina: Greenwood Press, 1902.

Brown, Douglas Summers. *The Catawba Indians: The People of the River*. Columbia, South Carolina: University of South Carolina Press, 1966.

Bull, Elias B. *Community and Neighborhood Names in Berkeley County, Part III*, in *Names in South Carolina*. Columbia, South Carolina: Department of English, University of South Carolina, 1966.

Butler, Jon. *The Huguenots in America: A Refugee People in a New World Society*. Cambridge, Massachusetts: Harvard University Press, 1983.

Brown, Richard Maxwell. *The South Carolina Regulators*. Cambridge, Massachusetts: Belknap Press of Harvard University, 1963.

Burney, Eugenia. *Colonial South Carolina*. Camden, New Jersey: Thomas Nelson Inc., 1970.

Calhoun, Jeanne. *The Scourging Wrath of God: Early Hurricanes in Charleston.* Leaflet No. 29. Charleston, South Carolina: The Charleston Museum, n.d.

Carman, Harry. *American Husbandry*. New York: Columbia University Press, 1939.

Chaplin, Joyce E. *An Anxious Pursuit: Agricultural Innovations and Modernity in the Lower South, 1730–1815.* Chapel Hill, North Carolina: University of North Carolina Press, 1993.

Childs, St. Julien Ravenel. *Malaria and Colonization in the Carolina Low Country, 1526–1969.* Baltimore: Johns Hopkins Press, 1940.

Clowse, Converse D. *Economic Beginnings in Colonial South Carolina, 1670–1730.* Columbia, South Carolina: University of South Carolina Press, 1971.

Coclanis, Peter A. *The Shadow of a Dream: Economic Life and Death in the South Carolina Low Country 1670–1920.* New York: Oxford University Press, 1989.

Coldham, Peter Wilson. *American Loyalists Claims.* Washington, D.C: National Geological Society, 1980.

Cooper, Thomas and David J. McCord. *The Statutes at Large of South Carolina, (1682–1838)*, 10 vols. Columbia, South Carolina: A.S. Johnson, 1838.

Correspondence of Ralph Izard of South Carolina for the Years 1774 to 1804, with a short memoir. New York: Charles Francis & Co., 1844.

Cote, Richard. N. and A.L. Baldwin. *Undated Medway Plantation, Back River: A Historical Outline,* 1684–1993. No publisher cited.

Crane, Verner W. *The Southern Frontier*, 1670–1752. Durham, North Carolina: Duke University Press, 1928.

Cross, Russell J. *Historic Ramblin's Through Berkeley*. Columbia, South Carolina: R.L. Bryan Company, 1985.

Dalcho, Frederick. *A Historic Account of the Protestant Episcopal Church in South Carolina.* Charleston, South Carolina: A.E. Miller, 1820, reprinted 1969.

Dargan, Hugh, and Mary Palmer Dargan. *The Gardens of Crowfield in South Carolina: First Example of the Early Picturesque Landscape Movement in America, c. 1730.* Charleston, South Carolina: Hugh Dargan Associates Inc., 1998.

Deas, Anne Simmons. *Points of Colonial Interests Around Summerville, South Carolina*. Columbia, South Carolina: Caroliniana Library, 1905.

Doar, David. *Rice and Rice Planting in the South Carolina Low Country*. Charleston, South Carolina: The Charleston Museum, 1936.

Dubose, Samuel David and Frederick A. Porcher. *A Contribution to the History of the Huguenots of South Carolina*. New York: The Knickerbocker Press, 1887. Reprinted from the original, Columbia, South Carolina: The R.L. Bryan Co. 1972.

Dwight, Henry Ravenel. *Some Historic Spots in Berkeley*. Pinopolis, South Carolina: Women's Auxiliary of Trinity Church, 1921; reprinted 1944.

Edgar, Walter B. *South Carolina a History*. Columbia, South Carolina: University of South Carolina Press, 1999.

Edgar, Walter B. and N. Louise Bailey. *Biographical Directory of the South Carolina House of Representatives: Volume I and Volumes II, III*. Columbia, South Carolina: University of South Carolina Press, 1974.

Fore, George. *Crowfield Plantation Ruins, Berkeley County, South Carolina Conservation Study*. Raleigh, North Carolina: George T. Fore and Associates, 1988.

Franklin, John Hope. *From Slavery to Freedom: A History of Negro Americans*. New York: Vantage Books, 1969.

Fraser, Charles. *A Charleston Sketchbook, 1796–1806*. Rutland, Vermont: Charles E. Tuttle Co. 1940.

Gibbes, Robert Wilson. *Documentary History of the American Revolution,* Volumes 2 and 3, 1776–1782. Spartanburg, South Carolina: The Reprint Company, 1972.

Gordon, Asa H. *Sketches of Negro Life and History in South Carolina*. Columbia, South Carolina: University of South Carolina Press, 1929.

Heitzler, Michael J. *Historic Goose Creek, South Carolina, 1670–1980*. Easley, South Carolina: Southern Historical Press, 1983.

Hewat, Alexander. *Historical Account of the Rise and Progress of the Colonies of South Carolina and Georgia (1779)*. In *Historical Collections of South Carolina*, B.R. Carroll, ed. New York: Harper & Brothers, 1836.

Hicks, Theresa M., ed. *South Carolina Indians, Indian Traders and Other Ethnic Connections Beginning in 1670*. Spartanburg, South Carolina: Peppercorn Publications Inc., 1998.

Hirsch, Arthur Henry. *The Huguenots of Colonial South Carolina.* London: Archon Books, 1962.

Hofstader, Richard. *The American Republic*. Englewood Cliffs, New Jersey: Prentice-Hall, 1959.

Holcomb, Brent H. *Petitions For Land From The South Carolina Council Journals Volume VI: 1766–1770*. Columbia: SCMAR, 1999.

———. *South Carolina Deed Abstracts: Books F-4 to X-4*. Volume5 1773–1776. Columbia, South Carolina: SCMAR, 1999.

———. *South Carolina Deed Abstracts: Books Y-4 to H-5*. Volume 7 1776–1783.Columbia, South Carolina: SCMAR, 1994.

———. *South Carolina Deed Abstracts: Books I-5 to Z-5*. 1783–1788. Columbia, South Carolina: SCMAR, 1996.

———. *South Carolina Deed Abstracts: Books F-4 to X4*. Volume 5 1778–1783. Easley, South Carolina: Southern Historical Press, 1993.

Hughson, Shirley C. *The Carolina Pirates and Colonial Commerce, 1670–1740*. Baltimore: Johns Hopkins Press, 1894.

Hrabowski, Richard. *Directory for the District of Charleston Comprising the places of residence and occupation of the White Inhabitants of the Following Parishes to wit…St. James (Goose Creek)*. Charleston, South Carolina: John Hobb, no. 6 Broad Street, 1809. The book is deposited with the South Carolina Historical Society, Charleston, South Carolina.

Irving, John Beaufain. *A Day on Cooper River*. Charleston, South Carolina: A.E. Miller, 1869.

———. *A Day on Cooper River*. Enlarged and edited by Louisa Cheves Stoney; reprinted with notes by Samuel Gaillard Stoney. Charleston, South Carolina: R.L. Bryan Co., 1932.

———. *The South Carolina Jockey Club*. Spartanburg, South Carolina: The Reprint Co., 1975.

Johnson, Joseph. *Traditions and Reminiscences, Chiefly of the American Revolution in South Carolina.* Charleston, South Carolina: Walker & James, 1851.

Joyner, C. *Down by the Riverside*. Urbana, Illinois: University of Chicago Press, 1984.

Klingberg, Frank J. *An Appraisal of the Negro in Colonial South Carolina.* Washington, D.C.: Associated Publishers, 1941.

———. *The Carolina Chronicle of Dr. Francis LeJau, 1706–1717.* Berkeley and Los Angeles: University of California Press, 1956.

———. Carolina Chronicle: *The Papers of Commissary Gideon Johnson, 1707–1716.* Berkeley and Los Angeles: University of California Press, 1946.

Koger, Larry. *Black Slave Owners, Free Black Masters in South Carolina, 1790–1860.* Columbia, South Carolina: University of South Carolina Press, 1995.

Langley, Clara A. *South Carolina Deed Abstracts, Vol. 1, 1719–1740, Books A through T.* Easley, South Carolina: Southern Historical Press, 1983.

———. *South Carolina Deed Abstracts, Vol. 2, 1740–1755, Books V-PP.* Easley, South Carolina: Southern Historical Press, 1984.

———. *South Carolina Deed Abstracts, Vol. 3, 1755–1768, Books QQ–HHH.* Easley, South Carolina: Southern Historical Press, 1983.

———. *South Carolina Deed Abstracts Vol. 4, 1767–1773, Books III–ZZZ.* Easley, South Carolina: Southern Historical Press, 1984.

Leiding, Henriette Kershaw. *Historic Houses of South Carolina.* Philadelphia: J.B. Lippincott, 1921.

Life in Carolina and New England during the Nineteenth Century, as Illustrated by Reminiscences and Letters of the DeWolf Family of Bristol, Rhode Island. Bristol, Rhode Island: privately printed, 1929.

Lind, Ivan. "Geography and Place Names," *Readings in Cultural Geography.* Chicago: University of Chicago Press, 1962.

Lieding, H.K. *Historic Houses of South Carolina.* Philadelphia: J.B. Lippincott, 1921.

McCowen, George Smith, Jr. *The British Occupation of Charleston, 1780–1782.* Columbia, South Carolina: University of South Carolina Press, 1972.

McCrady, Edward. *History of South Carolina.* 4 vols. New York: McMillan, 1897–1901.

———. *The History of South Carolina Under the Proprietary Government, 1670–1719.* New York: Macmillan, 1897.

McDowell, William L., ed. *Documents Relating to Indian Affairs, 1754–1765*. Columbia, South Carolina: University of South Carolina Press, 1970.

Milling, Chaplin. J. *Red Carolinians.* Chapel Hill, North Carolina: University of North Carolina Press, 1940.

Mills, Robert. *Statistics of South Carolina.* Spartanburg, South Carolina: The Reprint Press, 1973. Originally published in 1826, by Hurlbut and Lloyd, Charleston, South Carolina.

Moore, Alexander. *Biographical Directory of the South Carolina House of Representatives, Columbia: Vol. V: 1816–1828.* South Carolina Department of Archives and History, 1992.

Moore, Caroline T., ed. *Abstracts of the Wills of South Carolina.* Columbia, South Carolina: R.L. Bryan, 1960–1974.

Motes, Jesse Hogan III and Margaret Peckham Motes. *South Carolina Memorials: Abstracts of Land Titles.* Vol. 1 (1774–1776). Greenville, South Carolina: Southern Historical Press, 1996.

Nevins, Allan. *Slave Trading in the Old South.* New York: Frederick Ungar Publishing Co., 1959.

Neuffer, Claude, ed. *Names in South Carolina.* Volume XVI. Columbia, South Carolina: Department of English, University of South Carolina.

Newe, Thomas. "Letters from South Carolina in 1682." In *Narratives of Early Carolina.* New York: 1911.

O'Brien, Michael and David Moltke-Hanson. *Intellectual Life in Antebellum Charleston.* Knoxville: University of Tennessee Press. 1986.

Orvin, Maxwell Clayton. *Historic Berkeley County, S.C., 1671–1900.* Charleston, South Carolina: Comprint, 1973.

———. *A History of Monck's Corner, Berkeley County, South Carolina.* Charleston, South Carolina: 1961.

Parker, Ellen. *Record of the Parker family of the parish of St. James, Goose Creek and Charleston, South Carolina.* Charleston, South Carolina, 1930.

Pierre, C.E. *The Work of the Society for the Propagation of the Gospel in Foreign Parts in the Colonies.* Washington, D.C. From The Association for the Study of Negro Life and History Inc. From the Journal of Negro History 1, no. 4 (October 1916).

Poyas, E.A. *The Olden Times of South Carolina.* Charleston, South Carolina: S.G. Courtenay & Co., 1855.

Ramenofsky, A.P., PhD. *The Archaeology of Population Collapse: Native American Response to the Introduction of Infectious Disease.* Seattle: Department of Anthropology, University of Washington, 1982.

Ravenel, Mrs. St. Julien. *Charleston, the Place and the People.* New York: McMillan, 1912.

"Report of the Committee on Education," in *Acts, Reports and Regulations of the General Assembly of South Carolina.* Columbia, South Carolina: R.W. Gibbes, 1858.

Reynolds, Emily Bellinger, and Joan Reynolds Faunt. *The Biographical Dictionary of the Senate of South Carolina, 1776–1964.* Columbia, South Carolina: The Senate Research Committee. The South Carolina Department of Archives and History, 1964.

Rivers, William J. *A Sketch of the History of South Carolina.* Spartanburg, South Carolina: The Reprint Co., 1972.

Rogers, George C. Jr. *Charleston in the Age of the Pinckneys.* Norman, Oklahoma: University of Oklahoma Press, 1969.

———. *Evolution of a Federalist: William Laughton Smith of Charleston (1758–1812).* Columbia, South Carolina: University of South Carolina Press, 1962.

Rose, Mrs. Arthur Gordon, (Jeanne). *Little Mistress Chicken.* Reprinted by the Youth's Companion, n.d.

Rutledge, Anna Wells. *Artists in the Life of Charleston.* Philadelphia: American Philosophical Society, 1949.

Salley, Alexander S. Jr. *Narratives of Early Carolina.* 1911, reprinted. New York: Barnes & Noble, 1967.

Salley, Alexander S. Jr., ed. *Journals of the Commons House of Assembly.* Columbia, South Carolina: State Printing Company, 1907.

———. *Warrants for Land in South Carolina, 1672–1711 in 3 Volumes.* Columbia, South Carolina: Historical Commission of South Carolina, 1910–1915. Columbia, South Carolina. Reprinted in 1998. The State Company.

Sass, Herbert Ravenel. *The Story of the South Carolina Low Country.* West Columbia, South Carolina: J.F. Hyer Publishing Co., 1956.

Savell, Max. *A History of Colonial America*. New York: Holt, Rinehart & Winston, 1966.

Seeman, William. *Down Goose Creek.* New York: Fleming H. Revell Company, 1931.

Sellers, Leilla. *Charleston Business on the Eve of The American Revolution.* Chapel Hill, North Carolina: University of North Carolina Press, 1932.

Sellers, Hazel Crowson. *Old South Carolina Churches*. Columbia, South Carolina: Crowson Printing Co., 1941.

Shuler, Jay. *Had I the Wings: The Friendship of Bachman and Audubon*. Athens, Georgia: University of Georgia Press, 1993.

Sirmans, M. Eugene. *Colonial South Carolina: A Political History 1663–1763*. Chapel Hill, North Carolina: University of North Carolina Press, 1966.

Smith, H.A.M. *Rivers and Regions of Early South Carolina.* Spartanburg, South Carolina: the Reprint Press, 1988. Originally published in 1928, in the *South Carolina Historical and Genealogical Magazine*, Charleston, South Carolina.

Smith, W. Roy. *South Carolina as a Royal Province, 1719–1776*. New York: MacMillan, 1903.

Stockton, Robert P. *Historic Resources of Berkeley County.* Moncks Corner, South Carolina: Berkeley County Historical Society and South Carolina Department of Archives and History. 1990.

Stoney, Samuel Gaillard. *Plantations of the Carolina Low Country*. New York: Dover Publications Inc. 1938.

Swanton, John Reed. *Indians of the Southeastern United States*. Washington, D.C.: Government Printing Office, 1946.

Thompson, Theodora J., ed. *Journals of the South Carolina House of Representatives, 1783–1784*. Columbia: University of South Carolina Press, 1977.

Turner, Frederick Jackson. *The Frontier in American History*. New York: Henry Holt and Company, 1947.

Wallace, David Duncan. *South Carolina: A Short History*. Columbia, South Carolina: University of South Carolina Press, 1951.

———. *The History of South Carolina.* 4 vols. New York: American Historical Society Inc., 1934.

Waring, Joseph Ioor. *A History of Medicine in South Carolina, 1670–1825*. Charleston, South Carolina: South Carolina Medical Association, 1964.

———. *St. James' Church, Goose Creek, South Carolina: A Sketch of the Parish from 1706–1896*. Charleston, South Carolina: Lucas & Richardson Co. Printers and Engravers, 1897.

Writer's Program of the Works Project Administration (WPA). *Palmetto Place Names*. Spartanburg, South Carolina: The Reprint Co., 1975.

Waddell, Gene. *Indians of the South Carolina Low Country, 1562–1751*. Columbia, South Carolina: Southern Studies Program, University of South Carolina, 1980.

Wood, Peter. *Black Majority: Negroes in Colonial South Carolina from 1670 through the Stono Rebellion*. New York: Knopf, 1974.

Vipperman, Carl J. *The Rise of Rawlins Lowndes*. Columbia, South Carolina: University of South Carolina Press, 1976.

Index

Symbols

A

B

C

D

E

F

G

H

M

N

O

P

Y

About the Author

Michael James Heitzler was born in St. Louis, Missouri, in 1947. He is the son of Marine Corps Colonel Joseph S. Heitzler and Gentry Virginia Heitzler. He is the father of two sons, Andrew and Adam. He received his formal training in several public and private schools from Florida to Hawaii and holds a Doctor of Education degree from the University of South Carolina. He has served as a teacher and administrator in the Berkeley School District, South Carolina, since 1968, was elected to Goose Creek City Council in 1976, and has served as mayor of the City of Goose Creek since 1978. He is the author of *Historic Goose Creek, South Carolina, 1670–1980,* which was published in 1983 by Southern Historical Press, Easley, South Carolina.